Who Am I in the Lives of Children?

CALIFORNIA VERSION

ELEVENTH EDITION

Who Am I in the Lives of Children?

An Introduction to Early Childhood Education

Stephanie Feeney
University of Hawai'i at Mānoa, Emerita

Eva Moravcik
Honolulu Community College

Sherry Nolte
Honolulu Community College

 Pearson

330 Hudson Street, NY NY 10013

Director and Publisher: Kevin Davis
Executive Portfolio Manager: Julie Peters
Managing Content Producer: Megan Moffo
Portfolio Management Assistant: Maria Feliberty and Casey Coriell
Development Editor: Krista McMurray
Executive Product Marketing Manager: Christopher Barry
Executive Field Marketing Manager: Krista Clark
Manufacturing Buyer: Carol Melville
Cover Design: Carie Keller, Cenveo
Cover Art: Jeff Reese
Media Producer: Daniel Dwyer
Editorial Production and Composition Services: SPi Global, Inc.
Full-Service Project Manager: Jason Hammond
Text Font: Palatino LT Pro 9.5/13

Credits and acknowledgments for materials borrowed from other sources and reproduced, with permission, in this textbook appear on the appropriate page within the text.

Every effort has been made to provide accurate and current Internet information in this book. However, the Internet and information posted on it are constantly changing, so it is inevitable that some of the Internet addresses listed in this textbook will change.

Cataloging-in-Publication Data is on file at the Library of Congress
TK

ISBN 10:   0-13-487114-6
ISBN 13: 978-0-13-487114-1
REVEL
ISBN 10:   0-13-448844-X
ISBN 13: 978-0-13-448844-8
Package
ISBN 10:   0-13-448679-X
ISBN 13: 978-0-13-448679-6

A Letter to Readers

Dear Reader,

You are enrolled in a course that introduces you to the underlying theoretical principles of developmentally appropriate practices in early childhood care and education. Your textbook, *Who Am I in the Lives of Children? An Introduction to Early Childhood Education,* 11th ed., provides a rich overview of the field's past and present. It provides you with a wealth of information about the early care and education field and how to be a reflective, effective teacher of young children.

Who Am I in the Lives of Children? addresses how current trends and movements occurring nationally and internationally affect our field. This supplement provides you with additional information specific to California. California has a unique structure for

- teacher certification
- ensuring that its state-funded child care and development programs are of the highest quality, and
- easing your progress through the higher education system

Since the last edition of this text, the authors have added information and resources that will make this course more meaningful to you as you explore a career working with young children. Also since that last update, the California Department of Education, Early Learning and Support Division has also continued developing and implementing new documents, tools, and resources to support high-quality services to children and families. We have included those available at press time.

Both your text book and the California Early Learning System emphasize the important of reflective practice. Throughout the text you have many opportunities to reflect on your knowledge, skills, and experiences. You will see this emphasis on reflection in the various California tools and initiatives as well.

In keeping with the emphasis on reflective practice, *Who Am I in the Lives of Children?* includes digital opportunities for you to assess your own understanding of the text content. By using A Quick Check, A Final Check, Application Exercises, and Shared Writing, you can make sure you have mastered the content of the chapters. (*Note:* The new digital version of *Who Am I in the Lives of Children?* is available in REVEL, which has an accompanying app. Your instructor sets up the course in REVEL, shares an access code with you, and you gain access via your laptop, tablet or Pearson REVEL app.)

Another addition to both the text and the California Learning and Development System is the addition of video to enhance your understanding of important concepts. Links to video examples and video-based Application Exercises are included in every chapter of your text in REVEL. As you explore the programs and initiatives that comprise the Learning and Development System you will also find video clips to support your thinking and learning. The Competencies Self-Assessment Toolkit has an especially helpful collection of videos to help you think about the ways you implement the competencies in your work with children and families.

The Early Childhood Education field is fortunate to have access to a constructivist text as respectful to children, families, and educators as *Who Am I in the Lives of Children?* The text is described as being "a warm, comprehensive, child-centered approach to early childhood education," and I agree wholeheartedly. The California Learning and Development System is also child- and family-centered and supports the use of observation and reflection to meet the diverse needs of California's children and families. This text and the California system are companions in your learning. Together they will give you a wealth of knowledge and skills to become a capable and reflective educator of young children.

This supplement will enable you to see how national trends in early childhood education are being implemented in California. Early Childhood Education is a dynamic field. As the authors of *Who Am I in the Lives of Children?* explain, ". . . you have lots of learning challenges and joys ahead as you become an early childhood educator." Enjoy the journey!

Sydney Fisher Larson, Professor Emeritus
College of the Redwoods Eureka, CA

California's Learning and Development System

Note: Reprinted by permission from the California Department of Education, CDE Press, 1430 N Street, Sacramento, CA 95814.

California's Learning and Development System provides a comprehensive approach to ensuring California's children have access to high-quality child care and development services. According to State Superintendent of Public Instruction, Tom Torlakson, "We know that investments in early learning pay off for our state, our society, and for California's children."

The Learning Foundations are at the core of California's Learning and Development System and they will inform all other parts of the system including staff development, curriculum frameworks, program and child assessment, and guidelines and resources. These initiatives will help you when you become a teacher to make a contribution to an excellent system of early care and education programs for the children of California.

The supplement will introduce you to the following California Department of Education/Early Education and Support Division Initiatives and Documents. *Note: Websites do change and links break. If you encounter a broken link, simply search for the content using the website name and search words. Precede URLs with "http://www.". Full addresses are shown for those that do not include http://www*

Learning and Development Foundations

- California Infant/Toddler Learning and Development Foundations
  cde.ca.gov/sp/cd/re/documents/itfoundations2009.pdf

- California Preschool Learning Foundation, Volume 1
  cde.ca.gov/sp/cd/re/documents/preschoollf.pdf
- California Preschool Learning Foundation, Volume 2
  cde.ca.gov/sp/cd/re/documents/psfoundationsvol2.pdf
- California Preschool Learning Foundation, Volume 3
  cde.ca.gov/sp/cd/re/documents/preschoolfoundationsvol3.pdf

Curriculum Framework

- California Infant/Toddler Curriculum Framework
  cde.ca.gov/sp/cd/re/documents/itcurriculumframework.pdf
- California Preschool Curriculum Framework, Volume 1
  cde.ca.gov/sp/cd/re/documents/psframeworkkvol1.pdf
- California Preschool Curriculum Framework, Volume 2
  cde.ca.gov/sp/cd/re/documents/psframeworkvol2.pdf
- California Preschool Curriculum Framework, Volume 3
  cde.ca.gov/sp/cd/re/documents/preschoolframeworkvol3.pdf

Desired Results Assessment System

- DRDP System
  https://www.desiredresults.us/about-desired-results
- DRDP Tutorials
  https://www.desiredresults.us/drdp-tutorials
- Desired Results Developmental Profile for School-Age, Preschool, & Infant/Toddler

desiredresults.us/sites/default/files/docs/forms
/DRDP-SA%282011%29%20Complete100311.pdf
cde.ca.gov/sp/cd/ci/documents/drdp2015preschool.pdf
cde.ca.gov/sp/cd/ci/documents/drdp2015infanttod
dler.pdf

Professional Development

(Only programs with services for students/early childhood educators are included.)

- California Early Childhood Mentor Program
  ecementor.org
- California Preschool Instructional Network
  cpin.us
- Child Development Training Consortium
  https://www.childdevelopment.org
- California Early Childhood Online
  caearlychildhoodonline.org
- California School-Age Consortium
  https://calsac.org
- Family Child Care at Its Best
  humanservices.ucdavis.edu/ChildDev/Programs/
  FamilyChildCare.aspx?unit=CHLDEV
- Program for Infant/Toddler Care
  pitc.org/pub/pitc_docs/home.csp
- Child Development Permit Matrix
  ctc.ca.gov/credentials/CREDS/child-dev-permits.html
- California Early Childhood Educator Competencies
  cde.ca.gov/sp/cd/re/documents/ececompetencies
  2011.pdf
- CompSAT, Competencies-Based, Self-Assessment Toolkit
  ececompsat.org/about.html
- California Community College Curriculum Alignment
  Project
  https://www.childdevelopment.org/cs/cdtc/print
  /htdocs/services_cap.htm
- California Quality Rating and Improvement System (QRIS)
  cde.ca.gov/sp/cd/rt/californiaqris.asp

Program Guidelines and Resources

- California Infant/Toddler Learning and Development
  Guidelines
  cde.ca.gov/sp/cd/re/documents/itguidelines.pdf
- California Preschool Program Guidelines
  cde.ca.gov/sp/cd/re/documents/preschoolproggdlns
  2015.pdf
- The Integrated Nature of Learning (Best Practices for
  Planning Curriculum for Young Children)
  cde.ca.gov/sp/cd/re/documents/intnatureoflearning
  2016.pdf
- Family Partnerships and Culture (Best Practices for
  Planning Curriculum for Young Children)
  cde.ca.gov/sp/cd/re/documents/familypartnerships.pdf

- Preschool English Learners, Principles and Practices to
  Promote Language, Literacy, and Learning: A Resource
  Guide (2nd. ed)
  cde.ca.gov/sp/cd/re/documents/psenglearnersed2
  .pdf
- California's Best Practices for Young Dual Language
  Learners: Research Overview Papers
  cde.ca.gov/sp/cd/ce/documents/dllresearchpapers
  .pdf
- Inclusion Works! Promoting Child Care Programs That
  Promote Belonging for Children with Special Needs
  cde.ca.gov/sp/cd/re/documents/inclusionworks.pdf
- California Child Care Disaster Plan
  http://cchp.ucsf.edu/sites/cchp.ucsf.edu/files
  /CA-ChildCare-Disaster-Plan.pdf
- All About Young Children
  http://allaboutyoungchildren.org
- The Alignment of the California Preschool Learning
  Foundations with Key Early Education Resources
  (California Infant/Toddler Learning and Development
  Foundations, California Content Standards, the Com-
  mon Core State Standards, Head Start Child Develop-
  ment and Early Learning Framework)
  cde.ca.gov/sp/cd/re/documents/psalignment.pdf

Learning and Development Foundations

In 2002, the National Association for the Education of Young Children in collaboration with the National Association of Early Childhood Specialists in State Departments of Education adopted a joint position statement entitled "Early Learning Standards: Creating the Conditions for Success," recommending that states develop Early Learning Standards. California's response to this recommendation was to develop Early Learning Foundations.

"The term 'foundations' is used "because the focus on preschool learning in California includes the full range of domains, the term 'foundation' is used rather than 'standards' (PLF V1, p. xi–xii). This term is intended to convey that learning in every domain affects young children's readiness for school." California identifies nine domains in its Preschool Learning Foundations. Volume 1 of the California Preschool Learning Foundations covers social-emotional development, language and literacy, English-language development, and mathematics. Volume 2 addresses visual and performing arts, physical development, and health. Volume 3 includes history/social science and science. "The foundations describe competencies—knowledge and skills—that most children can be expected to exhibit in a high-quality program as they complete their first or second year of preschool" (PLF V3, p. xi).

"The foundations are designed to promote under-standing of young children's development of knowledge and skills and to help teachers, program administrators, families, and policymakers consider appropriate ways to support children's learning. In essence, the foundations serve as a cornerstone for informing early childhood educators about children's learning and development" (PLF V3 p. xvi).

California also developed the Infant/Toddler Learning and Development Foundations, which includes the early months (from 0 to 4 months), social-emotional development, language development, cognitive development, and perceptual and motor development.

The Infant/Toddler Foundations "describe competencies infants and toddlers typically attain during the birth-to-three-year period." The infant/toddler foundations are built on the belief that "during the infant/toddler years, all children depend on responsive, secure relationships to develop and learn" (I/TLDF, ix).

The Infant/Toddler Learning and Development Foundations address the following topics.

- Social Emotional Development
  - Interactions with Adults: The developing ability to respond to and engage with adults
  - Relationships with Adults: The development of close relationships with certain adults who provide consistent nurturance
  - Interactions with Peers: The developing ability to respond to and engage with other children
  - Relationships with Peers: The development of relationships with certain peers through interactions over time
  - Identity of Self in Relation to Others: The developing concept that the child is an individual operating within social relationships
  - Recognition of Ability: The developing understanding that the child can take action to influence the environment
  - Expression of Emotions: The developing ability to express a variety of feelings through facial expressions, movements, gestures, sounds, or words
  - Empathy: The developing ability to share in the emotional experiences of others
  - Emotion Regulation: The developing ability to manage emotional responses with assistance from others and independently
  - Impulse Control: The developing capacity to wait for needs to be met, to inhibit potentially hurtful behavior, and to act according to social expectations, including safety rules
  - Social Understanding: The developing understanding of the responses, communication, emotional expressions, and actions of other people

- Language Development
  - Receptive Language: The developing ability to understand words and increasingly complex utterances
  - Expressive Language: The developing ability to produce the sounds of language and use vocabulary and increasingly complex utterances
  - Communication Skills and Knowledge: The developing ability to communicate nonverbally and verbally
  - Interest in Print: The developing interest in engaging with print in books and in the environment

- Cognitive Development
  - Cause and Effect: The developing understanding that one event brings about another
  - Spatial Relationships: The developing understanding of how things move and fit in space
  - Problem Solving: The developing ability to engage in a purposeful effort to reach a goal or figure out how something works
  - Imitation: The developing ability to mirror, repeat, and practice the actions of others, either immediately or later
  - Memory: The developing ability to store and later retrieve information about past experiences
  - Number Sense: The developing under standing of number and quantity
  - Classification: The developing ability to group, sort, categorize, connect, and have expectations of objects and people according to their attributes
  - Symbolic Play: The developing ability to use actions, objects, or ideas to represent other actions, objects, or ideas
  - Attention Maintenance: The developing ability to attend to people and things while interacting with others and exploring the environment and play materials
  - Understanding Personal Care Routines: The developing ability to understand and participate in personal care routines

- Perceptual and Motor Development
  - Perceptual Development: The developing ability to become aware of the social and physical environment through the senses
  - Gross Motor: The developing ability to move the large muscles
  - Fine Motor: The developing ability to move the small muscles

The Preschool Learning Foundations Volume 1 covers these domains.

- Social Emotional Development—"The competencies covered by the social-emotional development foundations underscore the multiple ways in which young children's development in this domain influences their ability to adapt successfully to preschool and, later on, in school" (PLF V1, p. xii).

- Self
  - Self-Awareness
  - Self-Regulation
  - Social and Emotional Understanding
  - Empathy and Caring
  - Initiative in Learning
- Social Interaction
  - Interactions with Familiar Adults
  - Interactions with Peers
  - Group Participation
  - Cooperation and Responsibility
- Relationships
  - Attachment to Parents
  - Close Relationships with Teachers and Caregivers
  - Friendships

- Language and Literacy—"The foundations that were written for this domain reflect the field's growing interest in and understanding of the knowledge and skills that foster children's language and literacy learning during the preschool years" (PLF V1, p. xiii).
  - Listening and Speaking
    - Language Use and Conventions
    - Vocabulary
    - Grammar
  - Reading
    - Concepts about Print
    - Phonological Awareness
    - Alphabetics and Word/Print Recognition
    - Comprehension and Analysis of Age-Appropriate Text
    - Literacy Interest and Response
  - Writing
    - Writing Strategies

- English Language Development—"The English-language development foundations are specifically designed for children entering preschool with a home language other than English. Some English learners will begin preschool already having had some experience with English. For other English learners, preschool will offer them their first meaningful exposure to English. No matter how much background English learners have with English before they enter preschool, they will be on a path of acquiring a second language. As the English-language development foundations indicate, the learning task for English learners is sequential and multifaceted" (PLF V1 p. xiii).
  - Listening
    - Children Listen with Understanding
    - Beginning Words
    - Requests and Directions
    - Basic and Advanced Concepts
  - Speaking
    - Children Use Nonverbal and Verbal Strategies to Communicate with Others
      - Communication of Needs
      - Vocabulary Production
      - Conversation
      - Utterance Length and Complexity
      - Grammar
      - Inquiry
    - Children Begin to Understand and Use Social Conventions in English
      - Social Conventions
    - Children Use Language to Create Oral Narratives About Their Personal Experiences
      - Narrative Development
  - Reading
    - Children Demonstrate an Appreciation and Enjoyment of Reading and Literature
      - Participate in Read-Aloud Activity
      - Interest in Books and Reading
    - Children Show an Increasing Understanding of Book Reading
      - Personal Connection to the Story
      - Story Structure
    - Children Demonstrate an Understanding of Print Conventions
    - Children Demonstrate Awareness that Print Carries Meaning
      - Environmental Print
    - Children Demonstrate Progress in Their Knowledge of the Alphabet in English
      - Letter Awareness
      - Letter Recognition
    - Children Demonstrate Phonological Awareness
      - Rhyming
      - Onset (Initial Sound)
      - Sound Differences in Home Language and English
  - Writing
    - Children Use Writing to Communicate Their Ideas
      - Writing as Communication
      - Writing to Represent Words and Ideas
      - Writing Their Name

- Mathematics—"Young children's development of mathematics knowledge and skills is receiving increasing attention in research and practice" (PLF V1 p. xiii).
  - Number Sense
  - Algebra and Functions
  - Measurement
  - Geometry
  - Mathematical Reasoning

The Preschool Learning Foundations, Volume 2, addresses the following subjects.

- Visual and Performing Arts—"The foundations written for this domain reflect the many ways in which young children experience the joys of learning, creativity, self-expression, and playful exploration. The arts provide varied and meaningful opportunities for children to engage in integrated learning experiences that contribute to their development in all domains" (PLF V2, p. xiii).
  - Visual Art
    - Notice, Respond, and Engage
    - Develop Skills in Visual Art
    - Create, Invent, and Express through Visual Art
  - Music
    - Notice, Respond, and Engage
    - Develop Skills in Music
    - Create, Invent, and Express through Music
  - Drama
    - Notice, Respond, and Engage
    - Invent, and Express through Drama
  - Dance
    - Notice, Respond, and Engage
    - Develop Skills in Drama
    - Invent, and Express through Dance
- Physical Development—"The competencies covered by the physical development domain center on what preschool children do much of the day. This area of development describes many avenues for young children's play, engagement with others, exploration, and learning" (PLF V2, p. xiii).
  - Fundamental Movement Skills
    - Balance
    - Locomotor Skills
    - Manipulative Skills
  - Perceptual-Motor Skills and Movement Concepts
    - Body Awareness
    - Spatial Awareness
    - Directional Awareness
  - Active Physical Play
    - Active Participation
    - Cardiovascular Endurance
    - Muscular Strength, Muscular Endurance, and Flexibility
- Health—"Young children's development of health knowledge, attitudes, habits, and behaviors is receiving increasing attention in research and practice" (PLF V2, p. xiii).
  - Health Habits
    - Basic Hygiene
    - Oral Health
    - Knowledge of Wellness
    - Sun Safety

- Safety
  - Injury Prevention
- Nutrition
  - Nutrition Knowledge
  - Nutrition Choices
  - Self-Regulation of Eating

The Preschool Learning Foundations, Volume 3, covers these areas of development.

- History-Social Science—"The foundations for this domain reflect the many ways in which young children learn about basic concepts of history-social science" The history-social science foundations "center on young children's capacity to operate as members of a community" (PLF V3, p. xiii).
  - Self and Identity
    - Culture and Diversity
    - Relationships
    - Social Roles and Occupations
  - Becoming a Preschool Community Member (Civics)
    - Skills for Demographic participation
    - Responsible Conduct
    - Fairness and Respect for Other People
    - Conflict Resolution
  - Sense of Time (History)
    - Understanding Past Events
    - Anticipating and Planning Future Events
    - Personal History
    - Historical Changes in People and the World
  - Sense of Place (Geography and Ecology)
    - Navigating Familiar Locations
    - Caring for the Natural World
    - Understanding the Physical World through Drawings and Maps
  - Marketplace (Economics)
    - Exchange
- Science—"The competencies covered by the science domain center on content that connects with the natural curiosity of preschool children" (PLF V3 p. xiii).
  - Scientific Inquiry
    - Observation and Investigation
    - Documentation and Communication
  - Physical Sciences
    - Properties and Characteristics of Nonliving Objects and Materials
    - Changes in Nonliving Objects and Materials
  - Life Science
    - Properties and Characteristics of Living Things
    - Changes in Living Things
  - Earth Sciences
    - Properties and Characteristics of Earth Materials and Objects
    - Changes in the Earth

All three volumes of the California Learning and Development Foundations will support your learning as you read *Who Am I in the Lives of Children?* The authors of your text recognize the ways in which "each domain influences the others during every period of early childhood." Chapter 2 – The Field of Early Childhood Education will introduce you to Program Accountability and Program Standards, Chapter 6 – Relationships and Guidance provides a wealth of information about the social-emotional development of children including social interactions and relationships. Chapter 10 – The Curriculum and Chapter 11 – Curriculum Planning cover the role of standards (Foundations in California) in the curriculum and the curriculum planning and assessment process.

Curriculum Framework

The California Learning and Development System includes curriculum frameworks to "provide an overall approach for teachers to support children's learning through environments and experiences that are:

- developmentally appropriate,
- reflective of thoughtful observation and intentional planning,
- individually and culturally meaningful, and
- inclusive of children with disabilities or other special needs" (PCF V1, p. 2).

The frameworks are based on the Infant/Toddler and the Preschool Learning Foundations and continue to support the California Department of Education, Early Education and Support Division's philosophy that high quality child care and development programs can enhance children's learning in all the developmental domains.

The Infant/Toddler Curriculum Framework and the three volumes of the Preschool Curriculum Framework each cover the same learning domains as their corresponding foundations.

Each Curriculum Framework also includes overarching principles, a brief discussion of English-language development in all domains, universal design for learning, curriculum planning including supporting children as active meaning-makers, integrated curriculum, the environment and daily routines as curriculum, the daily schedule, and the curriculum planning process.

The are eight overarching principles for each age group that emphasize developmentally appropriate practice.

Infant/Toddler Curriculum Framework

"The purpose of the *California Infant/Toddler Curriculum Framework* is to provide early childhood professionals with a structure they can use to make informed decisions about curriculum practices. The framework is based on current research on how infants and toddlers learn and develop in four domains: social-emotional, language, cognitive, and perceptual and motor development. It presents principles

for supporting early learning, a planning process, and strategies to assist infant/toddler care teachers in their efforts to support children's from learning birth to age three" (I/TCF p.1).

The overarching principles for infants and toddlers focus on the unique needs of infants and toddlers.

- The family is at the core of a young child's learning and development.
- Infant/toddler learning and development is grounded in relationships.
- Emotions drive early learning and development.
- Responsiveness to children's self-initiated exploration fosters learning.
- Individualized teaching and care benefits all children.
- Responsiveness to culture and language supports children's learning.
- Intentional teaching and care enriches children's learning experiences.
- Time for reflection and planning enhances teaching and care (I/T CF, p.4).

The Infant/Toddler Curriculum Framework also emphasizes that "program policies that support effective infant/toddler curriculum planning and implementation include these elements:

- **Primary Care** —assigning a primary infant care teacher to each child and family
- **Small Groups** —creating small groups of children and caregivers
- **Continuity** —maintaining consistent teacher assignments and groups over time
- **Personalized Care** —responding to individual needs, abilities, and schedules
- **Cultural Continuity** —maintaining cultural consistency between home and program through dialogue and collaboration with families
- **Inclusion of Children with Special Needs** —providing appropriate accommodations and support for children with disabilities or other special needs" (I/TCF, p.12)

The Infant/Toddler Framework also points out, in planning and supporting learning for infants and toddlers programs must recognize:

1. Infants follow their own learning agenda.
2. Infants learn holistically.
3. Infants experience major developmental transitions in their first three years.
4. Infants are in the process of developing their first sense of self (I/TCF, p.13).

Another unique aspect to infant/toddler curriculum planning is that teachers must plan for these three contexts for learning.

1. **"The play environment as curriculum.** Curriculum plans include the selection of play materials that add interest and complexity to distinct areas where infants and toddlers freely play. A thoughtful selection of materials invites infants and toddlers to explore experiences that challenge their emerging skills, concepts, and ideas.
2. **Interactions and conversations as curriculum.** Curriculum plans address ways of being with infants and toddlers during interaction, including nonverbal interaction, conversations, cooperation, conflicts, and times when infants express strong feelings such as delight, sadness, anger, or frustration.
3. **Caregiving routines as curriculum.** Curriculum plans include care routines, particularly mealtimes, diaper changes, and naptimes. Intentional teaching invites infants and toddlers to participate in care routines that deepen their relationship experiences and open up possibilities for building emerging skills and concepts" (I/TCF, p. 20–21).

The authors of the Infant/Toddler Curriculum Framework point out, "Planning infant/toddler curriculum begins with teachers discovering, through careful listening and observation, each child's development. Observation is an essential teaching skill. When teachers mindfully observe, they find out how individual children make discoveries and make meaning within everyday moments of play and interactions" (I/TCF p. 26).

Preschool Curriculum Framework

The preschool curriculum frameworks are based on eight overarching principles. "Grounded in early childhood research and practice, the following eight principles emphasize offering young children individually, culturally, and linguistically responsive learning experiences and environments:

1. Relationships are central.
2. Play is a primary context for learning.
3. Learning is integrated.
4. Intentional teaching enhances children's learning experiences.
5. Family and community partnerships create meaningful connections.
6. Individualization of learning includes all children.
7. Responsiveness to culture and language supports children's learning.
8. Teachers need time for reflection and planning" (V1, p. 5).

The Preschool Curriculum Framework includes strategies to support English-language learners that focus on integration of learning in all domains. "In an integrated curriculum, the key to supporting all children is to plan learning activities and environments based on an ongoing understanding of each child's interests, needs, and family and cultural experiences. For young children who are learning English, this approach means focused attention to each child's unique experiences in acquiring a second language and an understanding of how to use a child's first language to help her understand a second language. In applying an integrated approach, teachers take advantage of every moment to provide children with opportunities to communicate with greater understanding and skill while engaged in play or in adult-guided learning activities" (PCF V3, p. 12).

There is also content on universal design which "provides for multiple means of representation, multiple means of expression, and multiple means of engagement" (PLF V3, p. 14).

The foundation suggests that "effective curriculum for young children engages their active minds and nurtures their enthusiastic search for meaning and understanding" (PCF V3, p. 15).

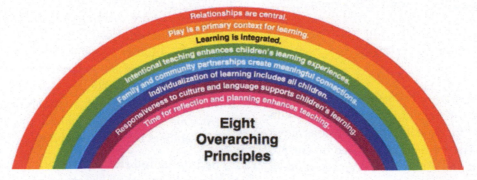

Eight Overarching Principles

Note: Reprinted by permission from the California Department of Education, CDE Press, 1430 N Street, Sacramento, CA 95814.

They identify four aspects of curriculum planning:

1. Curriculum planning to support children as active meaning makers
2. Integrated curriculum
3. The environment as curriculum: interest areas to support children's play and child-initiated learning
4. Daily routines as curriculum

The foundations also address a daily schedule including child-initiated play, teacher-guided activities in small groups, and teacher guided activities in large groups.

Each of the three Preschool Curriculum Frameworks has guiding principles and domain specific suggestion for environments and materials. This is followed by rich explorations of each domain with vignettes, teachable moments, interactions and strategies, and a section on bringing it all together.

The final aspect of curriculum, which is covered by the foundations, is partnering with families and making connections.

The foundations curriculum planning focuses on the reflective process shown below.

The Reflective Curriculum Planning Process

Note: Reprinted by permission from the California Department of Education, CDE Press, 1430 N Street, Sacramento, CA 95814.

Desired Results Assessment System

The California Department of Education (CDE) Early Education and Support Division (EESD) Desired Results (DR) system is designed to improve the quality of programs and services provided to all children, birth through 12 years of age, who are enrolled in early care and education programs and before-and after-school programs, and their families.

The Desired Results for Children and Families

DR1: Children are personally and socially competent

DR2: Children are effective learners

DR3: Children show physical and motor competence

DR4: Children are safe and healthy

DR5: Families support their child's learning and development

DR6: Families achieve their goals

The DR system implemented by the California Department of Education is a comprehensive approach that facilitates the achievement of the Desired Results identified for children and families. California is one of the very few states in the nation that has developed its own system designed specifically for measuring child progress toward desired outcomes. The system is aligned to both the state's learning and development foundations for early care and education programs and the content standards for kindergarten.

Components of the DR System

The DR system consists of the following components:

1. **Desired Results Developmental Profile© (2015) A Developmental Continuum from Early Infancy up to Kindergarten Entry**
   The DRDP© (2015) assessment instruments are designed for teachers to observe, document, and reflect on the learning, development, and progress of children, birth through 12 years of age, who are enrolled in early care and education programs and before- and after-school programs. The assessment results are intended to be used by the teacher to plan curriculum for indi-

---

Who Am I in the Lives of Children? provides an in-depth look at the role of early childhood education programs in facilitating children's learning and development. Based in constructivist theory, *Who Am I in the Lives of Children?* provides detailed information about child development as the foundation for early childhood education programs. The authors recognize that relationships are primary in meeting the developmental needs of children and that observation and assessment are necessary to provide developmentally appropriate programs. They explain the role of the classroom environments "to meet the needs of the children and support your educational values and developmental goals." *Who Am I in the Lives of Children?* also recognizes play as central to children's learning and development. The content of the curriculum and the curriculum planning in the California Curriculum Framework are consistent with the child-centered approach in *Who Am I in the Lives of Children?* The authors of your text and the California Curriculum Foundations emphasize the need to include all children and to develop partnerships with families. As you read *Who Am I in the Lives of Children?* and the California Curriculum Framework, you will find that both put children at the center.

Desired Results for Children and Families

1 Children are personally and socially competent.

2 Children are effective learners.

3 Children show physical and motor competence.

4 Children are safe and healthy.

5 Families support their child's learning and development.

6 Families achieve their goals.

Note: Reprinted by permission from the California Department of Education, CDE Press, 1430 N Street, Sacramento, CA 95814.

3. **Environment Rating Scales (ERS)**

The ERS are used to measure the quality of the program environment (e.g., child-teacher interactions, children's interactions and activities, use of language, health and safety practices, space, and materials). The ERS are required instruments for yearly program self-evaluation and used for the reviews conducted by CDE/EESD program staff.

4. **Program Self Evaluation**

The Program Self Evaluation addresses: family and community involvement; governance and administration; funding; standards, assessment, and accountability; staffing and professional growth; opportunity and equal educational access; and approaches to teaching and learning. Program quality is assessed annually through the required self-evaluation and the reviews conducted by CDE/EESD program staff.

Professional Development

The California Department of Education, Child Development Division recognizes that to ensure the implementation of its Learning and Development System it must address the professional development of those of you who are already working in the field and those of you considering a career in early care and education. The CDE/CDD has a variety of programs to support pre-service and in-service early childhood educators. Several programs are:

The **California Early Childhood Mentor Program**, also offered at community colleges throughout the state, provides stipends to selected teachers and directors who mentor early childhood education students in filed placements. The mentors are selected by local selection committees through a rigorous application process. When you are ready to enroll in your field experience course you may be able to work with a Mentor Teacher in your community. There are also Director Mentors available to work with directors throughout the community on request. http://www.ecementor.org/

California Preschool Instructional Network (CPIN) "provides high quality professional development for

vidual children and groups of children and to guide continuous program improvement.

2. **Desired Results Parent Survey**

The Parent Survey is designed to assist programs in gathering information from families about (1) the family members' satisfaction with their child's program and how it supports the child's learning and development; and (2) family members' perceptions of their progress toward reaching the two Desired Results identified for families. Families in the program are asked to complete the Parent Survey once a year and return it to their classroom. Families complete this survey anonymously to ensure that their opinions and concerns are kept confidential.

Who Am I in the Lives of Children? addresses program quality improvement throughout the text. The authors introduce the California Desired Results system in Chapter 5 – Observing and Assessing Young Children. You can deepen your understanding of California's assessment and accountability initiatives by considering the Desired Results for Children and Families as you explore the text. https://www.desiredresults.us Chapter 8 – The Learning Environment introduces you to environmental evaluation tools including the ECERS.

preschool administrators and teachers highlighting current research-based information, resources, and effective instructional practices which are focused on preparing children to flourish in early childhood and succeed in elementary school and beyond. CPIN is organized into 11 regions of the state that will disseminate information, training and resources to their particular region" (CPIN website).

The **Child Development Training Consortium** (CDTC) provides support to early childhood education and child development students in California colleges through tuition reimbursements or stipends, Child Development Permit application fees, and other services which vary campus to campus. These services focus on those of you currently employed in the child care and development field. http://childdevelopment.org

The **California Early Childhood Online** (CECO). CECO is an online learning portal. The CECO website explains, "To support early childhood teachers, the California Early Learning and Development System provides an integrated set of resources based on state-of-the-art information for early learning and development and best practices in early education." This site requires that you log in to create a student profile. It provides access to professional development. http://www.caearlychildhood online.org

Family Child Care at Its Best provides high-quality, university-based child development education to thousands of licensed family childcare providers throughout California. The program is funded by a contract from the state Department of Education, which enables the center to offer the courses free to participants who may otherwise be unable to afford them. http://humanservices.ucdavis.edu/ChildDev/Programs/FamilyChildCare.aspx?unit=CHLDEV

The **Program of Infant/Toddler Caregivers** (PITC), in collaboration with the California Department of Education offers Infant/Toddler Learning & Development Academies to provide an opportunity to learn about the California Department of Education's new learning and development system and how these resources can be used to support program quality and optimal child growth and development. http://www.pitc.org/pub/pitc_docs/home.csp

The **California School-Age Consortium (CalSAC)** supports the out-of-school time child care field with training, conferences, and projects specific to the needs of school-age children in child care. https://calsac.org

The **California Association for the Education of Young Children (CAEYC)** is the state affiliate of the National Association for the Education of Young Children, a professional membership organization that works to promote high-quality early learning for all young children, birth through age 8, by connecting early childhood practice, policy, and research. There are over 25 local affiliates of CAEYC throughout the state. https://caeyc.org

In both Chapter 1 – The Teacher and Chapter 14 – Becoming an Early Childhood Professional, *Who Am I in the Lives of Children?* emphasizes that early childhood education is a career with a code of ethical conduct and an obligation to ongoing professional development and participation in professional organizations. California provides many opportunities for you to increase your knowledge and skills and demonstrate your commitment to life-long learning.

Child Development Permit

The California Child Development Permits, currently issued in six levels, by the California Commission on Teacher Credentialing, authorizes individuals to work in child care and development programs. The six permits include:

- Associate Teacher Permit
- Assistant Teacher Permit
- Teacher Permit
- Master Teacher Permit
- Site Supervisor Permit
- Program Director Permit

The Child Development Permit is required for employees of child care and development programs funded through the California Department of Education, Child Development Division. The California Department of Social Services, Community Care Licensing (CDSS, CCL) accepts the Site Supervisor Permit and the Program Director Permit to qualify holders to be the Director of Title 22 licensed child care facilities. CDSS, CCL also accepts the Child Development Associate Teacher Permit, Child Development Teacher Permit, or Child Development Master Teacher Permit as verification of qualifications for a Teacher in a licensed facility.

In the 2014 Budget Act, the California Legislature issued a directive to the Commission on Teacher Credentialing to review the Child Development Permit Matrix. The matrix had not been reviewed or changed since 1994. A Child Development Permit Advisory Panel was convened with members selected from stakeholder groups throughout the state. After an intensive review and public comment period the panel has sent a proposal to the Commission on Teacher Credentialing for their consideration. The proposal suggests four permit levels (rather that the current six) including a 12 unit Associate, Associate Degree level Teacher, Bachelor Degree level Teacher Specialist, and a Post-Baccalaureate Degree Program Administrator. (The full report is available at this link: https://www.ctc.ca.gov/docs/default-source/commission/agendas/2017-02/2017-02-2a.pdf.)

The full commission has not adopted this proposal. If the proposal is adopted it will take time to fully develop and implement to new matrix. All current Child Development Permit holders will be "grandfathered" into the system and will be able to renew their permits as current regulations require.

Child Development Permit Matrix - *with Alternative Qualification Options Indicated*

Permit Title	Education Requirement (Option 1 for all permits)	Experience Requirement (Applies to Option 1 Only)	Alternative Qualifications (with option numbers indicated)	Authorization	Five Year Renewal
Assistant (Optional)	**Option 1:** 6 units of Early Childhood Education (ECE) or Child Development (CD)	None	**Option 2:** Accredited HERO program (including ROP)	Authorizes the holder to care for and assist in the development and instruction of children in a child care and development program under the supervision of an Associate Teacher, Teacher, Master Teacher, Site Supervisor of Program Director.	105 hours of professional growth*****
Associate Teacher	**Option 1:** 12 units ECE/CD including core courses**	50 days of 3+ hours per day within 2 years	**Option 2:** Child Development Associate (CDA) Credential	Authorizes the holder to provide service in the care, development, and instruction of children in a child care and development program, and supervise an Assistant and an aide.	Must complete 15 additional units toward a Teacher Permit. Must meet Teacher requirements within 10 years.
Teacher	**Option 1:** 24 units ECE/CD including core courses** plus 16 General Education (GE) units*	175 days of 3+ hours per day within 4 years	**Option 2:** AA or higher in ECE/CD or related field with 3 units supervised field experience in ECE/CD setting	Authorizes the holder to provide service in the care, development and instruction of children in a child care and development program, and supervise an Associate Teacher, Assistant and an aide.	105 hours of professional growth*****
Master Teacher	**Option 1:** 24 units ECE/CD including core courses** plus 16 GE units* plus 6 specializations units plus 2 adult supervision units	350 days of 3+ hours per day within 4 years	**Option 2:** BA or higher (does not have to be in ECE/CD) with 12 units of ECE/CD, plus 3 units supervised field experience in ECE/CD setting	Authorizes the holder to provide service in the care, development and instruction of children in a child care and development program, and supervise a Teacher, Associate Teacher, Assistant and aide. The permit also authorizes the holder to serve as a coordinator of curriculum and staff development.	105 hours of professional growth*****
Site Supervisor	**Option 1:** AA (or 60 units) which includes: • 24 ECE/CD units with core courses** plus 6 administration units plus 2 adult supervision units	350 days of 3+ hours per day within 4 years including at least 100 days of supervision adults	**Option 2:** BA or higher (does not have to be in ECE/CD) with 12 units of ECE/CD, plus 3 units supervised field experience in ECE/CD setting: **or** **Option 3:** Admin, credential*** with 12 units of ECE/CD, plus 3 units supervised field experience in ECE/CD setting; **or** **Option 4:** Teaching credential**** with 12 units of ECE/CD, plus 3 units supervised field experience in ECE/CD setting	Authorizes the holder to supervise a child care and development program operating at a single site; provide service in the care, development, and instruction of children in a child care and development program and serve as a coordinator of curriculum and staff development.	105 hours of professional growth*****
Program Director	**Option 1:** BA or higher (does not have to be in ECE/CD) including: • 24 ECE/CD units with core courses** plus 6 administration units plus 2 adult supervision units	One year of Site Supervisor experience	**Option 2:** Admin credential*** with 12 units of ECE/CD, plus 3 units supervised field experience in ECE/CD setting; **or** **Option 3:** Teaching credential**** with 12 units of ECE/CD, plus 3 units supervised field experience in ECE/CD setting, plus 6 units administration; **or** **Option 4:** Master's Degree in ECE/CD or Child/Human Development	Authorizes the holder to supervise a child care and development program operating in a single site or multiple sites; provide service in the care, development, and instruction of children in a child care and development program; and serve as coordinator of curriculum and staff development.	105 hours of professional growth*****

Note: All unit requirements listed above are semester units. All course work must be completed with a grade of C or better from a regionally accredited college. Spanish translation is available.

* One course in each of four general education categories, which are degree applicable. English/Language Arts; Math or Science; Social Sciences; Humanities and/or Fine Arts.

** Core courses include child/human growth & development, child/family/community or child and family relations; and programs/curriculum. You must have a minimum of three semester units or four quarter units in each of the core areas.

*** Holders of the Administrative Services Credential may serve as a Site Supervisor or Program Director.

**** A valid Multiple Subject or a Single Subject in Home Economics.

***** Professional growth hours must be completed under the guidance of a Professional Growth Advisor. Call (209) 572-6080 for assistance in locating an advisor.

This matrix was prepared by the Child Development Training Consortium. To obtain a permit application visit our website at www.childdevelopment.org or call (209) 572-6080.

You might want to look over the Child Development Permit matrix as you read, "Specialized Knowledge and Skills" and "Finding Your Path - Educational Requirements" in Chapter 1 – The Teacher and "Becoming a Professional" in Chapter 14. The following websites will be useful:

Child Development Training Consortium (click on Child Development Permit Matrix - right side of the page)
https://www.childdevelopment.org/cs/cdtc/print/htdocs/services_permit.htm
California Commission on Teacher Credentialing
https://www.ctc.ca.gov/credentials/req-child-dev

California Early Childhood Educator Competencies

The California Department of Education, Child Development Division, in collaboration with First 5 California developed and released the California Early Childhood Educators Competencies in 2011. This document supports the belief of the authors of *Who Am I in the Lives of Children*? In the introduction of the competencies, the authors state, "Early childhood educators who work directly with young children are doing the most important work of their profession. The early childhood education field's strength stems from the many professionals who dedicate their life's work to directly serving young children and their families."

The purpose of the Early Childhood Educator Competencies is explained as follows:

> *The ECE competencies serve several interrelated purposes. First, they provide coherent structure and content for efforts to foster the professional development of California's early childhood workforce. Second, they inform the course of study that early childhood educators follow as they pursue study in institutions of higher education. Third, they provide guidance in the definition of ECE credentials and certifications. And fourth, they give comprehensive descriptions of the knowledge, skills, and dispositions that early childhood educators need to support young children's learning and development across program types.*

The CA ECE Competencies identify 12 competency or performance areas including:

- Child Development and Learning
- Culture, Diversity, and Equity
- Relationships, Interactions, and Guidance
- Family and Community Engagement
- Dual-Language Development
- Observations, Screening, Assessment, and Documentation
- Special Needs and Inclusion
- Learning Environments and Curriculum
- Health, Safety, and Nutrition
- Leadership in Early Childhood Education
- Professionalism
- Administration and Supervision

In 2017, the California Department of Education, Early Learning and Support Division began work to add competencies related to Adult Learning and Coaching into the Professionalism competency.

There are differing levels of competencies depending on the context in which an early childhood educator works. Although where an educator falls on this context rubric may vary, one can assume that the first context would encompass an aide or teacher in a classroom, the second context, a lead or mentor teacher, the third, a site or program director, and the fourth, an agency director, child advocate, community professional trainer, or college/university faculty. All of the competencies build on the base knowledge, skills, and dispositions of the context before them.

Supporting Early Learning and Development

An early childhood educator who supports early learning and development experiences possesses and applies fundamental knowledge, usually in the immediate context of the group or classroom.

Planning and Guiding Early Learning and Development

An early childhood educator who plans and guides early learning and development experiences possesses and applies broad knowledge, usually in the immediate context of the group or classroom.

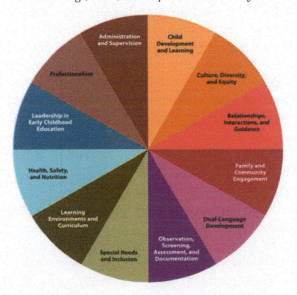

Note: Reprinted by permission from the California Department of Education, CDE Press, 1430 N Street, Sacramento, CA 95814.

Creating and Maintaining Program Policies and Practices

An early childhood educator who creates and maintains program policies and practices possesses and applies deep knowledge, usually in the broad context of a program or site, and supervises program staff.

Advancing the Early Childhood Profession

An early childhood educator who advances the early childhood profession models data-informed decision making that often has an impact on policy and practice across programs, or in the early care and education field. http://www.cde.ca.gov/sp/cd/re/documents/ececompetencies2011.pdf

Competencies Self-Assessment Toolkit (CompSAT)

CompSAT is *the* companion to the CA ECE Competencies. CompSAT guides early educators through a process of self-reflection and authentic assessment in the 12 competency areas detailed in the ECE Competencies. This tool allows you to engage in reflection and authentic self-assessment as part of the fabric of your daily practice with children and families, thus enriching and enhancing your work.

CompSAT offers you guidance and support through 12 modules, each one named for one of the CA ECE Competencies. The modules address many of the issues and challenges that come with providing high quality early care and education. http://www.ececompsat.org/about.html

---

Chapter 14 – Becoming an Early Childhood Professional in *Who Am I in the Lives of Children?* identifies nine areas of knowledge and skills which are included in standards for professional development. California has identified 12 competencies. California includes separate competencies for dual-language learners and children with special needs. The California Competencies also include Leadership in ECE and Administration and Supervision. Both the authors of your text and the California system recognize the wide range of knowledge and skills required to provide high-quality care to children and their families. Like the CompSAT, *Who Am I in the Lives of Children?* encourages you to reflect on your knowledge and skills and how to strengthen them.

Quality Rating and Improvement System (QRIS)

Throughout the country, states have developed Quality Rating and Improvement Systems and are using these to both rate the quality of child care and development programs and to identify areas which could be developed to enhance the experience for young children and their families. "The California QRIS (CA-QRIS) Consortium strives to improve the quality of early learning with a focus in three areas of program quality: child development and readiness for school; teachers and teaching; and program and environment quality." http://www.cde.ca.gov/sp/cd/rt/californiaqris.asp

Unlike other states, California has a collective of county and regional QRISs. The entire state includes some common tiers but each county or region may include tiers specific to their region of the state.

Each QRIS in California must:

- Assess program quality comparably across provider types (publicly and privately funded centers and family child care homes) throughout the state;
- Align program standards with early learning and practitioner standards;
- Support continuous quality improvement for participating programs and their staff; and
- Provide families with information about program quality to assist them in making informed choices.

Understanding the California Quality Rating and Improvement System will enhance your understanding of the section in Chapter 2 of the text regarding national Quality Rating and Improvement Systems as required by the Childcare and Development Block Grants.

Program Guidelines and Resources
Preschool Program Guidelines

In 2015, the California Department of Education, Child Development Division published the *Preschool Program Guidelines*. The guidelines were developed to update information included in the *Prekindergarten Learning and Development Guidelines* published in 2000. The guidelines are designed for those responsible for preschool program planning. These will include a DVD to deepen the understanding of administrators and other program planners. The guidelines include three parts. http://www.cde.ca.gov/sp/cd/re/documents/preschoolproggdlns2015.pdf

PART ONE: Setting the Stage for Program Quality
Chapter 1 **Current Issues in Early Childhood Education**
- Evidence from Research
- Need for High-Quality Preschool Programs
- Early Childhood Investments and Societal Impacts
- Recent Research on Brain Development
- School Readiness
- The California Context

California Quality Rating and Improvement System (CA-QRIS) Quality Continuum Framework -Rating Matrix with Elements and Points for Consortia Common Tiers 1, 3, and 4

Element	1 Point	2 Points	3 Points	4 Points	5 Points
CORE I: CHILD DEVELOPMENT AND SCHOOL READINESS					
1. Child Observation	• Not required	• Program uses evidence-based child assessment/observation tool annually that covers all five domains of development	• Program uses valid and reliable child assessment/ observation tool aligned with CA *Foundations & Frameworks*[1] twice a year	• DRDP (minimum twice a year) and results used to inform curriculum planning	• Program uses DRDP twice a year and uploads into DRDP Tech and results used to inform curriculum planning
2. Developmental and Health Screenings	• Meets Title 22 Regulations	• Health Screening Form (Community Care *Licensing form LIC 701 "Physician's Report -Child Care Centers" or equivalent*) used at entry, then: 1. Annually OR 2. Ensures vision and hearing screenings are conducted annually	• Program works with families to ensure screening of all children using a valid and reliable developmental screening tool at entry and as indicated by results thereafter AND • Meets Criteria from point level 2	• Program works with families to ensure screening of all children using the **ASQ** at entry and as indicated by results thereafter AND • Meets Criteria from point level 2	• Program works with families to ensure screening of all children using the **ASQ & ASQ-SE**, if indicated, at entry, then as indicated by results thereafter AND • Program staff uses children's screening results to make referrals and implement intervention strategies and adaptations as appropriate AND • Meets Criteria from point level 2
CORE II: TEACHERS AND TEACHING					
3. Minimum Qualifications for Lead Teacher/ Family Child Care Home (FCCH)	• Meets Title 22 Regulations [**Center:** 12 units of Early Childhood Education (ECE)/Child Development (CD) **FccH:** 15 hours of training on preventive health practices]	• **Center:** 24 units of ECE/CD[2] OR Associate Teacher Permit **FCCH:** 12 units of ECE/CD OR Associate Teacher Permit	• 24 units of ECE/CD + 16 units of General Education[2] OR Teacher Permit AND • 21 hours professional development (PD) annually	• Associate's degree (AA/AS) in ECE/CD (or closely related field) OR AA/AS in any field plus 24 units of ECE/CD OR Site Supervisor Permit AND • 21 hours PD annually	• Bachelor's degree in ECE/CD (or closely related field) OR BA/BS in any field plus/with 24 units of ECE/CD (or master's degree in ECE/CD) OR Program Director Permit AND • 21 hours PD annually
4. Effective Teacher-Child Interactions: CLASS Assessments (*use tool for appropriate age group as available)	• Not Required	• Familiarity with CLASS for appropriate age group as available by one representative from the site	• Independent CLASS assessment by reliable observer to inform the program's professional development/improvement plan	• Independent CLASS assessment by reliable observer with minimum CLASS scores: **Pre-K** • Emotional Support - 5 • Instructional Support - 3 • Classroom Organization - 5 **Toddler** • Emotional [[amp]] Behavioral Support - 5 • Engaged Support for Learning - 3.5 **Infant** • Responsive Caregiving (RC) - 5.0	• Independent assessment with CLASS with minimum CLASS scores: **Pre-K** • Emotional Support - 5.5 • Instructional Support - 3.5 • Classroom Organization - 5.5 **Toddler** • Emotional & Behavioral Support - 5.5 • Engaged Support for Learning - 4 **Infant** • Responsive Caregiving (RC) - 5.5

[1] Approved assessments are: Creative Curriculum GOLD, Early Learning Scale by National Institute of Early Education Research (NIEER), and Brigance Inventory of Early Development III.

[2] For all ECE/CD units, the core eight are desired but not required.

Note: Point values are not indicative of Tiers 1–5 but reflect a range of points that can be earned toward assigning a tier rating (see Total Point Range).

CORE III: PROGRAM AND ENVIRONMENT - Administration and Leadership

Element	1 Point	2 Points	3 Points	4 Points	5 Points
5. Ratios and Group Size (Centers Only beyond licensing regulations)	**Center:** Title 22 Regulations **Infant** Ratio of 1:4 **Toddler Option** Ratio of 1:6 **Preschool** Ratio of 1:12 **FCCH:** Title 22 Regulations (excluded from point values in ratio and group size)	**Center - Ratio: Group Size** **Infant/Toddler** - 4:16 **Toddler** - 3:18 **Preschool** - 3:36	**Center - Ratio: Group Size** **Infant/Toddler** - 3:12 **Toddler** - 2:12 **Preschool** - 2:24	**Center - Ratio: Group Size** **Infant/Toddler** - 3:12 or 2:8 **Toddler** - 2:10 **Preschool** - 3:24 or 2:20	**Center - Ratio: Group Size** **Infant/Toddler** - 3:9 or better **Toddler** - 3:12 or better **Preschool** - 1:8 ratio and group size of no more than 20
6. Program Environment Rating Scale(s) (Use tool for appropriate setting: ECERS-R, ITERS-R, FCCERS-R)	Not Required	Familiarity with ERS and every classroom uses ERS as a part of a Quality Improvement Plan	Assessment on the whole tool. Results used to inform the program's Quality Improvement Plan	Independent ERS assessment. All subscales completed and averaged to meet overall score level of 5.0	Independent ERS assessment. All subscales completed and averaged to meet overall score level of 5.5 OR Current National Accreditation approved by the California Department of Education
7. Director Qualifications (Centers Only)	12 units ECE/CD + 3 units management/administration	24 units ECE/CD + 16 units General Education +/with 3 units management/administration **OR** Master Teacher Permit	Associate's degree with 24 units ECE/CD +/with 6 units management/administration and 2 units supervision **OR** Site Supervisor Permit **AND** 21 hours PD annually	Bachelor's degree with 24 units ECE/CD +/with 8 units management/administration **OR** Program Director Permit **AND** 21 hours PD annually	Master's degree with 30 units ECE/CD including specialized courses +/with 8 units management/administration, **OR** Administrative Credential **AND** 21 hours PD annually

TOTAL POINT RANGES

Program Type	Common-Tier 1	Local-Tier 2[3]	Common-Tier 3	Common-Tier 4	Local-Tier 5[4]
Centers 7 Elements for 35 points	**Blocked** (7 points) - Must Meet All Elements	**Point Range** 8 to 19	**Point Range** 20 to 25	**Point Range** 26 to 31	**Point Range** 32 and above
FCCHs 5 Elements for 25 points	**Blocked** (5 points) - Must Meet All Elements	**Point Range** 6 to 13	**Point Range** 14 to 17	**Point Range** 18 to 21	**Point Range** 22 and above

[3] Local-Tier 2: Local decision if Blocked or Points and if there are additional elements.

[4] Local-Tier 5: Local decision if there are additional elements included California Department of Education, February 2014 updated on May 28, 2015; effective July 1, 2015.

This document is designed for program administrators who will look at the topics through a different lens from that of a classroom teacher. The topics, like those covered in the California Learning and Development Foundations and the Curriculum Framework, are addressed throughout *Who Am I in the Lives of Children?*

Infant/Toddler Learning and Development Program Guidelines

"This publication, *Infant/Toddler Learning and Development Program Guidelines*, presents information about how to provide high-quality early care and education, including recommendations for program policies and day-to-day practices that will improve program services to all infants and toddlers (children from birth to 36 months of age). It contains vitally important information about early learning and development. With this publication, the California Department of Education intends to provide a starting point for strengthening all programs that educate and care for infants and toddlers, including centers, family child care homes, and kith and kin care. The guidelines specifically address the concerns of program leaders, teachers, and family members. They also inform community organizations, policymakers, business leaders, and others interested in improving the care and education of California's youngest children.

The guidelines pay particular attention to the role of the family in early care and education, to the inclusion of children with disabilities or other special needs, and to collaboration between programs and families. Because high-quality programming cannot be attained without attention to these topics in all components of care, the topics are woven throughout the publication rather than treated separately. In addition, family child care and care by relatives are included in the main body of the guidelines and, when necessary for clarity, are addressed individually (I/TLDG, p. 2).

> *Who Am I in the Lives of Children?* identifies the specific needs of infants and toddler throughout the text.

The Integrated Nature of Learning

Although California divided the learning foundations and curriculum frameworks into domains (nine for preschool and four for infants and toddlers) the Early Education and Support Division recognizes that children's learning is integrated. *The Integrated Nature of Learning* focuses on this integration.

"The aim of this publication is to:

- explore what it means to teach when working with children birth to five, using current research evidence as the starting point;
- apply this understanding to a broad definition of *curriculum* that includes the learning that occurs within play, within the daily routines, and within conversations and interactions;
- provide examples of how teachers observe, document, and interpret children's play and interactions in order to plan and implement curriculum, to assess learning, and to engage children and families as partners in planning the learning experiences." (http://www.cde.ca.gov/sp/cd/re/documents/intnatureoflearning2016.pdf)

The document addresses the following topics:

Play, Learning, and Curriculum: How They Fit Together
- How Young Children Learn: What Science Reveals
- Play as a Context for Building Knowledge
- Integrated Curriculum

- Learning Occurs in Relationships
- How Teachers Support Children's Active Meaning-Making

Early Childhood Curriculum: A Broad Definition
- Curriculum Occurs Throughout the Day
- Play Spaces as Curriculum
- Daily Routines as Curriculum
- Interaction and Conversation as Curriculum
- Contexts for Written Plans

Reflective Planning
- A Cycle of Observing, Documenting, and Interpreting
- Observe and Reflect
- Document to Hold in Memory
- Interpret the Documentation

Curriculum That Reflects Children's Lives
- Dynamic
- Co-Constructed
- Responsive

Assessment
- Documentation as Ongoing Interpretation of Learning
- Documentation and Periodic Standardized Assessment

> The California document, *The Integrated Nature of Learning*, is consistent with Chapter 9 – Understanding and Supporting Play, Chapter 10 – Curriculum, and Chapter 11 - Curriculum Planning in the text. The authors of *Who Am I in the Lives of Children?* agree on the importance of play, of curriculum based on observation of children, and reflective practice by classroom teachers.

Family Partnerships and Culture

California is one of the most diverse states in our country (second only to Hawaii). While this diversity gives California its richness, it also makes it imperative that early education programs and families work together to provide children the most developmentally appropriate experience. California produced *Family Partnerships and Culture* because, "it is important for program staff to learn to collaborate effectively with families. To develop a partnership and to tap into the family as a primary resource, teachers and program staff must reach out to families, learn about, and develop strong partnerships with them. This process requires openness to learning and an effort to understand the individuality of each family and the diversity of the families from which the children come. Culturally competent practices are essential in the early learning setting or environment in order to form authentic partnerships with families that promote children's development. Specific knowledge of the child's cultural or multicultural background and life at home can be the key to effective teaching and learning." http://www.cde.ca.gov/sp/cd/re/documents/familyp-artnerships.pdf

This publication aims to assist early childhood professionals in the development of cultural competence in working with children and families from diverse cultural backgrounds, specifically to:

- value families and their contribution to children's learning
- approach cultural diversity with an open mind
- apply knowledge gained about families, including their values and beliefs, to teaching and learning

Guiding Principles for Developing Cultural Competence
- Cognitive Cultural Competence
- Affective Cultural Competence
- Cultural Responsiveness
- NAEYC Cultural Competence Project

Understanding Culture
- Definition of Culture
- Why an Understanding of Culture Is Important
- Distinguishing Between Ethnicity and Culture
- Learning About Cultures
- Exploring Dimensions of Culture
- Collectivist versus Individualist Cultures
- Myths About Cultures
- Support Development of the Home Language

Understanding Contemporary Families and Households
- Family Composition
- Culturally Based Family Strengths
- Family Strains

Culture, Family Life, and the Early Childhood Curricula
- Implications of Culture and Family
- Curriculum Frameworks

Who Am I in the Lives of Children? shares a belief with California's *Family Relationships and Culture* "that family members play a crucial role in young children's lives and are children's first and most important teachers." This document will heighten your understanding of program-family partnerships. Concepts of family collaboration and respect for home culture are infused throughout the text and are emphasized in Chapter 13 – Partnerships with Families.

California Preschool English Learners: A Resource Guide, 2nd ed.

"This guide is designed to help the reader understand the preschool English learner more fully. Each chapter provides important information about the development, abilities, and everyday experiences of the preschool English learner that is based on current and rigorously conducted research. The preschool English learner is (1) a child whose first language is other than English and as a result is learning English as a second language; or (2) a child who is developing two or more languages, one of which may be English. During the preschool years from birth through five years of age, most children are still acquiring the basic knowledge of their home language, even when that language is English. The purpose of this guide is to enrich the reader's understanding of the language and literacy development of young English learners" (PEL, 2nd ed., p. 2).

California's Best Practices for Young Dual Language Learners: Research Overview Papers

California's State Advisory Committee on Early Learning and Care released research overviews of topics specific to the unique needs of young dual-language learners in the state. These papers cover:

- Neuroscience Research: How Experience with One or More Languages Affects the Developing Brain
- Cognitive Consequences of Dual Language Learning: Cognitive Function, Language and Literacy, Science and Mathematics, and Social-Emotional Development
- Program Elements and Teaching Practices to Support Young Dual Language Learners
- Family Engagement in Early Childhood Programs: Serving Families of Dual Language Learners
- Assessment of Young Dual Language Learners in Preschool
- Early Intervention and Young Dual Language Learners with Special Needs

---

Who Am I in the Lives of Children? is an introduction to the Early Childhood Education field and does not cover English Language Learners in depth. It is sensitive to the needs of children and families developing their English skills and adapting to American culture. Topics related to serving dual language learners are covered in Chapter 1: The Teacher – Attitudes Towards Diversity, Chapter 10: The Curriculum – Language Curriculum, and Chapter12: Including All Children – Dual Language Learners.

Inclusion Works!

"The purpose of (Inclusion Works!) is to help child care providers learn strategies that promote inclusion of and a sense of belonging for all children.

Child care providers who are not accustomed to enrolling children with disabilities or other special needs into their programs will be reassured by the following considerations:

- Child care providers can successfully include children with disabilities or other special needs in the program while promoting belonging for all children.
- Major modifications to their program or facility probably will not be needed in order to include children with disabilities or other special needs.
- Assistance and support for more significant changes in their program or facility may be available.
- An inclusive child care program is rewarding for all the children, families, and staff in child care programs" (Inclusion Works, p. viii).

> Chapter 12 in *Who Am I in the Lives of Children?* provides a rich discussion of working with children with special needs. It addresses legal requirements for serving children with special needs (including IEPs and IFSPs), program types, identification, inclusion, characteristics of young children with specific disabilities, and it includes a section on working with families.

California Child Care Disaster Plan 2016

In cooperation with the University of California–San Francisco, the California State Department of Education published The California Child Care Disaster Plan. This document provides information and resources to support child care providers, children in their care, and their families before, during, and after an emergency or disaster. http://cchp.ucsf.edu/sites/cchp.ucsf.edu/files/CA-ChildCare-Disaster-Plan.pdf

> Chapter 7 – Health, Safety, and Well-Being in *Who Am I in the Lives of Children?* includes a reference to "Preparing for Emergencies." The California Child Care Disaster Plan 2016 supports and enhances that information.

All About Young Children

This is a series of videos created to provide families information on children's early development. It is available in eight languages. "As a parent, you are your child's first teacher. You have experienced how fascinating and how puzzling your young child can sometimes be. We invite you to explore with us information that can help you understand your child's learning and discover new ways to support your growing child." http://allaboutyoungchildren.org

> As you read Chapter 13 – Partnerships with Families in *Who Am I in the Lives of Children?* you will see how the information provided in the All About Young Children web pages will help parents understand their children and the work that you do in an early childhood education program.

The Alignment of the California Preschool Learning Foundations with Key Early Education Resources: *the California Infant/Toddler Learning and Development Foundations, California Content Standards, Common Core State Standards, and Head Start Child Development and Early Learning Framework*

"This online publication presents the developmental continuum of learning for children from birth through kindergarten. It shows the connections that the nine domains of the preschool learning foundations have with the content of these other important resources. This alignment demonstrates that early learning is a significant part of the educational system and that the knowledge and skills of young children are foundational to future learning" (Alignment p. 6).

> This information will deepen your understanding of the section on "Educational Standards" in Chapter 2 of *Who Am I in the Lives of Children?*

California Community College Curriculum Alignment Project

"The California Community Colleges Curriculum Alignment Project has engaged faculty from across the state to develop a lower-division program of study supporting early care and education teacher preparation. The Lower Division 8 represents evidence-based courses that are intended to become a foundational core for all early care and education professionals." http://www.childdevelopment.org/cs/cdtc/print/htdocs/services_cap.htm

This textbook aligns most closely with the Principles and Practices course. The matrix below shows you how the course student learning outcomes are addressed in *Who Am I in the Lives of Children?*, 11th ed.

Principles and Practices of Teaching Young Children

Course Descriptor: Historical context and theoretical perspectives of developmentally appropriate practice in early care and education. Examines the role of the early childhood educator, identification of best practices for environmental design, curriculum, and teaching strategies. Explores teacher–child relationships, professional ethics, career pathways, and professional standards.

Student Learning Outcomes	Where This Material Appears in *Who Am I in the Lives of Children?* 11th ed.
1. Compare and contrast historical and current early childhood education perspectives, theories, and program types and philosophies.	**Chapter 1: The Teacher** **Chapter 2: The Field of Early Childhood Education** **Chapter 3: History and Educational Models** **Chapter 4: Child Development**
2. Describe the role of the early childhood educator, including ethical conduct and professional pathways.	**Chapter 1: The Teacher** **Chapter 5: Observation and Assessment** **Chapter 6: Relationships and Guidance** **Chapter 14: Becoming an Early Childhood Professional** **Appendix A: NAEYC Code of Ethics**
3. Identify quality in early childhood programs related to environment, curriculum, and teaching strategies.	**Chapter 7: Health, Safety, and Well-Being** **Chapter 8: The Learning Environment** **Chapter 9: Understanding and Supporting Play** **Chapter 10: The Curriculum** **Chapter 11: Curriculum Planning** **Chapter 12: Including All Children** **Chapter 13: Partnerships with Families**

Features of this Book

New Contextualized Video Links

Classroom videos and videos of teachers help you to understand what it is like to teach young children and make practical connections between what you are reading and what teaching is really like. Try answering the question(s) that accompany these videos to deepen your understanding.

Video Example 9.1: Solitary Play

Watch the video to see an infant engaged in solitary play. What do you think was engaging to the baby about this play? What skills and concepts might he be developing?

New Comprehension Checks and Application Opportunities

A Quick Check

Click on A Quick Check to check your understanding of the major chapter section you've just read.

 A Quick Check 9.1
Gauge your understanding of the concepts in this section.

 Application Exercise 3.2 Final Reflection

Final Reflection

Respond to a question about chapter content with a short answer at the end of the chapter. This involves reflection and application.

Learning Outcomes

We had a purpose and specific learning outcomes in mind as we wrote each chapter of this book. Review this list to make sure that you are able to demonstrate the knowledge and skills that the items cover. Each outcome aligns with a major section of the chapter, and serves as a useful review of chapter content.

Chapter Learning Outcomes:

1.1 Explain the context in which early childhood education occurs and the most important tasks that characterize the work of the early childhood educator.

1.2 Discuss the importance of teachers' personal attributes, both those that are inborn and those that are learned from culture, family, and community.

1.3 Demonstrate understanding of what it means to be a professional with emphasis on the role of morality and ethics.

1.4 Describe educational pathways that are appropriate to a variety of career goals and identify some that you think might be appropriate for you.

Reflection Margin Notes

There are two types of reflection notes in the chapters of this book. These margin notes pose questions for you to think, write, and talk about.

"Reflect on . . . " Notes

These questions are intended to help you engage with what you are learning. Thinking and reflecting is a cornerstone of the learning process. Discussing and writing about these topics is a good way to focus your learning and clarify your thinking.

> **Reflect On**
> **Your Interest in Child Development**
> How did your interest in young children begin? What did you first notice about them? What interested you then? What intrigues you now about young children?

"Ethical Reflection" Notes

Early childhood educators often encounter ethical issues in their work. An overview of professional ethics and discussion of ethical dilemmas that teachers of young children might experience can be found in Chapter 1, "The Teacher." These notes describe ethical dilemmas and ask you to think about the conflicting responsibilities in each situation and to reflect on what the "good early childhood educator" might do to resolve it using guidance from the NAEYC Code of Ethical Conduct.

> **Reflect On**
> **Your Ethical Responsibilities and Confidentiality**
> A mother of a child in your class asks you to share how a relative's child (also in your class) is doing in school. She shares that she is concerned about this child's development. You've been worried about the child, too. Using the "Guidelines for Ethical Reflection" box in Chapter 1, reflect on your ethical responsibilities in this situation and think about an ethical response that you might make.

Related NAEYC Professional Preparation Standards

We show which professional standards apply to the chapter in this brief section.

> **The NAEYC Professional Preparation Standards**
> The NAEYC Professional Preparation Standard that applies to this chapter:
> Standard 6: Becoming a Professional (NAEYC, 2009).
>   Key element:
>   6a: Identifying and involving oneself with the early childhood field

> **Golden Rules**
> **for Interviewing a Child for Assessment**
> 1. Don't interrupt a child who is actively involved with friends or play activities; instead, invite the child to join you during an interlude after play.
> 2. Choose a quiet corner for the interview where you can sit at the child's level.
> 3. Plan a few questions in advance and relate them to your objectives for children—remember, you want to know what children understand and can do, not whether they liked an activity or the way you teach.
> 4. Use open-ended questions that have many possible answers to avoid the child feeling there is a "right" answer. Start with phrases like "Tell me about . . . " and "What do you think . . . ?"
> 5. Use language that is easy for the child to understand.
> 6. If the child doesn't answer a question, try rephrasing the question and asking it again.
> 7. Use the child's answers and interests to guide the interview.
> 8. Record children's behavior as well as their words.

Golden Rules

"Golden Rules" boxes contain important principles and practices for teaching, summarized and presented in a clear and useful format.

Connecting with Families

Another feature is guidelines or strategies contained in boxes that we call "Connecting with Families." These give you practical ideas for ways to include families in your program.

> **Connecting with Families**
> **On Assessment**
> Families have an important role in assessment. They are not merely "the audience" to whom you present a portfolio. They have valuable contributions to make. Invite families to participate in tangible ways. Have incoming families tell the child's story, describe what the child was like last year, and share who the child is in the family today. You might want to design a questionnaire for incoming families to complete to include in a portfolio.

> **Document Your Skill & Knowledge About the Learning Environment in Your Professional Portfolio**
> Include some or all of the following:
> - An evaluation of an existing early childhood environment using the Learning Environment Checklist in Appendix B. Include a short written analysis of the strengths of the environment as well as how you might change or modify it to better support children's development.
> - A photograph of a classroom, playscape, or learning center you have created with a brief description of why you designed it in this way.

Starting Your Professional Portfolio

Today, professionals in many fields create portfolios in which they document for employers and themselves their qualifications, skills, experiences, and unique qualities. Portfolios are "living documents" that will change as you grow, learn, and have new experiences.

End-of-Chapter Features

- **Final Reflection:** This is an interactive writing opportunity in the Pearson eText that permits you to demonstrate reflection and write about topics when prompted in this pop-up exercise with suggested feedback.

- **Demonstrate Your Understanding:** This section suggests activities and projects to help you learn more about the chapter's content—all organized by learning outcomes. In addition, the Final Check hyperlink is a pop-up multiple-choice quiz (in the Pearson eText) with feedback, designed to help you check your own learning.

- **Document Your Knowledge and Competence:** This section suggests items that you might wish to put in your professional portfolio. Today, professionals in many fields create portfolios in which they document for employers and themselves their qualifications, skills, experiences, and unique qualities.

Portfolios are "living documents" that will change as you grow, learn, and have new experiences. Guidelines for starting a portfolio can be found in Chapter 1.

- **To Learn More:** This section lists books and websites that might be of interest if you want to follow up on what you have learned.

- **Shared Writing:** At the end of each chapter is a shared writing exercise intended to give you an opportunity to share your thoughts on some aspect of the chapter with your classmates and instructor.

At the back of the book you will find a Bibliography, which lists the books and articles that we consulted as we wrote each chapter. We hope you will have the opportunity to read some of these references as you develop into a committed early childhood educator.

 Application Exercise 3.2 Final Reflection

 To Learn More

Read

Absorbent Mind, M. Montessori (1967)
Experimenting with the World: John Dewey and the Early Childhood Classroom, H. K. Cuffaro (1995)
Giants in the Nursery: A Biographical History of Developmentally Appropriate Practice, D. Elkind (2015)
Hidden History of Early Childhood Education, B. Hinitz (2013)
Hundred Languages of Children, C. Edwards, L. Gandini, & G. Forman (1998)

Visit a Website

The following agencies and organizations have websites related to the history of early childhood:

Froebel Foundation USA

Rachel McMillan Nursery School

The Association for Experiential Education: Progressive Education in the United States

High/Scope Educational Research Foundation

Bank Street College of Education

Why Waldorf Works (website of the Association of Waldorf Schools of North America)

American Montessori Society

Association Montessori Internationale

North American Reggio Emilia Alliance

Document Your Skill & Knowledge About the History of ECE in Your Professional Portfolio

Include some or all of the following:

Explore an Educational Approach

- Read about one of the educational approaches discussed in this chapter (High/Scope, DIA, Waldorf, Montessori, Reggio Emilia). Describe what you see as the major features of the program. Analyze how what you read reflects the history of early childhood education described in the chapter. Include your thoughts and reactions to what you learned and the implications for you as an early childhood educator.

Read and Review a Book

- Read a book about one of the historical figures or European educational approaches discussed in this chapter. Write a review of the book that includes your thoughts about what you learned, how it helped you understand themes in the history of early childhood education, and implications for you as an early childhood educator.

 Shared Writing 3.1 History of Early Childhood Education

Supplements to this Text

The supplements package for the tenth edition is revised and upgraded. All online ancillaries are available for download by adopting professors via pearsonhighered.com in the Instructor's Resource Center. Contact your Pearson sales representative for additional information.

Instructor's Resource Manual This manual contains chapter overviews and activity ideas for both in and out of class.

Online Test Bank The Test Bank includes a variety of test items, including multiple choice, true/false, and short essay, and is available in Word.

TestGen Computerized Test Bank TestGen is a powerful assessment generation program available exclusively from Pearson that helps instructors easily create quizzes and exams. You install TestGen on your personal computer (Windows or Macintosh) and create your own exams for print or online use. The items are the same as those in the Test Bank. The tests can be downloaded in a variety of learning management system formats.

Online PowerPoint Slides PowerPoint slides highlight key concepts and strategies in each chapter and enhance lectures and discussions.

Brief Contents

Contents

Special Features

Chapter 1
The Teacher

SOURCE: Jeff Reese

We teach who we are.

JOHN GARDNER

⌄ Chapter Learning Outcomes:

1.1 Explain the context in which early childhood education occurs and the most important tasks that characterize the work of the early childhood educator.

1.2 Discuss the importance of teachers' personal attributes, both those that are inborn and those that are learned from culture, family, and community.

1.3 Demonstrate understanding of what it means to be a professional with emphasis on the role of morality and ethics.

1.4 Describe educational pathways that are appropriate to a variety of career goals and identify some that you think might be appropriate for you.

NAEYC Professional Preparation Standards

The National Association for the Education of Young Children (NAEYC) Professional Preparation Standard that applies to this chapter:

Standard 6: Becoming a Professional (NAEYC, 2011).

Key elements:

6a: Identifying and involving oneself with the early childhood field

6b: Knowing about and upholding ethical standards and other professional guidelines

6c: Engaging in continuous, collaborative learning to inform practice

6d: Integrating knowledgeable, reflective, and critical perspectives on early education

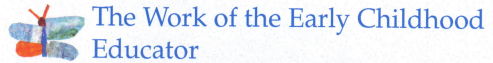

The Work of the Early Childhood Educator

Welcome to the field of early childhood education! You are embarking on the important career of educating and caring for young children. The kind of person you are and the kind of professional you become will have a lasting impact on children, families, and society. The purpose of this book is to help you become an educator who can nurture the growth of children, support families, work amicably with colleagues, advocate for children and families, and, in the future, make your own distinctive contributions to early childhood education.

This first chapter will introduce you to the field of early childhood education and the work of a teacher of young children. Before you learn what and how to teach, it is helpful to have some understanding of the teacher's role and responsibilities and the different kinds of teaching positions that are available to you.

In the process of learning more about yourself and about the field of early childhood education, you will acquire the knowledge, skills, and attitudes that will help you to grow into a dedicated early childhood educator who can provide nurturing experiences that support the learning and development of young children.

The Context

Because words create an image of who we are and what we do, what we call things is important. So we begin this first chapter with some basic definitions regarding who we serve and what we call the field and the people who work in it. **Early childhood** is generally defined as the period in the life span that includes birth through age 8. The field is generally referred to as "early childhood education," "early childhood education and care," or "early care and education" to emphasize the dual focus on learning and care that distinguishes early childhood programs and educators from other educators and schools.

In this book, we use the term **early childhood education (ECE)** to refer to education and care provided in all settings for children between birth and age 8. We use this term because education is a core function of the early childhood educator's work and because it brings our field into alignment with other arenas of education (elementary, secondary, and postsecondary) while suggesting the uniqueness of our field's focus on young children. Additionally, the role of education is the one most valued in our society. When programs are viewed as providing education, they are seen as worthy of respect, and the children who participate in them are viewed as learners. This term suggests that those who implement early childhood education support development and help children learn in the context of caring relationships.

Early childhood educators provide education and care for young children in a number of different kinds of settings with the goal of promoting positive development and learning, These programs are found in diverse facilities, in centers, schools, and homes. Programs for children under age 5 may be called **child care centers**, **preschools**, **child development centers**, or **prekindergartens** (a term often used for programs for children under age 5 housed in public schools). Programs for young children and their families may be called **family–child interaction** or **home-visitor programs**.

Programs for children 5 through 8 years of age (often housed in public schools) include kindergartens, primary grades, and **before- and after-school programs**. **Kindergarten** serves 5- and 6-year-olds and is the first year of formal schooling. **Primary grades** refers to grades 1 through 3 (and sometime includes kindergarten). Children with disabilities (birth to age 8) may be served in preschool, kindergarten, or primary grade classrooms, or may be taught in separate classrooms.

As you learn about and have experience in these different kinds of programs you are likely to notice differences in philosophy and practices between infant–toddler and preschool programs that serve children from birth through age 4 and kindergarten through third grade classrooms that serve children 5–8 years-of-age. Teachers in preschools are more likely to have training in child development and provide children with opportunities to explore and play in a planned learning environment. Preschool programs tend to emphasize child-choice and hands-on activity and base assessment on observations of children as they engage with learning experiences in the classroom.

In elementary programs, as you probably remember from your childhood, teachers tend to focus more on the acquisition of knowledge and skills in subjects like reading and math, science and social studies. Elementary classrooms are often furnished with desks and learning is likely to involve reading and verbal instruction. Children do more assigned paper-and-pencil work and are most often assessed with paper and pencil tests. There are, of course, exceptions to these generalizations in every community.

Reflect On

Your Ideas about Early Childhood Teachers*

What do you see in your mind when you think of a teacher of young children? What is the teacher like? What is the teacher doing? (Keep a copy of your response so you can refer to it later in this course or program.)

---

* This is the first of many reflections that you will find in this book. Thinking about the questions asked and writing down your ideas will help you to become a reflective teacher of young children.

Of all the terms that are used to describe people who provide care and education for young children, we choose to use **teacher** "because it is the broadest term, it captures most of the job responsibilities, commands society's respect, and is, after all, what children usually call the adults who care for and educate them no matter what the setting" (Bredekamp, 2011, p. 21). The term *teacher* emphasizes the things that unite us as a group of people who work with young children. It also is a term that the general public—people like your family and friends—will understand and about which they are likely to have positive associations. We call this chapter "The Teacher" because we believe this term best reflects you, a student using this text, and

SOURCE: Jeff Reese

your career aspirations, whether you are considering working with infants or 8-year-olds. We will also use the terms *caregiver, provider, practitioner,* and *early childhood educator* to refer to those who are employed to educate and care for children between birth and age 8 in infant–toddler programs, family–child interaction programs, home visiting programs, family child care homes, preschools, kindergartens, and primary grades.

Because programs for children under age 5 are most often found in preschools and child care centers while kindergarten through grade 3 programs are usually housed in elementary schools, it can be challenging to get a sense of the field of early childhood education as a whole. As you construct your understanding of the field, it may be helpful to keep in mind that programs for young children have the overarching purpose of supporting children's growth and development. No matter what they are called or where they are housed, all programs for young children provide both care and education. People who work in early childhood programs, regardless of their job title or the age of the children, strive to support all aspects of children's development, promote learning, and provide nurture and care.

Working with young children is varied and challenging; it demands knowledge, skill, sensitivity, creativity, and hard work. If these challenges inspire you, you have probably chosen the right field. Early childhood education is especially rewarding for those who enjoy the spontaneous teaching and learning opportunities that abound in daily life with young children. It may not be as gratifying for people who prefer dispensing subject matter or for those who like work that is tidy and predictable. Sometimes, college students who begin their careers with visions of shaping young minds become discouraged when they discover how much of their time is spent mixing paint, changing pants, arbitrating disputes, mopping floors, and wiping noses. But while working with young children can be demanding and tiring, it can also be invigorating, for, in addition to more mundane tasks, you will get to have conversations with children, tell and read stories, sing, observe nature, explore neighborhoods, plant gardens, and provide inspiration for creative art, music, and movement. You will have the opportunity every day to plan and implement interesting and meaningful learning experiences. We have found that this wide range of tasks makes work with young children endlessly interesting and challenging.

While your most important task as an early childhood educator is working with children, you will also interact with families, colleagues, and community agencies. If you embarked on a career in early childhood education because you enjoy being with young children, you might be surprised at the extent to which teachers work with adults as well. You will interact with families and work with other staff members daily. You might also communicate with people in agencies concerned with children and families (such as child welfare workers and early intervention specialists) and engage with other professionals in order to further your own professional development.

We hope that you, as one of tomorrow's early childhood educators, will make a commitment to providing high-quality programs for young children (the chapters of this book will help you learn to do that). Eventually, you may also want to develop knowledge of broader societal issues and become involved in policy decisions and advocating for the rights and needs of young children.

Working with Children

The first and most important of your tasks as an early childhood teacher is working with children. Each day you will communicate with them, teach them, play with them, care for their physical needs, and provide them with a sense of physical and psychological security. The younger the children you work with, the more you will be called on to provide physical care and nurture.

Your work with young children will begin before the first child arrives and will continue each day after the last child has gone home. Because the learning environment is the primary teaching tool in programs for children under age 5, you will set the stage for learning by creating a classroom that is safe, healthy, and stimulating. You will also plan the daily schedule, design learning experiences, create materials, and use resources. After children arrive, you will observe and support them as they learn and play, mediate relationships, model the way you want people to treat one another, and help them develop skills and learn about the world. In a single day, you might be doing the work of a teacher, friend, secretary, parent, reference librarian, interior designer, nurse, janitor, counselor, entertainer, and diplomat.

PRACTICE BASED ON KNOWLEDGE OF CHILDREN Because young children are vulnerable and dependent on adults, early childhood educators regard all areas of development—social, emotional, intellectual, and physical—as important and interconnected. As a teacher of young children, you will be called on to nurture and support all these aspects of development. Concern for development of the **whole child** is an idea you will encounter over and over in this book. Care and education that is responsive to and based on research on children's development is known as **developmentally appropriate practice (DAP)** (Bredekamp & Copple, 2009). On the pages of this book we explain how you can provide developmentally appropriate learning experiences for young children.

INTENTIONAL TEACHING Early childhood educators need to have a repertoire of teaching strategies that will effectively reach every child they encounter (Epstein, 2007; National Association for the Education of Young Children, 2009). According to Ann Epstein (2007), an **intentional teacher** has a purpose behind every decision and skill in articulating the reasons for actions. The intentional teacher decides on goals for children's development, thinks through alternatives, and then decides on strategies that will achieve these goals. This teacher also has a solid base of knowledge of development, research, **pedagogy**, and relevant standards. He or she knows how to use this knowledge to meet goals and adapt to individual differences in children. An important part of your preparation to be a teacher will be learning to select appropriate teaching strategies and to articulate why you chose them in ways that can be understood by children's family members, and colleagues.

ADDRESSING STANDARDS More and more, early childhood educators are being asked to pay attention to **early learning standards**. These standards are developed by states to specify developmental expectations for children from birth through entrance to first grade. As part of the current emphasis on standards, you will probably be expected to do the following:

- Know what standards are used in your program and in your state
- Design a curriculum that addresses early learning standards
- Assess what children have learned in terms of standards
- Identify how you are meeting standards

These tasks are very similar to what teachers have done in the past, but today you can expect your work to be more visible, more public, and more likely to be evaluated.

Application Exercise 1.1

Watch and Write About Working with Children

Working with Families

Young children cannot be separated from the context of their families, so building good relations with family members is an important part of the role of the early childhood educator. Because early childhood programs often provide the child's first experience in the larger world away from home, you will play an important role in the transition between home and school—helping families and children learn to be apart from one another for a period of time each day. In fact, you may be the second professional (the first is usually the pediatrician) who has a relationship with the family and the child. A close, respectful partnership between home and the early childhood program is absolutely essential in programs for infants, toddlers, and preschoolers. It is also important in programs for children over the age of five.

Just as your work with children brings with it diverse roles and demands, your work with families involves a range of attitudes and skills that are both similar to and different from those you need in your work with children. In your work with families, you may find yourself being a consultant, a social worker, an advocate, a teacher, a reporter, a librarian, a mediator, a translator, and a social director. These diverse roles provide another way that your job will be varied, engaging, and challenging.

Working as Part of a Team

An important feature of the role of most teachers is working collaboratively with other adults. Working as part of a team involves collaborating with coworkers, supervising volunteers, interacting with program administrators, and working with a host of other adults, ranging from custodians to counselors.

The ability to work productively on a team is an essential skill for an early childhood educator. In effective teams, people work together on behalf of a shared goal. They support and respect one another. They acknowledge and make the best use of one another's strengths and contributions. They understand their roles and fulfill their responsibilities. Perhaps most important, they communicate effectively and strive to resolve the conflicts that inevitably occur when people work together every day. For these reasons, many teachers find that participating in a team gives them support, stimulation, and a sense of belonging.

Being a part of a team is more than just turning up for work each day. It involves an understanding of team roles and responsibilities. It means being a good colleague by treating others with respect, honoring diverse values and communication styles, being sure that you do your share of the work, and appreciating your colleagues' contributions.

 A Quick Check 1.1

Gauge your understanding of the concepts in this section.

The Teacher as a Person

Because who you are as a person is the foundation for the professional you will become, we begin our exploration of the role of the teacher of young children by looking at personal characteristics. We will consider a personal quality that is inborn (temperament) and others that are shaped from infancy by a child's interaction with family, culture, and community. We will look at the kinds of personal characteristics that are desirable in teachers of young children and ask you to take a thoughtful look at who you are in relationship to the teacher you wish to become. As you enter the field the sum of your previous experiences will blend over time with your professional training and experiences working with children and families to forge your emerging professional identity as an early childhood educator.

There is no one "right" personality type, no single set of experiences or training, no single mold that produces a good teacher of young children. Although people from many different backgrounds can do a good job working with young children not everyone is right for this field. What makes a good early childhood teacher? What combination of attitudes, knowledge, skills, and personal qualities—including **dispositions** (tendencies to respond to experiences in certain ways)—contribute to the ability to work effectively with young children? Successful early childhood educators have been described as having a positive outlook, curiosity, openness to new ideas, enthusiasm, commitment, high energy, physical strength, a sense of humor, flexibility, self-awareness, the capacity for empathy, emotional stability, warmth, sensitivity, passion, perseverance, willingness to take risks, patience, integrity (honesty and moral uprightness), creativity, and love of learning (Cartwright, 1999; Colker, 2008; Feeney & Chun, 1985; Katz, 1993).

In addition all teachers of young children should love their work, communicate effectively, be good role models, and have deep appreciation and respect for children. Respect—the belief that every human being has value and deserves to be appreciated—is fundamental. It is not necessary (or possible) to love every child, but it is imperative that teachers respect the worth and value of every child and family member. It is also important for them to have the capacity to nurture and to be able to focus consistently on the best interests of others.

In 1948 child development scholar Barbara Biber wrote the following statement which we have included in the previous 10 editions of this book because it so eloquently describes aspects of psychological health that are important for teachers (Biber & Snyder, 1948).

> A teacher needs to be a person so secure within herself that she can function with principles rather than prescriptions, that she can exert authority without requiring submission, that she can work experimentally but not at random and that she can admit mistakes without feeling humiliated (p. 282).

We know that genuine liking and respect for children, paired with a caring nature and an inquiring mind and spirit, lead to a sense of commitment that can turn teaching young children from a job into a deeply held sense of mission (sometimes referred to as a **calling**).

SOURCE: Jeff Reese

People with a wide range of personal **attributes** can be effective as teachers of young children. What is important is for you to be willing to look at yourself as objectively as possible, understand your personal qualities and how they might impact your work, and be willing to try to overcome anything that could hinder your ability to work effectively with children and their families. Who you are as a person has a strong and lasting impact and is the first thing that should be considered as you embark on your career as a teacher.

Some personal attributes, like temperament, are inborn. Others are shaped by early experiences and the culture of a person's family and community. **Culture** refers to the way a group of people lives as well as their shared, learned system of values, beliefs, and attitudes (dictionary.cambridge.org. NAEYC, 2009). People are immersed in their culture the way a fish is immersed in water. Its impact is so pervasive that a person may not be aware of its influences. The culture that a person experiences as a child has a powerful impact on their thinking and behavior and influences decisions throughout life. Your culture has had a profound influence on you and culture has a similarly powerful influence on the children you will teach and their families.

Video Example 1.1: The Importance of Valuing Cultures

Watch this video on teaching culturally diverse students. Why it is important for teachers of young children to understand their own cultures?

Temperament

We have found the research of pediatricians Alexander Thomas and Stella Chess on the temperament of infants, adapted to adults by therapists Jayne Burks and Melvin Rubenstein (1979), a good place for our college students to begin to look at their personal attributes. Thomas and Chess refer to **temperament** as an individual's behavioral style and typical ways of responding. They found that newborns show definite differences in traits of temperament that tend to persist over time. Although they can be modified through life experiences, the nine dimensions of temperament are helpful in explaining personality differences in adults as well as children.

Figure 1.1 gives a brief description of the nine traits as they apply to adults and a continuum accompanying each trait. We have used these dimensions in our teaching as a tool for personal reflection. Traits of temperament are neither good nor bad; they are simply part of who you are. However, some characteristics, such as positive mood, a high activity level, and ease in adapting to new situations are helpful in working with young children.

Ruby and Michelle teach together in a classroom of 3- and 4-year-olds. Ruby arrives at school an hour before the children and families arrive; she likes to be alone in the classroom to gather her thoughts and get materials ready. Michelle rushes in at the last minute with

Figure 1.1 Thomas and Chess's Nine Dimensions of Temperament

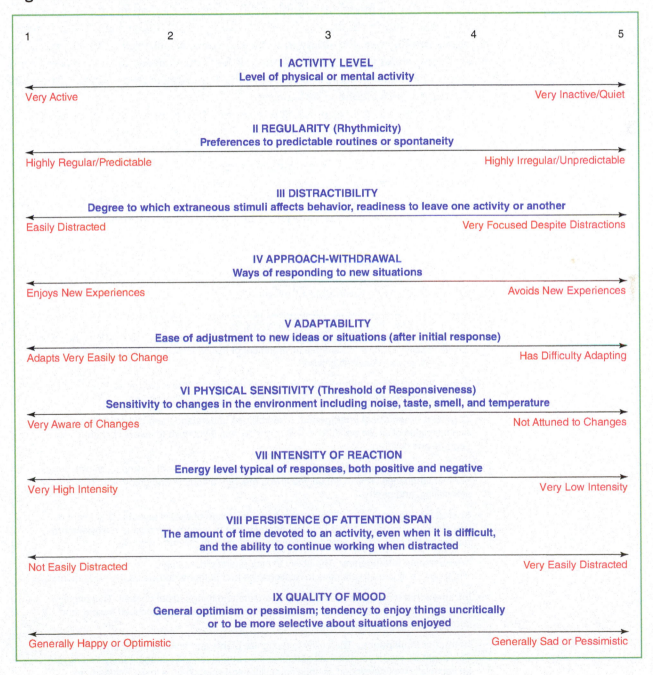

a bag of intriguing items she has gathered related to their curriculum on plants. A half-hour after the school has opened, Ruby is quietly reading to a few of the younger children, including Joshua, who has been having a hard time separating from his mom. Michelle is leading the rest of the children on a hunt through the yard for flowers.

Ruby and Michelle display some different temperamental qualities, particularly rhythmicity and intensity of reaction. Recognizing that a child, parent, or colleague has a temperament that is different from your own (as in the case of Ruby and Michelle) may keep you from finding his or her behavior negative or difficult. To heighten your awareness of your own temperament, you may wish to plot yourself on the continua in Figure 1.1 and think about the implications of what you find for working in an early childhood education program.

Multiple Intelligences

Howard Gardner's model of multiple intelligences is another tool that can be helpful in understanding children and understanding yourself (Gardner, 1983). Gardner describes **intelligence**, the ability to think and learn, as culturally defined, based on what is needed and valued within a society. When you realize your unique talents and strengths (your intelligences), you are better able to maximize them. Figure 1.2 presents the eight categories identified by Gardner.

Understanding that people can be intelligent in different ways can also be helpful in your work with colleagues. Ruby and Michelle, in the earlier example, would do well to build on one another's strengths and learn from one another. Ruby, with her inclination to reflect and her strong interpersonal intelligence, is likely to become the expert on addressing children's social-emotional needs, and Michelle, with her strong naturalist intelligence, will become the expert in inspiring children and creating science curricula. If they are wise, they will come to appreciate each other for these differences.

Figure 1.2 Gardner's Multiple Intelligences

- **Musical intelligence:** The ability to produce and respond to music. This might be you, if you are especially sensitive to the aural environment of the classroom and play instruments and sing easily as you work with children.

- **Bodily-kinesthetic intelligence:** The ability to use the body to solve problems. This might be you, if you demonstrate good coordination and play actively with children.

- **Logical-mathematical intelligence:** The ability to understand the basic properties of numbers and principles of cause and effect. This might be you, if you love to invent challenges for yourself and children.

- **Linguistic intelligence:** The ability to use language to express ideas and learn new words or other languages. This might be you, if you are very articulate and enjoy word play, books, storytelling, and poetry.

- **Spatial intelligence:** The ability to form a mental image of spatial layouts. This might be you, if you are sensitive to the physical arrangement of a room, are able to easily see how to rearrange the classroom, or especially enjoy working with children in blocks.

- **Interpersonal intelligence:** The ability to understand other people and work with them. This might be you, if you are attentive to relationships and demonstrate sociability and leadership.

- **Intrapersonal intelligence:** The ability to understand things about oneself. This might be you, if you have strong interests and goals, know yourself well, are focused inward, and demonstrate confidence.

- **Naturalist intelligence:** The ability to recognize plants and animals in the environment. This might be you, if you know all about the flora and fauna in your community and have an especially well developed science curriculum and science area in your classroom.

Learning more about yourself can help you be more sensitive to and accepting of differences among people, more aware of the impact of your personality on others, and better able to consider the kinds of work settings in which you might work most effectively.

Reflect On

Your Temperament and Intelligences

Use Thomas and Chess's temperament dimensions and Gardner's model of multiple intelligences to reflect on your temperament and intelligences. What do they tell you about yourself? What are your preferences for activity and setting? What are you good at? What is challenging for you? What might be the implications of what you learned about your personality for relating to children, families, and colleagues?

Personal Values and Morality

The decisions you make each day, the foods you eat, the place you live, the magazines and books you read, the television programs and videos you watch, and the work and play you choose are all influenced by your values. **Values** are principles or standards that a person believes to be important, desirable, or worthwhile and that are prized for themselves (e.g., truth, integrity, beauty, love, honesty, wisdom, loyalty, justice, and respect). You develop your values during a complex process of interaction between your family's culture, religion, and values, community views, and life experiences. Your professional values will evolve from these personal values in combination with professional experiences. If you spend some time reflecting, you will be able to identify your personal values and see the impact they have on your life.

You are very likely to have chosen early childhood education because you care deeply about children. You might be motivated by a concern for social justice, religious values, or a passion for learning. You might have a desire to help children enjoy fulfilling lives, to be successful students, or to become productive members of society. As part of your preparation for becoming a teacher of young children, it is worthwhile to consider what values brought you to the decision to enter this field and how these values might influence the ways you will work with young children.

Reflect On

Your Values and the Moral Messages You Received as a Child

Make a list of your values. How do you think you developed these values? Which values were directly taught in your home, place of worship, or community? Were some taught in indirect ways? What messages did you receive about behaviors that are right and wrong? How do these reflect your childhood and upbringing? Can you think of ways that your values have changed over time?

It is often surprising to discover that other people do not share the values that you hold dear—it is one of the reasons that the first year in a new community or a new relationship (e.g., with a new spouse) or the first year of working in a program can be difficult. Awareness can help you realize that values are very much a part of who you are and that your values might not be held by everyone you meet in your life and work.

Morality involves people's views of what is good, right, or proper; their beliefs about their obligations; and ideas about how they should behave (Kidder, 1995; Kipnis, 1987). Morality involves decisions about what is right and wrong. From an early age, people learn that moral issues are serious because they concern our duties and obligations to one another. We quickly learn, for example, how we ought to treat others and that adults expect even children to behave in these ways.

The roots of personal morality can be found in the early childhood years. You can probably identify the standards of behavior that were established by the adults you looked up to in your home, place of worship, and neighborhood. Telling the truth, helping others, being fair, respecting elders, putting family first, and respecting differences are examples of some of the earliest moral lessons that many of us learn from our families and community and religious leaders.

Attitudes about Diversity

Attitudes toward groups of people whose culture, religion, language, class, ethnicity, sexual orientation, appearance, or abilities are different from our own grow from our culture including the values and messages we get as children from the adults in our lives, and from our experiences (or lack of them) with different kinds of people. We all develop preferences and expectations about people. A **bias**—the inclination to favor or reject certain individuals or groups of people—may be based on the human tendency to feel comfortable with those who are similar to us. Unfortunately, these biases can lead to stereotypes and prejudices that may have a negative impact and even lead to unfair or unjust treatment of individuals or groups of people. A **stereotype** is an oversimplified generalization about a particular group of people, the belief that all people with a particular characteristic are the same. **Prejudice** is a prejudgment for or against any person or group that is not based on reason or direct experience. If you can recall the experience of having been rejected or negatively judged because of one of the characteristics listed above, you will be aware of the powerful effect of prejudice. We usually think of prejudice as negative feelings about a group, but it can also be harmful to be prejudiced in favor of a group. When this occurs, members of the favored group may get an unrealistic sense of entitlement, and those who are not favored may perceive themselves as unworthy (Derman-Sparks, 1989).

Many of us fail to recognize our own biases, but everyone has some. We may resist this awareness because it could be embarrassing or place us in an unfavorable light. But ignoring biases does not make them go away. They influence all of our relationships.

Working to identify your biases will help you recognize when they could have negative effects on children or their families. When you become aware of a bias, simple awareness may be enough to help you be more accepting of differences or correct a tendency to react negatively to a child or family. For example, you may realize that you have a tendency to pay more attention to children who are active and energetic than those who are quiet and withdrawn (or the opposite). This awareness might help remind you to pay more attention to the children you tend to overlook. Many fine teachers actively work to dispel negative feelings by identifying the things they like about a child or family member who triggers a negative reaction. When you focus on positives, you are more easily able to develop a special affection for a child or adult whom you were once inclined to dislike. Your newfound appreciation of a child or family can also influence your feelings about other members of a group.

As you prepare to be a teacher it is important to ask yourself if there are any kinds of children or groups of children with whom you prefer not to work. If you find that you have strong prejudices toward groups of children or families that you can't overcome, you may need to consider seriously whether it is a good idea for you to enter the field of early childhood education.

We live in an increasingly diverse world. As a teacher of young children, you are very likely to have close contact with people who have different racial, economic, cultural, and linguistic backgrounds and different sexual orientations, abilities, and lifestyles. This diversity offers both challenges and opportunities. Although you may have moments of discomfort, you also have the possibility of gaining new appreciation as you learn to value a wide range of human differences.

Reflect On

Your Attitudes Toward Diversity

Have you experienced bias or prejudice in your own life? What was the impact of that experience? Are there groups of people with whom you feel uncomfortable or whom you tend to dislike? What could be the impact of these experiences and attitudes on you as a future teacher of young children?

The Impact of Life Experiences

You bring your whole history to your work with children and their families. Who you are as a person includes influences on your early development, temperament, and the attitudes and values that grow from your culture and experiences. These things will have an impact on the early childhood professional you will become and it is important to reflect on them in order to understand yourself.

Cheryl grew up as an only child. Both of her parents were teachers, and she always pretended to be teacher to her dolls and toy animals. Cheryl loved school, but she was shy and did not make friends easily. She volunteered at a neighborhood preschool when she was in high school and discovered that she didn't feel shy with children. She decided to become a preschool teacher. She completed her degree in early childhood education and became a teacher in the preschool where she did a practicum placement. No one who meets her today can believe that she was ever shy and lacked friends.

Sue is a first-grade teacher who grew up in the inner city. Her parents did not speak English. She has vivid memories of her first unhappy days in kindergarten. But Sue soon loved school. When Sue was 8, her father died, soon after her brother died of a drug overdose. There was never enough money, and there were many sad days. But Sue did well in school and earned a scholarship to go to the state college. She was the first person in her family to earn a degree. Sue loves her job teaching in a Head Start program and often talks about the ways in which she feels she is making a difference to children from families like hers.

Sarah is a preschool teacher who came from an abusive family. She left home before she was 16, but Sarah managed to go to school and earned an AS degree. She is now a teacher of 3-year-olds. She is fiercely protective of the children in her class and says most parents don't deserve to have children. She is negative about authority figures like her director and the preschool board. She is frequently absent and often comments on the poor quality of her program. Sarah complains that she is paid too little to put in extra hours to fix up the classroom or meet with parents.

As you enter the early childhood field, remember that you were once a child and that the ways you feel about yourself and others were profoundly influenced by your early experiences. It is a good idea to reflect on these experiences and how they might impact your relationships before they crop up in unexpected and negative ways. Many fine early childhood educators, like Sue, dedicate themselves to giving children the positive early experiences that they missed. Some, like Sarah, are not able to overcome their early negative experiences and current challenges without assistance.

The capacity for caring and compassion is related to the ability to know and accept yourself. Self-knowledge grows from the ability to observe yourself in the same honest and nonjudgmental way that you will observe children and to realistically appraise your strengths and areas that need to be changed. Self-knowledge means recognizing that everyone experiences negative feelings and strong emotions such as anger and fear. These feelings need to be identified, accepted, and expressed in productive ways (e.g., in discussion with caring friends and relatives, with a counselor, or by writing about them), or they may become destructive. Self-knowledge and acceptance are cornerstones of the quality of *compassion* that is so important in a teacher of young children.

Part of the process of growing as a professional (and the central theme in this book) is to ask yourself, "Who am I in the lives of children? Who do I want to be?" It is not easy to be aware of how your culture and early experiences shape your attitudes toward children and families and your reactions to everyday situations. It is important to learn to look at yourself as objectively as you can and to accept feedback from others as valuable information that can help you grow instead of something to defend against or to use to belittle yourself.

Reflect On

Who You Are and Who You Want to Be in the Lives of Children

What events and experiences in your childhood most influence who you are today? What, if any, unhappy or difficult experiences have you had to work to overcome? What might be the connections between your childhood experiences and your desire to teach young children? Who do you want to be in the lives of children?

 A Quick Check 1.2

Gauge your understanding of the concepts in this section.

 The Teacher as a Professional

You are learning to be a teacher of young children, which means that you are planning to enter a *profession* and to become a *professional*. We hear these terms used every day, but their meanings are not always clear. A **profession** is an occupation that provides an essential service to society. A **professional** is an individual who has received training and who uses their specialized knowledge and skills to serve society through doing the work of the profession.

Discussion is under way today about whether early childhood education is a "true profession"—meaning whether it meets most of the criteria that are used by scholars to determine if an occupation is a profession. Some of these criteria are:

- A specialized body of knowledge and expertise
- Prolonged training
- Rigorous requirements for entry into training and admission to practice
- Agreed-on standards of practice
- Altruism—commitment to unselfish dedication to meeting the needs of others
- Recognition as the only group in the society who can perform its function
- Autonomy—self-regulation and internal control over the quality of the services provided
- A code of ethics that is enforced

Early childhood education is working to meet the criteria of a specialized body of knowledge and expertise. The American early childhood professional association, NAEYC, has developed a code of ethics that spells out moral obligations, identifies the distinctive values of the field (listed in Figure 1.4, in this chapter), and provides guidelines for ethical conduct. However, this code is not enforced as are those of recognized professions like medicine and law. We do not fully meet criteria regarding prolonged training and rigorous requirements for entry into the field. Training is often quite brief, and entry requirements are usually not rigorous. Early childhood programs are rarely autonomous or self-regulated because most private programs for children age 5 and younger are regulated by and licensed by social welfare agencies, and public school programs by elected boards of education. Early childhood educators are dedicated to meeting the needs of children. Altruism is the area in which we shine!

Although our field may not meet all of the criteria used to define a profession, there is no doubt that we make important contributions to society by nurturing and educating young children during a critically important period in the life cycle. Awareness of the value of our contributions is growing and efforts are under way to enhance our professional status. And whether or not we meet the criteria of a true profession, early childhood educators have a powerful impact on all aspects of children's development so it is imperative that our behavior reflects the professional ideals of dedication to service and provision of high-quality services.

Specialized Knowledge and Skills

Specialized knowledge and skills is the central defining feature of every profession. Over the past few years, a great deal of work has been done on defining the core knowledge of early childhood education. There is growing agreement and an extensive body of literature that describes what early childhood educators should know and be able to do to support young children's development and learning.

Knowledge and skills are described in teacher preparation standards that have been developed to ensure that teachers are prepared to work effectively with young children. These include Child Development Associate (CDA) competencies administered by the Council for Professional Recognition, Early Childhood Professional Preparation Standards developed by NAEYC,[1] Standards for Accomplished Early Childhood Teachers created by the National Board for Professional Teaching Standards, and Standards for Special Education Teachers of Early Childhood Students developed by the Council for Exceptional Children. In addition to the standards produced by national groups, most states have created professional development systems to increase the expertise of educators who work with children from birth through age 5 (Bellm, n.d.).

A new study *Transforming the Workforce for Children Birth Through Age 8* explores implications of child development research for the professional development of those who work with young children. It examines the current workforce and the policies that guide professional learning and makes recommendations to improve the quality of teaching in early childhood settings. The recommendations made in this study are designed to create a unifying foundation of child development and early learning, shared knowledge and competencies for care and education professionals, and principles for professional learning (Institute of Medicine and National Research Council, 2015). The report is intended to promote greater consistency of practice by focusing the competencies and professional learning that need to be shared by early childhood educators across roles and settings. Recommendations include: strengthening qualifications for all care and education professionals working with children birth through

---

[1] NAEYC is an association dedicated to improving the well-being of young children, with focus on the quality of educational and developmental services for children from birth through age 8. Founded in 1926, NAEYC is the world's largest organization working on behalf of young children.

SOURCE: Jeff Reese

age 8; developing pathways to help lead educators transition to bachelor's degrees; strengthening requirements for supervised practice for all lead educators; and developing better systems for evaluating and assessing performance of early childhood educators.

There is general consensus in all of the discussion of teacher preparation that the centerpiece of the knowledge base of the skilled early childhood educator is child development. The commitment to basing work on knowledge of child development goes back to the child study movement of the 1920s and is a characteristic that distinguishes early childhood educators from most other groups of educators. This and other essential knowledge is reflected in the chapters of this book.

The NAEYC Standards for Initial and Advanced Early Childhood Professional Preparation Programs (2009) address what graduates of early childhood training programs in 2-year, 4-year, and advanced programs need to know and be able to do. Figure 1.3 presents a summary of the NAEYC standards. It should come as no surprise to you that their content makes up much of the substance of this book. We will indicate at the end of each chapter which of the NAEYC standards it addresses.

Professional Conduct

Being a professional involves more than knowledge and skills. It also requires professional behavior including being a good employee, behaving ethically, and the willingness to continue to learn and grow.

The first important aspect of professional behavior is being a good employee. This means being punctual, dressing appropriately, having a positive attitude, communicating well, following through on responsibilities, keeping personal feelings and grievances out of the workplace and representing the workplace positively in the community.

Being a good employee also involves awareness of the legal responsibilities that accompany your position. Like every citizen, you must follow the laws of our country and community. In addition, you need to know the laws and policies that are applicable to work with children. If you plan to work in a preschool setting, you will need to know about the child care regulations in your community. In most states, child care is licensed by the department of health or the department of human services. The agency that regulates programs for young children is responsible for standards that include group size, ratios of adults to children, and teacher qualifications. You should also learn about state laws that pertain to early childhood education in your community.

In every state, early childhood educators are mandated reporters of child abuse or neglect. This means that you will have a legal as well as an ethical responsibility to report suspected abuse or neglect, such as a child who comes to school with symptoms that you suspect are the result of being physically or psychologically abused by a family member or other adult.

An important task for a new teacher is to find out the child abuse–reporting procedures for your workplace. Your employer is likely to provide the training. If this training is not offered, you should seek out the training that is available in most states. Although you may fervently wish to never have to use this information, it is critical that you know what to do in order to fulfill your legal and moral responsibilities to keep children safe from harm.

Professional Values and Ethics

Personal values and morality cannot always guide professional behavior because not everyone has the same values, or the same morality. Even those who have the same

Figure 1.3 Summary of NAEYC's Standards for Early Childhood Professional Preparation Programs

Standard 1. Promoting Child Development and Learning

Key elements of Standard 1

- 1a: Knowing and understanding young children's characteristics and needs, from birth through age 8
- 1b: Knowing and understanding the multiple influences on early development and learning
- 1c: Using developmental knowledge to create healthy, respectful, supportive, and challenging learning environments for young children

Standard 2. Building Family and Community Relationships

Key elements of Standard 2

- 2a: Knowing about and understanding diverse family and community characteristics
- 2b: Supporting and engaging families and communities through respectful, reciprocal relationships
- 2c: Involving families and communities in young children's development and learning

Standard 3. Observing, Documenting, and Assessing to Support Young Children and Families

Key elements of Standard 3

- 3a: Understanding the goals, benefits, and uses of assessment—including its use in development of appropriate goals, curriculum, and teaching strategies for young children
- 3b: Knowing about assessment partnerships with families and with professional colleagues to build effective learning environments
- 3c: Knowing about and using observation, documentation, and other appropriate assessment tools and approaches, including the use of technology in documentation, assessment, and data collection
- 3d: Understanding and practicing responsible assessment to promote positive outcomes for each child, including the use of assistive technology for children with disabilities

Standard 4. Using Developmentally Effective Approaches

Key elements of Standard 4

- 4a: Understanding positive relationships and supportive interactions as the foundation of their work with young children
- 4b: Knowing and understanding effective strategies and tools for early education, including appropriate uses of technology
- 4c: Using a broad repertoire of developmentally appropriate teaching /learning approaches
- 4d: Reflecting on own practice to promote positive outcomes for each child

Standard 5. Using Content Knowledge to Build Meaningful Curriculum

Key elements of Standard 5

- 5a: Understanding content knowledge and resources in academic disciplines: language and literacy; the arts—music, creative movement, dance, drama, visual arts; mathematics; science, physical activity, physical education, health and safety; and social studies
- 5b: Knowing and using the central concepts, inquiry tools, and structures of content areas or academic disciplines
- 5c: Using own knowledge, appropriate early learning standards, and other resources to design, implement, and evaluate developmentally meaningful and challenging curriculum for each child

Standard 6. Becoming a Professional

Key elements of Standard 6

- 6a: Identifying and involving oneself with the early childhood field
- 6b: Knowing about and upholding ethical standards and other early childhood professional guidelines
- 6c: Engaging in continuous, collaborative learning to inform practice; using technology effectively with young children, with peers, and as a professional resource
- 6d: Integrating knowledgeable, reflective, and critical perspectives on early education
- 6e: Engaging in informed advocacy for young children and the early childhood profession

Standard 7. Early Childhood Field Experiences

Key elements of Standard 7

- 7a: Opportunities to observe and practice in at least two of the three early childhood age groups (birth–age 3, 3–5, 5–8)
- 7b: Opportunities to observe and practice in at least two of the three main types of early education settings (early school grades, child care centers and homes, Head Start programs)

SOURCE: From NAEYC Standards for Early Childhood Professional Preparation Programs. Copyright © 2009 NAEYC®. Reprinted with permission.

values and moral commitments may not apply them in the same way in their work with children. As early childhood educators, our personal attitudes, values, and morality need to be supplemented with professional values that enable us to speak with one voice about our professional obligations and that give clear guidance about how to approach issues in the workplace that involve morality.

PROFESSIONAL VALUES   Professional values, as set forth in a **code of ethics**, spell out a profession's beliefs and commitments. These are not a matter of preference but are agreed-on statements that members believe to be the foundation of their work. NAEYC's Code of Ethical Conduct and Statement of Commitment (revised in April 2005 and reaffirmed and updated in May 2005/2011) is designed to guide moral professional practice. The Code identifies **core values**, presented in Figure 1.4, that express early childhood educators' central beliefs, commitment to society, and common purpose. These core values make it possible to reach agreement on issues of professional ethics by relying on professional *values* that apply to all early childhood educators rather than on personal values or beliefs.

Most people who choose early childhood education as a career find themselves in agreement with the spirit of these values. As you merge your personal values with the professional values of the field of early childhood education you will join other early childhood practitioners in their dedication to supporting the healthy growth and development of children and partnerships with their families.

Reflect On

Your Professional Values

Brainstorm a list of commitments that you think all early childhood educators should hold. Compare your list to the NAEYC core values in Figure 1.4. Think about why these lists are similar to or different from each other.

When Values Conflict   When you encounter conflicts in your work, they will often involve values. Sometimes these conflicts will be within yourself. For example, when working with children you may value freedom of expression (e.g., allowing children to engage in dramatic play about topics of interest to them) versus the value of peace (e.g., forbidding guns and war play in the classroom). Or you may face the predicament

Figure 1.4 Core Values in Early Childhood Education

Standards of ethical behavior in early childhood care and education are based on commitment to the following core values that are deeply rooted in the history of the field of early childhood care and education. We have made a commitment to:

- Appreciate childhood as a unique and valuable stage of the human life cycle
- Base our work on knowledge of how children develop and learn
- Appreciate and support the bond between the child and family
- Recognize that children are best understood and supported in the context of family, culture*, community, and society
- Respect the dignity, worth, and uniqueness of each individual (child, family member, and colleague)
- Respect diversity in children, families, and colleagues
- Recognize that children and adults achieve their full potential in the context of relationships that are based on trust and respect

*The term *culture* includes ethnicity, racial identity, economic level, family structure, language, and religious and political beliefs, which profoundly influence each child's development and relationship to the world.

SOURCE: Reprinted from the NAEYC Code of Ethical Conduct and Statement of Commitment, revised April 2005, reaffirmed and updated May 2011. Copyright © 2005 NAEYC®. Reprinted with permission.

of having to choose between work that pays well and work you love. In these situations, it will be helpful to analyze the conflict and try to prioritize which value is most important to you.

It is also important to be sure your actions are consistent with your values. Sometimes, teachers are not aware of the ways in which their behavior contradicts their values. A teacher we know thought that she valued independence and child-initiated learning. But when she looked carefully at her classroom, she realized children were not allowed to choose their own materials from the open shelves.

You are likely to encounter value conflicts with others. It helps to recognize that differences in values are a natural and healthy part of life in a diverse society. You can learn to address values conflicts thoughtfully, though it is not always easy to arrive at a solution. You may find yourself in a situation in which an administrator's actions (such as dealing with fear about allegations of sexual abuse by forbidding staff to hug children) are in direct conflict with an important value you hold (giving young children the affectionate physical contact that they need). You may find yourself in conflict with colleagues whose values lead them to different ideas about how to work with children (demanding quiet at mealtime while you think meals are a perfect time to develop conversational skills).

You are also likely to encounter value conflicts with families. At some time, you will probably have to deal with family members who want you to do something that you feel is not right for the child. For example, they may be anxious about their child's success in school and want them to master academic content that you think is not appropriate for the child's age, interests, or abilities.

When you encounter a conflict, it is helpful to decide whether it is about values. Values conflicts can be best handled by suspending judgment (the inner voice that says, "No! They're wrong! I'm right!") and listening carefully to the other person's viewpoint. Our friend and colleague, the late Jean Fargo, used to recommend that people learn to "be curious, not furious" about other people's differing viewpoints.

Often, values conflicts are based on cultural differences, for example, whether it is best to do something for a child or encourage the child to do it independently. When you listen carefully and work to communicate with a person with whom you have a values conflict, you can often arrive at a solution that is satisfactory to both parties. But when competing views are based on strongly held value differences you may simply have to agree to disagree.

Reflect On

A Values Conflict

Can you remember a time when you and another person had a disagreement based on values? What values did each of you hold? What did you do? Were your values or the relationship changed by the conflict?

Occasionally, values differences regarding teaching are so serious that you will find you do not want to continue to work in a program. For instance, one of our students chose to leave a good-paying job when the school adopted a paper-and-pencil curriculum that did not allow her to teach in ways that were consistent with her commitment to hands-on learning. Coming to this conclusion can be painful, but it may be the best alternative if the value difference is extreme. You might find that, like the student we just described, you are happier teaching in a setting that more closely reflects your strongly held beliefs about educational practices.

PROFESSIONAL ETHICS   **Ethics** is the study of right and wrong, duties and obligations. **Professional ethics** describe the moral commitments of a profession, extending the personal values and morality of individuals through shared, critical reflection about right and wrong actions in the workplace. Standards of ethical conduct provide a shared common ground for professionals who strive to do the right thing.

The ethical commitments of a profession are contained in its code of ethics. An ethical code is different from program policies, regulations, or laws. It describes the values of the field and the moral obligations of individual professionals. A code of ethics helps professionals do what is right—not what is easiest, what will bring the most personal benefit, or what will make them most popular. When followed by the members of a profession, a code of ethics assures the public that practice is based on moral standards and supports the best interests of those being served.

Codes of Ethics   There are several codes of ethics available for educators today. Those of the American Montessori Society and of the National Education Association apply to those who work with students preschool through grade 12. Codes developed by NAEYC and the Division for Early Childhood of the Council for Exceptional Children are specific to work with young children. If you live or work in a country other than the United States, you may have a code of ethics that reflects local values and culture. Early Childhood Australia, Canadian Child Care Federation, the British Association for Early Childhood Education, the New Zealand Teachers Council, and the Association of Early Childhood Educators, Singapore, have all developed codes of ethics for early childhood educators.

The most compelling reason for early childhood educators to have a code of ethics is that young children are vulnerable and lack the power to defend themselves. The adults who care for them are larger and stronger and control the resources that children need. Lilian Katz and Evangeline Ward (1978/1993) pointed out that the more powerless the client is, the more necessary it is for practitioners to behave ethically. Young children cannot defend themselves from teachers who are uncaring or abusive. For that reason, it is extremely important for those who work in early childhood programs to act fairly and responsibly on children's behalf.

Another reason that it is important for early childhood educators to have a code of ethics is that they serve a variety of client groups—children, families, and employing agencies. Most early childhood educators agree that their primary responsibility and loyalty is to the children. But it can be hard to keep sight of this when parents, agencies, or administrators demand that their concerns be given priority.

The Code of Ethics developed by the NAEYC is widely used in the United States and included in the curricula of many early childhood teacher education programs. The Code was designed to help teachers answer the question: "What should the good early childhood educator do when faced with a situation that involves ethics?" The Code is based on the core values of the early childhood field and organized into four sections describing professional responsibilities to children, families, colleagues, and community and society. The Code is designed to help practitioners make responsible ethical decisions. It includes **ideals** that describe exemplary practice and **principles** that describe practices that are required, prohibited, and permitted. (The NAEYC Code can be found in Appendix A.)

The NAEYC Code was adopted in 1989 and has been updated regularly since then, the most recent version being approved in 2011. The Code includes a supplement for teacher educators (2004) and a supplement for administrators (2006). It has been adopted by the National Association for Family Child Care and endorsed by the Association for Childhood Education International and the Southern Early Childhood Association. All educators who work with young children should identify the code that applies to their program, read it carefully to understand their ethical responsibilities, and refer to the code when ethical guidance is needed.

Video Example 1.2: Why a Code of Ethics Is Important for Early Childhood Educators

Watch this video (paying special attention to the first 3 minutes) of Stephanie Feeney discussing the importance of a Code of Ethics in early childhood education. Which of the reasons were most meaningful to you? What is your reaction to the idea of using a code of ethics to support moral behavior in early childhood programs?
https://www.youtube.com/watch?v=51jQ4wnSDag

Ethical Responsibilities **Ethical responsibilities** are those things that must or must not be done in work with young children. They are clear-cut and not subject to deliberation. The first and most important of the responsibilities spelled out in the NAEYC Code and most other codes of ethics is that the professional should do no harm. The first item in the NAEYC Code (P-1.1) reads, "Above all, we shall not harm children. We shall not participate in practices that are emotionally damaging, physically harmful, disrespectful, degrading, dangerous, exploitative, or intimidating to children. This principle has precedence over all others in this Code" (NAEYC, 2005/2011). This item in the Code tells us that the first priority of every early childhood educator must be the well-being of children and that every action and decision should first be considered in the light of potential harm.

A second very important responsibility is the obligation to keep information shared in the course of professional duties strictly confidential (**confidentiality** is a hallmark of every profession). This is a very important responsibility for early childhood educators and one that is too often violated because they work closely with children and family members and acquire a great deal of information about them. Nothing erodes trust faster than divulging private information given by a family member. An early childhood educator should never share confidential information, such as knowledge about an impending divorce shared by a parent, with a person who does not have a legitimate need to have it.

Other ethical responsibilities include being familiar with the knowledge base of early childhood education and basing practice on it; being familiar with laws and regulations that impact on children and programs; respecting families' culture, language, customs, beliefs, child-rearing values, and right to make decisions for their children; attempting to resolve concerns with coworkers and employers collegially; and assisting programs in providing a high quality of service.

Ethical Dilemmas When you encounter an issue or problem at work, one of the first things you need to do is determine whether it involves ethics. Ask yourself whether it has to do with right and wrong, rights and responsibilities, and human welfare. Not all conflicts that arise at work involve ethics. If the teacher next door keeps using the same outdated curriculum, she may not meet your standards or provide the best experiences for children, but she is not being unethical. If you decide that an issue involves ethics, however, you need to decide whether it involves a responsibility or if it is an ethical dilemma.

An **ethical dilemma** is a workplace issue that involves competing professional values and has more than one defensible resolution. Deciding on the right course of action can be difficult because a dilemma puts the interests of one person or group in conflict with those of another. For instance, it might mean placing the needs of a child above those of the parent. We have often used the example of a situation in which a parent asks a teacher to prevent her child from taking a nap even when it is clear that the child needs the nap to be able to function in the afternoon. Whatever choice you make in an ethical dilemma involves some benefits and some costs. In the nap situation, if the teacher decides not to let the child nap, she will be honoring the parent's wish, and the child may be able to fall asleep more easily at night. If she refuses the mother's request, the child will get much-needed sleep and will have a better experience in school in the afternoon. Either of these solutions could be justified using a code of ethics. There may not be ready resolutions for many of the dilemmas you face in your early childhood workplace in this or any other book. Rather, these dilemmas require careful deliberation, using guidance from a code of ethics in combination with good professional judgment. The first thing you must do when facing an ethical dilemma is to determine if there is potential that a child might be harmed. If this is the case, you must give priority to the needs of the child.

Guidance for addressing ethical dilemmas can be found in the NAEYC Code of Ethical Conduct. The "Guidelines for Ethical Reflection" box provides direction for thinking about the ethical dilemmas presented in this book.

Guidelines for Ethical Reflection

A feature in this book, "Reflect on Your Ethical Responsibilities," is designed to give you experience in thinking through how an early childhood educator should approach a professional ethical dilemma. When a dilemma occurs in the workplace, it is best if how you respond is based on the collective ethical wisdom of the profession, not on your personal view of the right thing to do. The question changes from "What should I do in this situation?" to "What should the good early childhood educator do in this situation?" Although it may not always tell you exactly what to do, the NAEYC Code of Ethical Conduct can help you think through the ethical issues that you encounter and remind you that the primary commitment of an early childhood educator is to the well-being of children. When faced with an ethical dilemma, the best course of action is sometimes obvious, but at other times you will need to think hard to come up with the best possible resolution. The NAEYC Code will help you clarify your responsibilities and prioritize values. Ethical reflections are found throughout the chapters in this book.

Once you have determined that you are facing an ethical dilemma, you can use the following steps to guide you in finding a satisfactory resolution:

- Who are the people involved in the situation? What are the conflicting responsibilities? What does each of the people involved need?

- Look for guidance in the NAEYC Code—what are the applicable ideals and principles and core values? Be sure to look at all of the sections of the Code that might apply.

- Based on your review of the Code and your reflection about the situation, what do you think would be the most ethical resolution to the dilemma?

✓ **A Quick Check 1.3**

Gauge your understanding of the concepts in this section.

Careers in Early Childhood Education: Finding Your Path

In this section, we will explore career options in early childhood education and look at training requirements for various roles and stages of professional development.

Every early childhood educator has a story.

Fred always enjoyed being with children. He took a child development class in high school and loved the time he spent with kids in a preschool. Like his older brother, Fred went into auto mechanics and became a certified mechanic. His family approved, and he made good money. But Fred was dissatisfied; working as a mechanic was not fulfilling. After 3 years, he decided to go back to school to train to be an early childhood educator. He realized that he wouldn't make as much money, but he knew this was what he wanted to do.

As a young mother, Ann enrolled her son in the campus child care center while working on her BA in French. She often stayed at the center and helped out. One day, the staff asked her if she wanted to work part-time at the center. The next semester, Ann changed her major to education. Today, she is a kindergarten teacher.

Ruth always knew she wanted to be a teacher. She enrolled in pre-ed classes as soon as she entered college. She worked in a child care program as a part-time aide while she was going to college. Ruth became a preschool teacher after she graduated and soon went on to graduate school. Today, she is the education director for a small preschool.

In college, Laurel had a double major in psychology and anthropology. She decided that she wanted to communicate her love of learning by becoming a teacher. Through a practicum placement in a preschool, she learned about the strong impact that early childhood education can have on children's development. She decided to become a preschool teacher because she wanted to make a difference. After teaching preschool for several years, she realized that she was fascinated by the philosophy and theory of early education. She decided that she could also serve young children by working with future teachers. She went back to school for a master's degree and now teaches early childhood education in a community college.

Roles

There are many settings in which you can work with young children and many roles you can take. Sue Bredekamp (2011) suggests that these roles can be divided into two broad groups. The first, "working *with* children," includes positions that involve direct responsibility for children's care and education. Positions include family child care providers and classroom teachers in infant–toddler programs (sometimes called caregivers), preschools, kindergarten, and primary grades (1 through 3) as well as bilingual and special education teachers.

The second category, "working *for* children," includes positions that support children's development and learning but does not involve day-to-day interaction with them. Roles that involve close proximity to children include child care center administrator, curriculum specialist, school principal, and counselor. Roles that are further removed from direct work with children are education specialist in a large agency, teacher educator, resource and referral specialist, and parent educator.

There are other roles in which a professional supports young children but that require significantly different training. These include child therapists, child care licensing workers, librarians, social workers, and school counselors. Those who fill these roles do important work for children and families but are not considered to be early childhood educators.

The great majority of the students who are reading this book are preparing to work directly with young children and many will find this work satisfying for their entire careers. Others may work with children for a period of time and then seek a new challenge or realize that they are more suited for other kinds of work. If you choose to move to another role, you are likely to find that what you learned about young children will prove to be valuable in your life in variety of ways.

Educational Requirements

You will gain the knowledge and skill you need to work effectively with young children through specialized training in child development and early childhood education.

Teaching experience alone or a degree in another field (even a related field like elementary education) does not provide the specific knowledge and skills needed to work successfully with young children.

Research has demonstrated that higher levels of teacher education result in better classroom quality and greater gains in children's cognitive and social development (Barnett, 2004; Early et al., 2007; Kontos & Wilcox-Herzog, 2001). This research has led to recent efforts to require more training, especially in the federally funded Head Start program and state-funded prekindergarten programs. It has also led to efforts to coordinate training requirements for everyone who works with children from birth to age 8 in all settings.

Educational requirements vary depending on the position, the age of the children, how the program is administered, and the community in which it is housed. Requirements for teachers who work in programs for younger children (birth through age 5) are almost always less rigorous than those for teachers who work in kindergarten through third grade classrooms. In some places, different training is required for those who work with children younger than 3 years than for those who work with 3- to 5-year-olds. Teachers in programs for children from birth to age 5 may receive a degree from a 2-year college while those who work in public school prekindergarten programs and kindergarten through third grade are required to complete a 4-year degree in education.

Preschool and child care programs for children from birth to age 5 generally require an associate's (2-year) degree in early childhood education or the *Child Development Associate (CDA)* credential. The CDA is a nationally awarded early childhood credential that requires that applicants have a high school diploma or GED, complete 120 hours of approved training in eight subject areas (from a community college, agency, or distance-learning organization), have 480 hours of experience working with young children, complete a professional portfolio, be observed in the classroom, and take an examination (Council for Professional Recognition, 2011).

Associate degrees in early childhood education require course work in education and child development; practical experience working with infants, toddlers, and preschoolers; and general education courses. Students who receive a bachelor's degree in education or child and family studies with specialized course work in early childhood education may also teach in programs for children younger than 5.

Within the early childhood community, the 2-year degree is regarded not as a terminal degree but as a step in a professional development continuum that is referred to as a career ladder or lattice (lattice suggests that movement can be across roles, as well as to higher levels of the same role). Since the 1980s, efforts have been under way to create a seamless system for early childhood professional development that begins with community-based training or a CDA, progresses to a 2-year degree, articulates to a 4-year degree, and, finally, leads to a graduate degree (NAEYC, 2009). This progression is designed to encourage each educator to find the role and training that best reflects his or her interests, abilities, and personal preferences.

Teaching prekindergarten through grade 3 in public schools requires a 4-year teacher preparation program that leads to a bachelor's degree in education. These programs follow an approved course of study that qualifies the student for a teaching certificate (also called a license). Training requirements for teaching young children vary from state to state. Some programs in 4-year institutions focus on preparing teachers to work with children birth to age 8; some focus on preschool and primary grades (4–8 years), and others on preparation for teaching kindergarten through sixth grade (5–12 years). Some programs offer a degree in early childhood education, others make it an endorsement to an elementary certificate.

Awareness of the importance of early childhood education in children's development has led to an increased interest in the qualifications of those who work with young children. For example, Head Start, a federally funded program for low-income children, has raised teacher requirements to ensure that all newly hired and half of current Head Start teachers must have a bachelor's degree in early childhood education or a related field.

Table 1.1 lays out recommended training for a variety of roles in early childhood settings.

Career Paths

People come to the field of early childhood education in a variety of ways. It is estimated that only 25% of early childhood educators began their careers in the "traditional" manner by majoring in early childhood education before they started working in the field. Some (about 25%) were introduced to the field as parents, observing the benefits of a good program for their young child and then going to school to get formally trained. Others (about 50%) have come by what can be called a serendipitous route, discovering the field as a happy accident, often after receiving a degree in another field and later obtaining the specialized training needed to become an early childhood educator (Bredekamp, 1992).

Table 1.1 Roles and Training Required to Work with Children in Early Childhood Programs

Setting	Role	Required Training
Homes	Family child care provider	Most states—no formal training required Infant/child CPR and first aid CDA credential in family child care and accreditation by the National Association for Family Child Care are desirable Small business administration training is desirable
	Nanny	Most states—no formal training required Nanny training programs in colleges and private agencies—can vary from 6 weeks to a year in length
	Home visitor	Most states—no formal training required CDA credential or higher degree required for some home visitor programs for low-income and at-risk children
Centers (early childhood programs for children under the age of 5 and after-school programs for elementary school children)	Teacher aide/assistant	Orientation and on-the-job training or CDA credential
	School-age program leader	High school diploma or equivalent Orientation and on-the-job training
	Assistant teacher/assistant caregiver	Some training in working with young children May require a CDA (infant and toddler, preschool, or bilingual) or a degree Usually less training or experience than the supervising teacher
	Teacher/caregiver	Specialized training in working with young children Most states—college degree required (sometimes in education, early childhood education, or child development) Some states—CDA accepted
	Master, lead, or head teacher in a program for children birth to age 5	Same as teachers Employer may require specialized training Positions involving staff supervision or curriculum development may require bachelor's or master's degree
	Special education preschool teacher	A bachelor's degree in education with specialized training in special education
Elementary schools	Educational assistant	Requirements vary from state to state—in some states 2 years of college required
	Teacher (pre-K, kindergarten, grades 1–3 in a public school)	Bachelor's degree and elementary teacher certification Specialized training may include training in early childhood education Licensure varies by state—may cover infancy through third grade, preschool through third grade, kindergarten through sixth grade, or early childhood or kindergarten endorsement in addition to an elementary certificate
	Resource teacher or specialist	Degree and teaching credential, plus training to prepare in subject area

SOURCE: LaFramboise/Pearson Education, Inc.

We, the authors of this book, reflect two of these typical paths. Stephanie did what we like to refer to as "worked her way up" to early childhood education. She got degrees in anthropology and teaching secondary school. After working as a social worker in a Head Start program she recognized the importance of early development and found her way to early childhood education. Eva and Sherry completed early childhood training before they entered the field. Eva always knew she wanted to become a preschool or kindergarten teacher and entered college with that as her career goal. As an undergraduate majoring in sociology, Sherry took a child development class as an elective and switched her major to child development when she became interested in learning more about young children.

Although there are diverse paths to entry, our observations over the years confirm Laura Colker's (2008) assertion that many early childhood educators enter the field because they feel that it is their "calling" and because they have a commitment to making a difference in children's lives and in the world.

Reflect On

Your Path

Have you always known you wanted to be a teacher? Did you receive training in another field and discover early education by happy accident? Did you come to early childhood education with your own children? How do you think the path that brought you to the field might influence your perspective as a teacher?

Video Example 1.3: Age Groups Teachers Prefer

Watch the video to see an example of teachers of young children discussing their career choices and the age group they prefer to work with. Reflect on which age group you feel most drawn to as you begin your career in early childhood education. Why does this age group appeal to you? Which group do you think you would find most challenging?

Stages of Professional Development

Just like the children with whom you will work, you will pass through developmental stages as you continue to grow as an educator. Like the children, you will need appropriate motivation and support to reach your full potential at each stage. Knowing about these stages can help you realize that you will have different professional needs at different times in your career. As a beginning teacher, you will focus on working directly with children and the network of relationships that go with it. With experience, day-to-day tasks get easier, and you will have different needs and seek new challenges.

Reflect On

Your Ideal Job

Imagine a perfect job for you in early childhood education. What would the job be like? Why does it appeal to you? What training would you need for this job?

Lilian Katz (1995) describes four stages in the development of teachers of young children that focus on changes in the need for professional support and education. Awareness of these stages may help you understand the progression of growth and learning in teachers:

- **Stage 1: Survival.**   The first year of working with young children is a time when you need to apply the knowledge that you gained in college. It can be stressful because everything is new and also because you may have unrealistically high expectations of yourself. As a beginning teacher, you are likely to need advice and lots of practical suggestions. You will want to feel appreciated and connected to other professionals.

- **Stage 2: Consolidation.**   When you have become adept at basic "survival" in the classroom, you begin to bring together what you know to create a more personal approach to working with children. During this time, you may find on-site assistance, consultation, and the advice of colleagues helpful.

- **Stage 3: Renewal.**   When you have been working with children for 3 to 5 years, you may begin to feel the need for new challenges. At this stage, you may enjoy doing professional reading, going to conferences or workshops, doing action research, and joining professional associations. Visits to other schools may renew your enthusiasm and give you new ideas as well as a greater sense of belonging and professionalism.

- **Stage 4: Maturity.**   After 5 or more years of working with children, you may find yourself less interested in practical details (which you have mastered) and more interested in consideration of the values, theories, issues, and philosophy that underlie your work. At this stage, attending seminars, working on advanced degrees, and more theoretical professional reading may renew your sense of excitement and provide new areas of interest and involvement.

A Quick Check 1.4

Gauge your understanding of the concepts in this section.

Final Thoughts

You are at the beginning of your career as an early childhood educator and have much to learn and many rewarding experiences ahead of you. You already know that you will need to work hard in your college classes. But you may not realize that this is just the beginning—you will continue to learn well after your college work is over. Good teachers are lifelong learners because they want to be and because it is essential to their work. If you aspire to be a good teacher—and we assume you do—you will continue to learn about children's development and how to teach them for your whole career.

A job becomes a *calling* when it involves an important purpose, deep values, and a strong sense of how one wants to contribute to the world. When you get paid to do work that has meaning in your life—work that you love—you have a calling. We hope that you will find that work in early childhood education will be your calling—a way you can experience personal fulfillment as you serve young children and their families.

The children are waiting.

 Application Exercise 1.2 Final Reflection

 ## To Learn More

Read

Bad Guys Don't Have Birthdays: Fantasy Play at Four, V. Paley (1991).
Good Morning Children: My First Years in Early Childhood Education, S. Pappas (2009).
My First Year as a Teacher, P. R. Kane (1991).
Teaching Four-Year-Olds: A Personal Journey, C. B. Hillman (Revised 2011).
The Boy Who Would Be a Helicopter, V. Paley (1990).
The Girl with the Brown Crayon, V. Paley (1997).
The Kindness of Children, V. Paley (1999).

Visit a Website

The following agencies and organizations have websites that are relevant to the study of teachers of young children:

National Association for the Education of Young Children
Association for Childhood Education International
Myers & Briggs Foundation
New York Early Childhood Professional Development Institute

 ## Starting Your Professional Portfolio

In order to document your growing knowledge and skill as an early childhood educator, we recommend that you keep a **professional portfolio**, as described in this section and update it regularly.

In education, as in many other fields, a good way to demonstrate your professional accomplishments is through the presentation of a professional portfolio. A portfolio documents your skills, knowledge, and training. In some colleges, you will be asked to create a portfolio for the purpose of assessing whether you have accomplished the required performance outcomes for a class or program.

Regardless of whether or not you are required to create a professional portfolio, we recommend that you keep one as a convenient way to keep track of your accomplishments to share with future employers as well as a tool for recording your growth as a teacher. At the end of each chapter, we suggest additions to your professional portfolio that relate to the content of the chapter and that demonstrate your learning. Here are some ideas to help you begin:

Start Your Portfolio.   Select an open, flexible format that is easy to organize and modify (such as a three-ring binder or a digital format of your choosing that will still be current when you interview for a job) to hold your portfolio.

Introduce Yourself.   Use the reflections in this chapter to help you get started—writing ideas you'd like to include (1) in a brief autobiography that outlines the significant events in your life that led you to choose early childhood education as your career, (2) in a personal mission statement that explains your vision for yourself as an early childhood educator and your hopes and dreams as a professional, and (3) in a statement of educational philosophy describing what you value in the education and care of young children. Remember, these will change as you progress from beginning student to beginning professional. Periodically go back to these to see how your ideas have evolved and make revisions that reflect new insights.

Collect Letters of Recommendation.   Letters of recommendation from people who know your work and your character are independent evidence of your ability. When an employer, supervisor, or college professor gives you a favorable evaluation or compliments you on your work, it is a good moment to ask that person to formalize his or her appreciation by writing you a letter for your portfolio.

Create a Résumé.   A résumé is a short outline of your qualifications and experience. It is useful to include an updated résumé in your portfolio if you plan to use the portfolio as a part of a job application. It gives a prospective employer a quick way to see if you are suitable for a position.

Document Your Qualifications.   Make a section in your portfolio for degrees, certificates, personnel registry cards, and diplomas. Remember that training in other fields (e.g., music, water safety) can be useful supplements to your formal training in early education.

Begin an Ongoing Training Record.   Over the course of your career, you will have many opportunities to engage in ongoing training. Your portfolio is an excellent place to keep track of this training and keep any certificates of attendance that you receive. For each training entry, be sure to note the date of the training, the name of the trainer and sponsoring organization, and the number of hours of training. You can also make a note of any ways in which you improved your practice as a result of the training.

Document Your Knowledge and Competence.   Use the statements of core knowledge and skills for your state, the CDA competency standards, or the NAEYC program standards as a framework for the knowledge and competency sections of your portfolio. In each section, provide examples of what you have learned and work you have done in this area. You can document your work through photographs (e.g., a photograph of children's work or a classroom environment that you designed), written descriptions (e.g., a description of a situation in which you successfully guided a child who was having difficulties), or a sample of your written work (e.g., a lesson plan, a paper that demonstrates your knowledge, or a newsletter for families).

Your portfolio should include only items that have a direct bearing on your professional abilities and growth. Each item for the knowledge and competence section of your portfolio should have a brief explanatory statement that ties your work to the standard that is being illustrated so that a reader can understand why it has been included.

Sample Portfolio Table of Contents

Introduction to a Teacher

Autobiography

Philosophy and mission

Professional letters of recommendation

Qualifications

Résumé of education and experience

Personnel registry card

College degrees and certificates

First aid and CPR certification

NAEYC or other professional association membership card

Ongoing Training Record

Certificates of attendance at workshops and conferences (be sure to include date)

Knowledge and Competence (This could be put in two columns labeled "Competency Area" and "Examples")

Growth and development (e.g., photograph of a toy you made for a child of a particular age)

Professionalism (a sample of a reflection you wrote after attending a workshop)

Diversity (a plan for a child with disabilities or who speaks a language other than English)

Observation and assessment (an observation you made and a plan based on it)

Health, safety, and nutrition (a plan for teaching children about health)

Learning environments (a sample floor plan for a classroom)

Relationships and guidance (a reflection on a situation in which you guided a child)

Planning learning experiences (a sample integrated study plan you created)

Working with families (a newsletter or family conference outline you wrote)

Program management (a sample of some ways that you maintain records)

Notes: Your portfolio should not include brochures or handouts that you have gathered—only those you have produced yourself. To ensure privacy, be sure that you do not include the names of children and family members in portfolio materials.

Document Your Skill & Knowledge About Teachers in Your Professional Portfolio

Include some or all of the following:

- Briefly describe yourself using Thomas and Chess's Nine Dimensions of Temperament, and Gardner's Multiple Intelligences. Reflect on how these characteristics might influence how you teach.

- Review the experiences and relationships in your life at home and in the world that led you to choose early childhood education as a career. Reflect on how these experiences might impact how you teach.

- Read one of the books about teachers and teaching listed in the "To Learn More" section of the chapter. Write a short review of the book as if you were writing for a newsletter or journal for teachers. Give the highlights of the book. Discuss what you learned about the teacher in the book as a person and a professional. Share the personal meaning for you.

- Explore the kinds of positions for early childhood educators available in your community. Look at community websites and newspaper advertisement for jobs. What did you learn about kinds of jobs and their availability?

Shared Writing 1.1 Educational Requirements and Licensure for Your State

---

Chapter 2
The Field of Early Childhood Education

It takes a village to raise a child.

AFRICAN PROVERB

 ## Chapter Learning Outcomes:

2.1 Describe the kinds of programs that are available for the education and care of children between birth and 5 years of age including those with disabilities and other special needs.

2.2 Describe the kinds of programs for the education and care of children ages 5 to 8 years of age including those with disabilities and other special needs.

2.3 Explain how different kinds of accountability measures are used to protect children and support quality in early childhood programs.

2.4 Discuss some of the educational standards that are in place today and their relationship to program quality.

2.5 Explain different views of school readiness and their implications for practice.

The NAEYC Professional Preparation Standards

The NAEYC Professional Preparation Standard that applies to this chapter:

Standard 6: Becoming a Professional (NAEYC, 2009).

Key element:

6a: Identifying and involving oneself with the early childhood field

Education and Care Programs for Children from Birth to Age 5

In this chapter, we present an overview of early childhood education as it exists in the United States today with an emphasis on programs and developments that we believe will be of interest to a beginning teacher seeking to find her or his place in the field. Early childhood education touches the lives of many people in our society. Those who are affected most are the children and families who are served by programs and the educators who work in them. Children's lives are enriched by early childhood programs that support their development and by teachers who are knowledgeable and who respect and care about them. Family members benefit when they are sure that their children are well cared for when they are away from home and from relationships with teachers who communicate effectively and offer guidance about how they can support their children's development. Teachers thrive on supportive workplaces and the opportunity to do work that makes a difference in the lives of children and families.

The field of early childhood education has grown and evolved greatly in the past 50 years in terms of the number of children served and the kinds of programs that are available for families to choose from. It is a good time for you to be entering the field because there is strong public support for early learning today and many new developments are under way. Before you turn your focus to how to engage with young children, it is helpful to acquire some basic information about the field that you are entering. In this section we describe programs that are most widely available today for children 5 years of age and younger.

As you become a teacher, you will learn about and work in different kinds of programs for young children. We recommend that you visit and participate in several programs to gain direct experience with a variety of ages and approaches available in early childhood education today. Your growing understanding of aspects of the field and the important contributions it makes in our society will contribute to your growth as an educator who supports the development of young children.

Ways to Classify Programs

There are many different kinds of programs designed to meet the diverse needs of children and families. Programs vary in the services they provide, in the length of the program day and year, and in the philosophy and goals that guide their practice. Programs for young children can be classified in terms of the ages and other characteristics of the children they serve, by their purposes, by the places in which they are housed, and by their sponsorship and funding.

CHILDREN SERVED **Early childhood** is a period in the life cycle that includes birth through age 8. This phase can be subdivided into four different age-groups:

- Infants and toddlers—birth to 36 months
- Preschoolers—3- and 4-year-olds
- Kindergartners—5- and 6-year-olds
- Primary age children—7- and 8- year-olds

The children served in early childhood programs include those who are typically developing and those who have a disability or other special need.

PURPOSES Early childhood education programs serve a number of interrelated purposes. The primary ones are to provide education for children—to support their learning, to stimulate development in all areas, and to prepare them to be successful in the next level of schooling. A second important purpose is to provide care for children in families where adults are working or in training. Care for children's physical and psychological needs and the provision of early education are inextricably linked—preschools, child development centers, early intervention programs, prekindergartens, and kindergartens, are the major ways care and education are delivered to children between birth and age 5. Another purpose is to provide children who are at risk for school failure with programs designed to ameliorate the effects of poverty through the provision of high quality programs and support services for their families. Yet another purpose is the revitalization of indigenous languages that has emerged as an important goal for members of communities who want to preserve their language for future generations. Some early childhood programs serve additional purposes, such as education of family members and the provision of health, nutrition, and social services to children and families.

SETTINGS Early childhood education and care programs can be found in settings that are dedicated to the care of children (centers and schools) and in homes.

SPONSORSHIP AND FUNDING Sponsorship and funding of early childhood programs may be public (federal, state, or county) or private. Over the years and continuing today, the greatest percentage of programs for children under age 5 are private and paid for by tuition paid by the families of the children who attend. Private programs may be not-for-profit, intended as a service to children and their families. Some of these programs are housed in religious facilities and may be partly subsidized by faith-based groups. Programs may also be for-profit, designed as a service-oriented business. Some of these centers are owned and operated by nationwide chains that attempt to make child care affordable and profitable by using standardized building plans, bulk purchase of equipment and supplies, and a standardized curriculum. These for-profit chains have become an increasingly common type of privately sponsored child care.

Child Care

The term **child care** refers to the provision of care for young children whose family members work or are in school or training programs. Historically, child care programs served the working poor with a minimal quality of care and little or no attention to education. Today, in recognition of the important development that occurs in the early years, child care programs provide early childhood education along with care for children while their family members are at work. It is important for a beginning teacher to understand that child care is an important delivery mechanism for early childhood education.

Child care is a fact of life for a significant portion of children and families in our country. Families face numerous decisions for balancing their work and home lives, including choosing the type of care to provide for their children while they are at work. Most families want a setting that is convenient to their home or workplace, that they know will provide safe and nurturing care for their children, and, of course, that they can afford.

Child care may be provided in centers and schools and in homes. Both kinds of programs have the challenging task of providing a safe, nurturing environment and worthwhile educational experiences, often for long hours each day. Today, the majority of programs provide care for children for a full day while members of their family are at work or engaged in other tasks.

The need for out-of-home care for children under age 5 has increased as growing numbers of mothers have entered the workforce. In 2014, the labor force participation rate of mothers with children under 6 years old was 64%. Participation of mothers with children under 3 years old was 62% (Bureau of Labor Statistics, 2015, Table 5). Even for children whose mothers were not working for pay, over a quarter were in some form of care (Laughlin, 2013, Table 2) Figure 2.1, illustrates this. In 2011, 61% of the 20.4 million children under 5 years of age were in some type of regular child care arrangement (Laughlin, 2013, Table 1).

Children tend to spend long hours each week in care settings. In 2011, preschoolers in child care (see footnote 7 pg. 6 of Laughlin) spent an average of 33 hours per week in care. Many children of working parents experience more than one child care placement. In 2011, 27% of preschoolers of employed mothers participated in two or more child care arrangements (Laughlin, 2013, Table 2).

Child care settings are diverse. Based on the 2011 census, (see Figure 2.2) the most recent statistics available, relatives regularly provided child care to almost half of the more than 20 million preschoolers. Nearly one-quarter of all preschoolers were cared for in organized facilities, with child care centers being the most common (Laughlin, 2013,Table 1). Some families choose care offered in a caregiver's home or provided by nannies who work in the child's home. Preschool-age children were more likely to be cared for by a relative (42%) than by a nonrelative (33%) (Laughlin, 2013, Table 1).

Because they have found that it contributes to a reliable and productive workforce, some corporations, hospitals, and government agencies provide child care programs for their employees. The U.S. Department of Defense—the largest employer sponsor of child care—offers programs for children of personnel who serve in the military. Colleges and universities may sponsor and subsidize early childhood programs that offer care and education for the children of faculty, staff, and students as well as serving as laboratories for teacher education and research. Some high schools sponsor early childhood programs to serve the children of students and/or as a place for students to learn about child development and how to work in early education programs.

Specialized care designed to meet the needs of working families is available in some communities. This includes programs that are available late hours for family members

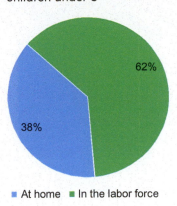

Figure 2.1 Mothers with children under 3

- At home   In the labor force

SOURCE: Women in the labor force: a databook as published by U.S. Bureau of Labor Statistics, 2016.

Figure 2.2 Who's Minding the Kids? Children under 5

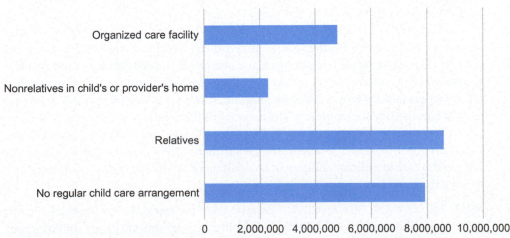

SOURCE: Who's Minding the Kids? Child Care Arrangements: Spring 2011, Household Economic Studies, as published by US Census Bureau, Lynda Laughlin, Issued April 2013

who work in hotels and factories; others, often housed in hospitals, care for children with mild, noncontagious illnesses.

CENTER-BASED EDUCATION AND CARE **Center-based education and care** for children between birth and 5 years of age may be located in sites that are specifically designed to provide care and education for groups of young children; religious facilities, community and recreational facilities, housing complexes; and workplaces. Programs include child care centers (also called child development centers), preschools, laboratory schools, parent co-ops, Head Start programs, and state-funded prekindergarten programs. Child care programs are sometimes referred to as day care—this term is left over from the 1900s, when it was used to distinguish care offered during the day from overnight boarding care. We prefer the term **child care**, which gives a more accurate description of what programs actually do.

Until the 1980s most early childhood programs served children between 2½ and 5 years of age. As more and more women entered the workforce, the demand for out-of-home care for infants and toddlers grew. In order to meet children's needs and ensure their safety, experts believe—and most states require—that programs for infants should have a ratio of one caregiver to every three or four children. For this reason, the cost of infant care in centers is much higher than care for older preschoolers. In 2014, the average annual cost of full-time care for an infant in center-based care ranged from $4,822 in Mississippi to $22,631 in the District of Columbia (Wood et al., 2015, Appendix 1). Even though infant–toddler care may be available in most areas, its high cost makes it inaccessible for many families (see Figure 2.3).

HOME-BASED EDUCATION AND CARE **Home-based education and care** is the least visible yet most common form of privately sponsored child care in the United States. Throughout history, children have been cared for in their own homes and in the homes of relatives, friends, and paid caregivers. Home-based care may be located in the home of the child or the home of a caregiver. It can be provided in licensed or unlicensed family child care homes (usually three to eight children), in licensed group child care homes (generally 12 to 15 children), in the homes of relatives or family friends (called family, friend, and neighbor care), or in the child's own home by either a trained caregiver, like a nanny, or an untrained caregiver.

Home-based care is typically less expensive than center-based care and nearly always more flexible with regard to schedule and provision of care for children who have mild illnesses. It may be available from early morning to early evening and may also be offered evenings and weekends. This kind of program is often chosen by families of infants and toddlers who prefer that their children be cared for in the small, intimate environment of a home. It is also employed as an alternative to a center-based care for preschool-age children whose families find these programs more convenient or more affordable, or who prefer a less structured setting.

Until recently, the expense of in-home care was borne by the families of the children served. In the early 1990s, the federal government reformed welfare programs that provide financial assistance to poor families, and child care subsidies became available to assist families who are leaving welfare rolls to enter the labor force. Under the Temporary Assistance for Needy Families program, funds are allocated to states to be used to help families pay for child care. The majority of these families choose informal care, which is generally more obtainable in low-income neighborhoods than licensed care, especially for infants and toddlers. The Department of Defense also offers the option of in-home care to military children in recognition of the fact that many families prefer to have their children cared for in home settings.

AVAILABILITY AND FINANCING Because there is no one system for financing and delivering child care, the availability and quality of programs varies greatly from community to community and from state to state. What is consistently true is that quality programs are expensive and therefore tend to be most accessible to affluent families.

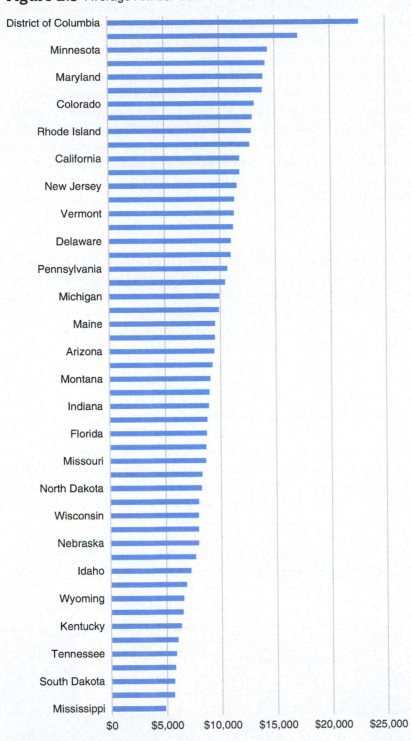

Figure 2.3 Average Annual Cost of Full Time Infant Care

Low-income families who meet eligibility requirements may have access to high-quality government-funded early childhood programs when spaces are available.

Families in poverty with an employed mother rely to a greater extent on grandparents and fathers than on child care centers or family child care providers for care for their children. Children in families above the poverty line are more likely to be cared for in a child care center or preschool than are children in poverty. This tendency can be attributed to the higher costs associated with organized care (Laughlin, 2013, Table 1).

The cost of child care continues to rise. In 2011, families with children under 5 paid, on average, over $9,300 a year for child care. Families in poverty spent a greater proportion of their monthly income on child care compared to families at or above the poverty level. In 2014, average center care cost for a 4-year-old varied between 26% of a median single parent family's income in Louisiana and 45% in New York State (Wood et al., 2015 Appendix III). However, for families who pay for care, the percentage of family monthly income actually spent on child care has remained relatively constant between 1987 and 2011, at around 7% (Laughlin, 2013, Figure 4).

Some families receive fee assistance from a local or state agency for a child care subsidy, such as the federal Child Care and Development Block Grant (CCDBG), to help pay for the child care. Unfortunately, Congressional funding of CCDBG has stayed flat since 2002, while demand for child care subsidies has risen. Some states have responded by cutting reimbursement rates to child care providers; increasing parents' co-payment, making care unaffordable for some; and tightening eligibility, so a program serves fewer children (Wood et al., 2015, p. 38).

Early Childhood Education

The term **early childhood education (ECE)** refers to education and care provided in all settings for children between birth and age 8. It is designed to support children's development and prepare them for later school experiences. The great majority of programs today also provide care for children while family members are at work or in school. Some programs last for only part of a day but most programs today are available for a full day to meet the needs of working families.

One of the first types of early childhood education offered in the United States was the **nursery school**, which was designed to give children opportunities to socialize and engage in creative activities. Historically nursery schools were part-day programs that focused on social and emotional development. The nursery schools of the past have evolved into today's preschool programs. **Preschool** is the term used to refer to programs that focus on supporting children's development. Most programs today combine education and care functions—they support children's development and learning and also provide care for children while their families are at work. This has led early childhood educators to emphasize that the two are linked by referring to the field as "early childhood education and care."

 Application Exercise 2.1

Watch and Write About Education and Care in Early Childhood Programs

High-quality programs for young children today embrace the dual focus of care and education as essential components. As a teacher entering the field, you will see that good programs for young children interweave these elements into all aspects of the program.

LABORATORY SCHOOLS **Laboratory schools** (sometimes called demonstration schools) are programs operated in association with a university, college, or other teacher education program. They supplement academic learning with a living laboratory in which college students observe children and acquire supervised teaching experience. In a lab school, students may participate in informal research and the development of curricula. These schools are used to show visitors exemplary educa-

SOURCE: Jeff Reese

tional practice and may also provide a setting for faculty and graduate student research in psychology or child development. Lab schools take several forms. Some serve a college's student, staff, and faculty children as well as provide opportunities for college students to gain experience working with children; others may extend services to the community at large. Lab schools may provide care for preschool-age children only or may include infants and toddlers and kindergarten, elementary, and high school students.

PARENT COOPERATIVES **Parent cooperatives** are preschool programs that are organized and run by family members who are expected to actively participate in all aspects of the school, including administration (including the hiring of teachers), operation, and maintenance of the facility; meetings related to the school program; and fund-raising. An important feature of these programs is that they give parents an opportunity to work directly with children under the guidance of a trained teacher. Learning effective guidance and teaching strategies helps them be better parents while bonding with and learning alongside their child. Originally, family members were expected to participate in the classroom on a regular basis. Today, in response to limitations posed by families' work schedules, this requirement may be modified and additional paid staff hired. Similarly, some part-day parent-cooperative programs have increased their hours of operation in response to family work schedules. Teachers in co-op programs need a high level of skill to be able to work effectively with children and, at the same time, guide family members in interacting with children and learning about child development.

Head Start

A significant landmark in the history of early childhood education in the United States was the creation of **Head Start**, a federally funded, comprehensive child development program that provides education and support services for eligible children from low-income families. The program was created to ameliorate the effects of poverty on young children and to help prepare them to engage successfully with school expectations. Head Start is dedicated to addressing all aspects of development. It includes an educational program, support for social-emotional development, physical and mental health services, and a nutrition component. It also emphasizes strengthening the family and involving the community.

Since it was created in 1965, Head Start has provided high-quality early education and comprehensive support services to 3-, 4-, and 5-year-olds from low-income families. Programs include services such as health screenings, referrals, and social services. It supports family members in learning about child development, parenting strategies, and how to be their child's first teacher. Head Start also encourages the involvement of parents in the administration of community programs.

Head Start serves a diverse group of children and families. Nearly half the children served are 4-year-olds, 37% are of Hispanic or Latino origin, 29% are African American, 29% are from families speaking a language other than English at home, and 12% have identified disabilities (see Figure 2.4). Most programs are housed in centers, and half are full rather than part day. A small percentage of Head Start spaces are in family child care programs (Administration for Children and Families, 2015). All Head Start programs must comply with federal Head Start Program Performance Standards designed to promote all areas of children's development.

Head Start has grown and changed over time. Soon after it started, Head Start programs for Native American and migrant farmworkers were added. In the 1990s, it was expanded from part day to full day in many places in response to provisions of national welfare reform that required parents who were receiving welfare assistance to pursue job training and employment opportunities.

In 2015, Head Start employed approximately 120,000 teachers, assistant teachers, home visitors, and family child care providers. In response to the requirement in the Head Start Act for higher levels of teacher education, in 2015, 73% of Head Start center-based preschool teachers had a baccalaureate degree or higher in early childhood education or a related field. Among child development staff, 30% were proficient in a language other than English (see Figure 2.5) (Administration for Children and Families, 2015).

EARLY HEAD START In 1994, in recognition of research demonstrating the importance of development from birth to age 3, **Early Head Start** was established to serve low-income pregnant women and families with infants and toddlers from birth to age 3. The Early Head Start program is designed to enhance all areas of children's development, to promote school readiness, and to enable parents to be better caregivers and teachers to their children. The program, conducted in both centers and homes, includes educational experiences, home visits, parent education, comprehensive health services, nutrition, support for parenting, and comprehensive services to pregnant women.

Since its inception in 1965, Head Start has served more than 33 million children throughout the country. In 2015, Head Start was funded to serve nearly 1 million children and pregnant women (Administration for Children and Families, 2015). Unfortunately, due to a lack of sufficient funding, only half of all eligible children in the United States are currently able to participate in the Head Start and Early Head Start programs (Schmit & Ewen, 2012).

RESEARCH ON HEAD START AND SIMILAR PROGRAMS FOR LOW-INCOME CHILDREN Since it was created, there has been a great deal of debate about the effectiveness of Head Start and other early childhood programs for low-income children. Many

Figure 2.4 Who's in Head Start?

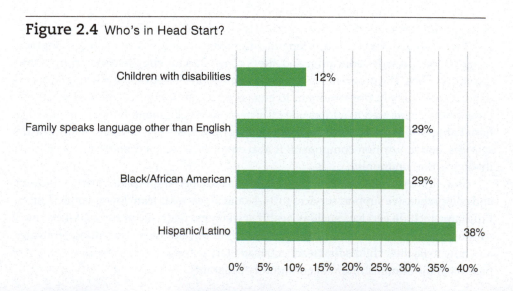

Figure 2.5 Education of Head Start Center-Based
Preschool Teachers

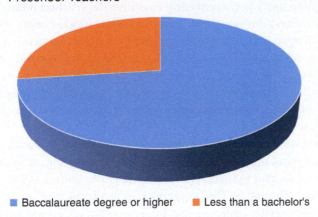

■ Baccalaureate degree or higher   ■ Less than a bachelor's

studies have been conducted, but until recently evidence regarding the long-term outcomes of these programs has been inconclusive (Barnett & Hustedt, 2005).

One national longitudinal study of the development of Head Start children was
conducted in 1997, using a battery of instruments called FACES (Family and Child
Experiences Survey). This study reported that children who attended Head Start
showed significant gains in vocabulary, writing skills, and social skills and that the
program had a positive impact on child health and readiness for school and families'
parenting practices. Follow-up studies in 2000, 2003, and 2006 documented significant
gains in vocabulary, early math, and early writing skills (Administration for Children,
Youth, and Families, 2001, 2003, 2006).

Barnett and Hustedt (2005) conclude from a review of research that the benefits of
the Head Start program are difficult to determine for a number of reasons related to
program implementation, funding, and the purpose and design of the studies. They
maintain that the best evidence for benefits comes from long-term studies of small
demonstration preschool programs that have shown significant and lasting impact on
children's cognitive development, social behavior, and health. These programs had
well-educated teachers, small classes, good supervision, and substantial resources.

The best known of these long-term studies, the Perry Preschool Program in Ypsilanti, Michigan, included home visiting and a well designed preschool program. This
program is still implemented today as the High Scope Model. A 2007 study that tracked
recipients to age 40 reported that those who attended the program were more likely
than other members of their peer group to be employed, earned better salaries, and
had lower rates of criminal behavior. The researchers concluded that for every dollar
spent, approximately $16 was saved in later remedial education programs, correctional
institutions, and other costs to society (Schweinhart, 2007).

The Abecedarian Study, conducted by researchers at the Frank Porter Graham Child
Development Center in North Carolina, also followed into adulthood the low-income
children who participated in an intensive program of home visiting and preschool education. Those who attended the program from infancy through age 5 scored higher on
all measures than members of the control group. At age 21, they had higher academic
achievement, a greater likelihood of going to college, fewer teenage pregnancies, and a
greater likelihood of obtaining skilled employment as a young adult (Pungello, Campbell, & Barnett, 2006). Positive results like these were linked to the high quality of the
programs studied—which included high ratios of adults to children, ongoing professional development, good salaries for staff, and individualized curricula for children.

A recent study on the impact of early intervention programs conducted in North
Carolina makes a strong case for the positive impact of carefully designed and well-
implemented programs on low-income children. Researchers studied two program
approaches designed to support the development of young children and ameliorate the

effects of poverty. Both programs served large numbers of children (more than one million children were included in the study). The first program, Smart Start, was designed for children birth to age 5 to prevent early cognitive deprivation related to the impact of poverty on children's development. It provided state funded supports in the form of high quality education and care, health and family support services, and professional development for educators. The second program, More at Four, offered high-quality preschool for 4-year-olds during the year before kindergarten. It focused on building reading and math skills and was designed to close achievement gaps and boost academic achievement. The classrooms were required to meet state standards and national quality standards.

The study found that state investments in early childhood education were associated with higher standardized test scores in math and reading, reductions in special education placements and reductions in the number of children being retained in the third, fourth, and fifth grades. The programs had positive effects on all of the groups studied but were especially strong for low-income children. The researchers concluded that the programs produced significant impacts that persist through the end of elementary school and that they warrant dissemination and continued government support (Dodge, Bai, Ladd, & Muschkin, 2016).

Early Childhood Family Education

Early childhood family education is delivered in programs that focus on support for families in their role as the children's first and most important teachers. These include home visiting programs and family–child interaction (sometimes called play and learn) programs (see Table 2.1).

Table 2.1 An Overview of Programs for Young Children

Type	Purpose	Population	Funding	Location
Child care centers (for-profit or not-for-profit)	Education and care while families work	Children birth through age 5; and before and after school and vacation care for elementary school children	Tuition paid by families and government child care subsidies for low-income families	Community-based facilities Some in public schools
Family–child care	Care and education while families work	Children birth through age 8	Tuition paid by families and some government child care subsidies for low-income families	Private homes
Early childhood family education (home visiting and family–child interaction programs)	Enrichment and education for parents and children together	Families and children birth through age 5	State and community agencies	Community-based facilities and public schools
Head Start and Early Head Start	Education, care, and family support	Head Start, ages 3 and 4 years; Early Head Start, ages 0–3 Families must have incomes below the poverty level	Primarily federal government, some state funding	Community-based facilities and public schools
Pre-K, public prekindergarten	Education with a focus on school readiness	Primarily 4-year-old children; may be targeted to low-income children or universal (serving all children), depending on the state	States	Public elementary schools or in partnership with community-based early childhood programs
Early intervention programs	Education	Children birth to age 3 with identified disabilities or at risk for disability	Combination of states and federal government	Community facilities
Programs for children with disabilities	Education	Children ages 3 to 8 with identified disabilities	Federal government and states	Public schools
Public schools	Education	Children ages 5 to 8	State governments	Public school facilities
Charter schools	Education	Children ages 5 to 8	State governments	Community facilities
Private schools	Education	Children ages 5 to 8	Tuition paid by families	School buildings or community facilities
Home schools	Education	Children ages 5 to 8	Families	Children's homes

HOME VISITING PROGRAMS   Home visiting is an approach to early education that provides services to children and family members in their homes. **Home visiting programs** may serve pregnant women or families with young children. Home visitors (who may be professionals like nurses or trained paraprofessionals from the community of the families served) interact with parents to improve child health and development, pregnancy outcomes, and parenting skills through providing information and parenting support. Some programs include developmental screening and activities for children. Widely implemented programs include HIPPY (Home Instruction for Parents of Preschoolers), Nurse Family Partnership, Healthy Families America, Healthy Start, Parents as Teachers (PAT), and Head Start and Early Head Start home-based options.

Research on these programs indicates that they offer an effective approach for providing services to support children's growth and learning as well as benefits for families. In response to these findings, the federal government has initiated a home visiting grant program, and states are developing support systems to oversee home visiting programs, assess program capacity, and prioritize areas for improvement.

FAMILY–CHILD INTERACTION PROGRAMS   **Family–child interaction programs** are based on the assumptions that the family provides the child's first learning environment and that parents are the child's first and most important teachers. The programs involve more than one generation—family members and children. They may be housed in public schools or community facilities. Program goals may include educational enrichment and school readiness for children; information for families about child development, child guidance, and how to get children ready to be successful in kindergarten; information about community resources; and sometimes support for the development of literacy in adults.

SOURCE: Jeff Reese

One example of this approach is the Early Childhood Family Education (ECFE) program in the state of Minnesota, which has been a pioneer in the provision of this type of program. The ECFE program is offered by school districts to all Minnesota families with children between the ages of birth and age 5. ECFE programs involve parents and children coming together for learning activities as well as parent discussion sessions facilitated by a parent educator and age-appropriate activities for children in an early childhood classroom.

Another approach, widely implemented in low-income communities in Hawaii, is family–child interactive learning. In this family-focused approach, teachers create an organized environment that encourages family members to engage with their children in a variety of learning experiences. Teachers offer coaching, modeling, and support as the family members practice interacting with their children in developmentally appropriate ways.

An example, the Tutu and Me Traveling Preschool program, is designed to help families prepare their young children for kindergarten. Adults (parents, grandparents, or other relatives) gain understanding of child development by engaging in activities with children. The program also includes parent education, books for children to take home, and field trips (Porter et al., 2010).

Similar programs are offered in other states, targeted to meet the needs of particular groups of young children and families. Research has demonstrated that two-generation programs, particularly those that include a high-quality program for children, are beneficial both to children and to family members (Barnett, 1995).

Family literacy programs are another kind of family-focused approach. These programs are designed to break the cycle of poverty and illiteracy and improve the opportunities of low-income families. This approach integrates a program of literacy instruction for children with additional literacy instruction and parenting education for family members. A review of research by Padak and Rasinski (2003) reported positive outcomes of these programs for both children and families. Some parent–child programs are designed for all young children; others may target particular populations (such as families at risk for child abuse, single parents, teen parents, or low-income parents), or a specific population of children (such as infants and toddlers or those with disabilities).

State-Funded Public Prekindergarten Programs

A significant development in programs for children under age 5 and one that plays an increasingly important role in the landscape of early childhood education is the growth of state-funded **prekindergarten (pre-K) programs** for 4-year-olds (and, in some places, 3-year-olds as well). The rapid increase in enrollment in these programs over the past decade can be attributed to public interest in the positive effects of early education on children's later academic performance. Educators and policymakers have concluded that children who attend pre-K programs will be better prepared to meet later school expectations. Information about the benefits also served to increase parental demand for pre-K programs. The 43 states that offer these programs have adopted quality standards to ensure that programs are effective.

Pre-K programs may be housed in public schools, in child care centers, and in some communities in both schools and centers. Availability and eligibility vary greatly between states. In some, the programs are intended for low-income children who are at risk for school failure; others attempt to serve all age-eligible children. The movement to make these programs available for all 4-year-olds before they enter kindergarten, essentially adding another year of elementary school, is referred to as universal pre-K.

In *The State of Preschool 2015*, Barnett et al. (2015) reported that the 2014–2015 school year showed some improvement in state-funded pre-K programs that they attribute to recovery from the recession. Enrollment, quality as measured by national benchmarks, and funding increased in many places. The most dramatic progress was in the state of New York which adopted universal preschool for all 4-year-olds in New York City. Unfortunately some states, notably Texas and Florida moved backward. Barnett and his colleagues conclude that access to high-quality preschool programs has remained unequal and that in some states the quality and availability of pre-K is at risk for many young learners because of efforts to reduce government spending.

Programs for Children Birth to Age 5 with Disabilities

Children birth to age 5 who have disabilities and those who are gifted and talented are not regarded as typically developing and may be served by a variety of specialized programs. Today, these programs and services are available in all states, supported by a combination of federal and state funding. Children from birth to 3 years of age who have been identified as having a serious developmental delay (or in some states children who are determined to be at risk for such a delay) may be eligible for **early intervention** services offered by community agencies. Since 1986, the federal law providing special education has also provided early intervention services designed to support the development of infants and toddlers with disabilities. The assumptions underlying these services are that families can learn to be more effective in meeting children's needs and that children who receive positive intervention when they are very young will need less remediation later. An eligible child receives a developmental evaluation, and a team of specialists works with family members to develop an **individualized family service plan (IFSP)** that determines services that will best support the child's development.

Preschool children with disabilities may be served in public school programs (either in separate "self-contained" classroom or in regular "inclusive" preschool classes), they may attend Head Start programs (10% of the children served can meet criteria for identifying disabilities), or they may attend private preschools. When a child meets state disability requirements and is identified as needing additional services, the school district is required to develop an **individualized education plan (IEP)** for the provision of an educational program and services to the child. It is preferable for children to be in classrooms with typically developing peers, something that is more likely to occur in schools that have preschool classrooms.

Reflect On

Programs for Children from Birth to Age 5

Think about a program for children under age 5 that you know. What are its purposes? How is it administered? Who pays for its services? Do you think it is a high-quality program? How can you tell? Would you enjoy working in it? Why?

✓ **A Quick Check 2.1**

Gauge your understanding of the concepts in this section.

Programs for Children 5–8 Years of Age

Children between 5 and 8 years of age attend kindergarten through third-grade programs whose primary purpose is to provide education. These programs are offered in public schools that are funded by state and local tax dollars and in private schools that are supported by tuition paid by families. Programs for children with disabilities are most often housed in public schools and receive a combination of state and federal funding. Although there is great diversity in programs for children under the age of 5, the majority of 5- to 8-year-olds attend kindergarten through third grade in government-funded public elementary schools. A small percentage of children attend private schools or are homeschooled.

Over 10% of prekindergarten through grade 8 students were in private schools in 2015–2016. Roughly three percent of elementary and secondary school students were homeschooled in 2012 (National Center for Education Statistics [NCES], 2016a, Tables 205.10 and 206.10). Before- and after-school programs are available in many school districts to provide assistance to families who need care for children outside of school hours (see Figure 2.6).

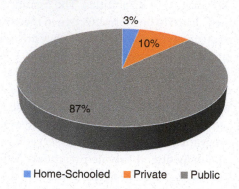

Figure 2.6 Where Are the Kids?
5–8 Year Olds

■ Home-Schooled   ■ Private   ■ Public

Public School Programs: Kindergarten Through Grade 3

Kindergarten, the first year of formal schooling, is provided for full or part day in almost every school district in the United States. Until recently, kindergarten served as a transition for 5-year-olds between home or an early childhood program and formal schooling. Today, it is much more academically demanding and increasingly involves content that was not taught in the past until first grade. According to the NCES, enrollment of 5- to 6-year-olds has been about 96% for several decades, drifting down to 94% in 2013 (NCES, 2015, Table 103.20). In most states, kindergarten is available for families who wish to send their children, but school attendance is not mandatory until first grade (NCES, 2016c, Table 5.3).

Nearly four million children entered kindergarten for the first time in the fall of 2010 (NCES, 2012, Table 136). Of these, 89% attended public kindergartens, and 11% attended private schools. A little more than half (55%) of these children had attended a center-based care program in the year prior to kindergarten (NCES, 2015, Table 202.65).

Until the 1970s, kindergarten was offered in most places as a half-day program; in the years since then, the percentage of full-day kindergartens has increased. In 2009, approximately 61% of all kindergarten programs nationwide were considered full day (NCES, 2013b). In 2014, 81% of 5-year-olds in kindergarten attended full-day (NCES, 2016a, Table 202.10). States are moving toward providing full day kindergarten because families need care for their children while they are at work, because full-day kindergarten gives children more time to acquire the academic skills that are required by state and national standards, and because it increases academic benefits for children from low-income and minority group families.

Although there have been kindergartens in public schools in the United States since the middle of the 19th century, there is less consensus than in other areas of education about what their goals should be or the kinds of educational experiences they should provide. It was pointed out by policy specialist Kristie Kauerz (2005) that, "Kindergarten is not firmly established either as an integral part of the K–12 system or as an integral part of states' emerging systems of early care and education. Kindergarten in the United States straddles both worlds" (p. 1). Kindergarten was introduced as a nurturing, play-based program intended to ease the transition from home or preschool into formal schooling. Today it is viewed as the beginning of the academic school program. Until recently, reading wasn't taught until first grade because children under the age of 6 were not considered "ready" to read. That has changed dramatically, and today literacy skills are regularly taught in kindergarten as well as in many preschool programs.

First grade has long been considered the beginning of the serious work of school. In the United States, school attendance is compulsory from 6 or 7 years of age. The

Video Example 2.1: Studying the Desert

Watch this video of a first grade teacher guiding a study of the desert. Think about how the children and instruction in this classroom are different from those in preschool programs.

primary grades—first through third—are an integral part of the public school system, though children in these grades are still included in the definition of early childhood. The curriculum in the primary grades has historically been and continues to be more academic than that of the preschool or the kindergarten.

Charter Schools

Growing concern with the ability of public schools to meet the needs of all children has led to the development of **charter schools**. Charter schools are independently operated, publicly funded programs that have greater flexibility than regular schools in meeting state or district regulations. A charter is a performance contract that describes the mission of the school, the educational programs it will follow, and the methods that will be used for assessing student progress and program effectiveness. If a program can demonstrate successful performance, the charter may be renewed. Charter schools have received grants from the U.S. Department of Education since 1995 and continue to be a focus of educational reform efforts. The underlying concept is that in exchange for being granted a higher degree of autonomy than other public schools, a program must demonstrate the effectiveness of its practices (U.S. Charter Schools, n.d.). Between school years 2003–04 and 2013–14, the percentage of all public schools that were public charter schools increased from 3.1 to 6.6 percent, and the total number of public charter schools increased from 3,000 to 6,500. The number of students enrolled in public charter schools between school years 2003–04 and 2013–14 increased from 0.8 million to 2.5 million—5.1 percent of public school students (NCES, 2016b).

Legislators and policymakers who think that public school systems are too slow to embrace change regard charter schools as a way to speed up the process and believe that they will improve public education. Advocates for charter schools maintain that they provide more choices for families, encourage innovative teaching, and improve education. Critics maintain that charter schools attract the best students, leave the regular public schools to deal with those who have the greatest needs, and take needed resources away from already overburdened public schools.

Home Schools

Some families in the United States choose to educate their children at home. **Homeschooling** refers to the practice of educating children at home rather than in public or private schools. The NCES (2016a, Table 206.10) reports that approximately 1,773,000 students were homeschooled in the United States in 2012—3.4% of the school-age population.

Prior to the advent of universal public education, teaching children at home was the only option for families who lived in isolated locations or could not afford to send their children to private school. Today, most families who homeschool children think they can give a child a better education at home. Some research suggests that homeschooled children do somewhat better on standardized tests than those who are educated in schools, and there is no reported evidence of negative consequences of homeschooling (Ray, 2006). The most common reasons that families give for homeschooling are (1) to teach a particular set of values and beliefs, (2) to increase academic achievement, (3) to individualize curriculum, (4) to enhance family relationships, and (5) to provide a safe environment.

Many states have established standards and requirements that families must meet in order to educate their children at home. These requirements vary greatly. Some states and school districts require a particular curriculum or adherence to an approved plan of instruction.

Programs for Children Ages 5–8 with Disabilities

The majority of 5- to 8-year-old children with disabilities are educated in public school classrooms. The services provided to them are guided by an Individualized Education Plan, IEP, a written plan developed by a team and reviewed and revised regularly. Historically these children were taught in classrooms that served only children who had been identified as disabled. Today, an increasing number are included in general education classrooms for at least part of the day. Many school districts implement full inclusion—which means that children with disabilities are placed in general education classrooms for the entire school day. Most educators today believe that this practice is beneficial for both children who have disabilities and their peers who are not disabled. When children with disabilities are included in regular classrooms, it is imperative that school districts provide adequate support services for the teachers involved.

Reflect On

Programs for 5- to 8-Year-Olds

Think about a kindergarten or primary grade classroom that you know. What is the program like? Do you think that it does a good job of supporting learning? Do you think it does a good job of supporting social and emotional development? Would you enjoy working in it? Why?

 A Quick Check 2.2

Gauge your understanding of the concepts in this section.

Educational Standards

A notable part of the landscape of early childhood education in the United States today is the prevalence of educational **standards**, written descriptions of the knowledge and skills that students should possess at specific stages in their schooling, and that teachers are expected to address in their work with children. Standards are created to assure educators, family members, and the public that programs that serve young children will provide content that is worthwhile and that will help children to succeed in later schooling.

Education in the United States was profoundly influenced by the movement for school reform that began in 1983 with the publication of the report *A Nation at Risk* (National Commission on Excellence in Education, 1983). This report examined the state of American education and declared that a "rising tide of mediocrity" threatened the nation. The authors reported that test scores were falling, that academic expectations were too low, and that students in the United States were not competing satisfactorily with those in other countries. Recommendations for addressing this problem included the development of high and measurable standards for academic performance and higher standards for teacher preparation.

In the years since *A Nation at Risk* was written, accountability for school performance has become a national priority. The federal government has become increasingly involved in educational policy, which until the 1980s had been the realm of state and local governments. In 1989, the National Educational Goals Panel (NEGP), a bipartisan group of political leaders, took up the cause of educational reform and initiated the creation of eight national education goals. In 1994, the NEGP was charged with monitoring and facilitating progress in reaching the eight goals (NEGP, 1997). This initiative resulted in the development of current state systems for linking standards, assessment, and accountability.

The NEGP promoted the development of standards intended to help states and school districts ensure that worthwhile subject matter would be taught. **Content standards** address goals and objectives for each subject area for each grade. These standards were originally developed by professional associations including the National Council for the Social Studies, the National Council for Teachers of Mathematics, the International Reading Association, and other associations that focused on subject matter taught in K–12 schools. States then developed their own standards, drawing on the national standards but tailoring them to their own educational priorities. **Performance standards** (also called achievement standards) and assessments, most often in the form of standardized tests, were later developed by states to determine the extent to which children had mastered the content prescribed in the standards. Standards and accountability systems are now a feature of every public school system in the United States.

Common Core Standards

The Common Core Standards Initiative, a state-led effort coordinated by the National Governors Association Center for Best Practices and the Council of Chief State School Officers, promotes the use of **Common Core Standards**—nationally agreed on literacy and math curriculum standards. These standards are intended to prepare kindergarten through 12th grade students to be college and career ready at high school graduation and to provide consistency of expectations across the country. The development of these standards was informed by existing state standards, the experience of teachers and educational leaders, and feedback from the public. With encouragement to do so from the federal government, most states are adopting these standards as the basis for their curriculum and assessment.

Video Example 2.2: A Teacher Discusses Common Core Standards

Watch the video of a second grade teacher and reflect on how she addresses Common Core Standards using the curriculum of her classroom. What was your reaction to the use of standards?

Some early childhood advocates, while supportive of core standards, are concerned that the standards as written focus on only two curriculum areas rather than on all development domains including social and emotional and physical development. They also question whether these standards are appropriate for young children because they are based on expectations for high school graduation that have been traced back to younger learners. Concerned educators fear that unrealistic expectations for kindergarten and primary-age children will lead to pressure for academic achievement at the expense of the hands-on experiential learning that is most appropriate for young children (Alliance for Childhood, 2011).

Early Learning Standards

When elementary school teachers and administrators realized that what children learned in preschool had an impact on their ability to meet kindergarten expectations, they began to call for early childhood educators to develop their own standards. **Early learning standards** (also called early learning guidelines) were created by states to describe what children should know and be able to do before they start kindergarten. These standards are intended to improve program quality by guiding educators in the design of worthwhile curricula for preschool programs. They include examples of what most children should be able to do at a particular age when exposed to appropriate learning experiences.

NAEYC and the National Association of Early Childhood Specialists in State Departments of Education (NAEYC/NAEC-SDE, 2009) have developed a joint position statement identifying principles for the development, adoption, and implementation of early learning standards. The position statement points out that expectations for the content of early learning experiences can help focus curriculum and instruction in order to provide appropriate, educationally beneficial opportunities for all children. This is true, of course, only if the standards adequately reflect what young children can be expected to know and do at an early age.

There has been tremendous growth in the development and implementation of early learning standards over the past decade. In 1999, only 10 states had standards for children's learning prior to entering kindergarten. By 2014, all 50 states; Washington, D.C.; American Samoa; Guam; the Virgin Islands; and Puerto Rico had early learning guidelines in place. The majority of these standards were developed for use by state-funded early childhood programs. States vary in the focus of their standards—some address only language and literacy, and others address all domains of development. While all states have early learning guidelines for programs for 3- to 5-year-olds, most (45) have also developed standards for children between birth and age 3 (National Center on Child Care Quality Improvement, 2013). In most places, early learning guidelines are linked to K–12 standards, though states vary in the extent to which their use is mandated.

The Zero to Three organization, a nonprofit group dedicated to promoting the healthy development of infants and toddlers, has developed recommendations intended to promote beneficial standards for the youngest children that will not be used to push academic expectations down to them. Some of their recommendations are that infant–toddler standards (1) address a range of developmental domains, (2) be inclusive of the culture and languages of the children's homes, and (3) incorporate items addressing the critical nature of relationships for infant and toddler development. Zero to Three also stresses that early learning guidelines for infants and toddlers should be aligned with pre-K and K–12 standards in a way that illustrates how foundations of learning are established in the first years of life (Zero to Three, 2008).

Standards are helpful when they are appropriate for the age of the child they are designed for and when they emphasize worthwhile content for the curriculum. Unfortunately, when they call for teaching young children using watered down content for older children, they can also lead to inappropriate expectations and narrowly focused teaching. It is important that early childhood educators and policymakers work together to ensure the effective development and use of standards so that they lead to positive outcomes for children and the field (Kagan, Scott-Little, & Stebbins Frelow, 2003).

Reflect On

Your Experience with Standards

Have you had experience with standards in a program for young children you have visited or worked in? What do you remember about the standards? What do you remember about the effect they had on students and teachers? How do you feel about using standards to guide curriculum and assessment when you begin your career as a teacher?

 A Quick Check 2.3

Gauge your understanding of the concepts in this section.

 ## Program Accountability Measures

Because young children are vulnerable and dependent on adults, families and society want to be assured that the programs that they attend will be concerned with their welfare and will protect them from harm. There are two types of regulations used to hold programs accountable—licensing of programs (usually required in programs for children from birth to age 5) and requirements for teacher qualifications (usually found in programs for children ages 5 and older and preschool programs in public schools). Licensing of preschool programs is a state requirement that assures families that their children are safe. Licensure (also called certification) of teachers is the way that children's safety is ensured and learning promoted in public school programs.

Programs, such as child development centers, for young children that are privately administered can be regulated because governments are able to regulate programs that are operated in the private market. Program licensure is the method used to ensure a minimal level of quality in private sector programs for children under age 5. If the program is housed in a community-based organization, it will be licensed by the state. If, like most special education and pre-K programs, it is located in a public school setting, it will fall under the regulations that govern educational programs for older children.

Licensure of Early Childhood Programs

Regulation of programs for children under 5 years-of-age is based on licensing standards that are developed in each state. **Licensing regulations** are designed to protect the health, safety, and well-being of children in care, largely by reducing the risk of injury, abuse, and communicable disease. Requirements for licensing typically include child-to-staff ratios and group size, minimum square footage per child indoors and outdoors, building safety, provisions for control of infectious diseases, food safety, child immunizations, teacher qualifications, and criminal background checks for staff members.

Because early childhood care and education programs have, until recently, been viewed as a social service for families, licensing is generally administered by health and human services departments rather than departments of education. Licensing originally focused on preschool programs, but now includes programs for infants and toddlers and before- and after-school care. Most states also have provisions for licensing or registering family child care homes, particularly those programs that serve children whose families pay for care using child care subsidies.

Rules about staff training requirements, guidelines for how many children can be cared for, and the kind of learning experiences that must be provided differ from state to state. In most states, licensing is intended to provide a "safety net" to ensure that the physical environment is safe and healthy and that there are enough adults available to supervise children. In some states, all programs must be licensed; in others, certain categories of programs are exempt. Standards for licensing and for enforcement of standards vary greatly, so licensure in itself is no guarantee of quality. In some states, standards are higher and educational guidelines are included in program requirements. Unlike many other Western nations, the United States has no nationally mandated child care standards, even for federally funded programs.

The National Association for the Education of Young Children (NAEYC, 1997) position statement on licensing and public regulation of early childhood programs emphasizes children's right to care in settings that protect them from harm and promote their healthy development. It states (1) that all facilities, including centers and family child care homes, should be licensed; (2) that licensing standards should be clear and reasonable and reflect current research; (3) that licensing standards should be vigorously and equitably enforced; and (4) that licensing agencies should have sufficient staff and resources to do their job.

Accreditation of Programs for Children

Some programs strive to reach a higher level of quality than that required for state licensing. In 1985, NAEYC established an **accreditation** system for recognizing programs that meet criteria for determining high quality. Accreditation is a voluntary process that enables programs to measure themselves against a set of national standards that indicate high-quality practice. The accreditation process requires extensive self-study and validation by professionals outside the program being reviewed.

As of December, 2016 there were 7,170 (National Association for the Education of Young Children Academy, 2017) programs accredited by NAEYC in all states, including child care centers, military programs, Head Start programs, and public school programs. Almost 500,000 children are currently served in accredited programs (Retrieved from http://www.naeyc.org/academy/accreditation/search).

Interest in accreditation as a way to improve program quality has led to the creation of a number of national accreditation systems in addition to that of NAEYC. These systems have been developed by the National Association for Family Child Care, National Early Childhood Program Accreditation, the American Montessori Society, the Association of Christian Schools International, and the National Lutheran Schools Association.

Some programs that receive government funds may be required to exceed state licensing standards through meeting accreditation standards. Child care facilities run by branches of the armed services for the children of military personnel are expected to meet accreditation standards that are higher than those required by most states. Family child care providers who serve military children are certified according to a set of military standards and are encouraged to obtain NAEYC accreditation (Hruska, 2009). Head Start programs are required to meet state licensing requirements and follow national Head Start performance standards. These standards address the broad categories of early childhood development and health services, family and community partnerships, and program design and management (Administration for Children and Families, 2016).

Quality Rating and Improvement Systems

A **Quality rating and improvement system (QRIS)** is a systemic approach to assessing, improving, and communicating the level of quality in early and school-age care and education programs. These systems are intended to support children's development by raising the quality of care and education in early childhood programs. Similar to rating systems for restaurants and hotels, QRIS grant quality ratings to early and school-age care and education programs that meet a set of defined program standards.

QRIS create, align, and strengthen the components of early care and education. These components include quality standards, a process for monitoring the extent to which these are met, a process for supporting quality improvement, a system that identifies pathways to professional development for those who work with young children, data management and reporting systems, provision of financial incentives, and other supports to meet higher standards. QRIS systems also include dissemination of information about program quality to parents and the public. Participation is usually voluntary, and many kinds of early childhood programs can participate, including center-based child care, family child care, school age, pre-K, and Head Start (QRIS National Learning Network, 2009).

States vary in their quality rating standards as well as the monitoring and support strategies, but there are some commonalities. Quality standards typically address the classroom learning environment, staff qualifications, family involvement, and classroom ratios and frequently include leadership and business practices and the utilization of curricula and child assessments (Tout et al., 2010). In most states QRIS are organized in tiers; the first of which recognizes programs that comply with or slightly exceed licensing standards, while higher tiers reflect increasingly higher levels of quality, above and beyond licensing standards.

As of 2016, most states had implemented a QRIS (Administration for Children and Families, 2016). The Office of Child Care (of the Federal Department of Health and Human Services, Administration for Children and Families) now requires states to report on their progress in developing or implementing QRIS in their annual Childcare and Development Block Grant Plans. These plans are mandatory in order for states to access federal funding for child care (Administration for Children and Families, 2016).

Workforce Qualifications

Workforce qualifications vary greatly for teachers who work in programs for children from infancy to age 5 and those who work in programs for 5- to 8-year-olds and state funded preschools. Requirements for licensure of early childhood programs that serve children between birth and age 5 focus, to a great extent, on characteristics of facilities and the provision of adequate supervision of children. They also include provisions for teacher and administrator education and experience that vary greatly from state to state. In many states, lead teachers may take responsibility for a group of children with as little as a high school diploma and a background check. A few states require teachers in programs for children from birth to age 5 to have a Child Development Associate (CDA) credential, an associate's (2-year) degree, or a bachelor's (4-year) degree in early childhood education. Most states require directors to have a CDA or more formal education (NACCRRA, Child Care Aware, 2013).

The qualifications of teachers and administrators who work in public school programs are recognized by a **teaching license** (also called certification) that is awarded to the individual teacher. Teaching pre-K through grade 3 and special education in public schools requires a teacher preparation program that leads to a bachelor's degree (or higher) in education. These programs follow an approved course of study that when completed qualifies the student for licensure.

Teacher preparation programs (in both two-year and four-year institutions) must demonstrate that they meet a set of national standards designed to ensure that their graduates have the knowledge and skills needed to be effective teachers. NAEYC has established the national standards and has developed **accreditation** a process of peer review that determines if the program meets a set of national standards for early childhood teacher education programs. Until recently only associate degree early childhood teacher preparation programs were eligible for accreditation by NAEYC. In 2017 the accreditation program was expanded to include baccalaureate and master's degree programs (NAEYC.org, Higher Education). We address these NAEYC Professional Preparation Standards in this book.

It is useful for a person entering the field of early childhood education to understand that preschools and public schools employ very different mechanisms for protecting children and controlling quality. In settings for children between birth and age 5, the approach that is used to ensure that programs will protect young children and that adults who work with them are adequately prepared is *licensure of programs*. In schools for children between 5 and 8 years of age, the mechanism that is used to ensure that the adults are well trained is individual *licensure of teachers*. In both systems, institutions that award degrees in early childhood education are required to follow national professional preparation standards.

 A Quick Check 2.4

Gauge your understanding of the concepts in this section.

 # School Readiness

As a teacher of young children, you are likely to hear the term *readiness* often and in a number of different contexts. Your friends or parents of a child in your school might ask if you think their child is "ready" for kindergarten. You might hear kindergarten or first-grade teachers complain that the children entering their classrooms are not as ready as they would like them to be. You may also hear preschool teachers worrying about whether the children they teach are going to be ready for kindergarten, and kindergarten teachers wondering whether their children will be adequately prepared for upcoming first-grade expectations. Having some background about what readiness means and how its definition has evolved over time may be helpful preparation for these discussions.

Readiness is a term used to describe preparation for what comes next. **School readiness** refers to children's preparation to function successfully at the next level of education. Early childhood educators may talk about the readiness of a child in an infant–toddler program for the 3-year-old program in the preschool or the 3-year-old's readiness for the 4-year-old class. But the term is most often used to describe the interface between the home or preschool and the kinder-

garten (which tends to be regarded as the "real school"). It refers to the state of early development that enables a child to engage with kindergarten learning experiences and to successfully meet school expectations. Readiness for kindergarten has long been a topic of interest to families and teachers, but it has taken on new urgency in recent years as academic expectations in the kindergarten have increased.

From the legal standpoint, children's readiness for school is determined by their birth date. Every state has a cutoff date for when children can enter kindergarten or requires that districts set this date. Forty-two states and Puerto Rico have kindergarten entrance cutoff dates between July 31 and October 16, meaning that children entering kindergarten are at least age 5 or will be turning 5 shortly after school starts (NCES 2016c, Table 5.3).

Another way to look at readiness has to do with the abilities that children have when they arrive in kindergarten. Elementary school teachers and administrators became concerned when they noticed that some children were having a hard time meeting the higher kindergarten expectations and were falling behind. They responded to this concern by redefining "readiness" to focus on what children need to know and be able to do in order to do well in kindergarten. In recent years, there has been a trend for states to adopt cutoff dates earlier in the year so that the cohort of children is older when they start kindergarten. School administrators chose to increase the age of kindergarten entry because they believed that older children would do better at meeting the academic expectations set out in standards. In some places, assessment tests have been used to exclude children who were judged to be "unready" for kindergarten. More and more children are retained in kindergarten because they aren't ready for the more rigorous expectations of first grade, and many families consider keeping a child out of kindergarten in the hope that he or she will be better able to succeed if he or she enters a year later. Postponing the date of kindergarten entry does not take into account that families need to find care for children who enter school a year later.

As a result of these concerns, educators began to discuss the question: "How should readiness be defined?" (Lewit & Baker, 1995). Most agree that school readiness "refers to the state of child competencies at the time of school entry that are important for later success" (Snow, 2006, p. 9). Where the viewpoints vary is in the type of skills, abilities, and knowledge that are considered to be important and the ideas about what needs to be done to help children become ready.

How readiness is defined in large measure determines where the responsibility for its improvement lies—with the child, the family, the school, or the community. The definition of readiness that is decided on has practical consequences. It affects decisions about assessment, about the kinds of investments that communities and states should make in early education, and about how to judge educational progress.

Reflect On

Readiness

Reflect on your first days of kindergarten and first grade. Were you "ready" for school? How did you know? What made it easy or hard for you when you started school? What did the school or teacher do to help or to hinder your first school experiences? What other experiences have you had with school readiness? How might knowledge of issues relating to school readiness be helpful as you begin to work with young children?

A general consensus regarding the broad components of readiness was put forth at the national level. The National Education Goals Panel (NEGP) (1997) recommended three components: (1) readiness in the child, (2) schools' readiness for children, and (3) family and community supports that contribute to children's readiness. Many states have been working to systematically define each of these components and to decide how progress in each one will be measured. Readiness initiatives in the states can include finding ways to provide high-quality preschool for more 4-year-olds (especially those from low-income and minority groups who may be at risk for school failure), using more developmentally appropriate curriculum in the kindergarten, educating families about things they can do to help their children in school, training teachers and principals in child development (including realistic academic expectations for young children), and developing procedures, including summer programs for helping children make a smooth transition from home or preschool to kindergarten.

NAEYC's (1995) position statement on school readiness states, "The nature of children's development and learning dictates two important school responsibilities. Schools must be able to respond to a diverse range of abilities within any group of children, and the curriculum in the early grades must provide meaningful contexts for children's learning rather than focusing primarily on isolated skills acquisition" (p. 3). In other words, schools should meet the needs of all the children who are age eligible to attend without consideration of their ability to perform academic tasks.

A Quick Check 2.5

Gauge your understanding of the concepts in this section.

Final Thoughts

As you can tell from reading this chapter, early childhood education is a diverse field with much to contribute to our society. Over the past century, our understanding of the needs of young children has changed dramatically. At the beginning of the 20th century, most people believed that children were not ready to learn anything important until the age of 6, when they entered school. Few people were aware of the impact of the early years, especially on children's cognitive development, and the work of early childhood educators was generally not understood or appreciated. Today, we have entered a new era of awareness of the impact of early experiences on human development. New studies of child development, especially brain development, have demonstrated that the early years are a critically important period in the development of a human being. Compelling research has shown the positive impact of high-quality early childhood programs, beginning as early as infancy, on children who are at risk for failure in school.

The public is discovering the value of early childhood education, and policymakers are acknowledging that investing in programs for young children can have significant social and economic benefits.

And while early education is receiving greater recognition than it has in the past, it is still subject to the economic forces that shape our society. For several years, we have seen positive movement in early childhood education: greater understanding of the importance of the early years, a call for more government-funded programs for 3- and 4-year olds, awareness of the importance of program quality, and calls for higher qualifications for teachers of young children. At the time of this writing we are concerned that progress will be slowed by economic concerns and an increasingly conservative political landscape.

Early childhood educators, more than any other group, have an obligation to consider children's well-being and to support them in growing into fully functioning human beings. Knowledgeable and caring teachers have much to offer to children, families, and society, and they *can* make a difference. Those of you who are entering the early childhood field now will see many changes and new developments. There will be opportunities, challenges, and important contributions that you can make.

 Application Exercise 2.2 Final Reflection

To Learn More

Visit a Website

The following agencies and organizations have websites that will help to introduce you to the field of early childhood education:

Association for Childhood Education International
Association for Supervision and Curriculum Development
Child Care Aware
Common Core Standards
Head Start/Early Head Start
National Association for the Education of Young Children
National Child Care Information Center
National Institute for Early Education Research
Pre-K Now
Southern Early Childhood Association
Zero to Three

Document Your Skill & Knowledge About the Field of Early Childhood Education in Your Professional Portfolio

Include some or all of the following:

- Survey your community and report on the programs that are available for children from birth to 8 years of age (preschools, child care centers, Head Start and Early Head Start, pre-K programs, public and private school programs, and programs for children with disabilities). What kinds of programs are best represented? Is there a needed program that is missing? How well do you think families in the community are served? Reflect and write about what you learned.

- Based on what you learned in your survey of programs, identify who is responsible for regulating each kind of program. What kinds of regulations did you find (licensing or teacher certification)? Are any programs in your community accredited by NAEYC? Reflect and write about what you learned.

- Research and write about what is being done in your state with regard to one or more of the following initiatives: state-funded pre-K programs for 3- and 4-year-olds, Quality Rating and Improvement Systems (QRIS), early learning standards, and school readiness initiatives.

- Explore some of the associations that serve young children, families, and educators listed in the "To Learn More" section.

 Shared Writing 2.1 Aspects of Early Childhood Education Program Quality

Chapter 3
History of Early Childhood Education

SOURCE: Jeff Reese

What is past is prologue.

WILLIAM SHAKESPEARE

∨ Chapter Learning Outcomes:

3.1 Discuss some of the significant ideas about early childhood education that emerged from ancient Greece and Rome through the Industrial Revolution.

3.2 Describe how Friedrich Froebel, the McMillan sisters, and John Dewey have influenced early childhood education today.

3.3 Explain the unique contributions to early childhood education made by Maria Montessori, Rudolf Steiner, and Loris Malaguzzi.

3.4 Discuss significant aspects of the history of child care in the United States and how it has evolved into today's early childhood programs.

NAEYC Professional Preparation Standards

The NAEYC Professional Preparation Standard that applies to this chapter:

Standard 6: Becoming a Professional (NAEYC, 2009).

 Key elements:

 6a: Identifying and involving oneself with the early childhood field

 6c: Engaging in continuous, collaborative learning to inform practice

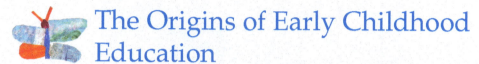 # The Origins of Early Childhood Education

Knowledge of the history of early childhood education gives you a sense of its roots in the past and an idea of how current approaches to working with children and families have grown out of previous thought and practice. Knowing about the history of the field can help you realize that much of what is called "innovation" in current practice has been thought about, written about, and tried before. Similarly, it may help you face the challenges you will encounter when you learn that current philosophical debates are not new—they mirror issues that have been debated for a long time. It can also give you a vantage point for looking at many of the things you will encounter as you begin to observe programs and learn to work with young children.

Early childhood education is a fairly new field, although it has old roots and emerges from a long historical tradition. In this chapter, we discuss the evolution of some of the important ideas and developments that have contributed to the field as it is today.

Many of our current ideas about early education were shaped by Western—largely European—views about children and education. We focus on how these views have evolved and continue to influence the field of early childhood education in the United States today. As you read this chapter, it is important to keep in mind that every country has its own history of early education and that some places and some ethnic groups and cultures in the United States have their own educational history and values.

It is helpful to remember that history is communicated in the voice and viewpoint of the people who write about it. In the case of early childhood education, women have tended to be the practitioners—educating and caring for children—while men have tended to be the theorists, philosophers, and writers. As you read, it may broaden your perspective to think about who is not represented and whose voices are not heard—and to think about how they might have told the story.

There is much more about the history of early childhood education than can be addressed in one chapter. Therefore, the history we present is selective and focuses on the origins of the ideas that led to what we call *developmentally appropriate practice* today. These ideas inform our work and this book.

The Roots of Developmentally Appropriate Practice

The field of early childhood education has its roots in **humanism**, a cultural and intellectual movement that focused on human needs and values rather than on religious authority. Humanist beliefs stress the value and goodness of human beings and highlight respect for human dignity, the right of people to shape their own lives, and concern for human values and well-being.

Humanistic ideals contributed to the development of the **child-centered approach** to education that continues to be implemented today in what we refer to today as *developmentally appropriate practice*. Some of the important ideas that guide this approach to education are:

- The importance of the early years
- Education based on the growing abilities, needs, and interests of the child
- Attention to all aspects of children's development
- The important role of play in children's development
- The connection between mind and body
- The value of learning about children through observation
- A commitment to **universal education**—available to all without regard to sex, ethnicity, or economic status
- The value of childhood as a time in its own right, not just as a preparation for adulthood
- The significant role of families in children's development

Child-centered approaches to working with young children were slow to be accepted, particularly during the lifetimes of their originators. Innovators who advocated new ways of working with young children were often regarded as radical and treated with suspicion and hostility. At only a few times in history has the dominant practice in teaching young children been based on the child centered approach.

In order to put this history into perspective, it helps to realize that today's concept of childhood is the product of centuries of social and economic change. In the past, there were many different and conflicting ideas about children and how they should be educated. A prevailing view for much of Western history was that children were like small adults and that childhood was something a person had to get through on the way to the much more desirable state of being a grown-up.

In Europe and North America in the past, the treatment of children was mainly harsh, and most education was based on rote learning. Physical punishment was the means by which adults controlled children's behavior. At different times and in different places, philosophers and educational innovators recognized shortcomings in the dominant approaches and suggested more humane alternatives. Although they influenced some educators and philosophers, none of these fundamentally changed the day-to-day education and treatment of most young children. However, the idea of educating young children in more humane and meaningful ways has been suggested or rediscovered over and over again by educators and philosophers discussed in this chapter. Taken together, they have pointed to the child-centered approach that early childhood educators endorse and implement in programs today.

Ancient Greece and Rome (400 B.C.–A.D. 200)

Our Western tradition of education can be traced back to ancient Greece. In ancient Mediterranean societies, children younger than 7 were usually cared for by their mothers and other members of their extended family. At about age 7, specific training for an occupation began. Such training differed widely between genders and among social classes.

The ideal of a well-rounded education was first clearly expressed in ancient Greece. The Greek word *paideia* (from which we get our words *pedagogy* and *encyclopedia*) was used to express this cultural ideal. The Greeks believed that free human beings should strive for excellence in body, mind, and spirit.

PLATO   The philosopher Plato (428–348 B.C.) believed that the early childhood years provided a splendid opportunity to shape a child's future social, cultural, and intellectual life. Plato suggested in the *Republic* (his book on the ideal state) that state nurseries should be established to foster a spirit of community. Plato recognized different stages of childhood (Lascarides & Hinitz, 2000) and proposed that the curriculum should include games, music, stories, and drama that would illustrate the values needed by all good citizens. In this ideal state, gifted children would be identified and provided with an enriched program. Plato believed that children came into the world with all essential knowledge dormant within them. Education helped children to "remember" this knowledge and apply it to their daily lives.

Plato broke with the tradition of his own time by insisting on the importance of the education of girls and by criticizing the use of corporal punishment. Plato's realization of the importance of early childhood in shaping future social and political views would come to influence many later educational thinkers. Plato's view that knowledge of geometry and geometrical shapes was essential to understanding the order of the cosmos would later play a role in the balls and blocks created for the first kindergartens.

Play was considered a worthwhile activity in Greece. Structured physical play in the form of games and gymnastics began in childhood and continued to be important as recreation for adult men. The free play of young children was viewed as necessary and a way of learning.

ARISTOTLE   Like his teacher Plato, Aristotle (384–322 B.C.) recognized the importance of beginning education with young children, believed in the potential of human beings, emphasized the development of mind and body, and valued children's play. But whereas Plato was interested primarily in leading students and society to the contemplation of "the Good," "the True," and "the Beautiful," Aristotle was interested in the world visible to the senses and the logical organization of thought. Aristotle valued the education of young children because he believed that good habits must be established early in life.

QUINTILIAN   In Rome, Quintilian (A.D. 35–95) was the foremost educator of his time. His ideas about education were similar to those of the Greek educational philosophers. From observation, he realized that children younger than 7 did not benefit from the customary educational practices. Accordingly, he encouraged parents to allow young children to play. He suggested that it was important to pick good nurses and tutors so that young children could learn correct speech and behavior by imitation rather than intimidation. Figure 3.1 highlights the ideas and impact of Plato, Aristotle, and Quintilian.

While these Greek and Roman philosophers played a role in advocating some new and humane forms of early childhood education, their views did not reflect the whole picture of Greek and Roman society. Both societies practiced slavery and tolerated infanticide.

The Middle Ages (500–1450)

The Middle Ages are generally defined as the period between the Roman Empire and the Renaissance. This period was characterized by a feudal economic system—the granting of land in exchange for military service and by the powerful influence of the church.

Figure 3.1 The Ideas and Impact of Plato, Aristotle, and Quintilian

The Ideas of Plato, Aristotle, and Quintilian

- Education should begin with the young child.
- Human beings are essentially good.
- Both boys and girls should be educated.
- Development of both mind and body are important.
- Play is a valuable tool for learning.

The Impact of Plato, Aristotle, and Quintilian on ECE

- Later educational philosophers incorporated these ideas in their work.

In the fourth century, the Roman emperor Constantine became a Christian and began a series of reforms that put Christian leaders and values in positions of moral and legal authority. Although most Christians believed that children were born in sin, the ritual of baptism was believed to restore their original goodness. Christian emperors soon made all forms of infanticide illegal. Land and money were given by the Roman state to the church so that it could provide social services for the poor.

The Western Roman Empire collapsed in the late fifth century. The church, under the leadership of the pope, managed to convert the barbarian tribes that had conquered western Europe. For the thousand years of the medieval era, the Catholic Church struggled to carry on the traditions of literacy and learning in an age of darkness.

SOURCE: Mondadori Porfolio/Getty Images/Newscom

In the later Middle Ages, new religious orders, such as the Franciscan friars, moved out of the monasteries and went into communities to work among the poor. They often provided care and education to abandoned or orphaned children. In the early 13th century, St. Francis emphasized devotion to the child Christ, helping to inspire more concern for the children of the poor.

Most people during that period were peasants who worked land that belonged to the rich and powerful. Peasants and poor people in towns needed the help of their young children. Boys and girls as young as 3 were expected to feed and tend animals and to work in kitchen gardens. Children in the towns were taught the basics of their parents' trade early and were formally apprenticed to a craft at age 7. However, toys and art depicting children at play are the tangible evidence that even in the Middle Ages, childhood and childhood pastimes were distinct from those of adults.

The Renaissance and the Reformation (1300–1600)

During the Renaissance and Reformation in Europe (which began in Italy in the 1300s and moved westward until the early 1600s), attention turned from the church to the individual and the arts, stimulating a revival of the literature of the ancient Greeks and Romans (Gutek, 1994). Renaissance men and women placed a high value on education. The invention of the printing press about 1485 helped make many books available so that knowledge was no longer the monopoly of the church. In order to help young children make a good beginning in their study of Latin (the universal language of educated Europeans), men such as Sir Thomas More of England (1478–1535) and Desiderius Erasmus (1466–1536) encouraged parents and teachers to avoid using severe physical punishments as a way to motivate children. Both men believed that children would want to learn if an effort was made to make the subject matter enjoyable.

MARTIN LUTHER   In the 16th-century Martin Luther (1483–1546), a former monk whose biblical scholarship caused him to break with the Catholic Church, began a movement of religious reform known as the Protestant Reformation. Luther was a strong advocate of universal education. He believed that boys and girls should be taught to read so that they could experience the Bible for themselves. An extensive school system was developed in Germany based on Luther's views that schools should develop the intellectual, religious, physical, emotional, and social qualities of children. But his goal of universal education did not become a reality until 19th-century America. Figure 3.2 highlights the ideas and impact of Martin Luther.

During the 16th and 17th centuries, efforts by the Catholic Church to respond to the Protestants led to a renewal of Catholic culture known to historians as the Counter-Reformation. This movement led to the creation of new religious societies dedicated to good works, including the education of orphans, children of the poor, and non-Christian peoples in the New World.

Figure 3.2 The Ideas and Impact of Martin Luther

The Ideas of Martin Luther
- Education should be for all children.
- Individual literacy is important.
- All aspects of development are important.

The Impact of Martin Luther on ECE
- Later educational philosophers, particularly Comenius, incorporated these ideas in their work.

JOHN AMOS COMENIUS—THE FATHER OF EARLY CHILDHOOD EDUCATION

John Amos Comenius (the Latinized version of Jan Amos Komensky) (1592–1670) was born and raised in what is now the Czech Republic and was a bishop in the Protestant Moravian Church. In the hope that he could help teachers provide effective and humane education, Comenius began to write about education, which he believed could be an important vehicle for improving society. He developed teaching methods that anticipated elements of modern early childhood education and produced some of the earliest materials for teaching young children.

Comenius's work was well received in Europe, and his books were widely translated. He thought that all people were equal before God and, therefore, that all individuals—rich or poor, common or noble, male or female—were entitled to the same education. Comenius believed that up to the age of 6, children should not leave the family and should be taught in their native languages, not in Latin. In his work *School of Infancy*, Comenius suggested that young children should develop simple practical knowledge consistent with what we still view as a good early childhood curriculum today, such as the names of body parts, words for the geography of their home (hill, river, and valley), simple arithmetic (many, few, and knowing that three is more than two), and simple short songs. He believed that schools should prepare children for life and for further education that he envisaged as taking place in a series of ascending grades, where at each level the child would be exposed to an ever-widening circle of knowledge. He hoped that providing universal education would bring about a world of peace and goodwill among those of differing faiths.

Long before the development of modern theories of child development, Comenius wrote about how young children learned. Based on close observation of children, he recognized that the period from birth to age 6 was of the highest importance for human development. Comenius believed that the foundation for learning about the arts and sciences began in the early years (Deasey, 1978). He believed that language was the foundation for later learning and designed programs for language and concept acquisition that were intended to begin in infancy and carry on through later childhood (Gutek, 1994). Schooling for the youngest began in the maternal school, the "school of the mother's knee." The mother was to attend to her child's physical needs and encourage play. She might show the child a book designed by Comenius that had woodcuts illustrating words and concepts. This book, *Orbis Pictus*, is considered to be the first picture book.

Comenius observed that learning seems to occur spontaneously when children are allowed to play. He encouraged classroom use of puzzles, building materials, and other concrete objects as learning tools. Contemporary evolution of these practices can be seen in the ideas that children learn best when knowledge is personally relevant and that concrete experiences must precede abstract tasks. These ideas are important today in what we refer to as **developmentally appropriate practice (DAP)**. The ideas and impact of Comenius are outlined in Figure 3.3.

Figure 3.3 The Ideas and Impact of Comenius

The Ideas of Comenius

- The period from birth to age 6 is of the highest importance for human development.
- Language is the foundation for later learning.
- Education begins with nurture at the "school of the mother's knee."
- Learning should be meaningful/personally relevant.

The Impact of Comenius on ECE

- Use of picture books
- Use of toys (puzzles, blocks) in education.
- Later educational philosophers, particularly Pestalozzi, incorporated these ideas.

The Age of Enlightenment (1700s)

During the 18th century, the scientific revolution led to a new emphasis on human understanding of the universe as a way to transform society. Philosophers and educators of the Enlightenment tended to emphasize human reason and to doubt traditional sources of authority. During this period, there were efforts to make education more practical and scientific.

JOHN LOCKE—THE CHILD IS A BLANK SLATE John Locke (1632–1704)—academic, doctor, philosopher, and political theorist—developed the theory that the child comes into the world with a mind like a blank slate (**tabula rasa**). He suggested that knowledge is received through the senses and is converted to understanding by the application of reason. This view was in direct contradiction to the opinion generally held during his time that people entered the world with some aspects of their character already formed. Locke's belief in the importance of "nurture" over "nature" in determining human development led him to emphasize the influence of early training and education and to advocate changes in the way that families cared for their children. He believed that infants should not be restricted by the common practice of swaddling them in tight strips of cloth, that young children should be allowed to engage in physical exploration, and that gentle forms of discipline rather than corporal punishment should be used. Locke believed that respectful, loving relationships are the best way to teach and that learning should never become a task imposed on the child. Locke's ideas, highlighted in Figure 3.4, anticipated the modern notion of the role of education in the shaping of human potential (Cleverley & Phillips, 1986; Weber, 1984).

JEAN JACQUES ROUSSEAU—THE CHILD IS INHERENTLY GOOD Jean Jacques Rousseau (1712–1778)—French philosopher, writer, and social theorist—challenged

Figure 3.4 The Ideas and Impact of Locke

The Ideas of Locke

- The child enters the world as a blank slate or "tabula rasa."
- Knowledge is received through the senses.
- Nurture more important than nature.
- Prolonged swaddling is not good for children.
- Respectful loving relationships are encouraged rather than corporal punishment.

The Impact of Locke on ECE

- Playful teaching.
- Focusing on the child in education.

Figure 3.5 The Ideas and Impact of Rousseau

The Ideas of Rousseau

- The child is inherently good.
- Education should begin at birth and continue into adulthood.
- Children learn best from direct experience and exploration of the environment.
- Children learn through their own natural, undirected play.
- There are developmental stages.

The Impact of Rousseau on ECE

- Focus on direct experience.
- Belief in free play.

the prevalent view of his time that children came into the world with original sin and needed to establish habits of obedience, even if it required that they be treated harshly. Rousseau believed not that people were born evil but rather that their inherent goodness was spoiled by civilization. He formulated a stage theory of development and believed that education should begin at birth and continue into adulthood. He believed in basing educational practice on knowledge of the nature of the child, whose ways of learning are different from those of adults. Educational practice, according to Rousseau, should be based on the understanding that children learn best from direct experience and exploration of the environment. He envisioned children learning through their own natural, undirected play, free of adult interference and guidance. He encouraged parents and educators to support the natural growth process by allowing for the interests and spontaneous activities of children. Rousseau's ideas—viewed as radical in his time and by many in ours—had a tremendous impact on the educators who followed and were a precursor to later research on developmental stages. Figure 3.5 outlines Rousseau's ideas and impact.

The Industrial Revolution (1800s)

During the 19th century, national school systems were evolving in Europe, and the beginning of public education was under way in the United States. New theories of education had widespread impact. Two notable contributors to education at that time were Johann Pestalozzi and Robert Owen.

JOHANN PESTALOZZI—EARLY CHILDHOOD EDUCATION BEGINS Early childhood education as a distinct discipline began with Johann Pestalozzi (1746–1827), a Swiss educator who had been influenced by the views of Rousseau. Pestalozzi experimented with teaching strategies advocated by Rousseau, found them ineffective, and concluded that he should develop his own teaching methods.

Pestalozzi believed that all children had the right to education and the capacity to profit from it. He devoted his life to education, particularly for the orphaned and poor, and established several schools in which his ideas could be implemented. He believed that education could help awaken the potential of each child and thereby lead to social reform. He wrote that the first

Figure 3.6 The Ideas and Impact of Pestalozzi

The Ideas of Pestalozzi

- All children have the right to education and the capacity to profit from it.
- Education can help to awaken the potential of each child.
- The first year of life is the most important in a child's development.
- Instruction should be adapted to each child's interests, abilities, and stage of development.

The Impact of Pestalozzi on ECE

- Focus on sensory exploration.
- Allowing self-paced learning.

year of life was the most important in a child's development. He proposed that instruction should be adapted to each child's interests, abilities, and stage of development. He rejected the practice of memorization and advocated sensory exploration and observation as the basis of learning. The learning experiences he designed were sequenced from concrete to abstract. He believed that children learned through self-discovery and could pace their own learning. Pestalozzi was also concerned with teaching human relationships. His ideas laid the foundation for the reform of 19th-century education and had a strong impact on development of progressive education in the United States and Europe.

Figure 3.6 highlights the ideas and impact of Pestalozzi.

ROBERT OWEN   Welsh industrialist and social reformer Robert Owen (1771–1858), a disciple of Pestalozzi, became concerned with the condition of families who worked in the cotton mills during the industrial revolution. Owen worked for reforms in labor practices and the establishment of schools to improve the lives of factory children who, from the age of 6, were required to labor for long hours in the mills. He provided humane living conditions and abolished child labor in his textile factory in Wales.

Owen believed that the education of young children, combined with an environment that allowed people to live by the principle of mutual consideration, could transform the nature of people and society. The **infant school** he developed, the first in England for children 3 to 10 years of age, offered a nurturing setting. Owen believed that the natural consequences of their actions would teach children right from wrong. Sensory learning, stories, singing, dance, nature study, and physical exercise were included in the school curriculum. Although the schools he created did not survive in England, ideas like free choice of activities, a caring and nonpunitive teacher, and the use of spontaneous play as a vehicle for learning can still be found in today's early childhood programs.

Both Pestalozzi and Owen, who were directly involved in the education of young children, have had a strong influence on later educational practice. They were idealists, deeply humanitarian, and concerned with social reform as it affected the poor. Owen's concern for the education of his factory workers' children led to the creation in Britain of the Infant School Society in 1825. This society later became a model for efforts to educate the children of working mothers in the United States. See Figure 3.7 for an outline of Owen's ideas and impact.

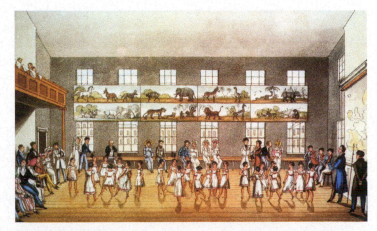

SOURCE: New Lanark Trust

Figure 3.7 The Ideas and Impact of Owen

The Ideas of Owen

- An "infant" school for children under 5 should be established.
- Education of young children (in combination with other factors) can transform the nature of people and society.
- Natural consequences will teach children right from wrong.
- Do not pressure children to learn.

The Impact of Owen on ECE

- Sensory learning, stories, singing, dance, nature study, and physical exercise
- Periods of time during which children choose their activities.
- Play valued as a vehicle for learning.
- Caring and nonpunitive teachers.
- Influence on later educational systems particularly in the American kindergarten, the Lanham Act schools, and the British Infant School.

A Quick Check 3.1

Gauge your understanding of the concepts in this section.

Educational Movements That Shaped Early Childhood Education

Some programs and ideas that originated at the beginning of the 20th century have had a profound and long-lasting impact on the field of early childhood education in the United States and in other places in the world. These include the kindergarten, created in Germany by Friedrich Froebel; the nursery school, founded in England by Margaret and Rachel McMillan; and progressive education, which began in the United States based on the progressive political movement and the educational philosophy of John Dewey. Although these programs originated in different places and in response to different societal needs, all three reflect the caring and respectful attitudes toward children that characterized many of the educational reforms that we described on the previous pages.

Froebel and the Kindergarten

Friedrich Wilhelm Froebel (1782–1852) established the first kindergarten program in Germany in 1837. After working in a number of different jobs, he discovered that he had a talent for teaching. After study in a training institute run by Pestalozzi and further education in science and linguistics, Froebel devoted his life to education. He developed a philosophy of education and a program for 4- to 6-year-olds that provided a transition between home and school and between infancy and childhood. Because this program was intended to be a place where children were nurtured and protected from outside influences, as plants might be in a garden, it was called **kindergarten** (child garden). This term is still used for all programs for young children in many parts of the world and for programs for 5-year-olds in the United States.

Like Comenius, Rousseau, and Pestalozzi, Froebel believed that children were social beings, that activity was the basis for knowing, and that play was an essential part of learning. Froebel thought that the education of young children should differ from that of older children and wanted children to have the opportunity to develop those positive impulses that came from within.

He also thought that the mother's relationship to the infant and young child had a significant impact on development.

THE KINDERGARTEN   Froebel described three forms of knowledge as the basis for all learning: knowledge of forms of life, such as gardening, care of animals, and domestic tasks; knowledge of forms of mathematics, such as geometric forms and their relationships with each other; and knowledge of forms of beauty, such as design with color and shape, harmonies, and movement.

Children's play in the kindergarten was guided by the teacher, who carefully presented materials and activities designed by Froebel to enhance sensory and spiritual development. The materials, called **gifts**, included yarn balls, blocks, wooden tablets, geometric shapes, and natural objects (see Figure 3.8). Among the gifts were the first

---

Figure 3.8 Froebel's Gifts

Gift 1:
Six colored balls of soft yarn or wool

Gift 2:
Wooden sphere, cylinder, and cube

Gift 3:
Eight cubes, presented together as a cube

Gift 4:
Eight rectangular pieces, presented as a cube

Gift 5:
Twenty-one cubes, six half-cubes, and twelve quarter-cubes

Gift 6:
Twenty-four rectangular pieces, six columns, and twelve caps

Gift 7:
Parquetry tablets derived from the surfaces of the gifts, including squares, equilateral triangles, right triangles, and obtuse triangles

Gift 8:
Straight sticks of wood, plastic, or metal in various lengths, plus rings and half-rings of various diameters made from wood, plastic, or metal

Gift 9:
Small points in various colors made of plastic, paper, or wood

Gift 10:
Materials that utilize rods and connectors, similar to Tinker Toys

wooden blocks used as tools for children's learning. These objects were intended to encourage discovery and manipulation and to lead children to an appreciation for people's unity with God. Froebel embraced the view that each child was inherently good and born with innate knowledge that could be awakened by exposure to the fundamental principles of Creation. The outward symbols of Creation were the basic shapes of geometry. Froebel's blocks and other gifts were designed to expose children to these shapes and allow for the exploration of their symbolic truths.

Handwork activities, called **occupations**, included molding, cutting, folding, bead stringing, and embroidery. They were intended to foster discovery, inventiveness, and skill. Songs and finger plays (many written by Froebel), stories, and games were selected to encourage learning the spiritual values underlying the program. Froebel held that education must begin with the concrete and move to greater abstraction and that perceptual development precedes thinking skills.

The early kindergartens emphasized the importance of cleanliness and courtesy, the development of manual skills, physical activity, and preparation for later schooling. Kindergarten children were not made to sit still, memorize, and recite as older children were. The teacher's role was that not of taskmaster but of affectionate leader.

THE KINDERGARTEN MOVEMENT Froebel proposed the idea of training young women to be kindergarten teachers. Educators from Europe and the United States studied his methods and returned to their homes to start kindergartens. Graduates of Froebel's teacher training institute brought the ideals and practices of the kindergarten to the United States and many other countries.

Two sisters, Bertha Meyer Ronge and Margarethe Meyer Shurz, brought the kindergarten to the English-speaking world. In 1851, Bertha started the first kindergarten in England. Margarethe founded the first American kindergarten in Watertown, Wisconsin, in 1856 (Lascarides & Hinitz, 2000). The early American kindergartens were private, often established in homes and taught in German by teachers who had studied with Froebel (Beatty, 1995).

Elizabeth Peabody founded the first English-speaking kindergarten in Boston in 1860 and later the first kindergarten teacher education program in the United States. She was influential in winning public support for kindergartens. The first publicly supported kindergarten was opened in St. Louis, Missouri, in 1873 and was followed by rapid expansion of kindergartens between that year and 1900. Peabody was also a social reformer who worked to provide education for the children of slaves in the South and Native American children and worked toward a free society for all people (Lascarides & Hinitz, 2000; Jones, 2002)

Two aspects of the society of the late 1800s appear to have contributed to the rapid growth of the kindergarten. The first was that the idea that children are inherently good was gaining wider acceptance at that time. If children are viewed in a positive way, it follows that they require a nurturing and benevolent environment in their early years. The second was a concern for the social issues created by the large influx of poor immigrants, which gave rise to the field of philanthropic social work. Mission kindergartens for children of the poor were established by social workers with the expectation that if children were taught the appropriate values and behaviors, they and their families would be more successful in assimilating into American society.

Many of the first professional associations concerned with early childhood education in the United States grew out of the kindergarten movement. Elizabeth Peabody established the American Froebel Union in 1878. The International Kindergarten Union, which began in 1892, merged with the National Council of Primary Education in 1930 to become the Association for Childhood Education International, which is still an active organization today. The National Kindergarten Association, founded in 1909 with the goal of supporting universal acceptance of the kindergarten, was disbanded in 1976 (Williams, 1992).

Patty Smith Hill (1868–1946), one of the founders of the Institute of Child Welfare Research at Columbia University Teachers College, worked to bring innovation to the Froebelian kindergarten when it came under fire for being rigid and teacher dominated. She combined ideas from a number of approaches and was able to move kindergartens in a direction more consistent with the progressive ideas of her time.

Kindergarten programs in the United States were influential in other countries. After visiting programs James Laughlin Hughes founded the first kindergarten in Canada in 1883. Margaret Windeyer founded the first kindergarten in Australia in 1895 and New Zealand's first free kindergarten was established in the 1880s (Prochner, 2009).

ISSUES RELATED TO THE KINDERGARTEN MOVEMENT   Froebel's ideas dominated the kindergarten movement in the United States until progressive educators challenged them at the beginning of the 20th century. Although the kindergarten allowed children to learn through play it had little resemblance to what we consider to be developmentally appropriate practice today. It was, however, profoundly influential in its day and is regarded as the beginning of contemporary early childhood practice in much of the world (Weber, 1969; Williams, 1992).

A period of ferment caused by conflicting philosophies began in the kindergarten movement in the 1890s and lasted for more than 20 years. Progressive educators challenged supporters of Froebel's approach and expressed the concern that kindergarten practices were rigid and didn't reflect their ideas about how children develop and learn. By 1920, the progressive approach had achieved dominance. The reformed kindergarten curriculum reflected many of Froebel's original ideas but added a new emphasis on free play, social interaction, art, music, nature study, and excursions. New unstructured materials, including large blocks and dollhouses, encouraged children's imaginative play. Books and songs reflected children's interests rather than conveying a religious message, and activities were inspired by events in the children's daily lives.

THE IMPACT OF KINDERGARTEN   Publicly supported kindergartens began in the United States in 1873, but were not widespread at first. As kindergartens gradually moved into public schools, they met with grudging acceptance. Today, school for 5-year-olds is accepted and universally available in the United States and most other countries, though it is not mandatory everywhere. In many countries, the word *kindergarten* is synonymous with early childhood education (Education Commission of the States, 2011).

SOURCE: Eva Moravcik

The child-centered approach of the kindergarten has had an impact on the education of young children in both primary grades and preschool programs. Originally the rigid atmosphere of the traditional primary schools, with their emphasis on drill and practice of academic skills, was very different from the approach of kindergartens. However, the gap gradually narrowed. Many kindergarten activities found their way into the primary grades, even as primary activities filtered down into the kindergarten. Today, kindergartens are increasingly academic and in most places quite similar to first-grade classrooms.

Froebel's kindergarten has also had an impact on preschools. The preschool curriculum that includes play, handwork, songs, and rhymes clearly is the descendant of Froebel's gifts and occupations. Figure 3.9 summarizes the goals, principles, and impact of the Froebelian kindergarten.

The McMillan Sisters and the Nursery School

Margaret McMillan (1860–1931) and her sister Rachel (1859–1917), whose parents were Scottish, were social reformers in England who spent their lives addressing the problems of poverty brought about by the industrial revolution. During the 1890s, they began to visit the homes of the poor, which led them to lives of social activism with a focus on improving the welfare of what was then referred to as the "slum child." They campaigned for school meals and opened Britain's first school health clinic.

In 1911, the sisters started the Open-Air Nursery School and Training Centre in London, attended by 30 children between the ages of 18 months and 7 years. This open-air, play-oriented nursery school was their response to health problems they observed in children who lived in poverty and was intended to be a model for other schools and a site for educating teachers. They called their new program a **nursery school** to show that they were concerned with care, nurture, and learning. The McMillan sisters recognized that many poor children in England needed both care and education in their first few years to give them a good foundation for later life. (In the 1980s, the **National Association for the Education of Young Children (NAEYC)** revived this notion by deciding to add the word *care* to *early childhood education*.) The nursery school was designed to identify and prevent health problems and to enhance children's physical and mental development before they entered formal schooling. The McMillan sisters were concerned with basing education on the child's "sense of wonder" and believed that teachers must know what attracts and engages children (Williams, 1992). They also wanted to help parents learn how to have positive interactions with their children.

Figure 3.9 The Goals, Principles, and Impact of the Froebelian Kindergarten

Goals of the Froebelian kindergarten:

- To awaken the child's senses to the perfection of the God-given structure underlying all of nature.
- To provide a common ground for all people and advance each individual and society into a realm of fundamental unity.*

Pedagogical principles of the Froebelian kindergarten that are still prevalent today:

- Activity is the basis for knowing.
- Play is an essential part of the educational process.
- The role of the teacher is to support the development of positive impulses in children.
- Teaching of young children should differ in content and process from teaching older children.
- The teacher is an affectionate leader.

Froebelian kindergarten practices that are still used today:

- Teaching materials and activities (Froebel called them *gifts* and *occupations*) including clay work, paper cutting, block building, finger plays, singing, and drawing.
- A preparation program for teachers.

*Brosterman, 1997, 12–13.

Margaret McMillan wrote a series of influential books that included *The Nursery School* (1919) and *Nursery Schools: A Practical Handbook* (1920). In 1930, Margaret established the Rachel McMillan College to train nurses and teachers.

In providing for children's physical needs, the McMillan sisters emphasized the value of active outdoor work and play, health and nutrition, perceptual-motor skills, aesthetics, and the development of imagination. A planned environment that children could explore was an important aspect of learning in the nursery school (McMillan, 1919). The nursery school included materials for sensory development, creative expression, gardening, nature study, and sand play. The teacher's role was both to nurture and to teach children in an informal way.

NURSERY SCHOOLS IN THE UNITED STATES   At the same time that kindergartens were gaining hold in the United States, the nursery school movement began as an effort to provide care and education to even younger children. Nursery schools in the United States were inspired by the nursery schools in England, by Sigmund Freud's ideas about psychosocial development, and by the philosophy of progressive education.

One of the first nursery schools in the United States was the City and Country School, established in New York City in 1913 by Caroline Pratt. In 1916, the Bureau of Educational Experiments opened a laboratory nursery school under the direction of Harriet Johnson. In the 1920s, a number of other laboratory nursery schools were established in the United States, including one organized by Patty Smith Hill at Columbia University Teachers College in New York City (Hill was also founder, in 1926, of the National Association for Nursery Education which evolved into the NAEYC) and the Ruggles Street Nursery School and Training Center directed by Abigail Eliot in Roxbury, Massachusetts.

Abigail Eliot studied with Margaret McMillan in England and was among the first women to receive a doctorate from Harvard University. She founded the Ruggles Street Nursery School, an early example of a full-day program for children in a low-income neighborhood. Eliot emphasized the creation of an intellectually stimulating, child-centered environment and she sought to involve parents in the school (Beatty, 1995).

In 1916 the University of Chicago established the first **parent cooperative nursery school**. Cooperative schools were like other nursery schools in that they provided supervised learning and socialization experiences for young children. They differed in that they were cooperatively run by a teacher and by parents who were expected to assist in the daily program. The benefits of these programs were low tuition, opportunities for mothers to gain new insights and skills in working with young children, a sense of community, and the development of new leaders. The schools became popular and spread rapidly throughout the United States (Byers, 1972). Parent cooperatives can still be found throughout the United States (as well as in Canada, Australia, New Zealand, and Great Britain), although the number of programs has declined since the 1970s, when women's participation in the labor force began its rapid growth.

Also founded in the 1900s were prominent child-study institutions with laboratory schools: Yale University's Clinic of Child Development, the Iowa Child Welfare Research Station, and in 1921 the Merrill-Palmer Institute in Detroit founded by Edna Noble White, who had visited the McMillans' nursery school in England (Beatty, 1995).

During the 1920s and 1930s, **laboratory preschools** were established in many college home economics departments to train future homemakers and teachers and to conduct child development research. These programs were multidisciplinary in orientation because the pioneers of early education came from a number of fields, including nursing, social work, medicine, psychology, and education. The earliest nursery schools emphasized children's social, emotional, and physical development—hence the beginning of the **whole-child approach** described in this book.

THE IMPACT OF THE NURSERY SCHOOL   Early childhood education still reflects the legacy of the nursery school. In these early programs (and in today's programs), children learn through interactions in a planned learning environment. The role of the school is to let children develop in their own unique ways of knowing. The daily schedule is characterized by blocks of time in which children are free to choose activities and engage in them for long periods. The classroom is divided into activity areas—typically those for block construction, dramatic play, art, water play, sand play, science, math, and language and literacy. The role of the teacher is to create an environment that facilitates development by giving children many things to represent, explore, think about, talk about, and read about. Teachers support children's social and emotional development by providing a safe and nurturing environment, valuing each child's contributions, encouraging children to work and play cooperatively, and to verbalize their feelings. In the early days of the nursery school, cognitive development was not emphasized because of the belief of that time that significant development in this area did not occur until children entered school at the age of 6. As scholars learned more, cognitive development was added to the conception of "the whole-child approach."

The nursery school has continued to evolve since the 1960s in response to the needs of disadvantaged children and in recognition of the importance of early experiences for cognitive development. What remains constant is the insistence that children can benefit from play in a carefully designed learning environment under the guidance of a caring and skilled teacher.

Today, the terms *nursery school*, *preschool*, and *child development center* are used in the United States to describe programs that evolved from the McMillan nursery school. Programs such as Head Start and state-funded preschools for low-income children embody the purpose of the original nursery schools and the McMillan sisters' vision and commitment to poor children. The Head Start program is the best contemporary example of this legacy. The comprehensive design of the Head Start program, which includes health and nutrition, reflects the commitment of early nursery education to children's health and well-being. See Figure 3.10 for an overview of the goals, principles, and impact of the nursery school.

Figure 3.10 The Goals, Principles, and Impact of the Nursery School

Goals of the nursery school:
- To provide nurture (loving care) to children.
- To support the health, nourishment, and physical welfare of children.
- To assist parents in improving their ways of caring for and interacting with their children.
- To provide a model for teachers of how to work with young children.*

Educational principles of the nursery school that are prevalent today:
- It is important to stimulate the child's sense of wonder and imagination.
- Play in a planned learning environment is an important vehicle for education.
- Outdoor work and play are important.
- Aesthetics are an important part of the curriculum.
- The teacher's role is to nurture and teach informally.
- Children need trained and qualified teachers.

Nursery school practices that are still used today:
- Programs like Head Start for low-income children.
- Sensory activities.
- Outdoor activities including sandbox and gardening.
- A focus on children's health, including personal hygiene and nutrition.
- Creative expression activities.

*Lascarides & Hinitz, 2000, 121.

John Dewey and Progressive Education

Progressive education evolved from a combination of the ideas of Rousseau, Pestalozzi, and Froebel and from 19th-century social reform movements (Williams, 1992). The founders of the movement desired a "progressive" society in which people could develop their full potential. Their goal was to improve society through fundamental changes in the schools. They attempted to transform dreary educational environments in which children learned by drill and recitation.

SOURCE: Library of Congress Prints and Photographs Division [LC-USZ62-51525]

JOHN DEWEY   John Dewey (1859–1952), though not the founder of the progressive movement, became its most influential spokesperson. Dewey taught at the University of Chicago, where he was instrumental in setting up a laboratory school for experimentation with innovative educational concepts. Later, he moved to Columbia University in New York and continued to write about education and philosophy for the rest of his career.

Dewey wanted schools to be places where children could grow physically, intellectually, and socially and be challenged to think independently. He called for classrooms to be places in which children investigated the world around them and expanded their natural curiosity. One of his most significant ideas was that schools should reflect the life of the society and that education should be viewed as the life of the child in the present, not just as preparation for the future. He also believed that, in addition to instruction, schools should play a role in helping immigrants learn to adapt to a new culture.

Progressive educators advocated techniques of instruction that were based on children's interests, involved hands-on activities, recognized individual differences, and were to the greatest extent possible initiated by the child, not the adult.

PROGRESSIVE EDUCATION   In Dewey's view, the school community offered children an opportunity to practice democratic ideals in a group setting and to learn through activities that were interesting and meaningful such as carpentry, weaving, cooking, and the study of local geography. An innovative instructional approach, still used today, was to have children in the elementary school work on collaborative projects related to their own interests.

In progressive programs children learned through doing—through experiencing and experimenting with materials and self-directed activities. In *My Pedagogic Creed*, Dewey (2010) wrote that the child's own instinct and powers furnish the material and give the starting points for all education. This mirrors today's view that children's needs and interests are essential components of curriculum planning. But Dewey cautioned that though educational activities could be enjoyable, they always needed to support children's development and learning.

Teachers were expected to provide a carefully designed learning environment and curriculum that prepared children to be members of a democratic society. They observed children and, based on their observations, asked questions and provided experiences designed to integrate different subject areas and help children expand their understanding of the world. The role of the teacher was to serve as a guide and observer, not lecturer and disciplinarian.

THE LEGACY OF PROGRESSIVE EDUCATION   The ideas of progressive education, combined with research in child development, triggered a great deal of educational experimentation. In New York in 1916, Harriet Johnson, Caroline Pratt, and Lucy Sprague Mitchell organized the Bureau of Educational Experiments, the forerunner of the Bank Street College of Education, as an agency for research on child development. Caroline Pratt's and Harriet Johnson's observations of preschool children at play led to the development of the wooden blocks (called **unit blocks**) that continue to be standard equipment in early childhood programs today. A significant contribution was Johnson's *The Art of Block Building* that described her observations of nursery school children's stages of skill in block building (Beatty, 1995).

Mitchell, a friend of John Dewey and a strong advocate of progressive education, directed the Bank Street School for Children and was influential in its evolution into a teacher training institution. Mitchell was deeply committed to young children's learning about their world through direct experience. Her book *Young Geographers* introduced the study of geography to young children through exploring in their communities. This community study still characterizes the curriculum of Bank Street School for Children and an educational model based on its practices.

A number of schools based on progressive ideas were established at the end of the 19th century and the beginning of the 20th. These included the Laboratory School at the University of Chicago, which began in 1896; the Francis Parker School in Chicago in 1883; the Horace Mann School in New York City in 1887; the Bureau of Educational Experiments (later called Bank Street School) in 1916; and the Lincoln School at Teachers College, Columbia University, in 1917. In 1914, Carolyn Pratt founded the Play School in Greenwich Village, emphasizing the arts, exploration of the environment, and children's active participation in their own education. The Play School developed into the City and Country School, which still serves children in New York today.

Principles of progressive education gained acceptance in American school systems during the first half of the 20th century and were also influential in European schools. From its beginnings, however, progressive education had its critics. Eventually it came under fire from those who felt that students were not gaining sufficient mastery of basic school subjects. The movement had become associated with permissiveness rather than with its guiding principles that the curriculum must challenge children intellectually and help them develop self-direction and responsibility. The progressive influence on American education waned after World War II as more academic, skill-based teaching practices became prevalent. It almost came to a halt after the launch of the Soviet satellite *Sputnik* in 1957, which changed the focus of American education to producing scientists who could compete with the Soviet Union.

Progressive education had a profound impact on American education, particularly on kindergartens and nursery schools, many of which remain more closely allied ideologically with progressive philosophy than with more skill-based academic approaches. A number of highly regarded private schools continue to implement the philosophy of progressive education. These programs are based on the beliefs that curriculum should be integrated instead of based on separate subject areas, that children should be active learners who have many opportunities to pursue their own interests, that schools should help children to understand their world, and that classrooms should be places where children can learn to live in a democratic society. See Figure 3.11 for an outline of progressive education goals, principles, and impact.

Two programs that are well known and widely implemented today have direct connection to the educational approaches that we just described. The High/Scope model, which embraces many of the goals of the McMillans' nursery school, and the Developmental-Interaction Approach, developed at Bank Street School and College, are present-day examples of progressive education.

High/Scope was one of the first programs designed in the 1960s to ameliorate the effects of poverty on young children's development. High/Scope, created by David Weikart and his colleagues in Ypsilanti, Michigan, draws its theoretical foundation from the work of Jean Piaget. The curriculum is based on key experiences related to the acquisition of concepts studied by Piaget, including classification, seriation, number, spatial relationships, and time. These key experiences provide the basis for planning and adapting the learning environment, making decisions about teacher-led group activities, and assessing children's progress.

The Bank Street School for Children (serving preschool through 8th grade) in New York City embodies the philosophy of progressive education. This approach emphasizes the interaction of different aspects of development, and the interaction of the child

Figure 3.11 The Goals, Principles, and Impact of Progressive Education

Promoted by John Dewey, Lucy Sprague Mitchell, Harriet Johnson, and Caroline Pratt in the United States in the 1890s

Goals:

- To improve society through schooling.
- To help people develop their full potential.
- To prepare citizens to live in a democratic society.

Progressive pedagogical principles that are still prevalent today:

- Education is the life of the child in the present, not just preparation for the future.
- Cooperation and problem solving are important aspects of the curriculum.
- Children learn through doing.
- All aspects of development are important.
- The role of the teacher is to be a guide.

Progressive teaching practices that are still used today:

- Curriculum based on children's interests and needs.
- Projects and active exploration as the core of the curriculum.
- The community as a source of curriculum.
- Unit blocks used to represent what is learned.

with other people and with the environment. In the 1970s, the name of this method was changed from the Bank Street approach to the **Developmental-Interaction Approach (DIA)** to focus on the importance of interactions in education rather than the location of the school (Goffin & Wilson, 2001).

A DIA classroom is viewed as a representation of society, with social studies and learning trips forming the core of the curriculum. Other subject areas are integrated into the exploration of social studies topics. Teachers are expected to provide children with the experience of living within a democratic community and to be sensitive facilitators who respond to the needs and interests of children (Cuffaro, 1995). A number of the curriculum examples we use in this book are based on pedagogy of the DIA.

Reflect On

Your Experience

Reflect on your experiences in preschools and kindergartens. How did the programs that you attended as a child or that you have observed or taught in seem to reflect the programs described here? How were they different? What were the programs like? What were your reactions to them?

 A Quick Check 3.2

Gauge your understanding of the concepts in this section.

 ## Three European Approaches

Three educational approaches that emerged in Europe in the 20th century reflect many of the ideas and values that were initiated in the kindergarten, the nursery school, and progressive education. Each of these programs was developed by an inspired and creative thinker, and each of these innovators added significant new elements to what had gone before. The programs are the **Montessori method**, developed in Italy by Dr. Maria Montessori; **Waldorf education**, conceived of in Germany by Rudolf Steiner; and the **Reggio**

Emilia approach, founded in Italy by Loris Malaguzzi. Many schools today implement these approaches, and all of them have had a profound impact on contemporary educational thought and practice. Each of these programs has its own educational philosophy, including ideas about the nature of the child, curriculum content, teaching methods, design of the learning environment, and the role of the teacher. As you study early childhood education and observe programs, you might hear someone say, "We base our program on Reggio," or "I work in a Montessori school," or "My child attends a Waldorf school." The descriptions that follow will help you understand what those statements mean. You can gain direct experience of these approaches by visiting or working in one or more of these kinds of programs.

The Montessori Method

Maria Montessori (1870–1952) overcame the opposition of her family and her society to become, in 1896, one of the first women in Italy to receive a medical degree. The foundation for her interest in education was her study of the writings of French physicians Édouard Séguin and Jean-Marc-Gaspard Itard about their humane methods for educating children with mental retardation. Early in her medical career, she devised effective approaches for teaching children with serious cognitive delays who had previously been regarded as incapable of learning. In 1907, she founded the *Casa dei Bambini* (Children's House) in Rome, where she explored the applicability of educational methods she designed for children with cognitive delays to typically developing children. The program she designed was based on her observations of young children and how they learned. She reached the conclusion that intelligence was not fixed and could be either stimulated or stifled by the child's experiences. Further, she believed that children learn best through their own direct sensory experience of the world. Although Montessori's training was in medicine, the contributions she made to education have been her lasting legacy.

Montessori was interested in the first years of life and believed that children went through sensitive periods during which they had interest and capacity for the development of particular knowledge and/or skills. She believed that children had an inherent desire to explore and understand the world in which they lived. She saw these young explorers as self-motivated and able to seek out the kinds of experiences most appropriate for their stage of development. She was concerned about preserving the dignity of the child, and she valued the development of independence and productivity.

MONTESSORI PROGRAMS   The provision of child-size furniture (first created by Montessori), carefully designed and sequenced learning materials, and learning experiences that actively involve the child characterize Montessori's educational approach. The role of the teacher is to observe, guide, and direct children's learning rather than to instruct. For this reason a Montessori teacher is referred to as a directress or director.

In a Montessori classroom, children are grouped in mixed ages and abilities: 0 to 3, 3 to 6, and 6 to 12. Children learn from firsthand experience—by observing and by doing. Practical life experiences, such as buttoning, zipping, cutting, and gardening, enable children to care for themselves and the environment while building skills that will be useful throughout their lives. All learning in a Montessori classroom is cumulative. Each activity paves the way to future, more complex experiences. Children move freely about the classroom and choose their own activities. These activities are organized primarily for individual work rather than for group interaction.

Montessori stressed the importance of an orderly environment that helps children to focus on their learning and develop the ability to concentrate. Classrooms are equipped with **didactic materials** designed by Montessori to help children develop their senses and learn concepts. These carefully crafted and aesthetically pleasing materials continue to be the basis of the curriculum in a Montessori school. They are treated with care and respect and are displayed on

SOURCE: Courtesy of Centenary of the Montessori Movement

open shelves so that children can use them independently. The materials are graded in difficulty, and sequenced from known to unknown and from concrete to abstract. Each concept to be taught is isolated from other concepts that might be confusing or distracting. For example, if the child is learning the concept of shape, the materials will be of uniform size and color so that the attribute of shape can be readily perceived. Materials are also designed to have immediate, self-correcting feedback so that children know if they have successfully completed a task.

Video Example 3.1: Montessori Classroom

Watch this video that provides a tour of the environment and learning materials in a Montessori classroom. What did you learn about the essential elements of Montessori's approach to early childhood education? Do you think you would enjoy working in a Montessori classroom? Why or why not?

Purposeful activity is a characteristic of a Montessori classroom. Children's work is taken seriously and is not considered play. Children can work on any material they have learned to use at any time. Teachers do not make assignments or dictate what activities children should engage in, nor do they set a limit as to how far a child can pursue an interest. Adults and children are expected to respect concentration and not interrupt someone who is working at a task. Children are free to move around the room. A child can work at an activity for an unlimited time but is expected to approach tasks in sequence.

THE IMPACT OF MONTESSORI PROGRAMS   Montessori's schools were successful in Italy and the Netherlands (where Montessori had her headquarters for many years), and they eventually spread throughout the world. Although private Montessori schools have operated in the United States since 1915, this method remains a separate movement that has not been integrated with other educational approaches.

Montessori carefully prescribed the teaching techniques and materials for her schools. Teachers who work in these programs are trained in the Montessori method including the philosophy and how to use the specialized materials. See Figure 3.12 for the goals, ideas, and features of Montessori schools.

Historically, Montessori education was controversial in the United States, probably because its foundational beliefs were quite different from those of the nursery school and

Figure 3.12 Characteristics of the Montessori Method

Goals:
- To preserve the dignity of the child.
- To develop the child's independence and productivity.
- To ensure the psychological health of the child.

Significant ideas:
- Education begins at birth—and the first 6 years are critical. There are sensitive periods for development of skills.
- Intelligence is stimulated by experience.
- Children learn best through sensory exploration.
- Children are intrinsically motivated and seek out appropriate learning experiences.
- Learning is sequential.

Distinctive features:
- Orderly, child-size learning environment.
- Self-correcting, sequenced materials designed to teach a concept or skill.
- Children work independently, choosing activities based on level of complexity.
- Space delineated by mats or trays.
- Mixed age grouping.
- Teacher (directress) is observer and guide.

progressive education. Montessori schools share with the nursery school and progressive education the view that children are inquisitive, self-motivated learners, capable of selecting activities appropriate for their needs and developmental stage. Montessori programs differ from these approaches in that they do not emphasize social interactions or the development of creativity through the arts. Montessori was an important educational innovator, and a number of her ideas—such as the provision of child-size furniture and the use of didactic materials and sensory experiences—have found their way into most contemporary early childhood programs.

Two major professional associations are involved in the training of teachers and accreditation of Montessori schools and teachers. The original organization, Association Montessori Internationale, has headquarters in the Netherlands. The second, the American Montessori Society, was founded in 1956 to adapt Montessori methods to an American style of working with children. Today, public and private Montessori programs can be found in the United States and in many other places throughout the world. The North American Montessori Teachers Association (2014) estimates that there are about 4,500 Montessori schools in the United States and approximately 20,000 worldwide. See Figure 3.12 for a summary of the characteristics of the Montessori method.

Waldorf Education

Rudolf Steiner (1861–1925) was a German philosopher, scientist, and educator whose method is known today as Waldorf education. Steiner studied mathematics, physics, chemistry, and philosophy. He was a prolific thinker and made contributions both to philosophy and education. He was deeply interested in the individual's search for self and the development of human potential and was the founder of a school of philosophy called *Anthroposophy*, which explores the role of spirituality in contemporary society.

After World War I, the owner of the Waldorf Astoria Cigarette factory in Germany invited Steiner to establish a school to serve the workers' children. The first Waldorf School was opened in 1919 with the goal of educating people to build a free, just, and collaborative society.

Steiner believed that childhood is a phase of life that is important in its own right. His theory of human development is based on 7-year cycles that combine physical, mental, and spiritual development. Steiner's philosophy emphasizes balanced development, imagination, and creativity. The schools he developed were designed to promote healthy, unhurried learning experiences for children based on their stage of development.

WALDORF PROGRAMS   Steiner's schools stressed the development of the child's body, mind, and spirit. The focus was on educating the "whole" child because Steiner believed that engaging with a variety of academic, artistic, and handicraft subject areas would, over time, help a child develop balance between thinking, feeling, and will.

Steiner believed that in the first 7 years of life, the most important development had to do with the child's body and will (inclination to activity) and that educational activities should, therefore, be practical, imitative, and hands-on in nature. The Steiner kindergarten program takes place in an ungraded setting for children 3 to 6 years of age. The curriculum consists of storytelling, puppetry, artistic activities (painting, drawing, and modeling), imaginative play, and practical work (finger knitting, bread baking, and gardening).

Steiner thought it was important for the young child to experience a feeling of warmth and security. Therefore, classroom environments for young children are like an extension of a home. Classrooms tend to feature soft colors, natural materials, and simple learning materials, such as homemade dolls, that encourage imaginative use. Early childhood classrooms are beautifully appointed and aesthetically pleasing; they do not include plastic toys, academic materials, or modern technology, such as computers and video players.

Video Example 3.2: Waldorf Classroom

Watch this video that gives you a tour of a Waldorf classroom and learning materials. What did you learn about the essential elements of Waldorf education? Do you think you would enjoy working in a Waldorf School? Why or why not?

Steiner believed that there is a time for every stage of development and that children under the age of 7 should not receive formal academic instruction and should remain childlike. Children in Waldorf schools are not taught to read and write until well after their peers in other kinds of schools. Waldorf educators maintain that they catch up in learning these subjects by second or third grade (Williams & Johnson, 2005).

Teachers in Waldorf schools stay with a group of young children for 3 years, allowing them to create a community of learners and promote continuity of experience.

Teachers in Reggio programs regard themselves as researchers who conduct systematic study of children's learning by documenting their work and sharing it with families and communities. Photographs of the children working and transcriptions of the children's questions and comments are mounted and displayed with their work so that children and parents can examine them. Documentation also includes portfolios of the children's work, tape-recordings of sessions with the children, and videotaping the children as they engage in activities.

Video Example 3.3: Reggio Educational Approach

Watch this video that gives you a brief introduction to the Reggio approach to early childhood education as it is implemented in an American classroom. What did you learn about the essential elements of the Reggio approach to early childhood education? Do you think you would enjoy working in a Reggio based school? Why or why not?

THE IMPACT OF REGGIO EMILIA   The early childhood programs of Reggio Emilia reflect a uniquely collaborative approach to working with children, families, and the community. This approach is consistent with the social and political systems of the city of Reggio Emilia and its province, Emilia Romagna, which embrace a socialist political philosophy and are among the most progressive and prosperous in Italy.

Unlike the Montessori and Waldorf educational approaches, there are no "Reggio" schools outside of Reggio Emilia, Italy. Leaders of the schools in Reggio caution against efforts to replicate their system or to follow its provisions without question (in fact, questioning, or provocation, is an essential component of the Reggio approach). They have avoided publishing curricula or teacher's manuals and insist that education must be constantly evolving and changing based on the unique characteristics of each community. Thus, while Reggio education cannot be directly exported, many delegations of educators from the United States have visited Reggio since the 1980s to seek inspiration for their programs at home. When you encounter a program that is based on this educational philosophy, you will probably hear teachers say they are "Reggio inspired" rather than a Reggio program. American interest in Reggio schools raises questions about whether educational practices from one country can retain their vitality when transplanted to another country that has a different educational history, traditions, and goals.

Reflect On

Three European Approaches to ECE

Think about the Waldorf, Montessori, and Reggio programs described here. What are your reactions to each of them? Which appeals to you the most? Have you had any experience with them or noticed their influence in programs you have observed and worked in?

Early childhood education in Reggio Emilia can be viewed as a reaffirmation of the progressive roots of American early childhood education, and it offers a reminder about how important it is for educators to thoughtfully examine and discuss their practices. The commitment of the municipal government of Reggio Emilia to the welfare of young children makes Reggio more than just another educational innovation. It is also an inspiring example of a society that has dedicated itself to caring for and nurturing the potential of young children. See Figure 3.14 for the characteristics of the Reggio Emilia approach.

Common Elements of the Three Approaches

Each of these educational approaches was created in Western Europe as a response to specific historical circumstances, and has qualities that made it appealing and that has led to ongoing interest in it. Each one is distinctive and has strong supporters. But there are important similarities between them. All of the founders viewed children as active participants in their own development and had a clear vision of how to improve society by helping children realize their full potential. Each of these programs involves a carefully prepared, aesthetically pleasing learning environment that communicates respect for children, values partnerships with families, and evaluates children through careful observation and documentation of their work and play rather than by traditional tests and grades (Edwards, 2002). These three programs epitomize the respect for and

Figure 3.14 Characteristics of the Reggio Emilia Approach

Goals:
- To work collaboratively in a community.
- To develop the child's potential.
- To develop children's symbolic languages.
- To ensure the young child is visible to community and society.

Significant ideas:
- Child is "strong, rich, and competent"; respect for the child is important.
- Systematic focus is on symbolic representation.
- The learning environment is a teacher.
- The teacher is learner, researcher, and co-collaborator.

Distinctive features:
- Aesthetic learning environment (light and transparency).
- Wide variety of open-ended materials.
- In-depth project work based on children's interests.
- Emphasis on using the arts to represent ideas.
- Looping (3 years with same teacher).
- Documentation of children's work shown throughout the school.
- Trained artist (*atelierista*) as guide in addition to teacher.

anyone to care for them. Some poor women pooled their resources to pay for care or had older children mind the younger ones. Others left their children to beg in the streets or even locked them indoors during the workday.

Quaker women in Philadelphia founded the Society for the Relief and Employment of the Poor in order to provide poor working women with child care. In 1798, this society built a house that provided religious education for children while their mothers worked at spinning in another portion of the house.

In l928 philanthropists in Boston who hoped to provide good care for the children of working mothers took Robert Owen's British infant schools as a model and founded the Boston Infant School. In the 1830s, other infant schools were established in several U.S. cities. Two cities established separate infant schools for African American children. Support for the infant schools was not sustained past 1850, however. By that time, most middle-class Americans thought that young children should stay at home with their mothers. They failed to realize that working outside the home was an urgent necessity for many women.

Although the infant schools did not survive, the day nurseries of the mid-19th century served the most needy of the great waves of immigrants arriving in the United States. The first of these programs was New York's Nursery for the Children of Poor Women, founded in 1854. Its mission was to provide care for the children of women temporarily forced to provide for their families (Michel, 1999). These privately run programs enabled immigrant parents employed in factories to keep their families together. Personnel in the day nurseries were largely untrained, worked long hours with large groups, and provided minimal care for children. These programs were concerned primarily with the health of children and not with educational goals.

In 1878, Pauline Agassiz Shaw, a wealthy Boston woman influenced by the success of the American kindergarten movement, established a day nursery with educational programs for children of different ages (Michel, 1999). Other day nurseries followed Shaw's trend in providing comprehensive services with long hours of operation, infant care, family education and training programs, and even counseling.

Unfortunately, most day nurseries did not include services for infants in addition to 3- to 6-year-olds. An attempt to meet the need for care of infants was made by Frances Willard as part of her work with the Women's Christian Temperance Union in the 1880s. Willard's day nurseries were provided free of charge to poor mothers. The day nurseries were not open to all racial and ethnic groups, however, and never to the children of unwed mothers. Such discrimination left many working mothers with no option but to send their children to orphanages or to unsatisfactory arrangements in the homes of strangers (Michel, 1999).

The National Association of Colored Women became active in the 1890s in establishing day nurseries for urban African American children. Many African American women had a history of domestic servitude, first as slaves before the Civil War and then as domestic servants. In most cases, they had been required to care for white children while leaving their own babies in the care of only slightly older children (Michel, 1999).

The 19th century witnessed a number of experiments in child care, enabling many women to avoid the worst extremes of poverty by working outside the home. The general attitude in American society was that child care was a stopgap measure that a decent mother would use only in the most dire of circumstances. While public schooling was winning acceptance as a necessary condition for the rights of citizenship, the provision of care for young children was frowned on because it was associated with social welfare (Michel, 1999).

Child Care in Times of National Emergency

Child care in the United States has never been seen as a basic benefit that government should help provide, except as a temporary response to families in need of aid or during times of national political or economic crisis. During the Depression in the 1930s, federal child care centers, called Emergency Nursery Schools, were established to provide relief work for teachers, custodians, cooks, nurses, and others who had lost their jobs and needed employment. These programs were terminated as the Depression ended.

During World War II, the U.S. government again became involved in the business of providing child care. This time, the purpose was to meet the need for child care of the large numbers of women employed in defense plants. Under the Lanham Act (1942–1946), federally funded centers served children in 41 states.

Employer-sponsored child care, which was common in Europe, also emerged as part of the response to the demand for women workers during the war. Notable were the two child care centers run from 1943 to 1945 by the Kaiser shipyards in Portland, Oregon. The Kaiser centers were outstanding for the comprehensive, high-quality services that were made available to employees with children ages 18 months to 6 years.

The Kaiser company hired Lois Meek Stolz, an early childhood expert who had been director of the Child Development Institute at Columbia University and professor of psychology at Stanford University, as director. James L. Hymes Jr., a graduate of the Child Development Institute and highly respected early childhood educator, was manager of the programs. Teachers trained in early childhood education were hired, and the centers were designed by an architect to serve young children. The centers functioned 24 hours a day, all year long (except Christmas). They included an infirmary, provided hot meals for mothers to take home when they picked up their children, and offered other services that helped families combine work in the defense industry with caring for their children. During the short time they were in operation, the Kaiser centers served almost 4,000 children (Hymes, 1996). The centers were closed down after the war when women workers were no longer needed, but their legacy reminds us that we as a nation can provide high-quality, comprehensive programs for children and families when we think it is worthwhile to do so.

Government- and industry-sponsored child care were temporary measures, intended only to support the war effort. They were largely phased out as peace brought a return to the image of the "traditional family" with mothers in the home, tending to their children. Of course, many mothers did not return home but continued their employment. As child care facilities either closed or were reduced to prewar levels, these employed mothers had limited options for child care. A patchwork of private arrangements was the common solution. The California Children's Centers were among the few survivors of the Lanham Act provisions and were eventually merged into California's child care system.

Developments after World War II

The postwar view that a woman's appropriate role was homemaker, combined with the idea that children of employed mothers suffered from a lack of essential maternal care, gave strength to the belief that child care was at best unnecessary and at worst harmful to children. Between 1950 and 1965, it received little attention or support. Meanwhile, family life in America started to undergo major changes. The extended family system began to disintegrate as family mobility increased and the divorce rate soared. More and more women entered the workforce either out of financial necessity or because of a desire to find meaningful work outside the home. Employed single parents no longer had enough time to provide full time care for their young children but had to share this responsibility with other caregivers, usually nonrelatives. As women continued to enter the workforce the need for more and better child care became apparent. Though the need was great there was little government interest in subsidizing programs for young children until research began to make it clear that significant cognitive development occurred in the early years.

Another purpose for early childhood education emerged in the 1960s—ameliorating the effects of poverty on young children. In 1964, President Lyndon B. Johnson declared a "War on Poverty." Born of the civil rights movement, the War on Poverty reflected the idea that the government should help disadvantaged groups to compensate for inequality in social or economic conditions. It was based on the belief that education could be a solution to poverty. **Head Start,** the program created in response to this need represented a new view of child development as a valuable end in itself and an unprecedented mobilization of resources on behalf of children. The Head Start program, which continues today, is a contemporary example of the weaving together of the themes that have characterized the history of early childhood education: attention to children's health, involvement of families in their children's education, a curriculum that addresses all areas of development, and early childhood education as a way to improve society by supporting the healthy development of young children who live in poverty. Many of the practices associated with high-quality child development programs today, including health screening, nutritious meals, and family education and involvement, grew from Head Start's comprehensive approach to supporting the development of young, low-income children and their families. And much as the word *kindergarten* became the generic term for early childhood programs in much of the world, so too *Head Start* has become synonymous with preschool programs for low-income children in many places.

A Quick Check 3.4

Gauge your understanding of the concepts in this section.

Final Thoughts

Today's early childhood education and care programs grew out of the innovative thinking of the historical figures we have just discussed and the programs that they created: the nursery school, which focused on the healthy development of the child; the kindergarten, which provided a nurturing transition between the home or preschool and the rigors of first grade; and the day nurseries that sought to provide a safe, nurturing environment for families who needed to participate in the workforce. In recent years, the terms *education* and *care* have been combined to define the early childhood field. This terminology reflects ongoing efforts to bring the historical strands together into a coherent system.

The field you are entering has a long history and a tradition of concern for the needs of children and their families. Its pioneers were often ahead of their time in their recognition that education had to address the "whole child," not just the child's mind, and in their treatment of children in ways that were respectful and based on knowledge of development. A unique feature of the field of ECE is that significant contributions came from disciplines as diverse as medicine, health, and philosophy. Many of its founders recognized the important role of play in learning, advocated for universal education, and recognized that the education of young children was a valuable strategy for ameliorating the effects of poverty. They were concerned with improving society and saw that the creation of a caring and humane world must begin with the children.

Respect for children and their development and the vision of a better, more humane world have been at the center of early childhood education since its beginning and are still embraced. The programs for young children that we describe in this chapter are part of this legacy. In his book *Giants in the Nursery* David Elkind points out that "beneath the appearance of diversity and discontinuity in the history of early childhood education, there is an underlying unity and continuity" (Elkind, 2015, p. 3). This unity is at the core of today's conception of developmentally appropriate practice.

Over the years, slow progress has resulted in programs for young children that are based on knowledge of development, as well as more humane and egalitarian treatment of young children. Our society has become more aware of children's needs and the importance of meeting them in their early years, we have learned more about how children grow and learn and how to provide educational experiences based on this knowledge, and we have learned more about the kind of support that families need in order to give their children a good beginning in life. The history of early childhood education is still being written, and as a person entering the field today you will have the opportunity to be part of it.

 Application Exercise 3.2 Final Reflection

 ## To Learn More

Read

Absorbent Mind, M. Montessori (1967)

Experimenting with the World: John Dewey and the Early Childhood Classroom, H. K. Cuffaro (1995)

Giants in the Nursery: A Biographical History of Developmentally Appropriate Practice, D. Elkind (2015)

Hidden History of Early Childhood Education, B. Hinitz (2013)

Hundred Languages of Children, C. Edwards, L. Gandini, & G. Forman (1998)

Visit a Website

The following agencies and organizations have websites related to the history of early childhood:

Froebel Foundation USA

Rachel McMillan Nursery School

The Association for Experiential Education: Progressive Education in the United States

High/Scope Educational Research Foundation

Bank Street College of Education

Why Waldorf Works (website of the Association of Waldorf Schools of North America)

American Montessori Society

Association Montessori Internationale

North American Reggio Emilia Alliance

Document Your Skill & Knowledge About the History of ECE in Your Professional Portfolio

Include some or all of the following:

Explore an Educational Approach

- Read about one of the educational approaches discussed in this chapter (High/ Scope, DIA, Waldorf, Montessori, Reggio Emilia). Describe what you see as the major features of the program. Analyze how what you read reflects the history of early childhood education described in the chapter. Include your thoughts and reactions to what you learned and the implications for you as an early childhood educator.

Read and Review a Book

- Read a book about one of the historical figures or European educational approaches discussed in this chapter. Write a review of the book that includes your thoughts about what you learned, how it helped you understand themes in the history of early childhood education, and implications for you as an early childhood educator.

 Shared Writing 3.1 History of Early Childhood Education

Chapter 4
Child Development

SOURCE: Jeff Reese

In all the world there is no other child exactly like you.
In the millions of years that have passed, there has
never been a child like you.

PABLO CASALS

⌄ Chapter Learning Outcomes:

4.1 Describe reasons that early childhood teachers need to know about child development.

4.2 Explain the principles (main beliefs) that are the framework for understanding child development.

4.3 Describe ways that children's development is influenced by heredity, by the environment, and by the interaction between the two.

4.4 Identify key elements of theories about how children grow and learn and apply these theories in your work with children.

4.5 Demonstrate understanding of the "whole-child" concept of child development and recognize typical developmental milestones and sequences of development in infants, toddlers, preschoolers, and young school-age children.

NAEYC Professional Preparation Standards

The NAEYC Professional Preparation Standard that applies to this chapter:

Standard 1: Promoting Child Development and Learning (NAEYC, 2011).

Key elements:

1a: Knowing and understanding young children's characteristics and needs

1b: Knowing and understanding the multiple influences on development and learning

1c: Using developmental knowledge to create healthy, respectful, supportive, and challenging learning environments

---

You are becoming a specialist in understanding and appreciating how young children grow and learn. You are learning about them today, and you will continue to learn about them throughout your career. Fascination with children's development is a trait shared by most early childhood teachers. They watch with excitement as a toddler tentatively reaches for, then plucks, spears of grass. They are intrigued as they listen to preschoolers in the dramatic play area trying to decide who will get to be the dad and as they watch a 7-year-old carefully create a complex LEGO structure. Knowledge of child development principles and theories, coupled with your experiences with young children, will spark your excitement about being a part of their growth and learning and will help you to provide meaningful experiences for them. As you increase your understanding of child development, you will also increase your appreciation for children and your joy in watching them grow. This may transform teaching from your job to your calling. It will also help you build skills and hone your craft as an early childhood educator.

Because knowing about children's growth and development is an essential part of being a competent early childhood teacher, in most teacher preparation programs, you will take one or more courses focused on child development. If you have completed such a course, this chapter is a review; if not, it serves as a reference.

Why Study Child Development?

People have studied children for centuries. Research on children's development conducted over the past 75 years has given educators insight into how children grow and learn and a greater understanding of the patterns and sequences of development. It has taught us to see similarities in children's development and how each individual is unique. It has encouraged us to identify the factors and circumstances that support children's growth as well as those that may impede it.

Child development research, both past and current, highlights the holistic nature of young children's growth and development. Studies continue to confirm the interrelationship between children's development in all **domains**—physical, social, emotional, and cognitive—as opposed to focusing on a single aspect of development.

Studying child development theory can be exciting! As you learn more, you will see how children you know display characteristics and **developmental milestones** related to what you have learned. You will find you are increasingly interested in observing children. Knowing about child development theory will help you understand and organize your observations of young children and help you plan activities and experiences that will support their development.

A part of the study of child development is learning about the characteristics of children at different ages. This knowledge is one of the foundations of developmentally appropriate practice (DAP). As a teacher of young children, you will strive to make your **practice** a good fit for the children you teach. When you know about milestones, are attentive to children's individual characteristics, and know about their family and culture, you can thoughtfully develop learning experiences that are meaningful, relevant, and respectful of children (Copple & Bredekamp, 2009).

Video Example 4.1: Children's Development and Individual Needs

Watch this video to learn more about how understanding children's development and their individual needs and interests increases your ability to provide developmentally appropriate experiences for children. What are some examples of how individual needs might influence a teacher's choice of activity? How does understanding typical development help teachers to keep children safe?

Reflect On

Your Interest in Child Development

How did your interest in young children begin? What did you first notice about them? What interested you then? What intrigues you now about young children?

Principles of Child Development

There are six underlying principles, or main beliefs, that serve as a framework for the contemporary study of child development.

The Child Develops as a Whole

In early childhood education, we often refer to the development of the **whole child**. By this, we mean that we consider all domains (or areas) of development as we look at how the child grows and learns.

> *Three-year-old Sterling is playing in the sand. As he digs and dumps, he demonstrates his* physical *ability. He cups his hand, stretches out his arm, scoops, and makes vrooming noises replicating the action of a backhoe. This shows his understanding of how things work and his* cognitive *skill. He engages* socially *as he calls to his friend and beckons him into the play. As Sterling plays, he reveals his* emotional *state—his eyes gleam with satisfaction and he uses his* language *skills to tell you, "I'm a backhoe man."*

Children use their bodies and their senses to move about and explore the world (physical development). They acquire and organize information and learn to reason and solve problems (cognitive development). They learn to talk with others about what they are thinking, experiencing, perceiving, and doing (language development). They learn to relate to others and make moral decisions (social development). They learn to trust and to recognize and express their feelings (emotional development). Early childhood educators recognize the importance of each of these areas of children's development and know that they are interconnected and influence one another. They believe that these areas cannot be addressed separately and that no single area is more important than another.

Development Follows Predictable Patterns

Children acquire skills and achieve milestones in a predictable sequence.

> *For the first time today, Sidney, 36 months, picks up the scissors. He holds them awkwardly, struggles to open and close the blades, and ineffectively cuts small snips in the paper, giving up after a few tries. Kim, his teacher, goes to the cupboard and gets out cotton balls and tongs. She invites Sidney to try to pick up the cotton with the tongs, and he experiences much greater success than he did with the scissors. Over the next weeks, Kim provides other tong activities and brings in a variety of sturdy paint sample cards that Sidney enthusiastically snips. Sidney is not yet a master cutter, but each day he gains skill and confidence in using scissors.*

Development is sequential and cumulative. In other words, milestones are achieved in a predictable sequence, and the skills acquired in one stage are the foundation for developing later milestones. For example, before children can learn to skip, they must have mastered the large-muscle coordination required to hop and run. New experiences that do not build from previous experiences can be meaningless or overwhelming to a child, while experiences that are not challenging or interesting may lead to boredom and restlessness. J. McVicker Hunt (1961) described the concept of an

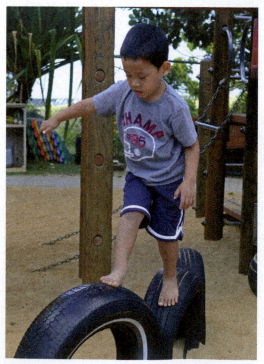

SOURCE: Jeff Reese

optimal match between a child's present level of understanding or skill and the acquisition of new knowledge or skill. New experiences need to provide just the right amount of novelty or challenge in order to engage the child.

You support and encourage children's development by planning experiences that provide challenge and by avoiding experiences that children find too frustrating (because they are too difficult) or boring (because they are too easy). Such planning requires that you know the sequence of typical development.

Rates of Development Vary

A child's age in years and months (**chronological age**) and the child's **stage of development** are only approximately related. The direction and sequence of development are similar for every child, but each individual develops at his or her own pace.

> *Ella was born 2 weeks after Shane. Both children started at a child development center when they were 6 months old. Shane's teeth emerged 3 months before Ella's, and he accomplished each milestone of physical development well ahead of Ella. Ella was a vocally responsive baby and by her first birthday had a vocabulary of about 25 words and syllables that she used skillfully in her interactions with people. Shane was cheerfully wordless until well into the middle of his second year. Now at 2½, both are healthy, verbal, active toddlers.*

Each infant enters the world with a unique set of inborn traits and biological characteristics (**heredity**). They interact with their environment in ways that are influenced both by that environment and by their heredity. Therefore, no two children (not even identical twins in the same family) are exactly alike.

What children can do and understand today is the basis of their future development. Understanding how children develop will help you plan a program that takes into account the wide variety of abilities you are likely to encounter, even among children who are close to the same age. In order to have appropriate expectations, you need to observe and become acquainted with the competencies of each child in your group and add that information to what you know about child development in general.

Development Is Influenced by Maturation and Experience

Development results from changes in the child based on the interplay of maturation and experience.

> *Gabriella, 22 months old, is taking apart a knobbed puzzle of farm animals. She has been dumping the pieces out of puzzles for several weeks now, then saying "Help!" to her caregiver, who patiently worked with her to pick up the pieces and fit them back in the spaces. Day after day, she repeated this activity. Today, without assistance, she manipulates each animal piece back in its space. "I did it!" she cheerfully announces.*

Gabriella learned to do the puzzle because she had many experiences with it, was physically and cognitively ready to successfully complete this task, and had support from an attentive adult.

Maturation is the unfolding of genetically determined potential that occurs as the child grows older. **Experience** is made up of a person's interactions with the environment, with people, and with things. The interaction between them influences children's development in all domains.

For example, in the **cognitive domain**, young infants lack the concept of **object permanence**—the awareness that even when an object is not in sight it still exists. As the child matures, this concept develops, but no amount of training seems to significantly accelerate its acquisition. However, a lack of experience with objects that can be seen, handled, and then removed may delay the development of this concept (Moore & Meltzoff, 2008 cited in Berk, 2016).

During the early childhood years, children's bodies increase in size and mass (maturation), and they gradually develop increasingly more complex physical responses and skills. Although it is not clear whether such development can be enhanced through special training, it can be delayed by factors such as poor nutrition, serious illness, and the lack of opportunities to explore the world (experiences).

As an early childhood educator, you will become skilled at providing safe and interesting environments and experiences based on your knowledge of each child's level of development, their past experiences, and their unique gifts and interests.

Development Proceeds from Top Down and from Center Outward

Physical development proceeds from the top downward (the **cephalocaudal pattern of development**), seen most clearly in the development of the fetus. In the early stages of fetal development, the head is half the total body length, whereas at birth the head is one-quarter the body length. This same top-down pattern is seen in **motor** development. Infants develop control of their heads before sitting and walking.

Growth and motor control proceed from the center of the body and move outward toward the hands and feet (the **proximodistal pattern of development**). The large muscles closest to the center of the body grow and develop coordinated functions before the small muscles of the hands and fingers.

When Monica was 3, she loved to paint. Each time she went to the easel, she covered her hands with paint and used them to swirl the colors around the paper. Now that Monica is 5, she draws detailed pictures of people, animals, houses, and objects using fine-tipped marking pens.

The proximodistal pattern is reflected in Monica's developing skills in painting and drawing. Younger children paint or draw using their whole arm in large circular motions. As they get older, they are better able to control the brush or pen and use their wrists and fingers to make more precise movements.

As children mature and engage in motor activities, they become more capable of coordinating their movements. It is important to be aware of physical capabilities at different ages so that you provide children with the challenges that they need to grow but do not frustrate them by expecting them to perform tasks for which they are not ready.

Culture Affects Development

SOURCE: Jeff Reese

Leanne, a teacher in a program with a large Samoan population, brings out a long rope to mark off a playground area. Four-year-olds Mele, Sione, and Talisa pick it up and skillfully begin to jump rope. Leanne looks on in amazement and comments to Sione's father, who has just dropped him off, that she has never seen preschool children jump rope. Sione's father smiles proudly and tells her that he always knew that young children could jump rope but was amazed when Sione began to talk so much after being in school a few months. He tells her that he did not expect children to talk that much until about age 8.

Children's development is influenced by the culture in which they live and grow. Values and beliefs of each culture and family determine many of the experiences and opportunities that are provided for children. Developmental expectations also have a cultural component.

Connecting with Families

Understanding Individual Development

Families want their children to do well. They want to know that their children are meeting developmental milestones in a timely fashion and accomplishing tasks at the same time as (or ahead of) other children of the same age. Family members may compare their child's progress to the achievements of others—siblings, cousins, or other children in the classroom or community. You can help families to have appropriate expectations for their children's development. Here are some strategies:

- Share information with families about children's successes and achievements. *"Connor was so excited this afternoon when he stacked 12 blocks into a tower."*

- Explain what is important about children's actions. *"Connor's fine motor skills and eye–hand coordination are growing quickly. These will be important later as he does more writing."*

- Document children's work for families through pictures and written observations. These help families to see children's progress. *Take a photograph of Serena as she successfully climbs to the top of the climber and share it with her father at pickup time.*

- Focus on the individual nature of development; remind families that when children are very focused on development in one area (such as climbing and/or socializing), they may show less interest in another area (such as language or fine motor practice). *"Lisa Marie is so focused on learning to stand. She'll begin babbling again once she masters learning to walk."*

- Remind families that every child develops at an individual pace and that most differences do not mean that a child is delayed or won't be successful. *"Bryson may not be reading yet, but he's showing such an interest in stories. Children develop skill in reading over time and with many opportunities to learn about words."*

- Let families know that all children have important individual skills and strengths and help them celebrate their child's unique talents. *"Alex is so thoughtful of other children. He always seems to know when someone is upset and shows them kindness and concern."*

For example, some cultures place a high value on independence and self-assertiveness. Young children in families with these values may show more skill in verbal interactions and may express feelings and ideas more frequently and skillfully than children from families who use more nonverbal interaction cues and who value a less assertive interaction style. Conversely, children whose families have taught them nonverbal communication skills may demonstrate more sophisticated ability to interpret feelings and to read social cues than children from more verbal home backgrounds. When you learn about these differences, you are equipped to meet the needs of each learner and to appropriately support development.

Applying Principles to Practice

Your understanding of these six principles of development will guide many of the choices that you make as a teacher. This knowledge provides a lens through which you view every experience you provide for children. You will choose materials and activities with knowledge of developmental principles and with understanding of the individual children in your classroom. This allows you to offer experiences that enhance the growth and development of *every* child. Over time, you will gain the ability to explain your reasons for making each choice.

✓ A Quick Check 4.2

Gauge your understanding of the concepts in this section.

SOURCE: Jeff Reese

Heredity and Environment

Throughout history, there have been shifts in beliefs about the relative impact of biological factors (heredity) versus environmental (external/experiential) forces on personality and behavior. Biological factors (sometimes referred to as *nature*) are genetic or inborn traits that influence growth and maturation. For example, a person's adult height is determined by his or her genetic inheritance. Environmental forces (referred to as *nurture*) have to do with the kinds of interactions and experiences that enhance or restrict the development of biological potential. For example, every child is born with the capacity to learn to speak any language but will learn only those that he or she hears spoken.

Historically, people have engaged in heated debate (often called the **nature–nurture controversy**) over whether the biological endowment or the environment is the primary force in shaping human behavior. Today, we know that both heredity and environment have powerful influences on the development of each individual. The way that children interact with their environment and organize their understanding from these interactions is determined by their biological attributes, their current stage of development, and their past experiences and interactions.

The Biological Basis of Development

Jonah and Megan are twins born into a large and loving biracial family. Their grandparents, aunts, uncles, cousins, and friends all visit the babies to see who they look like. Megan has her daddy's chin and her mommy's nose. Jonah has his mommy's eyes and daddy's nose. But somehow, both babies look uncannily like baby photos of their dad. During the first week home, their mom reports that Megan is a calmer, "sunnier" baby and Jonah is a fussier and more sensitive baby. Megan nurses easily; Jonah is harder to console.

Infants are born into the world with a complex combination of traits that derive from genetic inheritance. Each baby has some characteristics and needs that are universal and others that are unique.

INHERITED CHARACTERISTICS   No one questions that biological factors play an important role in development. The hereditary basis of development includes physical characteristics such as eye, hair, and skin color. Other characteristics—height, weight, predisposition to some diseases, and **temperament**—are significantly determined by individuals' biological inheritance but can be influenced by environmental factors as well. Studies of identical twins reared separately who select similar careers and lifestyles raise intriguing questions about the impact of heredity (Segal, 2012).

Although we do not know the extent to which genetics influence behavior and development, we do know that each young child comes with a unique genetic inheritance and no two are alike. In developmentally appropriate early childhood programs, children are not expected to be the same. Differences are respected and valued. The teachers offer a variety of learning activities to address children's interests and learning preferences, and adjustments are made constantly to meet individual needs. These programs welcome children with diverse characteristics and abilities. Adjustment to schedules, routines, and activities can allow typically developing children, those with disabilities, and those with special gifts and talents to grow and flourish in the same program.

Video Example 4.2: Meeting the Needs of Diverse Learners

Watch this video to see a second grade teacher adapt a science activity to meet the needs of diverse learners. Try to identify some of the ways the teacher made sure that all of the children in the classroom had a meaningful learning experience.

BASIC NEEDS

In their first weeks, Jonah's and Megan's lives consist of a host of needs expressed and met. They nurse, they sleep, they are held and rocked, and they are changed and bathed. Their mother nurses the babies, and her life is an almost constant pattern of feeding and caring for their needs. Their dad delights in caring for the babies. He holds, rocks, and sings to them, and he changes and bathes them.

An undeniable factor in development is **physiological** need. Every human being has basic needs for air, water, food, and shelter. If these needs go unmet, the individual will not survive. An additional prerequisite for an infant's healthy development is warm physical contact with a caregiver. A classic study conducted by Harry Harlow in the 1950s supports the importance of physically comforting experiences for all species. Harlow found that baby monkeys had a marked preference for contact with a terrycloth surrogate mother who provided contact comfort but no food over a wire mother who had the advantage of providing milk but little physical comfort to the baby monkeys (Harlow & Zimmerman, 1959).

Reflect On

Your Own Basic Needs

Think about a time when you were unhappy and under stress and another time when you were especially happy and productive. How well were your basic needs being met during these times? What made it possible for you to be happy and productive? What do these conclusions suggest for your work with young children?

SOURCE: Jeff Reese

The first and most important task of any early childhood program is to ensure that children's basic needs are met. Young children of any age thrive in programs that provide safe environments, nutritious and regular meals, appropriate physical activity and rest, and warm physical contact. Although the emphasis varies depending on the age of the children, all early childhood educators understand and devote a considerable amount of attention and time to making sure that needs are addressed.

TEMPERAMENT

By the time Megan and Jonah are 10 weeks old, they are clearly different individuals. Megan sleeps, eats, and eliminates on a predictable schedule. She is soothed by being rocked in a baby swing outside in a tree. She stares contentedly at the patterns of a mobile and rests quietly inside when she can hear the sound of people's voices.

Jonah's sleeping, eating, and elimination are much less regular than Megan's. He is calmed by a mechanical swing that does not vary in span or pace. He nurses and rests better if he is away from the sounds of people.

An aspect of development that has its basis in biology is called temperament. Temperament is "an observable, biologically based pattern of behavior and emotions, a characteristic way of experiencing and interacting with the world" (Kaiser & Rasminsky, 2012). Several researchers have constructed models of temperament. The most widely used and the one we find most useful was described by physicians Alexander Thomas and Stella Chess (1977) (see also Thomas, Chess, & Birch, 1970) based on the New York Longitudinal Study. Thomas and Chess reported that babies are not all alike at birth (something that parents have always known) and that distinct and observable differences in temperament are evident among newborn infants in their first days and weeks of life. According to Thomas and Chess, babies can be seen to differ in nine personality characteristics (see Figure 4.1).

The individual traits tend to cluster together in three basic types of temperament in children, labelled by Thomas and Chess as follows:

- The *Easy Child* (about 40%) quickly establishes regular routines in infancy, is generally cheerful, and adapts easily.

- The *Difficult Child* (about 10%) has irregular daily routines, is slow to accept new experiences, and tends to react negatively and intensely.

- The *Slow-to-Warm Child* (about 15%) has a low activity level, has mild or low-key reactions to stimuli, is negative in mood, and adjusts slowly.

Another 35% of children do not match any of these clusters but seem to have unique blends of temperamental traits. Megan, in the preceding examples, appears to fit the profile of an "easy" child, while Jonah has more of the characteristics of the "difficult" child.

Studies support the idea that temperament is genetic. For instance, one study found that Asian babies tend to be less active, irritable, and vocal but more easily soothed and better able to quiet themselves than Caucasian infants of the same age (Kagan et al., 1994; Lewis, Ramsay, & Kawakami, 1993). Infant boys tend to be more active and less fearful than infant girls (Berk, 2012). This supports the idea that some temperamental traits are present from birth.

The *longitudinal* (long-term) nature of the Thomas–Chess research shows that the characteristics are moderately stable throughout childhood and later in life. However, more recent research (Rothbart, Ahadi, & Evans, 2000) indicates that early

Figure 4.1 Thomas and Chess's Nine Dimensions of Temperament

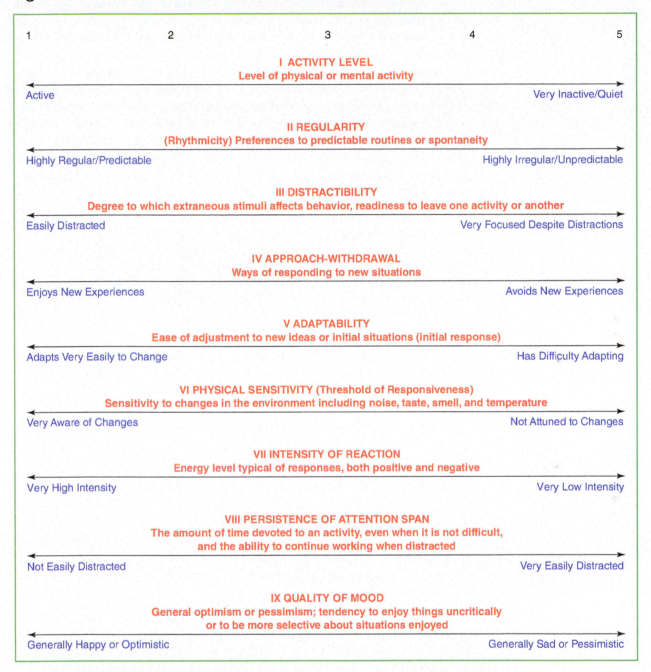

1	2	3	4	5

I ACTIVITY LEVEL
Level of physical or mental activity

Active ← → Very Inactive/Quiet

II REGULARITY
(Rhythmicity) Preferences to predictable routines or spontaneity

Highly Regular/Predictable ← → Highly Irregular/Unpredictable

III DISTRACTIBILITY
Degree to which extraneous stimuli affects behavior, readiness to leave one activity or another

Easily Distracted ← → Very Focused Despite Distractions

IV APPROACH-WITHDRAWAL
Ways of responding to new situations

Enjoys New Experiences ← → Avoids New Experiences

V ADAPTABILITY
Ease of adjustment to new ideas or initial situations (initial response)

Adapts Very Easily to Change ← → Has Difficulty Adapting

VI PHYSICAL SENSITIVITY (Threshold of Responsiveness)
Sensitivity to changes in the environment including noise, taste, smell, and temperature

Very Aware of Changes ← → Not Attuned to Changes

VII INTENSITY OF REACTION
Energy level typical of responses, both positive and negative

Very High Intensity ← → Very Low Intensity

VIII PERSISTENCE OF ATTENTION SPAN
The amount of time devoted to an activity, even when it is not difficult,
and the ability to continue working when distracted

Not Easily Distracted ← → Very Easily Distracted

IX QUALITY OF MOOD
General optimism or pessimism; tendency to enjoy things uncritically
or to be more selective about situations enjoyed

Generally Happy or Optimistic ← → Generally Sad or Pessimistic

behaviors tend to change somewhat over time and become established by age 2. This suggests the effect of the environment on children's temperamental dispositions. With repeated experiences, certain temperamental traits and patterns tend to become more stable.

Reflect On

A Child You Know

Think about a child you know well. Can you characterize him or her as easy, difficult, or slow to warm? How well do this child's characteristics fit with the expectations of his or her parents or caregivers? How do you respond to the child's temperament? What could you do to support this child if you were his or her teacher or caregiver?

We have found the concept of temperament valuable in helping us understand the wide range of personalities in the young children we have taught. We have also found the idea of "**goodness of fit**" (Thomas & Chess, 1977) very useful when considering the impact of temperament. Goodness of fit refers to the interaction between children's characteristics and the expectations of the adults who live and work with them. Children experience goodness of fit when teachers are aware of and sensitive to their temperament, accept characteristic temperamental behaviors, and help them adapt to their environment. Early childhood teachers who are respectful of temperamental difference will prepare routines and environments that support the needs of children with a range of characteristics. For example, teachers who recognize that some children have a very high activity level will arrange their schedules to ensure that these children have frequent opportunities for vigorous play rather than expecting them to sit quietly for long periods of time.

> *Max was a "difficult" infant and young child. His high energy level and his intense personality were often challenging for family members and teachers. Max's parents were careful to ensure that he had many opportunities to use physical energy in acceptable ways. They worked closely with his preschool and elementary teachers to encourage them to simultaneously hold high expectations and provide avenues for success that fit well with Max's personality and learning style. Max, at 17 years of age, is a relaxed young man, enthusiastic about his upcoming choices for college, and happy in his relationships with friends and family. His energy, drive, and enthusiasm are seen as assets.*

In this example, Max's family and teachers saw his individual traits as strengths and made sure to provide him with acceptable ways to express them. Understanding temperament will help you value and nurture children as individuals. It will enable you to respond flexibly to individual children and find ways to modify the environment and your own behavior to provide a good match for each child's temperament.

The Impact of Environment

The foundation for healthy development is laid down prenatally, before birth. There is a strong relationship between the health and well-being of the mother and other family members during pregnancy and the later development of the infant, child, and adult (Centers for Disease Control and Prevention, 2006). When infants and young children have their basic needs met, when they are nurtured by the adults in their environment, and when they have adequate opportunity to explore the world, they are most likely to grow and develop optimally.

> *Jonah and Megan's parents are able to give their babies attention, time, and a safe and healthy home. By the time the babies are 3 months old, Megan sleeps happily alone in the crib, while Jonah sleeps better in the family bed. Both babies love to be sung to and read to. Their sensitive and attentive parents have modified their lives in response to their children's needs. In addition, mom's Asian culture encourages the perspective that the child is the center of the home.*

Each baby is born into a particular family, culture, and set of circumstances. Children are shaped by and will shape their environment in a reciprocal dance that begins the first day of life.

THE CRITICAL NATURE OF NURTURING RELATIONSHIPS   A prerequisite for healthy development is a warm, intimate, continuous relationship between a child and his or her primary caregivers. Care given in the context of a loving relationship is essential to normal physical, cognitive, social, and emotional development and helps a child learn that the world is a safe and trustworthy place. A classic study of babies raised in an orphanage in Romania points to the vital importance of warm, nurturing relationships. While these children were fed, bathed, and changed regularly, they received limited interaction from adults and had few playthings or activities. Researchers found that their development was significantly delayed in all areas (Dennis, 1973). A central conclusion from the landmark report *From Neurons to Neighborhoods* (Shonkoff & Phillips, 2000) is that human relationships are the "building blocks of healthy development." The authors highlight the significance of responsive adult–child interactions, noting that caring adults are critical for healthy development and that children's achievements occur in the context of close relationships with others. Numerous studies confirm the crucial role of healthy relationships in fostering all areas of development, particularly development of the brain (Center on the Developing Child at Harvard University, 2016).

John Bowlby (1969) identified attachment to a primary caregiver (often the mother) as foundational to healthy social and emotional development. He defined **attachment** as a close emotional bond between two people and identified stages of infant attachment. Bowlby noted that from birth, infants behave in ways that engage adults and promote attached relationships. Crying, gazing, and smiling are all infant behaviors that tend to engage adults and help them form intense bonds with infants. Mary Ainsworth (1979) researched the degree of attachment between mothers and their children. She found that attachment ranged from securely attached to not attached at all. Securely attached infants were more likely to explore independently and exhibit positive interaction patterns than those with insecure attachments. More recent research indicates that secure attachment is strongly related to children's development in all domains. Securely attached infants may have strong multiple attachments rather than a single bond with only the mother. Fathers and other significant adults provide important nurturance (Center on the Developing Child at Harvard University, 2016).

While establishing positive relationships is pivotal for teaching young children of all ages, the significance of attachment is of particular concern to those who work with infants and toddlers. The work of Magda Gerber and the RIE (Resources for Infant Educators) Institute, as well as Ronald Lalley at the Center for Child and Family Studies, WestED/Far West Lab (Gerber 1997, Lalley 2009), affirms the critical nature of attachment for infants and toddlers both at home and in out-of-home care settings. Responsive interactions experienced by well-attached children have been shown to foster the development of strong neural pathways in children's brains and provide a foundation for all areas of development (Center on the Developing Child at Harvard University, 2010, 2016). Programs for very young children foster attachment when they use a **primary caregiving system**—a staffing plan where a very small group of infants and/or toddlers are assigned to one adult, their *primary caregiver*, who handles the majority of their care. Primary caregivers are able to learn the particular needs and styles of each child. Children and their primary caregivers form strong bonds and learn one another's ways of communicating. Primary care groups allow caregivers and children to develop warm relationships, one of the hallmarks of quality care for young children. Families sometimes worry that children in child care settings may become overly attached to caregivers and that these relationships interfere with family–child bonds. However, studies indicate that out-of-home care in quality programs for infants does not undermine children's attachment to their parents and that a secure attachment to a teacher may enhance infant–parent bonds (NICHD, 2006). In an ongoing longitudinal study of early child care and its effects on children's development, researchers from the National Institute of Child Health and Human Development found that higher-quality child care programs are positively related to better mother–child relationships (2006).

THE IMPORTANCE OF EARLY EXPERIENCES   Until the mid-1900s, the prevalent view of development was that people matured in predictable ways according to a biologically predetermined plan. In the classic work *Intelligence and Experience*, J. McVicker Hunt (1961) countered that view and cited many studies demonstrating the powerful effects of early experience on children's development. Contemporary research has validated these conclusions and demonstrated resoundingly that experiences in the early years of life have a critical impact on all areas of children's subsequent development (Center on the Developing Child at Harvard University, 2016; Shonkoff & Phillips, 2000).

In particular, numerous studies have shown that in order for infants and young children to develop normally, they need an environment that provides them with an appropriate amount of novelty and stimulation and includes opportunities for sensory exploration. Interactions with people and objects in the course of play—the important work of infancy and childhood—have positive effects on later development.

Resiliency   Inner strength and the ability to handle difficult circumstances with competence is called **resiliency**. Children who are resilient are able to "bounce back" from adversity and handle challenging life situations with competence.

> *Maureen is the first child in a family of six siblings. Both her parents used alcohol and drugs from the time that she was very young, and she assumed the role of caregiver for her younger siblings. She experienced regular episodes of parental anger and neglect. However, she was very close to her maternal grandparents, who visited her often and created special family events for her and her siblings. As an adult, Maureen is a successful executive of a large corporation. She is well liked by employees, friends, and associates. She is a loving wife and enjoys a warm relationship with her two teenage children.*

Studies suggest that inadequate nurture and stimulation in the early years does not necessarily cause irreversible deficiencies later in life (Kagan, 1984). A longitudinal study of children from the Hawaiian island of Kauai identified characteristics of children who are resilient in the face of adversity (Werner, Bierman, & French, 1971; Werner & Smith, 1992). Resilient children have a combination of inherited characteristics, such as a positive disposition, and significant environmental factors, the most important of which is a long-term, trusting relationship with a caring adult. In the preceding example, Maureen's relationship with her grandparents, coupled with her inborn easy temperament, contributed to her success both as a child and as an adult despite many challenges. Although repeated experiences of extreme and early deprivation can cause serious damage to the developing child, studies suggest that human beings can be remarkably resilient and that early deprivation does not necessarily result in lifelong problems.

The contemporary view is that the development of resilience is a dynamic process and that most children can learn to cope with some stress. Resilient children have a sense that they can control much of what happens to them and are willing to persist even when they encounter challenges. They are able to identify their strengths and use them to create positive outcomes. They usually display a sense of humor and playfulness (Breslin, 2005; Kersey & Malley, 2005). Resilient children are able to understand cause and effect and see the world as a positive place where events have reason and meaning. As a teacher, you support resilience in young children when you form meaningful personal relationships with each child and help each one identify his or her strengths. You can then use your knowledge to create experiences that encourage the children in your care to believe they are competent people and that the world is an interesting place (Gonzalez-Mena & Eyer, 2014).

Critical and Sensitive Periods   Animals generally exhibit critical periods, times during which the normal development of an organ or structural system must take place. If development does not occur during a critical period, permanent damage may occur or growth may be retarded. For example, research with kittens and monkeys shows that if their eyes are covered or they are kept in darkness during the early months of life, normal vision will not develop later, even when their eyes are uncovered or they are put into lighted environments. Human beings also have critical periods. For instance, during prenatal development, if the growing embryo or fetus is exposed to **teratogens**—environmental substances that cause prenatal damage—or to maternal diseases during particular times of growth, serious physical and/or mental impairments are likely.

Although critical periods in human beings are quite significant, there are relatively few of them.

More prevalent, however, are **sensitive periods**, times when an individual can most easily learn a particular skill or mental function (Center on the Developing Child at Harvard University, 2011). Recent studies of human neurological development suggest that these "windows of opportunity" are periods when the brain is rapidly developing and creating neurological circuits that are particularly related to the skills learned during that time. Sensitive periods that occur during the early years include a sensitive period for attachment (birth through age 3), language development (birth through age 5), and the ability to read social cues (birth through age 5) (National Scientific Council on the Developing Child, 2007). As an illustration, it is easiest for an individual to learn language during the first few years of life because this is the time when the brain circuitry for language is being built. It is possible to become fluent in languages learned later, but it will require more effort to master a language acquired after age 5 or 6.

Recent work by Courtney Stevens, Helen Neville, and others at the Institute of Neuroscience in Oregon supports the significance of sensitive periods for development of a variety of skills, including selective attention, the ability to remain focused on one thing even in the presence of distractions. This skill is foundational for learning and for school achievement (Stevens & Neville, 2013).

BRAIN RESEARCH AND ITS IMPLICATIONS FOR EARLY CHILDHOOD PROGRAMS   During the past thirty years, there has been a growing body of research on the development of the brain. Once it was assumed that the structure of the brain was genetically determined and fixed at birth. Today, we know that only the brain's main circuits are determined at birth. The brain of a newborn is only 25% of its adult weight. At birth, the baby's brain has all the **neurons** (the brain's nerve cells) that it will ever have. It will not grow more cells; instead, each neuron expands in size and develops more connections—called **synapses**—to other brain cells. Synaptic connections are what enable us to think and learn. The brain continues to grow and change significantly during the early years (and beyond) in response to experience.

Brain research has yielded a great deal of information about how young children develop and learn. Much of the information gathered from studies of the brain can be useful to you as you work with and plan for young children. Some of the points we have found most helpful follow:

- **The complex interaction between people's inborn biological traits (nature) and their experiences (nurture) profoundly affects all of human development, including brain development.**   This interplay begins before birth and continues throughout life. It is most significant during childhood. According to Shonkoff and Phillips (2000), "It is the ongoing communion between our heredity and our experiences that shapes us" (quoted in Galinsky, 2010). This complex interaction is especially important to brain development because as children interact with the people and objects in the environment, their brains create new synapses, thus becoming more dense and consequently better able to think and learn. The child's brain reaches a maximal density at about 3 years of age. This density is maintained during the first decade of life, after which a "pruning" of excess synapses occurs. The brain keeps the connections that have a purpose—those that are being used—while eliminating those that are not in use. Pruning increases the efficiency with which the brain can do what it needs to do. In this way, the brain actually "creates" itself based on the individual's experiences.

To increase your understanding of how children's brains are built, go to Harvard University's website, *Center on the Developing Child,* and view the video, "Experiences Build Brain Architecture."

- **Early experiences have a decisive and long-lasting impact on the architecture of the brain—the way it is built.**   The brain circuitry that is developed through early experiences controls children's ability to pay attention, learn, regulate emotions, and understand the social cues of others. According to the Center on the Developing Child at Harvard University, "The quality of a child's early environment and the availability of appropriate experiences at the right stages of development are crucial in determining the strength or weakness of the brain's architecture, which, in turn, determines how well he or she will be able to think and to regulate emotions." Research has found that the ways in which significant adults relate to children have a direct impact on the formation of neural pathways. Secure attachment to a nurturing, consistent caregiver who provides stimulating experiences supports brain development and helps a child learn impulse control and ways to handle stress. Conversely, when young children do not receive appropriate sensory, social, or emotional experience, brain development will be negatively influenced (National Scientific Council on the Developing Child, 2007). Further, when young children are repeatedly exposed to high levels of stress, brain development can be disrupted, putting children at risk for long-term cognitive delay, as well as emotional and physical illness (Center on the Developing Child at Harvard University, 2016).

- **The whole-child approach to understanding child development is supported by brain research.** Brain-imaging studies show that many areas of the brain are engaged when people complete specific tasks. For example, when infants' coos and babbles are responded to by adults, neurological pathways are built not only in the language area of the brain but also in the memory, motor, visual, emotional, and behavioral control centers. Researchers have determined that when children focus on cognitive tasks, the areas of the brain related to emotion are also activated (Galinsky, 2010). It is important that early childhood teachers understand how children's feelings are related to their cognitive skills and abilities and are aware of the interplay between developmental domains, particularly between cognitive and emotional learning.

- **Brain research helps us to understand the importance of the executive functions—the neurological processes people use to successfully engage in a range of important activities, such as planning, organizing, strategizing, paying attention, remembering details, and managing time and space.** Executive functions emerge during the preschool years but don't fully mature until early adulthood. **Executive functions** are intellectual skills and they also include the interplay between social, emotional, and intellectual abilities. When you are able to recall information and mentally manipulate it, control your feelings and behavior in order to meet goals, and change your thinking and actions appropriately in different situations, you are using executive functions (NCLD 2010, Center on the Developing Child at Harvard University, 2016).

In *Mind in the Making: The Seven Essential Life Skills Every Child Needs*, Ellen Galinsky (2010) offers an extensive and readable review of the research on children's learning and brain development. She notes that studies consistently find that executive function is strongly related to children's abilities to be successful in many arenas, including academics and relationships with others.

Figure 4.2 lists some of the tasks and behaviors that executive function supports.

To learn more about what scientists are learning about early brain development and its importance for children's overall well-being, go to Harvard University's website, *Center on the Developing Child* and view the video, "Executive Function."

- **Experiences can increase executive function.** A growing body of research indicates that teachers and parents can offer children experiences that increase executive function, specifically skill in understanding perspectives of others, paying attention, critical thinking, and self-control. Children who develop these skills during the preschool years and early in kindergarten have been shown to have

Figure 4.2 The Importance of Executive Functions of the Brain

Executive functions in the brain are what allow people to:

- Pay attention & focus on tasks
- Keep track of time and finish work on time
- Keep track of more than one thing at once
- Remember rules
- Inhibit a first response in order to meet a larger goal
- See another's point of view or perspective
- See connections between past events and new experiences; put ideas together in new ways
- Evaluate ideas and reflect on past work

SOURCES: Information from E. Galinsky, *Mind in the Making*, 2010; National Center for Learning Disabilities (NCLD), 2010.

stronger interpersonal skills as well as greater gains in literacy and math than children without these abilities (Galinsky, 2010). Neville et al. (2013) conducted several studies of Head Start children that indicate that providing specific training for children and for their families in attention and self-control has positive effects on both children and parents. Children who participated in this program were found to have increased brain function for attention as well as for language, intelligence, and behavior, while positive effects for parents included reductions in stress.

- **The developing brain is vulnerable.**   At certain times during childhood, negative experiences or the absence of appropriate stimulation are more likely to have serious and sustained effects on development than at other times. Trauma and neglect can lead to impairment of the brain's capacity. Excess cortisol, a hormone that increases when stress levels rise, can destroy brain cells and lessen brain density. Maternal depression, trauma, abuse, and/or prenatal exposure to substances such as cocaine, nicotine, and alcohol can all have harmful and long-lasting effects on brain development (Center on the Developing Child at Harvard University, 2016; National Scientific Council on the Developing Child, 2007; Shore, 1997). Studies indicate that when children are in high-stress situations for a prolonged period, they are less able to pay attention, to remember, and to have self-control (Galinsky, 2010).

- **Early intervention can promote healthy brain development.**   Evidence amassed over the past two decades indicates that early intervention promotes healthy brain development, increases cognitive abilities, and leads to more positive academic outcomes for infants and young children in high-risk circumstances. Intensive, timely, and well-designed intervention can create significant and long-lasting improvement for children who are at risk of impairment (Center on the Developing Child at Harvard University, 2016).

    The University of North Carolina's Abecedarian Project, a longitudinal study, demonstrated the positive effects of early intervention on children whose mothers had low income and low education levels (risk factors for cognitive impairment in children). Children who received an intensive 5-year program of full-day, full-year child care and whose families participated in parent involvement activities beginning in the first few months after the child's birth had dramatically higher IQs than those in a control group who received only free formula and diapers. The children receiving intervention demonstrated significantly better school achievement through elementary and high school. This intensive early intervention had a long-lasting impact on these children's lives (Ramey, Campbell, & Blair, 1998). Several other longitudinal studies, including the Chicago Longitudinal Study of the Chicago Child-Parent Centers, have demonstrated similar positive outcomes for children enrolled in high-quality early care and education programs (Reynolds & Ou, 2011).

Figure 4.3 Implications of Brain Research for Early Childhood Practice

1. Provide safe, healthy, stimulating environments and good nutrition to children.
2. Develop warm and caring relationships with children and support strong attachment between children and their families.
3. Ensure each small group of infants or young toddlers has a consistent primary caregiver.
4. Engage in frequent and warm verbal interaction with young children and read to them often.
5. Adopt a whole-child approach; focus on children's experiences and learning of physical, social, emotional, communication, and cognitive skills.
6. Design activities, environments, and routines to allow children of diverse abilities, backgrounds, interests, and temperaments to experience consistent acceptance and success.
7. Encourage exploration and play.
8. Involve families in the program in meaningful ways.
9. Limit television exposure (even "educational" TV) and encourage families to do the same.
10. Identify children who may have developmental delays or special needs; assist families in locating resources for support and early intervention.

Increased interest in the implications of brain development research has encouraged ongoing study and review by neuroscientists, psychologists, and linguists. The results of these studies consistently demonstrate that educational enrichment for children and families in the early years of life promotes healthy development in many domains from school entry to adulthood (Reynolds & Ou, 2011). See Figure 4.3 for further discussion of ways to apply findings from brain research to your work with children. To learn more about children's brain development, visit the Zero to Three website and explore the baby brain map.

A Quick Check 4.3

Gauge your understanding of the concepts in this section.

Theories of Development

Child development researchers and scholars have developed **theories**—a group of related ideas or principles that describe and explain how children grow and learn. Theories show us the relationship between facts (what has been observed) and a thoughtful interpretation of what these facts might mean. Theories help us understand the past and predict the future. Theories of child development offer frameworks for understanding children's growth and learning.

As you study theories of development, it is helpful to remember that theorists' research and conclusions were influenced by their own circumstances, including when and where they lived, their culture, and their values. As a student, you will study child development theories. You should reflect on them seriously, think about how they do and do not support what you have read and learned about children and families, and consider whether they are consistent with this learning and with your direct experiences with children. As you learn and gain insight, you may discover that your philosophy of education and teaching, as well as your practice, is changing.

Arnold Gesell and Maturational Theory

Arnold Gesell (1896–1961) and his associates, Frances L. Ilg and Louise B. Ames, pioneered the scientific study of child development in the 1930s. By gathering information on dozens of children at each age level, they identified typical characteristics, behaviors, and patterns of development (**developmental norms**) of children from birth through adolescence. The resulting guidelines for what can be expected of children at various ages and stages of development serve as the basis for many developmental charts (like the ones included in this chapter) and screening instruments that are in use today (Gesell, 1940; Gesell & Ilg, 1974).

SOURCE: Jeff Reese

Gesell claimed that genetic inheritance and maturation determined a major portion of an individual's development. This view, sometimes known as **maturationist theory**, proposes that genetic differences determine the rate at which children attain the growth and maturation necessary for learning skills and concepts. Without the required growth and maturation, they cannot progress. Therefore, attempts to hasten development are ineffective.

Gesell's work led to the concept of *readiness*, a period in development when a specific skill or response is most likely to occur. The notion of readiness is one that influences our thinking in many areas of children's growth and learning. Decisions about when children should be expected to learn to use the toilet, read, or drive an automobile are influenced by our understanding of and beliefs about readiness.

Critics of maturational theory have challenged Gesell's methods of data collection and have suggested that the small size and limited diversity of the children studied restrict the applicability of the conclusions. Other reviews have cautioned that the maturationist approach can be taken to mean that environmental stimulation is not important.

IMPLICATIONS OF MATURATIONAL THEORY FOR PRACTICE   Understanding that development follows a predictable sequence allows you to plan activities that encourage children to practice the skills they are building and to move on to the appropriate next steps when they are ready. Children grow and thrive in environments that invite the practice of emerging skills but avoid pushing children to reach new milestones before they have fully mastered prerequisite ones. One of the wonders of development is that when children engage in appropriate activity at any one stage, they are naturally building the skills needed to successfully enter the next. For example, the infant lying on her stomach, kicking vigorously, is strengthening the lower back muscles needed to begin to sit up.

Developmental norms can guide your decisions about when children can realistically be expected to acquire abilities and to learn skills. They can also provide guidelines for considering whether or not to be concerned with a child's progress or overall development. However, it will be imperative that you apply developmental norms with sensitivity to the children with whom you work. Take time to get to know the circumstances of the families whose children are in your care and to learn about the values that they hold for their children's achievements. This awareness will help you understand how individual family beliefs and circumstances influence the experiences they provide for their children. Knowing individual children and their families will help you apply information about developmental norms in ways that are appropriate.

Reflect On

Developmental Norms

What do you know from your family or from your memories about your own development? For example, when did you first walk? Talk? Ride a bike? Read? Was your development considered "typical" or "normal"? Did your development cause concern for your family? What might you imagine that families feel when they suspect their child's development is not proceeding on schedule?

Jean Piaget and Constructivist Theory

The process by which a helpless newborn becomes a talkative, reasoning child is immensely complex and not readily apparent. We cannot watch an idea grow or see thoughts develop. Understanding how children think and learn has been and continues to be a significant focus of study for educators and child development researchers.

Tomas (age 2½) and Janae (age 4) sit down at the table. Their teacher gives each of them a ball of play dough. Janae breaks up her dough into three small balls. Tomas looks over at Janae's dough and begins to wail, "I want plenty like Janae!"

Perhaps the best-known cognitive theorist is Jean Piaget (1896–1980). Piaget was originally trained as a psychologist. He specialized in understanding the nature of knowledge (epistemology). Piaget's interest in children began when he worked at the Binet Laboratory, studying intelligence testing. As part of this work, Piaget noticed and became intrigued with the consistency of children's incorrect answers to certain questions. This led him to focus his research on understanding how children think. From careful study of his own three children, he came to the significant conclusion that children actually think in ways that are substantially different from adults (Piaget, 1966). Earlier theorists had focused on opposing beliefs that knowledge is either *intrinsic* (coming from inside the child—nature) or *extrinsic* (coming from the external environment—nurture). Piaget thought that neither of these positions explained how children actually think and learn but instead that the interaction between the child's physical and genetic abilities (brain growth, reflexes, and motor skills) and the child's experiences (people and objects in the environment) created knowledge and understanding. Piaget's theory is based on his conclusion that children create or *construct* their own understanding of the world. They do this through their interactions with the people and things in their environment. As they grow and develop, they continue to revise and expand their understanding. Because of this core tenet, Piaget's theory is referred to as **constructivist theory**.

Piaget believed that children can create understanding only when they are engaged in interactions. Constructivist theory supports a hands-on, interactive approach to teaching as opposed to instruction that focuses on telling or showing. Piaget believed that understanding must be constructed by the activity of the child rather than through passive observation. His position supports the importance of play as the most relevant way for children to learn. Through play, children encounter a variety of opportunities to interact with their environment and create logical understanding of how the world works.

Josie holds a phone receiver to her ear, saying, "We want a big pizza with lots of cheeses and some pepperonis." At the table next to her, Gabriel pounds and rolls a piece of play dough and tells Josie, "I making 'dis one for you. We gotta make it and cook it, 'den I'll put it in the truck and bring it to your house."

As they engage in pretend play, children remember past experiences and re-create and expand on them. As they do, they increase their understanding of objects and situations in the world around them. They are beginning to use symbols—the block represents a telephone; the play dough a pizza. The ability to engage in symbolic thought is pivotal for reasoning, critical thinking, and later academic success. Frequent and repeated opportunities to engage in play allow children to build both the skills and the knowledge base needed for later academic success.

Reflect On

Symbolic Play

Think about a time when you have observed children engaged in pretend play. How did this play help them to explore their understanding of how the world works? How were they learning to use symbols?

KINDS OF KNOWLEDGE   Piaget postulated that children acquire three kinds of knowledge as they grow: physical, social, and logico-mathematical. *Physical knowledge*, the knowledge of external reality, is gained from acting on the physical world. For example, by holding and playing with a ball, children experience and learn about its properties—texture, shape, weight, squishiness, and tendency to roll away and bounce.

Social knowledge is learned from others. It includes language, rules, symbols, values, ideas about right and wrong, rituals, and myths. It is learned by observation, through being told, and, for older children and adults, by reading. For example, children learn that balls are used to play games, that certain kinds of balls are used for certain games, and that particular types of balls have particular names.

Logico-mathematical knowledge is the understanding of logical relationships constructed as children observe, compare, and reason. When children categorize, order, and observe the relationships between things, they are developing logico-mathematical knowledge. For example, children will observe the relationship between a tennis ball and a playground ball (similar shapes, roll and bounce but different size, color, texture, and weight). Through the experience of many balls, a child develops the idea of *ball* as a single category based on shared characteristics. Logico-mathematical knowledge requires direct experience but is based on the internal process of reflecting on what is experienced.

PROCESSES FOR CONSTRUCTION OF UNDERSTANDING   Piaget theorized that as children interact with the environment, they develop organized ways of making sense of experiences. Piaget referred to these organizing structures as **schemata** (sometimes called *schema* or *schemes*). Early schemata become the basis for more complex future mental frameworks. Infants use mostly behavioral or physical schemes, such as sucking, looking, grasping, and shaking. Older children move from physical or action-based schemes to the development of mental schemes that allow representational thought and the ability to solve problems. Piaget identified two processes—**assimilation** and **accommodation**—that children use to organize their experience into structures for thinking and problem solving. These processes are summarized in Table 4.1.

PIAGETIAN STAGES OF COGNITIVE DEVELOPMENT   Piaget proposed that children progress through a series of developmental stages that build from the interaction among three elements: existing mental structures, maturation, and experience. Stages occur in the same predictable sequence for everyone, although the exact age at which a

Table 4.1 Piaget's Model of Cognitive Change

Child's Experience	Cognitive Process/Adaptation	Child's State of Cognition
Child has many experiences with dogs.	Child creates a mental schema, a "dog scheme" that includes the information that dogs walk on 4 legs.	Equilibrium *Definition: A balanced and comfortable state.*
Child sees a sheep for the first time and calls it "dog."	Assimilates: Child includes the sheep into her existing "dog scheme." *Definition: Includes new information into existing schemes or behavior pattern, but does not change the existing mental structures or patterns.*	Equilibrium: Child has successfully adapted to the new information by including it into an existing mental structure.
Child notices that sheep have different characteristics from dogs. She has experiences with other 4-legged creatures.		Disequilibrium *Definition: A state of imbalance where new information does not fit into existing mental structures.*
She calls sheep "maa."	Accommodates Child makes a new mental structure for these 4-legged animals that do not bark or wag their tails. *Definition: Creates a new scheme, or rearranges one or more existing ones, so that new information will fit accurately into the mental structures.*	Equilibrium: By creating a new scheme, the child has successfully adapted her mental structures to new information.

Piaget's theory suggests that both the child's stage of cognitive development and previous social experiences contribute to moral development. His research demonstrated that children move from the view that rules are unchangeable and derived from higher authority to the more mature perspective that rules are made by people and can be changed. A number of other scholars have studied how children think about authority and fairness and how the development of morality can be supported by the adults in their lives (Damon, 1988; Edwards, 1986; Eisenberg, 1992; Lickona, Geis, & Kohlberg, 1976). See a discussion of Kohlberg's theory later in this chapter.

IMPLICATIONS OF CONSTRUCTIVIST THEORY FOR PRACTICE Piaget's work has helped parents and professionals become aware that children's thinking is fundamentally different from that of adults and that it relies on experience. As children have direct, repeated sensory experiences, they construct their understanding about the world. Constructivist theory has helped educators understand that children's cognitive development proceeds through stages, just as their physical development does. It is as foolish to attempt to rush a child into thinking like an adult as it would be to attempt to teach a crawling infant to high-jump. This understanding has helped educators refine the construct of readiness. Although cognitive development cannot be rushed, research suggests that it can be impaired. Children need intellectual stimulation to learn to think and reason (Healy, 1990; Shonkoff & Phillips, 2000).

Piaget's insistence that young children are always trying to construct a more coherent understanding of their world through their experience has led many educators to the belief that educational practices should allow ample opportunity for children to explore, experiment, and manipulate materials. Piaget was adamant that we cannot directly instruct children in the developmental hallmarks that characterize the next stage. As a teacher who has learned about constructivist theory, you will understand that you cannot pour knowledge into children. You will find that it is not effective to try to "cover" a concept in your teaching through lecture or demonstration. Instead, you will select materials and experiences that encourage each child to build his or her own understanding of important ideas. Piaget stressed that children are naturally curious; when you offer children opportunities to solve problems and search for their own meanings, you support them in constructing understanding.

Piaget's work has generated significant interest and debate among educators, child development specialists, and cognitive scientists. His careful observations of the strategies that children use in their thinking and his description of the processes and stages of development have made an important contribution to our understanding of how young children learn and have generated much fruitful thought and research about cognitive development. His studies have been replicated in many settings, and his work has been extensively critiqued. Later research has concluded that some of the cognitive milestones Piaget identified occur earlier than he determined. Some criticism focuses on Piaget's idea of distinct stages of cognitive development, suggesting that stages are not discrete and that skills develop gradually with experience and familiarity with particular materials and content. Nonetheless, his work has significantly shaped contemporary understanding of human intelligence and learning. Figure 4.4 lists some classroom practices that are based on Constructivist Theory.

Laurence Kohlberg and Moral Development Theory

Laurence Kohlberg's (1927–1987) work on moral reasoning elaborates on and extends Piaget's theory of children's moral development (Kohlberg, 1981, 1984). Kohlberg focused on how people make moral decisions across the life span. He described three stages of moral development that relate to developing views of moral conventions—the rules about what is right and wrong. In Kohlberg's view, people move from stage to stage as a result of their own reasoning, which grows with experience. As they mature,

Figure 4.4 Implications of Constructivist Theory for Practice

1. Provide materials for sensory play and exploration.

2. Offer open-ended materials that can be organized and combined in many ways.

3. Develop a daily schedule with large blocks of time for children to play.

4. Ask questions and encourage children to solve their own problems.

5. Provide meaningful experiences and opportunities for study based on children's real-world experiences.

they are able to see contradictions in their own beliefs. Like Piaget's stages, Kohlberg's model is a hierarchy—that is, each person must pass through each stage in order, and each is dependent on the preceding one. Kohlberg's model assumes that people move from making decisions about behavior based on external controls (punishments or negative consequences) to choosing behavior based on internal standards and principles (see Figure 4.5).

Carole Gilligan and others have been critical of Kohlberg's research because his subjects were primarily male and because the research was based on hypothetical, not real-life, situations. Gilligan did follow-up research that led her to conclude that males are oriented more toward fairness and justice in their moral decision making and females are concerned more with caring and responsibility (Gilligan, 1982). Further research offered compelling evidence that both males and females include a caring and a justice orientation in their moral decision making (Smetana, Killen, & Turiel, 1991; Walker, 1995). Others have noted that Kohlberg's theory emphasized the Western value of individual rights, ignoring other cultures' focus on group values (Berk, 2012).

Lev Vygotsky and Sociocultural Theory

Lev Semenovich Vygotsky (1896–1934) was a Russian psychologist whose work focused on the manner in which children develop thought and language. His **sociocultural theory** addresses the ways that children's development is influenced by their culture. A foundational tenet in this theory is that social and cognitive development are interactive and that language influences learning (Vygotsky, 1962, 1978).

Figure 4.5 Kohlberg's Stages of Moral Development

Level One: *Preconventional morality* (characteristic of children from 2 to 7)—moral decisions are based on self-interest—on emotion and what the child likes. At this stage children have no personal commitment to rules that they perceive as external. They will do something because they want to, or not do it because they want to avoid being punished. By age 4 children begin to understand reciprocity—if I am nice to you, you might respond by being nice to me.

Level Two: *Conventional morality* (characteristic of children between 7 and 12)—people choose to conform to and uphold the rules and conventions of society because they exist. They are concerned with group approval and consensus. Action is guided by concern with the general good and a desire to maintain the social order by doing one's duty.

Level Three: *Postconventional morality* (adolescent and older, though not everyone reaches this stage)—people accept rules and laws that are agreed on in society and based on underlying moral principles. When the highest level is reached, individuals may make decisions based on conscience, which places universal morality above law or custom.

SOURCE: Information from L. Kohlberg (ed.), *The Philosophy of Moral Development: Moral Stages and the Idea of Justice*, 1981.

Like Piaget, Vygotsky believed that children are active participants in their own learning and that they construct their understanding. However, unlike Piaget, who believed that children's development is bound by their maturational stage, Vygotsky suggested that children's learning is shaped by their social experiences and by interactions with and expectations from peers, older children, and adults, as demonstrated in the example below.

Skye, age 3, is building with blocks. She builds a low building with a roof. Her teacher, Val, sits down next to her and also constructs a building with a roof. Then Val says, "I think I need more space in my house." Val puts a unit block at each corner and places a roof board on top to create a second story. Skye looks on with great interest and tries to add a second story to her house using three units and a half-unit block for the corners. Her top floor collapses. Val says to her, "Help me find four that are just the same size for the next floor."

According to Vygotsky, **social context** (the circumstances of the family, the values of the school, and the geographic location of the community) influences both what children think about and the ways that their thinking is structured and focused (Bodrova & Leong, 2007). For example, children who live in rural settings may learn to think about time based on crop cycles, whereas those in urban settings may understand time based more on seasonal activities, such as playing in the wading pool or piling up autumn leaves. Children raised in families where spoken language is valued as the primary way to communicate will understand and organize experiences and information differently from a child raised in a family where nonverbal communication is more customary.

In Vygotsky's view, the development of language allows children to organize and integrate experiences and to develop concepts, making language central for thinking. Communication with others is vital because children develop language in relationships with more competent speakers (adults and older children). Whereas Piaget believed that cognitive development creates language, Vygotsky proposed that language is the means for developing thoughts and creating understanding. Like Piaget, Vygotsky observed the egocentric speech of childhood; however, he interpreted it as the *means* by which children develop concepts and plan actions. Most adults are aware of talking to themselves internally and may occasionally find themselves "thinking out loud," particularly when faced with a new or challenging task. For children, **private speech** is audible and gives them a tool for regulating their actions and their behaviors (Bodrova & Leong, 2007). As children get older, this audible speech diminishes and becomes internalized.

Vygotsky believed that every function in development occurs first at the social level and then at the individual level. Children develop through what he referred to as the **zone of proximal development (ZPD)**, the range of behaviors between what a child can accomplish independently and what the child can do with help. In *Thought and Language*, Vygotsky (1962, p. 199) wrote, "What the child can do in cooperation today he can do alone tomorrow." In this view, adults support learning by providing a small amount of assistance, or **scaffolding**, to allow children to successfully complete a task, as in the earlier example of Skye. As the child becomes more competent, less assistance is offered until the child can do it alone. For example, when children are first learning to ride a two-wheeled bicycle, they may use training wheels that are close to the ground. As skill and confidence increase, an adult may raise the wheels. After additional practice, the wheels are removed, and an adult holds the bike and runs as the child rides. Finally, the child is able to balance and pedal independently.

IMPLICATIONS OF SOCIOCULTURAL THEORY FOR PRACTICE   Vygotsky's theory helps us understand that adults play a vitally important role in young children's learning and development because they are actually helping them to construct understanding. Through relevant conversation, adults help each child find a personal meaning in the activities offered. This theory, which is very influential today, makes us aware of the importance of the social context for learning. Vygotsky's work helps

Video Example 4.3: Scaffolding Children's Learning

Watch this video of two children working on puzzles. What did you notice about how each teacher helped the children to be successful? Why are these examples of scaffolding?

early childhood educators appreciate that family and culture of the child must be a welcome part of the program.

Vygotsky's concept of a ZPD is immensely useful to early childhood educators. The practitioner who understands this concept knows how to support a child in a task, as illustrated in the example of Skye. Teachers apply this theory when they consider physical, emotional, social, and cognitive development when planning for children and identify goals that are both challenging and achievable (Copple & Bredekamp, 2006). This is a cornerstone of developmentally appropriate practice.

Vygotsky's belief that children's abilities should be analyzed both quantitatively and qualitatively supports careful observation of children as a valid assessment of their skills and abilities (Mooney, 2013). Teachers will identify children's skills, then guide their learning using a variety of techniques. They will also encourage cooperative learning by arranging activities where small groups of children with varying skills work and talk together to complete tasks. Time, materials, and support for fantasy and pretend play are also included in classrooms that embrace this theory.

Urie Bronfenbrenner and Ecological Theory

Urie Bronfenbrenner (1917–2005) was a psychologist and one of the founders of the Head Start program. His **ecological theory** describes systems of social and cultural contexts that influence development. Bronfenbrenner suggests that children's development can be understood only in the context of social, political, legal, and economic systems and that these can be thought of as nested layers around the child. Each of these systems influences the other as well as the growing child.

According to Bronfenbrenner's model, the *microsystem*, is where the child has the most interactions. This includes the family, school, and peers. These relationships influence the child, and the child influences others in the microsystem. The next layer, the *mesosystem*, involves the relationships between the microsystem and the broader environment, such as the family's relationships to the school or to children's peers. For example, a family's positive relationship with the child's school is likely to encourage academic success for children. Moving outward, the *exosystem* includes social settings that affect but do not directly include the child—for example, a parent's workplace or agencies that provide services to the family. Conditions experienced by a parent at work, such as a change from a day to an evening shift or a new and more demanding boss, are likely to cause changes in the parent–child relationship at home. The next layer, the *macrosystem*, is the culture in which the child lives—the behavior patterns, beliefs and values, and laws and customs that are transmitted from one generation to another. For example, the type of discipline families use is influenced by the values and beliefs that are part of their culture. Finally, the *chronosystem* refers to the timing of events and circumstances and how it affects individual development. For example, a young child will be influenced differently than an older one by the death of a parent or a divorce. Figure 4.6 illustrates this theory.

IMPLICATIONS OF ECOLOGICAL SYSTEMS THEORY FOR PRACTICE Ecological systems theory reminds us that children can be understood only within the context of their relationships to family, peers, the community, their culture, the society, and the time in which they live. Understanding that changes in family circumstance affect the child and that a

Figure 4.6 Bronfenbrenner's Ecological Theory

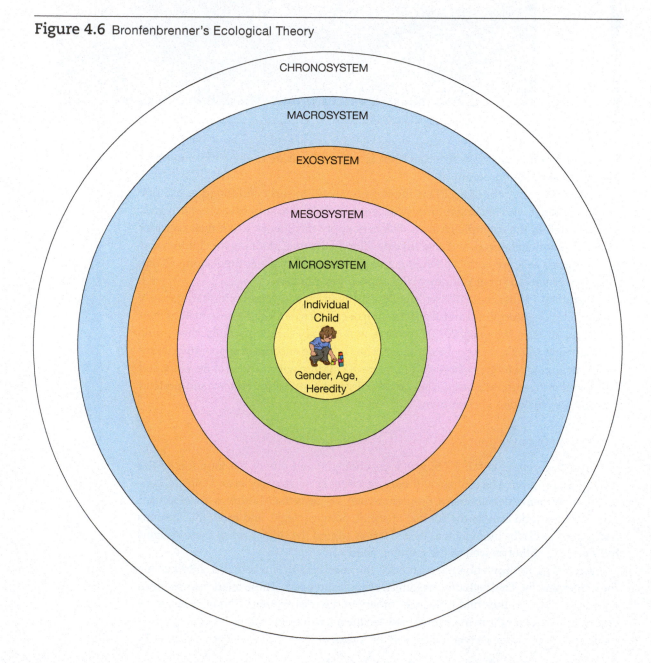

child's behavior and development also affect the family is helpful to teachers who want to support positive growth and learning. Ecological systems theory supports the practice of basing the curriculum on significant aspects of the child's family, neighborhood, and culture.

Erik Erikson and Psychosocial Theory

In his seminal work, *Childhood and Society* (1963), Erik Erikson (1902–1994) proposed a **psychosocial theory** of development. This theory, which remains influential today, describes eight stages of social and emotional development that cover the human life span. Erikson believed that basic attitudes are formed as individuals pass through these stages and that serious problems at any stage will lead to difficulty in mastering the next stage. Each stage is characterized by a major task or challenge. In infancy, the major task is the development of basic trust; for the toddler, the development of autonomy; for the preschooler, the development of initiative; and for the school-age child, the development of industriousness (Erikson, 1963). Figure 4.7 describes each of these stages.

For each stage, Erikson described a continuum with the potential for healthy development at one end and the potential for development of negative and self-defeating attitudes at the other. He saw development as a product of the tension between the two extremes, with more positive than negative experiences necessary for healthy progress. He believed that strengths developed at one stage allowed individuals to move successfully to the next and that it is possible for individuals to return to earlier stages and revisit and resolve those conflicts.

IMPLICATIONS OF PSYCHOSOCIAL THEORY FOR PRACTICE   Insights from psychosocial theory have important implications for early childhood educators. Because crucial aspects of development occur in the first 8 years, when a child is greatly dependent on adults, the relationships between children and significant adults in their lives are extremely important. Understanding that the young child is in the process of

---

Figure 4.7 Erikson's Stages of Childhood Psychosocial Development

Trust vs. Mistrust (Infant): During the first stage of development infants learn, or fail to learn, that people can be depended on and that they can depend on themselves to elicit nurturing responses from others. Nurturing, responsive relationships in the first year of life are essential to the development of basic trust. Through the love, nurture, and acceptance received, the infant learns that the world is a good and safe place. Infants who do not receive such care may lose hope and the ability to trust themselves or others.

Autonomy vs. Shame and Doubt (Toddler): During the second stage of life, which begins at 12 to 15 months, children develop a basic sense of autonomy that can be defined as self-governance and independent action. Rapidly growing toddlers are learning to coordinate many new patterns of action and to assert themselves as human beings. Conflict during this period centers on toilet training and self-help skills. If parents and caregivers are accepting and easygoing and if they recognize the child's developing need to assert independence, the child will move successfully through this stage. If adults are harsh and punitive and if the child is punished for assertive behavior, then shame and doubt may become stronger forces in the child's life.

Initiative vs. Guilt (Preschooler): This period is one of interest, active exploration, and readiness for learning. Children need to express their natural curiosity and creativity during this stage through opportunities to act on the environment. If explorations are regarded as naughtiness and if parents or teachers are overly concerned with preventing children from getting dirty or destroying things, a sense of initiative may not be developed and guilt may be the more prevalent attitude.

Industry vs. Inferiority (School Age): During this period, children are ready for the challenge of new and exciting ideas and of constructing things. They need opportunities for physical, intellectual, and social accomplishment. They need many and varied interactions with materials. Success and a feeling of "I can do it!" result in a sense of competence. When children's attempts to master new skills and situations result in repeated failure, they may develop a sense of inferiority.

SOURCE: Information from E. Erikson, *Childhood and Society* (rev. ed.), 1963.

becoming a distinct individual can help you understand and support children's conflicting needs for connectedness and independence.

Reflect On

The Role of Trust

Can you recall experiences from your childhood that helped you learn to trust or to mistrust others? How do you feel when you are with people you trust? What can you do when you are with individuals you trust that you cannot do when you are with those you do not trust? What would your life be like if you did not trust people?

Many practices found in high-quality early childhood programs support children in moving successfully through Erikson's developmental tasks. Low ratios of children to adults and the designation of a primary caregiver in programs for infants and toddlers are important because contact with a limited number of caring adults is a necessary condition for the development of trust. Infant caregivers who respond promptly and respectfully allow infants to develop a sense of safety needed to move to the next stage. Offering many opportunities for toddlers and young preschool-age children to make choices about play activities, materials, playmates, and self-help routines encourages the development of a sense of autonomy. Skilled toddler teachers accept the toddler's need to say no while maintaining clear and consistent limits. They encourage toddlers to demonstrate increasing independence and remain available to them for physical and emotional support. During the preschool and early elementary years, teachers must provide adequate time and resources to encourage children to explore, to plan, and to carry out play episodes so that the sense of initiative can develop. Initiative blossoms when children experience a curriculum that allows them to practice their emerging skills and provides them with tools and materials for success. And during the school-age years, providing opportunities for children to participate in many kinds of creative projects helps develop the sense of industry. Elementary teachers who deemphasize mistakes, focus on successes, and encourage children to try new things are fostering positive development for children in this stage.

As you build skill in helping children move through these developmental tasks, be aware that in many cultures, families place a high value on interdependence and support of the group. These families may not support developing autonomy and initiative in their young children and may prefer that you employ practices that focus on encouraging children to be supportive members of a group. Open and sensitive communication with families will help you determine their preferences and select practices that are congruent with families' culture and values.

B. F. Skinner and Behaviorist Theory

B. F. Skinner's (1904–1980) theory of **behaviorism** is among the most influential in shaping contemporary beliefs about how people learn. Unlike the developmental theories of Piaget, Vygotsky, Erikson, and others, which are based on age-related characteristics, the behaviorist theory assumes that its principles apply to all learners regardless of their age. Behaviorist theory is founded on the belief that behavior is changed as a result of the consequences individuals experience immediately following the behavior. For example, if a child is praised warmly by an important adult each time she returns toys to the shelf after play, she will learn to consistently pick up her toys.

Through a series of experiments with rats, Skinner and his colleagues developed the concept of **operant conditioning**, the belief that positive consequences encourage repetition of a behavior, while negative ones decrease its frequency. Behaviorists believe that using positive reinforcers, often called rewards, teaches people to repeat positive behaviors and that applying negative reinforcers, sometimes thought of as punishment, gradually eliminates unwanted behaviors.

IMPLICATIONS OF BEHAVIORIST THEORY   The work of behaviorists has helped us understand how people are shaped by past experiences and by their inner drives to experience positive stimulation. Virtually all educators and parents apply the concept of reinforcement when teaching young children. When you acknowledge a child's work, "Lamar, you spent so long building that tower; you really concentrated and worked hard," you are applying principles of behaviorism by offering positive reinforcement for desired behavior. Many professionals caution against overapplication of these principles, however. Behaviorism deals with isolated, observable behaviors and how they respond to individual stimuli. This is effective in controlled settings with very specific behaviors. However, human behavior is complex and occurs within diverse contexts. This makes isolating individual positive and negative consequences difficult. Additionally, behaviorism focuses on extrinsic motivators, teaching that behaviors should be repeated based on external rewards and punishments. Most contemporary early childhood educators believe that children are best served when they learn internal behavior control and self-motivation.

Children with disabilities or those with particular learning needs or challenging behaviors may benefit from judiciously applied systems of behavioral learning techniques, and all children can learn from the thoughtful use of appropriate acknowledgment and consequences. It is important to remember that good teachers use a variety of strategies and approaches that meet children's individual needs. Behaviorists' principles may be effective in teaching very specific behaviors in certain controlled situations. However, more complex, less observable behaviors, such as critical thinking and social awareness, are best taught using principles from constructivist and other developmental theories.

Howard Gardner and Multiple Intelligences Theory

Howard Gardner's research in cognitive development and neuroscience led to the creation of **multiple intelligences theory**. Like behaviorism, multiple intelligences theory is a learning theory rather than a developmental one. This theory suggests that, instead of a single general intelligence, each person's intellectual capacity is actually made up of different faculties that can work individually or in concert with one another.

Gardner (1991, 1993, 2011) has identified nine "intelligences" and believes that more may be identified in the future (see Figure 4.8). His original theory identified seven. His recent work includes Naturalist and Existentialist intelligences. However, he suggests that while the Existentialist category meets most of the criteria to be identified as an intelligence, unlike the other eight it is not associated with a specific region of the brain. Therefore he qualified its inclusion by referring to it as a 1/2-intelligence.

Intelligence is culturally defined based on what is needed and valued within a society. Imagine for a moment how different cultures may view diverse types of intelligence. For example, people from ancient Polynesian cultures used the stars to navigate from place to place. They put a high value on spatial intelligence. Individuals from cultures that were dependent on hunting for food valued those who had the bodily-kinesthetic intelligence necessary to be successful hunters. People who possessed these needed abilities were valued, and children were taught these skills. Euro-American societies have typically valued linguistic and logical-mathematical intelligences. American teachers have, to a great extent, emphasized the acquisition of language and math abilities.

IMPLICATIONS OF MULTIPLE INTELLIGENCES THEORY FOR PRACTICE   Multiple intelligences theory supports the idea that individuals have unique talents that should be acknowledged and maximized. It also reinforces the view that we should plan a

Figure 4.8 Gardner's Multiple Intelligences

Musical intelligence: The ability to produce and respond to music. It is seen in children who are especially sensitive to sound and who frequently play with instruments and music.

Bodily-kinesthetic intelligence: The ability to use the body to solve problems (e.g., in playing a game or dancing). Children who have high bodily-kinesthetic intelligence demonstrate good coordination at a young age, show expressiveness with their bodies, and have a hard time sitting still.

Logical-mathematical intelligence: The ability to understand the basic properties of numbers and principles of cause and effect. Children who love puzzles and show an early interest in numbers are demonstrating this intelligence.

Linguistic intelligence: The ability to use language to express ideas and learn new words or other languages. Children who have strength in linguistic intelligence may play with and be capable with language from an early age, love reading and rhymes, be imaginative, and be able to tell stories.

Spatial intelligence: The ability to be able to form a mental image of spatial layouts. A young child with good spatial intelligence may be able to read maps and draw at a young age, construct imaginatively with blocks, and be sensitive to the physical arrangement of a room.

Interpersonal intelligence: The ability to understand other people and work with them. A child who notices the relationships between others and demonstrates sociability and leadership is demonstrating interpersonal intelligence.

Intrapersonal intelligence: The ability to understand things about oneself. A child with intrapersonal intelligence has strong interests and goals, knows him- or herself well, is focused inward, and demonstrates confidence.

Naturalist intelligence: This more recently identified intelligence is the ability to recognize plants and animals in the environment. Children with this intelligence may want to collect animals and plants, long to be outdoors, and show a highly developed ability to discriminate between different animals and plants. They also show skills in identifying specific cars, planes, dinosaurs, and so forth.

Existential Intelligence: The newest intelligence, it is the capacity to think about and discuss deep questions about human existence, such as the meaning of life, why we die, what love is, and how we got here. Gardner refers to it as a 1/2-intelligence based on his understanding that unlike the other eight, existential intelligence does not appear to be connected to a particular region of the brain (Gardner, 2011).

variety of ways for children to learn the same skills and concepts. It encourages schools and teachers to expand their definition of success to go beyond traditional academic outcomes. When we have identified children's strengths, we can provide a number of effective ways to nurture their potential.

Educators who embrace the multiple intelligences constructs will ensure that children have learning opportunities that develop intelligence in all areas. Consideration of diverse intelligences could result in more attention to and funding for curriculum and programs that focus on the arts and physical education as well as use of assessment tools that allow children to demonstrate mastery of standard content in more than one way.

Reflect On

Your Own Multiple Intelligences

Consider the nine areas of intelligence that Gardner describes. Which are your areas of strength? What areas are most challenging for you? What were your best learning experiences in school? What were your worst? How might knowledge of multiple intelligences theory influence how you will provide learning experiences for young children?

Abraham Maslow and Self-Actualization Theory

Psychologist Abraham Maslow (1908–1970) developed a theory regarding the development of human motivation and potential. His **self-actualization** theory was based on the view that there is a hierarchy, or pyramid, of basic needs (Maslow, 1968, 1970). (See Figure 4.9) At the base of the pyramid are the physiological needs for air, water, food, and shelter. If these needs go unmet or are only partially met, individuals may not survive or may focus all their energy on meeting these needs. When basic physical needs are satisfied, security becomes a more pressing issue. According to Maslow, the highest human need is for self-actualization. When people are free from threats in their environment, when they are surrounded by others who are caring and predictable, they feel secure and can achieve self-actualization—the ability to focus on giving and receiving love, the pursuit of an understanding of the world, and self-knowledge. Maslow's model suggests that individuals who are self-actualized are able to perceive reality clearly, are open to new experiences and can make choices that support the growth of their own potential. They have the ability to be spontaneous and creative and to form and maintain positive relationships with others.

Maslow's theory has been promoted as universally applicable. However, it rests on a Western philosophy of individualism. Cultures that take a more collective perspective would argue that the needs of the family or group should take precedence over those for individual potential and personal growth.

IMPLICATIONS OF SELF-ACTUALIZATION THEORY FOR PRACTICE   Have you ever tried to study for a test or learn a new task at a time when you were tired, not

---

Figure 4.9 Maslow's Hierarchy of Human Needs

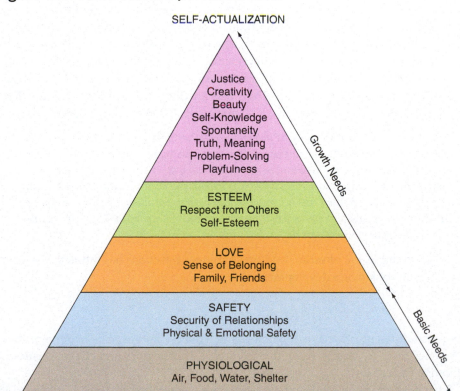

SELF-ACTUALIZATION

Justice
Creativity
Beauty
Self-Knowledge
Spontaneity
Truth, Meaning
Problem-Solving
Playfulness

ESTEEM
Respect from Others
Self-Esteem

LOVE
Sense of Belonging
Family, Friends

SAFETY
Security of Relationships
Physical & Emotional Safety

PHYSIOLOGICAL
Air, Food, Water, Shelter

Growth Needs

Basic Needs

SOURCE: From Maslow, Abraham H. Frager, Robert D., & Fadiman, James, *Motivation and Personality.* 3rd ed. © 1987. Reprinted and electronically reproduced by permission of Pearson Education Inc., Upper Saddle River, New Jersey.

feeling well, or worried about an important relationship? If so, you already know about applying Maslow's ideas. Awareness of this theory will remind you to be attentive to children's need for regular and nutritious meals and snacks. It will lead you to pay careful attention to creating and maintaining an environment that is safe and healthy. In addition, it will help you understand that children who do not feel loved and accepted may have difficulties learning. When children are isolated, you will take steps to help them experience social acceptance. You will foster children's feelings of self-esteem and approval from others by providing a variety of ways for them to achieve success. As you model curiosity, appreciation for aesthetics, and enthusiasm for learning, you support children's movements toward becoming self-actualized individuals.

> **A Quick Check 4.4**
> Gauge your understanding of the concepts in this section.

Development of the Whole Child

The study of early childhood development focuses on looking at all aspects of children's growth and development during the early childhood years. In other words, early childhood educators study children from before birth (the prenatal period) through their seventh year of life. We look at all domains or aspects of their development, and we learn about how each domain influences the others during every period of early childhood.

Domains of Development

To understand and define children's development, it is important to identify aspects or domains of development—physical, social/emotional, and cognitive (including language). These divisions are not universally agreed on—social and emotional development are sometimes considered as distinct domains, development of language is often separated from cognitive development, and creative development is sometimes identified as a separate domain. Regardless of how they are categorized by educators and theorists, in a real child they are parts of a whole that interact with and influence one another.

> *Five-year-old Janine has experienced frequent middle-ear infections, a physical condition that has limited her ability to hear since early infancy. Because of this, her speech and language development are not as advanced as those of many other 5-year-olds. She has fewer words than most, and it is sometimes difficult to understand what she says. This has limited her play with other children, and her social skills are not as advanced as many of her peers. Her delayed language also means that sometimes she doesn't understand spoken information as quickly as other children do.*

In this example, the physical condition of the ear infections has influenced a number of domains of Janine's development.

Periods of Development

Children at different ages have different characteristics. Studies of development, such as the ones done by Gesell, have identified typical behaviors and characteristics of children at each age.

Educators and child development specialists usually describe early childhood in terms of four distinct periods:

- **Infants** range in age from birth through approximately 12 months.
- **Toddlers** are 12 months through 36 months (1 to 3 years).

- **Preschoolers/kindergartners** range from 3 years to 6 years.
- **School-age children** are those whose ages are between 6 and 8.

Each of these stages of development has distinct milestones. Children achieve these hallmarks of development based on their own internal genetic clocks as well as the opportunities they have for experience and practice. Children with disabilities may achieve some milestones simultaneously with their peers while acquiring others later.

The charts of developmental milestones on the following pages are meant to give you a "snapshot" of development during each period of early childhood. When you use them, keep in mind the principles of development discussed at the beginning of this chapter and recall that every child is different and that each child's development is influenced by the unique circumstances of his or her life.

SOURCE: Jeff Reese

Understanding Infants' Development

During the first year of life, infants experience extremely rapid growth in all developmental domains. They move from being totally dependent at birth to being able to move independently, communicate, and engage in relationships with others. During their first 12 months, infants start to understand fundamental principles of cause and effect and ways to make sense of the world around them. They transform from babies who are usually eager to please adults to young toddlers who are taking their first steps toward independence.

INFANTS' PHYSICAL DEVELOPMENT   In the first year of life, children grow faster than they will at any other time of their lives. Their height increases by approximately 50%, their weight triples, and their brain size doubles (Berk, 2016). Several teeth emerge from their gums. They develop the ability to sit, crawl, stand, and perhaps take their first steps.

INFANTS' COGNITIVE AND LANGUAGE DEVELOPMENT   Infants explore the world using all of their senses and begin to organize these experiences into categories that have meaning. As they explore objects and people, they begin to identify characteristics and develop concepts—mental images that help them make sense of their experiences. Initially, they gaze at caregivers, attending to facial expressions and speech. They play with sounds themselves and begin to engage in sound dialogue with trusted adults. By the end of the first year, they understand many spoken words and may begin to name some familiar people and objects.

INFANTS' SOCIAL AND EMOTIONAL DEVELOPMENT   During the first year of life, infants develop attachments to important people in their lives. When their needs are met promptly—when they are nurtured, played with, and responded to—they develop a sense of trust, which is essential for healthy emotional and social development. From birth, babies carefully observe the actions of people around them. They begin to be aware of themselves as separate from others; they experience differences in their own emotions and become sensitive to the feelings of others around them. Table 4.3 shows milestones of infant development.

Understanding Toddlers' Development

During the toddler years children explore and learn about the world with great eagerness and curiosity. During this brief period, they acquire many skills, organize a great deal of information, and have a lot of energy. This constant on-the-go behavior and their need to demonstrate independence has resulted in the unfortunate label of "terrible

Table 4.3 Milestones of Development for Infants

Age	Domain		
	Physical and Motor	**Cognitive and Language**	**Social and Emotional**
Birth–5 Months	• Rapidly gains height and weight **Large Motor** • Lifts head • Sits with support • Rolls over **Small Motor** • Gazes at, then reaches for, objects • Examines hands and fingers • Grasps objects • Transfers objects from hand to hand	• Gazes at faces and objects • Tries to repeat behaviors that cause interesting results (e.g., kicks at a mobile when it moves) • Indicates recognition of familiar people, places, and things • Cries, coos, and responds to human language • Babbles strings of consonants and vowels • Begins to imitate sounds	• Smiles; uses smile to respond and get responses • Copies adult expressions • Responds actively to familiar people • Responds more to people than to objects • Begins to laugh • Cries when distressed • Begins to show emotions such as surprise, fear, and anger
6–12 Months	**Large Motor** • Sits unassisted • Crawls • Stands with assistance • Stands alone; cruises • Takes some steps **Small Motor** • Uses pincer grasp • Coordinates two hands	• Shows awareness of cause and effect by repeating actions to create an outcome • Imitates simple actions such as waving bye-bye • Demonstrates object permanence; searches for objects and people; protests when they disappear; locates a toy that has rolled behind something by removing the object • Understands familiar words; looks at objects when they are named • Responds appropriately to simple requests (e.g., "kiss mommy") • Speaks first words	• Engages in interactive games such as peek-a-boo • Demonstrates awareness of, then anxiety with, unfamiliar people • Shows awareness of caregivers' different moods • Demonstrates attachment to caregivers • Uses caregivers as "home base" to provide security • Shows anxiety when separated from familiar caregivers • Responds to other children; may touch them, verbalize, take or offer toys • Responds to others' distress

twos." As you observe toddlers and come to appreciate how fast they are growing and learning, you may decide, as many toddler teachers have, that this name should be replaced with "terrific twos."

TODDLERS' PHYSICAL DEVELOPMENT Although they are not growing as rapidly as they did as infants, toddlers experience significant height and weight gain and master many large motor skills. They progress from clumsy tottering to speedy running. It is easier for toddlers to begin moving than to stop or turn, so they often bump into objects and people as they move. As toddlers gain control of the small muscles of their hands and fingers, they learn to feed themselves with skill. They become masterful at undressing, although they still struggle with putting on clothes and shoes. As their growth slows, so does their appetite, and during this stage they may become fussy about what they eat. By the end of the third year, most children have mastered using the toilet during the daytime, although accidents are still common. Because they are practicing so many new motor skills and learning about the world with their senses, they are "into everything." This means that caregivers must be particularly attentive to ensuring that environments are safe for active exploration.

TODDLERS' COGNITIVE AND LANGUAGE DEVELOPMENT Like infants, toddlers are sensory learners. They learn about the world using all five senses. Their memory for objects and events increases dramatically. Younger toddlers enjoy imitating the actions of others and will hold a play phone to their ear and babble or pretend to drink coffee as they have seen adults do. As their memory and cognitive skills increase, they add their own ideas and plans to make-believe play events. For example, a toddler might use blocks as pretend food and invite an adult to taste the dinner. Their language skills expand rapidly as they engage with adults and with other children. Toddlers often use *overgeneralized speech*—the use of a single word for a variety of similar objects. For example, a toddler we know referred to the family cat as *mao* and overextended the word to label the neighbor's dog, a furry toy, and the lady across the street who had three cats.

TODDLERS' SOCIAL AND EMOTIONAL DEVELOPMENT The toddler years are a time of growing independence. As their physical and cognitive skills develop and mature, toddlers move away from being acquiescent infants and begin exerting autonomy. Shouts of "No!" and "Me do it!" are familiar to adults who spend time with toddlers. Opportunities to make choices and time to complete tasks successfully are crucial for developing toddlers. They often feel frustrated because their emerging but still immature skills lead to situations where they cannot yet accomplish what they wish to do. Toddlers usually experience higher expectations and more limits from adults than they did as infants; this often results in feelings of frustration. Consequently, tantrums are common during these years as toddlers struggle to learn to control their bodies and emotions. Table 4.4 outlines milestones of toddler development.

Table 4.4 Milestones of Development for Toddlers

Age	Domain		
	Physical and Motor	**Cognitive and Language**	**Social and Emotional**
12–24 Months	• Grows rapidly but slower than the first year **Large Motor** • Walks with increasing steadiness • Has a wide "tottering" stance • Climbs onto furniture • Squats to pick up objects • Begins to run with stiff gait • Walks up stairs with assistance, one step at a time • Uses riding toys by pushing feet on ground **Small Motor** • Picks up and drops small objects into containers • Scribbles • Turns pages in a book, 2–3 at a time • Feeds self with fingers or spoon • Stacks 2–3 small blocks	• Imitates simple adult behaviors when adult models • Uses sensory trial and error to solve problems • Points to objects in a storybook • Follows a one-step direction • Imitates behavior that has been seen in the past • Has 4–5 words at 15 months; 15–20 by 18 months; 200 by 24 months • Combines two words; simple sentences by 24 months • Uses words broadly (e.g., calls all beverages milk) • Fills in words in familiar stories	• Shows strong attachment to familiar caregivers and works to maintain physical closeness with them • Continues to use primary attachment figures as "home base" and is willing to venture further from them • Prefers to play alone (solitary play) • Begins to play beside others (parallel play) • Refers to self by name • Understands ownership of personal possessions, "mine" • May try to comfort someone in distress; hugs, pats, or brings a favorite toy to them
24–36 Months	**Large Motor** • Walks on tiptoe • Leans forward while running • Kicks large balls • Climbs • Throws a ball with two hands • Jumps in place • Begins to pedal a tricycle **Small Motor** • Hand preference is emerging but not stable • Stacks 6 or more blocks • Strings large beads • Uses a spoon and fork • Uses thumb and forefinger to draw with crayons or markers • Snips with scissors	• Identifies several objects in a single picture • Distinguishes one object from many • Begins to understand aspects of space and time (e.g., the park is near, Grandma's is far; we will go to the park tomorrow) • Overextends concepts such as calling all animals dogs • Begins to match objects by similar characteristics • Substitutes one object for another in make-believe play (e.g., uses a block for a telephone) • Uses telegraphic speech ("Daddy bye-bye") • Sings parts of familiar songs • Understands prepositions ("over, on, behind") and pronouns ("mine, his, yours") • Uses 3- to 5-word sentences • Uses question words ("who, what, why") • Begins to use past tense and plurals • Recognizes and repeats simple rhymes • Recognizes and names a few colors	• Enjoys playing alongside others; carefully observes other children • Engages in behaviors to elicit responses from others (e.g., runs from adults to engage them in chase games) • Insists on doing things independently • Identifies self as a boy or girl • Engages in simple role-playing games (e.g., pretends to drive to the store) • Begins to show preference for certain children as friends

Understanding Preschoolers'/Kindergartners' Development

The increasing physical and cognitive skills of children ages 3 to 5 allow them to be more self-sufficient than toddlers. Their interest in peer relationships has expanded, and they are starting to understand how the social world works. Preschoolers and kindergartners are unfailingly curious about both the physical and the social world and may exhaust adults with their many questions. Their rapidly developing sense of humor makes interactions with them lively and fun.

PRESCHOOLERS'/KINDERGARTNERS' PHYSICAL DEVELOPMENT   During the preschool/kindergarten years, children gain approximately 4 to 6 pounds and grow 2 to 3 inches each year. Their legs lengthen, and their physical appearance becomes leaner and more adultlike. Preschoolers' brains continue to grow and will reach 90% of adult size by age 5. Most enjoy using their rapidly developing large motor skills. Throwing, jumping, hopping, running, and skipping are favorite activities for most children of this age. Preschoolers are building dexterity in their hands and fingers so that by age 5 most use scissors and drawing materials with skill. At age 4, they typically start to write letters and numbers and include details in their drawing and painting. The many examples of children's art that you see in this book were created by 3-, 4-, and 5-year-olds. By age 5, most children have developed consistent hand preference, called **hand dominance**.

PRESCHOOLERS'/KINDERGARTNERS' COGNITIVE AND LANGUAGE DEVELOPMENT   Preschoolers and kindergartners learn about the world directly through their experiences; they are often referred to as concrete learners, meaning that they need many real interactions with people and objects to develop understanding. They can learn only what they can see, hear, and experience (known as **perceptually bound thinking**); logic and abstract thought develop only after many hands-on experiences. The 3-year-old who insists that her friend has more spaghetti because she has spread her mound around her plate is demonstrating this perceptually bound thinking. Children organize their experiences by sorting and classifying objects, people, and events. As they near age 5, children can begin to sort and order using two or more characteristics.

Both spoken (expressive) and understood (receptive) vocabularies are expanding rapidly in the preschool years, and children use words both to give and to ask for information. They use many rules of grammar but may occasionally overextend these. The child who tells you she "sitted" or "runned" is demonstrating understanding of how past tense is applied. Because language is closely tied to culture, it is important to remember that children from families who place high value on nonverbal learning and communication may not demonstrate the same type or quantity of expressive language as do children whose families use extensive spoken language. Dual language learners, children who are learning to speak English at the same time they learn their home language, may appear less verbal than their monolingual peers when they are first learning English, but given opportunities to use both languages, they will show similar language development to children who are only learning to speak English (Tabors, 2008; Youngquist & Martinez-Griego, 2009).

PRESCHOOLERS'/KINDERGARTNERS' SOCIAL AND EMOTIONAL DEVELOPMENT   Children's sense of initiative grows during this period. They take great pleasure in creating and carrying out plans, particularly during fantasy play. Sensitive teachers make sure that children have ample time and assistance for planning things; they provide interesting and functional materials to support children's projects and make-believe play. Preschoolers are interested in friendships with other children, although their concrete thinking often creates challenges in these first friendships. For young preschoolers, a friend is the child who is playing with them now, offers a desired toy, or sits by them at lunch. Older preschoolers and kindergartners develop decided preferences for certain peers—and conflict over friendship is common during this period. Children who are 3- through 5-year-olds develop increasing awareness of the needs and feelings of other people and are able to engage in more empathetic behaviors and play more cooperatively. They are learning to regulate their behavior but still need adult support to help them verbalize feelings and delay gratification. Table 4.5 summarizes the developmental milestones for this age-group.

Table 4.5 Milestones of Development for Preschoolers and Kindergartners (3–5 years)

Age	Domain		
	Physical and Motor	**Cognitive and Language**	**Social and Emotional**
3–4 Years	• Growth slows; body elongates **Large Motor** • Walks swinging arms • Balances on one foot • Pedals and steers a tricycle • Gallops • Climbs quickly and smoothly with alternating steps • Throws a ball overhand with accuracy • Bounces and catches a ball **Fine Motor** • Dresses with occasional assistance • Uses scissors to cut • Copies vertical lines and circles • Draws simple picture of a person	• Organizes and groups objects by a single characteristic (e.g., color, size, shape) • Judges quantity by appearance • Develops one-to-one correspondence • Rote counts to 10 • Understands that numbers refer to a specific amount • Attention span lengthens; notices increasing detail • Carries out a three-step direction • Distinguishes between day and night • Enjoys and attends to books and stories • Uses self-talk • Has rapidly expanding vocabulary • Uses "s" for plurals, "ed" for past tense, sometimes overgeneralizes (e.g. "I putted on my shoes") • Uses 4- to 5-word sentences • Understands relational words ("on, in, under")	• Begins to share and take turns • Engages in some small group and cooperative play • Wants to please adults • Understands that others have thoughts, ideas, and memories • May assume that what they know and feel is the same as what others know and feel • Shows gender-stereotyped beliefs and actions • Often expresses strong feelings physically (e.g., hits when angry)
4–5 Years	• Legs lengthen; body proportions become more adult-like **Large Motor** • Displays increased speed and agility in large-motor activity • Walks up and down stairs unassisted, alternating feet • Skips using alternating feet • Shows mature climbing and running patterns • Catches and throws balls using only hands and fingers • Dribbles and bounces balls **Fine Motor** • Cuts with scissors following a straight line • Copies a triangle and cross • Begins to show mature pencil grip • Demonstrates hand preference	• Visualizes space from the perspective of others • Is increasingly able to create a plan and predict outcomes of actions • Begins to categorize objects based on function • Begins to sort objects by more than one attribute (e.g., color size, shape, weight) • Begins to develop understanding of difference between reality and fantasy • Understands time concepts of yesterday, today, and tomorrow; begins to use clocks and calendars • Rote counts to 20; can count groups of objects up to 10 • Knows that letters and numbers are different • Recalls some letter and number sequences • Recognizes several printed words • Tells familiar stories • Defines some words • Asks questions and wants answers that give useful information • Has growing vocabulary of approximately 10,000 words	• Begins to prefer same-age peers to adults • May have special or best friends • Is able to express strong feelings using words • Shows rapid mood shifts • Becomes aware of the effect of their actions on others • Is increasingly cooperative in play and actions • Obeys rules in order to avoid negative consequences

Understanding Young School-Age Children's Development

Children ages 6 to 8 are increasingly social and are rapidly developing logic and reasoning skills. This is the time in childhood when peers become much more important and children define themselves increasingly by how other children relate to them. Most young school-age children enjoy physical activity, and participation in organized sports and competitions becomes important to many. Their early experiences in formal school settings will frame their beliefs about who they are as learners. Wise teachers will search for ways to ensure that all children experience success in their early academic endeavors. This requires that you attend to their different learning styles and diverse strengths and interests.

UNDERSTANDING SCHOOL-AGE CHILDREN'S PHYSICAL DEVELOPMENT   Healthy 6- to 8-year-olds grow 2 to 3 inches and gain approximately 5 pounds each year. Their legs are lengthening, giving them a somewhat "leggy" appearance. Their muscles are becoming stronger. Because their growing ligaments are not yet firmly attached to their bones, they are extremely flexible. They typically exhibit a high need for physical activity and may find it difficult to sit for extended periods of time. In addition to increased large-muscle strength and skill, they are gaining increasing control of the muscles in their hands and fingers. Their writing skill is growing, and their drawings and paintings include greater detail. This increased dexterity allows them to enjoy a wide range of crafts and construction projects.

UNDERSTANDING SCHOOL-AGE CHILDREN'S COGNITIVE AND LANGUAGE DEVELOPMENT   School-age children are typically enthusiastic and eager to learn new things. Their increasing attention span and memory allows them to focus on more complex concepts than younger children. They are beginning to use logic and reasoning to solve problems and can understand more abstract ideas. However, they still need many learning experiences that are related to what is familiar to them. They enjoy researching ideas and planning complex projects. They may collect such things as shells, rocks, beads, or sports-star cards, using their increasingly sophisticated classification and seriation skills as they sort and organize these collections. Their vocabulary is increasing at a faster rate than that of younger children, and many average 20 new words a day (Berk, 2012). They learn that words often have several meanings and take great delight in puns, riddles, and jokes. They are increasingly able to communicate in writing, often using invented spelling as they begin to understand rules of phonics.

UNDERSTANDING SCHOOL-AGE CHILDREN'S SOCIAL AND EMOTIONAL DEVELOPMENT   The years from 6 to 8 are a time of significant growth in social skills and competence. Children who have well-developed social abilities tend to do better in school than those who are less socially adept (Lin, Lawrence, & Gorrell, 2003). Peers are of vital importance, and children begin to define themselves by the ways they believe that others see them. It is important that children feel included and have ways to make contributions to the group. This is of particular importance for children of differing abilities.

Young school-age children understand the concept of fairness: everyone in the group should have the same resources and privileges. They begin to expand this concept to include the idea that those who work harder or show particular achievement merit additional rewards. As they near the end of this period of childhood, they begin to understand social justice in a broader way, and their social problem-solving skills expand. They may learn to value offering opportunities to those who are less advantaged or who have experienced losses or disabilities. Teachers of children in this age-group can help them to understand

SOURCE: Jeff Reese

Table 4.6 Milestones of Development for School-Age Children (6–8 years)

Domain		
Physical and Motor	**Cognitive and Language**	**Social and Emotional**
• Exhibits steady height and weight gains • Has high energy; strong need for physical activity **Large Motor** • Demonstrates increasing strength, flexibility, and agility in large-motor control • Shows increased balance; rides a two-wheeled bike, walks a balance beam, skates • Enjoys active games and activities requiring physical skill • Engages in rough and tumble play • Coordinates many movements and engages with increasing skill in sports **Fine Motor** • Prints clearly; few reversals • Includes more detail in drawings • Begins to include some depth cues in drawings • Eye-hand coordination matures; cursive writing begins	• Uses symbols as tools for thinking and for literacy • Develops conservation of quantity (e.g., realizes that quantity remains the same even if form changes) • Demonstrates logical thinking • Enjoys collections and organizes, sorts, and categorizes items in increasingly complex ways • Reads with increasing skill • Learns beginning number concepts • Begins to read for information • Has rapidly expanding vocabulary • Begins to grasp multiple meanings for words; puns, riddles, jokes, and metaphors are enjoyed • Changes speech and language patterns to be appropriate for individual listeners • Enjoys telling and writing stories	• Becomes increasingly influenced by peer relationships; peer pressure and a need for belonging are common • Has a growing interest in fairness, equality, and justice • Begins to evaluate self by what others think • Also views self in terms of own abilities • Recognizes that people can experience more than one emotion at a time • Shows increasing awareness of the subtleties of behavior; understands that actions do not always indicate thoughts and feelings • Has beginning understanding of social concepts such as laws and justice • Continues to need adult approval but may resist accepting it

and value **altruism**—unselfish concern for the welfare of others. School-age children can successfully plan and participate in community service projects and other activities that provide assistance to people in need—and they benefit when encouraged to do so. Table 4.6 summarizes school-age children's development.

 Application Exercise 4.3

Watch and Write About Children's Development

✓ **A Quick Check 4.5**
Gauge your understanding of the concepts in this section.

Final Thoughts

Understanding the ways that children grow and learn contributes to your growing skills as an early childhood educator. As you move ahead in your professional development, there are two important things to keep in mind. First, the information about children that you acquire as a college student is just the beginning. You will continue to learn about children throughout your career. Child development knowledge, like the children themselves, is always growing and changing. New research is being conducted—old theories are being refined and new ones created. Be aware of and keep an open mind about new information. Sometimes, you will discover information that is immensely helpful. At other times, a popular new theory will simply be a discredited old idea in a new guise. We find that an inquiring but somewhat cautious approach serves teachers and children best.

Second, keep in mind that you are in the process of personal and professional development. As you study and as you work directly with young children, your understanding will grow. Your daily experiences and observations of children will combine with what you read to give you an ever deeper and richer understanding. Working with young children involves a constant and dynamic interplay of information that combines the work of others with insight you develop based on your own observations. Keep watching and listening to children and know that your understanding will continue to grow and that you can supplement the conclusions of the experts with the knowledge you are gaining from experience.

 Application Exercise 4.4 Final Reflection

 To Learn More

Read

Born Together—Reared Apart: The Landmark Minnesota Twin Study, N. Segal (2012)
Just Babies: The Origins of Good and Evil, P. Bloom (2013)
Mind in the Making: The Seven Essential Life Skills Every Child Needs, E. Galinsky (2010)
The Scientist in the Crib: Minds, Brains, and How Children Learn, A. Gopnik, A. Meltzoff,
    and P. Kuhl (2009).
Theories of Childhood: An Introduction to Dewey, Montessori, Erikson, Piaget, and Vygotsky,
    C. Mooney (2013).

Visit a Website

The following agencies and organizations have websites related to child
    development:
Center on the Developing Child at Harvard University
Centers for Disease Control and Prevention (search for "child development")
Public Broadcasting Service (search for "child development")
Society for Research in Child Development (search for "publications: child
    development")
Zero to Three: National Center for Infants, Toddlers and Families

Document Your Skill & Knowledge About Child Development in Your Professional Portfolio

Include some or all of the following:

- **A child observation record** that you have completed following the suggestion below.

  Observe a child for 45 minutes to an hour. Write notes on what you see. Try to identify at least three behaviors for every domain of development. Create a grid like the following:

What You Observed	Developmental Domain the Behavior Illustrates
Example: S. climbed to the top of the climber, using alternating feet.	Physical

  Observe a second child who is in a different period of development and complete an observation record; note similarities and differences between the two children's behaviors.

- **An activity plan** that you have created for each of the two children that you observed; be sure to use information from your observation notes to select an appropriate activity for each.

- **A photo of a poster for parents** that you create to illustrate the milestones of development for one age-group of children (infants, toddlers, preschoolers, kindergarten, or primary children) in one area of development (social/emotional, physical, or cognitive/language).

Shared Writing 4.1 Explain Your Understanding of Child Development

---

Chapter 5
Observing and Assessing Young Children

*Bring with you a heart that watches
and receives.*

WILLIAM WORDSWORTH

 ## Chapter Learning Outcomes:

5.1 Describe the nature and purpose of observing and assessing children in early childhood programs.

5.2 Create and use observations for authentic assessment.

5.3 Create and use other authentic forms of assessment.

5.4 Explain how standardized assessment differs from authentic assessment.

NAEYC Professional Preparation Standards

The NAEYC Professional Preparation Standard that applies to this chapter:

Standard 3: Observing, Documenting, and Assessing to Support Young Children and Families (NAEYC, 2009).

Key elements:

3a: Understanding the goals, benefits, and uses of assessment

3b: Knowing about and using observation, documentation, and other appropriate assessment tools and approaches

3c: Understanding and practicing responsible assessment to promote positive outcomes for each child

3d: Knowing about assessment partnerships with families and with professional colleagues

Every day, you take in information, make comparisons, and evaluate situations. This helps you make decisions. Before you get dressed, you observe the weather, consider what you will be doing, and evaluate your clothing needs. Similarly, you will observe and assess the young children you teach in order to make appropriate decisions for their care and education. In education, **assessment** is a multipart process that is used for the purpose of evaluating young children's development and learning.

Historically, early childhood educators have believed that **observation** conducted during the course of daily life in the classroom is the best way to understand young children and authentically assess their strengths and needs. Such observation allows teachers to gain the information that is needed to understand children and thus design responsive and appropriate programs. We honor this history and reflect the high value we place on the skill of observation by placing observing first in the title of this chapter. Carefully and sensitively observing helps you understand, assess, and plan for children.

The Purpose of Assessment

The better you understand individual children, the more able you will be to provide a program that meets their needs. This is the ultimate goal of assessment—to better understand and thus better serve children. Keeping this goal in mind will help you understand and use observation and assessment appropriately.

If you watch a child on her first day of school and go to comfort her as she begins to look fearful, you will be using assessment to understand and meet the needs of an individual. If you observe a group of children and write notes on how they play and interact in a classroom and then use this information to modify the learning environment, you will be using assessment to guide your decision making. If you evaluate a child's abilities using a **checklist** and then make a plan that builds on these strengths, you will be using assessment to inform curriculum planning. If you conduct a **screening test** and use the results to refer a child for further testing, you will be using assessment to identify a child who may need special services. In each of these cases, assessment will help you support development and learning and meet the needs of children.

Assessment has other purposes as well. Assessment information is used to report to a child's family how the child is progressing in school and whether he or she has achieved learning goals. Giving a family information about the learning, growth, and development of their child enables them to better support their child at home. Administrators and policymakers also use assessment for program evaluation. It can guide them in determining goals for improvement and deciding how to allocate resources. These goals and resources may help create programs to better serve children. At this time in the history of education, **standardized assessment** (in the form of **test** scores) is often used to determine how effective teachers and schools are in achieving mandated goals.

Because assessment is part of early childhood program practice and state and national policy, it is essential for you to understand it. In fact, it is a part of your ethical responsibility to do so. As stated in the National Association for the Education of Young Children (NAEYC) (2011) Code of Ethical Conduct (see Appendix A),

> **P-1.5**—We shall use appropriate assessment systems, which include multiple sources of information, to provide information on children's learning and development.

> **P-4.5**—We shall be knowledgeable about the appropriate use of assessment strategies and instruments and interpret results accurately to families.

Components of Assessment

Assessment has three interconnected components (Jones, 2004; McAfee, Leong & Bodrova, 2016; McAfee, Leong, & Bodrova, 2004; Wortham, 2011). The first component is collecting and recording information about children's learning and development. The second component involves interpreting and evaluating the information gathered. The third part of the process has to do with using the information that you have acquired. This may involve making choices about instructional practice, providing information to families, deciding whether a child needs a referral for special services, or making a placement decision.

Formative and Summative Assessment

Assessment carried out while teaching, to inform and improve instruction, is called **formative assessment**. Teachers use formative assessment to tailor instruction to the individual needs of children. When teachers learn what children know and can do and then use this information as they work with them, they are using formative assessment.

Assessment that is designed to evaluate a child's acquisition of knowledge or skills after teaching is completed is called **summative assessment**. Summative assessments are often used as one-time **high-stakes tests**.

Authentic Assessment and Standardized Assessment

There are two broad categories of assessment: authentic and standardized assessment. Authentic means genuine. **Authentic assessment** refers to assessment based on what children do while engaged in everyday activities, including self-selected play, teacher-directed activities, routines, and transitions. In a natural or authentic approach to assessment, you observe and collect real-life examples of children demonstrating skills

and knowledge in activities that are meaningful to them. Authentic assessment is not a one-time event. Instead, it is an ongoing process. It uses the input of teacher, parent, and child. Thus, actual performance—rather than responses to artificial tasks on tests—is the way children's knowledge and skills are assessed.

In comparison, standardized assessment (sometimes called *formal assessment* or *standardized tests*) consists of tasks given to a child in a standard way and evaluated or scored using standard criteria. This is used because tests are intended to objectively compare children's development and learning to a norm. McAfee et al. (2004) point out, "We do assessment that is standardized when we do our best to be consistent and uniform, or standard in our methods so results can be compared. . . . Standardization saves time, as well as increases the reliability and fairness of our assessments" (p. 57).

SOURCE: Jeff Reese

Reflect On

Authentic Assessment

Consider one of your skills or accomplishments. It can be something simple like riding a bicycle or making a sandwich. Could you take a multiple choice quiz or a test to demonstrate this skill? How else could you demonstrate this achievement or ability to someone else? Is this demonstration more authentic (real) than taking a test?

CONFIDENTIALITY   When and how you share the information you collect with others, how you protect this information, and the uses to which you put it are all important issues. When you do share, it is important to consider your ethical and legal[1] obligations to children, families, and society.

Assessments are confidential and should be stored in such a way as to protect the privacy of children and families. Families have an undisputed right to access this information. And it is generally considered appropriate to share observations and assessment results with other teachers and administrators who work with the child. Who else has a "need to know"? Therapists, teachers in the next school, physicians, and others concerned with the child's welfare may have a genuine reason for being given information. Generally, before sharing information, you will get the written permission of the family. The NAEYC Code of Ethical Conduct provides you with guidance (P-2.12).

Reflect On

Your Ethical Responsibilities and Confidentiality

A mother of a child in your class asks you to share how a relative's child (also in your class) is doing in school. She shares that she is concerned about this child's development. You've been worried about the child, too. Using the "Guidelines for Ethical Reflection" box in Chapter 1, reflect on your ethical responsibilities in this situation and think about an ethical response that you might make.

Everyone enjoys telling a funny or endearing story about a child with whom they have worked. However, it is never acceptable to gossip or discuss a child in a way that may be injurious to the child or in a way that identifies the child to others. Even in your college observation papers, it is important to change the child's name or to use his or her initials to avoid breaching **confidentiality**. Specifically, here is what the NAEYC Code of Ethics states about confidentiality:

> **P-1.4**—We shall use two-way communications to involve all those with relevant knowledge (including families and staff) in decisions concerning a child, as appropriate, ensuring confidentiality of sensitive information.

and

> **P-2.13**—We shall maintain confidentiality and shall respect the family's right to privacy, refraining from disclosure of confidential information and intrusion into family life. However, when we have reason to believe that a child's welfare is at risk, it is permissible to share confidential information with agencies, as well as with individuals who have legal responsibility for intervening in the child's interest. (See Appendix A for the complete NAEYC Code of Ethical Conduct.)

---

[1] The Family Educational Rights and Privacy Act (FERPA) is a federal law that protects the privacy of student education records. The law applies to all schools that receive funds under an applicable program of the U.S. Department of Education. Generally, schools must have written permission from the parent or eligible student in order to release any information from a student's education record.

Observation

You see, but you do not observe.

Sir Arthur Conan Doyle

Observation is the first and most important form of authentic assessment. As a student of early childhood education, learning to observe is a part of your education. You use it to understand children's development, to make theory come alive. You observe teachers, learning environments, and activities to learn about teaching strategies and how these work (or don't work) in the real world.

As a teacher, you will observe to assess children and to assess your own teaching. So, observation is one of your most important tasks. However, the practice of observation is more than a task. It is a disposition, a habit of mind that you are cultivating in yourself. Once acquired, it will help to make you a better teacher and will bring you joy and satisfaction in your work.

How did you discover that you wanted to work with young children? You probably came to this field because you found children intriguing. You may have seen things about them that your friends didn't notice. The ability to observe—to "read" and understand children—is one of the most important and satisfying skills that you can develop. It is your most effective assessment technique because it will help you know and understand individuals, plan more effectively, and evaluate your teaching. More important, observation is the window that enables you to see into the world of the child.

> *Paul, a slender, just-turned 3-year-old, drags a laundry basket into the shade of a tree. He sits down in the basket and stretches his legs. "I fit! I'm 3!" he says, holding up three fingers. Paul rocks his body and the basket back and forth singing, "I'm rocking the cradle. I'm rocking the cradle." He rocks and rocks until the basket tips, his mouth and eyes open wide, and he spills onto the ground. Paul stands up and smiles. He turns the basket over and thumps it on the top several times making hollow drumming sounds. Then he lifts up the basket and crawls underneath. He crouches under the basket, peers out through the holes, and announces, "I'm going to hatch the cradle." He stands up wearing the basket like a turtle's shell. "I hatched!"*

By observing Paul with open heart and mind, you learn many things. You learn that, like many young 3-year-olds, he enjoys solitary play. You note that he uses language that is slightly more sophisticated than many 3-year-olds. You learn that he knows some things about cradles, drums, and eggs, and that he has a concept of "three," "fit," and "hatch." You see that he uses materials in innovative ways. You notice that he has the control of the large muscles in his arms, legs, and torso that you would expect in 3-year-olds. And you perceive that he handles a simple problem independently. Based on this, you might plan new experiences for Paul (perhaps use more rhymes and language games because he seems to be attuned to words). You may evaluate your own teaching (the rock-a-bye-baby activity seems to have taught a concept!). You gain an empathy toward Paul that helps you be his advocate and his friend. You develop insight into how Paul (and many 3-year-olds) feels about and understands the world—insight that you can share with other adults who did not observe Paul.

Observation can provide you with information that will help you respond effectively to the needs of a frustrated or angry child, to mediate problems between two children, to know what a child is experiencing as a member of a family, and much more!

It gives you increased understanding so that you:

- have empathy for children as a group and as individuals;
- have good relationships with children and foster good relationships between children;
- plan appropriate curriculum that meets children's needs and interests;
- know how to modify the learning environment so that it is responsive and appropriate for the particular children you teach;
- can effectively advocate for children;
- clearly communicate children's strengths, needs, and progress to others.

Observation lets you know what children are learning and experiencing today and helps you plan for tomorrow. It also helps you identify a child who needs more stimulation or who might be troubled, have special needs, or be abused or neglected and in need of help. Observation will help you communicate about children with other adults who share a concern about their well-being.

Observation is the basis for decision making in much of your work with young children and their families. You will observe children's characteristics, abilities, and interests and plan for their development. You will observe children as you teach and will modify your teaching and plans in response. You will observe children's interactions and modify your behavior to help them build good relationships. You will observe them with their families and help them build strong bonds with the most important people in their lives. When you observe that their needs significantly differ from other children, you will use observations to communicate with others to determine whether they require special services.

Reflect On

Observing

Remember a time when you observed something with fresh eyes (for example, a new home, a new city, or a new baby). What did you notice? How was this different from everyday looking? Look around at the place where you are right now and focus on the different colors and sounds in the environment. What do you notice? How is observation different when you focus? What might happen if you observed a child in this way?

Learning to Observe

To observe is to take notice, to watch attentively, to focus. Systematic observation means perceiving both the total picture and the significant detail. It is not nearly as easy as you might think! It requires training and practice. But the rewards are great; it will help you develop child sense—understanding and a sense of connection and empathy for individual children and groups.

To observe objectively and separate your feelings and reactions from what you actually see, it is useful to think of observation as a process with three parts:

1. **Observing.** Purposefully gathering information by watching and listening
2. **Recording.** Documenting what you have observed
3. **Interpreting.** Reflecting on what your observations might mean.

OBSERVING   The first and most essential step in the observation process is to consciously watch and listen. This is different from everyday seeing and from scanning the classroom to anticipate problems. It is most like the "fresh eyes" and heightened senses you bring when you travel to a new place.

Effective observers of young children see and hear what is really happening. They realize it is impossible to be completely **objective** because we all have biases, defenses, and preconceptions. They strive to quiet the inner voice that adds explanations, expectations, and judgments. Objectivity is difficult because you are used to making judgments about the world. It is also difficult because you are a participant in the classroom and you are influenced by the children, families, and setting. When you are aware of this, you can work toward being a more objective observer.

What do you notice when you walk into a room? Do you notice the sounds, the people, or the furniture? You have characteristics as an observer. When you realize what you tend to focus on, you can also get an idea of what you characteristically ignore. We have our college students observe a tank of fish and describe what they see. They are surprised at how different their observations of the same fish can be. Observation exercises like these help you become a better observer.

As you observe, notice your own biases. Are you drawn to children who are neat and tidy? Are you bored by children who are quiet and compliant? Do you prefer some children based on the way they look or their gender? One of the important benefits of observing is that it can help you discover things you like about every child you observe. It helps you appreciate diverse children and thus makes you a better teacher.

Skillful early childhood educators observe all the time. They know that children communicate as much through their facial expressions and body posture as through their spoken words and obvious actions. As you become an experienced observer you will learn to notice these and adjust what you do in response to what you see.

Karen observes 4-year-old Arisa during her third morning in school. Arisa does not talk to anyone but her eyes follow Shan, another 4-year-old, playing in the dramatic play area. With a sigh, Arisa lies down in the library corner and stares blankly into space. "Hey, come try the kitty-cat puzzle," Karen invites Arisa, remembering that yesterday she observed both Arisa and Shan playing with this puzzle at different times. Shan approaches the table and soon Shan and Arisa are playing together.

Observing will give you helpful information. Like Karen in the example above, you will sometimes use what you have observed immediately to respond to a child. At other times, you will observe purposefully with a specific focus over time to learn what a child can and cannot do, to plan curriculum, or to assess the environment.

RECORDING   Because few of us have good enough memories to accurately remember all that we observe, teachers also need to have skill in **recording**. You will record what you have observed so that you can remember, share, and make sense of it. Making a record turns observation into a powerful tool to use on behalf of children.

A number of techniques can be used to make a record of an observation. In the sections that follow, we describe three ways to record what you have observed: writing a **narrative observation**, using a simple **structured observation**, and using technology to make a **digital record**.

INTERPRETING   The third part of the observation process is making **interpretations** based on what you have seen and heard. It is best to be tentative in making interpretations. Although behavior is observable, the reasons for behavior can only be inferred. You can never truly know why a child behaves as he or she does. However, because every day you will make decisions based on what you have observed, you need to develop skill interpreting the relationship between the child's behavior you have observed and its unobservable cause.

Many factors determine how a child acts—stage of development, health, culture, and individual experience. One of the first things that you will consider in interpreting what you observe is what you know about children's development in general. This understanding, which will increase as you have more experience and education, helps you distinguish and interpret whether behavior is typical or unusual for the stage of development. For example, biting another child is typical of a toddler and unusual in a 4-year-old. Similarly, the same behavior can mean different things in children from different cultural backgrounds. Edwin's downcast eyes might mean he has been taught to show respect to adults by avoiding eye contact, while the same behavior from Joanie might mean she is avoiding acknowledging what you are saying. If your cultural background is the same as Edwin's, you are likely to understand his behavior, but if your background is more similar to Joanie's, you might mistakenly assume he is trying to avoid hearing or acknowledging what you are saying.

Each of us tends to notice different things. Becoming aware of different perspectives can help you realize how difficult it is to interpret accurately. Individuals can observe the same incident and make significantly different interpretations. For example, four of our college students noticed a little girl lying down in the shade of a play structure. One thought she was withdrawn and antisocial; another was convinced she was lonely, unhappy, and in need of comforting; the third felt she was tired and taking a few moments to relax; and another thought she was looking at bugs. Like the men in the fable of the blind men and the elephant, they needed more information about the child and the events that preceded their observation in order to make accurate, useful interpretations.

 ## Application Exercise 5.1

Watch and Write About Making Observations and Interpretations

Writing Observations

You will observe children all the time, but to accurately remember what you observe, you also need strategies to **document** or record your observations. Early childhood teachers typically rely on written observations, called narrative observations, to remember what they have observed. There are two types of narrative observations: **running records** and **anecdotal records**. When you hear early childhood educators talk about writing observations, they are referring to one of these.

Running records and anecdotal records have some key similarities. Either can be thought of as a story. It has a setting—where and when the observation occurred. It has characters—a child or children and the adults and materials with whom they interact. And it has action—the child's activities and interactions.

What belongs in a written observation? It can be hard to clearly separate what you observed (objective description) from what you think about it (subjective description). A good written observation gives specific, relevant details about what you saw and heard. As much as possible it includes the words children used. The three examples in Figure 5.1 demonstrate a range of narrative observations—one is objective, specific, and clear, one is lacking in detail, and the third is **subjective** and filled with personal opinions and

Figure 5.1 Three Contrasting Narrative Observations

Subjective
Sasha is a cute little girl with beautiful curly hair. She is happy because she is in the sandbox. Sasha is making birthday cakes. She sings "Happy Birthday." She wishes it was her birthday. Carson gets mad, he walks up to Sasha and says, "Hey it's not your birthday! It's my birthday!" He scares Sasha and kicks over her birthday cake. Sasha gets mad back and throws some sand at Carson. Carson and Sasha don't know how to be nice to one another.

Lacking in Detail
Sasha is playing in the sandbox. Carson walks up and yells at her. Sasha throws sand at him. Carson and Sasha cry.

Objective
Sasha sits in the sandbox playing with a bucket and shovel. She slowly fills the bucket with sand. After each scoop she peers into the bucket and pats the sand. When the bucket is filled to the brim she pats the top several times. She looks at the ground and picks up three small sticks that she pokes into the top of the bucket of sand. She sings, "Happy Birthday to Sasha." S. looks around the sandbox and smiles a wide smile. Carson, a classmate who turned 4 today, stomps up and says, "Hey it's not your birthday! It's my birthday!" He kicks over the bucket. S.'s eyes widen and fill with tears. She picks up a handful of sand and throws it at C. C. yells, "Teacher!" He and S. both burst into tears.

biases. For example, the statement lacking in detail *"Sasha is playing with sand"* does not tell the reader much. We have a better picture of the child and situation from the objective description, *"Sasha smiles and slowly fills the bucket with sand. After each scoop she peers into the bucket and pats the sand. When the bucket is filled to the brim she pats the top several times."* The details increase the reader's ability to understand Sasha and the situation. The subjective version tells you what the observer thinks was happening without telling you what was actually observed, *"Sasha is happily playing with sand. She is making birthday cakes."*

The objective version uses clear language to describe what was observed and enables the reader to visualize the children and their activity. It includes a detailed, precise description of what was observed (objective description) but it does not include words that reflect the observer's feelings, expectations, or opinions (subjective description).

As you can see from these examples, words that have a strong emotional impact or bias (happily, cute, mad, scares, nice) tell the reader what the observer thought rather than describing what was observed. Descriptive words and phrases (slowly, peers, a wide smile) tell what was observed and does not provide guesses about what the child might have felt, wished, or intended (things that cannot be seen). Opinions of children, such as "pretty," "cute," "bright," "attractive," "good," "messy," "slow," "mean," or "naughty," do not belong in written observations because they are value judgments. They tell more about the observer than the child. Because the descriptions you write may be shared with family members and other professionals, it is important to make sure they convey useful, objective information.

When you are learning to observe in a college class, you may be asked to write physical descriptions of children. This exercise is done to build your sensitivity to the unique qualities of individuals and to increase your ability to write descriptively and objectively. In writing physical descriptions, you will note basic physical attributes and write about them to help the reader visualize the child: age, gender, size, build, facial features, coloring, and distinguishing markings. A plain physical description gives little distinctiveness of a child: "She is a 4-year-old girl shorter than her peers." You will convey a better picture of the child as a unique individual if you elaborate with some of the child's unique qualities. The following additions convey a much more vivid sense of the child:

K. is a 4-year-old girl, shorter than her peers. She has black eyebrows, lashes, and hair, golden brown skin, a fair smooth complexion, thin lips, and a small upturned nose. She is slim and has a delicate build. She strolls from activity to activity with quick, light steps. Her arms hang slightly away from her body and swing with the rhythm of her stroll.

It is usually neither necessary nor desirable to describe specific details of children's clothing. They will be wearing something else the next time you observe!

Narrative descriptions are usually accompanied by statements of interpretation, sometimes called comments. These help you to share your understanding of what you observed with others. Comments should be clearly delineated from the narrative description. We encourage you to make liberal use of the words *might* and *seems to* in your interpretations to underscore the tentative nature of conclusions about children's needs, feelings, and motivation. Two people reading the same description will often have different perceptions.

RUNNING RECORDS   When you see a teacher or student teacher with a clipboard writing down everything a child says and does, that teacher is writing a running record. When you first learn to observe young children, you will usually learn to write a running record.

Running records are written while you are observing. Like a video recording they are open-ended (i.e., they continue as long as you are observing the child) and are detailed descriptions of everything a particular child does and says. You write what happens while it is happening, with as much fidelity as possible. Because it is written while it is happening, a running record is always written in the present tense. Learning to write a running record requires considerable practice.

When you are writing a running record you can do little else, so running records are rarely written by practitioners who are responsible for a group of children. As a student, you will have opportunities to practice the skill of writing running records in order to develop sensitivity to and knowledge about children. As a practicing professional, you may use this skill only when you need to do an in-depth study of a particular child and when you have assistance. For ordinary purposes, you will select more efficient and less time-consuming anecdotal or digital records.

Learning to Observe as a Student and Observing as a Teacher

Some Significant Differences

There are differences between observing as a student and observing as a teacher. As a student, you are learning to observe and are using observation to learn about children, programs, and teaching. You observe without having responsibility.

Teachers observe to gain information about individuals, to evaluate the effectiveness of instruction, and to give direction for future plans. They have responsibility for the well-being and education of the children while they are observing.

As a student observer, keep in mind the following guidelines:

Observe unobtrusively. Enter quietly and sit at children's eye level, close enough to see and hear but not so close that you distract the children with your presence.

- Briefly answer children's questions ("I am learning about what children do") and don't engage in extended conversations.

- Don't get involved while observing unless it is necessary to protect a child.

- Let the staff know you are practicing observation and will protect the confidentiality of children, families, professionals, and programs.

- After the observation, use child development information, such as tables of developmental milestones, to help you interpret what you have observed. As you do, you will be consolidating your knowledge of child development—one of the main reasons you are being asked to observe!

Figure 5.2 shows an example of a running record using a typical form. Before you start to observe, you note the date and the child's name at the top. While you observe you note the time and location in the left hand column and you write what you see in the middle column. As soon after observing as possible, you review what you have written and add comments, impressions, or conclusions (interpretations) in the right-hand column.

ANECDOTAL RECORDS   You may be asking yourself, "If observations are important but practitioners rarely write running records, what do they do instead?" The most frequently used form of written observation is an anecdotal record. Like a running record, an anecdotal record is an open-ended narrative describing behaviors and interactions. Unlike a running record, it is brief and describes a single incident. If a running record is like a video recording, an anecdotal record is more like a photograph. An anecdotal record is written after the fact. Teachers write an anecdotal record after they have observed something they want to remember. For this reason, anecdotal records are written in the past tense. Figure 5.3 (p. 148) shows an example of an anecdotal record using a typical form.

Early childhood teachers use anecdotal records to document children's skills or behaviors. It is important to learn how to write them and to develop strategies to make them a part of your daily work with children.

Figure 5.2 Example of a Running Record

Child: John A.	Date: 10/10	Observer: Lisa L.
Time/Setting	**Observation**	**Comment**
10:30 art area New play dough set out on table. Each chair has a plastic place mat, ball of dough, apron hanging over back of chair. Teacher has told children new play dough available.	J. runs to table and sits down without putting on an apron. Starts to pinch the ball of dough apart. Teacher says, "Hey J., I think you forgot something." J. smiles, "Oh yeah." Stands up and takes yellow plastic apron and pulls it over head—wearing it backwards (long part behind). Teacher makes no comment. J. sits back down and picks up the dough.	Complies with reasonable requests
	J. rolls a teaspoon-sized "pinch" of dough into a ball. Eyes are fixed on the dough and his hands as he rolls. He rolls the dough with his right hand against the mat. He rolls and rolls the ball until it is a nearly perfect sphere. With a little smile, he picks it up and places it on the edge of his mat and glances up at other children.	Shows good fine motor coordination and persistence
10:35	J. continues pinching and rolling little balls of dough, placing them along the edge of the mat. His eyes stay fixed on the dough. J. glances up after completing each ball but does not interact with other children who are chattering to one another.	Doesn't seem too interested in the other children
10:45	When entire big ball of dough has been turned into little balls, J. stands up and walks to the collage shelf. He picks up container of straws and toothpicks and carries back to table.	Seems to have a plan
	J. pokes a toothpick into first ball of dough. Then he pokes another ball of dough onto the other end of the toothpick. He sticks a second toothpick into the second ball of dough and continues to link the balls with toothpicks.	Attempting to symbolize?
	He gets to the fourth ball of dough and it falls apart. J. says to the teacher, "Help me." Teacher says, "What are you trying to do?"	Uses adults as resources

🐝 Application Exercise 5.2

Watch and Write About a Running Record

What belongs in an anecdotal record? Like a running record, an anecdotal record should include the date and the name(s) of the child(ren) and the observer. It should give the context (place/time). Because anecdotal records are brief and are usually read by those who know the child already, it is unnecessary to give much background information. Instead the observer writes what the children said and did briefly but completely. They then note why they wrote this observation, as you see in the examples that follow:

Behavior or interactions that seem typical for a child:
9/5—During outside play Bryce (4 years) walked quickly up a plank. Then he jumped across a tire to another plank. He walked across that plank and down the final plank. "Ta-da!" he said holding his arms out. "That's how you do it!"

Comment: Demonstrates a good sense of balance. Enjoys large-motor challenges.

Behavior or interactions that seem atypical for a child:
9/4—At circle time, a teacher sang "Old MacDonald" with finger puppets. The teacher held up one of the puppets and sang, "On this farm he had a cow." Emily (3 1/2 years) protested, "It's not a cow! It's a donkey." She lay on the carpet and cried while the group sang the song.

Comment: Unusual behavior—angry/unhappy and upset. Emily is usually very enthusiastic at circle time.

The achievement of a developmental milestone:
8/23—At 10:00 this morning, Tevin (10 months) was on his hands and knees next to a low table. He sat back on his heels and reached up so that he was grasping the edge of the table. He pulled himself to a standing position. His eyes grew wide, he grinned, and then his knees buckled and he sat down fast. He repeated this five more times during the next half hour.

Comment: First time Tevin has pulled himself up at the center.

Incidents and interactions that convey the child's strengths, interests, and needs:
9/20—After lunch at his desk, Ethan (5 1/2 years) drew a detailed picture of a car. The drawing included a tailpipe with exhaust, a spoiler, door handles,

Figure 5.3 Example of an Anecdotal Record Form

Observations of N.L.	
Domain I: Physical Development Secondary Domain: *Personal/Social* Date: 01/30 At the woodworking table NL used both hands to hold a hammer. She hammered repeatedly until the nail was securely in the wood. Comment: *Demonstrates physical strength and coordination. Shows persistence in completing tasks.*	**Domain II: Personal/Social Development** Secondary Domain: *Cognitive* Date: 01/31 NL and V. were playing with a big cardboard box. They took turns getting in the box. When V. was in the box and it was closed up tight NL told V. that she was going to tell the other children that no one was inside. "Don't say a word," she cautioned V. Then she said to other children, "There's no one inside, there's only air." Comment: *Plans for play. Engages in cooperative play. Able to take viewpoint of others.*
Domain III: Communication (Language/Literacy) Secondary Domain: *Cognitive* Date: 01/30 The children and teacher were observing a monarch caterpillar. The teacher asked why the caterpillar appeared to have two sets of antennae. NL said, "Maybe it's two caterpillars." Then the teacher said she didn't know but that she was going to find out. NL suggested, "Check on the computer." Comment: *Literacy: Demonstrates awareness of different sources of information.* *Science: Hypothesizes*	**Domain IV: Cognitive Development** Secondary Domain: *Personal/Social* Date: 02/01 NL said, "I want a booster. But, you know, my mom won't let me. She said I have to stay in my car seat. But V. is only four and <u>she</u> has a booster." Comment: *Seems to understand that rules should have a logical foundation. Makes logical arguments.* *Advocates for herself. Has concepts of fairness.*
Domain V: Creative Development Secondary Domain: *Personal/Social* Date: 02/05 NL mixed colors on her palette. With the colors she mixed she painted a scene that included a rainbow, sun, grass, and rain. When she was through she took her painting to each teacher and showed her work. Then she placed the painting on the drying rack. Comment: *Purposefully expresses ideas through art. Uses work to communicate with others. Takes responsibility for her own work.*	

headlights, and tires with elaborate hubcaps. Ethan wrote "RASG CR" on his drawing.

Comment: Shows understanding of and interest in cars. Is able to make detailed representations in drawings. Uses inventive spelling.

Incidents and interactions that convey the nature of social relationships and emotional reactions:

11/14—During outside play this afternoon, Bryan (4 years) was riding on the rickshaw trike. He zoomed past Kengo (4 years), who was shoveling sand into a bucket. He stopped and said to Kengo, "The garbage truck is collecting the garbage. You want to be a garbage man?" Kengo answered by picking up his bucket, sitting on the rickshaw seat, and yelling, "Let's go!" The two boys drove to one end of the yard, where they filled the bucket with leaves, which they packed to the other end of the yard. They continued to play garbage man until Bryan's mom came, about 20 minutes.

Comment: Cooperative friendships.

Behavior or interactions relating to an area of special concern:
3/3—While working on an addition exercise Stanley (6 years) put his head down on his desk. The teacher asked, "What's up, Stanley?" He said, "I'm just so dumb."

Comment: This is the second or third time that Stanley has said this in the last 2 weeks—each time it was associated with seat work.

Anecdotal records can also be made with special emphasis on children about whom you have questions or concerns and those children who sometimes seem "invisible"— so inconspicuous that they tend to be forgotten.

Golden Rules
for Writing Anecdotal Records

1. Write after you observe a typical behavior or interaction.
2. Write after you observe a new behavior or interaction.
3. Write after you observe an unusual behavior or interaction.
4. Describe what happened. Include only what you saw, heard, or otherwise experienced through your senses. Avoid generalizations (*always, usually, never*).
5. Omit the words *I* and *me* unless the child spoke those words (remember that the observation is about the child, not you).
6. Refrain from saying why you think the child behaved or interacted in this way.
7. Exclude your opinions of the child, the behavior, or interaction (remember, it's not about you).
8. Leave out your feelings about what happened.
9. Write a separate comment that explains why you thought this behavior or interaction was important to record and what you think it might mean in terms of this child's development and program goals for children.
10. Keep anecdotal records confidential.

Note: You may want to copy the "Golden Rules for Writing Anecdotal Records" and keep them close at hand when you are writing anecdotal records.

Making Anecdotal Record Writing a Part of Every Day   To understand the children in your class and how they are developing, it is important to have anecdotal records over time. So you need to create anecdotal records on a regular basis. Some teachers write while they are working with children. Some write at naptime, or on their break time. If you believe in the value of observations and make a commitment to writing them you will write consistently. The practice of creating anecdotal observations will then turn into a habit, a part of your daily routine like washing your hands and brushing your teeth. To do this, it is necessary to have a convenient and systematic way to write and keep them organized. We have used and seen a number of ways to make anecdotal records a part of everyday practice, including the following:

- *Clipboards or binders throughout the classroom.*   Place clipboards or binders with pencils throughout the classroom with an anecdotal record sheet for each child. You then can reach for the clipboard/binder and make a few notes right after you have observed

SOURCE: Jeff Reese

SOURCE: Jeff Reese

something of significance. In this method, an anecdotal record like the one shown in Figure 5.4 is helpful. The observations are filed weekly or when the forms are filled up. When you have forms on a clipboard, it is important to use a cover sheet to ensure confidentiality.

- *Self-stick labels, index cards, or notebooks.* Teachers wear aprons with pockets or waist packs and keep a pen and a stack of large self-stick labels, index cards, or a small notebook in the pocket. Anecdotal records are made with the child's name and the date. At the end of the day or week, notes are filed. They can be organized chronologically and/or by developmental domain. Some teachers later add selected self-stick labels directly to the child's portfolio. (See the section on portfolios later in this chapter.)

- *Notebooks.* Each child has a notebook in which teachers write anecdotal records. Notebooks are kept in the classroom. Sometimes, they are used as the basis of a portfolio, and at other times, they are kept where families can read them every day.

- *Digital voice recorders.* Digital voice recorders are kept in a pocket to dictate observations. These allow teachers to describe what they see happening and capture children's words verbatim. Because recordings must be transcribed and organized, they may be more time consuming than on-the-spot written observation.

- *Laptops, tablet computers, iPods, or smartphones.* These are carried in pockets, aprons, or waist packs or are kept in the classroom and are used to write or dictate observations while on the floor with children or after an observation has been made, at a time that is convenient and appropriate. Because these have the capacity to take a photograph, video, or audio clip, they serve a dual purpose. There are many apps available for inputting observations (e.g. TS GOLD, KIDS, DLRP, Evidence for Learning). While these can be time-saving, the process of inputting information can be distracting to both teachers and children. A convenient location in the classroom to keep the device safe and ready to use is required.

Whether you use a pencil and paper, a tape recorder, or an iPod as your tool, the content of an anecdotal record will be very similar. The anecdotal records you create in the course of your day may be just a few words or fragments of information with details that you fill in later (when written these are sometimes referred to as jottings). It is important to go back on the same day to any that are incomplete, or you will lose the details that make records useful. Anecdotal records, like all observations, are a part

---

Figure 5.4 Example of an Anecdotal Observation

Physical Development, Health, and Safety
Secondary Area Creative and Aesthetic Development
Observer: JR Date: 03/14/16
Ellie held scissors in her right hand and cut straight across a sheet of paper that she held in her left hand. She cut one of the pieces in half. She took the papers and set them next to each other, cut several pieces of tape, and taped the papers together.
Comment: *Shows fine motor strength and coordination.* *Displays right hand dominance.*

of your collection of information about each child. They need to be carefully monitored and filed with all other confidential records.

USING WRITTEN OBSERVATIONS   The point of writing observations is to improve the quality of the educational experience you provide for children. They help you understand and be more responsive to individuals. They are the most useful kind of observation to guide you in planning curriculum and assessing whether the curriculum is currently meeting children's needs. To use written observations for curriculum planning, bring together the observations and read through them to help determine children's strengths, interests, and needs. Plan curriculum that builds on the strengths and interests and that provides opportunities to address the needs.

Written observations also form the foundation of the child portfolio described later in this chapter. In a portfolio, you assemble observations, organize them, and summarize them to present a coherent picture of the child in school.

Digital Observation

People have been taking photographs of children in school for almost as long as cameras have existed. Today, digital technology (tablets, self-contained cameras and audio recorders, scanners, and computers) can help you record children's activities and work. Creating a video or audio record of a child engaged in school serves much the same purpose as other forms of observation and requires the same level of understanding of its purpose. Just as written observations require skill and practice that goes beyond writing, creating digital records is more than taking selfies.

ANNOTATED PHOTOGRAPHS   Is a picture worth a thousand words? Photographs are valuable when they show something meaningful. They can document something that is difficult to describe, such as an elaborate block structure. However, photographs are only valuable when they show what children do, not when they are posed. They are also not particularly useful when they record an event that is not meaningful, such as an entire class dressed up for Halloween or children eating gooey cupcakes and getting icing on their faces. Exercise the same criteria for taking photographs that you use for writing observations. Photograph children engaged in something typical, something new (a milestone), or something that is of concern.

The term **annotated photograph** (McAfee et al., 2004) is used to describe a photograph that is accompanied by an anecdotal record, as shown in Figure 5.5. The annotation should include the child's name and the date of the photograph, the setting or context of the photograph (e.g., in the dramatic play area), an anecdote explaining what happened (e.g., what you observed when the photograph was taken), and what the photo tells about this child. Without annotation, a photograph may not be enough to help another person understand its significance. It is valuable to take several pictures of a child engaged in an activity to show the process as the child engages in play or works to create a product.

Figure 5.5 Example of an Annotated Photograph

SOURCE: Jeff Reese

02/13 N. pedaled the rickshaw trike with two friends on the back demonstrating large-motor strength

VIDEO AND AUDIO RECORDINGS   **Video and audio records** are valuable when they show something happening or provide a record of a child's ability. They are particularly useful in documenting movement, language, and interactions. They allow a number of observers to view or hear the same child engaged in the same activity. They are not dependent on writing skill and are not as subject to the bias of the observer. You may notice detail in a recording that you would not have noted while writing an observation.

Video and audio recordings have some disadvantages, however. Equipment can be distracting to children and teachers. Recordings made in a typically noisy classroom environment can be difficult to understand. It can be time consuming to cull the few significant minutes or seconds from larger recordings.

In order to use video or audio records effectively, decide in advance what activity or interaction you want to record. Give children time to get used to the camera, phone, tablet, or tape recorder before you try to capture the significant event. Record a few children away from the rest of the group if possible. Ask another teacher, a volunteer, or a parent to help you video if you are recording while you are teaching. Finally, be sure to select only short relevant sections to share with others. Editing in this way can make the resulting video or audio records useful as **documentation**.

 Application Exercise 5.3

Watch and Write About Using Video Observations for Planning

 A Quick Check 5.2

Gauge your understanding of the concepts in this section.

 # Other Methods of Authentic Assessment

Teachers' observations of children engaged in meaningful activities is the most important form of authentic assessment. However, there are other ways to authentically assess a child's understanding and ability.

Structured Observation

When you need to quickly learn something specific about a child in order to make a referral or work on a problem, a structured observation can help. **Time samples**, **event samples**, checklists, **rating scales**, and **rubrics** are structured observation techniques. All aid in gathering information that will help you to know if your impressions of children's behavior and ability are accurate. The particular technique that you select will depend on what you want to know.

TIME SAMPLES   A time sample (also known as a **frequency count**) is an efficient way to find out how often a behavior (e.g., trike riding, social interaction, hitting, thumb sucking) is actually occurring. It is used for tracking behavior that occurs at regular intervals or in rapid succession and can be used for observing more than one child at a time. Teachers often conduct time samples to find out if their impressions of children's behaviour are accurate.

SOURCE: Jeff Reese

To conduct a time sample you create a grid, develop a simple code, and then observe for a specified time in a specified place, and record what is occurring. We once designed a time sample to understand 4-year-old Michael. Several staff members felt that they spent a great deal of time each day intervening in the conflicts that he provoked. Another teacher had difficulty understanding this frustration because she perceived Michael as very positive and cooperative. The time sample was simple. They agreed to track how frequently Michael initiated interaction with two friends and whether it was positive (play or conversation with another child) or negative (physical or verbal argument). They conducted three 15-minute time samples on different days and in different classroom areas that showed that while Michael had many more positive than negative interactions, he initiated interactions three times more frequently than his two playmates. This helped explain the teachers' different perceptions. Their increased understanding helped them to appreciate Michael. They were comfortable refraining from intervening because they understood that Michael's play was generally positive. Figure 5.6 shows an example of a time sample.

EVENT SAMPLES   An event sample is used to help you understand the relationship between a child's behavior and the context of the behavior so that you can understand the reason for the behavior. To conduct an event sample you identify a behavior you want to understand. Then you watch for the behavior (called the event) and record what preceded it, what happened while it was occurring, and what happened afterwards. It is made as soon as possible during or after the behavior occurs.

Like a running record, an event sample relies on your skill in making detailed observations. For example, if you think a child has been engaging in a lot of hitting, you would note what preceded hitting, what happened while the child hit, and what teachers and other children, as well as the child, did after hitting occurred. You may discover

Figure 5.6 Example of a Time Sample

Children: <u>Michael, Teddy, Philip</u>   Date: <u>3/3</u>

Time: <u>Outdoor choice time</u>   Space: <u>hollow block and sand area</u>

* = initiates interaction   Δ = responds to interaction
✓ = positive interaction   X = negative interaction
0 = plays alone/does not respond

	Michael	Teddy	Philip
0–3 min	*✓ *✓	0 Δ ✓	Δ ✓ Δ X
3–6 min	Δ ✓ *X	✓ Δ *X	Δ ✓ *✓
6–9 min	Δ X *✓	*X	0 Δ X
9–12 min	*✓ *✓	0	Δ ✓ Δ ✓
12–15 min	Δ X *✓	Δ ✓ 0	*X

that hitting is happening only before lunch or nap or at the end of the day. It might be triggered by interaction with one child or group, or you may discover that there are unintended consequences that are encouraging the continuation of hitting. While an event sampling is not time consuming, it requires you to focus on one child and the behavior of concern. It can provide useful information for figuring out the causes of behavior and can be the basis for generating plans to change the behavior. Figure 5.7 shows an example of an event sample.

CHECKLISTS, RATING SCALES, AND RUBRICS Checklists, rating scales, and rubrics are other ways to make a record of children's skills and knowledge. They all include lists of behaviors, concepts, traits, and/or skills. To illustrate how checklists, rating scales, and rubrics differ, the examples we use here all focus on gross motor skills often assessed in preschoolers.

A *checklist* is a list of observable behaviors or skills usually arranged sequentially in areas of development. There is a place to indicate (✓) that the behavior or skill was observed. A checklist can be used on an on-going basis with a place to note the date on which each behavior or skill is first observed or at a designated time such as the first month of the school year. Some programs create their own checklists based on milestones of development, their goals for children, or curriculum standards.

When teachers complete checklists during the school year, analyze what children can and cannot do, identify goals, and then plan curriculum based on their analysis they are using checklists as formative assessment. When they complete checklists at the end of all or part of the year, analyze what skills or knowledge children have acquired,

Figure 5.7 Example of an Event Sample

Child's Name Mari	Age 4.5		Date(s) Sept.–Oct.
Date/Time	**Preceding Event**	**Behavior**	**Consequence**
9.24/7:48	M. was pouring juice from pitcher at the snack table. She tipped over the paper cup and spilled a small amount.	M. set down the pitcher and struck out at a stack of paper cups, knocking them from the table.	Jim quickly grabbed M. in his arms and said, "It's OK, it was just a little spill."
9.26/8:07	M. entered the block area and began placing trucks from the shelf on the structure Pua and Jenny were building. Pua said, "You can't play."	M. ran from the block area past the art area on her way out the back door. On her way past the watercolor table, she made a wide sweep with her arm and knocked over a cup of water.	Ginger, who witnessed the block corner scene, followed her out. She took M. in her arms and told her "I bet it made you mad when Pua told you that you could not build with them."
10.6/7:51	M. placed her blanket in her cubby on top of a plastic container. The blanket fell out as she turned to walk away.	M. shoved the blanket back into the cubby and pulled the entire contents of the cubby onto the floor and ran out the door to the gate.	Jim, who was greeting the children, followed M. out and said, "Please let me help you get your blanket in straight."
10.8/8:15	M. was playing with the tinker toys. Jenny joined her and accidentally bumped her construction and several pieces fell off.	M. screamed at Jenny and said she was stupid. With a single sweep of her arm M. knocked the pieces to the floor and threw herself on the rug.	Ginger gently rubbed M.'s back until she calmed.

Figure 5.8 Example of a Checklist for Motor Development Skills

Date Observed	Motor Development Skills
	Walks forward and backward
	Stands on one foot
	Walks upstairs and downstairs
	Kicks ball
	Throws ball
	Catches ball
	Rides trike

they are using checklists as summative assessment for both children and the program. Figure 5.8 provides an example of a checklist for motor development skills.

A *rating scale* is nearly identical to a checklist in purpose and uses (see Figure 5.9). The significant difference is that a rating scale provides a mechanism for indicating the degree to which a skill or concept is present or the frequency with which it is demonstrated. A rating scale depends on the teacher's perception of the child's ability. Because people differ in their interpretation of words like *completely* and *partially* a rating scale may not be accurate.

You are probably familiar with a *rubric* from your college classes. In early childhood settings, rubrics are similar to rating scales. Both provide a way to indicate the extent to which a skill or concept has been demonstrated. As you can see from the example in Figure 5.10, a rubric differs from a rating scale in that it provides very specific criteria for different levels so it is likely to be more accurate.

INTERVIEWS   A formal **interview** is a structured observation technique. Informal conversations that provide you with insight into children's ideas and learning can be documented in anecdotal records. When you want to target a particular skill or area of understanding, a formal interview allows you to compare children's responses and better understand individual children. Children's answers can give you insight into language, social-emotional development, understanding of concepts, and perception of the world. You select a focus (e.g., math concepts, feelings about friends, language development) and then plan a series of questions and ask them of all the children. An interview may be repeated after an interval of time to help you understand and document a child's growth.

If you decide to conduct an interview, consider what you want to discover and how to communicate it to the children. For example, if you were trying to assess the value of a trip to the zoo during a study of birds, you might interview children as a group by

Figure 5.9 Example of a Rating Scale

Motor Development Skills	Consistently/ Completely	Sometimes/Partially	Does Not Demonstrate
Walks forward and backward			
Stands on one foot			
Walks upstairs and downstairs			
Kicks ball			
Throws ball			
Catches ball			
Rides trike			

Figure 5.10 Example of a Rubric for Motor Development Skills

Walking	Walks forward and backward legs widely spaced	Walks forward and backward with heel-toe pattern	Walks forward with legs close together, toes point forward, arms swing
Balancing	Balances briefly on one foot	Stands on one foot for 5 seconds	Stands on one foot for 10 seconds
Hopping	Hops once	Hops 5 times on same foot	Hops 10 or more times on same foot
Cimbing stairs	Walks down stairs placing both feet on each step	Walks up stairs alternating feet with support	Walks up and down stairs without support
Kicking	Kicks ball without backswing	Kicks ball with backswing	Kicks ball with backswing and follow-through
Throwing	Throws ball overhand without torso rotation	Throws ball overhand with torso rotation	Throws ball overhand with backswing and forward step on same side as throwing arm
Catching	Catches bounced ball passively	Catches ball passively with arms fully extended	Catches balls actively with hands at face height
Riding trikes	Sits on trike and pushes with feet on ground	Pedals and steers trike	Pedals trike rapidly, steering smoothly

asking a broad open-ended question ("What do you remember about the birds we saw at the zoo?") to find out whether they had acquired the concept. *"There are many different birds with many colors, shapes, and sizes."* Children's responses could then be recorded on a chart kept in the form of a **facsimile** (e.g., a rewritten chart on letter-size paper or a photograph). An audio or video recording also works well for documenting interviews. You might interview children individually to elicit a more targeted response aimed at a specific skill, such as the ability to observe and describe, by asking a child, "Tell me what you noticed about the toucan and the hornbill." Thus, like all assessment, interviews serve a dual purpose; in this case assessing children's understanding and advancing their learning. The box "Golden Rules for Interviewing a Child for Assessment" gives you ideas for ways to make interviews with children successful.

Golden Rules

for Interviewing a Child for Assessment

1. Don't interrupt a child who is actively involved with friends or play activities; instead, invite the child to join you during an interlude after play.
2. Choose a quiet corner for the interview where you can sit at the child's level.
3. Plan a few questions in advance and relate them to your objectives for children—remember, you want to know what children understand and can do, not whether they liked an activity or the way you teach.
4. Use open-ended questions that have many possible answers to avoid the child feeling there is a "right" answer. Start with phrases like "Tell me about . . . " and "What do you think . . . ?"
5. Use language that is easy for the child to understand.
6. If the child doesn't answer a question, try rephrasing the question and asking it again.
7. Use the child's answers and interests to guide the interview.
8. Record children's behavior as well as their words.

SELECTING AN OBSERVATION TECHNIQUE   Each of the techniques described in the preceding sections is particularly useful for one or more purposes. You are likely to use all of them at different times. Remembering what you are trying to accomplish can help you select an observation recording technique. Table 5.1 is designed to help you choose.

Work Samples

Work samples (children's drawings, paintings, cutting, writing, journals, dictated stories, maps, computer work, word banks, and so forth) serve as a tangible form of authentic assessment. Work samples are more than the accumulated contents of a child's art folder. Instead they are work of significance that shows a child's growing ability and understanding. Like photographs, work samples should be annotated and include the child's name and the date, the setting or context in which it was created, a written description explaining what happened (e.g., when it was created), and your interpretation of what it tells about this child. Some teachers prefer to scan children's work so that they have an electronic copy. Large or three-dimensional work samples (like easel paintings and woodworking projects) can more easily be captured and stored in a photograph.

Collect samples of each child's work on a regular basis. Remember to collect a variety of items. Be sure to label, date, and annotate all work samples before storing them (see Figure 5.11).

Portfolio Assessment

One of the most common ways to meaningfully organize the rich data that authentic assessment provides is in a **portfolio**. Portfolios are flexible, organized compilations of evidence of a child's learning, ability, and development (observations, work samples, photographs, and so on) collected over time. A child's portfolio presents a picture of who the child is and what the child knows and can do.

The term portfolio is also used in reference to a **professional portfolio**, a **program portfolio**, and a **classroom portfolio**, each of which provide documentation of a person or program's ability or quality. In this chapter, however, we are talking about children's portfolios. In preschool programs, a child's portfolio is sometimes called a **developmental portfolio** to reflect its purpose (to illustrate a child's development) and organization (by developmental domains). Portfolios for older students are usually designed to show achievement of academic objectives and so are organized by academic subject areas.

Portfolios are a logical extension of the observational approaches traditionally used in early childhood programs. A portfolio becomes a **portfolio assessment** when

Table 5.1 Selecting an Authentic Assessment Technique

In order to . . .	Use . . .
Create a vivid record of a child's activity	Running record; video
Record a behavior or interaction or the achievement of a milestone	Anecdotal record; annotated paragraph
Ascertain how often a type of behavior occurs	Time sample
Understand why or when a particular behavior occurs	Event sample
Gather information about children's play preferences, individual progress, how materials and equipment are being used	Checklist
Evaluate the extent to which a child has reached particular milestones	Rating scale; rubric
Compare how different children understand a specific concept	Interviews
Quickly and accurately document something that is difficult to describe	Annotated photographs; video
Document movement, language, or interactions (or related abilities, such as musical skill) in order to share them with others	Running record; video or audio recording

Figure 5.11 Example of an Annotated Work Sample

10/13 Using her right hand, Aria drew with a pink marker. She made a circle, then added smaller circles, dots, and lines. She said, "This is Lala." She asked, "Can you write the word that means love?"

Comment: Aria makes intentional representational drawings that symbolize people she knows. She understands that both print and drawings have meaning and that there is a difference between the two.

SOURCE: Reprinted with permission from Robyn. S. B. Chun.

it contains evidence to evaluate whether and to what degree a child has acquired skills, knowledge, and dispositions. In elementary school settings, portfolios are an alternative to tests, report cards, and letter grades. Portfolios focus on what children actually do so they provide a far more complete and authentic picture of a child than a checklist or a test.

Portfolios help you look at children's work over time and gauge how they are developing—socially, emotionally, physically, and cognitively. They give you a deeper understanding of a child and can help to guide your planning. Portfolios also assist you as you share your understanding with families and other professionals; they represent the child's strengths and potential and can be shared with the staff of the next program to which the child moves.

CREATING PORTFOLIOS   A folder full of random and disorganized "stuff" is not a portfolio, nor is a "scrapbook" decorated with stickers and posed photos. To turn a collection into a portfolio, you need to mindfully collect, organize, and interpret collected evidence. Each item should be meaningful and informative—it should tell something about the child's development, abilities, and learning. It should create a complete and authentic representation of the child's understanding and skill.

Portfolios can include narrative, structured, and electronic observation records, and work samples. What you collect for each child's portfolio will depend on program goals and your purpose in creating portfolios. For example, if a program goal is the enhancement of literacy, you might collect work samples in which a child has incorporated print or print-like marks, keep records of books read to or by the child, and write anecdotal records when the child talks about reading and writing, participates in story time, or uses pens or pencils to communicate. Many programs ask teachers to:

- Collect **core items** at the same time from all children, for example a drawing from the first week of school and another from the last week of school.
- Collect evidence of ability, for example an observation of a social interaction, a written or taped language sample, a photograph of a block building, or a writing sample.
- Have children select a favorite or "best" work to include.

Because a portfolio documents the individual child's development, evidence will not be the same for every child. However, having a list of items to collect will help. Figure 5.12 is a basic list of items to collect for a preschool child's portfolio. Your list will reflect the age of the children you teach as well as your program's goals and values.

Creating portfolios for a class of children is a lot of work! It is easier if you have a system for compiling items to be included. Some teachers use file boxes, some use accordion folders, and others organize materials in notebooks. Large items that must be stored elsewhere can be indicated with a note about where they are stored. Some teachers construct cardboard or wooden files sized to fit the easel paintings.

Once the evidence is collected, teachers reflect on what has been gathered, analyze what it means, and finally write a description of the child's abilities and characteristics. This description can be called a developmental summary, developmental description, individual profile, or summary statement. The portfolio example widget included here shows you an example of a preschool portfolio. Figure 5.13 shows you an example of a portfolio.

The individual profile provides a picture of what makes this child unique. It should include a general description of the child's ability, interests, progress, and ways of engaging in each of the areas included in the portfolio. It should incorporate the teacher's appraisal of where the child is in terms of program goals and note any areas

Figure 5.12 Sample Portfolio List for a Preschool Child

Background Information		
Child's date of birth	Date started school/class	
Language(s) spoken in the home	Ethnic/racial/cultural identification	

Evidence of Physical Development and Health: *Observations, photographs, work samples that show . . .*		
Size/weight compared to others of his/her age	Typical food intake/preferences	
Toileting routines/accidents	Length of typical nap	
Large-motor activity	Fine-motor activity	
Sensory activity	Preferred hand and grip	

Evidence of Personal/Social Development: *Observations, photographs, work samples, or recordings that show . . .*		
Self-regulation and self-help	Self-initiated activities	Friendships (also child-reports)
Making choices	Showing awareness of feelings	Interactions w/ others
Separation from family	Cooperative behavior	Solving a social problem
Pretend play		Formal group activity

Evidence of Language and Cognitive Development: *Observations, photographs, work samples, or recordings that show . . .*		
Reading or writing	Dictated notes or stories	Writing samples (one per month)
Listening to or telling stories	Talking or storytelling	Conversations with others

Evidence of Cognitive Development: *Observations, photographs, work samples, or recordings that show . . .*		
Noticing a natural phenomenon	Discovery or exploration	Sorting, counting, or classifying
Examples of maps or illustrations		Identifying a problem

Evidence of Creative Ability and Aesthetic Awareness: *Observations, photographs, work samples, or recordings that show . . .*		
Engaged in music	Painting (one per month)	Musical expression in song
Engaged in movement	Creative art or construction	Drawing (one per month)

Figure 5.13 A Portfolio of a Five-Year-Old's Development and Learning

The portfolio cover and the over-all developmental summary of the portfolio

Portfolio of the Development and Learning of

G. K.

May 20**

SUMMARY OF DEVELOPMENT

In her final year of preschool, G. is active and competent. She exudes confidence and a disposition to learn and play.

Physical Development
G. shows stamina, whole body balance, strength, control, and coordination. She has above-age object control and eye-hand coordination. She uses a mature pencil grasp and can cut a line with accuracy.

Social-Emotional Development
G. is independent and cares for her own needs. She has interests, and passions. She expresses feelings and preferences and stands up for her rights. She has a clear and positive self-image. She is a leader. She assists younger children and is sensitive to the feelings of others. She knows how to be a friend and has positive strategies for initiating play. G. has good relationships with teachers. She seeks help when needed. She understands and follows rules. She enjoys group activities, can wait her turn, sit quietly, and listen to the teacher.

Communication Development
G. has a large vocabulary and talks about words. She plays with language, makes up rhymes, defines words and makes analogies.
G. listens to and answers questions. She can read words that are important to her. She understands the purpose of print and knows the sounds of many letters. She writes words she knows. G. often looks at books and is attentive at story time. She knows titles and plots of many stories and is able to retell a familiar book.

Cognitive Development
G. uses inquiry skills to find answers. She can rote count to 8, understands principles of counting, addition, and subtraction. She is learning number symbols (numerals). G. often creates spatial challenges for herself with blocks and puzzles. She can see parts and wholes. She is full of curiosity about the world and has enjoyed our curriculum study of seeds. She asks questions, and makes logical statements. G. is interested in people in the community.
She shows this in her play and in her comments about other people. She also shows this as a participant in the classroom community.

Creative and Aesthetic Development
G. builds with blocks, participates in movement and music, and creates elaborate dramatic play scenarios. She uses language with sensitivity and beauty. She has excellent art skills. She draws and makes beautiful collages. Her first choice of subject matter is flowers, hearts, and stars. A goal for G. is to develop the confidence and self-assurance needed to use her creativity more innovatively and expressively, without as much need for the approval of others.
In summary, G. K. is a child with skills and dispositions needed to make a good transition to kindergarten. She has been a delight to her teachers in preschool and will, we trust, continue to be a delight to her teachers in kindergarten.

Description of Child's Social-Emotional Development and observations and photographs that provide evidence.

SOCIAL-EMOTIONAL DEVELOPMENT

April • G. and A. work together to set a table (with leaves and sand) and then clean it off—engaging in cooperative play.

Independence, Self-Awareness, & Self-Esteem
G. is independent and cares for her own needs. She has strong feelings and a sense of her own power (Girls Rule!) and ability (I can do it!). She has interests and passions (I love volleyball!). She can express feelings and preferences and stand up for her rights. She has a clear and positive self-image. Her grandmother's illness and death necessitated many trips, and much missed school. This had an impact on G. There were days when she was unhappy. Separation and small failures or disappointments often led to tears and withdrawal. Now at the end of the semester G. has returned to her formerly cheerful self.

Relationships with Peers

G. cares for her own needs and for the needs of other children. She occupies a leadership role in the classroom. She assists younger children. She is sensitive to the feelings and needs of others. G. knows how to have a friend and how to be a friend. She has positive strategies for initiating play and has a preference for social play. She has a continuing friendship with A. and T., new friendships with H.H. and S., and growing friendships with H.O. and M. Her friendships can be rocky when another child vies for leadership. She has some difficulty understanding the viewpoint of others. We see a growth in G.'s ability to follow the suggestions of others.

School Behaviors

G. has positive relationships with teachers. She knows how to seek help when she needs it. She understands and follows rules and expectations and has a good grasp of social conventions like saying please and thank-you. She enjoys group activities. She has the self-control necessary to wait her turn, can sit quietly for story, raise her hand, listen to the teacher, and handle disappointment. G. is sensitive and there are times when a disappointment will cause her much distress. At these times staff will ask her to take time to be away from the group to recover.

SOCIAL-EMOTIONAL DEVELOPMENT OBSERVATIONS

03/20
G. asked a teacher, "Can I choose the bunny feeder job please?" The teacher gave her her "job card." G. turned to the teacher and asked, "Do you want to choose a job with me?"
Participates in school routines and responsibilities. Uses social conventions (manners) appropriately. Has friendships. Initiates interactions with peers.

03/21
The children were opening and examining shelled peanuts. G. exclaimed, "I'm really good at opening peanuts!"
Has positive self-image. Realistically and positively evaluates own abilities.

03/27
G. stepped on another child's foot. The other child cried. G. leaned over to her, gently touched her and asked, "Are you okay? Are you okay?"
Shows caring/concern for others.

04/02
H.O. was building with blocks. G. approached her and asked, "Can I play with you?" H.O. and G. played together. They built a structure which H.O. called a zoo. G. got the zoo animals from the shelf to add to the structure.
Initiates interactions with peers. Engages in cooperative symbolic play. Is able to take follower role.

04/04
Beans from the sensory table spilled on the sidewalk. G. got the dustpan and broom and swept them up.
Takes responsibility. Shows independence.

04/11
"I just love volleyball!" G. announced.
Has interests and passions. Expresses feelings clearly.

Description of Child's Cognitive Development with observations and photographs that provide evidence

**COGNITIVE DEVELOPMENT
(MATH, SCIENCE, & SOCIAL STUDIES)**

Like most five-year-olds G. is a scientist, mathematician, philosopher, and sociologist. She asks "big questions"— "I want to learn about how God made me." "How could the very first person be born if they didn't have a mommy or daddy?" She observes and experiments with the world, has many concepts, and uses both her understanding and her inquiry skills to find the answers.

Mathematics: Numeracy, Patterns, and Logic
One way that G. learns about the world is through mathematics. G. has good beginning numeracy skills. She can rote count easily to 8 and beyond, understands the principles of simple operations (counting, addition, and subtraction). She is learning the number symbols (numerals) although at times she finds distinguishing them frustrating. G. uses her awareness of shape and space in her play. She often creates spatial challenges for herself such as building with blocks and putting together puzzles. This requires being able to see parts and wholes, skills she will use when she learns to do math problems in school.

Science: Learning About the Natural World
G. is full of interest and curiosity about the natural world. She wonders about the things she finds in the garden and yard—the bugs, plants, rocks, and weather. She has been an alert participant in our formal curriculum study of seeds. She demonstrates these interests by asking questions, making logical statements, and creating interesting challenges for herself.

Social Studies: Learning About People and Their Interactions

G. is also very interested in people, in their relationships with one another and the communities in which they live. She shows this in her play and in her comments about other people. She also shows this as a participant in the classroom community. As she moves into the larger world of elementary school she will learn more about how people in larger communities work together.

G. investigates discovery bottles.

COGNITIVE DEVELOPMENT OBSERVATIONS

04/08
G. noticed a praying mantis egg sac on the fence. She brought it to the attention of a teacher and asked, "What is this?"
Shows curiosity and interest in the natural world

04/10
While eating edamame, G. announced, "Look! I found the seed coat of the edamame!"
Makes connections to study. Generalizes concepts.

04/15
"Is macaroni a seed?" G. asked. "No," a teacher responded, "But it's made from wheat and wheat is a kind of seed."
Makes connections to study. Asks relevant questions. Demonstrates curiosity.

04/15
G. worked on a 12-piece frame puzzle. She took the pieces out one-by-one and built the puzzle outside of the frame on the table.
Invents challenges for herself. Shows awareness of spatial relationships.

04/16
Playing with a math workjob G. held up a card and accurately counted 8 birds on the card (placing her finger on each bird). She looked at the cards with numerals on them but was not able to identify the 8. She began to cry.
Counts accurately to 8.

05/09

G. selected this 100 grid to play with. She found 100 stones and seeds!
Numeracy awareness.

Golden Rules

for Creating Child Portfolios

1. Decide on domains or subject areas to be used as a structure.
2. Involve families in the portfolio process from the start by explaining what you plan to do and having them participate when possible.
3. Set aside a special place for collecting portfolio evidence. It should have a section for each child and be large enough to hold larger examples of children's work.
4. Establish a time line for collecting evidence and writing summaries, including how and when the portfolio will be shared and passed on.
5. Identify evidence you will collect for each child, such as a drawing, an observation of a social interaction, an observation or taped language sample, a photograph of a block building, or a writing sample.
6. Collect core items at the same time from all children, such as a drawing or writing sample from the first week of school and another from the last week of school.
7. Create a checklist to ensure you collect observations and samples of work in every domain for each child on a regular basis.
8. Annotate each item you collect with the date and a note of its significance.
9. Have older children select examples of a favorite or "best" work to include in their portfolios.
10. Find a colleague to be your portfolio partner so that you can share, edit, and review one another's work.

of concern that need to be monitored. School-age children can begin to take a role in this process. They can consider their own strengths, interests, and weaknesses, select work samples, and add their point of view to the summary (see "Golden Rules for Creating Child Portfolios").

Digital Portfolios   Some teachers create **digital portfolios** without physical materials. Instead, photos, observations, and work samples are entered or scanned into a computer. These are then assembled into a document that can be shared electronically. Digital portfolios (sometimes called **electronic portfolios or e-portfolios**) require no physical space, storage boxes, binders, sheet protectors, toner, or photo paper. They can include video and audio clips.

The disadvantage of a digital portfolio is that it requires technical expertise and equipment on the part of both teacher and family. Lack of computer access may place it out of reach for some families. As with all forms of digital storage, the application that created the portfolio will eventually be outdated, rendering the portfolio difficult, if not impossible, to access.

Software such as PowerPoint and Keynote; "cloud-based" programs such as Smilebox, Prezi, and Pearltrees; and apps such as DRDP Portfolio, TS Gold, and Three Ring can be used to construct digital portfolios.

Using Portfolios   How do you use the portrait of a child that the portfolio provides? One of the most valuable things you can do is to use it to share your understanding of the child with families and other professionals. The portfolio itself vividly depicts the child and his or her work. It provides a focal point for a conference with the family or other professionals. The summary description that you write for the portfolio can be used as part of a narrative report given to families at a conference.

The portfolio can also be used to guide planning for the child and for the group. The individual profile includes the child's abilities, strengths, interests, and challenges. These will help you plan for this specific child. Taken together, portfolios created for all the children in a group give you a picture of what curriculum content might benefit the class as a whole.

Portfolios are not static documents. They are updated at specific times. You might, for example, begin a portfolio at the start of the year, write an initial profile at midyear, add items throughout the year, and review and update it at the end of the year. Finally, the portfolio becomes a part of the documentation that moves with the child to the next class or into the archives of his or her family.

PORTFOLIO SYSTEMS   A number of products have been designed to aid early childhood educators in creating portfolios. They systematize and guide teachers in observing, organizing, and interpreting children's work. They stand at the border between authentic assessment (based on children's natural behavior in the classroom) and standardized assessment in which a consistent, uniform (i.e., standard) method is used so that results can be compared.

All **portfolio systems** require teacher training, and all ask you to collect data about children in natural and nonintrusive ways such as by anecdotal observations, work samples, annotated photographs, or video. They provide computer-generated reports and/or lesson plans through software or online programs. The following are a few of the better-known systems.

The High/Scope Child Observation Record   The High/Scope Child Observation Record Advantage (COR Advantage) (High/Scope, 2014) is designed for assessing children from infancy through kindergarten. It covers nine content areas: Approaches to Learning; Social and Emotional Development; Physical Development and Health; Language, Literacy, and Communication; Mathematics; Creative Arts; Science and Technology; Social Studies; and (if appropriate) English Language Learning (ELL). There are a total of 34 items scored on an 8-level scale. It is designed to include children with special needs and developmental delays, as well as those who are advanced.

Activities that typically occur in a day are used for assessment. The teacher, caregiver, or family member takes a series of brief notes over several months. Scores are interpreted by a trained test administrator. There are online alternatives for recording observations and generating reports and plans. To find out more, go to the High/Scope website and click on "Assessment."

The Work Sampling System   The Work Sampling System (Meisels, Marsden, Jablon, & Dichtelmiller, 2013) is a comprehensive performance-based assessment system designed to be used from preschool through the primary years (ages 3 to 11). It consists of three components: (1) developmental guidelines and checklists, (2) portfolios, and (3) summary reports. The guidelines and checklists are designed to assist teachers in observing and documenting children's growth and progress. They are structured around developmentally appropriate activities and are based on national, state, and local curriculum standards. Each checklist covers seven domains: (1) personal and social development, (2) language and literacy, (3) mathematical thinking, (4) scientific thinking, (5) social studies, (6) the arts, and (7) physical development. Checklists, observations, and digitized work samples are entered online, and a digital portfolio is created as a means of communicating children's progress to families. They include performance and progress ratings in each domain, along with teachers' comments about the child's development. To find out more, go to the Work Sampling System Online website.

The Ounce Scale (Meisels, Dombro, Marsden, Weston, & Jewkes, 2003) is the infant–toddler companion to the Work Sampling System. It includes three components: (1) an observation record; (2) a family album in which families collect observations, photos, and mementos of their child's growth and development; and (3) a rating scale to evaluate children's growth and development. The online version generates ideas for families to try at home.

The Ounce Scale has six areas of development: (1) personal connections, (2) feelings about self, (3) relationships with other children, (4) understanding and communicating (language development), (5) exploration and problem solving, and (6) movement and coordination. Family involvement is an integral part of the Ounce Scale. It is designed to be used in group programs, home visiting programs, and family support programs. To find out more, go to the Ounce Scale Online website.

Teaching Strategies GOLD   Teaching Strategies GOLD (also called TS GOLD) is designed to accompany *The Creative Curriculum for Preschool*, Sixth Edition (Dodge, Colker, & Heroman, 2015), and *The Creative Curriculum for Infants, Toddlers & Twos*, Third Edition (Dodge, Rudick, & Berke, 2014). It is a preschool and infant–toddler observational assessment system based on skills related to development (e.g., understands and follows directions). It uses a rating scale that includes examples of ways in which children might demonstrate the skills. These range from "forerunner" behaviors (associates words with actions—says "throw" when sees a ball thrown) to "mastery" behaviors that would typically occur when children have mastered the specific skill (follows directions with more than two steps—for example, follows directions to put clay in container, wipe table, and wash hands when the activity is finished).

Teachers using Teaching Strategies GOLD use a web-based system for recording and interpreting observations that are then used for the development of portfolios and curriculum plans. Because it is tied to a curriculum manual, it makes a clear connection between assessment and planning. To find out more, go to the TeachingStrategies website and click on "Assess."

Desired Results for Children and Families   The Desired Results Developmental Profile (2015) system is designed for early care and education programs and before- and after-school programs for children, birth through 12 years of age. While it was designed for programs in California, it is freely available to educators in other states. The DRDP system was developed by WestEd for the California Department of Education Child Development Division. The system is aligned to the state's learning and development foundations for early care and education programs and the content standards for kindergarten.

Desired Results are defined as conditions of well-being for children and families. The system is based on six Desired Results (four for children and two for their families): (1) personal and social competence, (2) effective learning, (3) physical and motor competence, (4) health and safety, (5) family support of child learning and development, and (6) family goals. The system consists of assessment instruments, a parent survey, environment rating scales, and program self-evaluation. To find out more, go to the Desired Results for Children and Families website.

PORTFOLIOS IN KINDERGARTEN AND THE PRIMARY GRADES   While portfolios and the authentic assessment strategies described here are not new, they are not universally used in programs for primary school–age children, particularly in public schools. If you come to teach in a public school setting, authentic assessment may feel like a time-consuming luxury that you have difficulty justifying. Your school may require you to write report cards. With the greater emphasis on accountability and testing requirements, you may have to administer standardized tests and may feel obliged to focus on the content and process of taking tests. What should you do?

Remembering that the purpose of assessment is to improve instruction, you can observe, document, and interpret what you observe in addition to administering standardized tests and completing report cards. You can use the information you gain from authentic assessment as a way to support developmentally appropriate practices in your classroom. See Figure 5.14 to guide your creation of a portfolio if you teach in a primary school.

In their thoughtful article "Joyful Learning and Assessment in Kindergarten," Hughes and Gullo (2010) suggest some ways to think about authentic assessment to ensure both accountability and joyful, appropriate learning:

1. View assessment as a continuous process—in other words, use ongoing authentic assessment of children's activities as a vehicle for assessing their growth and informing your teaching.

Figure 5.14 Sample Portfolio Contents for a Primary School-Age Child

For each subject area (typically reading, writing, math) include:

1. Statement describing the standards, program goals, curriculum objectives, and expectations in this subject area for this grade level
2. Representative work samples/formal assessments from the beginning, middle, and end of the year
3. Key assignments and related rubrics
4. Notable work samples chosen by child or teacher
5. Observations, jottings, captioned photographs, and video related to the subject area
6. Child reflections/summaries (from first grade); e.g., "One thing I'm good at is _____. One thing I want to work on is _____."
7. Summary statement by the teacher

2. Understand assessment as a comprehensive process—in other words, realize that true assessment needs to include children learning in different ways—not just on a test.

3. Consider assessment as an integrative process—that is, authentic assessment shows the effectiveness of instruction. When children use what they have learned in lessons and self-selected activity and you document their responses, you are powerfully assessing the children and your teaching.

While this understanding does not give you more time, it provides you with a powerful justification for both developmentally appropriate practices and authentic assessment. As Hughes and Gullo (2010) note, "Appropriate assessment can lead to joyful learning and joyful teaching" (p. 59).

SHARING PORTFOLIOS   Because all families want to know how their child is growing and learning in the early childhood program, all programs have some system for sharing information with families. In most early childhood programs, conferences, along with portfolios and other forms of authentic assessment, are used to regularly report on a child's progress.

In a conference, both family members and teachers share information and plan how to mutually support the child's development. A portfolio with written summaries or separate observations, photographs, work samples, and video clips are shared at the conference. Teachers often write a report with a summary of decisions made at the conference, and this is then added to the child's file or portfolio.

In programs that do not use portfolios, written narrative reports and report cards are the primary way families receive information about their child's progress. Report cards, most commonly used in programs for primary-age children, are often criticized because they distill large quantities of information about a child into a single letter grade.

Connecting with Families

On Assessment

Families have an important role in assessment. They are not merely "the audience" to whom you present a portfolio. They have valuable contributions to make. Invite families to participate in tangible ways. Have incoming families tell the child's story, describe what the child was like last year, and share who the child is in the family today. You might want to design a questionnaire for incoming families to complete to include in a portfolio.

Documentation Panels and Presentations

Documentation panels and **documentation presentations** are ways to authentically assess and share your program and curriculum. Documentation panels are associated with the preschool programs of Reggio Emilia, Italy. They are posters in which photographs, children's work, observations, and teacher-authored text are put together to illustrate an aspect of the program.

Often (though not always), documentation panels and presentations are used to present how curriculum studies/projects led to children's growth and learning. They can also be used to show how the questions of a group of children led to investigation, how children learn by using a particular piece of equipment or participation in an activity, or how children learn from their interactions with others.

Documentation panels and presentations can be displayed in school hallways, classrooms, and entryways and shared at family and community events. However, they are more than decorations for family night. They serve as advocacy for children and early childhood programs because they powerfully illustrate the depth of children's learning within the early childhood curriculum. They demonstrate our respect for children and make visible to families and the community that "real" education is going on in early childhood programs.

Before displaying documentation panels and presentations, it is crucial that you obtain written permission from children's families. As described in the section on confidentiality, you have a legal and ethical responsibility to get the written permission of families before any sharing of documentation. Figure 5.15 shows an example of a curriculum documentation panel.

Figure 5.15 Curriculum Documentation Panel

SOURCE: Stephanie Feeney

A Quick Check 5.3

Gauge your understanding of the concepts in this section.

Standardized Assessment

Childhood is a journey, not a race.

Anonymous

We have devoted the bulk of this chapter to authentic assessment because early childhood educators have historically been committed to using it as their primary means for learning about children. In this section, we tell you about standardized assessment. An **assessment instrument** or tool (the terms are interchangeable) is a systematic means of collecting and recording information.

What Is Standardized Assessment?

In standardized assessment, all children are given the same tasks in the same way and are evaluated or scored using the same criteria. A **standardized test** is a systematic procedure for sampling a child's behavior and knowledge that summarizes the child's performance with a score. Standardized assessments are intended to objectively evaluate children's development and learning.

Items on a standardized test are carefully constructed to establish their (1) **validity**, the degree to which they measure what they claim to measure, and (2) **reliability** or consistency, how often the same or similar results are obtained. For example, a test of a child's *ability* to jump over a low object would not be *valid* if it was based on whether or not the child followed a verbal instruction to jump. Similarly the test would not be *reliable* if the height of the object to be jumped was not specified.

There are two main types of standardized tests. **Criterion-referenced tests** relate a child's performance to a pre-determined criteria (for example, whether a child can identify five letters of the alphabet). **Norm-referenced tests** compare a child's performance score to the scores of a group of same-age peers (norm group) established by administering the test to a large number of children (for example, whether the child identifies as many letters of the alphabet as most children of the same age).

Standardized assessments are used for different purposes. Some may be used to identify children who may need specialized services and to identify children with delays and disabilities for the purpose of making decisions about instruction. Other types of assessment give teachers information to assist in the design of curriculum, predict if a child will succeed in a particular grade or program, or measure what a child has learned for the purpose of assessing the child or the program.

Reflect On

Testing in Your Life as a Student

Think about experiences you have had as a student (child or adult) with testing. How did you feel when you had to take a test? Did the test benefit you? Did it have any negative effects? Have you had any experiences with testing in early childhood programs? What did you notice? Why might it be important for you, as an early childhood educator, to know about tests?

Kinds of Standardized Assessments

Standardized assessments are used for different purposes. *Screening* is used to identify children who may need specialized services. **Developmental assessments** give teachers information to assist in the design of curriculum. **Diagnostic tests** identify children with delays and disabilities for the purpose of making decisions about instruction. **Readiness tests** predict if a child will succeed in a particular grade or program. **Achievement tests** measure what a child has learned in something that has been taught for the purpose of assessing the child or the program.

SCREENING   Screening instruments are designed to identify children who may need specialized services. Screening is a relatively fast and efficient way to assess the developmental status of children. It compares a child's development to that of other children of the same age. Every child is screened, in some way, beginning at birth. Simple screening, such as observation and testing of heart rate, muscle tone, and respiration, occur in the first few minutes after birth. As children grow and develop, they are screened in the course of regular medical care.

SOURCE: Jeff Reese

Another important kind of screening occurs in school settings to identify children who might have developmental delays or medical conditions requiring correction, such as a vision or hearing impairment. Appropriate screening can bring about improvements in children's lives. Generations of children entering Head Start have been screened. Many with hearing losses, vision impairments, and other medical problems have been identified and given appropriate treatment.

Video Example 5.1: Preparing Children for Hearing and Vision Screenings

Watch the video to see an example of a hearing and vision screening conducted in a Head Start program. How did the teachers prepare the children for the screening? Why do you think they did this? What does this suggest for teachers of young children?

Educational screening instruments are relatively short, have few items, address a number of developmental areas, and can be administered and interpreted by trained professionals or trained volunteers. Screening identifies children who may have possible developmental problems that need to be looked at more carefully. Screening cannot predict future success or failure, prescribe specific treatment or curriculum, or diagnose special conditions. For this reason, it should not be used to label a child, determine individual development plans, or be used as the basis for curriculum planning.

Good developmental screening instruments are valid and reliable and focus on performance in a wide range of developmental areas (speech, understanding of language, and large and small motor skills). They involve information from families who know the child best and have important information to contribute. Screening instruments are most likely to appropriately identify children if they use the language or dialect of the child's family. Children who are not tested in their first language will not be able to communicate their true abilities. Similarly, instruments should reflect the experiences and cultural background of the children.

No screening instrument is foolproof. Some children with developmental delays will remain undetected, while others who have no serious delays will be identified as needing further evaluation. For this reason, it is important that screening instruments be chosen carefully and that great care is taken in reporting results to families.

All communities in the United States are mandated to have Child Find programs to find children who have disabilities and need services. Most schools and many preschools provide screening when children enter the program. As an early childhood educator, you may participate in choosing or administering a screening instrument and be involved in follow-up. If formal screening is not available in your school your sensitive observations can also help you identify children who need further assessment.

DEVELOPMENTAL ASSESSMENT Developmental assessments evaluate children's skills and abilities. They are designed to help you learn about children's functioning in the classroom by identifying patterns of strengths and weaknesses in a number of developmental domains. They are criterion referenced—that is, they reflect a child's degree of mastery over a skill or sequence of skills rather than comparing achievement to a norm. Developmental assessments give you information so that you can design appropriate experiences for individual children and groups. They are not meant to label children.

A developmental assessment is usually administered, interpreted, and used by program staff. It may take weeks or even months to complete. It may be administered early in the year to identify skills the child already has and then used as the basis for designing experiences and activities to help the child move to the next step. The child may be assessed again later in the year.

Developmental assessments often include guidelines for lessons and materials that are designed to develop specific skills. Although these may provide good ideas, teachers should never teach assessment items in isolation or use them as the basis for curriculum. Developmental assessment may also serve a screening purpose, especially if no other screening has been done. If a delay is noted, the child is observed, provided with additional support, and given a diagnostic evaluation if the delay persists.

A developmental assessment instrument that is appropriate for your program will have goals for children that are similar to or compatible with program goals. It will include guidelines for use, be easily administered, and give clear criteria for success. It should be administered in the language or dialect of your program's population and reflect the culture and typical experiences of the children.

DIAGNOSTIC ASSESSMENT Diagnostic tests are in-depth evaluations of development and/or learning for the purpose of identifying learning difficulties, delays, disabilities, and specific skill deficits. These serve as the basis for making decisions about instructional strategies and specialized placements and are administered by a specialist such as a speech-language pathologist or a psychologist.

Diagnostic tests are often conducted as part of the comprehensive evaluation process carried out by an interdisciplinary team which may include physicians, therapists, family members, and teachers. The team will evaluate whether a serious problem exists, what it seems to be (diagnosis), and the kind of strategies, placement, and services that would be most appropriate for the child (treatment).

READINESS AND ACHIEVEMENT TESTS   Readiness and achievement tests examine children (individually or in groups) to make judgments regarding their performance in comparison to a standard. They are standardized tests that are administered and scored using a prescribed procedure that is not a part of the regular program activity.

Readiness tests focus on a child's existing levels of skills, performance, and knowledge. Their proper purpose is to facilitate program planning. Achievement tests measure what a child has learned—the extent to which he or she has acquired information or mastered identified skills that have been taught. Achievement tests are designed to determine the effectiveness of instruction and are often used as part of program evaluation.

Concerns with Standardized Testing

The dramatic increase in the use of standardized testing of young children in recent years raises a number of concerns (Graves, 2002; Kohn, 2000; Wortham, 2011):

- It is difficult to administer tests to young children because of their developmental capabilities, so test results may not be valid or reliable.

- Tests typically measure a narrow range of academic objectives and miss objectives considered important in early childhood education.

- Testing can have a negative impact on teaching because it takes time and resources and sometimes results in the elimination of recess, play, story reading, art, music, and physical education.

- Testing can have a negative impact on children, some of whom experience stress, anxiety, and a sense of incompetence during a test.

- Tests often are biased in terms of language and cultural assumptions. When instruments do not reflect their language, experiences, and background children do not communicate their true abilities.

Standardized tests can be used to make appropriate decisions about teaching and learning, identify concerns that may require intervention for individual children, and help programs improve. When they are used to deny children opportunities or services or to assign a child to remedial or special education unnecessarily, they are being misused. This is called **high-stakes testing**, and early childhood educators strenuously object to it.

The Alliance for Childhood, NAEYC, the National Association of Early Childhood Specialists in State Departments of Education (NAECS-SDE), and the Southern Early Childhood Association (SECA) (2013) have all developed position statements on testing. You can access these online by going to the organizations' websites.

As a teacher of young children, you need to be aware of different ways of gathering and using information, know the strengths and limitations of a range of assessment options, and remain sensitive and flexible in the ways you learn about children. No single technique or instrument will disclose everything that you need to know about a child. Understanding the uses and abuses of assessment and what constitutes effective assessment practices can help you become a better teacher and an advocate for children. The following is a list of some guidelines for effective assessment.

- Be familiar with ethical guidelines related to assessment (see Appendix A NAEYC Code of Ethical Conduct P-1.5, P-1.6, P-2.2, P-2-7, P-2.8, P-4.5).
- Use multiple sources of assessment gathered over time.
- Use assessment instruments for their intended purposes—e.g. If the instrument is designed to screen for potential problems do not use it to design curriculum.
- Gather assessment from realistic settings and situations that reflect children's actual performance.
- Use appropriate assessments for the ages and other characteristics of children being assessed (e.g. use English language assessments only with children who speak English).
- Ensure that what is assessed is developmentally and educationally significant.
- Use assessment data to understand and improve teaching.
- Always link screening to follow-up.
- Ensure that assessment instruments are in compliance with professional criteria for quality.
- Limit use of individually administered, norm-referenced tests.

A Quick Check 5.4

Gauge your understanding of the concepts in this section.

 # Final Thoughts

You are becoming an early childhood educator, someone who understands and supports the development of children. You will learn about children in many ways through reading, study, practice, and discussions with others. However, the authentic assessment of children, particularly through observation, will teach you the most. The rewards of authentic assessment are great. As you hone your skills, you will discover that you feel more joy and compassion in your work, teach with enhanced skill, and communicate with greater clarity.

Your ability to understand and use the range of observation and assessment strategies discussed in this chapter will help you better understand children and make sound educational decisions. It will make you a more competent professional and provides the basis for becoming an advocate for children.

 Application Exercise 5.6 Final Reflection

 ## To Learn More

Read

Assessing and Guiding Young Children's Development and Learning (6th ed.), O. McAfee, D. Leong, & E. Bodrova (2016).

Basics of Assessment: A Primer for Early Childhood Educators, O. McAfee, D. Leong, & E. Bodrova (2004).

Creating and Presenting an Early Childhood Portfolio: A Reflective Approach, D. Friedman (2012).

The Art of Awareness: How Observation Can Transform Your Teaching (2nd ed.), D. Curtis & M. Carter (2012).

Windows on Learning: Documenting Young Children's Work (2nd ed.), J. Helm, S. Beneke, & K. Steinheimer (2008).

Visit a Website

The following agencies and organizations have websites that are relevant to the study of teachers of young children:

High Stakes Testing (Alliance for Childhood)

Early Childhood Assessment: Why, What, and How (The National Academies Press)

Where We Stand on Curriculum, Assessment, and Program Evaluation (NAEYC)

Straight Talk About Kindergarten Readiness Assessment (Defending the Early Years)

FairTest: The National Center for Fair & Open Testing

Preschool Assessment: A Guide to Developing a Balanced Approach (NIEER)

Assessing Development and Learning in Young Children (SECA)

Document Your Skill & Knowledge About Observing and Assessing Young Children in Your Professional Portfolio

Whether your professional portfolio is a physical document or a digital one you can document your skill and knowledge of observing and assessing young children in the following ways:

- A narrative observation you have written with a short statement describing how you used or might use the information from this observation to meet this child's needs.

- A structured observation you completed on a child or group of children with a short statement describing how you used or might use the information to meet children's needs.

- A photograph of a child's portfolio you created with a short paragraph explaining how you used or might use the portfolio to share information in a conference or guide planning for the child.

 Shared Writing 5.1 Ethical Responsibilities in Observation and Assessment

Chapter 6
Relationships and Guidance

Nothing I have ever learned of value was taught to me by an ogre. Nothing do I regret more in my life than that my teachers were not my friends. Nothing ever heightened my being or deepened my learning more than being loved.

J. T. DILLON

 Chapter Learning Outcomes:

6.1 Describe the meaning of the term *child guidance* and discuss the ways that positive relationships form its foundation.

6.2 Explain appropriate goals of child guidance.

6.3 Identify communication tools that promote positive child guidance.

6.4 Describe appropriate strategies for guiding groups of young children.

172

6.5   Choose effective strategies for dealing with inappropriate behavior.

6.6   Discuss methods for managing challenging behaviors.

Child guidance is about supporting young children as they learn to build relationships and about helping them learn the difficult skills required to direct and manage their own behavior. When you guide young children, you lead them toward understanding themselves and developing self-control. You help them understand the effects of their behavior on others, and you teach them the skills they need for engaging in satisfying relationships—both with peers and adults.

In this chapter, we discuss strategies for guiding children in ways that will help them build these important life skills.

The Foundations of Child Guidance

You are learning about children's development and the ways it affects their behavior. You will learn to use this specialized understanding of child development to guide your expectations about how children should behave and it may enhance your pleasure in sharing time and experiences with them. Early childhood teachers value and enjoy childhood behaviors and believe children have a right to be childlike. They provide supportive guidance based on the understanding that children learn through experiences appropriate to age, and to individual temperament, learning style, culture, and family. They know that children learn social skills through being part of a group and by interacting with people and they understand that children are careful observers of the adults in their lives. Skilled teachers treat children with respect and welcome them into a classroom community. When you engage with children in these ways, you guide them to become cooperative, productive people.

The Meaning of Child Guidance

Child guidance refers to the practices that adults use to help children learn to choose acceptable behaviors and to understand the feelings of others and of themselves. Early childhood educators often use the term *child guidance* rather than *behavior management* or *discipline*. Guidance means assisting or leading another person to reach a destination. A guide accompanies others in order to show points of interest and to explain meaning. Effective early childhood teachers guide young children, helping them to learn to control and choose their actions based on what they are learning about living in a community and about their own values and beliefs.

In contrast, **punishment** teaches children to behave on the basis of fear rather than on inner control or self-discipline. Teachers and other adults use punishment based on the belief that children will stop unwanted behaviors in order to avoid pain, loneliness, or humiliation. While punishment may achieve immediate results, it will not teach children alternative behaviors or help them learn what should be done in similar future situations (Gartrell, 1987). Additionally, although children who have been physically punished may behave appropriately when an adult is watching them, at later times they tend to show increased aggressive behavior (Honig, 1985). Physical punishment demonstrates that it is okay to hurt someone if you are big or powerful enough. It damages children's emotional well-being and violates their trust in the teacher–child relationship. It should never be used in any form in early childhood programs. Child guidance, however, focuses on teaching children how to control themselves rather than on adults controlling children. When you use appropriate child guidance, children feel secure and can learn important life skills, such as problem solving, cooperation, and empathy.

Reflect On

Guidance and Punishment in Your School Experiences

How was misbehavior dealt with in the schools you attended? What strategies were used? Were they effective? What were your feelings about them? Recall an incident in which you were punished in school. What happened? How did you feel? What were the effects on you? What do you wish had happened? How did the teachers' ways of handling problems affect how you felt about your teachers and school?

Relationships

Warm, positive relationships between young children and the important adults in their lives are the foundation for healthy growth and learning. As an early childhood teacher, you will come to understand that the relationships you build with each child are your most effective guidance tools. When children experience genuine and caring relationships with their teachers, they learn the social skills necessary to become engaged members of the classroom community, and their teachers learn to appreciate their individual strengths and challenges. Within this safe relationship, both children and teachers grow to like and trust one another. When children trust their teachers and feel that they are liked and respected by them, they use teachers' behaviors as models for how to interact with others. They accept the teacher's guidance for how to respond appropriately to their strong emotions.

The relationship between child and teacher is a significant factor in how children feel about school and in their later academic success. Research supports the fact that "children who develop warm, positive relationships with their kindergarten teachers are more excited about learning, more positive about coming to school, more self-confident and achieve more in the classroom" (National Scientific Council on the Developing Child, 2004). Although most young children enter early childhood programs with lively and inquisitive minds, only some come to feel successful as students and to regard education as a rewarding experience. Children are most likely to retain

SOURCE: Jeff Reese

their eagerness and curiosity when they experience teachers who appreciate them and who base their actions on knowledge about how children grow and learn.

When children experience relationships with adults who meet their needs and respond to them with care, they build feelings of trust and learn that the world is a safe and welcoming place. Trust is foundational to all social and emotional growth. Many researchers have validated the importance of adult–child attachment for the mental health of infants and very young children. Work by Howes and Ritchie (2002) applies the premises of attachment theory (Bowlby, 1982) to teacher–child relationships. These researchers stress that for children of all ages and life circumstances, a trusting relationship with the teacher is necessary for children to learn. Further, their research indicates that the quality of the attachment relationship between teachers and children significantly influences children's long- and short-term development. When children trust their teachers, they are able to use them as resources to support their learning. In classrooms where teachers create strong teacher–child relationships and support positive peer interactions, children are more likely to behave in socially acceptable ways. In these settings, "classroom management" is about positive relationships rather than finding ways to manage conflict and suppress difficult behaviors (Howes & Ritchie, 2002).

Relationships are built on the small, shared individual experiences you have with children each day. Reading a story, feeding the guinea pig, discussing the planets, digging in the sand, taking a walk around the yard to look for bugs, or singing a song together—these are the kinds of experiences from which relationships grow. The most effective early childhood educators we know genuinely enjoy their interactions with children and gain children's cooperation without demanding unquestioning obedience. They see children as partners, not adversaries, and view the process of guiding children, through pleasant and difficult times, as central to their job. They are careful to promote positive relationships with and between children, families, and staff. This perspective is the basis of effective child guidance.

Understanding and Honoring Differences

Each child and teacher brings to the classroom a unique set of life experiences. Your own family, your past experiences, and your individual characteristics will influence how you relate to young children and the choices you make about how to guide their behavior. Your understanding of the diverse values and beliefs that families hold and your awareness of the primacy of the family in the child's life will play a key role in your ability to guide children appropriately.

Connecting with Families

About Guidance Practices

Families use a variety of ways to teach their children about their expectations and how they want them to behave. Some of these may be similar to what you know about and understand; others may be quite different. Here are some ways you can get to know more about their values and discipline practices:

- Make time for a get-to-know-you meeting during the child's first days and ask them about their discipline methods; share ways that you handle inappropriate behaviors in your classroom.
- Ask what social skills they most wish their child to master and invite them to share ideas for how you can support them in teaching these.
- Include a question in your enrollment packet asking families to tell you about ways they handle inappropriate behavior at home.
- Plan family meetings around discussion of common challenges, such as bedtime, meals, saying no, and so on. Ask for their input regarding what the topic should be.
- Invite professionals with expertise in child guidance or knowledge of the cultures of the families in your program to lead a family meeting or to offer a parenting class.

Families' discipline and guidance practices reflect their values about what is important for children to learn and their beliefs about how individuals should behave. Families most often choose guidance strategies based on what they have been taught by their parents and grandparents. These strategies vary widely. While they are different from one another, no one is better than another; all support children within the context of the family and its beliefs.

In some families and cultures, respect for authority is a core value. Families with this value expect children to do what they are told promptly, politely, and without questions. Their children often learn that obedience is expected and disobedience is punished. Other families value individual decision making and teach their children to question authority. Their children may experience that making choices and asking questions are behaviors that are expected and rewarded. Some families value the interdependence of group members. They may teach their children that conformity is important and that most decisions should be made based on what is best for the group—the family, the classroom, or the society. These families may discourage independence and engage in practices that limit children's autonomous actions. For example, they might hand-feed or carry an older toddler or dress a preschooler who is able to manage this task. Children from these families may develop self-help skills later than children from families who place a high value on independence.

Just like the families of the children in your class, you have values and beliefs about child rearing. Your family and your culture have taught you expectations for children's behavior and adults' roles in guiding them. You bring these values, beliefs, and expectations into the classroom with you, and they influence your expectations of children and the teaching and guidance practices you use.

Reflect On

Your Family's Expectations

What did your family expect of you when you were a child? How did your family want children to behave in public places and in gatherings with other adults? What did they expect from you at school? How did they let you know when they were pleased with what you did? How did they communicate disapproval?

At times, what you believe or what you have been taught (and are learning) about child guidance will be in conflict with the beliefs and values of children's families. In these instances, it is important to remember that competent early childhood educators learn to honor the values of the families of all children in their care. This does not mean that you will engage in practices that you believe to be inappropriate or unethical. Rather, you will listen thoughtfully when families tell you their views, and you will respectfully share your own. When teachers are insensitive to the differences in values between home and school, children may receive messages that indicate to them that their families' ways are "wrong" or "bad." All children deserve to feel that their family is respected and valued by their teachers.

Two-and-a-half-year-old Ajut has been enrolled in a full-day program for 4 months. Despite his teacher's warm overtures, he has not spoken directly to her. She has heard him speak to other children during playtime. When his teacher looks at him, Ajut looks away quickly and resists her invitations to talk or to play with her.

You are likely to have children in your classroom whose families have taught them behaviors that are different from the ones that are familiar to you. Because they are unfamiliar, these differences in behavior styles and ways of relating to others may make you feel uncomfortable or upset. As a teacher, you may encounter differences such as those described in Table 6.1.

Use these examples, along with others you will experience, to think about your acceptance of differences and to increase your awareness of family practices that feel

Table 6.1 Children's School Responses to Family Guidance Practices

What Families May Do at Home	How Children May Respond at School	Some Ways to Honor This Difference
Give directions; discourage or forbid questions Require unquestioning obedience	Confused when you ask them to make choices Unwilling to express personal wants or to ask questions Test limits often	Offer two options: "Do you want red or yellow paper?" Describe what you think a child may be wondering: "It looks like you are wondering why he had the first turn." Expect limit testing; be patient. Point out that home and school expectation can be different: "Sometimes we do things differently at school than at home. That can be confusing."
Expect children to ask questions Encourage children to make independent decisions	Question adult decisions and reasons Take initiative; may seem to "get into everything"	Explain reasons for the decisions that you make: "Children cannot use these large scissors because they may hurt themselves. Adults have larger hands and can control the scissors better." Offer many opportunities for exploration; encourage curiosity.
Use discipline that is harsh and may include spanking or other kinds of physical punishment	Appear to ignore or disregard verbal requests	Make eye contact and ensure that the child is attending when giving verbal directions. Ask the child to restate your words so you can check for comprehension: "Tell me what I said that I need you to do next."
Have very few limits for or expectations of young children	Distressed or confused when told "no" by adults	Clearly explain reasons. Stay with children while they follow through with requests: "I know you don't want to go inside yet. It's lunchtime now. I'll hold your hand, and we will walk in together."
May see young children as "babies" and enjoy interacting with them in this manner	Stressed and upset when separating from family members Limited self-help skills Resist or be upset when teachers expect them to feed, dress, and/or toilet independently	Work with families to establish a daily "good-bye" ritual. Remind children often that their parent will come back. State the expected return time: "Dad will be here to pick you up right after nap time today." Let them watch as other children dress, wash, and toilet. Gradually invite them to participate in these tasks. Do part of the task, then ask them to finish up: "I put your sock on your toes; now you can pull it up over your foot and ankle."
Expect independence	Difficulty sharing space, materials, or play activities Act without permission (e.g., leave the classroom or take food from serving bowls or other's plates)	Have some "alone" spaces in your classroom where children can choose solitary play. Ask children to identify which toys they can share with others before a conflict begins. Establish "teacher jobs" and "children jobs": "Your job is to feed the fish this morning; mine is to get the juice out of the refrigerator for snack."
Express feelings openly and often	Yell, scream, or throw a tantrum	Provide words to use to express strong feelings: "You are really mad. You can let me know that with words."
Encourage self-restraint and control of expression	Appear shy, reticent, and quiet Reluctant to speak in a group Unwilling to share ideas or opinions	Describe what you think a child is feeling and wanting: "It looks like Julie would like to play in the pretend center. She likes to rock the babies." Never force group sharing; invite children to share in small groups.
Encourage strong sense of family pride, honor, and respect	Extremely fearful when they feel they may have misbehaved or disappointed an adult; have a high need for adult approval	Emphasize that everyone makes mistakes sometimes; point out small successes and invite them to self-evaluate their progress: "Looks like you tried hard; that's higher than you jumped last time." "What are some things you like about your project?"
Discourage children from calling attention to themselves; require children to demonstrate a humble or modest attitude	Reluctant to speak in group settings; uncomfortable when called on by the adult	Avoid asking the child to respond in a group while everyone waits. Encourage conversation by all children during meals and other small-group times. Describe nonverbal communications: "I really love this spaghetti. Your face tells me that you might like it too."
Use language that may appear to "put children down" or avoid emphasizing their strengths and skills as a way to avoid bragging (e.g., "my lazy daughter")	Uncomfortable when praised or acknowledged	Avoid praising children. Speak to these children privately and express pleasure about their successes in a low-key manner. Ask them to tell you something they like about their work.
Insist that children assertively defend themselves or their property	Strike out at children who infringe on what they perceive as their personal possessions or space	Let children know it is never okay to hurt others and that you won't let others hurt them. Explain that you will help them protect toys, materials, or space that is being taken unfairly. Give them words to say to other children: "I won't let you hit Jeremy. Tell him you had the truck first and that you don't want to share it right now." Talk with families about the importance of preventing any kind of aggression at school. Ask them to help you think of ways that their child can be assertive without hurting others.

uncomfortable to you. Engaging in dialogues with families about their child-rearing beliefs and practices will help you build relationships and expand your understanding of appropriate guidance practices.

Knowledge of Development

You will base your expectations for children's behavior and your choices of guidance practices on the age and developmental stage as well as the individual circumstances of each child. Just as you would not expect a 1-year-old to ride a bicycle, you should not expect a 5-year-old to be able to sit quietly at a desk for an extended period of time.

All early childhood practitioners need to learn to tell the difference between an unacceptable behavior and one that may be annoying but is age appropriate. The following behaviors are typical, although they may be trying to adults:

Infants:	Sob when parent is out of sight
	Refuse to communicate with unfamiliar adults
Toddlers:	Joyfully empty containers
	Respond to most requests with a forceful "No!"
	Treat all objects as "mine"
Preschoolers:	Resist adult schedules; dawdle through routines
	Do not always tell the truth
	Tell others, "You're not my friend" or "You can't play"
School-age:	Become very competitive; love to be the winner
	Boss other children
	Say, "You can't make me" or "I hate you"

When you offer a toddler many opportunities to fill and dump or provide school-age children with chances to be leaders and to make decisions, you are using guidance practices that reflect your knowledge of child development.

A Quick Check 6.1

Gauge your understanding of the concepts in this section.

Goals for Guidance

Skilled early childhood teachers reflect carefully on their goals for children. They think about long- and short-term goals and consciously choose practices that are congruent with these goals.

Long-Term Goals

Most teachers will agree that the following are appropriate long-term goals for child guidance:

- To foster social and emotional intelligence
- To build inner control, self-discipline, and the ability to self-regulate
- To develop positive self-identity and resiliency
- To teach the skills needed to be an effective member of a community

It is important to make sure there is a good fit between what you actually do in daily practice and your long-term goals for children. For example, if you handle conflicts over toys by taking the disputed toy away, children will learn that adults solve problems; they do not learn how to negotiate or share materials. This may conflict with long-term goals of building inner control and developing skills for living in a community. Without this awareness, you can accumulate a grab bag of techniques that "work" (i.e., control immediate behavior problems) but that fail to teach the skills needed to meet long-term goals for children.

SOCIAL AND EMOTIONAL INTELLIGENCE   A long-term goal of guidance is to help children develop social and emotional intelligence. **Emotional intelligence** is the understanding of feelings, both one's own and those of others, and the ability to use this knowledge to guide thinking and decision making. **Social intelligence** is the ability to understand what others are doing, thinking, and feeling and to respond to that understanding in a socially effective manner (Livergood, n.d.). This includes the ability to understand the social cues of others, to resolve conflicts, and to engage in **prosocial behaviors**—behaviors that demonstrate empathy, cooperation, and **altruism**.

Effective guidance practices promote the growth of social and emotional intelligence by supporting children's growing abilities to:

- Identify their feelings and the feelings of others
- Demonstrate care and concern for others
- Develop warm and caring relationships
- Handle challenging situations constructively

Young children are just learning to deal with their own feelings and to read and respond to the feelings of others. Consequently, you will want to develop ways to help children learn to calm themselves when angry, make friends with other children, resolve conflicts successfully, and make socially appropriate choices (CASEL Forum Report, 2011).

Reflect On

Your Long-Term Goals for Children

What do you feel are the most important long-term social and emotional goals for educators to have for the young children they teach? Why did you choose these? How might they affect the types of guidance practices that you use?

Sometimes, teachers lament the amount of time they need to spend helping children learn to deal with upsets, to resolve social problems, and to cooperate. They may view this as time away from planned learning experiences. Teachers who value social and emotional learning and who recognize the importance of these skills believe that they are an integral part of the curriculum of equal if not greater importance than literacy, math, or other curriculum areas. Findings from a large study conducted in 2011 indicate that when children receive specific instruction in social and emotional competence, they not only demonstrate significantly improved skills in these areas but also show meaningful gains in academic achievement (Durlak, Weissberg, Dymnicki, Taylor, & Schellinger, 2011).

Researchers and early childhood specialists at the Center on Social and Emotional Foundations for Early Learning (CSEFEL) have identified a number of classroom practices that teach these skills and promote positive behavior. This model is based on the principle that when teachers put the majority of their time and energy into foundational relationships and a supportive classroom environment, less will need to be expended on more intensive intervention. In fact, research has shown that only about 4% of the children in a classroom or program will require more intensive support when foundational relationships and classroom environment are attended to (Sugai et al., 2000). Figure 6.1 illustrates this model.

Figure 6.1 The Teaching Pyramid for Supporting Social Competence and Preventing Challenging Behavior in Young Children

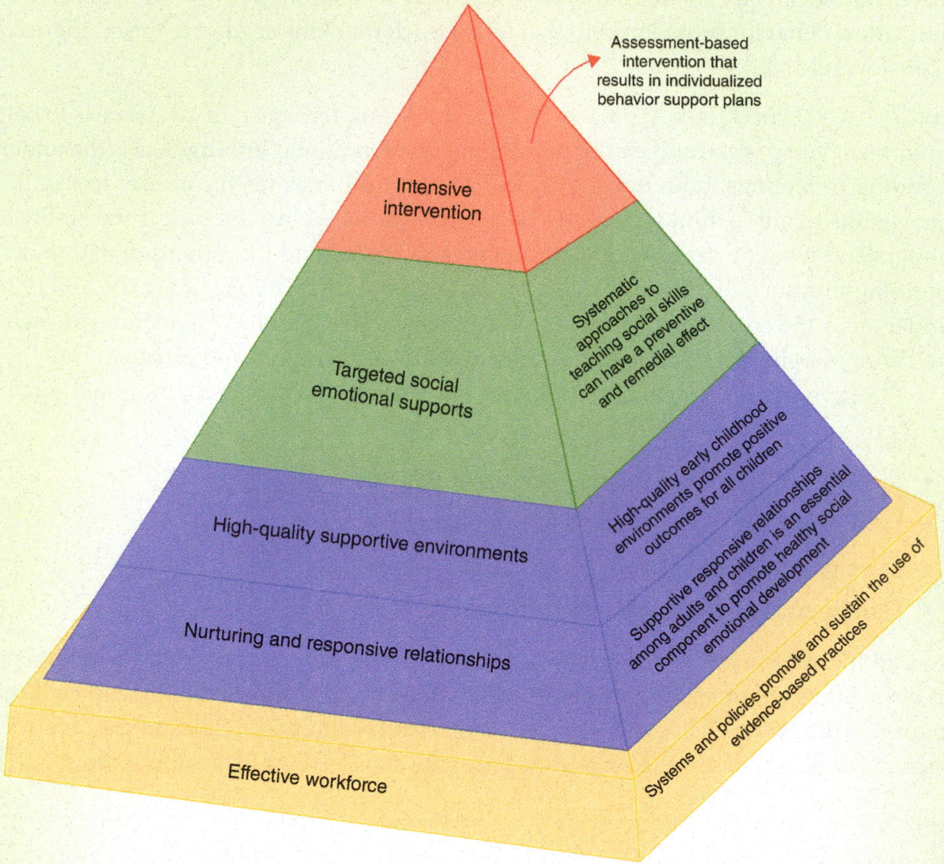

This model is based on the principle that when teachers put the majority of their time and energy into the foundational tiers—relationships and classroom environment—less will need to be expended on the ascending levels.

Foundation—Effective Workforce: The foundation of all succeeding tiers of the pyramid is the relationships that teachers build with young children. Warm and positive relationships are the key to supporting children's growing ability to relate to others in a positive and cooperative manner, and to preventing negative behavior.

Tier 1—Positive Relationships: The foundation of all succeeding tiers of the pyramid is the relationships that teachers build with young children. Warm and positive relationships are the key to supporting children's growing ability to relate to others in a positive and cooperative manner and to preventing negative behavior.

Tier 2—Supportive Classroom Environments: The ways teachers structure the physical space, the daily schedule, classroom routines, and the methods used to present curriculum all have a strong influence on children's sense of self-confidence and their growing ability to manage their emotions and behavior competently.

Tier 3—Social and Emotional Teaching Strategies: Many young children need specific instruction in ways to manage their emotions and to interact cooperatively with others. Teachers develop activities and select literature that helps children identify and talk about emotions. Positive communication strategies and skills for cooperative play and problem solving are a prominent part of the planned curriculum.

Tier 4—Intensive Individualized Intervention: The smallest portion of the pyramid, this illustrates the use of carefully planned intervention strategies for children whose behavior is challenging. Teachers, families, and administrators work with a trained behavior support specialist to develop a plan for teaching the child socially acceptable behaviors to replace behaviors that are challenging.

SOURCE: Center on the Emotional Foundations for Early Learning at Vanderbilt University.

SELF-REGULATION   **Self-regulation** is another long-term goal of guidance. It is the ability to control impulses—to stop doing something or to start doing something, even when one prefers not to do so. Self-regulation is a part of a set of skills referred to as **executive functions**, the mental processes that enable us to plan, focus attention, remember instructions, and juggle multiple tasks successfully. Children aren't born with these abilities. As their brains develop and when they experience positive relationships with others, they very gradually develop the skills needed to control their impulses and to choose acceptable behaviors.

Self-regulation is different from obedience; people who are genuinely self-regulated control their behavior whether or not someone else is watching. Children who have learned to self-regulate can think about the possible consequences of an action and choose appropriately. Self-regulation includes social/emotional skills, such as waiting for a turn or sharing a toy, as well as cognitive abilities, such as paying attention during circle time or recalling information about a story. Researchers have verified that self-regulation skills affect children's abilities to be successful in school. Social-emotional self-regulation allows children to follow rules and get along with others, and cognitive self-regulation allows children to solve problems and pay attention to cognitive tasks (Bodrova & Leong, 2007).

Self-regulation and executive function emerge as a result of both maturation and experiences in which children learn to take deliberate actions, plan ahead, and consciously control their responses. (Bronson, 2000; Bodrova & Leong, 2008). When children have repeated positive experiences with nurturing adults, their brains show stronger neural connections in the frontal cortex, the region of the brain that determines executive function (Galinksy, 2010). There are particular practices you can use to support the development of self-regulation at each stage of development (see Table 6.2).

Intentionally teaching young children skills for self-regulation along with helping them develop social and emotional intelligence has been shown to significantly influence children's readiness for elementary school and to be foundational for developing cognitive skills (Hyson, 2002; Mitchell & Glossop, 2005, cited in Willis & Schiller, 2011).

Reflect On

Self-Regulation

Think about a time when you felt very angry. Did you control or regulate your feelings? How? What were the consequences? What experiences have you had that have helped you learn to control your feelings?

SELF-IDENTITY AND RESILIENCY   Another long-term guidance goal is to help children develop a positive **self-identity**—how they define and feel about themselves (Epstein, 2014). As children grow and have experiences with others, they develop a set of beliefs about who they are based on their perceptions of how others see them. This is sometimes referred to as **self-concept** and includes perceptions of one's physical self, social and cognitive qualities, and competence. Self-identity or self-concept is greatly influenced by the "mirror" held up by significant people—family members, other important adults, and peers. It begins to develop in the first days of life and continues to grow and change.

Families are children's first and most influential sources of information about who they are. It is from families that children begin to establish their identities as individuals of a gender, race, and culture. As they get older, messages from peers become important to children's emerging concepts of themselves. When most of the messages that children receive indicate that they are valued and competent, they begin to build a sense of

themselves and to motivate learning and good behavior. But there is research that indicates that the consistent use of praise actually has the reverse effect; when children are praised repeatedly, they may become anxious about their ability to perform and may be less likely to repeat positive actions (Hitz & Driscoll, 1988; Kohn, 2001).

During a 1-hour classroom visit, one of us heard more than 30 instances where adults praised children. The teachers used phrases such as "I like how nicely Desiree is waiting for circle time," "You're our best cleaner, Bernie," "You're a great artist, Lorenzo," "Madison, that's a beautiful drawing," "Great building, Danisha," and, repeatedly, "Good job. Good job. Good job!"

Praise is often not genuine. Sometimes teachers use it not as a way to express genuine acknowledgment of a child's actions but rather as a means to manipulate future behavior or the behavior of other children (Meece & Soderman, 2010). The teacher who commented on Desiree's "nice sitting" was probably more interested in using words to encourage other children to come to circle than on giving Desiree meaningful feedback about her behavior. In other instances, praise is intended to encourage children to repeat a positive action in the future, not as a sincere acknowledgment of effort or skill. Used this way, praise becomes an external reward.

If your goal is to help children build self-regulation skills, then praise is generally not an effective practice. Praise can teach children to act to receive approval from adults, not because they feel an action is correct or worthy. In some cases, children become so dependent on external evaluation from adults that they can't determine what they like or value. We have known children who ask for adult approval constantly: "Do you like my picture?" "Am I climbing good?" "Am I a good helper, too?" These children appear to be "praise junkies," dependent on praise as the only way to feel good about themselves.

Several studies have indicated that although praise may encourage children to continue an activity while an adult is watching, children are less likely to continue the activity when the adult leaves or to repeat the activity in the future (Kohn, 2001). Rather than increasing children's commitment to positive behavior, praise encourages children to find ways to get future verbal "goodies" from important adults. Less obvious but equally important is the fact that praise can diminish children's sense of pride and self-worth. Those who are praised excessively may lose the ability to evaluate their own progress or to feel intrinsic delight in an activity.

Praise is like the large pink icing rose in the center of a cake. It is appealing, and at first bite its sweetness tastes wonderful. A couple more bites still might taste good, but it quickly becomes overly sweet. It has only one simple flavor; we soon tire of it, and if we eat very much at any one time, we might even feel slightly ill. It may provide some quick energy, but it provides no nourishment and doesn't support growth or health. Encouragement, on the other hand, is like a warm soup. It has many complex flavors, and eating it gives us nutrients we need to feel strong and to have sustained energy. While it may not have the initial appeal of the sweet icing, its long-term effects strengthen us and encourage our growth. Teachers use encouragement when they use R&R statements to comment on children's efforts ("You spent such a long time working on that drawing.") rather than evaluating the product ("That picture is just beautiful."). Encouragement helps children identify their own strengths and interests ("It seems like you enjoy building very tall towers.") rather than relying on adults' assessments ("You are one of the best builders."). For a comparison of encouragement versus praise, see Figure 6.3.

I-MESSAGES "Listen!" "Don't!" "Stop that!" "That's not nice!" Some of the language that we hear often in classrooms does little to help children learn positive behavior. Learning to effectively communicate when there is a problem with a child's behavior is a skill that you will need on your first day working with children. An **I-message** (Gordon, 2003) is one way to communicate concerns without blaming the

Figure 6.3 Differences between Encouragement and Praise

Encouragement is . . .	Praise is . . .
Specific:	General:
"Thank you. You helped pick up all the blocks and put them away where they belonged."	*"That's beautiful."*
Descriptive and nonjudgmental:	Making a judgment:
"You did the pilot puzzle. It's a tricky one."	*"You're a great puzzle solver."*
About feelings and motivation:	About external products or rewards:
"It's really satisfying when you finish a painting that you have worked on so hard, isn't it?"	*"I'll put the best paintings on the bulletin board to show the parents."*
Thoughtful and individual:	The same for all and holds little meaning for the individual:
"That was the first time you slid down the twisting slide by yourself."	*"Good job."*
Encouragement focuses on . . .	**Praise focuses on . . .**
The process, experience, and effort:	The person or outcome:
"You really worked hard on scrubbing that table."	*"That's the best job of cleanup I ever saw."*
Growth of the individual:	Comparison of children:
"You wrote the names of everyone in our class. I remember when you could only write your name."	*"You're the best printer in our class."*
Self-evaluation:	Judgment from others:
"It looks like you feel proud of that picture."	*"I love your picture!"*
"How did you feel about finishing your science project?"	*"Good work!"*

child. An I-message invites a child to participate in solving a problem rather than telling him or her what to do.

An effective I-message has three elements:

1. It states the specific condition or behavior that is problematic.
2. It expresses your feelings.
3. It explains how the behavior affects you.

I-messages communicate that, although you don't like a particular behavior or situation, you trust that the child is capable of dealing with it. Often, the behavior will stop once the child knows that it causes a problem. The order and wording of an I-message is not as critical as communicating the three pieces—behavior, feelings, and effect—and the implied invitation to the child to find a mutually acceptable solution. For example, if a child is disruptive at story time, you might use one of the following I-messages:

"It's hard for everyone to hear when there's so much noise."

"I feel frustrated when I have to shout so others can hear the story."

"I'm disappointed. This is a great story, but there's too much noise for everyone to hear it."

A more common response might be to use a directive: "Stop talking! You are bothering others. You have to leave the circle." Such a "you-message" denies the child the opportunity to solve the problem. It focuses on the child in a blaming, shaming, or evaluating manner and imposes a solution on the child rather than allowing him or her to solve the problem.

When you use an I-message, be careful to avoid overstating your feelings or attempting to make the child feel guilty with your statement. Use feeling words that accurately state your feelings but avoid strong statements telling children that they "hurt your feelings" or "made you sad," as these tend to be more manipulative than expressive of a true emotion.

Children will learn to use I-messages as a way to communicate with one another when they hear this model used frequently. The use of I-messages is helpful in teaching children to resolve problems and conflicts with one another. Teachers who use R&R statements and active listening create a foundation for the use of I-messages because they have modelled ways to describe situations and label feelings.

Reflect On

Your Relationship with a Teacher

Recall a teacher with whom you had a positive relationship. Recall another teacher relationship that you felt was negative. What contributed to your positive or negative feelings about each teacher? How did each teacher communicate with you? How did these relationships affect how you felt about teachers and school?

RESPONSIVE CAREGIVING: THE ART OF COMMUNICATING WITH INFANTS AND TODDLERS Communicating with very young children requires some particular skills and strategies in addition to those we have discussed. When you relate to infants and toddlers, you communicate with your whole being—voice, body, and heart. A relationship with an infant involves being attentive and responsive by returning coos, smiles, and babbles. The best educators of infants relate to even the youngest child with respect.

> *"Time for lunch," Darcy says to 8-month-old Reiko, who is sitting on the carpet exploring a box of rattles. Reiko looks briefly at Darcy, then returns her attention to the rattles. Darcy walks over to her, stoops, and watches her quietly for a few minutes. "You're really busy listening to those sounds," she tells her. She watches for another minute and then says, "It's lunchtime now. I'm going to pick you up and take you to wash hands, then eat lunch. We have carrots today—your favorite!" Darcy watches as Reiko looks up and reaches an arm toward her. "You're ready—up we go," says Darcy, lifting Reiko to her shoulder.*

Darcy was careful to acknowledge that the play Reiko was engaged in was interesting. She made sure to let her know what was coming and gave her time to respond before lifting her. In play as well as during care routines, skilled infant–toddler teachers give time and attention to communicating with each child. They learn each child's communication style and respond appropriately. It is impossible to "spoil" a baby by responding to his or her needs—something some adults fear. When you learn the meaning of a cry, a gurgle, a gesture, or a stare, you know what is needed and can act appropriately. This responsive caregiving tells the baby that you care about her and that her needs and wishes are valued. Responsive caregiving does not mean jumping at every cry. Instead, by knowing the infant and his or her typical behavior, you can acknowledge feelings and create routines and activities that meet the baby's needs.

Speak to infants and toddlers as you would speak to other people you know and care about. Although the conversation may be one-sided, the relationship is mutual. Just as you do with older children, build a relationship based on the things you do together. Learn to read nonverbal messages and to acknowledge and interpret their meanings. As their babbles and sounds increase, your language will provide a scaffold for the sounds to become talk. Not only does this verbal interaction build relationships, but it is also the way that human beings learn language.

The I-messages that we discussed earlier are useful with infants and toddlers as well as preschool- and school-age children. For example, a toddler with minimal language who pulls your hair can be told "Ouch!"—with an exaggerated sad expression— "It hurts when you pull my hair," followed by a gentle guiding of the hand in a patting motion and a smile: "I like it when you touch me gently." When a toddler behaves in an unacceptable way or an infant's action must be stopped, teachers who understand development will gently and clearly explain what must be done and why: "I can't let you pull my hair. That hurts me. Here, you can pull the raggedy doll's hair." Do the children understand? Infants and toddlers, like the rest of us, understand kindness and respect; understanding the words will come later.

✓ **A Quick Check 6.3**

Gauge your understanding of the concepts in this section.

Guiding Groups

Guiding a group of young children, sometimes called *classroom management*, is an art that requires knowledge, skill, sensitivity, and self-confidence. Like any art, it is one that you will acquire through learning and experience, and it becomes easier with practice. As your skill increases and you become comfortable using some of the strategies discussed in this chapter, you will find that you will need to devote less of your time to "managing" and will be able to spend more of your time focusing on relationships and learning experiences.

Use Authority

By virtue of your role as an educator, society confers on you a certain authority—the right to exercise power, make decisions, take actions, give commands, and expect obedience. The most obvious source of this authority is adulthood. You are larger, stronger, and older, so most children acknowledge your right to give direction. Although authority is given by society as part of your role, it is strengthened by your education, knowledge, skills, and commitment.

You have probably experienced teachers, bosses, family members, or others in authority who treated you fairly and kindly. It is also likely that you have encountered those who were harsh, punitive, or unfair. You may have experienced people in authority who were unclear and inconsistent, unable to provide direction about what you were supposed to do. When adults use authority in ways that are unkind or ambiguous, children feel confused, upset, and sometimes resentful and angry. Early childhood educators should strive to use authority humanely, fairly, and with clarity. We call this use of authority *authoritative* to distinguish it from unfair or harsh *authoritarian* uses of power.

> *In his first weeks as a practicum student in a kindergarten class, Miguel actively engaged in play with the children. On the playground, he took the role of the chasing monster, resulting in many giggles and calls of "Catch me, catch me, Mr. Miguel." His tickles and jokes and high-fives were enthusiastically welcomed by the children, and he became their favorite play partner. In sharing his experiences in his college seminar, Miguel expressed frustration. While the children were delighted to play with him, they ignored his directions and seemed to completely disregard his requests for them to engage in academic tasks.*

Becoming comfortable with authority is one of the first issues that any prospective educator faces. Our college students often struggle with authority as they learn to work with children. The way they approach authority involves their values and expectations. Some try to deny their authority. Like Miguel, they behave as if they were one of the kids and become confused and frustrated when children do not respect them or cooperate with them. Others expect children to grant them authority simply because they are the teacher. They make demands without first building a respectful relationship and are surprised when children are rebellious and resistant.

Authority that is authentic and lasting is based on mutual respect; it is used wisely and with compassion. There is no single right way to exercise authority and no one way that is appropriate for each age and individual. Some early childhood teachers invite children's cooperation with a shared joke and a smile, and children seem delighted to join them. This practice may be particularly effective with boys, who tend to respond well to judiciously applied humor. Other teachers calmly state appropriate expectations in a friendly, no-nonsense voice and gain willing compliance. Still others almost silently step in to redirect children with a word or gesture that prevents a blow, encourages a friendship, or assists in a routine. Each of these approaches is grounded in respect and knowledge of children.

> *Dana, a student teacher, is working with a small group of children to solve math problems. Across the room, Wayne, age 6, picks up a folder and shouts gleefully as it flies across the room. Dana leaves the group and reminds him, "We don't toss things in school. You are bothering the other children."*
>
> *Later that morning, Wayne says to another child, "C'mon!" as he grabs a LEGO from the table and runs with it to the library area, giggling and looking back at Dana, who is calling, "We don't do that."*

Your first experiences in trying to manage a group of children are likely to be somewhat challenging. Children will test you to find out what they can expect from you. They may intentionally "misbehave" to see how you will respond. With experience, teachers usually become more clear about their expectations and communicate them with kind authority. They clearly state what is expected rather than telling children what not to do or offering vague messages like Dana used in the vignette above when she told the children, "We don't do that." Less experienced teachers often hesitate and send mixed messages. Children respond with more testing. Authority comes with time, practice, and patience.

Reflect On

Teacher Authority

Think about a teacher you liked and a teacher you didn't like. How did each exercise authority? Did he or she win your respect and gain your cooperation? If so, how? If not, why not? What were the implications of this experience?

Create Guidelines for Behavior

It is important for all people—adults and children—to understand what is expected of them in particular situations. Understanding expectations creates a sense of safety. It allows people to make informed choices about how to act and to feel a sense of control. Young children feel safe when they know that there are boundaries that allow for personal choice within the confines of safety and respect for others.

We find that children are best served when teachers develop a set of **guidelines**—positively stated expectations that help them choose appropriate behaviors in a variety of situations. While many teachers call these *rules*, we prefer the term *guidelines*, which implies personal responsibility and individual problem solving. Guidelines need to be simple enough to be easily understood, few enough to remember, and general enough to apply to a wide variety of situations:

- Take care of others, take care of yourself, and take care of our things—toys, books, tools, and the environment.

- Treat yourself gently, treat one another kindly, and treat our environment with care.
- Be safe, be kind, and be thoughtful.

Using any of these, adults and children together can decide what constitutes safe, kind, thoughtful care for people and the environment they share. Guidelines should always be stated in the positive; they should provide direction about what *to* do rather than what *not* to do. More limited rules, such as "don't run" or "don't hurt," can be confusing to young children, who may recall and focus only on the last word they hear. These types of rules tell children what not to do but offer little if any information about appropriate behavior. They focus on adult enforcement rather than on child responsibility and learning. And imagine the length of the rule list if a teacher must note each behavior to be avoided in every situation! You will need to communicate guidelines with clarity and simplicity. Children are more likely to respect and follow the guidelines when they understand the reasons for them and when the behavior required is within their ability.

Older preschool and primary children can participate in creating and modifying classroom guidelines and creating group agreements about desirable behavior. This can be done quite successfully in class meetings. A good way to start this process is to ask the children, "What do we all need to agree to do so that everyone feels safe and can focus on learning in school?" Agreements created by the group are not permanent; instead, the group considers them and changes them in response to different situations. When children actively participate in creating and changing agreements, they become increasingly committed to following them and build understanding of principles of living in a group. Table 6.3 illustrates ways to use guidelines meaningfully when talking with children.

Guidelines are not just permissive rules—a misconception held by some adults. In fact, when applied in firm but friendly ways, guidelines help children learn to regulate their own behavior. They teach children to respect one another and to care for property and for the environment. They offer choice within the safety of limits. Within this framework, children learn to make decisions about what is right and learn skills for participating successfully in a community.

Anticipate Problems

Your growing knowledge of child development can help you anticipate children's needs and probable behaviors. This will go a long way toward ensuring smooth classroom experiences. Make sure children have worthwhile and interesting things to do, sufficient time to engage in activities, and experiences that require no more adult supervision than you have available. A particularly useful skill is to develop what we call "teacher eyes"—an awareness of what is taking place throughout the classroom. This means attending to a number of things simultaneously. You must learn to be aware of what is happening with the entire group while paying attention to small groups and individuals.

Table 6.3 Appropriate Classroom Guidelines

Situation	Guideline	Application	Reason
When a child hurts another child.	"Treat each other kindly."	"Use words to tell her you want a turn."	"It is hard to work and play if you are afraid of getting hurt."
When a child doesn't take care of toys or materials.	"Use materials carefully."	"Put the puzzles on the shelf when you finish using them."	"When toys are left on the floor, they might get damaged, or pieces could get lost. Then we would not have them to play with anymore."
When children's actions are dangerous to themselves or to others.	"Be safe."	"Slide down when there is no one on the sliding board."	"Everyone needs to be safe at school."

For example, in a typical preschool or kindergarten class, you might need to attend to all of the following situations at once:

> *Yusuke and Monte are building a large block structure and wearing the construction hats they use for playing police, which sometimes leads to rough-and-tumble play.*
>
> *Amena and Harrison are painting at the easel, giggling with one another as they look at one another's work. Harrison holds up a wet paintbrush and drips purple paint on the floor.*
>
> *Luciana, Tyrone, Dominic, and Emilia are listening to a story read by Dominic's mom in the library corner.*
>
> *Kellen, Max, and Nermeen are in the dramatic play area, dressed up in finery, feeding the dolls, when Kellen announces, "No boys!"*
>
> *Jon and Tiffany are staring intently at Squeakers, the mouse, while Tiffany pokes a piece of Tinkertoy at Squeakers.*
>
> *Anna, Mishka, and Colin are at the writing center, enthusiastically calling you to come write their words.*

As the teacher in this classroom, you would need to make on-the-spot decisions in response to what children need, what will help individuals, and what is needed for the class as a whole. You would have to continue to attend to the rest of the group after you have made your decision, and you would need to have an interesting alternative ready for each group of children as they were ready for a change.

Golden Rules

for Guiding Groups

1. Position yourself so you can see what is happening throughout the room.
2. Get children's attention by moving close to them, crouching down, and speaking directly to them. Avoid shouting across the room or yard.
3. Use children's names positively and frequently in conversation so they don't fear something negative when you address them by name.
4. Indicate what to do rather than what not to do when correcting behavior and include a reason for your direction. Children often feel rebellious and challenged when told what not to do. For example:

Instead of saying:	Substitute:
"Don't run inside."	"Please walk when you are indoors. That way you won't get hurt and neither will your friends."
"Don't sit down until you wash."	"Wash your hands before you sit down to eat so you can stay healthy."
"Don't tear the book."	"Turn the pages carefully so they won't tear."
"Don't poke the guinea pig."	"Use very gentle pats and quiet voices so you don't scare the guinea pig. We want him to feel safe at school."

5. Offer children two acceptable choices as a way to help them respond positively to adult requests. Choices help children to feel powerful and in control. For example:
   "Please walk when you carry scissors so no one will get hurt. I'd be happy to carry the scissors while you go outside to run."
   "Wear a smock so you won't get paint on your clothes. You may use pens or crayons if you don't want to cover up your new shirt today."
   "Touch the poster gently—you can use newspaper if you'd like to tear."
   - Avoid giving children choices that you are unwilling or unable to allow. "Would you like to give me the knife?" is not appropriate when you mean "I must have the knife right now—it is dangerous."
   - Use choices to help children comply with adult requests and retain a sense of independence: "Would you like to walk inside using great big giant steps or tiny quiet baby steps?" Notice that the choice is not whether or not to come inside but how to move your body to get there.

Orchestrate Transitions

Transitions are times when children are asked to move between types of activities and sometimes from one location to another. Throughout a typical day, preschoolers move from meals to center time, from centers to group activities, from group time to outside, and so on. Elementary children will transition between the classroom, lunchroom, and playground and sometimes between types of classrooms—art, music, and so forth. Because teachers are often busy and distracted at these times, aggressive and destructive behaviors often escalate. However, with advance planning, transitions need not be times of peril.

> *Reading time is over for the kindergarten class. Mrs. Lester has asked the children to put away their books and line up quietly in the area in front of the door so they can go outside. She gathers her materials from the circle area, then goes to the table where the children did an art activity earlier in the day. She begins wiping the table, telling the children to get ready to go outside in just a few minutes. As she is cleaning, the children are becoming increasingly restless. Jackson grabs Lexi's ponytail and tugs on it as she steps on his toes trying to cut into the line. Sasha is shouting at Jerome, who is insisting that it is his turn, not hers, to be the line leader. Liane and Juan Carlos are singing loudly and beginning to do a vigorous dance. Liane's elbow accidentally pokes Jacob's eye, and he shouts at her, "Cut that out now, you dummy!" Lely, who has been struggling with her sweater, starts to cry when a sleeve rips. As the commotion level rises, Mrs. Lester raises her voice and says loudly, "I said to wait quietly in the line by the door! If you can't line up quietly, you will miss recess."*

It is all too easy for situations like this one to occur when transition times are not planned with thought and care. The following strategies can help you to orchestrate peaceful classroom transitions:

- **Let children know before a transition will occur.** Young children do not understand time well and have difficulty predicting when one event will end and another will begin. It helps them take control of their actions if they know when a change is coming. For younger children, a reminder just a few minutes before a transition is helpful. It is best if the reminder is made in terms of something concrete that the child can understand: "You have time to ride the tricycle around the path two more times before we go inside." Telling very young children that a transition will occur in 5 minutes is less helpful. It alerts them that the change is coming, but because 5 minutes is a very abstract concept, it is not especially useful in helping them plan their remaining time in an activity. Older preschoolers and primary-age children are developing a sense of time. They appreciate a longer advance reminder and can understand when you tell them that they have 10 minutes before a change is coming. This allows them to organize how they will complete an activity.

- **Use music, movement, and/or fantasy.** It's much easier to help children move from a classroom to a playground when they fly like birds or swim like dolphins than when they must walk quietly in a straight line. Singing or pretending to be construction vehicles as you pick up blocks makes the activity more fun and encourages participation.

- **Keep transitions as short as possible.** Children are not good at waiting. Once you begin the movement from one activity to the next, do it as quickly and with as much focus as possible. In the example at the beginning of this section, Mrs. Lester's class would have handled the transition much more easily had she been present to assist them and then taken them outside as soon as all were assembled. When children are asked to wait, upsets are likely to occur.

- **Plan games or transition activities.** These help children focus and can encourage them to move individually rather than in a large, disorganized mass. The accompanying box, "Transition Activities," offers more suggestions.

Transition Activities

These ideas are especially useful when dismissing children from circle time or a group activity and helping them move to another location.

- **Clues and riddles.**   Give a clue about the child's family, vacation, pet, or home: "A child whose mom is named Donna and whose dad is named Skip can go." Ask a riddle about something related to the curriculum theme: "Asha, what grows in the ground, gives shade to sit in, makes a good place to climb, and is a place for birds to build their nests?" When Asha responds, allow him to move to the next place and ask another question to a different child.

- **Create a verse.**   Sing "Old MacDonald" (or a similar song with endless verses). Ask children to think of a verse, and they can go when their verse has been sung.

- **Props.**   To help children move into learning centers or activity time, bring items from the various centers—more than enough for each child. As you bring out the item, ask a child to describe it, name its place, and take it there to play.

- **Activity choices.**   Bring an example of the activity available in each center and lay a card on top, stating the number of children who may play there at any one time. Have children individually place their name tags on the activity of their choice and then move to their chosen play area. If the limit is reached, a child must select another activity for his or her first stop for the day.

- **Friends.**   Select a child to pick a friend with whom to leave the group.

- **Games.**   For example, the Lost-and-Found game: Choose a child. Say, "Helper Maya, there's a lost child who's wearing blue shorts and a Batman T-shirt. Can you help me find him?" When Maya finds the child, she leaves, and the found child becomes the helper.

- **Name songs.**   Sing a name song, such as "Get on Board Everybody" or "Hello," and have children leave when their name is sung.

To help children move all together as a group, invite them to do the following:

- **Choose an animal.**   Ask children to soar like eagles, walk like giraffes, or glide like butterflies from the playground to the inside table.

- **Play the "Can you . . . ?" game.**   Ask the children if they can take the smallest baby steps possible to get to the circle place, move past the room next door so quietly that no one will ever guess they were there, or pretend to be a boat that glides smoothly over the top of the water as they sail outside.

- **Plan for children who struggle with transition.**   Almost every class has children who have difficulty with transition. You'll quickly learn who these children are. You can help them by assigning them a role during the transitions and, when possible, remaining near them until they are re-engaged in the next activity.

When visiting a preschool classroom, we were pleased to hear a teacher say, "Duncan, we'll be going outside soon, and I would really appreciate it if you could help me take the hoops outside today. They're kind of large, so it would be great if you could carry them with me." We had seen Duncan struggle during transitions on previous days, but with this guidance, he moved from indoors to outdoors with success.

Manage Large Group Times

Particular skills are needed when you lead a large group (often at a daily event called "circle time," "morning circle," "morning meeting," or "group time"). Group times work best when they have a wide appeal, allow children to be active, and are relatively short—10 to 15 minutes for younger preschoolers. As children grow older, their ability to participate for longer periods of time increases, and kindergarteners and primary school children may be able to sit attentively for up to half an hour. Structured group activities are not appropriate for infants and toddlers, although a group may gather spontaneously if you do something interesting, such as playing a guitar, reading a story, or bringing in a puppy to visit. Teachers of toddlers and 2-year-olds will have much

Video Example 6.1: Transition from Circle to Handwashing

Watch this video on a transition from circle to handwashing to see a teacher orchestrating a transition. Why does the teacher have the children go in pairs instead of individually? What does she do to hold the children's attention while they are waiting for their turn?

more effective group experiences if they are prepared for spur-of-the-moment gatherings rather than spending time herding resistant toddlers to a group area and insisting that they sit down.

Group times work when children are comfortable (which means not too hungry, tired, or crowded) and when group size and teacher–child ratios are appropriate to their age and abilities. Consider children's development and interests in selecting group activities that match their ability to participate. For example, a typical group of 3-year-olds will be more interested in moving and making noises like animals than in discussions and pictures about animal habitats and eating patterns. A group of 7-year-olds might be exactly the opposite.

Appropriate group activities for preschool and primary children have the following characteristics:

- They encourage active participation. *Let's all make a sound like an elephant.*
- They include physical activity. *When I call your name, show us how you think the elephant would move.*
- They involve something to look at and to explore with other senses, such as touch, hearing or smell. *I am going to pass around a box of grass. Elephants love to eat grasses. Use your nose and tell me what it smells like.*
- They contain an element of novelty. *If you had an elephant, where could you keep him?*

Singing songs, doing finger plays, reading stories, presenting flannelboard stories or puppets, engaging in creative movement activities, creating group stories, playing games, and short discussions of something that is of interest are all potentially good activities for group time.

When leading a large group, you are the center of the learning experience, and the children respond to your direction. Your sensitivity to their mood and energy and your ability to respond to it will determine whether the children stay involved and are

Video Example 6.2: Group Time for Babies and Young Toddlers

Watch this video to see an example of an appropriate group time for infants and toddlers. How does the teacher ensure that all children are included in the group? How does she keep the youngest child safe? How does she teach the meaning of "nice"?

cooperative. A large group will fail if it requires too much waiting or if children lack interest. When you reach the limits of children's attention, you need to say, "That's all for today," and dismiss children appropriately. Do so cheerfully and without blaming children or showing disappointment. Learning to read children's cues and to respond to a group takes time, experience, and self-confidence.

Young children who are not ready for group experiences will tell you by wiggling, getting up, lying down, or walking away. These behaviors give you valuable feedback—something (e.g., the activity or the timing) is not appropriate to their needs. Sometimes, one or two children have difficulty while the rest enjoy group time. If so, provide an alternative activity for these children. Both you and the children will have a better time if expectations are appropriate and clear and if non-punitive alternatives are available for children who aren't ready for group experiences. Another successful strategy for some children is to allow them to hold something in their hands during group time, such as a small toy car or stuffed animal. While this may seem distracting, it actually may help them focus and participate. The "Golden Rules for Group Times" box offers some suggestions for making group times successful.

Golden Rules
for Group Times

1. **Make a plan.**   Plan the activities you will do in advance; have a backup activity to do if something you planned doesn't work.
2. **Have an "attention grabber."**   Start group times with something you know will capture children's interest: a new action song, a large shell, or a picture of an anteater. Gaining children's interest at the beginning helps ensure a successful group time.

3. **Be organized.** Have all your materials gathered and ready so that when you bring the children together, they do not have to wait while you locate needed items.
4. **Demonstrate enthusiasm.** If you present a group activity as something that is fun and desirable and you expect everyone to cooperate, the children are likely to believe you're right and act accordingly.
5. **Mix it up.** Focus children's attention by keeping the activities moving without long pauses. Include lots of movement and do different things.
6. **Be flexible.** Make changes in response to what children do. Skip a planned activity, add movement, or insert a song or finger play as you notice children's responses.
7. **Be positive.** Focus on things children do right—don't focus on the negative.
8. **Be dramatic.** Use your voice for effect (change volume and pitch to catch interest). Use your face to communicate—eyes, eyebrows, and mouth can express feelings and ideas without words. Some teachers even dress to interest children. A teacher we know has a collection of T-shirts and earrings that she wears to go with the day's activity.
9. **Use the unexpected.** See the classroom from a child's point of view; anticipate what's going to interest children and incorporate it into what you are doing. If a fire truck drives by or a visitor walks in, make this a part of the group activity.
10. **Quit while you're ahead.** Group times often fall apart when they go on too long. When children's interest flags, save your activity for another day.

Build a Positive Classroom Climate

"Classroom climate" refers to the overall atmosphere you create for the children in your group. Do they feel respected? Safe? Are they encouraged to take appropriate risks, to build relationships, and to work cooperatively? Are their unique talents and individual differences included in meaningful ways? A positive classroom climate ensures children's physical and psychological well-being. It helps them learn how to work and play with others and to care for themselves. It promotes our long-term goals for child guidance. You build this type of classroom climate when you use the teaching practices discussed below.

CREATE A SUPPORTIVE ENVIRONMENT The physical environment of a classroom sends strong messages to children about how they are expected to act and whether they are welcome and accepted. A carefully arranged environment can help you set up physical spaces that invite children to work and play together in harmonious ways. A daily schedule that allows adequate time for active and quiet play, along with time for relaxed routines such as meals and rest, helps children feel comfortable and behave appropriately. When you notice that children are having difficulties, it is useful to look at the environment and the daily schedule to determine whether either one is the source of the problems.

For example, in a preschool class we know, the block center was in the middle of the room. To get to any other area, children had to walk through the block center, often bumping into structures. Children whose buildings were knocked down responded angrily, often using blocks as defensive weapons. Children who walked through the block area regularly picked up blocks as props for other centers and deposited them far away. Creating a more sheltered block area reduced these problems. In a toddler program we observed, staff provided few duplicate materials, and toddlers were often in conflict over toys. Replacing highly prized single toys with two to four similar toys minimized conflicts. In a primary program, children's behavior improved noticeably after the schedule was changed from two consecutive and lengthy seated activity periods to a routine where quiet seat work was interspersed with time outside and in learning centers.

ENCOURAGE FRIENDSHIPS Young children are naturally interested in others. Even very young babies show interest in peers and will vocalize to get their attention. Early childhood teachers support developing friendships when they understand some characteristics of typical social development and use this knowledge to help children build meaningful friendships. Teachers of babies support this when they engage in warm and nurturing interactions with each child, setting the stage for them to develop later

SOURCE: Jeff Reese

relationships with peers. Toddlers are quite interested in the actions of others and often wish to play near them with similar toys and materials. Teachers help toddlers learn about friendships by creating small spaces where two or three children can comfortably play near one another. Duplicates of favorite toys help toddlers resolve issues of "mine!" Because they are egocentric and don't understand feelings of others, it is helpful when teachers interpret toddlers' behavior to one another. "She's pulling on the rabbit because she doesn't want you to take it." "He's waving at you; I think he wants to play with you." Three-year-olds show increasing interest in peers and begin to show preference for particular playmates. The familiar "He's not my friend" is often heard in preschool classrooms as children struggle to understand the concept of friendship. For 3-year-olds, a friend is someone playing with them at the play dough table, riding near on the trike path, or asking to sit with them at lunch. Four-year-olds tend to show more stable preferences for particular children, often based on shared interests and recalled past interactions. Because preschoolers focus mostly on what is happening right now, when a playmate chooses a new activity or a different person to sit with, the child feels the friend is lost. Young children quickly learn that friendship is important and may use the bestowing or removal of friendship to attempt to manipulate others. "If you let me have that shovel, I'll be your best friend!" School-age children are increasingly motivated by friendship with peers, and this is the age when exclusive cliques may emerge. Elementary-age boys often base friendships around common interests and activities; girls are more likely to focus on personal characteristics and shared feelings.

You will help children build meaningful friendships when you:

1. Create small, cozy spaces in the classroom where two or three children can interact comfortably and create some larger spaces, particularly in popular areas, so that more children can play together without feeling crowded.

2. Include items in your environment that need two or more people to operate, such as large planks or boxes to lift, trikes for two riders, or games for two or more players.

3. Describe friendly behavior: "He asked if you wanted to play; that was friendly."

4. Comment on friendly interactions: "It seemed like you and Brett really enjoyed pretending to be tigers when you were outside this morning."

5. Pair or create small groups of children to complete a task: "Robyn, Moonif, and Mathias will set up the outdoor activities for today."

6. Teach children skills for entering play groups; when needed, stay with them to facilitate successful play interactions. "Ask if the grocery store needs a shopper."

7. Show you value differences and point out similarities as well: "Some children like to play with blocks; others like to use play dough." "Some of us have brown eyes; others have green ones, but we all have eyes."

8. Allow children to choose playmates but insist that they show kindness and respect. It is not acceptable to say, "Go away, you aren't my friend." However, it is okay to say, "I want to play by myself right now. Maybe we can play later." Help children learn words that aren't hurtful and exclusive.

During the preschool years, children often begin to show gender preferences in their choices of playmates, and the focus of their play may take on more gender-stereotyped roles. You may hear, "Only girls can be in this boat" or "No girls can run with us!" This is typical behavior as children look for friends who share similar interests and activity levels. Gender differences in interests and in styles of communication may contribute to same-gender friendship preferences. Be sure to support these emerging friendships while avoiding gender stereotypes. Include books and posters that show both men and women in a wide variety of work roles and encourage both boys and girls to build, play with dolls, use cars and trucks, throw balls, and engage in many types of pretend play.

MODEL AND TEACH RESPECT AND FAIRNESS   When children learn to treat others with respect and to resolve disputes fairly, they are developing the skills they will need to be successful members of a community. You teach these skills most meaningfully through the words and behaviors you choose. Listen attentively to the words you use with children: Are you polite? Respectful? Are you careful that everyone is included in classroom routines and activities? Do you manage materials in fair and equitable ways—does everyone get the same opportunities to go first or use a preferred toy? Are children who are less appealing, less skilled, or more challenging welcomed into discussions and activities with the same warmth as easy, well-mannered youngsters? Are those with disabilities given meaningful ways to participate? Are children of all nationalities welcomed and included equally? Do you speak with colleagues, families, and other adults with courtesy?

Children learn to treat others with respect and fairness when teachers value, model, and teach these practices. Many teachers use daily class meetings as a means of teaching fairness, respect, and cooperation. When meetings are structured so that everyone is encouraged to talk and share feelings honestly but with kindness, children learn the skills they need as communicators, negotiators, and problem solvers. Class meetings help teachers create an environment where children feel emotionally safe and as a result are able to concentrate and learn (Gartrell, 2012; Vance & Weaver, 2002).

Many teachers ask older preschoolers and school-age children to resolve disputes by meeting together for a discussion. This method of social problem solving is congruent with those used in Hawaiian and other native cultures. In Hawaii some classrooms include a *ho'oponopono*, a time and place for individuals to gather to talk through differences when they arise. Classrooms in other places might have "A Talking Place" or "The Peace Center." Such practices strengthen the sense of community and teach children that they can learn to negotiate disputes.

Take time to notice kindness and fairness when you see it and to point it out to the children. "Jeremy's mom mended our painting aprons for us. That was so generous of her." "I saw our custodian, Mrs. Curtis, stop to help Tricia up when she slipped in the hallway. That was a kind thing to do." "Celene noticed that Santiago was waiting for a turn and offered him the ball first. That was a fair way to act." Gently and consistently insist that all members of the classroom community treat each other kindly and with respect.

Teach Children to Deal with Conflict

As a teacher of young children, an important part of your job is to ensure that children have productive group experiences and learn the skills necessary for thriving in a group. You will want to create a safe and positive social environment in the classroom, help children learn to get along with each other, and address the problems that inevitably arise in any group of young children.

> *"But I need to have them now; they are mine!" Nadia sobbed, pointing to the shiny red shoes that Vivian was dancing in.*

SOURCE: Jeff Reese

"I have them; you can't use them," Vivian said, dancing away.

"But I really, really need them! I need them right now," Nadia cried, running after Vivian. *"I can't do my dance without those shoes. You have to give them to me!"*

Problems and conflicts are an inevitable aspect of group life, both in and outside of early childhood programs. The way that teachers deal with conflict provides an important model for young children. When teachers view conflict as a learning opportunity, children can learn that it is a part of life and they can learn skills for problem resolution.

How you feel about conflict is a reflection of your experiences, values, and culture. Reflecting on how you feel about and deal with conflict in your own life may be helpful in considering what you will model for children.

Reflect On

Your Feelings about Conflict

How do you tend to deal with conflict in your life? Do the ways you deal with disputes and upsets usually work well for you? What do you want children to learn about conflict resolution?

SOURCE: Jeff Reese

HELP CHILDREN IDENTIFY AND EXPRESS THEIR FEELINGS Conflict is often accompanied by anger, a powerful emotion that can be hard to understand and express. Anger is a second-level reaction—a response to hurt, threat, frustration, or anxiety. Young children may not have words to express the feelings behind their conflicts or may have been taught not to express feelings. Before you can help children learn to resolve conflicts peacefully, you must help them identify and acknowledge their feelings. Even very young children benefit when teachers give names to the emotions they are feeling. As they get older, this helps children build a vocabulary for expressing and understanding feelings.

The accompanying box, "Ways to Help Children Understand and Express Feelings," suggests some ways to help children learn and talk about their feelings as a prelude to conflict resolution.

Ways to Help Children Understand and Express Feelings

- Accept and name children's feelings for them: "You feel unhappy that Calder has the ball you wanted."

- Model expressing your own feelings: "I'm so disappointed that it is raining on the day we planned to have a picnic!"

- Invite children to talk to you and to one another about how they feel: "Your face looks sad. Would you like to tell me how you are feeling?"

- Point out similarities and differences in feelings: "You both like to write stories. Briana likes to write by herself. Aaron prefers to work with a writing team."

- Provide opportunities for children to identify and express feelings through conversations, art, music, movement, dramatic play, and writing: "Would you like to make a painting that shows how you felt after you watched the sad movie about the dog?"

- Rehearse expressing feelings through activities like role-playing: "Let's pretend that it is time to clean up and you aren't finished with your construction project. How would you feel? Show me some of the things that you could do."

Be sensitive to the fact that, in some cultures, it is considered rude to show feelings. If children are uncomfortable with labeling or discussing feelings, never insist that they do so. Discussions with families regarding their preferences about expressing feelings and handling conflict can help you select strategies that meet the needs of all children in the group.

ENCOURAGE CHILDREN TO SOLVE PROBLEMS   When disputes between young children occur, it is wise to watch first and refrain from intervening too soon. Children who are not hurting one another can often work out their own solutions. Although it is tempting to step in to solve problems for them, this intervention does not help them learn to be problem solvers. Recall that two of the long-term goals for child guidance are building self-regulation and developing skills for living in a community. If children learn that the teacher is always going to solve problems for them, they will neither learn these skills nor be motivated to do so. Teachers who support these guidance goals allow children the time, space, and authority to resolve problems independently. We find it helpful to remember this phrase: "You can't teach children to think by telling them what to do" (source unknown). With practice, children can learn to tell each other how they feel and what they want instead of striking out or running to an adult when a confrontation occurs.

When children are "stuck" and cannot reach a solution on their own, a well-timed word can sometimes help them resolve the conflict. Here are some examples of things to say when you are talking with children who are in conflict situations:

"Stop. I won't let you hurt Gabriel. You can tell him that it makes you mad when he takes your truck. Ask him to give it back to you."

"I can see you're angry about what happened. What do you want to tell her?"

"Hitting hurts. Let's think of some other ways to handle this problem."

"You have different ideas about how to construct the model. What can you do to decide how to get back to building?"

"That hurt Alethea's feelings and she's really sad now. Please stay with me—maybe we can help her feel better."

"There isn't room for five children in the tire swing. Would you like to choose who goes first? Shall I help?"

"What can you do to solve this problem so you can go back to playing restaurant?"

It is important to know the individual temperaments of the children in your group. For some children, particularly boys, conflicts may quickly escalate into physical aggression. In these situations, be prepared to step in quickly and defuse the situation by gently explaining what happened—"Jeremiah didn't mean to hurt you; he was moving the plank over to his building and accidently bumped your leg." A light touch of humor—"Those builders sure make some loud grumbles!"—may also help to defuse a potential conflict (Gartrell, 2012).

When conflict threatens to cause hurt, you must act. Intervene swiftly and place your body between children who are hurting one another or threatening to do so. If the conflict involves a struggle over a toy, let the children know that you will hold it until the conflict is resolved. Talk with the children to help them begin to identify a solution. It is more effective to ask *what* can be done so that children can return to their activities than to ask *why* they are arguing, *who* had the toy first, or *who* hit first. Focus on a solution—"What can we do?" This helps the children resolve their problem rather than concentrating on who is right and who is wrong. "How can you get a turn with the trike?" and "What's another way to ask if you can play?" are more supportive of problem solving than "Who had it first?" and "Why did you hit him?"

Even very young children can be given time and opportunity to deal with conflict. We recently observed a teacher who simply put her arm between two toddlers who were hurting one another. She kept her arm there, saying little except, "You both want the white purse, but there's just one here" and "I can't let you hurt one another." Very quickly one child found another purse, and peaceful play resumed.

INCLUDE CONFLICT RESOLUTION IN YOUR TEACHING AND YOUR ACTIVITY PLANNING   We want children to learn to be cooperative and to solve problems constructively even when we are not present. By guiding them repeatedly through the process of peaceful conflict resolution, we can enable them to reach this goal. Refer to the accompanying box, "The Conflict Resolution Process," to help you learn and teach the steps in this process.

The Conflict Resolution Process

Jayson and Youssef are happily playing a game of Pokémon in the pretend area. Olivia and Stacey come in and sit at the table, starting to pretend that they are getting ready for a party. "Hey," Jayson shouts, "You can't be there. That's the Pokémon house."

"Yeah, get away," Youssef says. "We are playing here and no girls can come here."

"Uh-un," Stacey says. "We can play here if we want to. You've been here a long time and Olivia and I want to get our dresses on and play party."

As the teacher:
Approach the children calmly.
Get down to their level.
If a toy is involved, explain that you will *hold the toy* until the problem is resolved. Then lead the children through these steps.

Teach the children to:	Example:
Cool down. Everyone involved may need a moment to take several deep breaths and relax, particularly if the conflict has included children hurting one another.	"I can hear that you are all upset. Let's figure out what we can do. Take three big breaths to get calm, then we'll talk about how we can solve this problem."
Identify the problem. Figure out what the problem is and what needs to be solved without making judgments.	"Olivia and Stacey want to play in the home area. Jayson and Youssef say 'No' because they're playing Pokémon."
Describe the underlying feelings, worries, concerns, and values. These must be acknowledged before solutions can be generated	"Olivia and Stacey are worried they might not get a turn if they don't play now. Jayson and Youssef like playing here, too. They're afraid they won't get to play Pokémon if you join them."
Brainstorm solutions. Ask the children what they can think of to solve this problem.	"Olivia has thought of two plans. Jayson and Youssef can play Pokémon outside, or she and Stacey can play Pokémon, too. Youssef has thought of two plans also. He thinks that Olivia and Stacey can play in the block area now and play in the pretend area tomorrow, or they can play in the pretend area in 10 minutes."
Choose one and try it. Ask children to decide what they want to try and what they think will work for everyone. Encourage the children to follow one of the suggested solutions.	"Okay, Olivia and Stacey will try playing Pokémon in the home area for 10 minutes with Jayson and Youssef. Then they will play another game."
Follow up. If necessary, encourage and support children as they try the solution. At a later time, invite children to reflect on what could be done to prevent problems in the future and on how their solutions worked.	"What do you think we could do so that this problem doesn't happen again?" or "How did it work out when all of you played Pokémon?"

We find that young children are interested in this process and, with patient facilitation from adults, they quickly start to use it effectively on their own. In addition to being consistent with the goals of developing self-regulation and cooperation skills, teaching children this process relieves the teacher of the onerous role of being the "classroom police."

Many teachers include learning about ways to solve problems as part of their teaching plans. You might create a puppet show where two frogs are struggling over a place to sit on a log and encourage the children to help them solve this issue. There are many excellent children's books that deal with social problems and conflicts. Consider reading one or more of them and leading class discussions about ways to resolve these issues fairly and kindly. It is also helpful to notice times when children have resolved a conflict; ask them how they felt when they did this successfully, and invite them to share about it in conversation, a story, or a drawing. Help them recall this success when future conflicts arise.

 ## Application Exercise 6.2

Watch and Write About Helping Children Learn to Resolve Conflicts

✓ **A Quick Check 6.4**

Gauge your understanding of the concepts in this section.

 # Managing Inappropriate Behaviors

Building positive relationships, communicating respectfully, guiding groups effectively, and creating a positive classroom climate will go a long way toward helping children behave in cooperative and productive ways. However, even when you do all these things, there will still be times when a child or children behave in ways that disrupt the group, upset other children, and irritate or annoy adults. In this section, we offer strategies for guiding children whose behavior is difficult or inappropriate.

Reframing Misbehavior as "Mistaken Behavior"

Dan Gartrell (1995, 2001, 2012) suggests that it is helpful for teachers to think about unacceptable behavior as **mistaken behavior** instead of labeling it with the more familiar term *misbehavior*. He suggests that misbehavior implies the behavior is intentional and that children must therefore be punished for their "bad" actions. Teachers who think of misbehavior in this way may label children as naughty and punish them in an attempt to get them to stop the misbehavior.

Mistaken behavior, on the other hand, suggests that children are learning to behave acceptably and are therefore subject to making mistakes. A teacher who adopts this viewpoint can act as a guide who helps children rather than taking on the role of a judge who scolds and criticizes.

> Mikayla and Cherise are in the dramatic play area. Mikayla puts on a lacy tutu and turns to sit on a small sofa next to Cherise. Cherise sees the skirt and shrieks, "That is mine!" She begins tugging on the tutu as Mikayla holds it tightly around her. Mikayla stands and starts to try to move away, and as she does, Cherise reaches over and slaps her face.

The girls' teacher can choose to view Cherise's behavior as "mistaken." She knows that it is hard to learn ways to get what you want. While she does not condone or accept behavior that hurts others, she does not judge Mikayla as "bad" because she hasn't yet learned more cooperative ways. As she moves to assist the girls, she asks herself, "What can Cherise and Mikayla learn from this experience?"

> Walking quickly to the dramatic play area, the teacher stoops and places an arm around each girl. She asks Mikayla, who is crying, to show her where it hurts. She asks both children to tell her what has happened. She empathizes with each, telling Mikayla, "You felt upset when Cherise tried to take the tutu, and it hurt when she hit you." She is also empathetic to Cherise: "You were using the tutu earlier, and you did not want Mikayla to take it." She says, "Cherise, I can see that you really want to use that tutu. You were trying to let Mikayla know that you did not want her to have a turn. Mikayla is crying now because her face is hurting where you hit it."

She includes both girls by asking, "What do you think you can do now?" After the negotiations are concluded, the teacher ensures that both Cherise and Mikayla are reengaged in an activity before moving to other responsibilities.

Application Exercise 6.3 Managing Inappropriate Behaviors

Understanding behavior as "mistaken" encourages the conflict resolution approach that we discussed earlier in this chapter. It also has the following characteristics of effective guidance:

- It avoids judging, labeling, or victimizing either child.
- It does not require a forced apology but invites the child who offended to make amends if he or she so chooses.
- It takes a learning-focused approach; the situation is viewed as an opportunity for each child to learn behaviors that work well in relationships.

DIFFERENTIATE THE CHILD FROM THE BEHAVIOR

There are several points to keep in mind when dealing with children whose behaviors are mistaken. First, always remember that the *behavior*, not the *child*, is the problem. When children's behavior is upsetting, it is easy to confuse *what* the child does with *who* the child is. It's tempting sometimes to think of Lucia as an annoying child, Jillette as the naughty one, Mateo as cooperative, and Aaron as a good boy. Some teachers begin to think of the child as characterized by the behavior. Rory is a "biter." Yun Mi is a "talker." Children are better served if we avoid these labels. Lucia's behavior has been upsetting. Rory has been biting lately. Even positive labels like "good girl" put adults in the role of judges and may not have positive results. It helps children make appropriate choices about how to behave when you view them as good, worthy, and lovable people who sometimes make mistakes and need help choosing appropriate behavior.

Another thing to remember is that all behavior has a reason. Even though you may not be able to identify it, there is a reason for everything a child does. Your job is to be a detective and find out how a mistaken behavior is serving a particular child. Once you understand the purpose, it is easier to help the child find a less disturbing way to get his or her needs met.

RECOGNIZE YOUR "BUTTON PUSHERS"   Each teacher has behaviors that he or she finds difficult to deal with. One teacher may be upset when children spit. Another may deal with spitting easily but be unnerved when children swear or whine. The difference in your acceptance of children's behavior comes from your own experiences and beliefs about how children should behave. It's helpful to identify behaviors that you find particularly upsetting. This is sometimes called "finding your button pushers." *Button pushers* are actions that cause you to become angry or upset very quickly. Many children seem skilled in identifying those buttons and pushing them. It gives children a sense of power when their actions create an immediate and strong response in adults. If you know which behaviors cause you to have a strong reaction, you can plan how you will react to them. A calm response lacks drama, is thoughtful, and is much less interesting for children than an unplanned outburst. Because of this, they may be less motivated to repeat the behavior. A thoughtfully worded and simple message is the key: "Spitting spreads germs. Instead of spitting, please use words to let me know how you are feeling."

Reflect On

Your "Button Pushers"

Think about a particular behavior that causes you to become upset and angry. What are you likely to do when a child acts in this way? Would this response help the child to choose a more appropriate, less annoying behavior? Does it show anger? Is it punitive? Plan a more reasoned response you might make when a child "pushes your buttons."

Strategies for Dealing with Mistaken Behavior

Every child will occasionally make a mistake and behave in a way that is disruptive. And every teacher of young children needs a repertoire of strategies for dealing with children's mistaken behavior. The accompanying box, "Golden Rules for Responding to Mistaken Behavior," offers a starting place for learning about these practices. The sections that follow describe some specific strategies in greater depth.

Golden Rules

for Responding to Mistaken Behavior

1. **Observe the child closely and think carefully about what the behavior means.**   There is always a reason for it.
2. **Emphasize that school is a safe place.**   Let children know that you will not allow anyone to hurt them or permit them to hurt others.
3. **Offer two acceptable choices when you want children to change their behavior.**   "You can paint at the easel or at the table."
4. **Give real choices.**   If it is time to clean up, an appropriate choice might be, "Would you rather put the blocks away or help clean up the pretend area?" Don't ask, "Do you want to put your toys away now?"
5. **Allow children to save face.**   For example, if a child has loudly proclaimed that he won't hold your hand as you cross the street, allow him to hold the hand of another adult or the child next to him.
6. **Focus on solutions rather than causes.**   Ask, "What can we do since you both want to lead the reading group today?" instead of "Why did you take the leader badge away from her?"

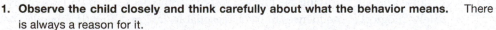

REDIRECTION   When children behave in ways that are unsafe or damaging to the environment, a good strategy is to redirect their energy and attention to an activity similar to the one that is unacceptable.

> *Eighteen-month-old Kea stands at the sink, pouring water from a cup onto the floor. Her teacher says, "You are really enjoying pouring that water. Someone might slip when water is on the floor—let's get out the water table and do some pouring there."*

In this example, Kea's teacher respects her interest in pouring. She offers her a similar activity that will allow her to continue her interest in a way that is safe. Children who are running in a block area can be directed to a movement activity; shouting can be refocused by playing a game with voice sounds, including whispers and songs.

Redirection is a more respectful technique than distracting a child by offering an activity that has no relationship to what the child is interested in. Distraction tells children that their interests are not worthy or valued; redirection respects children's focus and energy while helping them engage in an activity that is acceptable.

NATURAL AND LOGICAL CONSEQUENCES   Children learn to behave appropriately when they have opportunities to make connections between their behavior and the outcomes that it produces. The use of natural and logical consequences can help children make this association. This approach is based on the work of Alfred Adler as interpreted and applied to classrooms by Rudolf Dreikurs (1969). Dreikurs suggests that helping children make connections between what they *do* and the outcome or consequence of their action teaches them to take responsibility and become responsible members of a family or classroom group. This approach is often referred to as the *democratic approach* to guidance.

Natural consequences allow a child to learn from experience and require no adult intervention. For example, if a child pours his paint down the drain, the natural consequence is that there is no paint for him to use. This approach is appropriate when the consequence does not endanger a child and when it does not unfairly penalize another person or the group. You should describe what has happened in a matter-of-fact manner. For example, to a toddler who has dumped her juice onto the table: "You wish you had more juice, but it's all gone." Or to a 5-year-old who has thrown the balls over the fence: "You would really like it if we had more balls to play with." Your task is not to fix the situation or sympathize with the child. Be careful to refrain from voicing a smug "I told you so." when a child experiences natural consequences that you foretold and allow the child to experience the circumstances and feelings related to his or her own actions.

Some negative behavior does not lead to any natural or acceptably safe consequences. In this situation, you may choose to create **logical consequences** that are closely related to the behavior. Children can benefit from situations where teachers use clearly related consequences, such as "Because you are breaking crayons, you will need to leave the art area and find another place to play." In following through on a consequence, you need to be calm and simply say, "You may not be in the block area now because you are throwing the blocks. You can come back when you are ready to play safely." Logical consequences must be reasonable, fair, and directly related to behavior: "You threw the books off the shelf. When you are calm you can put them back on the shelf." Such consequences are consistent with the values of fairness and responsibility. Be sure to apply them calmly and to avoid using them in a punitive manner or one that isolates children. A logical consequence becomes a punishment when you angrily shout, "No books for you; you tore the pages!"

AVOID TIME-OUT   For many years, teachers were taught that time-out was a logical consequence that could be used to help children learn appropriate behaviors. The premise of time-out is that children will learn that if they misbehave, they will be separated from the group. Children are sent to a "time-out" chair where they are instructed to sit and "think about" their behavior. While this may offer the teacher a respite from dealing with the child, this type of isolation does not help children learn how to behave (Gartrell, 2001; Schreiber, 1999). Lilian Katz (1984) notes that time-out confuses young children because they cannot understand the relationship between their "bad" behaviors and the forced removal to the chair.

Although many teachers who use time-out intend it to be a strategy that helps children learn appropriate social behaviors, there are some undesirable outcomes of time-out:

- Because it is imposed by others ("go sit in the chair"), time-out does not encourage children to develop internal control or self-regulation skills.

- Children in time-out are not learning about alternative strategies for handling upset or dealing with social situations.

- Other children may view the child in time-out as "bad" or a troublemaker.

We recall a classroom visit where a child who pointed to another and said, "That's Vince; he's bad. He has to go to time-out every day." Vince's recurring mistaken behaviors during the observation confirmed that the practice of time-out was not effective in helping him learn productive ways of interacting with others. We prefer strategies that include children in the group and offer them ways to learn acceptable behavior.

Providing a safe, comfortable space for a child to regain composure can be helpful. Different from time-out, offering a place for calm reflection and "cooling off" can be an effective way to help children gain self-control. It is particularly useful when teachers help children learn to take themselves there at times when they are upset or need a quiet place. The differences between this practice and time-out are that offering a place to calm down is not punitive and that it is self-regulated—the child determines when to go and when to return to the group. Dragging a kicking and screaming child to the "calm place" is not effective. Sometimes you may need to forcibly (and as gently as possible) remove a child from an emotional or physically aggressive situation. When this happens, remain with the child, offering encouragement and support as he or she works to regain enough self-control to return to the group. You can offer the child some criteria to determine readiness: "When your body is relaxed and you can keep your hands from hitting other people, then you will be ready to come back." Be sure to offer a returning child some assistance in re-entering the group. Contrast these practices with those of traditional time-out where children hear, "Sit in the time-out chair and think about what you did until I tell you to get up."

REINFORCEMENT Reinforcement techniques—offering rewards or reinforcement for positive behaviors—have been used in many classrooms over the years. Based on the theory of **behaviorism** created by John Watson (1878–1958) and B. F. Skinner (1904–1990), these practices center on the belief that children misbehave because they have been taught to do so by improper rewards, or reinforcement; in order to change or extinguish old behaviors, new ones must be taught and rewarded.

All early childhood educators use behaviorist principles some of the time. When you smile at a shy child who attempts a new activity, you are providing reinforcement. When you ignore a child whose demanding behavior is disruptive, you are choosing not to reinforce it. The phrase "catch them being good" is a simple way of suggesting that you encourage, reward, or provide social reinforcement to children for desired behavior.

Behaviorist techniques have been used successfully in classrooms that serve children with disabilities. When applied with care, they can be helpful when dealing with extreme or challenging behavior. They are sometimes used to help children with cognitive disabilities learn appropriate ways to behave. However, for typically developing children, we do not believe that systematically using external rewards as a method for teaching positive behavior is either effective or appropriate. It does little to support the development of self-regulation skills and may teach children to behave in ways that are manipulative and self-serving.

PHYSICAL PUNISHMENT: WHY IT IS NEVER A CHOICE   Neither spanking nor any other type of physical punishment is ever appropriate in early childhood programs. Not only are such practices illegal in most states, but they also have harmful effects on children and are in direct opposition to the long-term goals of teaching children to be self-regulated individuals who can resolve conflicts peacefully. Research has shown that adults who were regularly spanked as children are more likely than those who were not spanked to be depressed, to use alcohol or drugs, to engage in crime and violence, and to hit their spouses and their own children (American Academy of Pediatrics, 2009). When children are spanked, they learn that it is acceptable to hurt people who are younger, smaller, or more vulnerable. They learn that hands are more powerful than words. Because children imitate the important adults in their lives, children who have been spanked are more likely to deal with problems in an aggressive manner than those who have consistently experienced other forms of discipline (Straus, Sugarman, & Giles-Sims, 1997).

The National Association for the Education of Young Children (NAEYC) Code of Ethical Conduct (2011) strongly supports this position. "Above all, we shall not harm children. We shall not participate in practices that are emotionally damaging, physically harmful, disrespectful, degrading, dangerous, exploitative, or intimidating to children. This principle has precedence over all others in this Code" (NAEYC, 2011, Section P-1.1).

Bullying

Bullying is a topic that has received significant attention both in the popular press and in articles targeted to educators. Bullying is a set of hurtful behaviors that are done with the intent to harm or intimidate a person. When a child repeatedly hurts or frightens another child, especially when the targeted child is perceived as being weaker or less powerful, these actions are bullying. Young children do not yet have well-developed social skills, and many behaviors that are associated with bullying—name-calling, threatening, excluding, and physical aggression—are typical behaviors for children who are just learning to get along in groups. A hurtful preschool behavior becomes bullying when it is repeated, intense, and targeted to a particular child. Although bullying most often begins in primary grades, research indicates that it can begin in preschool.

Bullying is damaging not only for the victim but also for the child who bullies and the children who observe bullying (Kaiser & Rasminsky, 2012). Children who bully have learned this behavior from others, perhaps from home situations with adults or older siblings who bully them. Because the bullying is meeting underlying emotional needs, they will continue to bully if adults do not intervene. It is your responsibility as the teacher to stop bullying immediately and to implement strategies to teach the child who bullies replacement behaviors that will meet their needs and help them effectively interact with peers. Here are some things you can do:

1. **Intervene immediately.**   School must be a physically and emotionally safe place for everyone. Remove the child who bullies from the play area *every time* bullying occurs. Explain that the behavior is not acceptable. Always remind bullying children that they will have another chance to play if they can do so without being unkind and that you will remove them if they hurt others.

2. **Set clear guidelines**—"Be kind" and "Be safe"—and apply them to the behavior. *"Name-calling is unkind and hurts others." "Everyone may play with blocks." "No one is allowed to tell other people who they can play with."*

3. **Intentionally teach social skills**   and focus on creating a classroom community. Use class meetings and other group times to discuss ways to work together and strategies for preventing hurtful behavior.

4. **Ensure that adults in your classroom never threaten, shame, punish,** or use their power in ways that bully children. Children learn to bully when they are bullied.

5. **Avoid labeling** the child as a bully. Bullying is a set of harmful behaviors, not who the child is; focus on teaching the child appropriate ways to interact.

6. **Actively teach alternative social behaviors;** look for how the bullying is serving the child's needs and teach other ways to get those need met.

7. **Follow each directive with positive interactions:** "Jaylyn, make space for everyone at the pretend table. It looks like you are preparing a delicious meal. I'm glad I can join you for tea. It's fun to play when everyone is included."

A Quick Check 6.5

Gauge your understanding of the concepts in this section.

Challenging Behaviors

Some children exhibit **challenging behaviors**—persistent behaviors that prevent them from being able to function in a group or that threaten their own safety or the safety of others. These are distinguished from the "difficult" behaviors we discussed in the previous section, as they are usually more severe and harmful. Generally, the term *challenging behavior* refers to behaviors that persist over time and are disruptive, damaging to others or to the environment, and resistant to teacher intervention. Kaiser and Rasminsky (2012) identify challenging behaviors as those that:

- Interfere with children's cognitive, social, or emotional development;
- Are harmful to the child, to other children, or to adults;
- Put a child at high risk for later social problems or school failure.

These behaviors are challenging for the children themselves, who are unable to be successful in a group and who probably feel unable to control their behavior. They are also challenging for the adults who deal with them daily and who may feel helpless and overwhelmed by such behaviors.

It is important to remember that many young children engage in challenging behaviors at some time in their lives and that, in most instances, consistent use of the positive guidance techniques discussed in this chapter will help them learn more acceptable behavior. In some cases, however, challenging behavior indicates ongoing difficulties that may require intervention strategies.

Causes of challenging behaviors are complex. Children with developmental delays and attention deficit disorders have a higher biological risk for developing challenging behaviors than other children. Certain temperamental traits tend to be associated with challenging behavior. Children whose mothers used drugs and alcohol during pregnancy may also be at risk. Environmental factors that increase children's risk of developing challenging behavior include poverty, exposure to violence, neglect, frequent exposure to harsh, inconsistent discipline, family interactions that model antisocial dispute resolution, viewing violent television, and low-quality child care (Kaiser & Rasminsky, 2012).

SOURCE: Jeff Reese

Children who are aggressive to others need to know that you will not allow them to hurt themselves or other people. Children who are destructive need to know that you will not allow them to destroy materials, hurt pets, or harm the environment. These points need to be emphasized each time aggressive or destructive incidents occur or appear imminent; for example:

"It's my job to keep everyone safe at school. I won't let you hurt Freddie, and I won't let anyone hurt you."

"I won't let you tear children's artwork. Everyone's work is cared for at school."

"Even though you are very mad, it is never okay to hurt someone. I will help you calm down."

"I'll help you find a way to safely put the trikes in the shed; they get dented when you slam them against the wall."

"Come with me to find a place where you can calm down and get control of your body. I can't let you hurt other children."

As children learn that their feelings will be respected, that their needs will be met, and that they will be protected from retaliation and isolation, they may turn less to aggressive and destructive behaviors. The techniques you have been studying will help you guide children with challenging behavior—but they will take time and a "stick-to-it" disposition. Change does not happen overnight, and you may find that you need support as you help these children become functional members of the group.

Dealing with challenging behavior is increasingly identified as a source of concern for early educators (Gilliam, 2005; Hemmeter, 2007). In response to this need, the Center on the Social and Emotional Foundations for Early Learning (CSEFEL) at Vanderbilt University developed the Pyramid Model for Supporting Social Emotional Competence, discussed earlier in this chapter. The authors of this model suggest that children with consistently challenging behavior (the top level of the pyramid) can be helped when teachers, parents, and administrators work with a trained behavior support specialist. Working collectively, this team can develop a plan that includes teaching the child skills and behaviors to replace the challenging ones. They can also use consistent strategies to prevent the challenging behaviors from occurring (Hemmeter, 2007). Additional information about positive behavior support plans can be found at the CSEFEL website.

Assistance for children who need intensive support may be available from state offices of child development, special education services in public schools, and state departments of health. For children under age 3, support may be available from early intervention services, often administered by departments of health or education. Remember, it is never helpful or productive to blame the child or the parents for the challenging behavior. All children deserve opportunities to learn the skills they need to function in our society. The box, "Dealing with Challenging Behaviors" discusses some strategies that may be helpful when you have a child with challenging behavior in your classroom.

Dealing with Challenging Behaviors

- Identify what you genuinely like about the child and tell team members, the family, and the child.
- Identify for the child what he or she is doing right.
- Let the child know you are committed to helping him or her make it in the classroom and that you believe it will happen.
- Have sincere, positive physical contact with the child every day.
- Recognize your own aggravation and find ways to release it away from the child.
- Find a coworker to talk to during the days when the child's behavior is upsetting you.

Often, teachers and administrators struggle to meet the needs of a child with challenging behavior and simultaneously teach and care for other children in the group. In such cases, it may be helpful to refer to the NAEYC Code of Ethical Conduct for guidance about how to proceed.

 Application Exercise 6.4 Classroom Newsletter

 ✓ **A Quick Check 6.6**
Gauge your understanding of the concepts in this section.

 # Final Thoughts

As you make decisions about the practices you will use to build relationships and to guide children, we urge you to give thoughtful consideration to your values, the ways you use authority, and your long-term goals for children. We encourage you to be aware of cultural and individual differences, both your own and those of families and colleagues. We remind you that it takes many years and much practice for children to build the complex skills needed to control strong feelings and to cooperate with others. We hope that you will find joy in your relationships with the young children you teach and that you will use encouraging practices to promote their social and emotional growth. Working with young children is a voyage of discovery. Your thoughtful use of appropriate guidance practices can help ensure that it is a peaceful voyage taken with friends.

 Application Exercise 6.5 Final Reflection

 # To Learn More

Read

A Matter of Trust: Connecting Teachers and Learners in the Early Childhood Classroom, C. Howes & S. Ritchie (2002).

Challenging Behavior in Young Children: Understanding, Preventing, and Responding Effectively, B. Kaiser & J. S. Rasminsky (2011).

Class Meetings: Young Children Solving Problems Together, E. Vance & P. J. Weaver (2014).

Education for a Civil Society: How Guidance Teaches Young Children Democratic Life Skills, D. Gartrell (2012).

Me, You, Us: Social-Emotional Learning in Preschool, A. S. Epstein (2009).

The Emotional Development of Young Children: Building an Emotion-Centered Curriculum, M. Hyson (2004).

The Importance of Being Little: What Preschoolers Really Need from Grownups, Erika Christakis (2016).

The Irreducible Needs of Children: What Every Child Must Have to Grow, Learn, and Flourish, T. B. Brazelton & S. I. Greenspan (2000).

Visit a Website

The following agencies and organizations have websites related to positive child guidance:

Center on the Social and Emotional Foundations for Early Learning

Collaborative for Academic, Social, and Emotional Learning (CASEL)

Never Hit a Child

Technical Assistance Center on Social Emotional Intervention for Young Children

Document Your Skill & Knowledge About Child Guidance in Your Professional Portfolio

Include some or all of the following:

- Your Child Guidance Philosophy Statement consisting of one or two paragraphs that describe your beliefs about relating to and guiding young children, your long term goals for them, and a brief discussion of the communication and guidance practices you use or plan to use.

- A list of agencies in your state or city that provide support and assistance for families and teachers of children with challenging behavior. Record contact information about these programs. You may wish to include a copy of this list in your Community Resource file.

- An annotated bibliography of children's books about dealing with feelings and handling upset and conflict.

Shared Writing 6.1 Your Ethical Responsibilities Related to Supporting Children with Challenging Behavior

---

Chapter 7
Health, Safety, and Well-Being

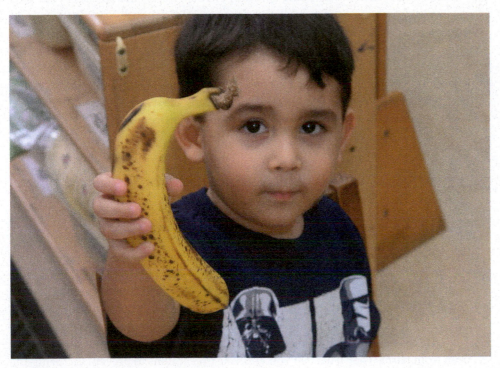

The greatest wealth is health.

VIRGIL

⌄ Chapter Learning Outcomes:

7.1 Create and maintain safe indoor and outdoor environments for young children.

7.2 Implement routines and practices that limit the spread of disease and support health.

7.3 Provide a curriculum that teaches children about health and safety.

7.4 Promote children's emotional health and overall well-being.

NAEYC Professional Preparation Standards

The NAEYC Professional Preparation Standard that applies to this chapter:

Standard 1: Promoting Child Development and Learning (NAEYC, 2011).

Key elements:

1a: Knowing and understanding young children's characteristics and needs

1b: Knowing and understanding the multiple influences on development and learning

1c: Using developmental knowledge to create healthy, respectful, supportive, and challenging learning environments

Ensuring children's **well-being**—(health of body, mind, and spirit) is your most important job as an early childhood teacher. Children's well-being is the foundation for their growth, learning, and overall quality of life. As an early childhood educator, you will implement practices to ensure that children are safe and healthy. You will create environments and routines that safeguard wellness and promote physical and emotional health. When you supervise attentively, provide appropriate challenges, nurture positive relationships, and encourage healthy lifestyle choices you make significant contributions to young children's current and future health.

Safe Places for Children

Young children spend a significant part of their lives in early childhood settings. Approximately 11 million children in the United States under age 5 are in some type of child care arrangement (Child Care Aware, 2016), and most children over the age of 5 are enrolled in an elementary school program. Many are also enrolled in after-school care programs. Whatever the setting, young children need programs that promote their safety, **health**, and well-being. When a family sends their child to an early childhood program, they assume that the program will have policies to ensure that their child will not be hurt. They trust that you, the teacher, are knowledgeable and skilled in selecting safe equipment, materials, and activities and that you follow procedures to protect children from harm. They trust that you will take precautions to prevent accidents and supervise children carefully in order to ensure their safety.

Keeping children safe and well is, in large measure, a matter of common sense. Protect children from hazards. Supervise them attentively. Make sure they have nutritious food, water, and clean facilities. Teach them how to follow routines that will keep them safe and well. Although at first glance these things appear simple, they are actually somewhat complex, and implementing them can be challenging.

If you teach in a program for children 5 years of age and under, you will have particular responsibilities to implement health and safety practices. Special care must be taken with infants and toddlers, who are especially vulnerable. As children enter kindergarten and move into the primary grades, they are better able to attend to their own health and safety needs. However, kindergarten and primary teachers still need to practice routines for safety and wellness.

Standards for promoting children's health and safety change often as new information becomes available. To ensure you are using the most current practices, we recommend that you consult *Stepping Stones to Caring for Our Children: National Health and Safety Performance Standards: Guidelines for Early Care & Education Programs*, 3rd edition, (American Academy of Pediatrics [AAP], American Public Health Association, & National Resource Center for Health and Safety in Child Care and Early Education, 2013). This manual, which we will refer to here as SS3, provides comprehensive health and safety guidelines for early childhood programs. It is available both online and in hard copy. The online version is updated frequently as new information becomes available. References listed at the end of the chapter offer additional information regarding health and safety.

Risks vs Hazards

Young children build skill and strength as they engage in activities that challenge their abilities. Learning to walk, climbing on playground structures, riding a bicycle, and using scissors, knives, and other tools are skills that children can master with support from adults and with opportunities to practice. All involve a certain amount of **risk**. Risk is defined as exposure to the chance of injury or loss. While we want to protect children from injury, we know that children learn from challenging activities that require developmentally appropriate risk taking. Children's natural inclination to learn through exploration encourages risk-taking behavior. Your role is to ensure that activities are well matched to children's skill and ability level.

You must also make sure that the environment is free of **hazards**. A hazard—as differentiated from a risk—is a danger a child cannot anticipate or see and, therefore, cannot evaluate. A sharp table edge, a hot metal slide, a broken stair, and a balloon fragment are examples of hazards. Young children do not have the experience to know that these things may be harmful. Consequently, you must protect children from hazards by promptly repairing them, or removing them. When this is not possible, be certain to block children's access to these dangers. Your knowledge about children's development and about their individual circumstances will guide you as you make decisions about appropriate risks and ways to protect children from hazards.

Developmental Differences and Safety

Characteristics of children at each stage of development determine decisions about their safety. Infants and toddlers explore the world by putting things in their mouths, so small objects in the environment are a choking hazard. Toddlers' rapidly developing large motor skills encourage climbing—both on climbers and on furniture—so sturdy furniture and close supervision are a must. Three- and 4-year-olds are curious and active, and bruises and scrapes are common during vigorous exploratory play even in safe environments. Kindergarten and primary-age children usually have well-developed motor skills and growing confidence in their own abilities, so injuries may occur during their investigations of materials, equipment, and their own emerging physical skills. Children with disabilities may explore and play in ways that are more characteristic of younger children and may need more supervision and protection than their typically developing peers.

Part of your job will be to eliminate hazards, keeping the characteristics of the children in mind. This does not mean eliminating appropriate risks. Jim Greenman (2007) reminds us, "There are often serious consequences if a program eliminates opportunities for children to use their bodies and materials in ways that involve some risk. . . . In a sterile, padded world with insufficient stimulation or challenge, humans either turn themselves off or turn to and on each other for stimulation" (p. 103). In settings where there is little opportunity for physical challenge or appropriate risk taking, children will invent these experiences for themselves. When you notice children climbing on railings, jumping from shelves, or balancing atop slide rims, they are telling you that they need additional large motor challenges. Ensuring safety is important, but it is also important to provide opportunities for children to test their own abilities and begin to learn to assess danger accurately. If you remove most challenges from children's environments, you deprive them of opportunities to build confidence and learn ways to keep themselves safe.

Safe Outdoor Environments

The outdoor environment provides children with rich and varied learning opportunities. In fact, the SS3 guidelines state that all children, including infants and toddlers, should have two or three outdoor play periods every day except when weather and air quality conditions create a significant health danger (AAP et al., 2013). Outdoor environments must be free of hazards and outfitted with equipment that is safe and age and stage appropriate. Although you may have little control over the characteristics of your program's outdoor environment, it is important that safety guides your decisions about how you use the space and the types of outdoor experiences you plan for children.

PLAYGROUNDS   Play yards for children should be:

Secure: Sturdy fences with gates and childproof latches ensure that children do not leave without supervision. Remind families that only adults are allowed to open gates. When possible, locate latches out of children's reach. Playgrounds for school-age children may use less structured boundaries, such as plants and hedges, to define outdoor play spaces.

Hazard Free: Check for and remove dangerous items such as broken glass or cigarette butts. Be sure that chemicals, fertilizers, tools, and other dangerous equipment or substances are locked out of children's reach. Because many common plants are toxic, it is important to know about the plants that grow in the play yard. Ask your local poison control center or cooperative extension service for information about poisonous plants and, if necessary, arrange for their removal.

Safely Equipped: Playground equipment (e.g., swings, slides, and climbers) provides opportunities for children to develop physical skills. This equipment should be appropriate for the size and skills of the children using it and should meet guidelines for safety. The U.S. Consumer Product Safety Commission's (2015) *Public Playground Safety Handbook* provides comprehensive standards for outdoor play structures.

Each year, more than 200,000 children go to U.S. hospital emergency rooms with injuries associated with playground equipment (Consumer Product Safety Commission, 2015). Many of these injuries occur when a child falls from the equipment onto the ground. The risk of injury from falls is reduced when play structures are surrounded by railings and have the proper type, depth, and area coverage of impact-absorbing materials beneath them.

The Consumer Product Safety Commission provides information about playground surfacing and requirements for its installation and maintenance. Grass, concrete, asphalt, soil, turf, and carpeting are unacceptable as impact-reducing surfacing. Sand, wood chips, pea gravel, shredded/recycled rubber mulch and commercially installed soft surfaces are the types of materials recommended for cushioning falls. If your playground has sand or wood chips, part of your job may be to turn and rake them regularly. If your playground does not have appropriate impact-reducing material, you can advocate for improving this important safety feature. See Chapter 6.2.3.1 of SS3 for further discussion of safe surfacing materials.

PRACTICES THAT PROMOTE OUTDOOR SAFETY   Established safety practices can go a long way toward ensuring that children's outdoor experiences are safe. You can work with administrators and other teachers to establish and follow such routines:

Complete regular safety checks.   Outdoor play areas should be checked daily for dangerous substances and these should be removed. Use a checklist such as the one included in Appendix B to regularly check outdoor equipment to ensure safety.

Check weather conditions.   Unless there is a wind chill below minus 15°F, a heat index above 90°F, or local health authorities report an air quality risk, plan to take children outside for some part of every day (SS3, 3.1.3.2).

See Figure 7.1 for more information about safe outdoor play in warm and cold weather.

Supervise attentively.   Even the safest playgrounds can't protect children from injury. Constant, attentive supervision by adults at all times is absolutely necessary. We have visited schools where teachers spent much of the outdoor time talking with one another instead of supervising the children. This puts children at risk and limits teachers' opportunities for enhancing learning. Early childhood staff should develop a plan for outdoor supervision that will ensure that adults are close to play structures and alert to children's activity at all times. While this careful attention can't prevent all injuries, it will ensure that in most instances children will be as safe as possible during outdoor play. Additionally, when you are engaged with children during outdoor time, you have many opportunities to capitalize on learning and promote development of a variety of skills.

Help children learn to be safe.   When young children play outside, they run, jump, and climb. They test themselves. Most of the time, their activity is safe and appropriate—but not always. It is important for teachers to work together to determine acceptable behaviors that ensure safe outdoor play in their setting. Develop guidelines (some teachers call them rules) that are stated positively—so that they tell children what *to* do—and worded so that each has a reason that a young child can understand. Use the suggestions in "Guidelines to Help Children Learn to Use Outdoor Equipment Safely" to talk to children about outdoor safety. Teach children there are two basic guidelines that everyone needs to follow—*keep yourself safe* and *keep other people safe*. It is also important to teach children to keep all plants and plant materials, such as seeds or flowers, out of their mouths and to bring broken or damaged toys to an adult right away.

Figure 7.1 Guidelines for Safe Outdoor Play in Warm and Cold Weather

The American Academy of Pediatrics recommends that young children have two to three periods for outdoor play each day, weather permitting.

For safe play in warm weather (a heat index of 90°F or less):

- Play outside before 10:00 or after 2:00.
- Offer water frequently.
- Check equipment to be certain that it will not burn children's skin and prevent access to equipment that is too hot.
- Ask families to provide hats with brims for sun protection and encourage children to wear them. Wear a hat yourself to model safe sun practices and to protect your own skin.
- With parental permission, apply sunscreen about 30 minutes prior to outdoor play; use sunscreen with a UVB and UVA ray protection factor (SPF) of 15 or higher. Keep infants younger than 6 months in shaded areas and dress them in wide brimmed hats and light clothing that covers their bodies completely. Limit use of sunscreen to small areas such as the face and the back of the hands (AAP, 5/3/16).

For safe play in cold weather (a wind chill no colder than minus 15°F):

- Ensure that children have dry, warm clothing; layers work well for active play, as children can remove clothing if they become too warm.
- Be sure scarves are tucked into jackets.
- Ensure that hoods do not have strings, as these can get caught on playground equipment and cause strangulation.
- When there is snow, encourage children to enjoy digging, exploring, and playing with it but do not allow them to eat it.

Guidelines to Help Children Learn to Use Outdoor Equipment Safely

Swings

So that you won't fall . . .

- Sit on swings.
- Hold on with both hands.
- Stop the swing before you get off.
- Allow only one person at a time to use a swing.

Slides

So that no one will get hurt . . .

- Hold on with both hands while climbing up.
- Wait until no one is on the slide in front of you before you go down.
- After you slide down, move away from the bottom of the slide.

Climbing Structures

So that no one will fall . . .

- Use both hands and a whole-fist grip when climbing.
- Keep toys and balls off of climbing structures and out of fall zones.
- Only _____ people at a time can use the climber (fill in a safe number).
- When it is wet, choose somewhere else to play.

Tricycles

So everyone can be safe . . .

- Sit on the seats.
- Stop before you bump into other people.
- Only one child at a time may ride on single-seat tricycles.

Vehicle and Trip Safety

Learning trips extend children's educational opportunities beyond the program site and should be a regular part of the curriculum. Whether you travel by school bus to visit a farm, take the city bus to a nearby shopping mall, or go on a neighborhood walk to find leaves and insects, you need to take precautions for children's safety.

Safe learning trips require a low adult–child ratio and small group size. The age and characteristics of the children determine the ratio and group size required to ensure their safety. A walk that includes crossing a busy street with a group of six 7-year-olds and one teacher may be safe and reasonable. That same walk with six toddlers and one teacher would be unsafe.

Plan trips carefully. Visit the site before the trip so that you will be aware of possible hazards as well as points of interest. Locate crosswalks, bathrooms, and sources of water. Carefully prepare children before the trip to be certain that they know the safety rules. We find that pretending to go on a trip before the actual event helps children follow rules and know what to expect. Notify families in advance of each excursion and, if possible, invite them to join you. Extra adult hands can be a welcome addition on excursions!

Always take a well-stocked first-aid kit and current emergency contact information for each child and adult. Develop an agreed-on plan for how to manage emergencies and take a working cell phone. Diapers and clothing changes for younger children will be needed. Be sure that children have access to drinking water and bring a meal or snack if the trip is during a time when children usually eat. Plan drop-off and pickup spots to minimize exposure to traffic.

All vehicles used to transport children should run well, be fitted with appropriate safety restraint systems (based on children's height and weight), and have all safety features operational. Child safety seats should be appropriate for the children's size and meet the Federal Motor Vehicle Safety Standards. The use of child safety seats reduces risk of death by 71% for children younger than 1 year of age and by 54% for children ages 1 to 4 (AAP et al., 2013).

Walking trips are a wonderful way of enriching the curriculum and helping children learn to be safe as pedestrians. Walk the route on your own before walking it with children. Determine hazards on the route and plan accordingly. Buggies or strollers with seat belts are a good way to take infants and young toddlers on walks around the neighborhood. Like all equipment, buggies and strollers should be checked before each trip to ensure that they are in good repair.

Safe Indoor Environments

Indoor environments need to be safe as well as attractive and functional. In order to create a classroom that is safe for children, you need to be aware of common hazards and do all that is possible to eliminate them. However, like the outdoor environment, some will be created by the building structure or design and will be beyond your control. When this is the case, it is your responsibility to safeguard children, make administrators aware of the hazards, and work with them to plan ways to minimize them. The box, "Common Classroom Hazards," identifies some types of hazards that are often present in classrooms for young children.

MATERIAL SAFETY   As a teacher, you will have more control over which toys and materials you offer to children than you do over the conditions of the building and its furnishings. You increase children's safety when you are attentive to manufacturer recommendations regarding the intended age-group for a toy and to notifications from government agencies and consumer groups that are concerned with toy safety. You can

Common Classroom Hazards

Hazard	Solution
Loose, slippery rugs and carpets	Eliminate throw rugs Install anti-slip rug underlay to area carpets Secure carpet edges with tape
Flammable fabrics	Install flame-resistant rugs and draperies or treat with child-safe flame retardant
Glass windows and doors	Check to make sure windows and glass doors are made of tempered or safety glass (you will be able to tell because there will be a small code etched into the glass located in one of the corners of the glass) If glass is not tempered, establish barriers that limit children's access. Install vision strips at both children's and adults' eye levels to protect against collisions
Electrical outlets	In classrooms for children under age 5, cover with safety plugs
Fans	Locate out of the reach of children
Radiators and heaters	Ensure that children do not have access to radiators or heaters Keep them away from curtains or other flammable materials
Hot water	Block access to water heaters Keep hot water temperatures below 120°F
Cleaning products, medications, knives and other sharp tools	Lock away in a sturdy, lockable cabinet
Blocked or cluttered exits	Keep areas around doors free from toys and other materials

keep up-to-date on new information on recalled toys at the U.S. Consumer Product Safety Commission's website.

Classrooms should be checked daily to ensure that all items accessible to children are safe for them to use. Because young children, particularly infants and toddlers, explore objects with their mouths, you must be especially aware of potential choking hazards. Small toys, broken pieces of toys, buttons, coins, and other small objects are choking hazards. Balloons are a particular choking danger for young children who are likely to put them into their mouths in an attempt to inflate them. Balloons should never be brought into an early childhood program, not even for birthdays or celebrations. Latex or vinyl gloves should also be kept out of children's reach. Foods that can pose choking risks will be discussed later in this chapter.

The suggestions in the "Golden Rules for Ensuring Safe Toys and Materials" box will help you select safe items.

SAFE EQUIPMENT AND FURNISHINGS   Furniture and equipment in early childhood programs should be comfortable, durable, and appropriately sized. Chairs should allow children's feet to touch the floor, and tables should be at a comfortable height for eating and working. Young toddlers need chairs that prevent them from falling out; cube chairs are well suited for this younger age-group. School-age children are most comfortable at tables with movable chairs. Shelving should be sturdy, stable, and low enough for you to see over. Corners and edges should be rounded. If you have an indoor climber, be careful to position it in an open area away from furniture and place large foam mats under and around it to cushion falls. All cribs used in child care centers must meet the Consumer Product Safety Commission (2011) crib standards.

SOURCE: Jeff Reese

Infant walkers and "jumpers" (seats attached to a door frame or ceiling that encourage the infants to jump or bounce) are prohibited by the SS3 standards. There have been several reports of

Golden Rules

for Ensuring Safe Toys and Materials

1. Choose toys and art materials that are labeled nontoxic. Crayons and paints should say "ASTM D-4236" on the package, meaning that they've been evaluated by the American Society for Testing and Materials.
2. Choose water-based paint, glue, and markers.
3. Avoid electrical toys that can cause shock.
4. Avoid battery-operated toys, as batteries and battery fluid can cause choking, internal bleeding, and chemical burns.
5. Do not use toys with strings or cords longer than 7 inches.
6. Check all toys regularly to ensure that they are in good repair with no cracks, rips, sharp edges, or loose parts.
7. Avoid materials with small removable parts that could be swallowed; for children under 3, choose toys that are larger than 1.25 inches in diameter and 2.5 inches in length; also avoid balls that are smaller than 1.75 inches in diameter. Remove button or google eyes from stuffed toys.
8. Avoid toy chests, which may trap children or pinch limbs.

springs or clamps breaking on various models of jumpers. Many injuries, some fatal, have been associated with infant walkers. They are dangerous because their upright position can cause children to tip over. Children in walkers can move around very fast, causing injury when they bump into furniture, objects, or people (AAP et al., 2013).

Practices That Promote Safety

Safety requires constant attention to the ways children interact with the program environment. The practices you adopt and the routines you implement will help keep children in your program safe.

PUT INFANTS TO SLEEP SAFELY   **Sudden infant death syndrome (SIDS)** is a tragedy that occurs when a seemingly healthy infant dies of no apparent cause while sleeping. No one knows exactly what causes SIDS, but research strongly supports the fact that SIDS deaths are significantly decreased when babies are put to sleep on their backs. You lessen the risk of SIDS when everyone caring for the infant follows a "safe sleep" policy. Guidelines are available from the American Academy of Pediatrics (AAP, 2016b). Families need information about safe sleep for babies. Check with a local health clinic or department of health for brochures or visit the website of the National Institute of Child Health and Human Development's Safe to Sleep campaign.

ESTABLISH SYSTEMS TO ENSURE THAT EQUIPMENT AND FACILITIES ARE SAFE   Every day that you work with young children, you will be aware of hazards and act immediately to remove them from your classroom. In addition, regularly completing safety inspections will help you and your teaching team ensure that less obvious hazards are noticed and removed or repaired. Use a checklist once a month to assess the safety of furnishings and equipment. See Appendix B for recommended intervals for inspections and for sample checklists.

SUPERVISE FOR SAFETY   An important way to keep children safe is to arrange your classroom so that you can see children at all times. When supervising children, it is important to be aware of individual differences and supervise appropriately—Monica may need a guiding hand and watchful eye when she snips with scissors, while Enrico is able to use them safely. As children grow and develop, your supervision strategies will need to evolve.

Attentive supervision will also limit injuries that occur as a result of children's conflicts. If you are paying close attention, you may be able to intervene before a child throws a block or bites another child.

SAFE GROUP SIZES AND TEACHER–CHILD RATIOS   It is difficult to keep children safe if the group is too large or if there are not enough adults to provide adequate supervision. Licensing requirements in most states include regulations for group size and ratios. Although as a teacher you may have little control over group size, it is important for you to know the standards so you can advocate for safe group sizes. The Early Childhood Program Standards and Accreditation Criteria developed by National Association for the Education of Young Children (NAEYC, 2015) offer guidelines for group size and teacher–child ratios for each age-group (see Table 7.1).

MONITOR ACCESS   Another way you protect children is by monitoring the people who enter your program. A system must be in place to ensure that only authorized adults pick up children. In most programs for children under age 5 and in some kindergartens, families must sign their children in and out. If an unfamiliar person arrives to pick up a child in your classroom, be certain to politely ask to see identification and then check the child's record to be sure the family has given this person permission to pick up the child. Sometimes, new teachers feel embarrassed or uncomfortable when asking for identification; however, in most cases, adults will be appreciative of your attention to children's safety.

Table 7.1 Teacher–Child Ratios within Group Size

Age Category	Age Range[1]	Group Size[2]										
		6	8	10	12	14	16	18	20	22	24	30
Infant	Birth to 15 months	1:3	1:4									
Toddler/Two	12 to 28 months	1:3	1:4	1:4[3]	1:4							
	21 to 36 months		1:4	1:5	1:6							
Preschool	30 to 48 months (2½ to 4 years)				1:6	1:7	1:8	1:9				
	48 to 60 months (4 to 5 years)						1:8	1:9	1:10			
	60 months to Kindergarten Enrollment (5 years to Kindergarten Enrollment)						1:8	1:9	1:10			
Kindergarten	Enrolled in any public or private kindergarten								1:10	1:11	1:12	

1 These age ranges purposefully overlap. If a group includes children whose ages range beyond the overlapping portion of two age categories, then the group is a mixed-age group. For mixed-age groups, universal criteria and criteria relevant to the age categories for that group apply.

2 Group sizes as stated are ceilings, regardless of the number of staff.

3 Group size of 10 is permissible for this age range, but an additional adult is required to stay within the best practice ratio.

Source: NAEYC, 2015. *New guidance on NAEYC accreditation criteria effective April 1, 2015*. Reprinted with permission from the National Association for the Education of Young Children (NAEYC).

PREPARE FOR EMERGENCIES   Advance preparation can limit the number or the seriousness of injuries that occur as a result of an emergency. You, your coworkers, and your administrator should have plans for emergencies including fire, weather emergencies such as earthquakes, hurricanes, or tsunamis, and threats from terrorism and other violence. You can prepare for emergencies by following the steps listed in Figure 7.2.

Teach Children to Be Safe

In order to help children learn to keep themselves safe, you need to view the world through their eyes. You can help them recognize hazards and notice when activities

Figure 7.2 Prepare for Emergencies

- Post current telephone numbers for emergency services and poison control centers near the telephone.
- Keep emergency contact telephone numbers for children's family members and have a system for regularly updating contact information.
- Maintain a well-stocked first-aid kit and keep it in a visibly marked and accessible place; if you place it in a clearly labeled backpack, it is easy to carry with you in the event of an emergency.
- Complete and maintain current first aid and CPR training certification. NAEYC Accreditation Guidelines (April 2015) require that at least one staff member with current CPR and pediatric first-aid training is always present with each group of children.
- Learn how to use fire extinguishers and make sure they are checked regularly to be certain that they are charged.
- Become familiar with your school's Disaster Action Plan; such a plan helps to ensure that both staff and families know what to do in the event of an emergency, such as weather, national defense, or terrorism, and are prepared to deal with these emergencies in an efficient way.
- Hold regular practice drills for evacuation during fire and other emergencies.
- Have in place plans for the following:
  - What to do if someone (child or adult) needs emergency medical treatment.
  - Supervision of children if someone must attend to an injured or ill child.
  - What to do when a child is missing.

Video Example 7.1: Preparing for Emergencies

Watch the video that explains some important practices to follow in the event that an emergency evacuation is needed. What are some points that should be included in an emergency evacuation plan? What should be kept in an emergency bag?

may be dangerous. Children need to know about unfamiliar situations, experiences, and equipment. It is important to give them information that they can remember and to teach them safety skills that they can master through practice. Teach them procedures for handling tools and materials safely. For example, we have discussed using a knife with 4-, 5-, and 6-year-olds in this way: "This is a knife. One side is sharp, and the other side isn't. When you cut with a knife, it's important to have the sharp side down and to make sure that your fingers aren't under the cutting blade. Hold onto the handle with one hand and use the other hand to push down—that way you won't accidentally get cut."

Safety explanations for toddlers must be simple and accompanied with close supervision and physical protection: "The pot is hot. Let's just look until it cools down." Place the pot out of reach and place your body between the pot and the toddlers.

Young children learn about safety in the context of daily life. As you prepare for a trip or a fire drill, have children help you create safety rules and procedures. Safety concepts can be integrated into activities that you are already doing. For example:

- Sing a song, such as Woody Guthrie's "Riding in My Car," and add a verse about wearing a seat belt.
- Add a painted crosswalk to the trike path for practice.
- Place some obviously broken toys around the classroom and send children on a broken-toy hunt as a way to teach them to always bring broken items to an adult.
- Include props and pictures of firefighters in full regalia in the dramatic play area to help children be unafraid of them in a real emergency. (Young children have been known to hide during a real fire!)

You can also teach children about safety through planned curriculum on fire, home, and traffic safety and on caring for themselves. Help children become familiar with the people and procedures to follow in disasters (such as fires and tornadoes). Teach them to always come to an adult when they hear a siren or see something that may be dangerous.

It is tempting to teach safety as a series of warnings—don't play with matches, don't go near the water, don't run in the street, don't talk to strangers. It is more effective, however, to teach children things they *can* do and help them understand why they should do them. For example, always bring matches to a grown-up, walk across the street in the crosswalk, and talk only with people you know. Let children know that you are pleased to see their growing ability to care for themselves.

Reflect On

Childhood Dangers

What do you recall from your childhood about things that were dangerous? How did adults teach you to deal with these risks? Think about children you know today. What are some risks that they encounter? What are some appropriate ways you can teach them to be safe?

Protecting Children from Abuse and Neglect

As an early childhood educator, you have legal and ethical responsibilities to identify and report child abuse and neglect. Your responsibilities include the following:

- Be aware of the indicators of abuse and neglect. (See Figure 7.3 for a description of these.)
- Report suspected cases to the appropriate agency so that the child and family can receive assistance.

Figure 7.3 "Red Flags": Possible Indicators of Child Abuse and Neglect*

Physical Abuse

- Has unexplained burns, bites, bruises, broken bones, or black eyes
- Has fading bruises or other marks noticeable after an absence from school
- Protests or cries when it is time to go home; seems frightened of the parents
- Shrinks at the approach of adults
- Reports injury by a parent or another adult caregiver

Emotional Maltreatment

- Shows extremes in behavior, such as overly compliant or demanding behavior, extreme passivity, or aggression
- Is either inappropriately adult (parenting other children, for example) or inappropriately infantile (frequently rocking or head-banging, for example)
- Is delayed in physical or emotional development
- Reports a lack of attachment to the parent

Sexual Abuse

- Has difficulty walking or sitting
- Expresses fear or reluctance to use the toilet
- Shows a sudden change in appetite
- Demonstrates bizarre, sophisticated, or unusual sexual knowledge or behavior
- Runs away
- Reports sexual abuse by a parent or another adult or older child

Neglect

- Frequently absent from school
- Seems excessively hungry
- Begs, steals or hides food
- Lacks needed medical or dental care, immunizations, or glasses
- Is consistently dirty and has severe body odor; frequently arrives in soiled diapers
- Lacks sufficient clothing for the weather
- States that there is no one at home to provide care

* These signs may signal a variety of circumstances and situations and any one taken alone may not be indicative of child abuse or neglect. Often children will exhibit more than one sign of abuse and they will occur in more than one instance.

SOURCE: Based on information from Child Welfare Information Gateway (2013).

- Inform families of your reporting obligation as part of their orientation to the program.

- Know about and use resources such as your local child protective service and the NAEYC Code of Ethical Conduct.

- Know what is available in your community for educating families about how to interact with their children in constructive, non-abusive ways.

A part of helping children to be safe includes teaching them some ways to avoid abuse and to get help if abuse does occur. When you listen to children with respect, you help them build a sense of confidence and self-worth. They learn that they can share concerns and feelings with trusted adults. Let children know that it is *never* okay for someone else to hurt them and they can ask for help if they are being harmed in any way. The "Golden Rules for Helping Children Protect Themselves from Abuse" box offers some additional suggestions.

It is impossible to "abuse-proof" very young children. No lesson, curriculum approach, or strategy will guarantee children's safety. Several well-publicized approaches are designed to prevent child abuse. However, their focus may alarm or mislead children. They tend to place responsibility on the relatively powerless child instead of on the adult. Effective child abuse prevention is an ongoing part of children's learning, not a one-time "inoculation."

Golden Rules

for Helping Children Protect Themselves from Abuse

1. **Provide choices.**   Offer children opportunities to make choices, including the choice to say no to an activity, food, or suggestion. This includes the right to reject physical contact. You offer choices by asking or alerting children before you touch or pick them up by saying things like, "May I give you a hug?" "Would you like me to rub your back?" or "I'm going to pick you up and put you on the changing table" rather than doing so without warning.

2. **Teach children to say "no."**   Let children know that it is okay for them to resist physical intrusion and to say, "No, I don't want you to do that to me!" to other children and to adults. This requires that you respect children's feelings and invite their cooperation rather than insisting on their compliance. You show respect for children when you avoid using physical force (e.g., picking children up and forcing them to be where they do not want to be) except in situations where a child's immediate safety is at stake.

3. **Develop body awareness and appreciation.**   Provide many ways for children to appreciate their bodies through routines, games, songs, movement, and stories. Use correct names for body parts. Children who value their bodies are likely to avoid harming themselves or letting others harm them.

4. **Encourage children to express needs and feelings.**   Help children understand feelings and encourage self-expression through words, stories, music, art, movement, and puppetry. Children who can express their ideas, needs, and feelings are better equipped to handle situations in which they are uncomfortable.

5. **Integrate safety education.**   Include safety in classroom activities through discussion, role-playing, and dramatization so children learn things they can do to be safe in a variety of settings (e.g., crossing the street, riding in cars, playing at the beach, shopping at the mall, answering the phone, or being with a stranger or with a friend).

6. **Distinguish surprises from secrets.**   Explore differences between secrets and surprises to help children understand that surprises are things you are waiting to share to make someone happy (like a birthday present) and that secrets are things someone wants you to hide that feels dangerous or wrong.

7. **Build positive self-esteem.**   Help children feel good about themselves—their characteristics, abilities, and potential. Recognizing and valuing differences and affirming individuality through song, celebration, and activities helps children feel they are worthy of protection.

Reflect On

Your Ethical Responsibilities

You have a 6-year-old in your class who is frequently absent from school. When you ask her about her many absences, she tells you that she had to stay home to take care of her baby sister because her mom was sick or had to work. Using the guidelines in Chapter 1, reflect on your ethical responsibilities in this situation.

A Quick Check 7.1

Gauge your understanding of the concepts in this section.

Healthy Places for Children

What could be more critical for children's overall welfare than being healthy? As a teacher, you will have many opportunities to involve children in regular routines that teach them to keep themselves healthy. You will also ensure that classroom environments are maintained in a manner that promotes health.

What is health? Health is a state of overall well-being—physical, mental, and social. It is more than just the absence of disease, it is a state of holistic wellness (WHO, 1948). We keep children healthy when we provide for all aspects of their development and well-being—their mental health, their developing social abilities, their growing bodies and brains, and their intellectual development. *Healthy People 2020*, a national initiative of the U.S. Department of Health and Human Services (2014), stresses the important relationships between children's health and their ability to learn.

Part of your job as an early childhood teacher is to know and use practices that promote the health of each child. Take precautions each day to limit the spread of disease. Ensure that all children, including those with disabilities and those with chronic health conditions, have a healthy classroom. Learn to identify health risks and act promptly to limit them. With administrators and health care professionals, implement policies and procedures that address health routines and health emergencies. Equally important, develop curricula that help children learn to care for their bodies and that engage them in daily exercise and healthy routines.

Understand How Illness Spreads

When Jasmine's dad comes to pick her up at school, her teacher tells him that Jasmine has a runny nose and is starting to cough. "She has a cold again!" her dad exclaims. "It seems like since Jasmine started school she is sick all the time."

Families and teachers alike are concerned about infectious diseases. Both want to ensure that early childhood programs are doing all they can to prevent and control the spread of illness. Learning to do this effectively will be an important part of your job. You control illness by eliminating **pathogens**—tiny organisms such as bacteria, viruses, or parasites that cause disease—and by limiting the ways that they can be spread from one person to another. You also do this by helping to improve children's overall health. Good nutrition, exercise, and good psychological health all improve resistance and decrease susceptibility to disease.

The close contact that people have with one another in early childhood programs increases opportunities for pathogens to be transmitted. Respiratory diseases such as colds and flu are spread when secretions from the mouth, nose, eyes, and lungs pass from one person to the other. This can happen through direct touching; sharing of toys, objects, and food; or contact with droplets in the air when individuals cough or sneeze. Diarrhea and other diseases of the intestinal tract are caused by viruses, bacteria, or parasites that are spread through contact with fecal matter. This happens when hand-washing or diapering practices are inadequate. Hepatitis B and HIV/AIDS are serious infections that are spread when the blood of an infected person comes in contact with a mucous membrane (lining of the mouth, eyes, nose, rectum, or genitals) or with a cut or break in the skin of another individual. Ensuring healthy routines can limit the spread of these diseases.

Follow Healthy Routines

In a healthy environment, routines established and maintained by the adults limit the spread of disease. Children are protected from many pathogens when sanitary hand-washing, diapering, and toileting practices are followed.

HAND WASHING   The most effective measure for preventing the spread of disease in early childhood programs is frequent and thorough hand washing (AAP et al., 2013).

All early childhood practitioners, particularly those who work with infants and toddlers, need to wash their hands many times a day. By doing so, they limit the spread of disease and protect their own health. Young children also need to wash their hands after activities that may put them into contact with pathogens. See Figure 7.4 for recommended times for hand washing.

To make hand washing effective in preventing disease, you should use running water and liquid soap, rub your hands together vigorously for at least 20 seconds, wash all over from fingertips to wrists, rinse thoroughly, dry hands on a disposable paper towel, and turn off the faucet using the towel to hold the faucet handle so as not to contaminate clean hands (AAP et al., 2013). Take time to teach children hand-washing routines and insist that hands

SOURCE: Jeff Reese

Figure 7.4 When to Wash Hands

You keep yourself and children healthy when everyone engages in frequent hand washing.

Teachers should wash their hands . . .
- When first entering the classroom
- Before and after handling food
- Before and after eating or feeding children
- Before and after changing diapers, assisting a child with toileting or using the toilet
- After contact with body fluids (e.g., wiping a nose, bandaging a cut, cleaning up a toilet accident, or cleaning up vomit)
- After handling pets
- After playing or cleaning up sand or water play areas
- Before giving a child medication
- After cleaning or handling garbage

Children should wash their hands . . .
- When first entering the classroom
- Before and after handling food
- Before and after eating
- After diapering or using the toilet
- After contact with body fluids (e.g., wiping a nose or bandaging a cut)
- After handling pets
- After sand or water play

Video Example 7.2: Learning to Wash Hands

Watch the video to see a teacher assisting a toddler with hand washing. What did the teacher do in the video to help the child learn appropriate hand-washing? What would have been different if the child had been older?

be washed thoroughly and regularly. Children can sing a song such as "Twinkle, Twinkle, Little Star" or a hand-washing song that lasts for approximately 20 seconds. Assist younger children and those who are just learning the hand-washing process. Hold infants and young toddlers at the sink, gently assisting them to rub hands together and rinse.

DIAPERING AND TOILETING   Because diapering and toileting are some of the most prevalent ways of spreading communicable illnesses, great care must be taken in managing them. Healthy diapering procedures can be more easily followed if the changing area is well set up and maintained. A diapering area needs a changing table with a washable mat. Procedures for sanitary diapering should be posted at adult eye level. Paper to cover the changing surface, plastic bags for soiled diapers, a pedal-operated lidded wastebasket, soap solution, sanitizing solution, and each child's diapers and supplies need to be within easy reach. To protect yourself from contact with feces, wear disposable vinyl gloves. The sink used to wash hands after diapering needs to be separate from food preparation areas. Most programs require each family to bring a supply of disposable diapers for their child. Because children's skin may be sensitive to diaper wipes, creams, and lotions, use only those provided by the family. When the diaper change is complete, be sure to record information about the change on the child's daily record. Guidelines for sanitary diapering procedures are provided in Standard 3.2.1.4 of SS3. If you work in a program in which children wear diapers, you need to receive training in how to diaper children in a caring and sanitary manner.

Toilet areas must be cleaned and sanitized daily, and additional sanitizing may be necessary during the day. To encourage both independence and sanitary use of toilets and sinks, it is best if they are child-sized. Otherwise, stable stools or wooden platforms will make them accessible. Use of potty chairs in group care settings is prohibited by SS3 because they are difficult to sanitize. Toilet tissue, running water, soap, and paper towels

Video Example 7.3: Sanitary Diapering

Watch the video that shows a teacher who is careful to use appropriate sanitation practices while she engages the toddler in the diapering process. What did you notice that she did to limit the spread of germs? How did she involve the child in the process? Why do you think she did this?

need to be within the reach of the children. Staff should carefully supervise toddlers' and preschoolers' use of the toilet. Older children will want privacy but may occasionally need assistance in the event of an accident. In some cases, children with disabilities will require special assistance for toileting. Use gloves when you help children and when cleaning up after accidents. Clothing soiled with feces should be tightly bagged and sent home for laundering.

TOOTHBRUSHING Children should to be taught how to brush teeth effectively and must be supervised during toothbrushing. Toothbrushes require careful storage and sanitizing. If your program includes toothbrushing, consult a health care professional or review Standard 3.1.5.1: Routine Oral Hygiene Activities in SS3 to ensure you are using best practices for in-school toothbrushing.

SOURCE: Jeff Reese

CLEAN, SANITIZE, AND DISINFECT Regular cleaning, disinfecting, and sanitizing of classroom equipment and materials effectively limits the spread of illness in early childhood programs. Classrooms must be **clean**—free of dirt and debris. Classroom furnishings, such as diaper change tables, countertops, door and cabinet handles, toilets, and rest mats, must also be **disinfected**—treated with a solution that destroys germs. Items that come in contact with food, such as countertops, cutting boards, and serving utensils, as well as toys that children put into their mouths, should be **sanitized**—treated with a product that reduces germs on surfaces to levels considered safe by public health regulations. Review "Appendix J: Selecting an Appropriate Sanitizer or Disinfectant" in SS3 to learn more about selecting and using these products as well as appropriate dilutions of chlorine bleach. Ensure that personal items, such as bedding, clothing, and comfort objects, are stored in individual storage units, such as a cubby, locker, plastic tub, or box, labeled with the child's name. Bedding should be washed at least weekly either in program facilities or in family homes.

USE STANDARD PRECAUTIONS   Learn about and follow standard precautions—safety measures that help prevent the transmission of illnesses that are carried in the body fluids. This includes when you clean a scrape, help a child with toileting or care for a bloody nose. See Figure 7.5.

PREPARE AND STORE FOOD SAFELY   Attention to food preparation—both what is prepared and how it is prepared—is important to children's health. If you are involved in food preparation (even slicing apples for snack), you will have the responsibility for making sure that surfaces and utensils are kept scrupulously clean and sanitized. All trash must be disposed of in tightly covered containers that are emptied at least daily. Perishable foods must be refrigerated at or below 40 degrees, and hot foods kept at 140 degrees until they are served. State departments of health regulations require anyone who prepares and/or serves food to be free of communicable diseases and use frequent and thorough hand washing to reduce the spread of pathogens.

FOLLOW GUIDELINES FOR EXCLUDING SICK CHILDREN   Recognizing early signs of illness in children and having policies and procedures for exclusion also help prevent the spread of disease. All programs need to have clearly written policies that address when children must be excluded due to illness and when they may return to the program. *Managing Infectious Diseases in Child Care and Schools: A Quick Reference Guide* (Aronson & Shope, 2013) gives useful information about the symptoms of childhood illnesses and those that require exclusion. In *Healthy Young Children* (2012), Susan Aronson (2012, p.14) notes, "Contrary to popular belief and practice, only a *few* illnesses require exclusion of sick children to ensure protection of other children and staff." If children are able to engage in their usual activities, they may remain in school even if they have symptoms of mild illness. Children who have colds are most contagious before symptoms appear, so exclusion does little to limit the spread of this common illness. Children should not be in school, however, when they are not able to participate comfortably in school activities or when they need more care than the staff can provide while also caring for the other children in the group (SS3 Standard 3.6.1.1: Inclusion/Exclusion/Dismissal of Children; AAP et al., 2013). Most states have guidelines for when children

---

Figure 7.5 Standard Precautions for Handling Body Fluids

When handling body fluids (blood, saliva, vomit, feces):

- Wear disposable vinyl or latex gloves.
- Remove glove by grasping the inner cuff and pulling it off inside out.
- Dispose in covered waste can lined with a disposable plastic bag.
- Wash hands thoroughly; lather for at least 30 seconds.
- Place soiled clothing and bedding in plastic bags and send home for laundering.
- Dispose of all blood-contaminated items such as towels, rags, and bandages and band-aids, as well as soiled diapers, by placing them in plastic bags and tying securely.
- Clean all contaminated surfaces by first using detergent followed by a rinse and use of a disinfectant solution.

SOURCE: Based on information from American Academy of Pediatrics, American Public Health Association, and National Resource Center for Health and Safety in Child Care and Early Education, *Caring for Our Children: National Health and Safety Performance Standards: Guidelines for Early Care and Education Programs*, 2013.

should be excluded from programs. Consult your local health agency or health care consultant if you have questions regarding an appropriate illness policy for your program.

It is important to have basic training for handling common symptoms of illness, such as fevers and vomiting, and for determining when a child should be isolated from others for health reasons. In some schools, a nurse or health aide will attend to health-related matters; in others, teachers or administrators will be responsible.

Reflect On

Your Ethical Responsibilities

A single mom drops her 4-year-old child off with you after he has been out of school for 2 days with a fever, constant runny nose, and cough. The mother reports that the child is feeling much better and that her boss has informed her that she will lose her job if she misses any more work this month. By 10:00 a.m., the child is running a fever of 101, coughing continuously, and complaining of a headache. He goes to the library corner and falls asleep. You do not have a school nurse in your program. Using the guidelines in Chapter 1, reflect on your ethical responsibilities in this situation.

Work with a Health Care Professional

There are so many issues related to children's health needs that early childhood educators cannot possibly know about all of them. The SS3 standards (AAP et al., 2013) and the NAEYC Early Childhood Accreditation Criteria (NAEYC, 2017) recommend that every program have a **health care consultant**—a licensed pediatric health professional or a health professional with specific training in health consultation for early childhood programs. Health care consultants can assist you in developing and implementing policies and procedures to promote children's and adults' health. Many states have received funding from the Healthy Child Care America campaign to support increased resources for health consultation for early childhood programs. You can visit the Healthy Child Care America website to learn about resources in your state.

Know About Conditions That Affect Health

There are many circumstances that affect children's health. Learning about these and ways to help children and families stay healthy is part of your job as an early childhood teacher.

CHILDHOOD OBESITY According to the Centers for Disease Control and Prevention (CDC, 2015), childhood obesity has more than doubled in the past 30 years. In fact, a report from the White House Task Force on Childhood Obesity (2010) found that one in every five children today will be overweight or obese by the time that they reach their sixth birthday. This puts them at risk for developing significant health problems such as high blood pressure, heart disease, and type 2 diabetes. See Figure 7.6 for more information about childhood obesity.

Studies indicate that three trends in contemporary lifestyles have influenced the rapid increase in overweight children:

- Decreased opportunity for active play and a more sedentary lifestyle

SOURCE: Jeff Reese

Figure 7.6 Some Facts About Childhood Obesity

- Childhood obesity has more than doubled in children and quadrupled in adolescents in the past 30 years.
- In 2012, more than one third of children and adolescents were overweight or obese.
- Obesity rates among preschoolers ages 2 to 5 have doubled in the past four decades.
- One in four children are overweight or obese by the time they enter kindergarten.
- Over half of obese children first become overweight at or before age 2.
- Only 25% of children ages 2 to 11 years consume three servings of vegetables a day, and less than 50% consume two daily servings of fruit.
- Preschool children spend over 4 hours a day watching television and videos, including time in child care.
- 64% of children 3 to 5 years of age are in some form of child care and spend an average of 29 hours per week in that child care setting; consequently early childhood programs have opportunities to affect children's food intake and their activities levels.

SOURCES: Based on information from *CDC Healthy Schools: Childhood Obesity Facts*, 2015; *CDC Overweight and Obesity Early Care and Education Indicator Report*, 2016; *White House Task Force on Childhood Obesity: Report to the President*, 2010.

- Increased "screen time," including television, video games, computers and cell phones
- Increased calorie consumption, including significantly more fast food and sugar-sweetened beverages.

The *Let's Move* campaign (letsmove.obamawhitehouse.archives.gov/) was launched in 2011 through the combined efforts of private, nonprofit, and government groups. This initiative provides a variety of tools and educational strategies geared toward ending obesity within this generation. It has expanded to include *Let's Move! Child Care*, which offers goals that early childhood programs can adopt as a focus for promoting children's health along with a variety of other tools that teachers and programs can use. Figure 7.7 shows a checklist of healthy practices developed by the *Let's Move! Child Care* initiative.

A study published in the *Journal of the American Medical Association* showed declines in obesity rates among children ages 2 to 5, indicating that current programs to improve young children's nutritional health are having a positive effect (CDC, 2014). You can contribute to this positive trend by including the goals of the *Let's Move! Child Care* initiative in your program and by implementing some of their strategies into your regular routines.

LEAD POISONING Childhood lead poisoning is a serious health problem. The CDC (2013a) estimates that 500,000 young children in the United States have elevated lead levels. Children who ingest or inhale even small amounts of lead are at risk for

Figure 7.7 Let's Move! Child Care Checklist

- **Get Children Moving:** Provide 2 hours of active play time throughout the day, including outside play when possible; include both teacher-led/structured activities and free play.
- **Limit Screen time:** No screen time for children under 2 years. For children age 2 and older, limit screen time to no more than 30 minutes per week during child care, and work with parents and caregivers to ensure children have no more than 1 hour of quality screen time per day, the amount recommended by the American Academy of Pediatrics.
- **Nurture Healthy Eaters:** Serve fruits or vegetables at every meal; eat meals family style when possible; avoid fried foods.
- **Provide Healthy Beverages:** Provide water during meals and throughout the day and do not serve sugary drinks. For children age 2 and older, serve low-fat (1%) or nonfat milk and no more than one 4- to 6-ounce serving of 100% juice per day.
- **Support Breastfeeding:** For mothers who want to continue breastfeeding, provide their milk to their infants and welcome them to breastfeed during the child care day; support all new parents in their decisions about infant feeding.

SOURCE: Based on information from Let's Move! Child Care (2017).

decreased bone and muscle growth, developmental delays, and behavior and learning problems. Children who come in contact with lead from either paint or plumbing are at risk. Buildings constructed before 1978 may contain lead-based paint. If your classroom is in an older building, work with other staff and administrators to ensure that paint has been tested by a licensed inspector to determine whether lead is present. If it is, your program will need to follow local guidelines to remove lead-based paint from all surfaces or completely cover it with nonleaded paint. Older buildings may also have lead pipes. As with paint, ask your administration to consult with your local health department to determine if your water should be tested for possible lead contamination.

Research indicates that the incidence of lead poisoning is highest in children who live in low-income areas and who consume a nutrient-deficient diet, which increases lead absorption (Marotz, 2015). If children in your program are at risk for exposure to lead in their homes, you can offer families information about the potential dangers from lead poisoning and encourage them to ask their health care providers to screen children for possible lead poisoning. To obtain brochures and information about lead poisoning, visit the Environmental Protection Agency's website.

FOOD ALLERGIES AND INTOLERANCES   The Centers for Disease Control reports that food allergies among children increased approximately 50% between 1997 and 2011 and that 4-6% of children have one or more food allergies (CDC, 2013b). Certain foods—nuts and nut products, eggs, wheat and gluten, soy, milk and milk products, fish and shellfish—are most likely to be the source of food allergies. (healthychildren. org, 2015; CDC, 2013b) A severe allergic reaction to food (or other allergens such as bee stings) can cause *anaphylaxis*—swelling of the airway, serious breathing difficulty, a drop in blood pressure, loss of consciousness, and, in some cases, even death. Food intolerances, different from food allergies, are experienced by some children and can cause stomach upset, rashes, or hives.

Children who have a history of severe allergic reactions (to either food or other allergens) may need to have an **Epi-Pen** kept at school. If you have a child in your class who may need this treatment, you will need to consult a health care provider about the proper way to administer this medication.

Most programs have systems in place to prevent teachers from accidently serving prohibited food to children with food allergies. Because of the increasing prevalence of nut allergies, many schools have adopted a "no-nuts" policy, which means that no one can bring to school any food containing nuts or nut oils.

ASTHMA AND ENVIRONMENTAL ALLERGIES   Asthma, a respiratory disease that causes intermittent episodes of wheezing and difficulty breathing, is the most common chronic childhood disease (Ball, Bindler, & Cowen, 2011). Children who live in impoverished neighborhoods, minorities, and children who live in urban areas are most at risk for developing childhood asthma (Moorman et al., 2015). Asthma attacks can be triggered by a variety of circumstances and irritants, including pollen, mold, traffic exhaust, cleaning products, fragrances, weather changes, and emotions (Ball et al., 2011). Asthma attacks can be severe and, if untreated, may be life threatening. Children who experience asthma attacks may require medication while they are in your care. If you have a child in your class who suffers from asthma, it is important that you learn the signs of an asthma attack and receive training on how to administer medications prescribed for symptom management.

Some children experience headaches, runny noses, coughs, watery eyes, and fatigue as a result of sensitivity to environmental allergens, including pollen, dust, mildew, and pet dander. According to the American Academy of Asthma, Allergy, and Immunology, 10% of American children under age 17 have a sensitivity to environmental allergens. It is important to know which children in your class have allergies so that you can remove as many potential allergens as possible from the environment. Understanding their symptoms will also prevent you from mistakenly thinking that an allergic child has a cold or other infectious illness.

> **A Quick Check 7.2**
>
> Gauge your understanding of the concepts in this section.

Help Children Learn to Be Healthy

Young children are intrigued with learning about themselves and their bodies. If you make it interesting, they will enjoy learning about the vital topics of health and nutrition. This will lay the foundation for habits that will promote health throughout their lives.

Children can learn good health habits during classroom routines and activities. When the day is scheduled to include periods of both planned and spontaneous movement activities, children learn to appreciate the value of being physically active. When they help plan healthy snacks and meals and participate in healthful routines, they begin to appreciate their bodies and acquire important attitudes and skills. A carefully planned curriculum can help them understand human growth and development, body parts and functions, and the value of cleanliness, medical and dental care, exercise, rest, and good nutrition.

Promote Physical Activity and Movement

Most children enjoy movement and physical activity. You can support this natural inclination by including exercise and fitness activities in your daily curriculum and helping children value physical activity as an important aspect of health.

Reflect On

Physical Activity

What types of physical activity do you enjoy? How do you include physical activity in your life? Is being active pleasurable for you? In what ways? How can you help children to enjoy being active?

The Society of Health and Physical Educators (SHAPE, 2009) recommends that all children participate in age-appropriate activities that have been designed to help them acquire movement skills, fitness, and overall wellness. Further, the SHAPE recommends that toddlers and preschool-age children *should not be sedentary* (inactive) *for more than an hour* except when sleeping and that school-age children *should have not more than 2 hours of inactivity*. Additionally, preschoolers and school-age children should accumulate at least 60 minutes each day of structured physical activity and toddlers should have up to 30. All age-groups need at least 60 minutes and up to several hours per day of unstructured physical activity.

These recommendations have important implications for program planning. You will need to find ways to plan structured movement activities and to design your schedule so that children are encouraged to be active. See the "Golden Rules for Supporting Movement" box for suggestions on how to help children become physically fit.

Golden Rules

for Supporting Movement

1. **Make movement activities part of each day's plan.**   Include action games, dance, yoga, creative movement, or other active events in your daily planning.
2. **Arrange your classroom so that you can easily include movement activities.**   Organize classrooms so that you have (or can easily move furniture to create) a space for active games and movement.
3. **Create movement stations.**   These are areas set up either indoors or outside that encourage particular kinds of movement, e.g. walking a balance beam, tossing beanbags into a bucket, jumping over two blocks or ropes set up in a v-shape, etc.
4. **Plan daily outdoor time.**   If there are no open areas outdoors for running, jumping, rolling, and other active play, take children to nearby parks for part of each day.
5. **Select equipment that encourages movement and active play.**   Choose materials such as hoops, ropes, scarves, ribbon sticks, stepping-stones, and balls of all sizes.
6. **Show children that you enjoy being active.**   Children learn from what you model. Let them see your enthusiasm for physical activity. Make active play engaging and fun and participate with them.
7. **Surprise children with new or unexpected movement activities.**   Encourage everyone to run around the playground three times before coming inside. During choice time, ring a chime and have everyone jump in place for 2 minutes before resuming indoor play. Before starting circle, engage with them in a dance to lively music that you enjoy.
8. **Help children understand why movement is important.**   Let children know why you are encouraging physical activities: "When you jumped like rabbits, that got your heart moving fast! Do you feel it? It's good for your heart to give it a workout like that sometimes."
9. **Offer children choices for active play.**   Let them choose ones that they enjoy and acknowledge the pleasure they show as they engage in them. This lays a foundation for lifelong fitness.

Source: Based on Pica (2006) and Moravcik & Nolte (2017).

Encourage Healthy Food Choices

We know that food choices are a significant factor in childhood obesity. This includes both the types of foods selected and the amounts eaten. From infancy, children begin to make choices about food. They decide which foods they like. They learn about how much they should eat, when and where they will eat, which foods are "treats," and which are good for them. Many of children's food preferences are established in early childhood. You can help children learn that their health is affected by the food they eat and that they can make food choices that will help them grow and be healthy. You help them learn about healthy eating when you follow the suggestions described in "Golden Rules for Supporting Children's Healthy Eating."

Golden Rules

for Supporting Children's Healthy Eating

1. **Never use food as a reward or withhold food as a punishment.**   This teaches children that food is about feeling good, not about nourishment, and can lead to later eating disorders. It may also teach that less healthy treats like candy are better than healthier choices. All children have a basic right to food. When it is withheld, their trust in adults is compromised.
2. **Create a relaxed and pleasant eating environment.**   Children thrive when meals are non-hurried times to enjoy food and the company of others. Plan so that mealtimes are not rushed. Make tables attractive. Sit with children during meals and snacks.

(continued)

classroom, you ensure that every child you work with has opportunities to experience overall health and wellness.

 Application Exercise 7.2 Final Reflection

 ## To Learn More

Read

Basic Health and Safety Practices: Child Care Provider's Guide, University of Hawai'i Center on the Family (2015).

Beyond Remote-Controlled Childhood: Teaching Young Children in the Media Age, D. Levin (2013).

Cooking Is Cool: Heat-Free Recipes for Kids to Cook, M. Dambra (2013).

Cup Cooking: Individual Child Portion Picture Recipes, B. Foote (2001).

Everybody Has a Body: Science from Head to Toe, R. Rockwell & R. Williams (1992).

Growing, Growing Strong: A Whole Health Curriculum for Young Children, C. Smith, C. Hendricks, & B. Bennet (2014).

Here We Go . . . Watch Me Grow, C. Hendricks & C. Smith (1991).

Pretend Soup and Other Real Recipes: A Cookbook for Preschoolers and Up, M. Katzen & A. Henderson (1997).

Rethinking Nutrition: Connecting Science and Practice in Early Childhood Settings, S. Nitzke, D. Riley, A. Ramminger & G. Jacobs (2015)

Salad People and More Real Recipes: A New Cookbook for Preschoolers and Up, M. Katzen (2005).

The Cooking Book: Fostering Young Children's Learning and Delight, L. Colker (2005).

Visit a Website

The following agencies and organizations have websites related to children's health and safety:

Action for Healthy Kids

American Academy of Pediatrics

Centers for Disease Control and Prevention

Child Health Alert

Healthy Child Care America

Healthy People 2020

KidsHealth

Let's Move! Child Care

National Resource Center for Health and Safety in Child Care and Early Education

Prevent Child Abuse America

U.S. Consumer Product Safety Commission

U.S. Department of Agriculture

Document Your Skill & Knowledge About Promoting Children's Health, Safety, and Well-Being in Your Professional Portfolio

Include some or all of the following:

- A safety or health checklist that you have completed with a written plan to correct any hazards or deficiencies that you discovered

- A recipe file for healthy snacks that you can make with children

- An activity plan that teaches young children something meaningful about keeping themselves safe and well

- An action plan to promote children's fitness and nutrition that follows the five goals outlined on the *Let's Move! Child Care* website.

Shared Writing 7.1 Your Ethical Responsibilities Related to Promoting Children's Health, Safety, and Wellbeing

The Learning Environment

A wonderful place to be a child is a place where a child can fall in love with the world.

ELIZABETH PRESCOTT

There is no behavior apart from environment.

ROBERT SOMMER

 Chapter Learning Outcomes:

8.1 Identify the essential elements of a good learning environment for young children.

8.2 Describe ways to arrange space and materials in the indoor learning environment.

8.3 Describe ways to arrange space and materials in an outdoor learning environment.

8.4 Recognize how environments should vary for children at different stages of development.

8.5 Identify how schedules are organized to promote learning in early childhood programs.

NAEYC Professional Preparation Standards

The NAEYC Professional Preparation Standard that applies to this chapter:

Standard 1: Promoting Child Development and Learning (NAEYC, 2009).

Key element:

1c: Using developmental knowledge to create healthy, respectful, supportive, and challenging learning environments

 # A Great Place for Young Children

The **learning environment** speaks to children. When children enter your classroom, they will be able to tell whether it is a place for them and how you intend them to use it. A cozy corner with a rug, cushions, and books says, "Sit down here and look at books." When they enter the yard, a **climbing structure** with stairs, tunnels, ramps, slides, platforms, and a bridge suggests, "Climb up, find a way across, and come down a different way." An environment with light, color, warmth, and interesting materials to be explored sends a clear message: "We care—this is a place for children."

> *It is the first morning of a new school year. The teachers have carefully set up the indoor and outdoor environment. There are trikes to ride, easels with paint, tubs of water, sand, blocks, puzzles, building toys, picture books, a rabbit, pens and crayons, and a dramatic play area with dolls, clothes, and props, including hats, shoes, and lengths of cloth. Four-year-old Cordell and his mother enter the classroom and look around. Cordell makes a beeline for the dramatic play area, finds a construction hat, and puts it on. He slings a shiny beaded purse over his shoulder. He goes up to Kaito, who is wearing a cowboy hat, and says, "We're police guys, right?" He turns and smiles at his mom and then turns to play with his new friend.*

When you become a teacher, you will create a learning environment. You will arrange space and select **equipment** and **materials**. You will design a schedule that ensures children's basic needs are met and they have enough time for activities that support learning. Your knowledge of children will help you design a program that provides opportunities to move, explore, represent, create, and manipulate.

A unique characteristic of the field of early childhood education and care is the careful attention teachers pay to designing learning environments. The philosophers and educators whose work forms the foundation of our field have long recognized the critical role of the environment in children's development. When you look at a well-designed environment for young children, you will see the following:

- Opportunities for children to play, as suggested by Jan Amos Comenius
- Child-size furniture and accessible and orderly shelves, as recommended by Maria Montessori
- Inviting hands-on materials like pattern blocks and paper with scissors, based on the gifts and occupations of Friedrich Froebel
- Wood unit blocks that match children's size and abilities designed by Caroline Pratt

- Daily opportunities for play outdoors with mud, sand, and water, as suggested by Margaret and Rachel McMillan
- Play objects made of natural materials, as described by Rudolph Steiner
- Environments filled with light and beauty, as suggested by Loris Malaguzzi.

Reflect On

The Environment of Your First School

Remember your first school (or any school that was important to you during your childhood). What about the environment stands out in your memory: the classroom, the playground, the equipment and materials, and the storage and distribution of materials? Was anything wonderful or magical for you? Why? How was the school similar to or different from your home? Did it reflect your culture and family in any way? What do you wish had been different? How do you think the environment affected your learning and relationships?

The learning environment you establish should mirror your values for children as well as the values of the program and children's families. It should confirm children's sense of identity, connection, and belonging. More than that, it should engage children in learning by awakening their senses, provoking curiosity and wonder, and stimulating their intellect.

Young children are learning all the time. In the eyes of the educators of Reggio Emilia, the environment is the children's **"third teacher"** (Edwards, Gandini, & Forman, 2012). The learning environment is both a powerful teaching tool and a visible sign to families that you are caring for, and providing appropriate experiences for their children. Because it is so important, teachers of young children spend a great deal of time carefully arranging their learning environments.

Learning environments should meet the needs of children and support your educational values and developmental goals. The choices you make as you design the environment influence the quality of children's relationships with other people and learning materials. In making these choices, you need to ask yourself three very basic questions:

1. Is it appropriate for these children? Is it safe and healthy? Does it reflect their age, stage of development, and characteristics as well as their community, families, and culture?

2. Does it engage children physically, socially, emotionally, and intellectually? Does it include elements that develop a sense of wonder?

3. Does it support relationships between children, between adults and children, and between adults?

Jim Greenman (2005) suggests there are nine overarching aspects of good early childhood learning environments. They are places:

1. to live, where children feel welcomed, competent, and relaxed with a sense of familiarity and order;

2. of beauty that engage all of the senses;

3. that promote strong diverse families;

4. with spaces for gathering and ways to see from place to place in the program;

5. with spaces for working independently and with others;

6. for exploration and discovery indoors and out, with room to move, modeled on laboratories, studios, gardens, libraries, gymnasiums, and playgrounds;

7. that develop responsibility, compassion, and community by giving children access to resources and encouraging them to work together;

8. to connect to the natural world, the larger community, and the world beyond; and

9. for staff to learn and work with space, Internet access, professional journals, and books.

✓ **A Quick Check 8.1**

Gauge your understanding of the concepts in this section.

The Indoor Learning Environment

What is important in the indoor learning environment? Space to move, comfortable child-size furnishings, inviting materials, and an arrangement that suggests how materials can be used provide a feeling of comfort and security. Materials and images that reflect children, their families, their cultures, and their community let children and families know that they belong. Soft lighting as well as natural and man-made items of beauty tell them that they are valued and that you care enough to provide an attractive place for them. Comfortable places for big and little people to sit tell them that they are welcome. All of these create an atmosphere of warmth and informality that meets the social-emotional needs of young children and their families and enables them to interact with people and materials in ways that support their development and learning.

Sally has been hired to teach a class of 15 5-year-olds for a summer enrichment program in a neighborhood church. She was given little to set up the learning environment. She surveys the room. Daylight streams in through the windows. In one corner, she has draped a carton of hymnals with a pretty tablecloth. On it, she has placed a small vase of flowers, a purple cup full of marking pens, a new box of crayons, and a basket of recycled paper. In a corner marked off by a pew, she has created a dramatic play corner with furniture made out of cardboard boxes, her childhood dolls, and dress-up clothes from the rummage sale bin. She has posted a print of a mother and child painted by Mary Cassatt from a calendar she saved. Dishpans and baskets with LEGO, wooden beads, and blocks gleaned from friends' closets fill a board-and-brick shelf next to a small carpet. Sheltered by the piano, a cozy corner has been created with a pile of pillows re-covered with remnant fabrics and a basket full of books from the public library. Tables and chairs from the Sunday school and a garage sale easel complete the classroom. There's water in a portable cooler and a bathroom a few steps away. It's not ideal, but Sally feels sure that she can provide a good experience for children here.

Space

The indoor learning environment will be influenced by many things but first by the building and the grounds that surround it. You may find yourself working in a space that is "**purpose-built**" to be an early childhood program. However, like Sally in the preceding vignette, you may find yourself in a building created for other purposes. Many different kinds of buildings can be turned into safe, workable, and even charming

SOURCE: Jeff Reese

early childhood learning environments. We have known and loved classrooms in converted homes, church sanctuaries, basements, apartment units, offices, and storefronts.

All groups of young children need a clearly defined "home" space. Enough space is needed. In most states, many countries, and the National Association for the Education of Young Children standard is 35 square feet usable space per child. However, The American Academy of Pediatrics, American Public Health Association, and National Resource Center for Health and Safety in Child Care and Early Education, (2011) recommend a minimum of 42 square feet per child and the U.S. General Services Administration's (GSA) child care design standards require a minimum of 48½ square feet per child in the classroom.

Children need secure, ongoing access to drinking water, toilets or diaper-changing space, and sinks for hand washing. There needs to be access for individuals (children, family members, visitors, or staff) who use walkers or wheelchairs.

Early childhood classrooms must be well lit. The classrooms of your childhood probably were lit with overhead fluorescent lights. You may have had classrooms without windows. Views on classroom lighting have changed. Natural lighting (i.e., windows) has been shown to have an impact on school achievement (Heschong Mahone Group, Inc., 2003), and it contributes to the aesthetic quality of the environment (National Institute of Building Sciences, 2017). Natural light is considered so crucial that it is included in accreditation standards and in the regulations that govern all federal government child care programs: "Natural lighting is essential in childcare centers. It is the hallmark of nurturing, quality environments" (U.S. General Services Administration, 2003). Homelike lighting, such as wall sconces, track lights, dimmers, and table lamps, are often recommended (Bergman & Gainer, 2002; Deviney et al., 2010a).

Reflect On

A Place You Like to Be

Think of a place where you like to be. What do you do there? What do you like about it? Why? How could you add some of these things to the learning environment you create for children?

SELF-CONTAINED AND OPEN-DESIGN CLASSROOMS One type of early childhood program building has **self-contained classrooms**. Each class spends most of the time in "their" room. Another type of building has an **open design** constructed so that several classes share one room most of the time. Designers of open-design buildings expect teachers to arrange **interest centers** throughout the room, with a large multifunction or large motor space in the middle. Facilities need not be used as they were designed. For example, in a school with self-contained classrooms, a team of teachers might decide to use their rooms together, giving each a particular function (e.g., one room may be the messy activity room for art and sensory activities). Open rooms are often turned into self-contained "classrooms" using dividers, furniture, hanging banners, and taped lines on the floor to suggest walls.

Self-contained classrooms offer a homelike atmosphere, a feeling of security and belonging. This is good for all children, especially very young children. However, very small classrooms don't provide space for children to move or allow teachers to provide a rich variety of learning experiences at all times. Large open-design classrooms with many children offer space for movement and allow teachers to create more and more diverse learning centers. They are inevitably noisier and less homey. Smaller group size has a positive effect on children. Large rooms with many children are less appropriate for younger children and inappropriate for infants and toddlers, who thrive in environments that are more sheltered from stimulation and are more like homes.

Reflect On

An Early Childhood Classroom You Have Known

Think about an early childhood classroom you have observed. Was it a self-contained classroom or part of an open-design building? What advantages for children or teachers were evident to you in this kind of classroom? What were its drawbacks? If you were a teacher in this setting, how would you change the learning environment? Why?

Principles for Arranging Space

Even though you are unlikely to design your building or construct your play yard, you will have many choices in designing an environment that supports children's learning and well-being. It will be a reflection of who you are and who the children are. Although your environment will be unique, it should follow some basic principles. The principles discussed below can be thought of as general guidelines or rules for action.

Arrange the Environment for Safe Supervision   Every environment for young children must be safe and meet the needs of their age and stage. Ensuring safety is the first principle of learning environment design. Your classroom and outdoor play space must be arranged so that areas can be easily supervised.

In a program for infants and toddlers, an adult must be able to see all of the children all of the time. Drinking water, diapering, sinks, and sleep areas must be accessible and supervised whenever they are in use. In a program for preschoolers, teachers have greater latitude. If there are no environmental hazards, a preschooler may be safely playing in one area while teachers work with other children a few feet away, supervising all the children by sight and sound. While standing, the teacher should be able to see the whole preschool room or yard and all the children in it. Water to drink, toilets and sinks, and quiet places for resting must be accessible and easy to supervise throughout the day. School-age children can safely have more independence. It is desirable, especially for kindergartners, to have toilets and drinking water in the classroom or yard. However, first and second graders can—and often must—walk to nearby bathrooms, drinking fountains, playgrounds, or classrooms with minimal supervision.

Although supervision is important, it should not overwhelm you. There is an unfortunate tendency in our society to worry so much about safety that we fail to take into account other concerns. Children need to run and play vigorously. They need to have opportunities for messy play. They need to take reasonable risks, such as rolling down a hill, climbing up a slide, or jumping off a low platform. Denying them these opportunities in the name of health or safety unnecessarily limits exploration and learning. A skinned knee or a stubbed toe can be an important part of the learning process.

Organize in Areas   Another principle for the design of the early childhood learning environment is to organize it in areas, **learning centers** (terms we use interchangeably to describe well-defined spaces in classrooms where a particular type of activity takes place), or **zones** (a term we use to describe larger, more flexibly defined parts of a room or yard). Anita Olds (2001) suggests thinking of a classroom for young children as having two "regions": a wet region (for activities like eating, art, and coming in with muddy boots) and a dry region for the remaining classroom activities, which she subdivides into active and quiet zones. The areas or zones that are included in an environment will vary with the age of the children and with the geographic locale of the program. Jim Greenman (2005) suggests thinking of serious work spaces (laboratories, artists' studios, gardens, parks, libraries, and gymnasiums) as models for the areas we provide for children.

Infants and toddlers need care or routine areas in which to be changed and washed and in which they can sleep, eat, and play. Preschoolers and kindergartners need areas for books, blocks, manipulative toys, sensory experiences, inquiry activities, art, writing, dramatic play, vigorous physical play, and both small- and large-group gathering. Primary-age children need spaces to work on their own and with others, to work on and display projects, for play, and for whole-group meeting.

In geographic areas that have extreme weather conditions, you will also need an indoor area for active play. In mild climates, you can use the outdoors for a wide variety of activities and may place some centers outside.

Place Areas with Special Requirements First   In both the indoor and the outdoor environment, some areas or zones have particular requirements that can be accommodated in only one or two places. Art, eating, sensory play, science, and diapering areas need to be near water and have an easy-to-clean uncarpeted floor. A library area requires good lighting. A science area, cooking area, or music center may need access to electricity. Wheeled vehicles like trikes and wagons require a hard surface, such as asphalt or cement. If equipment needs to be stored at the end of the day, it's best to place those areas near the storage. Once you know where these special areas need to go, you can plan the remaining centers or zones around them.

Equipment and Materials

The materials in early childhood programs are essential tools for learning. Harriet Cuffaro (1995) likens them to textbooks for older children: "Materials are the texts of the early childhood classroom. Unlike books filled with facts and printed words, materials are more like outlines. They offer openings or pathways by and through which children may enter the ordered knowledge of the adult world. Materials also become the tools with which children give form to and express their understanding of the world and of the meanings they have constructed" (p. 33). Equipment and materials suggest direction and provide raw material for children's exploration, development, and learning. Generally, equipment refers to furniture and other large and expensive items, such as easels and climbing structures. The term materials usually refers to smaller, less expensive items, such as puzzles, books, games, and toys. Consumables like paint, paper, glue, and tape are referred to as **supplies**.

Have you ever sat at a table that wobbled? Have you ever had a tool that broke when you tried to use it? It is frustrating and often unsafe to work with equipment and materials that are poorly made. Ensuring that the learning environment has safe equipment and materials is an important part of your job. Whenever possible, select good-quality, sturdy equipment and materials; discard those that are broken, unsafe, damaged, or can't be fixed; and maintain and fix the equipment and materials you have. Creatively recycle. And when you have money to spend, purchase materials that will last.

The furniture and equipment in an early childhood program should support classroom activities and respond to the needs of children. We favor wood because of its beauty and sturdiness and because it is easy to maintain. Appropriate furniture for young children fits their bodies, is stable and portable, and has rounded corners and edges. Infants need low, stable chairs that offer back and side support. Cube chairs that can double as stools for adults work well. Older children can be comfortable and can focus when seated at tables if their feet touch the floor and their elbows can rest on tabletops. Small tables provide greater flexibility than large tables and leave more space free for diverse activity.

Low, open shelves are good for storage of materials that children use independently. They allow children to make choices and make it easier for them to participate in clean-up. A shelf especially designed for books invites reading by displaying the books with their covers facing the children. Every child needs space for the storage of personal belongings. **Cubbyholes** (often shortened to cubbies) meet this need. Cubbies can be manufactured or improvised using such materials as dish tubs, sweater boxes, cardboard boxes, or commercial 5-gallon ice cream tubs. Where children come to school in coats and boots, hooks and storage shelves for these garments need to be provided.

Because teachers and parents also spend time in the classroom, it is important to have comfortable places for an adult and child to sit together. This contributes to the homelike feeling that is so important for young children in group settings.

Good materials are attractive. They have sensory appeal and feel good to touch and hold. Because they are children's tools for learning, the materials in a classroom must be kept in good repair, work properly, and fit children's size, abilities, and interests. They must be nontoxic, clean, and free of hazards. They should be sturdy and not easily broken.

Every classroom should have enough appropriate materials for the number of children who work and play there to have several options. A classroom for 10 children might have 50 choices spread throughout eight centers, while a classroom for 20 children might have 100 choices. There is no precise formula—there should be enough choices in each area so that the number of children who play there can be actively engaged.

It is valuable to rotate materials on the shelves. The same materials left out week after week will lose their allure. A toy that has been put away in the cupboard for a few weeks will be more inviting and will encourage more creative play.

It is a basic principle of good learning environment design to remove broken toys, dolls with missing limbs, torn or scribbled-on books, tattered dress-up clothes, or puzzles and games with missing pieces. By leaving these in the classroom, you give this message to children: "We don't respect the toys, and you don't have to either—it's okay to break or damage play materials here." Classrooms with damaged materials inevitably become home to even more damaged materials. They show children and parents that you don't care.

When a book is torn, a puzzle piece is missing, or a block is scribbled on, you can model respect for these resources by mending, refurbishing, or cleaning them. We like to do this with children, encouraging them to participate in the process (particularly if the children were party to the damage). Using broken toys, puzzle pieces, or children's books as the raw materials of art projects is not recycling to a young child. Instead, it sends an unclear message that implies that it is acceptable to cut up books or glue puzzle pieces. Similarly, using a triangular block as a doorstop or a hollow block as a stepstool in the bathroom suggests that you do not respect these play materials and don't expect children to do so.

Reflect On

A Plaything

Think of a plaything you loved when you were a child. What did it look like? How did it feel when you held it? What could you do with it? Where is it today? Why do you remember it? Think about what makes a good toy. What good toys do you want to make sure you have in your classroom?

MAKING THE INDOOR ENVIRONMENT WORK   Designing a learning environment is not a one-time event; it is an ongoing process. Children's needs change as they grow and learn. Any setting can be modified and improved. The perfect arrangement for this year's class of children may not work as well for a new group.

Plan on regularly reevaluating and changing the environment. When problems arise—for example, if children consistently fail to get involved in activities—you may want to look first at the environment to see whether it is part of the cause of the problem. Robert Sommer (1975), a psychologist who has studied the effect of environment on behavior, has said, "There is no behavior apart from environment, even in utero" (p. 19).

Before you finish arranging your indoor space and whenever you are about to change the environment, observe from the viewpoint of a child by sitting on the floor or the ground. From this perspective, observe from the entrance and each of the areas. Notice what you can see in each location, what is most attractive, and what is most distracting. This view may be quite different from what you perceive from your standing height and will help you design an environment that works for children.

Pay Attention to Organization and Aesthetics

At Children's Place Learning Center, visitors are struck by the difference between two classrooms. Lynn's room is cluttered—shelves are stuffed with toys stored in a miscellaneous assortment of cardboard boxes and dirty dish tubs. Children shout at one another over a loud recording of raucous music for children. The odor of Zippy the rabbit scents the air. The shelf tops are a jumble of paper for art products, recycled materials, and stacks of books. Tattered posters adorn the walls. In contrast, Summer's room is an oasis. The furniture has been arranged so chairs and tables color coordinate; plants divide and define some learning centers. Shelves are filled with toys in baskets or on trays, and there is space between items. Most shelf tops are clear of clutter. The carpets, pillows, and window fabrics complement each other; art posters and children's art decorate the walls. Sammy the guinea pig is contentedly chewing his fresh bedding. Instrumental music plays softly, and the noise of children talking and laughing is the dominant sound.

Make the Environment Beautiful   We believe that children's environments should be beautiful places. This means looking for ways to make aspects of the classroom harmonious by paying attention to design, light, color, and texture in the selection and arrangement of furnishings, equipment, and materials. Aesthetics is often overlooked in early childhood classrooms and playgrounds.

Choose Neutral and Soft Colors   Although we like color, we believe it's best to select soft, light, neutral colors for classroom walls and furniture. Why? Brightly colored walls dominate a room. The children, their artwork, and the toys, books, and art prints in a classroom bring color. The walls and furniture provide the backdrop. If they are neutral, they don't clash or dominate, and they focus children's attention on the learning materials on the shelves.

If you don't have a choice about color, coordinate tablecloths, posters, pillows, curtains, and storage containers with the walls and furniture. Color coordinate within centers (e.g., put all the blue chairs at the writing center and all the green chairs in the science center) so that children begin to see them as wholes rather than as parts. Avoid garish and contrasting patterns because they can be overstimulating.

If you must paint furniture, use one neutral color for everything so that you have greater flexibility in moving it from space to space. Make sure that marks from crayons, paints, and markers are cleaned up right away. We like to give children brushes and warm soapy water and let them scrub the furniture on a sunny, warm day.

Display Artwork   Mount and display children's art and artists' prints and avoid cartoons, advertisements, and garish, stereotyped, faded, or tattered posters. Make sure that much of the artwork (both by children and adult artists) is displayed at children's eye level. Use shelf tops sparingly for displaying sculpture, framed photos, plants, and items of natural beauty, like shells, stones, and fish tanks.

Enhance the Environment with Natural Objects and Materials   Look for ways to bring the beauty of natural materials and objects into your classroom and yard. Use plants, stone, wood, shells, and seeds as learning materials indoors. Outdoors, add small details, like a planter box or a rock arrangement, to show that the outdoors is also a place that deserves attention and care.

Make Storage Attractive and Functional   Storage areas can contribute to the smooth functioning of a program as well as to its aesthetic quality. Making storage functional, organized, and attractive is a principle of good design in early childhood programs, just as it is in homes, kitchens, stores, and offices. A thoughtfully organized environment helps children understand and maintain order and contributes to making your environment a pleasant place in which to spend time and work.

Store Materials for Children's Use in Sight and Reach   When children scan the environment, they should be able to tell at a glance what materials are available to them. Things stored on low, open shelves tell children that they are available for their use. Items for adult use only should be stored out of children's reach and view. Cleaning supplies, files, first-aid equipment, sharp tools, and staff personal belongings should be in locked or inaccessible storage.

Use Attractive Storage Containers   Baskets and wooden bowls are appealing choices. If you use plastic storage tubs, use the same kind and color on one shelf. If you use cardboard boxes, cover them with plain-colored paper or paint them. Avoid storing teachers' materials on the tops of shelves. If no other choice is possible, create a teacher "cubby" using a covered box or storage tub.

Avoid Clutter   Crowded shelves look unattractive and are hard for children to maintain. Keep most shelf tops empty. Design your space so that everything has a place. Get into the habit of returning materials after each use and teach children to do the same.

Rotate Materials Regularly   **Rotate** materials rather than having everything out at once. When you take something out, put something else away. The added benefit is that children have new and interesting things to try and familiar materials take on new life when they are brought out again.

Label Shelves   Children will be more self-sufficient if shelves and other storage areas are marked to indicate where to put things away. Even in rooms for infants and toddlers, it is helpful to the adults if shelves and containers are labeled with pictures of the contents. Some teachers code shelves and materials with self-adhesive colored dots to indicate the learning center in which they are stored (red dots for table toys, yellow dots for the writing area, and so on). Silhouettes of materials on shelves help children match an item to its proper place. Remember that your goal is to keep your environment functionally organized and pleasing to the eye.

There are several resources available to help you think about creating beautiful, inspiring spaces for children, including books (such as those by Bullard, 2014; Curtis & Carter, 2014; and Deviney et al., 2010a) and videos (Inspiring Spaces for Young Children and Bambini Creativi).

SOURCE: Jeff Reese

Reflect the Children—Reflect the Place

We live in a diverse society, so early childhood learning environments need to reflect and honor that diversity. Select books, artwork, software, and dramatic play props that reflect differences in culture, gender, race, ability, language, and family structure. Choose materials that portray the specific culture, community, and locale of the children and families who attend your program. An early childhood program in rural South Carolina should look different from a program in Chicago, Alaska, or Delaware. Doing this is a tenet of **place-based education**, an education approach that is designed to connect children with their social and natural environment. You can reflect the children in your environment in many ways.

When children see photographs of themselves and their families in the classroom, they know that it is a place that is for them. Use pictures of the children and the families to mark cubbies, make books, and create games. Families can be invited to share a family photo and a picture of their child. When you are selecting dolls, books, puzzles, and posters, be sure to look for those that resemble the children and their families.

Some of the ways that you can create an environment with a sense of place is to include natural materials and art from your local area and community. For example, in Hawaii, teachers often use lauhala baskets for storage; pandanus seeds as brushes; Aloha shirts, lei, and muumuu for dress-up clothes; and dry coconuts for pounding nails. They also display the work of Hawaii artists depicting Hawaiian scenes on the walls. Similarly, we have seen programs in Alaska where the dramatic play area was turned into a fishing camp.

The "Golden Rules for Creating Indoor Learning Environments" box summarizes the important things to remember in creating a classroom for young children.

AVOID BEING CUTE For many years, we have opposed the pervasive tendency to make environments for young children cute. What do we mean by cute? Cute is not the naturally appealing qualities of children. Rather, it is the affected, stereotyped falseness of an advertisement or a cartoon. What's wrong with cute? Jim Greenman (1998) speaks against what he calls the Unbearable Lightness of Cuteness: "Cuteness robs wonder of its evocative power, pasteurizing awe and delight into one-dimensional chuckles and fuzzy glows" (p. 28).

Overly cute materials are trivial. They suggest that because children are younger and less accomplished than adults, they also are less individual and less worthy of respect and that their learning is neither serious nor important. It is overly cute to have

Golden Rules
for Creating Indoor Learning Environments

1. Arrange the environment so it can be easily supervised, cleaned, and maintained.
2. Make sure there is water to drink, toilets/diapering facilities, sinks, and quiet places for resting.
3. Choose child-size furniture and include comfortable seating for adults.
4. Organize the classroom in areas.
5. Select safe, good-quality, sturdy equipment and materials and discard or repair broken, incomplete ones.
6. Store materials that children can use at their eye level on low, open, uncrowded shelves and store teacher materials out of reach.
7. Rotate play materials.
8. Regularly reevaluate and change the environment.
9. Add items of beauty to the environment.
10. Include materials that reflect the children, their families, and their geographic location.

posters of wide-eyed ladybugs instead of books about insects and opportunities to observe them. It is excessively cute when the walls of a school are covered with cartoon murals instead of displaying children's work.

Children are endearing, attractive, and charming. They are also human beings who are individual, strong, and worthy of our respect. They have intense, real feelings and desires. Appropriate early childhood learning environments and their contents are similarly endearing, attractive, and charming. They are also real. They are not cute.

 ## Application Exercise 8.1

Watch and Write About Early Childhood Classrooms

EVALUATE THE ENVIRONMENT   Using a checklist like those we provide in Appendix B, the Harms–Clifford Early Childhood Environment Rating Scale (Harms & Clifford, 2014), the checklists in Designs for Living and Learning (Curtis & Carter, 2014), or the Rating Observation Scale for Inspiring Environments (Deviney et al., 2010b) can help you take a systematic approach to the design of a learning environment.

Over the years, we have found it helpful to use specific dimensions or attributes described by Jones and Prescott (1984) as another kind of lens through which to observe and evaluate our environments (see Figure 8.1).

CONSIDER THE ADULTS   Although your program is first and foremost a place for children, it is important not to forget about adults when you design the environment (Greenman, 2007). This is especially important in a classroom for infants, where adults must cradle infants to help them to eat and sleep.

Create a place where you and other adults can sit comfortably. You may want to put this near the sign-in area or the library so that parents feel invited to participate. Be sure to include an outdoor bench or chairs for family members who may be uncomfortable sitting on the ground. If you have space, it is wonderful to include a family area in the classroom. Because you, too, spend long hours here away from your home, the environment contributes to how you feel about your work. You will also need a place where you can keep your own things safely, keep confidential records, and prepare materials.

Figure 8.1 Dimensions of Teaching–Learning Environments

- **Hard–Soft:** Comfortable furniture, pillows, rugs, grass, sand, furry animals, soft toys, sling and tire swings, dough, finger paint, clay, mud, water, and warm physical contact soften environments. Softness changes an environment, what happens, and how secure and comfortable people feel. Early childhood classrooms need to have soft furnishings, carpets, decorations, and lighting similar to homes. Hard environments, with indestructible materials like cement, unattractive colors, and harsh lighting are uncomfortable and indicate a lack of respect for children.
- **Open–Closed** (the degree to which the environment and materials restrict): Open materials inspire innovation. Materials that are closed can be rewarding when they provide appropriate challenge. Overly difficult materials cause frustration. Younger or less experienced children require more open materials. Older, more experienced children need and enjoy open materials but also enjoy closed challenges. When children appear bored or frustrated, the cause might be in the balance of open–closed experiences.
- **Low mobility–High mobility:** High mobility involves active motion. Low mobility involves sedentary activities. Both are important, both indoors and outdoors, throughout the day.
- **Simple–Complex:** Simple materials have one obvious use—they do not encourage children to manipulate or improvise. They include trikes, slides, puzzles, and concept games such as Chutes and Ladders. Complex materials allow children to use two different play materials together, making play less predictable and more interesting. They hold children's attention for a longer period of time—for example, a sandbox with tools, blocks with props, collage with paint. Super materials offer an even larger number of possibilities and hold children's attention much longer. They include sand with tools and water, or dramatic play areas equipped with furnishings, clothes, and props. Classrooms for inexperienced or less mature children need to be simple to help them focus and make choices. Older children can handle more complexity, which can be added by materials or people.
- **Intrusion–Seclusion** (who and what crosses boundaries between spaces): Intrusion adds novelty and stimulation that enrich learning—visitors, trips, and other experiences with the world outside the classroom. Seclusion from stimulation provides the opportunity to concentrate, think, and be alone. Tables or easels set up against walls provide partial seclusion; insulated spaces with protection on three sides allow privacy; hiding spaces, cozy closed places in crates, lofts, or under a table allow children to escape the stimulus of the classroom. When opportunities for seclusion do not exist, children often create their own seclusion by hiding or by withdrawing emotionally.

Based on E. Jones & E. Prescott, *Dimensions of Teaching-Learning Environments*, 1984.

A Quick Check 8.2

Gauge your understanding of the concepts in this section.

The Outdoor Learning Environment

Every program for young children needs an outdoor play area. Inside, children are restricted—walk slowly, talk softly, be careful, keep it clean. But outside, the loud, active, enthusiastic play of children is safe, permitted, and encouraged. Because many young children spend most of their time indoors regular play in the natural world is vital. As a society we are increasingly aware that children are suffering from a "nature-deficit" (Louv, 2008). During outside play children have the real experiences with the natural world that are vital to learning concepts that cannot be learned indoors. Lack of time outdoors affects both children and, ultimately, the planet. Cook (Robin C. Moore, Nature Play & Learning Places, 2014) describes this well, "Children must spend more time outdoors—for their good health and the health of our planet. . . . If children don't grow up engaged with nature, chances are they will never understand human dependency on the natural world."

Unfortunately, spacious playgrounds or **playscapes** (a term coined by landscape architects to join the idea of play with the concept of architectural landscapes) carefully designed for young children are the exception rather than the rule. In a large elementary school, the outside play area may consist of a jungle gym on the edge of the athletic field; in a school located in the business district of a big city, play space may be a rooftop or a paved parking lot. A suburban or rural setting is likely to have a grassy yard with some play equipment. Although none may be perfect, any outdoor learning environment can be enriched.

Because children are learning all the time, not just when they are in the classroom, outdoor space and equipment should support a range of developmental goals: physical, social, cognitive, and creative. The outdoors can be used for an endless variety of learning activities.

SOURCE: Jeff Reese

Outdoor Activity Zones

You can think about the outdoor environment as having zones with distinct purposes. Thinking of it in this way makes it easier to plan and make improvements.

TRANSITION ZONE The **transition zone** is where children enter and exit the playground. It should allow children to see what is available and make choices. It may be where equipment like balls, trikes, and wagons are waiting and where other activities can be seen, considered, and chosen by a child. It is important to provide a place for children to safely wait or gather. Benches, large tires, steps, or the edge of a low wall make good places to wait.

ACTIVE PLAY ZONE Every outdoor environment needs space—to run, jump, skip, roll hoops, throw balls, and ride and pull wheeled vehicles. Big areas, grassy if possible, are needed for children to safely run and play games. Preschoolers and primary-age children need a place to climb up high so they can see things from a different perspective. They need equipment for sliding and swinging to allow them to experience different kinesthetic sensations. The climbing structure, or **superstructure**, is the current evolution of what used to be called the "jungle gym." Superstructures often include platforms, slides, tunnels, nets, and ramps.

Although you may have little control over the size of the **active play zone** or the fixed equipment it contains, one thing that you can do is to create **visual boundaries**. Visual boundaries such as a low border of used tires (available at a tire store—choose only tires that have no exposed steel belts/wires) or potted plants give a visual signal that helps keep children safe. They encourage children to avoid an area that might be hazardous, such as the space where another child is swinging or riding a trike. When **wheeled vehicles** such as trikes, scooters, and wagons are provided, an asphalt or pavement pathway is needed.

School-age children benefit from greater challenge in the active play zone. They are able to climb and swing higher, jump farther, and learn new skills, such as sliding down long poles, balancing along high balance beams, and turning on parallel bars. Primary-age children also need movable equipment, such as hoops, bats, and balls, for organized games and hard surfaces for rope jumping and ball bouncing.

NATURAL ELEMENTS ZONE Every outdoor environment needs a **natural elements zone** where there are plants, dirt, rocks, trees, grass, water, and living creatures. Mud and sand for digging and water for pouring are soothing and provide important learning experiences. Nurture and protect the natural elements in your playground. If they are missing, add them by planting a garden, putting up a bird feeder, or housing a pet.

When the outside play area is a rooftop or parking lot, nature can be included by adding potted plants, garden boxes, pets, and sand tables (to fill with sand, water, or dirt). Regular walks to parks can supplement, but do not substitute for, daily experience with nature in the playground.

MANIPULATIVE–CREATIVE ZONE   Table activities like art and woodworking can take place outdoors. Messy art materials, such as clay and finger paint, are especially well suited to outdoor use. Manipulative–creative activities may often be found on playgrounds. In some programs, table games and books are brought into the **manipulative–creative zone**.

SOCIAL–DRAMATIC ZONE   Children create their own opportunities for social and dramatic play in the outdoor environment whether or not equipment is provided. Their play is richer when you add a playhouse, dress-up clothes, and pots and pans and **"loose parts**," such as hollow blocks, sheets, small tires, planks, and other movable pieces that children can arrange. A **social–dramatic zone** can be placed near a vehicle path to extend dramatic play with the use of trikes, carts, and wagons to use as cars, delivery vans, buses, and garbage trucks.

Using the Outdoor Environment

Almost every activity that happens indoors can come outside at least once in a while. In places where the climate is mild most of the year, it can be the primary location for sand and water play, pets, art activities, woodworking, and hollow blocks. Even where the climate is often cold, wet, or hot, there are still times when indoor activities can and should be taken outside.

Learning experiences take on new dimensions when they move outdoors. A story about trees, for example, read in the shade of an oak carries new meaning. Painting a picture with nature in view is different, and aesthetically richer than painting in a classroom. Singing songs outside feels different from singing inside. Dressing up and pretending outside is more adventurous than doing so inside. We all enjoy a picnic now and again. For toddlers, just like older children, there are things that feel different outside—a story, a song, or a snack. Make sure there is space to dream, think, and relax in the yard as well as inside. In the outdoor environment, just as in the indoor environment, children need a place to dream, think, and relax—to escape the noise and activity of the group. A playhouse, a secluded nook under the play structure, or a quiet place under a low tree can provide this kind of opportunity. If the landscaping and permanent equipment don't provide these kinds of places, you can add them temporarily with a wooden crate or a big cardboard appliance box. We recently visited a program where the teacher had created a "peace garden" in which she had placed many potted plants, a low bench, a birdbath, and a bird feeder around the base of a small tree.

Children need challenge. The outdoor environment is a good place to provide this. Once a challenge has been met, a new one must be found. Once a child has learned to climb up and slide down a slide, a new way to slide will be sought. There should be some things outdoors that take time and persistence to master. If your outdoor environment does not have challenges, children will invent their own. To make sure these are safe, you can add equipment and activities to fill this need. For example, a row of tires half buried in the sand can create a balancing challenge. A pathway of cones on the sidewalk is a challenge for the driver of a tricycle. One of the important things that teachers can do is to think of new ways to create challenge in the outdoor environment.

Whether the equipment is purchased or improvised, your outdoor environment requires thoughtful evaluation, planning, and change on a regular basis. The accompanying box, "Golden Rules for Outdoor Playscapes," summarizes the guidelines

Golden Rules

for Outdoor Playscapes

1. Organize in zones.
2. Create visual boundaries for safety and to protect children's play.
3. Provide physical development challenges.
4. Include natural elements in the outdoor play area.
5. Make sure there is space to dream, think, and relax.
6. Take indoor activities outside at times.
7. Observe children and add new experiences and challenges regularly.

presented here. You also may wish to look at a tool like POEMS: Preschool Outdoor Environment Measurement Scale (2005) to evaluate the outdoor environment.

As a classroom teacher, you cannot independently create a wonderful playscape for children. If you are fortunate, you will have colleagues, administrators, and families who value the outdoor learning environment, and together you can work to make it a wonderful place for children. If so, there are resources that will help you to think about how to do this (we recommend Keeler's [2008] *Natural Playscapes* and Elliott's [2008] *The Outdoor Playspace Naturally*). However, every teacher can plan for and work to enhance the outdoor environment that is available (see Figure 8.2).

NATURE PRESCHOOLS AND FOREST SCHOOLS   While it is typical for the outdoor learning environment to be an adjunct to the indoor classroom, sometimes outdoor learning is central to programs. In **nature preschools** (preschool programs with a primary focus on nature and outdoors activities) and forest schools (school held outdoors in natural areas), children play, explore, and learn in a forest or natural environment, whatever the weather. **Forest schools** reflect a growing concern with the extent to which children in industrialized countries lack consistent experience with nature and have few chances to learn and take risks outdoors. These schools are designed to build self-esteem, skills, and values and to solve what has been dubbed nature-deficit disorder (Louv, 2008). Forest schools began in Sweden in the 1950s and are common today in

Figure 8.2 Simple Ways to Enhance an Outdoor Play Space

1. Add plants for sight and smell—make daily watering a classroom job.
   - Bring in big sturdy pots of plants—position them so children can play near them.
   - Create a garden bed and plant flowers to attract butterflies, beneficial bugs, and hummingbirds—marigold, cornflower, dill, hyssop, chives, zinnia, sage, viola, alyssum, basil, lavender.
   - Create a sunflower house by planting a circle of sunflowers.

2. Add animals.
   - Hang bird feeders—make filling the bird feeder a classroom job.
   - Add a birdbath.
   - Make a home for a rabbit.

3. Add sound.
   - Hang wind chimes.
   - Create a drumming stand with big, recycled, and cleaned plastic barrels.
   - Hang pots and pan lids on the fence.

4. Personalize it.
   - Have children or families create concrete stepping stones (using ready-to-use concrete from the hardware store).
   - Let children paint the sidewalk or tires; or with administrator permission, invite them to create a temporary easel paint mural on the wall of the building or a storage shed.

Scandinavia, Germany, the Czech Republic, and the United Kingdom (Warden, 2012). There are a handful of nature preschools and forest schools in the United States, Canada, and Australia.

There are several formats for nature preschools/forest schools. Some are conducted outdoors each and every day. Others have a physical facility and children spend half of each day outdoors. In other programs, a single day of the week is designated as "forest day." If you are interested in learning more about forest schools there are a number of websites and videos posted on the web which you will find by searching for forest school in your web browser.

> ✓ **A Quick Check 8.3**
>
> Gauge your understanding of the concepts in this section.

 # Different Children—Different Places

As an early childhood educator you know that children at different ages and stages have different needs. This is as true in the environments we design as in the activities we provide.

Infant–Toddler Environments: A Place Like Home

Polly and Carol are teachers in a room for six infants ages 5 to 15 months. Coming in one Wednesday morning at 10:30, you see play materials on low, stable shelves placed along the walls near a large open space where Polly is sitting on cushions on the clean, soft carpeted floor looking at books with Shane, Lissa, and Guga. To the side, low, wide, cushioned steps make a place to sit or crawl. The diapering area is on one side of the room near the sink, under high cubbies out of the reach of children. Carol is changing Olivia. Olivia's eyes move from Carol's face to the mobile hanging above the changing table. In a corner in a padded glider rocking chair, Matthew's mom is nursing Matthew. And in the sleeping room just off the main activity area, Chris is sleeping in a crib covered with his own special blanket.

Imagine a place that is made for babies and toddlers, a place where the floor is clean, the furniture is low and soft, and everything is within reach for the youngest children.

Learning environments for infants and toddlers are designed differently from learning environments for older children. Infants and toddlers thrive in homes, so it is a principle of good infant–toddler environmental design to create the feeling of a home rather than a school. What makes a place "like home"? Most homes have the qualities that we can use as design principles: They are comfortable, functional, and flexible.

DESIGN FOR COMFORT An environment for infants or toddlers needs to be comfortable and calm so neither the children nor their teachers are stressed. A stable, adult-size chair or couch with soft cushions is essential. It provides a place where adults can cuddle up with children, good climbing experiences, and excellent handholds for beginning walkers. Because most infants and

SOURCE: Jeff Reese

toddlers are comforted by motion, a **glider rocker** (designed so that fingers cannot be pinched) or other chair that allows motion is important. Most activity in infant and toddler rooms takes place on the floor, so soft, clean carpets are critical.

DESIGN FOR ROUTINES   Indoor environments for infants and toddlers should be designed so that all of the important routines can happen safely in the available space. To accomplish this, most infant–toddler rooms include the areas discussed in the following sections.

An Arrival and Departure Area   Here, family members sign in, bring in supplies, and read notes on their child's day. For toddlers, it is a place to say good-bye. Separation can be hard for very young children, so it is important to make this a comfortable place for parents to spend a few minutes with their child. A good-bye window (a window at child level to watch a departing parent) is desirable in this area.

A Diapering Area   Because diaper changing is a prominent feature of the daily program, a changing area with a sink and hot water must be close at hand and separate from eating and play areas. Infant–toddler environments require a sturdy changing table at a comfortable height for adults (we prefer tables with stairs that roll in and out to encourage toddler independence and save the backs of staff). Diapering is a time to interact, and the diapering area should be pleasant. Toddlers may want to socialize with one another during diaper changing routines, so space should be available for a nearby friend. Because some toddlers and twos are beginning toilet learning, it is important there be an adjacent toileting area. Children have an easier time using toilets when fixtures are child size. Stable step stools or platforms that enable children to comfortably reach toilets and washbasins are essential if toilets and sinks are adult size.

An Eating Area   There should be a low table with stable chairs for eating that is somewhat separate from the activity area.

In infant rooms, it is also important to include these things:

- A comfortable chair for sitting while bottle feeding babies. This can also be used by mothers who come to nurse their children.

- A food storage and preparation area. The area should include a sink and counter, a refrigerator, equipment to warm food, and storage for food and utensils near the eating area but not within children's play areas.

- A sleeping area. This area should be shielded from the stimulus of the play area but easily supervised.

DESIGN FOR FLEXIBILITY   Homes are flexible, and programs for infants and toddlers need to provide this same kind of flexible space for the activities that take place each day. A sensible design principle is to center an infant or toddler room around an open, flexible activity zone/play area where materials and equipment can be moved in and out.

In an infant room, materials for play and exploration can be placed along the perimeter of this area so they are easy to find and bring into the larger space. Along the perimeter, there should be several play spaces for mobile children and different levels on which they can crawl and climb. If the room includes both nonmobile and mobile infants, provide low barriers for protection for nonmobile infants.

In a toddlers' room, the central activity area is a gathering place. Although structured group times are not appropriate for toddlers, it is not uncommon for a group to gather when you read or sing with them. This gathering place is also a good place for a movable climber or platform.

DESIGN FOR MOVEMENT   A room for infants is defined by words like safe, cozy, and secure—a small and beautiful space with light, color, and air and room for a small number of caring adults. But toddlers are movers. They run, jump, dance, and climb, so safe places to move indoors are a must. Short squat slides or small, low climbers are good for toddlers and 2-year-olds. Risers and low ramps that allow children to view the world from a higher perspective are also worthwhile. It is essential to assume that anything that can be climbed will be climbed—therefore, high, unstable shelves must be eliminated from toddler environments. Even relatively low shelves should be secured so that they do not tip. Avoid using shelves with wheels unless the wheels lock.

Around the perimeter of the gathering area, you can position a few different areas, including the following:

- A **toys area** for puzzles, simple manipulatives that are easily put together, nesting cups, pull toys, and animal figures. For infants and toddlers, toys and games must be large enough so they do not present a choking hazard and sturdy enough to withstand frequent sanitizing. They must have safe, smooth edges and be large enough to be easily grasped, light enough to be lifted, soft enough not to hurt, and strong enough to be dropped, stepped on, or thrown. They can include home-made toys, such as plastic bottles with clothespins to drop inside, and commercially made equipment, such as busy boxes. Duplicate toys placed side by side on the shelf will encourage parallel play and reduce conflicts. Infants and toddlers often interpret everyday objects as manipulative toys, so it is essential to keep unsafe or inappropriate items out of their reach. Two-year-olds can enjoy regular unit blocks and foam or cardboard large blocks.

- A **table area** for eating, tasting, and preparing food and exploring art materials, such as finger paint, play dough, and crayons. For infants and toddlers, art is primarily a sensory experience. They explore the raw materials of the artist through all their senses. Appropriate materials for toddlers include large, stubby crayons and watercolor markers with big pieces of paper, finger painting, paste and paper, and play dough. Toddlers and 2-year-olds can also enjoy easel painting with one or two colors at a time on an easel that has been adjusted to their size or on large sheets of paper hung on a wall or fence.

- A **book area** with baskets, low shelves, or wall pockets filled with high-quality, sturdy, appealing books and soft places to sit and enjoy them. In programs for infants, age-appropriate books can be provided in different places in the classroom. Small baskets provide accessible storage for sturdy board books. Bookshelves, such as those found in most rooms for preschoolers, present a hazard in a toddler room because they invite climbing.

- A **pretending area** for make-believe play. Toddlers need simple, realistic, dramatic play materials. A good selection might contain hats, shoes, clothes with few fasteners, bags, baby dolls, plastic dishes, lightweight aluminum pots, and wooden or plastic stirring spoons. It is important to include duplicates of all items. Expect toddlers to bring blocks and other small toys to the pretend area and use them as part of their play.

- A **sensory table** for water, sand, and other safe materials, such as bubbles. Natural materials are generally safe and are particularly satisfying for infants and toddlers. The younger the children, however, the more you will need to supervise. Because very young children are likely to put things in their mouths, you may wish to substitute dough for clay and flour, cornmeal, oatmeal, or rice for sand.

AN OUTDOOR PLAYSCAPE FOR INFANTS AND TODDLERS Have you ever seen a play yard designed just for infants and toddlers? The chances are good that you haven't. Outdoor learning environments for infants and toddlers have typically not received as much space, attention, and resources as outdoor environments for older

Video Example 8.1: Infant Environment

Watch the two videos of environments for infants and toddlers. Notice how teachers in each of the videos have provided for comfort, routines, and flexibility. What differences do you see between the environments? What similarities do they have?

children. This is unfortunate because the outside learning environment is important for the youngest children, and the design of a good outdoor playscape for infants and toddlers is somewhat different from one for older children. If you teach infants and toddlers, it is best if you have an area that is separate and different from the one for older children.

SAFETY Because they are more likely to sunburn, infants and toddlers need shade from the sun. Because they learn by putting things in their mouths, attention must

Figure 8.3 Floor Plan for Infant Classroom

be paid to removing potential hazards (small stones and sharp or toxic plants) and bringing out toys that can be safely mouthed. Because they crawl, there must be safe surfaces and knee protection for crawlers. Because they fall as they learn to walk, hard edges must be padded.

MOVEMENT   Infants and toddlers need to move and they are learning new ways to move. They need different surfaces to crawl and walk on, low objects to crawl over and through, sturdy objects to pull up on, smooth surfaces for beginning walkers, rocking toys, low sling swings to use belly down, riding toys to push with their feet, and small slides that are safe to go down head first as well as feet first. For an example of a classroom floor plan for an infant classroom, see Figure 8.3.

🐝 **Application Exercise 8.2** Figure 8.3: Infant Room Floor Plan

For an example of a classroom floor plan and outdoor playscape for toddlers, see Figure 8.4.

🐝 **Application Exercise 8.3** Figure 8.4: Floor Plan for Toddler Classroom and Outdoor Playscape

Figure 8.4 Floor Plan for Toddler Classroom and Outdoor Playscape

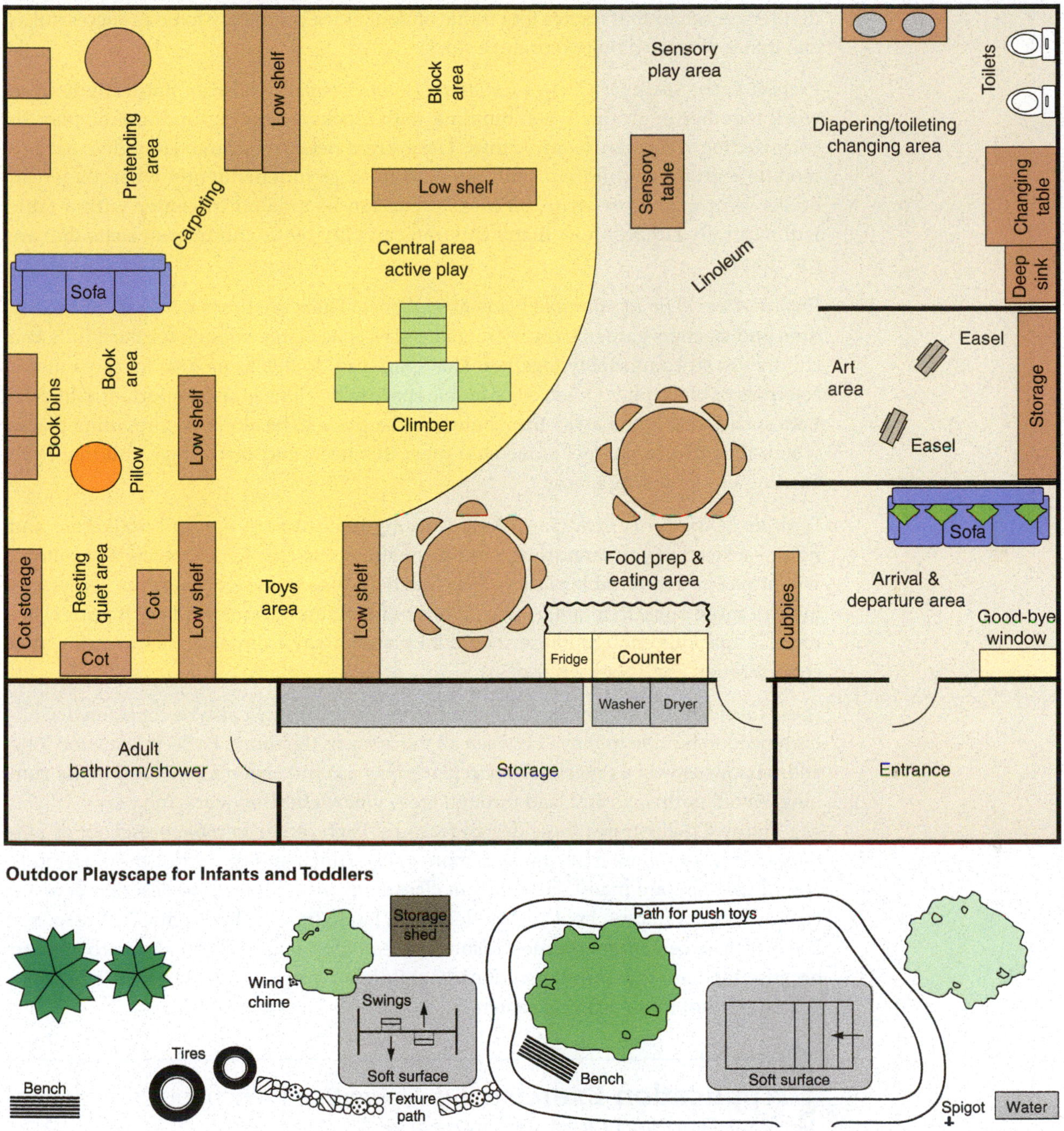

Toilets

Sensory
play area

Diapering/toileting
changing area

Changing table

Pretending
area

Low shelf

Block
area

Sensory
table

Low shelf

Carpeting

Deep sink

Central area
active play

Linoleum

Sofa

Storage

Art
area

Easel

Easel

Book
area

Book bins

Low shelf

Climber

Pillow

Sofa

Low shelf

Resting
quiet area

Food prep &
eating area

Arrival &
departure area

Cubbies

Good-bye
window

Cot storage

Cot

Low shelf

Toys
area

Low shelf

Cot

Fridge

Counter

Washer   Dryer

Adult
bathroom/shower

Storage

Entrance

Outdoor Playscape for Infants and Toddlers

Storage
shed

Path for push toys

Wind
chime

Swings

Soft surface

Tires

Soft surface

Bench

Texture
path

Bench

Spigot

Water

Preschool and Kindergarten Classrooms: A Child's Place

Envision a place where children are looking at books, building with blocks, painting at easels, playing with LEGO, putting together puzzles, dressing up, and playing with dolls. You are imagining the learning environment of a preschool or kindergarten that is based on their interests and developmental stage.

DESIGNING A PRESCHOOL OR KINDERGARTEN CLASSROOM   Designing a classroom where all this (and more) happens with little conflict or confusion requires knowledge and skill. The following principles will help you design a functional and inviting learning environment.

Use Partial Seclusion   Most learning centers in a preschool are devoted to particular purposes and need **partial seclusion** from the rest of the classroom with shelves and dividers. A center that invites foot traffic on four sides is unlikely to be as successful as one that is protected on two or three sides.

Provide Extra Space for Centers Children Use in Groups   Children naturally tend to work together in groups when building with blocks, engaging in dramatic play, or constructing with manipulative toys. These areas need to be large enough to accommodate a group of children. Children tend to work independently when they read books, do puzzles, or write, so these areas can be smaller. A center with a table will naturally suggest how many children can play by the number of seats that are provided.

Provide Areas to Be Together and Places to Be Alone   There are times when all of the children and teachers gather, so every room needs a space large enough for the adults and children to sit comfortably together. This space can double as an area for large motor activities or block play. Quiet, comfortable space to be alone is also important. Children who spend long hours away from home need a place to be alone. By providing places where they can safely feel alone, you meet this need and discourage children from creating unsafe hiding places.

Separate Noisy Areas from Quiet Areas   Young children are naturally talkative and noisy—a fact that you cannot and should not attempt to change. Carpeting and pillows will provide a comfortable place to relax and help absorb noise. Some areas necessarily involve more noise than others (e.g., block building and dramatic play). If your classroom is spacious enough, these should be placed away from areas that require quiet concentration (e.g., books, puzzles).

Avoid Corridors and Racetracks   The space between areas must also be considered. Children need to be able to move between all the areas in the room. Paths that are too long and narrow as well as **racetracks** (circular paths around shelves or tables) invite running. Avoid pathways that lead through areas where children work and play.

Figure 8.5 illustrates these design features. Each center in most preschool or kindergarten classrooms is set up as a more or less unchanging part of the classroom. Although there are many variations in classrooms, the centers we describe here are typically found in preschool and kindergarten (and some primary school) classrooms. Because these centers are the most distinctive feature of early childhood classrooms and because they are the foundation of early childhood curriculum, we provide detailed descriptions of these learning centers.

Application Exercise 8.4 Figure 8.5: Preschool Kindergarten Floor Plan and Outdoor Playscape

BLOCKS   Since the time of Froebel (and probably before), blocks have been used as toys for young children. There are many kinds of blocks available today, from giant hollow blocks to small interlocking plastic LEGO. However, when an early childhood educator says "blocks," he or she is referring to the hardwood **unit blocks** (designed by Caroline Pratt and Harriet Johnson) and their larger cousins: hollow blocks. Today, a set of hardwood unit blocks is considered an essential part of a preschool or kindergarten learning environment. Blocks occupy a special place in early childhood curriculum. As Kalyanee (2011) notes, "The power of blocks is that blocks have complete openness—total ambiguity. Blocks are the most indeterminate toy that can become the determinate thing. In other words, blocks can change from something completely open to something closed. When a child looks at a block, very quickly the openness can become

Figure 8.5 Preschool/Kindergarten Floor Plan—could be widget with hotspots

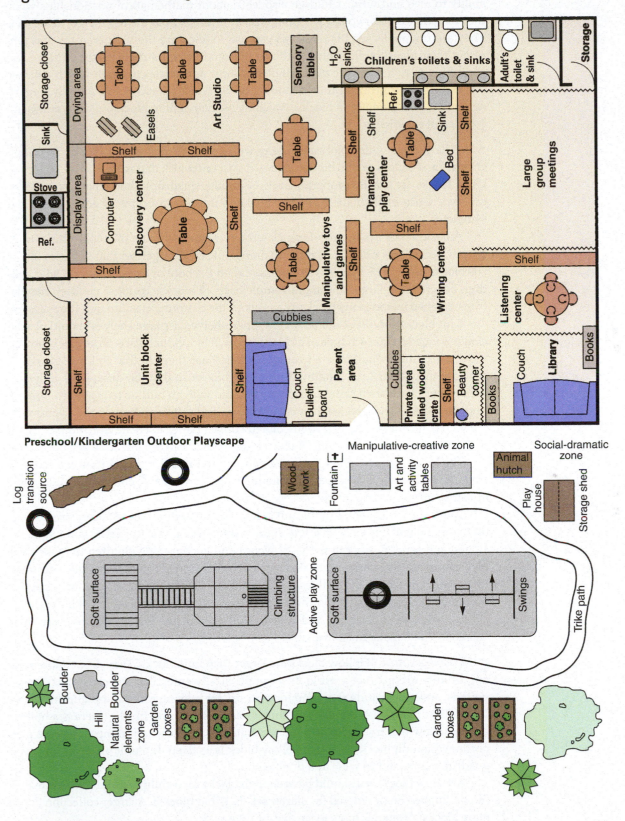

'something' (a bumper, a handle, a seat and so on); it can turn itself into something by the child's 'seeing'."

Unit blocks and **hollow blocks** help develop motor coordination and strength, enhance imagination, and provide opportunities for children to work together. They provide learning experiences in measurement, ratio, and problem solving. Children building with blocks gain experience in abstract representation that contributes to the ability to read and write. Children also learn about mathematical relationships when they experience that two blocks of one size are equivalent to the next-larger size block. They are raw materials that children can use to re-create their experiences and represent their ideas. Hollow blocks allow children to build structures that inspire and contribute to rich dramatic play. All blocks serve as vehicles through which children can express their growing understanding of the world. Preschoolers and kindergartners make extensive use of blocks. Watching as their skill in block building grows is a wonderful experience.

A Unit Block Area   A unit block area begins with a set of hardwood unit blocks. The different sizes and shapes of unit blocks are based on a unit block that is 5½ × 2¾ × 1⅜ inches. Other blocks are exactly proportional (½, ¼ double, quadruple, and so on), so children can experience mathematical relationships and develop concepts of equivalence and symmetry.

A basic set of unit blocks for a classroom includes 100 to 150 blocks in 14 to 20 shapes, sometimes called a nursery or preschool set. A larger set that includes 200 to 700 blocks in 20 to 25 shapes is sometimes called a school or classroom set. Older children benefit from larger and more complex sets of blocks. Younger children may be overwhelmed by too many blocks as well as by the daunting cleanup task they present.

Unit blocks should be stored on low, open shelves. Storage shelves should be spacious enough so that each type of block has its own individual place. Store blocks so that those with similar qualities are near each other. Place them so that children can easily see how they differ (e.g., lengthwise for long blocks so that the differences in length are evident). Each shelf should be clearly marked with an outline to enable children to find the blocks they need for their constructions and put them back in the appropriate places (we recommend using solid-colored contact paper to create the outline). Much of the benefit of block play is lost if they are stored without organization in a box or bin.

The block area should be large enough so several children at a time can build. A smooth floor or low-pile carpet will minimize noise and enable children to build without structures tumbling down.

You can enhance and extend unit block play by adding toy vehicles, street signs, dollhouses, small human and animal figures, and other props (carpet or fabric squares, stones, and sanded, smooth pieces of wood) and encouraging children to make their own props using materials available in the art area. Provide storage baskets and separate labeled space on the shelves for props. Posters, photographs, and books about buildings can be displayed in the block area. Older preschoolers and kindergarten children will use paper, pens, and tape for sign making and writing stories about their creations if you make them available.

A Hollow Block Area   Hollow blocks are larger than unit blocks. They give children the opportunity to construct a world they can physically enter. Each block weighs several pounds, and sets include short and long boards for making roofs and platforms.

Hollow blocks use the same module dimensions as unit blocks (there is a hollow unit, a hollow half unit, a hollow quarter unit, and a hollow unit ramp). They are proportioned to unit blocks (a single hollow block is as deep as a unit block, as long as a quadruple unit, and as wide as a double unit).

A hollow block area should have enough blocks for a child to build a structure that can be climbed on or entered (a "starter set" is 17 big blocks). A larger collection (50 or more blocks) promotes more extensive creative play.

Hollow blocks are expensive and require a good deal of space. When you set up a hollow block area, carpeting or other soft surfacing is essential to limit noise and to prevent damage to the blocks. Hollow blocks can be stored on shelves or can be stacked against a wall for storage. If you do not have indoor space for a hollow block area, it can be set up on a porch or in the play yard if sheltered storage is available.

Video Example 8.2: Building with Blocks

Watch the video of children playing with unit blocks. What do you notice about how the blocks are stored on the shelves and how props are integrated into the play?

We find that hollow blocks are used for more elaborate building and for more social–dramatic play if they are separated from unit blocks. If possible, locate the hollow block area near the dramatic play area so that children can coordinate hollow block building with social–dramatic play. For instance, the firefighters in the hollow block area may be called to extinguish a fire in the dramatic play area, or the carpenters in the hollow block area may build an addition or a garage onto the house. Good props for hollow blocks include hats, sheets, and lengths of colorful chiffon or gauze, which you can store in bins, boxes, or baskets nearby.

DRAMATIC PLAY AREA   **Dramatic play** is one of the most important activities for young children. Children imitate the actions of the important grown-ups in their lives and thus enact how different roles might feel. When they take on roles and use materials to pretend, they learn to symbolize and practice the skills of daily living. Manipulating the physical environment (e.g., putting on clothes with buttons and zippers) and managing relationships are skills learned in part through dramatic play.

A dramatic play area requires sheltered space and simple child-size furniture, typically including a pretend stove, a sink, and a table with chairs for two to four children. The addition of dress-up clothes motivates children to act out different roles. Dress-up clothes for both boys and girls should reflect different kinds of work and play, different cultures, and different ages. You may have to seek out props for the dramatic play area that reflect the families, cultures, and community of your children. Dolls representing

SOURCE: Jeff Reese

a variety of racial backgrounds and common objects of daily life such as kitchenware, books, furnishings, and tools also form a part of the equipment of the dramatic play area. Open shelves with bins or baskets or hooks on the wall provide storage for dramatic play clothing and props. Arrange materials so they are easy to find. Make picture labels for the storage shelves for materials that are always available.

Dramatic play centers are frequently referred to as a "home" area, emphasizing domestic activity. The home theme relates to the most common and powerful experiences in children's lives, but children find new ways to vary this theme. In one classroom, we observed children become a family of spiders when they spread a crocheted shawl between chairs to become a giant web. Dramatic play areas can be changed to present other options: post office, hospital, store, bus, farm, camp, or restaurant. For this reason, when we talk to children about this part of the classroom, we call it "the pretend area." Simple sturdy furniture that can be reconfigured to create different scenarios furthers this broader vision of a dramatic play area.

Because it is not possible or desirable to have all the props available at all times, it is a good idea to organize and rotate props in the dramatic play area. You can respond to children's dramatic play by adding appropriate materials when you observe a new interest developing or when you begin a new topic of study—for example, contributing fire hats, a rain slicker, boots, and a length of hose when the children are pretending to be firefighters. To prevent clutter, props can be stored in sturdy, attractive, lidded boxes organized by occupation, situation, or role.

 ## Application Exercise 8.5

Watch and Write About the Restaurant

MANIPULATIVE TOYS AND GAMES   Toys and games[1] (sometimes called **manipulative toys** or just **manipulatives**), such as puzzles, beads, LEGO, Bristle Blocks, and pegboards, give children practice in hand-eye coordination and help develop the small muscles of their fingers and hands. These experiences are important preparation for writing, and they expose children to such concepts as color, size, and shape, which help in the ability to recognize letters and words. In play with manipulative toys, children also have opportunities to create, cooperate, and solve problems.

---

[1] Because the term *manipulative* is not very meaningful to young children, we refer to this area as the "toys and games" or "table toys" area when we work with children.

There are several distinct types of manipulative toys, including these:

- *Building/construction toys*, such as LEGO blocks, parquetry blocks, Cuisenaire rods, hexagonal builders, and interlocking cubes. These are open-ended, have many pieces, and usually are used by more than one child at a time.

- *Puzzles and fit-together toys* like stacking cups. These are closed-ended, designed to be taken apart and put together in one or two ways, and usually used by one child alone.

- *Collections of materials*, such as buttons, shells, seeds, bottle caps and lids, keys, or pebbles. Safe recycled materials are very appropriate. These are open-ended materials that children can use for a wide variety of purposes, including sorting (a cognitive task), creating designs (an aesthetic activity), or pretending. We encourage you to include collectibles that reflect the children's cultures, community, and environment.

- *Games*, including those that are manufactured (such as pegboards, lottos, geoboards, and board games) and those made by the teacher, sometimes called **workjobs**. Games have simple rules. Older children will enjoy following the rules of the game, while younger children are more likely to ignore the intended use and build or pretend with the game's pieces. Board games like checkers or Chutes and Ladders can be well used by children from age 5. We do not recommend battery-operated toys of any kind, even those that have an "educational" purpose, because these tend to prescribe and limit children's play.

If you have adequate space, it is useful to have separate areas for the open-ended building toys that inspire noisier group play and puzzles and games that require greater concentration and tend to be used by children alone or in pairs.

Because manipulative toys have many pieces that are easy to lose or mix up, storage in this area is especially important. An organized and clearly marked manipulative toy area invites children to play productively. Children can use the materials on tables or on a carpet. Attractive place mats or small carpet pieces can define individual workspaces. Labeled bins or boxes are essential for storage of loose pieces.

SENSORY PLAY CENTER   Natural materials such as sand and water suit all stages and abilities. They are open-ended, can be used in many ways and are satisfying play materials. Children are soothed by the responsiveness of the materials and can safely vent strong emotions in their play with them. They help children learn about the properties of substances and develop math concepts. Cooperative and imaginative play is fostered as children work together with open-ended materials.

If you have room, create a dedicated center for sensory play—otherwise, include sensory materials in the art area and outdoors in good weather. The center needs space near a sink with an easy-to-clean floor. The heart of a sensory play center is a **sensory table**, often called a **water or sand table**, although it can hold much more than sand or water (dirt, salt, aquarium gravel, sawdust, birdseed, used coffee grounds, soapy water, ice, cornstarch goop). If you do not have a sensory table use plastic dishpans, baby baths, wading pools, or tubs from the hardware or garden supply store. Along with the sensory table, provide props (bowls, cups, scoops, spoons, buckets), aprons, and plastic tablecloths or shower curtains. A place to hang smocks and a dedicated, labeled shelf for storage will also be needed.

To keep young children healthy when playing with water in a sensory table, have children wash their hands before and after play. After each group is done, the sensory table should be emptied and the table and toys should be sanitized. Children with open cuts or sores should not participate in group water play (an individual tub makes a good alternative).

Salt and flour dough (play dough), potter's clay, or other kinds of malleable materials (e.g., plasticine) are important sensory materials. A sturdy table and chairs, along with storage containers, aprons, mats, and tools, are needed for play with dough or clay.

A **light table** or **panel** is another kind of sensory exploration equipment. A light table/tablet consists of a translucent surface with a light source recessed underneath it. Originally used by photographers to view slides and negatives, these were introduced to the larger world by the educators of Reggio Emilia. On a light table/panel children explore transparent or translucent materials, build with manipulative toys of colored plastic, and explore natural materials. A light table can also be used for watercolor painting, tissue collage, and other art activities.

ART AREA OR STUDIO   The heart of the art curriculum in your classroom will be the art area. Teachers influenced by early childhood programs in the city of Reggio Emilia often call this area a studio or **atelier** (the French word for "workshop"). In the art area, children can work with materials that are developmentally appropriate, functional, and satisfying to use. Art materials provide opportunities for creative expression, problem solving, and physical and sensory development.

A few built-in features will determine where to place the art area. Art is often messy, so the area should be in the "wet zone," near a sink if at all possible, on tile or linoleum that is easily cleaned. Choose an area in which there is good light from either natural (preferable) or artificial sources.

An art area requires worktables and easels sized to the children. We prefer children to stand at an easel so that they can utilize the full range of motion of their arms, so we do not place chairs at easels. Old or secondhand furniture, smocks, and a good supply of plastic tablecloths minimize concerns about the paint and glue spills. It is helpful to have open shelves for supplies that children can access and closed storage for adults-only supplies. A place for drying finished work is important. A drying rack with wire shelves is best for this purpose, but a clothesline makes an acceptable substitute.

In addition to furniture, an art area needs good tools and supplies, including the following:

- Different kinds of paint (tempera, cake and liquid watercolors, and finger paint or finger paint base)
- Brushes in a variety of widths and lengths and other things to paint with, such as sponges, Q-tips, and feathers
- Small containers to hold water and paint
- Paper in different sizes, colors, and weights (from tissue paper to cardboard)
- Things to draw with (crayons, markers, pencil crayons, and chalk)
- Clay and dough and tools like rollers and wooden or plastic knives for cutting
- Scissors
- Place mats and trays to define spaces and limit mess
- Glue and paste and spreaders to use with them
- Assorted materials to glue together (wood, paper, magazines, natural items like shells and leaves, and recycled items like ribbon and cloth scraps—one or two types at a time!)

Recycled materials can be used in art—old shirts for smocks, wrapping paper and ribbons, cloth scraps, old magazines, or paper that is too old for the copy machine. However, it is important to buy good-quality basic supplies, especially brushes, paint, markers, crayons, and scissors.

Art materials need to be stored so you can easily find them and put them away. Closed, well-marked storage for materials that only adults may access is especially important in the art area so that paints, glue, scissors, and bottles of food color or liquid water color are kept ordered and secure. Paying attention to organizing this each day will make your job easier and more pleasant.

We suggest having a place in the art area where interesting objects (like a vase of flowers or a bowl with goldfish) can be placed temporarily to inspire observation and artistic endeavors.

LIBRARY The best way to help children learn the joy of reading and become motivated to read is to have a large selection of good books available. Nothing is more important to support children in gaining literacy skills than to create the desire to read books. Having a good library area in your classroom is essential.

Source: Jeff Reese

Children feel invited to use books displayed with the covers visible on an uncrowded bookshelf at their eye level. Locate the classroom library area in the best-lit, quietest corner of the classroom. Include soft pillows and an adult-size chair or sofa. Decorate it with book posters, alphabet posters, or book covers. If there is room include a listening center with books on tape, puppets, a flannelboard for storytelling, and a private area for one or two children to enjoy a book.

In a spacious classroom, we like to combine the library with the writing center to create a literacy center. Besides books, storytelling, writing, and bookmaking materials, a literacy center can include literacy games.

A Story-Reading Place A library is a cozy place to read to one or two children; however, most teachers read stories to a group at least once a day. A group story-reading place needs good lighting. It needs to be sheltered from noise with relatively few distractions so that children remain attentive. There needs to be comfortable seating and space for children to move as they listen to a story. You will probably need to use an area that serves another purpose such as the block area as your story-reading place. To limit distractions and signal to children that an area has become the story-reading place, you might hang curtains over shelves or place dividers in front of shelves to keep tempting toys out of small hands. Some teachers set out mats, blankets, carpet squares, or pillows to establish boundaries and make sitting more comfortable.

WRITING CENTER Preschool and kindergarten classrooms need a writing center where children can draw, write messages and stories, and illustrate their writing. A writing center needs a table and chairs sized correctly for the children (feet should comfortably touch on the floor, and elbows should rest easily on the table). It also needs low shelves to store materials and supplies. Supplies should be set out so they are easy for children to find. Baskets or boxes with different types and sizes of paper, envelopes, note cards, paper notepads, pencils, erasers, markers, crayons, string, and hole punches. Other useful materials include a children's dictionary, clipboards, chalkboards with chalk, carbon paper, collections of words on index cards, letter-stamps, and wood or plastic letters for constructing words and for tracing.

DISCOVERY CENTER Discovery centers are laboratories for exploration. Although it is often called a science center, we prefer *discovery* because children understand the word and to suggest that the center is a place where discoveries of many different kinds can occur. In a discovery center, children solve problems based on observations and research, using tools and books you provide. Define the discovery center with low, open shelves and one or two low tables or counters. An electrical outlet is essential for a light, aquarium, or incubator. Set tables for displays against a taller shelf or wall.

Focus on Science   A discovery center is a home for science when you provide tools for exploration and for ongoing projects, such as aquariums and terrariums, animal families, and plants. Include science games, collections of objects and pictures, and science reference books. Set up a shelf with tools for investigation: sorting trays, plastic tubs and pitchers, aquariums, insect and animal cages, airtight containers for storage, balances, scales, measuring cups and spoons, and magnifying glasses. Select materials for investigation, sorting, collections (like shells or rocks), machinery to investigate and disassemble, information books, and photographs and posters that illustrate science concepts.

Focus on Math   A discovery center is a home for math when it contains materials that encourage children to experiment and think about math-related experiences such as math manipulatives (**Unifix cubes**, sorting and matching games, measurement tools, number rods) math picture books, and displays of math-related group work, such as graphs.

Focus on Social Studies   A discovery center is a home for social studies when you include displays, artifacts, games, maps and globes, and books about the attributes of the human and natural environments. Pictures, posters, and children's work (e.g., maps children have drawn) relating to social studies can be exhibited here.

WOODWORKING AREA   If you have adequate space and staffing, woodworking can be a wonderful addition to a classroom. A woodworking area requires a specially built workbench and proper tools (not pretend, child-size tools, which are usually of poor quality and therefore hazardous). If you feel uncomfortable having a woodworking area in your environment you might begin by learning about woodworking—by reading *Woodworking for Young Children* (Garner, Skeen, & Cartwright, 1984), by taking a class, or by inviting someone who is familiar with woodworking materials into your program to teach you and the children how to use them.

Primary Classrooms: A Place Called School

Do you remember your first-grade classroom? Did you sit in rows? Did you sit at tables? Was there a place to play? Did you have a pet? Did you have a desk? However it was structured, you probably remember it. It was your first experience of "real school."

Classrooms for primary-age children (first through third grade) can be quite similar to the preschool and kindergarten classrooms just described. However, they are more

Connecting with Families

Through the Learning Environment

Busy families of young children have very little time to spend in the classroom. Some may not feel that they are wanted or needed. But we know that greater engagement of families has benefits for children, families, and teachers. There are some simple things you can do as you design the learning environment and schedule that will encourage families to participate:

- Create a family corner in the classroom with comfortable adult seating and interesting things to read. This welcomes family members and tells them the classroom is a place for them as well. If there isn't enough space make sure there is a place for grown-ups to sit.

- Have short, interesting reading materials available for families in the classroom.

- Invite families to contribute to the environment through workdays, shared materials, simple take-home tasks (e.g. making play dough. Be sure to visibly and enthusiastically acknowledge families who contribute.

- Create a dedicated time in the schedule for a family activity—a once-a-week sign-up to read a story, a once-a-month, end-of-the-day play activity, or an end-of-a study sharing.

often more like classrooms for older children, with desks in rows and few interest centers. Available resources make a difference, of course, but the most important variable is the philosophy of the teacher and the school. Although you can set up learning centers in any room (as Sally, the teacher in the example at the beginning of this chapter, did in a church basement), as a new teacher you may be unwilling to make your room too different from the classrooms that surround you. If you teach in an after-school program for primary children, you may not even have a classroom and may need to set up a temporary environment each day in a gym or all-purpose room.

We started this chapter by saying that the learning environment speaks to children: What do you want your room to say to the primary-age children you teach? If you want it to say, "This is your room—you belong here—we make decisions together—we are on a learning adventure," you will do what you can to design a classroom that is quite a bit like a good preschool or kindergarten classroom. Instead of desks in rows, there will be clusters of worktables, a place for group meetings, and comfortable learning centers for reading, exploring, experimenting, and playing (see Figure 8.6). You can have some of the same learning centers you might see in a preschool, but their size and proportion may be different. And to make them appropriate to these older children, you will include some different things, specifically the following:

- In the library, you will have more books to match a range of reading skills, and they can be shelved with only the spines showing.

- In the writing center, classroom computers are a boon to beginning authors.

- A dictionary and other reference books that match the children's reading level, and a printer for publishing can be available in the writing center.

- Discovery areas can hold more fragile artifacts (objects). Also make available reference books that match children's reading level, Internet access that children can use independently, maps, globes, and educational games geared to the ability level of the group.

- A shelf for toys and games can hold math manipulatives; more complex construction toys like K'NEX and Lincoln Logs; board games that require greater ability like Hi Ho! Cherry-O, Mouse Trap, and Monopoly Junior; and smaller, more complex jigsaw puzzles with 50 to 300 pieces.

- If you have space, blocks are a wonderful material for primary school classrooms. Primary-age children skillfully use blocks to reproduce structures they know. Blocks can be integrated into curriculum and used particularly to support social studies and math learning.

 Application Exercise 8.6   Figure 8.6: School-Age Floor Plan

Technology in the Early Childhood Classroom

Technology is a part of our lives. We use technology when we drive a car, make toast, watch television, use a search engine, listen to a podcast, or make a phone call—even when we hammer in a nail we are using technology to augment our strength. Technology in early childhood classrooms is ubiquitous. Young children are gaining technological skills when they learn to turn on the lights, use scissors, and push the buttons on a blender. So the question is not whether to use technology in your classroom. You will be using it. But though most of us agree that every child should learn to use light switches and scissors we are not in similar agreement about digital technology.

Digital technology in the form of the Internet, computers, tablets, e-readers, and smartphones are an integral part of the way we live, learn, and teach today. You may be

Figure 8.6 School-Age Floor Plan

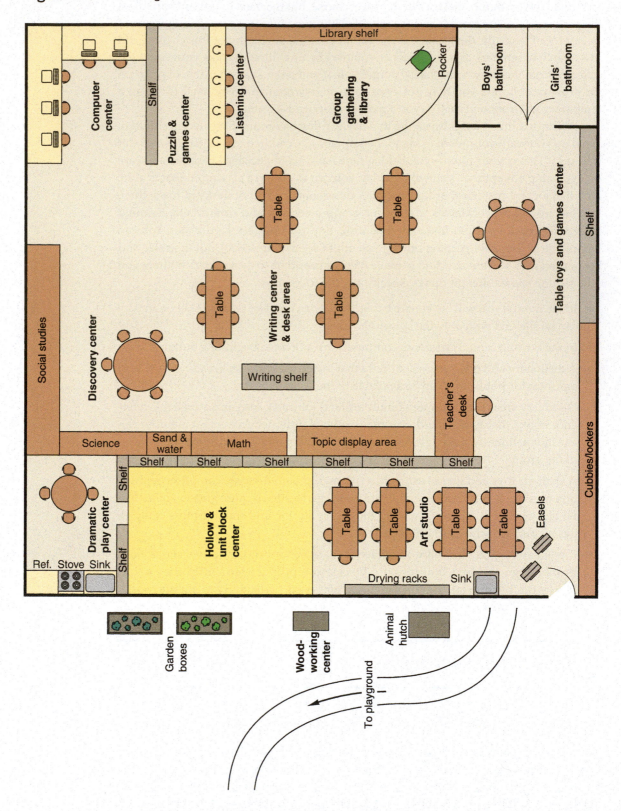

reading this book on your smartphone or taking the class for which it is a text online. As a teacher, digital technology will help you create learning materials, do research, document children's learning, and communicate with families.

In our enthusiasm for the very real value of digital technology we sometimes forget to ask some important questions about its role in our classrooms and in the lives of the young children. What digital technology is appropriate at different stages of development and what is not? How can we use it to support children's growth and learning? Are there any dangers or problems with the use of digital media?

Young children are in our care during the years from 0 to 5, a critical time for brain development, building secure relationships, and establishing healthy behaviors. What do children need during this time? They need hands-on experience with real things and social interaction to develop their cognitive, language, motor, and social-emotional skills. It is impossible for media to provide these things. The American Academy of Pediatrics (2016) tells us that there are other reasons to be concerned with the use of digital media. Several of these speak directly to teachers.

1. Applications designed for young children mostly target rote learning not thinking skills and executive functions essential for school success (e.g., task persistence, impulse control, flexible thinking). These skills are best taught through unstructured and social play.

2. Interactive enhancements in e-books may decrease the child's comprehension of content.

3. Heavy media use during preschool years is associated with increases in BMI, and sets the stage for weight gain later in childhood.

4. There are associations between excessive television viewing in early childhood and cognitive, language, and social/emotional delays.

For these reasons the American Academy of Pediatrics (2016) and the White House Task Force on Childhood Obesity (2010) discourage any digital media time for children under 2 years of age and recommend no more than 1 daily hour of "screen time" of any kind for children under the age of 5.

It is our strong belief (as well as that of many other educators) that while brief use of digital media can occasionally supplement the curriculum, it must not replace the traditional play materials and activities of the early childhood classroom (Levin, 2011). We concur with Jane Healy who says, "There are few things that can be done better on a computer and many that fail miserably by comparison. Teachers and parents must understand that if young children are allowed too much access to computers, they are missing a golden opportunity to develop the personal, social, and emotional skills they will need to function effectively in adulthood" (Early Childhood Today, 2013).

Computers   Primary-grade children learning to write are often much more fluent with the assistance of computers than without. Because computers are tools for gaining information it makes sense to place one in or near the discovery center. The computers should be located out of the flow of traffic where they will not distract children at play, against a wall or partition to prevent tripping over wires, near a light source and away from sources of glare, and away from art, sand and water, or cooking activities. Laptop and tablet computers offer greater flexibility in terms of space. Because they are smaller and more fragile, they require more adult control.

A computer area must have hardware (computer, printer, keyboard, etc.) and recent and developmentally appropriate software. The computer should be placed on a child-size table with several chairs so that several children can work together. Whereas using a computer is usually a solitary activity for adults, many children prefer to work with others as they use a computer.

Although some software for children is intriguing, many are simply electronic workbooks that provide drill and practice, in other words, rote learning, not thinking, skills. Appropriate applications help children develop critical thinking skills and creativity. What makes an appropriate application for a young child?

• The concepts are developmentally appropriate—that is, relevant and concrete. For example, children learn how to create a picture or initiate activity rather than to repeat a correct answer.

- They are open-ended. They allow a great deal of child choice and child direction.
- The pace is set by the child, not by the application.
- They have an intrinsically appealing process (such as exploring an environment) rather than an extrinsic reward (such as a smiling face for giving the correct answer).
- They invite collaborative decision making and cooperation rather than competition.
- They provide models of prosocial behavior and are violence free.

Another classroom use of computers that holds greater value, in our opinion, is the use of computers as portals to information. Accessing the Web is not an "adults-only" activity. However, like using the encyclopedia, it does require adult assistance. Many preschool and kindergarten children understand that the Internet is a valuable source of information. Why does that caterpillar appear to have two heads? Why does cream turn into butter? Why are stop signs red? What do chameleons eat? What will the weather be like tomorrow? When and where did mastodons live? Young children are filled with questions. We have been pleased to observe teachers using the Internet as a tool to help children find the answers to their questions. This helps them develop the desire to become scholars who understand and use technology well. And that is the real goal of using computers with young children.

Computer technology changes at a rapid pace. The skills and programs that children learn to use today may be obsolete tomorrow. To make appropriate use of the current computer technologies, you need to know how to use them in ways that are consistent with our knowledge of how children learn.

Television and Video   Most children will spend far more time in their lives watching television than they will in school. A debate is ongoing about the negative effects of television. A study published in the journal *Pediatrics* (Christakis, Zimmerman, DiGuiseppe, & McCarty, 2004) recommends that children under the age of 2 not watch television because of its potentially damaging effects. The same study points to growing evidence suggesting that television viewing by preschoolers is linked to an increase in occurrence of attention deficit disorders. Whether television programs created for children are thoughtfully produced or merely marketing devices for toys appears to be irrelevant to television's harmful effects. For this reason, we believe that television should never be used in programs for infants and toddlers and should be used rarely, if at all, in classrooms for preschoolers.

Used carefully as a tool with appropriate content and active teacher involvement, television and video programs may be acceptable for kindergarten and primary school children if they meet the following criteria:

- It is shown to children in short (under 15-minute) segments that you have previewed.
- It contributes to educational goals.
- You sit and watch with a small group of children and talk with them about what they have viewed.
- It addresses children respectfully and is geared to their age.
- It is used infrequently as a supplement to more concrete activities and experiences.

Digital Photography/Videography   Digital photography/videography is a wonderful tool for teachers. Whether with a class camera or tablet you are able to document and personalize the classroom, share children's learning and discovery with families, and reflect on your own practice (Luckenbill, 2012; Neumann-Hinds, 2007). We believe every teacher should make a habit of carrying a pocket-sized camera, iPod, or smartphone (with the sound turned off) along with a notepad for observations. Because digital photographs and video can be easily shared it is important to be scrupulous in safeguarding these images and never, ever share them on social media.

Reflect On

Your Ethical Responsibilities and Technology

You are a teacher of toddlers. The families in your classroom make a gift of a giant tablet computer for use in the classroom. You know that the American Academy of Pediatrics says that use of digital technology is not appropriate for children under the age of two. You also are aware that many of the children spend time each day with a television, smart phone, or tablet computer. Using the "Guidelines for Ethical Reflection" on page 22 reflect on your ethical responsibilities in this situation and think about an ethical response that you might make.

Including Children with Disabilities

All children deserve a classroom in which they can fully participate. Creating a classroom where children, regardless of ability can participate is called **universal design**. Universal design means that entries, pathways, centers, tables, climbing structures, and play materials are created with the needs of all children in mind so that they are flexible and easily adapted to accommodate all children. Other adaptations, such as creating additional alone spaces for a child with autism are less obvious but equally important parts of universal design. Often, small rearrangements of the furniture or schedule are enough to make your environment a good place for all children.

The outside environment, equipment, and activities must allow children with physical challenges to participate fully. Adaptations can be relatively simple. For example, creating walkways across grass and sand (recycled conveyer belts work well for this) will extend the range of a child in a walker or wheelchair. A sling swing or hammock can be used by a child who does not have the upper-body strength required to use a conventional swing. It is required by law that children with disabilities, like typically developing children, be provided with access to playgrounds and equipment.

A Quick Check 8.4

Gauge your understanding of the concepts in this section.

Time

The final element to consider when planning a learning environment for young children is time. A typical day in any early childhood program is an artful blend of routines and learning experiences linked by smooth transitions. We think of the daily ebb and flow of learning activities and routines as being part of a larger experience of living and learning with children.

The Daily Schedule

A day for children in a good early childhood program has a relaxed and flexible pace. Children are not rushed from activity to activity. Perhaps this is why in some programs it is called the flow of the

SOURCE: Jeff Reese

day rather than the schedule. Although there are many schedule differences, depending on children's age and other factors, schedules in good early childhood programs share two similarities: Children are offered choices and large blocks of time in which to fully explore the chosen activities, and routines and transitions are thoughtfully planned. Nine-month-old Camille—delightedly crawling from shelf to shelf and exploring toys until she tires and crawls to her teacher for a cuddle—and 7-year-old Harrison—writing a story about tigers during learning center time over several days—are each making choices and governing their own use of time.

Both spontaneous and planned activities occur daily in a carefully prepared program for young children, although the amount of each varies. Your role as a teacher is to include time for engagement with the materials you have provided, routines that allow for increasing mastery, and rituals that bring a sense of security for the children.

INFLUENCES ON THE FLOW OF THE DAY   The structure of a program day is influenced by the needs and developmental stage of the children, your observations of individuals, and your values and the values and concerns of parents, community, and the school administration. It is also influenced by the length of the program day, the physical setting, and the time of year.

Values and Goals   If you value creativity, independence, and the development of responsibility, you will allow large blocks of time (1 to 2 hours) during which children choose their own activities while you work with individuals and small groups. If you want to ensure that all children engage with all materials, you might have shorter play periods of assigned time in each area (for example, we have known programs with special art, block, and woodworking rooms where all children had assigned time each week).

Children's Needs and Developmental Stage   A schedule for a group of young children must include provisions for physical needs and take into account developmental differences. All children need time for rest, nourishment, and hygiene. They need time for vigorous activity, quiet times, and daily times when choice is permitted. Because younger children's needs vary greatly, the younger the children, the more flexible the schedule needs to be. During a 10:00 visit to a group of toddlers, we saw Aimee lying down and drinking a bottle, Ian having a nap, Walden looking at books, Nadine cuddling on a teacher's lap, and Jonathan using the toilet. A rigid schedule could not meet such diverse needs and would inevitably lead to frustration for adults and children. A skilled infant teacher whom we know creates a written individual schedule for each child and posts it in the classroom. This allows everyone in the care setting to be aware of each child's routine. By reviewing these schedules weekly, caregivers ensure that they are adapting their routines and expectations to meet the needs of each child.

Typical schedules for different age-groups have the following characteristics:

- Infants. Each child regulates him- or herself—meals, rest, toileting, and active/quiet times.

- Toddlers and young preschoolers. Regular meals, snacks, and rest, with toileting and active/quiet times occurring in response to children's needs and interests.

- Older preschoolers and kindergartners. Scheduled eating, rest, group activity, and outdoor times with some flexibility based on children's needs on any given day. As children mature, more structured plans for group and activity times are appropriate. A good way to start each day is with a group gathering to share news, sing a song, and map out the day's direction.

- Primary children. Similar to older preschoolers and kindergartners but with more structured group and activity times. A good way to finish each day is listening to a chapter from a book.

The Program Day   Children in a full-day early childhood program spend up to 60% of their waking hours out of their home. This is a significant portion of a young child's life, and the program is like a second home. In full-day settings, it is especially important to pay close attention to the quality of relationships, the design of the environment, and scheduling. For an example of scheduling, see Figure 8.7.

All early childhood programs must provide for the needs of children. A full-day program must offer lunch, a midday rest, and snack periods to avoid having overstimulated, hungry children. Because their stomachs are relatively small, young children need to eat every 2 to 3 hours (Aronson, 2012), so schedules must be adjusted accordingly.

Children in full-day programs may stay 6 to 11 hours, but the staff in such programs generally remain for only 6 to 8 hours. So children may spend significant time with two separate groups of staff members. Taking care to coordinate the transition between the shifts will help children maintain the sense of trust they need. Some people hold the misperception that anyone who cares for young children in the afternoon has a less important job than those who perform similar tasks in the morning. Children do not make this distinction. They learn and need nurturing throughout the day. Involving afternoon staff in planning and recognizing the vital tasks they accomplish is one way to maintain program quality throughout the day.

In part-day programs, it is likely that staff will remain consistent throughout the program day. Scheduled rest time is probably unnecessary, may meet with resistance, and is a waste of limited time. In a short program, a good blend of outdoor activity and indoor activities with a short snack break will provide for a pleasant, productive half-day experience.

Before- and after-school programs for kindergarten and primary children are designed to ensure children's well-being while parents are at work and to provide appropriate activities for children before and after school. Children need high-quality care and education throughout the day, and after-school programs should offer more than custodial care. However, children who are in structured school settings all day require a different, more relaxed program before and after school. Good after-school programs provide opportunities for play, socialization, and self-selected work. Although some homework can be incorporated, primary school children also need the opportunity to play in the second half of their days away from home.

The Physical Facility The building in which the program is housed will influence how you structure the day. If it contains only your program and has sufficient space for

Figure 8.7 Daily Schedule for a Full-Day Preschool

7:00–8:00	Arrival and child-chosen indoor activities
8:00–8:30	Breakfast—children may clean up their eating space and look at a book as they wait for the beginning of group meeting
8:30–8:45	Group meeting—staff and children gather to sing songs, discuss the events of the prior day, and share plans for the day
8:45–10:30	Learning center time—indoor activities are available and small groups may meet for part of the time for project work or teacher-led activities
10:30–11:30	Outdoor activity time
11:30–12:15	Lunch—hand washing, setting of tables, family-style service, and individual cleanup as each child finishes eating
12:15–12:30	Nap preparation—children toilet, wash hands, brush teeth, take out their mats or place nap bedding on cots, and settle down with a book while others prepare for nap
12:30–1:00	Book time—an adult reads several books aloud to children who wish to join the group while others continue to remain on their mats with their own book
1:00–2:30	Nap time—the lights are dimmed, soft instrumental music plays, and the staff are available to pat backs (from 1:30 on snacks and quiet activities are available for children who wake up or who do not wish to rest longer)
2:30–4:30	Indoor/outdoor activities—children may select from a variety of activities indoors and outdoors with special activities and ongoing projects available
4:30–5:00	Closure—materials are put away; children wash up, settle down for songs, stories, and quiet activities as they wait for their families

younger children to be separated from older ones, it is relatively easy to schedule the day to meet the basic needs of all age-groups. Where space is limited or facilities are shared, you may need to work out ways to accommodate different groups of children. If the bathroom or playground is located at a distance from the classroom, you will have to take this into account in planning.

Staff–Child Ratio and Group Size   The number of staff members in relation to the number of children is another factor of the physical setting that influences how you structure the day. Events, routines, and activities can be scheduled with more flexibility if there are lots of adults available to supervise. Teachers are free to be spontaneous and to plan for activities that have a variable time frame or that require more intense adult–child interaction. The size of the group will influence the flexibility of the daily schedule. Larger groups require more advance planning for the use of facilities, such as playgrounds, vans, and lunchrooms, and the daily schedule must be more tightly planned.

Time of Year   During the first days and weeks of school, your program must allow time to help children become accustomed to routines and new activities. As the year progresses, they will have mastered routines and become accustomed to program expectations. They will have developed new skills and abilities. Your schedule can be adjusted to their new competencies, cooperativeness, and skills. Group times may last longer, scheduled routines, such as toileting, may be omitted as children become independent and no longer require supervision, naptime may shorten as children grow out of the need for a lengthy nap.

Classroom Routines   Carefully designed and implemented routines support the important goal of having young children to develop competence in independently meeting their physical and social needs. As an early childhood practitioner, you will want to give routines attention and thoughtful planning, just as you do the other aspects of the program. The accompanying box, "Golden Rules for a Good Day for Young Children," summarizes the information that follows.

Arrival   Arrival each day should be a friendly, predictable event in which every child is greeted. An arrival period during which you greet and talk briefly with families and children sets a relaxed tone. It may be one of the few regular contacts you will have with children's families and is a good time for exchanging information.

Diapering and Toileting   Diapering is an important part of caregiving for infants and toddlers. You will respond to infants' diapering needs individually. However, in a classroom for toddlers and 2-year-olds diapering will be a part of the daily schedule. If you teach 2-year-olds or young 3-year-olds, or teach a mixed-age class, or a class with

Golden Rules

for a Good Day for Young Children

1. Use large blocks of time (at least 1 hour long) for indoor and outdoor self-selected activities.
2. Alternate quiet sedentary activities with active play.
3. Keep structured group times short.
4. Include times for nourishment, rest, and personal care.
5. Maintain a relaxed pace. Avoid rushing children from activity to activity or area to area.
6. Use meaningful, enjoyable activities to create smooth transitions.
7. Allow children to govern their own use of time (how long to work, play, eat, nap, and so on) as much as possible.
8. Build rituals into the day (e.g., a morning song or a nap-time story).

children with special needs, the daily schedule needs to include regular trips to the toilet for those who need this support.

Mealtimes and Snacks   Some of the most pleasant times in an early childhood program occur when adults and children sit down and eat together. Virtually all early childhood programs include a morning breakfast or snack. In full-day programs, they also include a midday meal and an afternoon snack. Programs with a long day schedule an additional snack toward the end of the day so that children do not go more than 3 hours without an opportunity to eat. This snack helps children and families have more pleasant departure times without the "arsenic hour" syndrome of tired parents and hungry, whining children.

Cleanup   Cleanup is a natural and necessary part of living with others. Children begin to understand that they are members of a community and that they need to share in the responsibility for maintaining cleanliness and order. Even though you will ask children to participate in clean-up you will find yourself doing a good deal of tidying of toys and equipment each day. As you straighten and reorder the environment, you are helping children see learning possibilities. In doing so, you also help children understand the process of maintaining order.

Rest Time   If children are tired, if the environment is restful, and if children feel secure, rest time in an early childhood program is a positive experience. If children are fearful, or angry, they will be unable to relax. Most children under the age of 5 (and many 5-year-olds) nap if the environment is comfortable.

Every child in a full-day preschool or kindergarten needs a mat or cot for sleeping. Infants need the protection of an individual crib or other sheltered sleeping space, such as a mat surrounded by pillows. To create an atmosphere conducive to rest and sleep, dim the lights and allow children to cuddle personal comfort objects. We like to play quiet music for nap, and there is research to suggest that the practice of playing quiet music helps children fall asleep more quickly (Field, 1999).

The length of nap and rest periods should be based on children's needs. It may also provide a quiet period for teachers to collect themselves and do some planning or preparation—but it is not the primary purpose. The length of rest for children who do not sleep should be based on their ability to relax. We suggest that children who have not fallen asleep be allowed to get up and play after 30 or 40 minutes of quiet time. Children 5 to 8 years old also benefit from short quiet times in their day that may be combined with an opportunity for reading. Kindergarten children who have not had a nap during the school day may need a time and place for napping or quiet resting in their after-school programs.

Reflect On

Routines

What routines do you have in your own life? How do you feel when the rhythm of daily routines is disrupted? What do you like about your routines?

What routines have you observed or implemented in programs for young children? When did these routines seem to harmonize with the activity of the classroom? When did they seem to be a disruption?

Transitions   Each time a scheduled activity or routine ends, it is followed by a transition, a time of gathering children or of movement into a new activity. Transitions can be smooth and relaxed if they are well planned and if children are prepared for them. Suggestions for meaningful and interesting activities that will help you to orchestrate smooth transitions can be found in Chapter 6.

Departure   The end of the program day should provide a smooth transition back into life at home. If all the children leave at the same time, departure can be structured to provide closure. You may read a story, go over events of the day, and plan for tomorrow. If children leave at different times throughout the afternoon, you may complete these routines early in the afternoon and then provide open-ended activities that children can easily leave as they are picked up. In all programs, a staff member should be available to share information with families and say farewell to children as they leave.

✔️ **A Quick Check 8.5**

Gauge your understanding of the concepts in this section.

 # Final Thoughts

What do you want your environment to say to children and their families? How can you make it say, "Welcome! I care. This is a place for you"? The environment communicates your caring and competence to families. When you design a learning environment (the space, the equipment, and the time), you are creating a resource that helps you do your job, and you are creating your own work environment.

Your home changes as you change. It reflects your needs, tastes, activity, and lifestyle. It changes as your family changes. Creating an environment for children and making it work is also a process of change. It allows you to use your knowledge of children's development, your sensitivity in observation, and your creativity. As you gain more knowledge and skill and as you devote time, energy, and resources to the environment, it will better meet children's needs. This kind of creation is a challenging and satisfying aspect of the work of a teacher of young children.

 Application Exercise 8.7 Final Reflection

 ## To Learn More

Read

A Place for Me: Including Children with Special Needs in Early Care and Education Settings, P. A. Chandler (1994).

Child Care Design Guide, A. R. Olds (2001).

Creating Environments for Learning: Birth to Age Eight, 2nd ed., J. Bullard (2014).

Creating Rooms of Wonder, C. Seefeldt (2002).

Designs for Living and Learning: Transforming Early Childhood Environments, 2nd ed., D. Curtis & M. Carter (2014).

Inspiring Spaces for Young Children, J. Deviney et al. (2010).

Last Child in the Woods: Saving Our Children from Nature-Deficit Disorder, R. Louv (2008).

Loose Parts: Inspiring Play in Young Children, L. Daly (2014)

Loose Parts 2: Inspiring Play with Infants and Toddlers, L. Daly & M. Beloglovsky (2016).

National Guidelines Nature Play & Learning Places: Creating and Managing Places Where Children Engage with Nature. R. C. Moore (2014)

Natural Playscapes: Creating Outdoor Play Environments for the Soul, R. Keeler (2008).

Places for Childhoods: Making Quality Happen in the Real World, J. Greenman (1998).

Visit a Website

The following agencies and organizations have websites related to early childhood learning environments:

American Montessori Association

Community Playthings: Videos and articles on learning environments for young children

Early Childhood Australia

Forest School Association

North Carolina State Natural Learning Initiative

The Department of Defense Child Development Virtual Lab School at The Ohio State University

 # Document Your Skill & Knowledge About the Learning Environment in Your Professional Portfolio

Include some or all of the following:

- An evaluation of an existing early childhood environment using the Learning Environment Checklist in Appendix B. Include a short written analysis of the strengths of the environment as well as how you might change or modify it to better support children's development.

- A photograph of a classroom, playscape, or learning center you have created with a brief description of why you designed it in this way.

Shared Writing 8.1 Adding Natural Elements to an Urban Play Space

Chapter 9
Understanding and Supporting Play

Through play, children learn what no one can teach them.

LAWRENCE FRANK

 ## Chapter Learning Outcomes:

9.1 Describe the nature of play and explain some theories that help us understand it.

9.2 Explain some ways that play contributes to development.

9.3 Develop strategies for facilitating children's play.

9.4 Identify some issues related to play.

NAEYC Professional Preparation Standards

The NAEYC Professional Preparation Standard that applies to this chapter:

Standard 1: Promoting Child Development and Learning (NAEYC, 2009).

Key elements:

1a: Knowing and understanding young children's characteristics and needs

1b: Knowing and understanding the multiple influences on development and learning

1c: Using developmental knowledge to create healthy, respectful, supportive, and challenging learning environments

D o you remember the dizzy joy of rolling down a hill, the focused effort of building an elaborate structure with blocks, the satisfaction of learning to jump rope, or the concentration of pretending with friends? Whether rich or poor, in town or country, you played. Children all over the world play; they have always played. Play is the ultimate realization of the early childhood educator's maxim of "learning by doing." Since the field began, early childhood educators have sought to understand and support this most natural of activities. Today, as in the past, belief in the value of play is a distinguishing characteristic of early childhood educators. It is a link to our past and a bond between early childhood professionals.

"Why do they play all day? When are you going to start teaching them something?" You will be asked these questions and will need to explain the importance of play to families, program administrators, and other educators. In the current era of "push-down academics" and standards-based instruction, it is crucial that you are able to explain how children learn through play and why play is essential for their development and learning. Because play is how children learn, it is the heart of developmentally appropriate early childhood curriculum. It is the medium through which children learn about the world, and an important way that you will achieve your goals for children's learning.

Play supports all aspects of children's development. It provides an avenue for them to practice skills and solidify concepts. Observing children at play is the basis of authentic assessment. Through these observations you will learn a great deal about what they understand and can do. You will also come to appreciate their interests and unique characteristics and know what they are like as individuals.

Because of the impressive power of play to lead the development of social, emotional, and cognitive competence, it is important that you understand play—what it is, how it develops, its function in growth and learning, the controversies surrounding it, and the role of the early childhood educator in supporting children's play.

 # Understanding Play

What is **play**? What is its significance? Why is play so compelling to children? Reflecting on the play of children and your own childhood play can help you realize that many things can be play. As you observe a child at play, you may notice the characteristics of play. As you watch children of different ages, you will see that play changes as children grow. And as you observe boys and girls with different temperaments, experiences, and abilities, you will see some of the individual differences in children's play. The characteristics and stages of play described by theorists and researchers can help you understand what you see.

Characteristics of Play

As the 4-year-olds gather, Ashley, the teacher, invites each child to select a center where he or she would like to begin the morning. Kaitlin, Bryce, and Ema select the dramatic play

area. Kaitlin announces, "Let's play farm. I'm the lamb, and Bryce, you be the farmer." Ema protests, "You got to be the lamb last time. I get to be the lamb this time." Kaitlin concedes and claims the role of the mommy lamb as she puts a blanket in the doll bed to serve as a bed for her baby lamb. Bryce follows with a carton of eggs (large beads) and says, "I'm the mommy chicken, and I'm making eggs." As he places the eggs in the doll bed, Kaitlin pushes him away, proclaiming that chickens use nests, not beds. Ashley observes the interaction and responds by offering a shawl as nest material.

Ask adults how they can distinguish children at play and they will likely tell you "when they are having fun" or even "when I can't get their attention." Perhaps there is no single agreed-on definition because no single activity is play. Is gardening play or work? Is running a joy or a punishment? Although no definition captures the essence of play, theorists, researchers, and educators have identified characteristics that distinguish play from other behaviors. These characteristics enable you to understand what play is—and what it is not. Knowing this can help you make decisions and take actions that support children's play and avoid interrupting or misguiding it. Although the exact wording varies, specialists on play (Brown & Vaughn, 2009; Johnson, Christie, & Wardle, 2005; Saracho & Spodek, 1998) include the following characteristics as necessary for play:

- Play is **intrinsically motivated**. It is its own reward. Children play because it is satisfying, not because it meets a basic need or receives an external reward. It is the motivation, rather than the activity, that makes something play. Walking on a balance beam as you cross the playground is play; walking a balance beam as part of a gymnastics routine because your parents want you to win a prize is most likely work. The pleasure and focus that Kaitlin, Ema, and Bryce brought to play in the preceding example is a sign of this personal motivation. Had Ashley (the teacher in the example) rewarded them for playing farm, it would have been work.

- Play is *freely chosen*. Children choose play. The play opportunity beckons, and children answer the call of play. Ashley invited the children to play, but she could not have required children to pretend in this way. The moment compulsion enters, it becomes work, not play.

- Play is *pleasurable*. Pleasurable, focused pursuit of an activity is a hallmark of play in children and adults. Although play can be seriously pursued and can include challenges, fears, and frustrations, it is the quality of joy that stands out when we think of play. Activity that is not enjoyable most of the time will not be chosen as play.

- Play is *done for its own sake*. The play, rather than an end product, motivates. Children are more involved in discovery and creation (the process) than the eventual outcome. Play can have a product or goal, but this will be spontaneously decided by the players as part of play and may change as the play progresses. Bryce, Ema, and Kaitlin were not putting on a lamb-and-chicken show—they were deeply involved in the process of pretending.

- Play is *active*. Play requires physical, verbal, or mental engagement with people, objects, or ideas. Although we clearly recognize the rough-and-tumble actions of the young child as play, quieter activities, such as drawing, molding play dough, or even daydreaming, are play when the child is actively engaged.

- Play is *self-oriented* rather than object oriented. In play, the basic question is "What can I do with this object?" In contrast, when confronted with a new or unusual object, the first order of business for most children is to answer the basic question "What is this object and what can it do?" Play theorists and researchers call this exploration and distinguish it from play (Johnson, Christie, & Wardle, 2005).

- Play is often *nonliteral*. Many activities are playful, but it is nonliteral pretending—when children suspend and alter reality for make-believe—that is the pinnacle of play. Children alter reality for make-believe—"Let's play farm—I'll be the mommy and you be the baby" or (holding an egg carton full of beads) "I'm the mommy chicken, and I'm making eggs." This temporary setting aside of the external world for internal exploration and imagining allows children to create realities and engage in symbolic representation.

- Play is *focused*. Mihaly Csikszentmihalyi (2008), a professor of psychology noted for his study of happiness and creativity, calls this **flow**—complete and energized focus. Focused play creates a sense of timelessness and living in the moment.

Children at play are powerful creators compelled by forces from within to create a world. Although the raw materials of their creations are life experiences, the shape of their creations is individual. Play is simultaneously an attachment to and a detachment from the world—a time during which children can act autonomously and freely and experience themselves and the world with intensity.

Scott Eberle, the vice president for interpretation at the Strong National Museum of Play in Rochester, New York, suggests that both children and adults go through a six-step process when they play: anticipation, surprise, pleasure, understanding, strength (or mastery), and poise (or grace and a sense of balance). When we experience all of these, we are playing (Eberle, in Brown & Vaughn, 2009).

Reflect On

Your Memories of Play

When you were a young child, how did you play? What made it play? What was your play like as you got older? How did the play change?

Kinds of Play

Babies play in different ways from preschoolers. Children play in different ways from adults. Although play changes across the life span, some types of play remain the same. As we consider play in early childhood, it is useful to remember that different types of play are not restricted to young children.

Body and movement play. Physical play is easy to identify. It is part of play from the first days of life. Whether you see a baby sucking his toes, a preschooler riding a trike, a kindergartner jumping rope, a fifth grader playing four-square, an adult dancing, or a kitten chasing a ball of yarn, you know they are playing. Freely chosen body movement is innately pleasurable and playful.

Rough-and-tumble play. Play fighting without intent to harm, called **rough-and-tumble play**, is characteristic of almost all mammals. If you have ever watched a litter of puppies or a group of 4-year-old boys on a playground, you have seen rough-and-tumble play (also called **big-body play**). Despite its near universality in homes, allowing rough-and-tumble play in formal programs is controversial. While it is often discouraged or banned outright, there is a growing recognition of the value of rough-and-tumble play (Carlson, 2011).

Object play. Exploring and manipulating objects is another early-to-develop, easy-to-recognize form of play. We have a special word for play objects (toys), special industries that make toys, and special stores that sell them. However, play objects can be as simple as a cup to bang on or a box to climb in. They can be as complex as an old machine to take apart or an iPad with interactive apps to play with.

Imaginative play. Pretend, dramatic, or imaginative play involves the creation of a story or narrative. In imaginative play, the players become immersed in acting out the story as they create it. Both a child dressed up in her mother's

SOURCE: Jeff Reese

hat and shoes and an adult who is a knight in the Society for Creative Anachronism are involved in imaginative play. Perhaps the most intellectually engaging form of play, imaginative play is considered by many to be the most important form of play for children to master (Bodrova & Leong, 2003; Brown & Vaughn, 2009; Elkind, 2007; Smilansky & Shefatya, 1990).

Games. Structured play that has a goal, rules, and a specific challenge is called a **game**. Games can be solitary but are more often interactive and involve competition. Games usually involve some kind of equipment (like board games and ball games). There are many different types of games, ranging from individual and sedentary (like solitaire and most computer games) to active group games played in teams. Games cross the boundary between play and work when a player is employed or rewarded for play, as happens in professional sports.

Why Children Play

Philosophers, theorists, educators, and psychologists have observed children at play for centuries and speculated about play's nature and purpose. Many of the philosophers and educators who have influenced early childhood education viewed play as worthy of serious consideration. Plato and Socrates wrote about play. John Locke suggested that it contributes to children's health, good spirits, and motivation. Friedrich Froebel, the "father of the kindergarten," believed that children learned through play and created toys (gifts) and play activities (occupations) to be used in a play-based curriculum (Frost, Wortham, & Reifel, 2011).

During the 19th and early 20th centuries, a number of writers studied play and formulated explanations for the role of play in human development. In 1938, Johan Huizinga proposed that play was a special separate sphere of human activity that existed outside ordinary life and that it was necessary for the creation of culture (Huizinga, 1971). The *surplus energy theory of play*, introduced by British philosopher Herbert Spencer (1963), suggested that the purpose of play was to help human beings use energy they no longer needed for basic survival. Adults have work to do, but children need to expend their energy in play. G. Stanley Hall (1904) formulated the *recapitulation theory* of child development, which suggests that during childhood, the history of evolution is relived. In Hall's theory, play serves to rid children of primitive and unnecessary instinctual traits carried over by heredity from past generations. Hall was the founder of the child study movement and influenced the creation of laboratory schools, where research could be done to form a scientific basis for teaching. John Dewey founded the Chicago laboratory school, an outgrowth of this movement. Dewey (1910) disagreed with Hall. He saw play as the way children construct understanding. *Instinct or practice theory*, developed by German philosopher and naturalist Karl Groos (1901), suggested that play was a natural instinct, necessary for children's growth and development. Groos argued that lower animals do not play but that more highly evolved species do. This theory suggested that play was practice for adulthood. Children at play practice the tasks and roles of adults. The *relaxation or recreation theory* of G. T. W. Patrick (1916) held that play was an essential mechanism to relieve tension and fatigue (Frost et al., 2011; Hughes, 2009). Today, we know that play is important to development of all kinds and essential to brain development. It is one of the ways that neurons develop connections, in other words, how the brain builds itself (Brown & Vaughn, 2009; Elkind, 2007).

When we observe a group of children, it is easy to see how these theories evolved. A group of energetic preschoolers cooped up on a rainy day certainly seem to have surplus energy. That same group, after an opportunity to run and yell outside, is much more relaxed when they come back in. A jungle gym full of climbing children is humorously reminiscent of our primate cousins and can seem to be replaying evolution. And it can be frighteningly apparent when we watch children playing house, school, or war that they are practicing adult roles.

Reflect On

Play in Your Life

Think of a way you play as an adult. What makes this activity play for you? How much and how often do you get to play? How important is play in your life? If you were being described by your friends or family, would they talk about the things you do as play? Why or why not?

More recent theorists, researchers, and educators have expanded our understanding of why children play. We know that play is both a natural and an instinctive activity that helps children's development. Current theories of play strongly reflect the influence of Freud, Piaget, and Vygotsky.

Freud and his followers, particularly his daughter Anna Freud and Erik Erikson, felt that play provided a catharsis, an emotional cleansing, to help children deal with negative experiences. According to these theorists, in play, children feel more grown up and powerful, can exert some control over their environments, and thus relieve anxiety created by real-life conflicts. Play therapy (psychotherapy for children) uses play and play materials in the diagnosis and treatment of children who have psychological conflicts and problems (Hughes, 2009).

SOURCE: Jeff Reese

Piaget and his followers believed that play is the medium through which children develop cognitively (Reifel & Sutterby, 2009). Based on his observations, Piaget described a set of stages in the development of children's play. Many of today's early childhood programs have a Piagetian orientation to play. Children are allowed time and materials to play, and their teachers trust that it will help them "construct" their own understanding of the world.

Theorist Lev Vygotsky also believed that play served as a vehicle for development. Unlike other theorists, Vygotsky thought play promoted several areas of development: cognitive, emotional, and social. He saw the special role of play as a bridge between what children already know and can do and what they will soon be able to understand and do. Vygotsky called this space between what the child knows and what she or he will soon comprehend the zone of proximal development. In Vygotsky's view, play provides an anchor between real objects and the ability to symbolize (Van Hoorn, Monighan Nourot, Scales, & Alward, 2014). He also believed that play facilitates the development of self-regulation, motivation, and **decentration** (the ability to consider multiple aspects of a stimulus or situation) (Bodrova & Leong, 2007).

Theorists have consistently confirmed the role of play in development. On-going research has recognized the ways that play helps children learn to self-regulate—to control their physical, emotional, social, and cognitive behaviors (Bodrova & Leong, 2003; Bronson, 2000). It confirms the pivotal role of play in children's learning of competencies and skills that lead to the development of proficiency, mastery, and self-control.

Application Exercise 9.1 Play Theorists and Their Theories

Stages of Play

As children grow and develop, they engage in different and increasingly complex types or stages of play. The ability to understand and identify the various stages of play is a valuable tool in your work with children of all ages. If you know that two 5-year-olds can play happily together building a road with blocks and sharing a single vehicle but anticipate that two toddlers will play separately and each will need his or her own truck, you will be able to make sensitive judgments of what behaviors are reasonable to expect from the children, and you will know how to provide developmentally appropriate opportunities for each child in your setting.

SOURCE: Jeff Reese

Stages of play have been described from several perspectives by developmental theorists. Parten studied the social dimensions of play and identified types that typified different age-groups. Piaget and Smilansky focused on the cognitive aspects of play. Elkonin, a student of Lev Vygotsky, identified levels of make-believe play.

PARTEN: STAGES OF SOCIAL PLAY   In the early 1930s, Mildred Parten developed categories of play that described the nature of the relationships among the players (Parten, 1932). Her categories of play continue to be used by early childhood educators. Parten identified six stages of social play that can be viewed along a continuum from minimal to maximal social involvement. The first two (unoccupied behavior and onlooker) are periods of observation preceding the venture into a new situation. Each of the four remaining stages dominates a particular

Video Example 9.1: Solitary Play

Watch the video to see an infant engaged in solitary play. What do you think was engaging to the baby about this play? What skills and concepts might he be developing?

age (although they occur at other ages as well), with children tending toward more and more social play as they get older. These four stages are as follows:

Solitary play (dominant in infancy). During **solitary play**, children play alone and independently with objects. Other children playing nearby go unnoticed. Although solitary play is dominant in infancy and is more typical in younger children, older children also select and benefit from solitary play.

Parallel play (typical of toddlers). In **parallel play**, children play side by side but still are engaged with their own play objects. Little interpersonal interaction occurs, but each may be aware of and pleased by the company of a nearby companion engaged in similar activity.

Associative play (seen most in young preschool-age children). Parten identified two forms of group play. The first, **associative play**, involves pairs and groups of children playing in the same area and sharing materials. Interaction may be brisk, but true cooperation and negotiation are rare. Two children, each building a zoo in the block area, sharing animal props, and talking about their zoo but not creating a joint zoo or negotiating what will happen at their zoo, are involved in associative play.

Cooperative play (characteristic of older preschool and kindergarten/primary-age children). **Cooperative play** is the most social form of group play. In it, children work together to create sustained play episodes with joint themes. They plan, negotiate, and share responsibility and leadership. For example, a group of children pretending to go on a picnic might cooperatively decide what food to take, who should attend the event, how to get there, who will drive, and what joys and catastrophes await them on their outing.

PIAGET AND SMILANSKY: COGNITIVE STAGES OF PLAY   Unlike Parten, who was concerned with the social aspects of play, Jean Piaget (1962) looked at how play supports cognitive development. He developed a framework with three stages of play development that are parallel to his stages of cognitive development. Sara Smilansky adapted Piaget's stages of play, based on her observations of young children

Video Example 9.2: Parallel Play

Watch this video to see toddlers engaged in parallel play. What do you notice about each boy's play? Why is this parallel rather than solitary play?

Video Example 9.3: Associative Play

Watch this video to see children engaged in associative play. What is different about this play compared to the parallel play you observed earlier?

Video Example 9.4: Cooperative Play

Watch the video to see cooperative play. Notice that some children are engaged and some are onlookers. How is the play different from the play in the earlier videos that you watched? What specific actions did you notice that indicated cooperative play?

from diverse cultural and economic backgrounds (Smilansky & Shefatya, 1990). She categorized play into four types, similar to those of Piaget, and added an additional type—constructive play. Piaget's and Smilansky's stages provide only slightly different ways of looking at similar play behaviors. Smilansky's work can be seen as building on Piaget's. Here is a summary that combines their cognitive play stages:

Practice or functional play (dominant from infancy to 2 years of age). In **practice play** or **functional play**, children explore the sensory qualities of objects and practice motor skills. This stage parallels Piaget's sensorimotor stage of development. Children who are engaged in functional play repeat actions over and over again as if practicing them. Both a baby who repeatedly drops a toy over the side of the crib for you to pick up and a toddler who dumps and refills a bucket over and over are engaged in practice play. These actions are viewed as explorations to learn about objects. Although this type of play is most common in the first 2 years, it does not disappear. Both a preschooler repeatedly pouring water from one container to another and a teenager repeatedly combing his already perfect coiffure in front of the mirror are involved in practice play.

Symbolic play (dominant from 2 to 7 years of age). In **symbolic play**, children use one object to represent another object and use make-believe actions and roles to represent familiar or imagined situations. Symbolic play emerges during the preoperational period as the child begins to be able to use mental symbols or imagery.

The different forms of symbolic play are further separated by Smilansky into two categories: **constructive play**, in which the child uses real objects to build a representation of something according to a plan (e.g., creating a bird's nest with play dough), and **dramatic play** and **sociodramatic play**, in which children create imaginary roles and interactions where they pretend to be someone or something (mommy, doctor, dog, and so on) and use actions, objects, or words to represent things or situations (a block for an iron, arm movements for steering a truck, or "woof woof" for the bark of a dog).

Video Example 9.5: Sociodramatic Play

Watch the video to see children engaged in sociodramatic play. How are they using objects as part of their play? What do the objects seem to symbolize? What is important to the children in the play?

Table 9.1: Stages of Play and Stages of Development

Age and Stage of Development	Stage/Level of Play According to . . .			
	Parten	**Piaget**	**Smilansky**	**Vygotsky/Elkonin**
Infants (0–15 months) Piaget **Sensorimotor** (birth–2 years) Erikson **Trust vs. mistrust**	**Solitary play** Children play alone other children unnoticed.	**Practice play** Children explore sensations and motor skills.	**Functional play** Children engage in exploration to learn.	
Toddlers (15–35 months) Piaget **Preoperational** (2–7 years) Erikson **Autonomy vs. shame and doubt**	**Parallel play** Children play side by side. Aware of, pleased by the company of others--little interaction.	**Symbolic play** Children represent reality and familiar or imagined situations.	**Constructive play** Children manipulate objects to create something.	**Level 1 Object Centered** Roles not named. Actions object centered, stereotyped, repeated w/o order. No "rules" for roles.
Young preschool children (3–4 years) Piaget **Preoperational** (2–7 years) Erikson **Initiative vs. guilt**	**Associative play** Pairs/groups play together sharing materials. Cooperation/negotiation rare.		**Dramatic play** Children pretend roles and use actions, objects, words to represent things or situations.	**Level 2** Roles named, actions sequenced. No negotiation, argument or explanation.
Older preschool and **kindergarten** children (4–6 years) Piaget **Preoperational** (2–7 years) Erikson **Initiative vs. guilt**	**Cooperative play** Groups engage in sustained play. They plan, negotiate, share.			**Level 3** Roles named before play. Role speech used. Inconsistent roles pointed out some actions explained.
Primary school children (6–8 years) Piaget **Concrete operational** (7–11 years) Erikson's **Industry vs. inferiority**		**Games with rules** Children recognize and follow rules that conform to expectations and goals of game.	**Games with rules** Children behave according to rules to sustain play.	**Level 4 Mature Play** Roles well defined. Action planned. Children stay in character. Rules for roles explained.

Make-believe with regard to actions and situations. Verbal descriptions are substituted for actions and situations. (Miriam acts out being scared of another child who she says is a mean lady who wants to steal puppies.)

Persistence. The child continues playing in a specific episode for at least 10 minutes. (Even though activity time is over, Miriam continues in the role of puppy and comes to circle time on all fours. She barks for the first song.)

Interaction. At least two players respond to each other in the context of a play episode. (Miriam and Rivera both are pets, but Rivera is a kitty. They play together and meow, hiss, whine, purr, and bark to one another.)

Verbal communication. Some of the verbal interaction relates to the play episode. (Periodically, Rivera gives Miriam directions on the next event in the play, such as, "It's nighttime, and the puppies and kitties have to go to sleep for 100 minutes.")

These elements of play can be used as a basis for evaluating the play skills of individual children. When a particular play skill is not seen, play skill training can be used to teach it to the child. (See Figure 9.3 later in the chapter.)

A Quick Check 9.1

Gauge your understanding of the concepts in this section.

The Role of Play in Development

Play isn't the enemy of learning, it's learning's partner. Play is like fertilizer for brain growth. It's crazy not to use it.

Stuart Brown, Christopher Vaughan

Children need to play. Play supports the development of the whole child—a person able to sense, move, think, relate to others, communicate, and create. It is important to healthy brain development (Brown & Vaughn, 2009; Frost, 2008; Shonkoff & Phillips, 2000). The importance of play was recognized by the UN General Assembly in November 1989, when they approved the Convention on the Rights of the Child, which asserts that every child has the right to play and must have the opportunity to do so.

Early childhood educators have long been able to justify play's value in supporting physical, social, and emotional development. In recent decades, they have met with ever-increasing pressure to justify play in terms of how it contributes to cognitive and language development. It is of particular interest that researchers have found positive relationships between the play abilities of children and their subsequent academic achievement and school adjustment (Brown & Vaughn, 2009). Current animal research indicates that frequent play, especially rough-and-tumble play, enhances brain development and social ability (Pellis and Pellis, 2013). Play researchers continue to discover ways that play facilitates all areas of development.

The Role of Play in Physical Development

Play contributes to physical development and health throughout life. Children at play develop physical competence efficiently and comprehensively. The vigorous activity of children's spontaneous play builds the strength, stamina, and skills they need to succeed as learners. Children learn best when they have bodies that are strong, healthy, flexible, and coordinated and when all of their senses are operating. From infancy on, children display an innate drive to gain physical control of their arms and legs as they strive to reach for and eventually grasp and manipulate objects (Bodrova & Leong, 2003; Bronson, 2000).

Children have an inborn drive to explore, discover, and master skills. The concentrated play of childhood leads naturally to the physical mastery that was probably essential to our survival as a species. Running, jumping, climbing, throwing balls, and riding bikes—the activities we most commonly think of as play—are of prime importance in the development of **perceptual-motor coordination** (the ability to use sensory information to direct motor activity) and in the attainment and maintenance of good health.

A growing body of research identifies specific benefits of play on health and physical development. Playful manipulation of objects in infancy provides the basis for object control skills, such as throwing, in the preschool years (Trawick-Smith, 2010). Mastery of locomotor skills is related to the frequency and quality of play experiences (Adolph, Vereijken, & Shrout, 2003). Preschool children as young as 4 who exhibit low levels of play activity have been found to have greater health risk factors, such as higher blood pressure and body mass index (Sääkslahti, Numminen, Varstala, Helenius, Tammi, et al., 2004).

The Role of Play in Emotional Development

Therapists and educators have long appreciated the rich emotional value of play. Freud and his followers identified play as a primary avenue through which children express and deal with their fears, anxieties, and desires. Contemporary therapists still use play as the medium for helping children deal with the feelings associated with traumatic events and disturbing situations in their lives.

Children at play devise and confront challenges and anticipate changes. In the process, they master their fears; resolve internal conflicts; act out anger, hostility, and frustration; and resolve personal problems for which the "real" world offers no apparent solutions. It is no wonder children are motivated to play all day.

Children at play feel they are in control of their world, practicing important skills that lead them to a sense of mastery over their environment and themselves. They discover ways to express emotions and to communicate their inner state that enable them to maintain the self-control necessary for a cooperative relationship with other players.

The Role of Play in Social Development

From birth, children are enmeshed in a social environment. They need to develop ways of expressing emotions and develop behaviors that enable them to create positive relationships with others (Bronson, 2000). Survival depends on adult care from the moment of birth. Caregivers play with infants in a way that is unlike anything adults do in any other life situation. They address questions to an infant and then take the infant's part to answer. An ordinarily dignified adult will make undignified noises and facial expressions ("ZZZZZZZZZZZZ Gotcha!") and respond with the greatest joy when the baby laughs aloud for the first time. Infant–adult play progresses to games like pat-a-cake and this-little-piggy (which have their equivalents in every culture).

Social play leads to increased social interaction skills. Children learn how to initiate play with relatives, family, friends, and peers. They develop awareness of others, and learn to cooperate, take turns, and use social language. They learn to be a part of a group, develop a social identity, and learn about the rules and values governing their family, community, and culture. The play becomes increasingly complex and is sustained for greater periods of time. By the time children reach their second birthday, most portray social relationships through dramatic play, such as pretending to feed a favorite doll or toy animal. By age 4 or 5, almost all will have learned the things they need to know to enact complex social relationships with their peers in sociodramatic play, for example, pretending to be customers and workers in an ice cream store. Soon after, they become able to play rule-governed games like tag. Through this play, social concepts such as fairness, justice, and cooperation evolve and influence play behavior and other social relationships.

The social competence developed in sociodramatic play leads to the development of cooperative attitudes and behaviors. Most peers, families, and educators prize the sharing, helpful, and cooperative behaviors associated with high levels of social competence developed through this kind of play.

The Role of Play in Cognitive Development

A major task of the early childhood years is the development of skills for learning and problem solving. In play, children learn to set goals, plan how to proceed, develop the ability to focus, and create ways to organize their approach to cognitive tasks (Bronson, 2000). Play is the primary medium through which young

SOURCE: Jeff Reese

children make sense of their experiences and construct ideas about how the physical and social worlds work. The functional play that begins in infancy and persists through life is basic to the process of learning about the properties of objects and how things work.

Constructive play, typical of the toddler, is the mode we use throughout life for discovering and practicing how to use unfamiliar tools and materials (as you may have done learning to use a smartphone or a map). The dramatic (pretend) play of preschool children has a critical role in the development of representational or symbolic thought and the eventual ability to think abstractly. In sociodramatic play, children develop understanding of the world by reenacting with playmates experiences they have had or observed (e.g., a trip to the grocery store). They alter their understanding based on the response and ideas of their friends ("I'm the store man, and you have to give me 50 dollars for that orange. Oranges cost lots of money!"), and then use the new meaning as they again experience the real world ("Mom, do we have enough money for oranges?"). This circular process is one in which information is constantly being gathered, organized, and used. It is one of the primary ways in which children come to understand the world. Jones & Reynolds (1992) suggest that young children engage in dramatic play in order to master the routines and sequences (referred to as 'life scripts') that adults encounter in daily life, for example, eating at a restaurant, attending a party or social event, participating in a faith-based ritual, driving, etc. "The familiarity of life's scripts is what makes the daily life of adults efficient. . . . We are free to think about other things. . . . We recognize this only when we find ourselves in an unfamiliar setting—driving a borrowed car . . . placing a phone call in a foreign country. Young children . . . play in order to find their way around in what is for them the foreign country of adults, to master its daily scripts" (Jones & Reynolds, 1992, p. 10).

Sociodramatic play is of particular interest to play researchers and educators because of its significance in cognitive development. Sociodramatic play involves symbols, and the ability to use and manipulate symbols is the foundation for later learning, particularly literacy skills. In their book *Facilitating Play: A Medium for Promoting Cognitive, Socio-Emotional, and Academic Development in Young Children*, Sara Smilansky and Leah Shefatya (1990) describe many studies in which competence at sociodramatic play is highly correlated with cognitive maturity and creative and social abilities.

The Role of Play in Integrating Development

Throughout this book, we refer to the development of the whole child. At play, more than at any other time, children engage all aspects of themselves and most fully express who they are, what they are able to do, and what they know and feel. Blocks, dramatic play props, construction toys, art materials, books, puzzles, climbing structures, sand, and water—the play equipment and materials found in almost every early childhood program—are rich in their potential for supporting all aspects of development.

 Application Exercise 9.3 Play Scenario with Development

Reflect On

More Memories of Play

Reflect on a time when you developed or improved a skill or learned through play. Did the activity take energy and work? Was it still play?

Video Example 9.6: Building a Boat with Blocks

Watch the video of children building with blocks. Which areas of development are children using as they play?

The Special Role of Outdoor Play

It is likely that some of your most poignant memories of play involve playing outdoors. Why? While all play is important, there is something special about playing outdoors. Perhaps it is the freedom to run, to yell, and to discover the limits of your physical abilities. Maybe it's the challenge of learning to use equipment like trikes, swings, and wagons or the excitement of overcoming your fear at the top of a slide. Perhaps it is the opportunity to experience the adventure of nature. It might be feeling the joy of play that is not as bound by adult rules. Whatever the reason, outdoor play has a special role in programs for young children and deserves special consideration.

What is different about outdoor play? It is obvious that the outdoors affords children the opportunity for a wider range of large motor activity than a classroom can. It is where rough-and-tumble big-body play is most likely to be accepted by adults and least likely to cause damage to people and furniture. Similarly, it is the place where children can engage in messy, sensory play with water, dirt, and sand without the mess-avoiding precautions needed indoors. And, of course, the outdoors is the best place to explore and learn about the natural world and its animals, plants, and weather.

There are additional, less obvious reasons that outdoor play is important. Young children's social development is enhanced when they play outside. Away from the restrictions of the indoor classroom, children have more space to develop friendships. They learn to be leaders, learn to be a part of a group, and learn to be alone. Children play differently outdoors than they do indoors. As well as involving more gross motor play, they engage in play that is more complex, filled with language, and less stereotyped by gender (Frost et al., 2011).

Children's lives and children's play in the 21st century are generally more restricted than they were in the past. Because of this, the children in your care may have few opportunities to play outdoors in their home lives. Knowing this, it is important to advocate for young children, whatever their age and wherever they live, to have time each day to play outdoors.

Explaining Play

As an early childhood educator whose program provides opportunities for children to play, you are likely to have many occasions in which you will need to understand and explain the role of play in children's development. Figure 9.1 provides you with a summary of some of the things that children develop through play and its relationship to academic success. You may also find the publication *Play in the Early Years: Key to School Success* useful when developing your explanation. You may also wish to keep it available to share. You can download it from the website of the Alliance for Childhood.

Figure 9.1 What Children Develop Through Play

- **Increased physical competence:** development of both fine and gross motor skill. This provides the foundation for a range of abilities from keyboarding to dancing.
- **Increased physical fitness and decreased health risks:** including reduced obesity.
- **Representational competence:** the ability to represent objects, people, and ideas. This provides the foundation for reading and math.
- **Oral language competence and narrative understanding:** the ability to understand and use language to talk to others and think in stories necessary for reading and the ability to understand subjects like history and science.
- **Positive approaches to learning:** curiosity, motivation, and a sense of mastery—attitudes that are key to school success.
- **Skills in logic:** concepts of cause and effect, the ability to classify, quantify, order, and solve problems that form the basis for higher order thinking in math, science, and other subjects.
- **Self-regulation and social negotiation:** the ability to negotiate, cooperate, advocate, listen, handle frustration, and empathize. This has been shown to contribute to emotional health and school success.

Connecting with Families

About Play

Families care about what their children do at school (that's their job!). But the value and power of play is not obvious to many families. Make it visible to them in many ways so that they come to understand why play is a part of your programs. Here are some ideas for how you might do this:

- Create a documentation panel with photographs or create a slide show that shows children learning through play.
- Plan a "play night" where families get to experience play activities and reflect on why they are fun and how they help children learn.
- Create a "guided tour" with posters or handouts to help a visiting family member see how the play they observe is contributing to development. Use descriptions from your college textbooks or online resources (allianceforchildhood.org, ipausa.org, or acei.org) to help you write the content.
- Feature a type of play and its importance in each issue of your newsletter.
- Create play backpacks for weekend borrowing. Each backpack can include play materials and a laminated sheet that explains how the activity supports development and suggests ways that a parent might use the materials with children.
- Involve families in the creation of play spaces and play materials for children. As they participate in creating play opportunities, they will gain insight into and appreciation for play.

A Quick Check 9.2

Gauge your understanding of the concepts in this section.

Facilitating Play

It is a happy talent to know how to play.

Ralph Waldo Emerson

You are learning about play and have come to understand it as a natural and powerful way for children to develop. As an early childhood educator, you have a significant role in children's play. By your attitudes and your actions, you can support or discourage play. What you do will influence the nature of children's play. Your next step is to learn a variety of techniques to support development through play.

Supportive Attitudes

When you understand play's role in children's development and learning, you approach children at play with an attitude of respect and appreciation. When you understand that you have an important role in facilitating children's play, you approach it with an attitude of serious attention. You see play as your ally and the support of play as an important part of your job.

Some practitioners in early childhood education and care accept play as part of the "care" aspect of their work but fail to trust it as a primary process in their "educator" role. These individuals might feel uncomfortable when children play in the educational part of the program and may try to intervene in play to make it seem more like "school." They don't understand play's role in children's development.

Your view of play will be influenced by your professional setting. Those who work with infants and toddlers generally receive support and approval for giving play an important role in their programs. The same is true for many (though not all) who work with 3- to 5-year-olds. If you teach in an elementary school, you may find that play is not understood or supported by your colleagues or the families of the children you teach. In this case, your appreciation for play must be coupled with information that supports its importance.

Supportive Roles

Mirah and Aiden are in the dramatic play area playing with the dishes. Granette, the teacher, enters, sits down, and asks, "Is this the House of Dragon restaurant?" (naming a recently visited restaurant). "Can I have some noodles with black beans?" Mirah looks quickly around the area and then says to Granette, "Can we get the restaurant stuff?" Granette smiles and nods as she lifts the restaurant kit from the nearby storage cabinet.

Children play regardless of the circumstances. What you do before and during their play can make a vital difference in the quality of play and in what children gain in the process. Appreciation for children's play brings with it the realization that in play, children—not adults—are the stars. You can, however, fulfill many supporting roles that facilitate their play.

STAGE MANAGER The essential elements of play are *time*, *space*, *equipment*, and *materials*. Your first supporting role in children's play is providing these elements. Elizabeth Jones and Gretchen Reynolds (1992) refer to this important role as that of **stage manager**. Being a stage manager involves more than simply setting out materials for play. It includes selecting and organizing materials,

SOURCE: Jeff Reese

space, and equipment so that they suggest play that is meaningful to the children. Children of all ages must have time to play. Early childhood educators who value play are flexible about time. They view children's play as more important than strict adherence to a schedule.

Part of the role of the stage manager is the artful arrangement of equipment and materials. This assists children in what Jones and Reynolds (1992) refer to as distinguishing figure–ground relationships—in other words, distinguishing what you are looking at from the background. Contemporary research suggests that a carefully organized play environment promotes children's abilities to explore activities and learn predictive skills (Weisberg et al., 2014, cited in Hassinger-Das, Hirsh-Pasek, & Golinkoff, 2017). If your classroom has too much equipment or if what you have is disorganized, it may be overwhelming or confusing to children and inhibit play. The cycle of setting up, playing, and reordering the environment is an ongoing process in early childhood settings. When you understand it and participate in it willingly, you communicate that you value play.

OBSERVER   Another important role you will have in children's play is that of observer. When you observe carefully and assess what you see based on what you know about child development and play, you are better able to understand what is happening for children, what children might need, and how you can support them in play.

> Emily filled several buckets with sand and water. She sat them in the sand and then went to get more water. Kenese and Sage sat down and began to play with the bucket of sand and water. Emily turned around and yelled, "Hey! That's my lab. I don't want anyone to work in my lab."

If you have observed that Emily still functions best in a parallel play mode, you might offer Kenese and Sage additional buckets and a space to play near her. Or, if you have observed that Emily is ready to move into cooperative play, you could provide her with additional containers and suggest that she give them to the scientists in the next-door laboratory.

Structured observation records can yield important insight about play. Checklists or scales have been developed for looking at play behavior. These tools can be used to increase your understanding of play. The social-cognitive play scale (see Figure 9.2) codes

Figure 9.2 Parten-Piaget Social-Cognitive Play Profile

Parten-Piaget Social-Cognitive Play Profile

Child: _____   Observation Dates: _____

Piaget Cognitive Play Stage		Parten Social Play Stage			
		Solitary alone with toys; other children unnoticed	**Parallel** side by side with little interaction	**Associative** playing with one or more children—they are sharing materials	**Cooperative** sustained play with a group of children—they plan, negotiate, and share
	Practice/Functional sensory and motor exploration of toys, materials, and people				
	Symbolic: Constructive manipulation of objects to create something				
	Symbolic: Dramatic pretending to be something/someone using actions, objects, or words.				
	Games with Rules structured play that has a goal, rules, and a specific challenge				

Instructions: Observe child every 10 minutes for 15 seconds during a freely chosen activity time. Check the box that best describes the child's type of play AND social involvement. Repeat on subsequent days over 1 or 2 weeks to create a profile of the child's typical play.

play on its social and cognitive dimensions and enables you to get a quick look at a child's stage of play development.

To develop a profile on the play behavior of each child in your class, you can use a sampling system over a period of several days. To begin, you make a gridded sheet like the one in Figure 9.3 for each child in the class, shuffle the sheets so they will have a random order, start your sample with the top sheet, observe the child, and then place it on the bottom of the pile to be used for subsequent samples on the same day. Observe the child for approximately 15 seconds, mark the play behavior on the sheet, and then move on to the next child. You can sample three children each minute, so if you had a group of 15, you could take six samples of each child in a half hour. After 4 or 5 days, you would have enough material to see typical patterns of play behavior for each child. In a classroom of infants, you would probably find more play occurrences marked in the solitary-functional grid. If you were to shadow an 8-year-old for a day, many of the play behaviors would likely fall in the lower-right-hand corner, indicating games played with groups of peers. This information is useful to you in making decisions about what intervention might be needed to support the play of individual children.

MEDIATOR AND PROTECTOR Children's play is most productive when they feel safe from harm and relatively free from interference. Because group play has the potential for disorder and disruption, you will sometimes take the role of play protector and play mediator. As opposed to a limit setter, a disciplinarian, or a rule enforcer, a mediator collaborates with children. As a mediator, you help individuals work out conflicts and concerns when a neutral third party is needed. A mediator does not intervene when the participants can handle a problem. Children's conflicts in play can give you an opportunity to teach peaceful conflict resolution skills that will assist children in handling problems on their own.

As a play protector, you maintain the delicate balance between guidelines that support and sustain play and excessive control that interferes with play. It's important

Figure 9.3 Group Sociodramatic Play Profile

Name	Imitative Role-Play	Make-Believe with Objects	Make-Believe with Actions	Persistence in Role-Playing	Interactions with Others	Verbal Communication
	child undertakes a role using action and/or words imitating familiar experiences	toys and materials substituted for real objects	words/descriptions substituted for actions	role continues for at least 10 minutes	with other players child responds in role	has verbal interaction related to the role and play scene

To develop a profile of the group's sociodramatic play skills, observe children over several days during both indoor and outdoor play. For each child check off the different types of sociodramatic play that you observe.

to encourage play but not let it get dangerous or uncontrolled. The way you enter children's play to ensure safety and order needs to be respectful of the play ("Excuse me, birds, would you like me to help you move your nest here under the table? I'm afraid it might fall out of the tree and the eggs will crack.") rather than intrusive and thus interrupting the play ("Get down from the table. Tables are not for playing on; someone might get hurt.").

Dramatic play episodes that are prolonged and engrossing often attract latecomers who wish to join in. In this situation, the play protector and mediator can observe carefully and assist shy or anxious children in entering the play. It is best if you can unobtrusively help the child find a role. For example, in a camp scene, you might say, "Would you like to get wood for the campfire? I think I know where we can find some." If the entering child is disruptive, you may help by giving the child a task that makes use of high energy in the scene, such as chopping the wood.

SOURCE: Jeff Reese

The hallmark of highly developed dramatic play is that the children use objects to represent things: A bowl becomes a hat, a plate becomes a steering wheel, and a block becomes a telephone. Therefore, play can be a disorderly process, as play materials for one type of activity are transformed in children's imaginative pretending. This tendency can present a dilemma. If you are overly concerned about the proper use of equipment, you may curtail play and important learning; if you provide no limits, the resulting disorder can be overwhelming for both you and the children. Deciding on the best course requires sensitivity. Notice what children are doing with the materials. If they are being used as part of the play it is best to let the play continue or to provide an appropriate substitute. For example, in a classroom we know, when manipulative toys were being used as "food" in the nearby dramatic play area, the teachers added pretend food. On another day in that same classroom children scattered and walked on the pretend food and played dog family. The teachers removed much of the food and left the bowls being used as dog food dishes.

Sometimes you might decide to allow play that would normally be restricted, as happened in a classroom we visited once when a child was dealing with a family move. When the child began to move dramatic play area materials across the room, the teacher observed and asked questions and then made moving a legitimate activity, explaining to the children, "We're pretend moving today, so the library is going to be our new pretend home, for a while."

PARTICIPANT   The conventional wisdom in early childhood education once was that teachers should not become directly involved in the play of children. Play was seen as the arena in which children were to be left free to work out their inner conflicts and exercise power over their environment. It was regarded as the duty of an adult to keep out of the child's play world so as not to interfere with important psychological development. The only valid roles allocated to the adult were those of stage manager and observer. In recent decades, however, research has pointed to reasons for joining in children's play as a participant.

Why should adults play with children? When adults play, they lend support to the amount and quality of the play. Your participation gives children a strong message that play is a valuable activity in its own right, so they play longer and learn new play behaviors from observing you. It also builds rapport with the children. As you learn more about their interests and characteristics, you are better able to interact with them. When you participate, play may last longer and become more elaborate.

Of course, your participation must harmonize with the play of the children or else it will disrupt or end the play. When you play with children, take your cues from them and allow them to maintain control of the play. Limit your role to actions and comments that extend and enrich the play. When you join in, it is important that you do so in a way that supports ongoing play. Sometimes, children offer a role to an adult. "Would you like a cup of coffee?" is an invitation to join a restaurant scene being enacted. If not invited, you might observe and then approach the player who seems to be taking leadership and ask to be seated as a customer and in this way gain entry into the play. As a customer, you might inquire about the price of a cup of coffee, ask for cream to put in it, and praise the chef for the delicious pancakes he or she has prepared. By asking questions, requesting service, and responding to things children have done, you introduce new elements into the play without taking over.

When joining babies' or young toddlers' play, becoming a parallel player is usually the least intrusive and most supportive way to connect with them. Sit near the toddler stacking the cups and begin to stack some yourself or pat the floor in imitation of a baby who is patting; this imitative action tells the young child that you are interested and encourages further exploration and play.

Sometimes, teachers think they should intervene in children's play to teach concepts or vocabulary. We once observed a teacher stepping into a play scenario to question children about the colors and shapes of the food being consumed at a pretend picnic. Just as this interjection might interrupt the conversational flow at a real picnic, the interruption did not lead to a meaningful discussion of colors and shapes, and it stopped two players who were having a lively interchange on the merits of feeding hamburgers to the pretend dog. It is possible to help children be aware of new ideas in play, but it takes skill to do so without manipulating and diverting the activity. For example, when joining the group at a pretend picnic, it would be possible to comment, "Could you please pass me that red apple? It looks very tasty," rather than, "What color is this apple?" It is appropriate to include specific vocabulary words that you wish children to learn into your play interactions as long as this is done in a natural rather than a quizzing or instructional manner. "I think that eggplant is a *delicious* vegetable!" instead of, "Eggplant is delicious; what does delicious mean?"

Why play with children? Perhaps the best reason is because it is a way to share their world, to demonstrate your respect, and to renew your appreciation of the complexities and importance of children's play.

TUTOR Although children play naturally, not all children have fully developed play skills. Children who have been deprived of opportunities to play, whose families do not value play, or who are traumatized may need the help of a tutor in learning to play.

 Application Exercise 9.4

Watch and Write About Teacher Participation in Sociodramatic Play

A study conducted by Smilansky (1968) in Israel found that children from low-income families in which parents lacked a high school education engaged less often in dramatic and sociodramatic play than did children from more affluent families. Since then, other researchers have found the same pattern in other countries. Intervention strategies have been designed to teach the play skills that a child lacks. In this play tutoring, you demonstrate or model a missing skill until the child begins to use the skill in spontaneous play situations. For example, if a child is dependent on realistic props, you might offer substitution ideas—"Let's pretend that these jar lids are our plates" or "Let's pretend that the sand is salt"—until the child begins to do so independently. It is important to note that the goal of play tutoring is to teach play skills in the context of the spontaneous play episode. The adult should not change the content of the play by taking a directing role. Play tutoring has proven effective in improving the dramatic and sociodramatic play skills of children, which in turn has brought about gains in cognitive and social development.

GUIDE   Recent studies of the relationship between play and development indicate that *guided play*, play that "maintains the joyful child-directed aspects of play but adds an additional focus on learning goals through light adult scaffolding," can build specific language, mathematics, and spatial skills (Weisberg, D.S., K. Hirsh-Pasek, R.M. Golinkoff, A.K. Kittredge, & D. Klahr, 2017).

> *Fatima, Tucker, and Noah are playing with table blocks. "This one is a triangle," Fatima tells the boys. "I'm gonna put it on top of this part to make my roof." "I want a triangle, too," Tucker says, searching through the blocks on the table. The children move some blocks around, putting various shapes on top of their structures. "I can't find one," Tucker says. Their teacher, Lucas, approaches and asks "I wonder if you could make a triangle using some other blocks?" Noah says, "I can make one with these!" He puts three square pieces into a triangle shape. "You found a way" Lucas says. "You figured out that this triangle has 3 sides that are all the same length; then you found some other pieces to make one." "Yeah," Noah says happily. "Let's make some more triangles."*

In this scene the teacher followed the children's play. He didn't interrupt what they were doing or quiz them about shape names. Rather he provided materials that allowed children to explore the properties of shape, modelled language to build vocabulary, and encouraged them to discover properties of shapes through active engagement with materials. This type of light scaffolding can prevent children from becoming frustrated and promote attention and longer periods of engagement.

Golden Rules

for Supporting Children's Play

1. Provide enough time—45 minutes to 1 hour of uninterrupted playtime several times a day, both indoors and outdoors whenever possible, even if the weather is less than perfect.
2. Choose play materials to meet needs and interests of the particular children.
3. Observe children as they play—to learn, to support, and to enjoy.
4. Add materials or equipment to support play as it happens.
5. Help children who have difficulty entering play by assisting them to find a role in play (e.g., "It looks like you need a fire dog in your fire station. Joe is good at barking—can he be the fire dog?").
6. Participate in children's play, but let children take the lead.
7. Observe and think twice before stopping play, unless a child is in danger.
8. Be playful and child-oriented when you guide or participate in children's play.
9. Avoid interjecting adult concepts or judgments into children's play (e.g., "How many are there? Was that nice?").
10. Redirect play (when necessary) in a way that supports rather than stops it.

Just as some children lack play skills because they are deprived of a safe physical and emotional environment in which to play, other children do not develop play skills because they are deprived of time to play. They are compelled to conform to adult standards of behavior, to excel academically at an early age, and to master skills typically developed by older children. To them, playtime is something they must "steal" from their busy schedule of dance lessons, soccer practice, math practice, and full-day school (Elkind, 1981). When you include play as a key feature in your early childhood classroom, support it skillfully, and learn to describe its value to others, you may help families to feel comfortable including more play into their children's daily experiences.

Reflect On

Playing in School

Reflect on a time when you played in school. Where did you play? Who supported your play? How much time did you have for play? What do you think your teachers thought about play? Why do you still remember this play today?

> ✔ **A Quick Check 9.3**
>
> Gauge your understanding of the concepts in this section.

Issues in Play

A number of issues affect children's play in the United States today. Because play is the cornerstone of early childhood curriculum, these issues will affect your work, and it is important that you are aware of them.

Diversity and Play

> *Drew, a 4-year-old, African-American child, enters the big playground running and calls to his Caucasian friend Jason, "Come on!" Both scramble up the big climbing structure and slide down the fireman's pole, then crawl into the tunnel made of tires. Siow Ping, whose family immigrated from Asia, sits in the shade of a tree. She has collected all the pebbles she can find and has lined them up from biggest to smallest. As she observes them, their teacher, Dena, is aware that the children are each playing in their preferred ways.*

Play researchers and practitioners have studied play in a variety of settings and found that cultural background, social class, and gender are factors, along with stage of development, that interact in dynamic ways to influence the types, amount, and quality of play that children engage in. In the preceding vignette, the differences in play preferences and activity level could be attributed to cultural or gender differences or to a combination of both.

Understanding that there are different play preferences, abilities, and styles among children will increase your sensitivity to individuals and help you be more supportive of the play of all children. It is wise to assume that all children want to and can play. Given that assumption, you can use your ability to observe, your understanding of individual children, your ability to create environments, and your skill in supporting play to help each child engage in productive play.

CULTURE, SOCIAL CLASS, AND PLAY In Euro-American culture, play is often seen as the means by which children learn about the physical and social world and develop language. In some cultures, it is valued as entertainment, and in others, it is seen as a needless distraction from work in which children are expected to participate. The value a culture places on play influences how much support the adults provide. Where play is assumed to contribute to learning, the adults are more likely to make available the materials, settings, and time for play. If it is seen as relief from boredom or a waste of time, children may be left on their own to improvise times, places, and materials for play. Whatever the case, children in all cultures play (Johnson, Christie, & Wardle, 2005; Rogers, 2011).

It is important to provide play props and other materials that represent the experience and cultural background of all of the children. Children from different cultures may not respond to the play props found in the typical early childhood program designed for middle-class American children. When the play props relate more closely to their life experiences, their play is likely to become richer and more complex.

How can toys and props represent cultural diversity? The makers of educational equipment strive to do this by selling elaborate ethnic costumes, musical instruments, and plastic ethnic food. Many of these props may be as exotic to the children in your class as they are to you. When selecting dramatic play materials it's important to know the families in your program and what their lives and cultures are like. For example, some cultural groups (Native American, African American, Mexican, and Asian, to name a few) value the extended family, and elders play a significant role. So props that represent the elders of the family (hats, bags, shawls, scarves, jackets, books, and cooking utensils) might increase dramatic play by children from these cultures (Trawick-Smith, 1994). How do the families of children in your classroom dress? What do they eat? What do they carry? If children's parents and grandparents dress like the rest of the population, it is unlikely that adding a happi coat or dashiki will contribute to richer, more meaningful play. As you communicate with family members and pay attention to the ways in which their daily lives are influenced by their culture, you will be able to bring this information into the play environment. For example, in Hawaii, where lei are given for most major events, it makes sense to have artificial flower lei in the dramatic play area. The same prop in Minnesota or New Brunswick would be decorative rather than meaningful for most of the children.

Cultures differ in their approach to relationships among people, and these differences can affect the play abilities of children. A child whose cultural background emphasizes cooperation and inclusiveness may be intimidated by children who have been taught to be competitive and exclusive. As an educator, you may need to assist such a child to learn how to enter a play situation dominated by children who may exclude others or not think to include them in their play ("Ask them if they need someone to hold the firefighters' hose."). And, similarly, you may need to support the child from the more competitive culture in finding ways to be more inclusive of others ("Firefighters always need a crew to put out fires. Ask firefighter David to be part of the crew.").

Early research on play and development often identified play deficits and linked them to cultural background or the deprivations of poverty. More recent work has uncovered bias in the prior work (Johnson et al., 2005). When children of different cultural and social class backgrounds are observed at play in settings and with materials with which they are familiar, they too display rich, complex play behaviors (Johnson et al., 2005). Your job as an early childhood educator is to find ways to bridge the differences between your classroom and the children's home environments. You can do this by thinking beyond the usual middle-class housekeeping material found in the dramatic play area. As you come to know the children in your group, you can introduce play materials and props throughout your program that relate to their life experiences. In a program we know located on a Marine base, the teacher asked families to help create child size "cammies" the working uniform worn by marines. In another program that enrolled many children from Latino and Hispanic families, a tortilla press was included with the kitchen tools.

- Violent dramatic play involves fast action and a thrilling chase. Adults find this exciting, and so do children.

- Toy weapons and accessories are often realistic. This realism is tantalizing and often creates a strong response in other children and adults.

- Sophisticated television marketing aimed at children evokes intense interest.

Reflect On

Your Ethical Responsibilities

You disagree with the other teachers in your school over whether to allow children to engage in violent pretend play. As a staff, you have decided that all forms of pretend guns and fighting are forbidden. A child in your class often pretends to shoot other children. You know this child has gone through some rough times, and you feel this play is important to him. Using the Guidelines for Ethical Reflection in Chapter 1 of this book, reflect on your ethical responsibilities in this situation.

Several strategies may help you in coping with violent dramatic play in your program:

- Observe the play to help you understand what it means to the children.

- Come to some basic agreements with your coworkers over the limits you will place on violent dramatic play in your setting. Even if you disagree, it's important for there to be consistency in how teachers respond. Whatever your decisions, it is never acceptable to allow children to hurt or bully one another.

- Facilitate children's play by asking questions to increase empathy, such as, "How does the bad guy feel? Who does he play with when he goes home? What does he do on his birthday?" In doing so, it is possible to help children to think beyond stereotypes.

- Encourage children to play pretend roles of powerful people who help or rescue without violence such as firefighters, ambulance drivers, and emergency medical technicians.

- Whatever decision you reach about the acceptability of dramatic play depicting violence, guide children in understanding when, where, and what behaviors will not interfere with the group. Just as yelling and shouting disturbs others indoors, shooting and crashing is also disruptive. Help children to think of where and when this kind of play will not disturb other people.

In a society where violence is prevalent, we cannot eliminate children's fascination with violence. We can provide children with alternatives (ask the bad guys why they want to shoot you up) and help them learn to be responsible and thoughtful members of their community.

Rough-and-Tumble Play

Physically vigorous play that involves actions such as chasing, jumping, and play fighting, accompanied by positive affect from the players toward one another, is known as rough-and-tumble, or big-body, play (Carlson, 2009; Pellegrini, 1995). As we have previously noted, rough-and-tumble play is nearly universal in young human males and among the young of other mammals, particularly primates (Brown & Vaughn, 2009; Pellis and Pellis, 2013). If this is true, and because we generally support children's natural play behaviors, you may wonder why we have placed rough-and-tumble play with play issues.

Rough-and-tumble play is often discouraged or banned in programs for young children because educators have many fears about it. Teachers fear that play fighting is the same as, or will lead to, real fighting. They worry that rough-and-tumble play will dominate and overshadow other kinds of play. Most of all, they fear that a child may be hurt during rough-and-tumble play. We share some of these concerns. We have seen an inadvertent poke during play fighting turn into a real fight. We have witnessed children so entranced by rough-and-tumble play that they do little else. We have seen children bruised in rough-and-tumble play.

So why would you allow rough-and-tumble play in your program? Play researchers point to a number of benefits (Pellis & Pellis, 2007). By its very nature, rough-and-tumble play is physically active, so it builds health as well as providing a way for children to meet their needs for touch. Perhaps more important, children learn the give-and-take of social interactions in rough-and-tumble play. They learn to detect and read social signals and to alternate and change roles as we do in other social interactions. So it may be that by forbidding this natural avenue for social learning, we deny it to the very children who need it most. This dichotomy makes rough-and-tumble play an issue and whether to allow it a dilemma.

Should you choose to allow rough-and-tumble play in your classroom (and we do not advocate that you do), be prepared to justify it to families, other staff, and administrators and gain their support. Those who support rough-and-tumble play suggest that you learn to differentiate it from real fighting (in play fighting, children smile and laugh, join the play readily and eagerly, and keep returning for more). Finally, you must ensure children's safety and well-being by providing an appropriate environment (enough space, padded surfaces, and no tripping hazards), guidelines (e.g., no kicking, choking, or hair pulling and listen to others' bodies and words), teaching (e.g., "Tell him, 'That hurts. Please let go.' "), and supervision. If these requirements are possible in your setting, you can safely allow this natural form of play. If they are not possible, then you will need to explain to children that rough-and-tumble play is not safe at school.

Exclusion—You Can't Say You Can't Play

Exclusion is another issue that arises in early childhood classrooms. Exclusion takes a number of forms. Children may overtly exclude one another because of gender (girls only), age (you're too little), or visible differences, such as race or ability (you don't know how to climb, so you can't play). More subtle exclusion may occur when one child is obviously not welcomed into play. What should a teacher do?

Some educators believe no child should be excluded from the play of other children. They think that it is important to have a rule like the one phrased by Vivien Paley (1993): "You can't say you can't play." Such a rule is designed to ensure equity and build empathy as children are asked to consider the feelings of children who are excluded. Others feel that this is interfering in the natural play choices of children and thus in the development of social skills. While there is no definitive way of handling exclusion in early childhood programs, there are some things you can do when children are being excluded from play:

- Be clear and unambiguous about exclusion that is unacceptable and create scripts that match your beliefs and values. "This classroom (material, area) is for everyone in our class. Boys get to play and girls get to play. Everyone gets a turn."

- Help children include others in the play: "Tell Lydia how to be a space alien so that she can play too. Show her how to get in your spaceship without knocking it down."

- If one child is regularly excluded, find ways to give that child particularly desirable responsibilities: "I need someone to help me get the lunch from the kitchen. Ethan, can you come with me, and can you choose one friend to go with us?"

- Teach excluded children to handle disappointments and find alternatives: "Cielo and Jasmine are friends. Right now they don't want to play with anyone else. That makes you sad, but there are other things for you to do. Would you like to draw with me and Soullee or help Baylor with his block structure?"

Reflect On

Play You've Observed

Think about a classroom you recently observed. How did the children play? How did the adults facilitate play? What seemed to be their attitudes toward play? Did you observe violent dramatic play or gender-stereotyped play? How did it make you feel? How did the adults respond? What impact did this have on children?

Shrinking Opportunities for Play

When you think of the play you engaged in during your childhood, you might remember hours spent climbing, sliding, pretending, swinging, running, and riding bikes. But the quantity and quality of play available to children today has changed. Factors that have limited or changed young children's play include families' hurried lifestyles, changes in family structure, changes in the availability and characteristics of play environments, increased focus on academics and enrichment activities at the expense of play, the substitution of television and video games for active play (Ginsberg, Committee on Communications, & Committee on Psychosocial Aspects of Child and Family Health, 2007), and a prevalent fear of children being harmed in communities in which neighbors no longer know one another.

Children play less today because there are safety issues. In many communities, particularly in areas that are unsafe because of violence or other environmental dangers, children cannot play safely outside the home unless they are under close adult supervision and protection.

Children play less because there are fewer places for them to play. In 1981, concerns with safety and liability in public places resulted in standards for public playground safety (Frost et al., 2011). Although guidelines can help create safe and wonderful playgrounds, implementing guidelines can be costly. In some communities, play structures were removed rather than improved.

Children play less because they tend to spend their time being passively entertained through television or computer/video games. According to a 2013 study by Common Sense Media, children ages 0–8 spend just under 2 hours/day engaged with in screen-media.

Time spent engaged with smartphones or other screen activities, time spent in organized enrichment, and time spent preparing for tests and on other academics leaves little time for the active and creative play that contributes to children's development. The increase in childhood obesity may be one result of less time for play. Data from two National Health and Nutrition Examination surveys (1976–1980 and 2003–2004) show that childhood obesity is increasing (Centers for Disease Control, 2007). A variety of studies have linked growing obesity rates with increased screen time (Strasburger et al., 2011). The issue of childhood obesity provides a strong argument for the inclusion of active play in the curriculum, particularly outdoor play.

Reflect On

Your Ethical Responsibilities

The principal of your school has decided that with the importance of testing mandates, it is essential to devote more time to preparing children. To this end, recess and physical education have been eliminated. You believe that this is inappropriate and harmful. Using the Guidelines for Ethical Reflection in Chapter 1 of this book, reflect on your ethical responsibilities in this situation.

A Quick Check 9.4

Gauge your understanding of the concepts in this section.

Final Thoughts

Understanding the importance of play in supporting and enhancing children's overall growth and learning ensures that you will value it in its own right and make full use of it in your work with children. It is also important not to lose sight of the exuberant, joyful, and nonsensical aspects of play. Treasure the creativity in fantasy and see worlds open up as children pretend. Appreciate the bravery, joy, and exhilaration as children take risks, laugh hysterically, run, fall, tumble, and roll without restraint. The uninhibited, imaginative quality of play distinguishes child from adult, and play from all other activities. Teachers who appreciate and understand the power of play can help children realize their human potential.

You may need to become an advocate for children and play. This role can be hard if other educators and children's families don't understand its value. We urge you to continue to learn about play and help others understand play's importance not only in learning and health but also as an inoculation against the pressures that society imposes on children. The children in your care need the opportunity to play now. You can speak to support them and safeguard this right. When you do, you give them a precious gift.

Application Exercise 9.5 Final Reflection

To Learn More

Read

A Child's Work: The Importance of Fantasy Play, V. Paley (2004).

A Mandate for Playful Learning in Preschool: Presenting the Evidence. K. Hirsh-Pasek, R. M. Golinkoff, L. E. Berk, & D. G. Singer (2009).

Play: How It Shapes the Brain, Opens the Imagination, and Invigorates the Soul, S. Brown with C. Vaughn (2009).

The Importance of Being Little: What Preschoolers Really Need From Grownups, E. Christakis (2016).

The Play's the Thing: Teachers' Roles in Children's Play, E. Jones & G. Reynolds (1992).

The Power of Play: Learning What Comes Naturally, D. Elkind (2007).

The War Play Dilemma: What Every Parent and Teacher Needs to Know, D. Levin & N. Carlsson-Paige (2006).

Visit a Website

The following agencies and organizations have websites related to play:

Alliance for Childhood (includes links and articles on play, playgrounds, and play policy)

Association for Play Therapy (includes videos and information on the value of play in general and in emotional development)

Defending the Early Years (search for "Play")

International Play Association (IPA)

The Strong National Museum of Play

National Institute for Play

Additionally, most early childhood professional associations have information, position statements, and publications on play.

Association for Childhood Education International

National Association for the Education of Young Children

Southern Early Childhood Association

Zero to Three: National Center for Infants, Toddlers, and Their Families

Document Your Skill & Knowledge About Play in Your Professional Portfolio

Include some or all of the following:

- Photos or a videotape of you as you engage with children and assume one of the supportive roles—stage manager, observer, protector/mediator, participant, tutor or guide—described in the text. Include a written description of how children responded to you and how your actions enhanced their play.

- A poster or brochure that you have designed to teach noneducators (such as children's family members) about the value of play. Choose a play material (e.g., play dough), a type of play (e.g., dramatic play), or a play experience (e.g., jumping rope) and create a brochure or poster that shows how this kind of play experience contributes to young children's development.

- A Structured Play Observation Record that you have completed. Observe a child at play and use the Parten-Piaget Social-Cognitive Play Profile (Figure 9.2) to develop a profile of the type of play you observed. Include this record and a description of your findings regarding the ages and stages of play; or observe a group of children and use the Group Sociodramatic Play Profile (Figure 9.3) to develop a profile of the elements of sociodramatic play most prevalent in that group. Include a description of your findings and what these suggest in terms of Smilansky's theories regarding sociodramatic play.

Shared Writing 9.1 Helping Families Understand Play

Chapter 10
The Curriculum

SOURCE: Jeff Reese

The belief that all genuine education comes
about through experience does not mean that
all experiences are genuinely or equally educative.

JOHN DEWEY, *EXPERIENCE AND EDUCATION,* 1938

 ## Chapter Learning Outcomes:

10.1 Explain what curriculum is in early childhood programs and how and why it is different from curriculum for older children.

10.2 Summarize the components of the physical development curriculum: gross and fine motor development and sensory awareness.

10.3 Describe the communication curriculum areas: language, literacy, and literature.

curriculum mirrors the cultural diversity that is prevalent and valued today. It also echoes society's concerns with violence, values, school readiness, standards, and the acquisition of basic content, especially literacy. Tomorrow's curriculum will address new concerns in ways we may not anticipate today.

We can think of these changes as an **educational pendulum** that swings between emphasis on the nature and interests of the learner and emphasis on subject matter. Each swing reflects a reaction to perceptions of the shortcomings of the current educational approach. Early childhood educators have long been committed to providing experiences that are meaningful, that engage children, develop curiosity, and support positive attitudes about learning and school. They believe that learning should be joyful and meaningful. This makes them somewhat different from many other educators.

The swinging pendulum of popular opinion has some important implications for you. One is that you must be aware that there will be shifts in views of curriculum and teaching during your career. For example, views of developmentally appropriate practice at the end of the 20th century focused early childhood programs on the needs and interests of children. Predictably, there was a shift toward **content standards**, accountability, and test scores. If you find yourself disagreeing with today's outlook on education, you are likely to find yourself agreeing with the views that will be favored in another 5 or 10 years (and vice versa, of course).

Knowledge is powerful. When you know about arts, sciences, and humanities and you understand how young children learn, you are able to make informed assessments of new views of early childhood curriculum. We urge you to keep an open mind so you can learn but to have a healthy sense of skepticism. You can rely on the combination of what research tells us about how children learn and your own observations. Your own stance will then be firm enough to withstand the inevitable shifts of popular opinion.

Reflect On

The Curriculum of the Schools You Attended

What was taught in the schools of your childhood? What do you remember most about the curriculum? When were you motivated to learn more? Do any of these experiences influence you today? What are the implications of these experiences for you as an early childhood educator?

The second implication of the swinging pendulum is the realization that early childhood education stands somewhat apart. Respect for the individual, a belief in the value of play, and a vision of education as helping children become self-directed and creative are consistent beliefs that have guided early childhood educators over time. You can hear this view in the words of the historical founders of our field:

> *The proper education of the young does not consist in stuffing their heads with a mass of words, sentences, and ideas dragged together out of various authors, but in opening up their understanding to the outer world, so that a living stream may flow from their own minds, just as leaves, flowers, and fruit spring from the bud on a tree.* (Comenius, 1896)

> *Play is the highest expression of human development in childhood for it alone is the free expression of what is in a child's soul.* (Fröebel, 1885)

Our goal is to help you learn to design curriculum that reflects these views. As you develop your own educational philosophy, we hope that you will see yourself as part of a long line of educators who put children first.

How Young Children Learn

Young children are learning all the time, from all their experiences, both in and out of school. Because of this, early childhood educators need to ask themselves, "How, when, and in what ways do I want to participate in this natural process?"

In order to design and implement meaningful and appropriate learning experiences, you need to know about young children and how they learn. You need to understand that all aspects of development are interdependent. This means that curriculum subjects are not distinct entities but rather natural parts of the life of the child. A few basic principles that guide early childhood teaching are outlined in Figure 10.2.

Curriculum in Early Childhood Education

What do early childhood educators teach? Every functioning adult knows more about the world than a young child. You have physical skills; you know how to take care of yourself and relate to others; you can read, write, and compute; and you know things about science and nature, the structure of society, and the arts. You know how to find out the answers to questions. These things will help you teach—but you need to know more than these basics to be an effective teacher of young children. You need to be educated. All early childhood college programs require that you study arts, sciences, and humanities because you need this broad education to effectively teach young children. You also need to know about children and how they learn so that you can design and implement meaningful and appropriate learning experiences. And you definitely need to understand curriculum **content**.

Most states, territories, and national organizations have early childhood **curriculum content standards**, also called **early learning standards** (goals for what children should know and be able to do at different ages) or **early learning guidelines**. Many of these align with the **Common Core Standards** for kindergarten through grade 12 (national standards for English language arts/literacy and mathematics) that have been adopted by most states. Standards, particularly the Common Core Standards, are controversial. They are designed to ensure that all children reach educational goals and are prepared for the next level of school. They also may lead to pressure on children and teachers. There is particular concern that content once taught in second or third grade now is "pushed down" to kindergarten and even preschool.

Figure 10.2 Principles of Early Childhood Teaching

Principle #1: Children learn by doing—through play and through concrete, sensory experience. Concepts are learned best when they are directly experienced.

Principle #2: Children learn best when they have many direct experiences with the world around them. Real experience through trips, visitors, and real-world activities are essential for learning.

Principle #3: Children need to reflect on their actions and experiences by playing, painting, building, singing, dancing, and discussing their observations and experiences. This is how they *reconstruct* their experiences and *construct* concepts (see Figure 10.3).

Principle #4: Children formulate concepts over time and through repeated experiences. Teachers who understand how children learn are careful to plan so that children can repeat experiences, many times.

Principle #5: Each child learns in a unique way and at an individual pace so we must teach them in diverse ways. Children learn best when they can choose activities that are appropriate and meaningful to them.

Principle #6: Children learn best when adults provide support to help them become more capable. Your job as a teacher is to know many ways to provide support, observe with an open mind and heart, and provide the support needed for each individual child.

Principle #7: Children learn best when there is communication and consistency between home and school. When you involve families in the curriculum, you make it meaningful.

BASED ON: E. Moravcik, S. Nolte, & S. Feeney, *Meaningful Curriculum for Young Children*, © 2013, p. 26. Reprinted and Electronically reproduced by permission of Pearson Education, Inc., Upper Saddle River, New Jersey.

Figure 10.3 Flying
Cockroach with Golden Wings

SOURCE: Reprinted with permission from
Melanie C. Nishimura.

Because most state early learning and development standards were created with the input of early childhood educators they include all areas of curriculum, not just English and math. Most include standards for children from birth through age 3 as well as standards for 3- to 5-year-olds. Early learning standards vary from state to state and have widely varying names and acronyms. You can type the name of your state or territory and the words "early learning standards" or "preschool content standards" into a search engine; in most cases, you will find a document specific to the state in which you live. The national Head Start Early Learning Outcomes Framework also provides standards that are used throughout the United States and its territories.

When thoughtfully constructed and well written, standards can help you identify what content is valuable for children at a particular age and stage of learning. They reflect what many early childhood educators believe to be essential curriculum content and can provide important information to help you design curriculum. It is important to remember there are many things content standards do not address. We agree with Lilian Katz, who suggests that a more appropriate approach would be to look at standards of experience. Katz suggests that we ask if young children have frequent opportunities to experience things such as intellectual engagement, absorbing and challenging activities, taking initiative and accepting responsibilities, overcoming obstacles and solving problems, and applying literacy and numeracy in purposeful ways (Katz, 2007).

> The 4-year-old class took a trip to the zoo yesterday. Today, Kurt, Shauna, Max, and Kauri go to the block area. Their teacher, Kelsey, suggests that they might build the zoo. They create enclosures around the animals and make a path on which several dollhouse people are placed. Shauna picks up a zebra and puts it in with the lions, and Kauri says, "No! The lions will bite the zebras!" The two argue about the placement of the zebras. Kelsey asks the children to think of some ways to put the lions and the zebras together so the zebras won't get hurt. The girls build a nearby enclosure for zebras. Kurt and Max create a wall of blocks that encircles the entire block area. Another child stumbles over it. Max and Kurt yell, and Kelsey asks, "What could you do so people would know that they should be more careful?" Max goes to the writing center and makes a sign that says ZU! STP! He tapes it to the wall and Kelsey suggests that he tell the other children about the sign and what it means.

These children were engaged in an activity designed to help them build an awareness of a social studies concept. But they were also engaged in a satisfying creative endeavor during which they were building motor coordination, using language, developing social problem-solving abilities, and gaining literacy skills.

> On a hot, sunny day on the toddler playground, Georgia, the teacher, brings a bucket full of crushed ice and dumps it in the water table. Immediately, Sango, Noah, and two other children rush to the table. Noah plunges his hands into the mountain of ice. His eyes widen. Georgia, who is crouched near the children, says, "It's really cold!" As the group plays, Sango stands hesitantly a foot away. Georgia says, "You can touch it, Sango." Noah finds a cup that Georgia has placed nearby and scoops the ice and dumps it into a pail also conveniently set nearby. He scoops and scoops until the pail is full. Sango picks up a tiny scrap of ice and holds it in her hands. In a few seconds, it is nothing but a drop of water. Sango looks at Georgia, who says, "What happened to the ice?" Sango says, "Wada." "Your ice melted into water," Georgia expands. Meanwhile, Noah is placing little hills of ice on the sidewalk that quickly melt away.

Just like the 4-year-olds, these toddlers were engaged in a planned discovery activity. They were using their senses, building physical coordination, and learning concepts about the world. Their learning was skillfully guided by a teacher who knows about how toddlers learn. In addition, they were developing language, confidence, and a sense of self-reliance.

> It is morning work time in the kindergarten class. Five children are working on their 100th-day collections (making trays with 100 things on them). Four more are constructing a block

model of the path from their classroom to the cafeteria. Two sit on pillows in the library corner, reading books. Two more are finishing their morning journal assignment. One is painting using watercolors. Kit and Sierra are examining Checkers, a tortoise that was recently added to the classroom discovery center. They are looking at a book on tortoises. They ask Ms. Narvaez, their teacher, "Can Checkers eat hamburger?" She says, "That's a good question. I see you have the tortoise book. What did you find out?" The children continue searching with some guidance from Ms. Narvaez. When the book fails to answer the question, she asks them to write their question on a chart hanging in the discovery area. The class will try to find out the answer in some other way.

The skillful design of curriculum includes ensuring that, in addition to planned activities, there will be time, space, and interesting things to explore. Ms. Narvaez clearly knows children can be self-directed learners. She has structured the environment, the time, the relationships, and the planned learning experiences to help these 5- and 6-year-olds develop knowledge and skills in math, science, social studies, language, literacy, and art. Perhaps more important, she is helping them become active, collaborative learners with a disposition to inquire.

Curriculum includes planned opportunities for learning provided as choices. It also includes guided activities that you implement with individuals or groups. The planned curriculum can address all domains of development, and it can be designed to help children develop understanding and skill in one or more subject areas. Each early childhood subject area can contribute to all domains of the child's development but can be seen as primarily emphasizing one or two areas, as illustrated in Figure 10.4. In this chapter, we talk about subject areas in clusters that relate to each domain of development.

Figure 10.4 Curriculum Contributions to Development

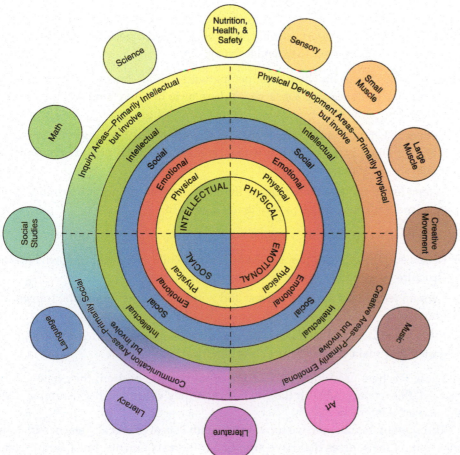

SOURCE: Jeff Reese

Each curriculum area is a specialty in itself. You may have an area in which you have particular talent or skill, and others in which you feel less sure. This should not stop you from planning and teaching every curriculum area. Early childhood teachers are, of necessity, "general practitioners." You can use your skill in one area to teach content with which you are less comfortable. An excellent storyteller with a math phobia, for example, might teach children and overcome his or her own fears by finding ways to incorporate math in storytelling!

How Early Childhood Teachers Teach

When you envision a teacher, you may think of someone standing in front of a class and talking. Yet, because young children learn in different ways from older children and adults, teachers in early childhood programs teach in significantly different ways.

Early childhood teachers teach by arranging the environment. They teach by supporting children in play. They teach by providing a challenge with a question or adjusting the environment to support a child's development of a skill or concept (called **scaffolding**). They teach through thoughtful, **intentional** interactions with children throughout the day. Learning to teach in this way requires you to be mindful, creative, and open. Whether you are helping a child understand a concept or teaching a social skill, good early childhood teaching is focused.

Dombro, Jablon, and Stetson (2011) offer a framework for structuring your interactions with children to support learning. They suggest three steps for consciously connecting with a child in order to extend learning:

1. **Be present.** Focus on what is happening with a child. Pay attention and tune in to what the child is doing. Observe what seems to be interesting and important to the child.

2. **Connect.** Let the child know you see and appreciate his or her interest. Connect by smiling, joining in the activity, listening carefully to what the child says, or asking a relevant question.

3. **Extend learning.** Use knowledge of the child and your connection to build knowledge and understanding in a way that is a good fit.

The vignettes that preceded this section were examples of powerful interactions:

- Kelsey encouraged Max to solve the problem of children knocking down his block structure by using his emerging writing skill.
- Georgia recognized Sango's interest and pointed her attention to the transformation of ice.
- Ms. Narvaez listened to children trying to find out what a tortoise eats and suggested they make it a topic for a class investigation.

These teachers used their knowledge of particular children, they listened and observed, they connected with the children, and they extended their learning. These were powerful interactions.

Throughout this chapter, we provide you with lists of practical, "teacher-friendly" books and online sources that have articles, position statements, links, and practical information on curriculum (see Figure 10.5).

Figure 10.5 Teacher-Friendly General Curriculum Books and Internet Resources

BOOKS

Basics of Developmentally Appropriate Practice, by Carol Copple & Sue Bredekamp (NAEYC)

Basics of Developmentally Appropriate Practice: An Introduction for Teachers of Infants & Toddlers by Carol Copple and Sue Bredekamp With Janet Gonzalez-Mena (NAEYC)

The Creative Curriculum for Preschool (6th ed.) and *The Creative Curriculum for Infants and Toddlers* (3rd ed.) (Teaching Strategies)

Developmentally Appropriate Practice in Early Childhood Programs (3rd ed.), by Sue Bredekamp & Carol Copple (eds.) (NAEYC)

Enthusiastic and Engaged Learners, by Mary Lou Hyson (Teachers College Press)

The Intentional Teacher: Choosing the Best Strategies for Young Children's Learning, revised edition by Ann Epstein (NAEYC)

Learning Together with Young Children: A Curriculum Framework for Reflective Teachers, by Deb Curtis and Margie Carter (Redleaf Press)

Meaningful Curriculum for Young Children, by Eva Moravcik and Sherry Nolte (Pearson)

Tools of the Mind: The Vygotskian Approach to Early Childhood Education, 2nd edition by Elena Bodrova & Deborah Leong (Pearson)

INTERNET RESOURCES

Association for Childhood Education International for teachers of children birth through early adolescence with a focus on primary school children.

National Association for the Education of Young Children

Southern Early Childhood Association

Thinkfinity.org contains free, comprehensive standards-based K–12 lesson plans, materials, tools, and reference materials reviewed by education organizations (AAAS, IRA, NCTE, NCTM, NCEE etc.).

Early childhood educators of other nations also have associations with online curriculum resources. Here are a few you may wish to explore:

Association For Early Childhood Educators (Singapore)

British Association for Early Childhood Education

Canadian Child Care Federation

Early Childhood Australia

European Early Childhood Education Research Association (EECERA)

Learning and Teaching Scotland

Te Tari Puna Ora o Aeotearoa *(New Zealand Child Care Association)*

Connecting with Families

About Curriculum

Families can contribute to the curriculum. They can be your partners. Invite families to participate in the curriculum. Survey incoming families to find out their skills and interests. Then invite them to come as honored guests to cook a dish, tell a story, teach a song, or demonstrate a skill. Those who prefer to work behind the scenes can make playdough, borrow books from the library, and sew pillows for the book corner. Find ways to regularly and meaningfully involve them in their children's learning.

✓ **A Quick Check 10.1**

Gauge your understanding of the concepts in this section.

The Physical Development Curriculum

The body is a young child's connection to the world. Sensory and motor development are prerequisite to learning. To learn to read and write, children must first develop the ability to make fine visual and auditory discriminations. Playing an instrument or

SOURCE: Jeff Reese

using a computer requires fine motor skill that emerges from practice in the control of the muscles of the fingers and hands. Discovering that blue and yellow paint mix together to make green requires eyes that see and fingers that respond. Hiking to see the ocean from the top of a nearby hill requires strength and stamina. To appreciate the order and beauty of the world, children must be able to experience it with their senses.

Gross Motor Curriculum

The **gross motor curriculum**—concerned with the development of arms, legs, and torso—helps children develop and maintain physical skills and abilities. Children must learn to move and must also move in order to learn.

Physical activity is essential for health. In the past, it was assumed that physical inactivity and its attendant health problems—obesity, diabetes, high blood pressure, and cancer—were of concern only in adults. Today, these are also problems in children, including children under the age of 6 (Ogden & Carroll, 2010). Attention span and concentration increase as children use their bodies in challenging physical movements. Exercise helps release tension and promotes relaxation. Children's early physical development experiences influence how competent they feel and whether they will enjoy physical activity throughout life. Large muscle curriculum activities help children develop strength and endurance, retain flexibility, and develop coordination and agility.

There are predictable patterns in children's development of large muscle skill. *Strength* and *stamina* (the capacity for the sustained use of strength) increase with age. Older children generally are stronger and have greater endurance. *Flexibility* (ease and range of movement) lessens with age as the muscle system becomes less elastic. Infants easily bring toes to mouth, but this flexibility wanes as children get older. *Coordination*—the ability to move body parts in relation to one another—grows with experience. *Agility*—the ability to move with control and precision—develops as children gain flexibility, strength, coordination, and kinesthetic sense. As children gain speed, grace, and precision, they feel a sense of mastery. Much of the pleasure children find in large muscle play stems from the enjoyment of their growing agility.

Early childhood curriculum includes helping children develop fundamental or basic movement skills. Movement skills that transport a child from one place to another (by walking, jumping, running, skipping, and so on) are called **locomotor skills**. Movement skills that involve bending, balancing, and twisting while staying in one spot are called **nonlocomotor skills**. Another category of large motor skills developed during early childhood years involves the use of arms, hands, and feet to move objects like balls. These are called **object control skills**.

It used to be considered sufficient physical development curriculum to send young children outside to play and occasionally organize a game of Duck, Duck, Goose. Today, we know we can do much more to help young children become fit individuals who have a positive attitude toward physical activity. Children need time for large motor play several times a day. They need optimal challenge—equipment, materials, and activities that provide the right degree of difficulty. The National Association for Sport and Physical Education (NASPE, 2004) recommends that toddlers and preschoolers engage in unstructured physical activity whenever possible—and that preschoolers have at least 60 minutes of structured physical activity each day. The Council on Physical Education for Children (COPEC, 2000) recommends 30 to 60 minutes daily. We believe preschool children should have significant blocks of time (45 minutes to an hour) daily for vigorous physical activity, in both the morning and the afternoon, and not be sedentary for more than 1 hour at a time. In addition to time for unstructured large motor play, all programs for young children should include guided large motor activity. NASPE (2004) recommends daily structured physical activity for preschool children and suggests structured physical education totaling 150 minutes per week for elementary age children.

As a teacher in a preschool or kindergarten, you will have a good deal of responsibility for planning and providing large motor curriculum opportunities. As a primary school teacher, you may have less control and responsibility. Eliminating recess—as is being done in some elementary schools to create more time for "work"—deprives children of needed opportunities for physical activity. In a nation in which obesity and inactivity are epidemic, even among children, this trend is foolish.

Many children develop physical competence from their self-directed play, but others need encouragement and support. All direct physical training and intervention needs to be carried out in pleasurable play situations so that the child's attitude will be positive and physical activity will be gratifying. Children may be discouraged if you are overly concerned about safety. If children are willing to attempt using a piece of equipment, they can usually manage it if you are prepared to provide careful supervision and occasional assistance and instruction.

Reflect On

Your School Experiences with Physical Education

Remember a time when you were a child in a physical education class in school. Why do you remember this experience? How did the teacher encourage or discourage you? Did you feel successful in physical education or unsuccessful? What physical activity do you do as an adult? Did your childhood experience influence this in any way?

Teaching young children to develop large muscle skills does not mean physical education as you remember it. Instead, it means things like placing a balance beam a little higher than before and holding children's hands as they take their first steps across, playing Ring-Around-the-Rosy, Follow the Leader, or Red Rover, tossing a ball as they learn to bat, and sharing their triumph as they learn to use a hula hoop. By encouraging and playing with children, you support their activity and provide a powerful demonstration that being active is natural and pleasurable. Adult-led activities, such as creative movement, simple yoga, group games, and exercises, provide focused practice

Video Example 10.1: Developing Large Motor Skills

Watch the following video to see some examples of ways young children develop large motor skills in early childhood settings. Notice how many different kinds of activities are provided for children and how these vary for different ages.

in developing physical competencies. All children, not just those who are physically competent, will participate if you minimize competition and win–lose situations in physical activities. **Cooperative games** are particularly appropriate for young children and encourage children who are reluctant to participate for fear of losing.

Fine Motor Curriculum

Learning to coordinate the hands and fingers begins when babies in their cribs reach out to feel, grasp, and manipulate. Those initial impulses eventually lead to the competent use of tools such as spoons, crayons, pens, and keyboards. Fine motor skills are the ability to control fingers, hands, and arms. These skills include reaching, grasping, manipulating objects, and using different tools like crayons and scissors. Fine motor (or small muscle) curriculum involves activities that build control, agility, strength, and coordination of the hands, fingers, wrists, and arms. As fine motor skills develop, neural pathways spread, making the brain more complex and flexible. There is research to suggest that children's fine motor skills relate to cognitive skills and can predict reading, mathematics, and general school achievement (West, Denton, & Germino-Hausken, 2000).

Time, practice, and many experiences develop fine motor competence. These skills involve **hand–eye coordination** and coordination of the two hands. Children growing up with typical abilities and opportunities to use their hands develop the strength, coordination, and agility required to do most small muscle activities.

Fine motor curriculum is a part of many activities that require the controlled use of hands and fingers. It can be helpful to think about categories of activities and skills to plan for small muscle development.

As with every other area of curriculum, you will support fine motor development when you understand development, observe children, and are sensitive to their differences. Then you interpret each child's level of development and provide materials and activities that present optimal challenge. Fine motor skills include grasp, eye–hand coordination, finger dexterity (quickly moving fingers), in-hand manipulation (positioning and moving an object within a hand), and hand or bilateral coordination (moving both hands together). Three aspects of fine motor development are often given consideration in fine motor curriculum: hand preference, the ability to use a pencil ("pencil grasp"), and the ability to use scissors. Figure 10.6 describes these.

It is essential that children have materials and adequate time to engage with them using their small muscles. Puzzles, manipulative toys, table games, drawing and painting, sensory activities like playing with play dough, woodworking, blocks, and daily living activities all help children develop small motor skills. Primary school children continue to enjoy manipulative toys but may be more motivated by more productive, grown-up, fine motor activities, such as cooking, crafts, and woodworking.

If a child becomes frustrated or bored with a small muscle activity, you can support his or her continued involvement by offering assistance, encouragement, or a different challenge. For example, if a child is having trouble cutting, you might say, "I see that paper is hard to cut. Would you like to use construction paper? Maybe it won't flop so much." You might also be sure to stock the shelf with a variety of different weights of paper and see whether more functional scissors are needed.

Reflect On

Your Fine Motor Skills

What is your most highly developed fine motor skill? Is it something you do for work (like using a computer keyboard), for pleasure (like knitting), or for daily living (like cooking)? How did you develop the fine motor coordination for doing this? Trace your fine motor history back to the experiences in your childhood that led to your development of this ability.

Figure 10.6 Three Fine Motor Abilities

Hand preference: Around 2 years of age hand preference emerges, though children frequently alternate hands. By 3, one hand will often lead activities and the other hand will assist. Though some switching will continue, by age 4 a strong preference for a lead and dominant hand is clear. And between 4 and 6 years, hand preference will be consistent and the roles of lead and assist hands established. The skill of the dominant hand will exceed the nondominant hand.

Grasp: By 4 months babies gain control over their arms and progress from reaching with both hands to reaching with one hand. They become capable of grasping and holding objects and can squeeze and hold objects in a closed fist. By 6 months they can pick up small items and by 12 months can hold small objects between their thumbs and index fingers, transfer objects from one hand to the other, and release objects voluntarily. At 12 months babies can make marks with crayons and markers, stack toys, turn pages, and roll a ball. Between 1 and 2 years they begin to move fingers independently and can poke and point. When using crayons they use whole-arm movements and hold a crayon in a closed fist with thumb pointing up. By 2 years of age coloring progresses from circular scribbles to horizontal or vertical scribbles and a crayon or pencil is held with fingers pointing toward the paper—called a pronated grasp. Between 3 and 4 years children hold a crayon in their lead hand while the assist hand stabilizes the paper. By 4 years of age, many children hold crayons pinched between thumb and index fingers, resting on their middle finger like most adults—called a *tripod, mature,* or *efficient pencil grasp.*

Scissors: At 2 years children use both hands to open and close scissors. By 3 years most can snip paper with the scissors in one hand and can cut a piece of paper into two pieces, but cannot cut along a line. By age 4 children typically move the scissors in a forward direction and can cut along a straight line and along simple curves with the assist hand turning the paper. By 5 years most children make smaller, more precise cuts and are able to cut out simple straight-edged shapes. When they cut, they hold the scissors in a thumbs-up position perpendicular to the floor. By age 6 most children hold scissors in a mature fashion.

SOURCE: Summarized from Skill Builders Pediatric Occupational Therapy, *Fine Motor Development 0 to 6 Years,* 2008. Copyright © 2008 by Skill Builders Pediatric Occupational Therapy. Used with permission.

It is important to design experiences that will build prerequisite skills for more challenging small motor tasks, such as cutting. The child who hasn't yet mastered scissors needs plenty of grasping, tension/release, coordination, and strength-building experiences. Providing play dough or clay to build strength and tools such as tongs, hole punches, tweezers, and staplers that require similar motor action will contribute to this emerging skill. You may sometimes need to demonstrate and instruct to help children learn complex fine motor skills.

Sensory Development Curriculum

Learning depends on sensory input—hearing, smelling, seeing, touching, moving, and tasting. We are not born with the ability to fully discriminate sensations but must learn to distinguish. If a child's ability to receive and use sensory input is impeded, normal development will be delayed. In addition to helping children learn, the senses are the source of appreciation and pleasure. For all of these reasons, good early childhood programs include a strong sensory component.

Two processes are needed for receiving and organizing sensory data. The first is sensation, that is, stimulation of the sensory receptors—eyes, ears, skin, and so on. The second is perception, attending to, discriminating, and interpreting sensation based on past experiences. The brain integrates the information that comes from the senses and uses it in a wide array of physical and cognitive tasks.

The sense we most associate with learning is *sight*. Like other senses, it requires opportunities for practice. In the early years, children learn to see details (acuity), track and recognize objects (constancy), judge distance (depth perception), distinguish an object from its background (figure–ground perception), and visually direct their own movement (visual motor coordination). The auditory sense, *hearing*, involves learning

Video Example 10.2: Developing Fine Motor Skills

Watch this video to see some examples of ways young children develop fine motor skills in early childhood settings. Which different activities for fine motor development were shown? Can you think of any others that might have been included?

to screen and attend—exclude irrelevant sounds and pay attention to what is meaningful. In addition, children learn to tell where sound is coming from (localization) and to hear differences between sounds (discrimination). The *kinesthetic* sense is awareness of movement and position that children develop as they crawl, walk, jump, climb, and balance. It includes the ability to detect differences in weight, force, distance, and speed (discrimination). The sense of *touch* is a primary mode of learning. Localization (identifying where a touch occurs on the body) and discrimination (differentiating stimulation) are two tactile abilities. We make many decisions based on the sense of *smell*; even newborns are highly sensitive to some smells. The sense of *taste* provides information about a few qualities: sweet, salty, sour, bitter, and umami (savory). The sense of taste, combined with smell, provides a critical guide to the edibility of food (toxins are often bitter, fruit is sweet, and salt is appealing).

To support the development of the senses, make sure that you regularly provide experiences that use and develop each one. However, it is important to realize that the senses are integrated, not isolated.

> The "Elephant Groovers" (a group of 3-year-olds) are involved in making banana pancakes. Sheyden touches the flour and salt as he pours it in. Torie smells the banana as she peels it. Emily experiences resistance when she stirs the batter. Keila comments on the bubbles she sees forming as air is beaten in. Their teacher, Jackie, says, "Listen to the sizzle as batter is poured in the pan." And all of the Elephant Groovers eat the finished product with gusto, commenting on its warmth and delicious taste.

Which sense was being developed? Separating these individual sensations would be difficult and unnecessary. The children learned from the entire experience.

Children develop their senses as they paint; manipulate clay and dough; play in sand, water, and mud; build with blocks; observe fish in the aquarium; feel the rabbit's fur; listen to stories; move to music; sort objects; and cook and taste. Play activities offer many opportunities for sensory development. You can provide space and materials that

Figure 10.7 Materials to Explore and Pour in the Sensory Table

- Sand—dry or wet
- Water—plain or with added color, aroma, soap
- Ice—blocks, crushed, with salt
- Mud
- Whipped soap or shaving cream
- Aquarium gravel (inappropriate for infants and toddlers)
- Bird seed
- Recycled dried coffee grounds
- Cornstarch and water
- Flour, rice, or beans (may be restricted in some programs, particularly programs with low-income or homeless families)

Other activities with a strong sensory component:

- Finger painting
- Collage
- Play dough
- Clay work
- Using musical instruments
- Cooking
- Tasting—compare different varieties of one thing such as cheese, apples, bread, vegetables
- Gardening
- Almost any field trips but especially to natural environments (e.g., a field, the beach, forest)

can be fully explored and help children focus on sensory experiences (see Figure 10.7). For example, you might help children notice the sensory qualities of the pancake batter by saying things like "How does it smell as it cooks?" "What do you notice when you mash the banana?" and "Can you think of something else that tastes like this?"

Although sensory development is vital to children's learning, it is not often addressed in content standards for older children. In early learning guidelines, it is included in either physical development or science standards. Figure 10.8 lists some books and Internet resources that can help you learn more about the physical development curriculum.

Figure 10.8 Books and Internet Resources for Physical Development Curriculum

BOOKS

Active for Life: Developmentally Appropriate Movement Programs for Young Children, by Stephen W. Sanders (NAEYC)

Active Start: A Statement of Physical Activity Guidelines for Children Birth to Five Years, by the National Association for Sport and Physical Education

Developmental Physical Education for All Children, by D. L. Gallahue & F. C. Donnelly (Human Kinetics)

Essential Touch: Meeting the Needs of Young Children, by F. M. Carlson (NAEYC)

Experiences In Movement, by Rae Pica (Delmar)

Follow Me Too: A Handbook of Movement Activities for Three- to Five-Year-Olds, by M. Torbert & L. B. Schneider (NAEYC)

Jump, Wiggle, Twirl & Giggle!, by Roberta Altman (Bank St. College and Scholastic Books)

Lifelong Motor Development, by C. P. Gabbard (Benjamin Cummings/Pearson Education)

Mighty Fine Motor Fun: Fine Motor Activities for Young Children, by C. Isbell (Gryphon House)

More Than Graham Crackers, by N. Wanamaker, K. Hearn, & S. Richarz, (NAEYC)

Mud, Sand, and Water, by D. M. Hill (NAEYC)

The Outside Play and Learning Book: Activities for Young Children, by K. Miller (Gryphon House)

Woodworking for Young Children, by P. Skeen et al. (NAEYC)

INTERNET RESOURCES

Appropriate Practices in Movement Programs for Young Children Ages 3–5 *Position Statement from the National Association for Sport and Physical Education*

Handedness Research Institute

Kids Health Information: Fact Sheets from the Royal Children's Hospital in Melbourne

NOVA: Taste, Our Body's Gustatory Gatekeeper

PBS: Sensory Play and Early Child Development

SHAPE America (Society of Health and Physical Educators)

Skill Builders Online—Skill Builders Occupational Therapy

The Smell Report—Social Issues Research Centre

To understand how the physical development curriculum is addressed in standards, check out your state's early learning guidelines or search for position statements from the National Association for Sport and Physical Education's *Appropriate Practices in Movement Programs for Children Ages 3–5* or *Appropriate Instructional Practice Guidelines for Elementary School Physical Education*.

A Quick Check 10.2

Gauge your understanding of the concepts in this section.

The Communication Curriculum

To understand the world and function in it, we need to be able to communicate with others. Learning language is one of the characteristics that unites people and one of our most important challenges. *Language* (both talking and listening) is of primary importance in the communication curriculum. **Literacy** (the developmental process of learning to write and read) is the tool that extends language over distance and time. *Literature* is the art form that uses language. All are dependent on language.

The goal of the communication curriculum is to help children become enthusiastic, competent users of spoken and written language. Your job is to provide relationships that are filled with language in all its forms. As you speak to children honestly and respectfully and listen to them attentively, you encourage language use. As you use language to mediate problems, communicate information, and share feelings and ideas, you demonstrate the usefulness and value of language. As you sing songs, tell jokes, recite rhymes and poems, and play verbal games with children, you help them find joy in talking. In a similar way, the value of written language is demonstrated as you write a note, a grocery list, or a thank-you letter, or read a recipe, story, poem, or book. As you introduce children to wonderful children's books, you give them a gift they will carry throughout their lives.

Reflect On

Communicating as a Child

Remember yourself as a young child. Was it easy for you to talk to other people, or did you feel shy or uncomfortable? When, where, and with whom did you feel most comfortable expressing yourself? Why? How did your family or teachers support you or discourage you from communicating?

Language Curriculum

Learning to understand and use language is one of the most significant tasks of early childhood. Without any formal teaching, almost all children acquire language at about the same age and in about the same way. It is a skill that appears to be "caught, not taught." As they forge their language, children develop an inseparable part of themselves as well as a tool for communication, self-expression, and learning.

Children learn the complex structure, rules, and meanings of language and develop the ability to create speech through processes that are still not completely understood. In their homes and communities they learn customs for language, to select appropriate speech for different settings and people, gestures, facial expressions, and intonation.

They come to understand the signals for turn taking in conversations. These unspoken ways of communicating are highly dependent on culture.

You will teach children whose culture and language are very different from your own. Some will come from families for whom English is not the home language, referred to as **dual language learners** or English language learners. Some will have different nonverbal customs, such as whether to make eye contact with adults. Your role requires sensitivity to and respect for communication differences. Hesitant or shy children, those who have less home language experience, or those who speak a different language may require time to become full participants in the language life of the classroom. Give these children time and lots of opportunities to communicate both verbally and nonverbally.

You will teach language in both incidental and planned activities, primarily through language-rich relationships. When you have conversations with children, you are teaching language. When you play with children, listen to them, sing songs, tell stories, and recite poems, you are teaching language. In structured group activities, such as discussions you are also teaching language.

As you do these things you are helping children master five aspects of language: (1) syntax or grammar, the "rules" of language; (2) morphology, the structure of words; (3) semantics, the meaning of words; (4) phonology, the sounds of words; and (5) pragmatics, the social conventions of language. Because children learn language by hearing you speak, it is important that you use clear, rich language and correct syntax. When you speak clearly, they hear the distinct sounds of words. As they hear you use new words, they add them to their vocabulary. Young children internalize syntax by hearing others speak. Mistakes like *knowed* and *eated* show that they have internalized language rules and are over-generalizing them. As they hear you using standard language they eventually correct themselves. Avoid correcting children's speech or drilling them in language or vocabulary; focus instead on providing meaningful opportunities for them to engage in dialogue.

You will not actually instruct children in "language" (a discipline studied by linguists and other scholars). Instead, you will help children develop language by *modeling* and *interacting*, as well as *planning* playful language activities. When children have a chance to talk about the things they know and that are important to them they learn to talk. You provide these opportunities when you ask questions, listen carefully to children, and respond to their questions. You may find it useful to look at the Head Start Early Learning Outcomes Framework for Language Development. It provides guidelines for curriculum planning and assessment that align with most state early learning and development standards.

Children acquire and build language in *conversations*. What is a conversation? It is an exchange of ideas, a dialogue. Because there are more children and fewer adults, there are fewer opportunities for conversation in early childhood programs than in most homes. In language-rich homes, conversations are complex and related to the child's life. By contrast, conversations in most schools tend to be brief, less complex, and more adult oriented. Like all conversations, a dialogue with a young child involves mutual interests and requires that you have a topic and take turns. It is different because of experience, size, status, and skills. It is an art that you will develop with experience (see the "Golden Rules for Having a Conversation with a Young Child"). As you have conversations with children, you will help them to *use abstract language* or **decontextualized speech**: talking about ideas and experiences that are not present—people, places, and events of the past or future, imagined and actual.

As you plan for language, remember that all children have language facility you can nurture. Talk to them, listen to them, and trust them. They need and want to communicate.

SOURCE: Jeff Reese

Golden Rules

for Having a Conversation with a Young Child

1. **Crouch or sit at the child's eye level.** This minimizes both the physical and the social differences between an adult and a child.
2. **Show attention physically as well as verbally.** Use eye contact, smiles, nods, or a gentle hand on a shoulder or back.
3. **Take turns and participate.** Otherwise, it's not a conversation.
4. **Read nonverbal communication.** Notice and put into words what you think the child is feeling and thinking: "It sounds like you're really happy." "That's very exciting." "It's a little scary."
5. **Respect the child's language.** Don't correct the child's speech or ideas. Don't hurry or interrupt. If you don't understand, say, "Show me" or "Tell me more about that."
6. **Listen.** Focus on what the child says. Remember this is about the child, not about you. Ask clarifying questions. Help the child extend: "What did your mom do when the eggs all spilled on the floor?"
7. **Select what to say carefully.** Make it brief and to the point—a child cannot concentrate for as long as an adult. Use a vocabulary that is simple but with a few words that are new and interesting.
8. **Remember, it's not a quiz or a lecture.** Questions can be conversation stoppers, so ask them sparingly; instead, say simple things: "I like to do that too" or "I didn't know that."

Video Example 10.3: Using Activities to Support Language Development and Build Vocabulary

Watch this video to see teachers engaged in meaningful group activities that support language development. How did these teachers introduce new vocabulary? What kinds of questions did they ask?

Literacy Curriculum

In everyday speech, literacy means the state of being able to read and write. When educators talk about early literacy, they mean the skills that are the foundation for reading and writing. **Emergent literacy** is the evolving process by which children become literate. The period between a child's birth and the time when he or she reads and writes in ways similar to literate adults (Teale & Sulzby, 1986).

Children who live in a print-filled world have early awareness of written language and develop concepts about it. Learning about reading and writing does not wait for children to go to school. The foundations for literacy start long before formal teaching begins.

Early literacy experiences are critical. By providing children with thoughtfully planned language and literacy opportunities before first grade, we are helping to prevent later reading problems.

The stages of emergent literacy, like the stages of language development, occur in a predictable order and unfold according to an individual timetable. The phrase *literacy begins at birth* expresses the idea that experiences in infancy with language, books, and reading are important parts of becoming literate. Each child learns to read and write as an individual, putting together ideas in ways that make sense.

Your approach to teaching literacy will vary with children's developmental needs, family, and interests. Reading and writing foundational skills and knowledge include **oral language** (talking), *vocabulary* (words), **phonological awareness** (realization that there are sounds in words such as rhymes and initial sounds), **alphabetic knowledge** (familiarity with the shapes and sounds of letters and awareness that there is a relationship between letters and sounds), **print knowledge** (understanding print rules, such as we read from left to right and that print always says the same thing), and **book knowledge** (how to use books). These are built through meaningful experiences presented in ways that are engaging. Having children participate in word and letter drills, irrelevant worksheets, and repetitive exercises lessens literacy learning rather than enhances it (Neuman & Roskos, 2005).

Reflect On

Your Ethical Responsibilities

The administrator of your school has decided that the children in second grade will no longer be allowed to read picture books because she believes picture books do not promote reading skills. You believe this is inappropriate and will damage children's motivation to learn to read. Using the "Guidelines for Ethical Reflection" found in chapter one, reflect on your ethical responsibilities in this situation and think about an ethical response that you might make.

There is strong evidence to suggest that children who have lots of real-world experiences, coupled with rich and varied language, are more likely to become readers (Bowman, 2003). Experiences with functional print (print that has a purpose, such as a recipe) and reading and writing used as a medium of pleasurable entertainment (i.e., stories) are also important. These experiences are sometimes referred to as "predictors" of reading success.

Children show their awareness of written language in many ways. Some take an interest in favorite storybooks and read along, point to the words, or retell the story. Familiar books may be "read" to a group by a child who pretends to be "teacher." Other children talk about the signs and labels around them—traffic signs, logos for products on packages, and advertisements. Children's first interest is often their own names, which they recognize and may wish to write.

Supporting children in becoming literate requires a watchful eye and sensitive ear. Whatever the age of children you work with, it is important to visibly enjoy reading and writing yourself. Write and read in front of children often and comment:

"I wonder what ingredients we'll need for the lasagna. I'm going to look it up here in my cookbook. Oh, mozzarella cheese. I'd better write that down on our shopping list." Share your writing with children so they will begin to understand adult purposes for writing.

Every classroom needs many appealing books. Every child needs to be read to. Planned and spontaneous reading to individuals, to a small group, and to the whole class is an essential part of every early childhood teacher's day. A program for even the youngest children should have books and words throughout. Your appreciation of children's literature and your visible enjoyment is one of the most important ways you demonstrate that reading is a worthwhile experience. The box "Golden Rules for Helping Children Develop Concepts About Print" includes ideas for how to put literacy into your daily life with children.

You may find it useful to look at the Head Start Early Learning Outcomes Framework for Literacy Development (search for the Head Start Early Learning Outcomes Framework). It provides guidelines for curriculum planning and assessment that align with most states' early learning and development standards.

Literature Curriculum

Children who love books come to love reading. Children who have many positive experiences with literature come to love books. Literature is not merely the carrot with which we motivate children to read; it is the most important reason for learning to read. Through good literature, children experience language and art, and learn about the world, themselves, and other people. Literature provides information, motivates exploration, builds concern for others, and creates a love of reading.

Because young children are not able to purchase books or use the library on their own, it is up to you to present a range of quality literature from which children can make choices. The sense of adventure that accompanies opening a new book creates active, eager readers. Every classroom needs a variety of different kinds of books

Golden Rules

for Helping Children Develop Concepts About Print

1. **Be joyful.** Read to children frequently with obvious pleasure.
2. **Be bountiful.** Fill the room with books—in the library and in other places that make sense.
3. **Have favorites.** Reread children's favorite stories over and over.
4. **Let children help.** Ask a child to choose the book, read the title, turn the page, or read the story their own way.
5. **Be enthusiastic.** Show and talk about about print, point out the message, comment on the font, the words, the parts of the book, even the punctuation.
6. **Be playful.** Do silly things—turn the book upside down and talk about why it can't be read like that.
7. **Be practical.** Use print for authentic, practical reasons in front of children. Read directions, write notes and letters, make signs for children, parents, other teachers. Write lists, create recipes, and write what you want to recall.
8. **Be curious in the presence of children.** Look things up in an encyclopedia, a cookbook, an informational book, or on the Internet.
9. **Be neat.** Label shelves and containers, puzzles and games, and charts and posters. Make signs that are permanent (The Block Area) and signs that are temporary (Bailey's Blocks—Please Don't Knock Them Down).
10. **Be creative.** Let children play with print. Provide time, space, and materials for writing. Make a writing center with lots of print to copy, cut, and play with.
11. **Be helpful.** Help children write, illustrate, and bind books for the classroom library.
12. **Be appreciative of children's print, including scribble writing, pretend writing, and inventive spelling.**

Video Example 10.4: Developing Literacy Skills

Watch this short video to see a teacher engaged in a literacy activity with preschool children. How could you tell the children were interested in the process of writing down their ideas? What else could the teacher do to build literacy understanding for these children?

that change regularly. The different kinds of books are called the **genres of children's literature**. These include fiction, informational books, mood and concept books, and poetry (see Figure 10.9). Although it is certainly possible to read other kinds of books (especially to children in second and third grade), in the early childhood years we rely on picture books and oral literature.

Figure 10.9 Genres of Children's Literature

Fiction (fantasy, folklore, and realistic fiction) for young children should have believable characters and the illusion of reality in time and place. In a good story the plot encourages children to understand reasons behind events. It is important that diverse race, ethnicity, and culture are represented. An example of a great fantasy is *Where the Wild Things Are* by Maurice Sendak. *Anansi the Spider* by Gerald McDermott is a delightful example of folklore. *When Sophie Gets Angry . . . Really, Really Angry* by Molly Bang is a good example of realistic fiction.

Informational books, sometimes called nonfiction, should be appealing and accurate. They must be well paced and skillfully presented. Illustrations convey more than the words alone can. *An Egg Is Quiet* by Dianna Hutts Aston and Sylvia Long is an example of a good informational book for young children.

Mood and concept books sensitize children to language, ideas, feelings, and build awareness. They include wordless books and books that use an organizing concept such as the alphabet. *Rain, Rain Rivers* by Uri Shulevitz is an example of a mood book. *Z Is for Moose* by Kelly Bingham is an entertaining example of a concept book.

Poetry collections (like *My Very First Mother Goose* by Iona Opie and Rosemary Wells) and picture books that feature a single poem (like *The Owl and the Pussycat* by Edward Lear, illustrated by Jan Brett) present mood and melody in language. They enhance children's understanding of the world and develop their sensitivity to language. This heightened awareness of the sounds of language is an important part of literacy.

Good children's literature has the following qualities:

- It shows respect for the reader (is not condescending and does not stereotype by gender, race, culture, etc.).
- It is written and illustrated with care and craftsmanship. The language and illustrations are created with artistry and are appropriate to the content.
- It has integrity (honesty and truthfulness within the context of the story).
- It teaches by example—it does not preach or moralize.
- It helps the reader to understand and feel more deeply.
- It interests and delights children—the children want you to read it again.
- It is not based on shows or products on movies, television shows, or other products—the purpose of books is to promote and sell them to children.

In the past, children's literature failed to include minorities, individuals with disabilities, and other groups. If we are to lead all children to a love of reading, we need to include people who are like them. To help children appreciate the humanity they share with people who are different, they need books that include diversity. Make sure that the books you choose represent diverse ethnicities, lifestyles, cultures, appearances, race, ages, and activities.

Good programs provide large blocks of time each day during which children and teachers can read, as well as a scheduled 10- to 20-minute story time at least twice in a full day. If you work with children younger than 3, it is best to read stories to individuals or groups of two or three. This is also usually the most comfortable when you first begin to read stories, even to older children. Reading a story to a group requires skill you will develop through practice. See "Golden Rules for Reading a Story to a Group" for tips that will help you develop skill as a story reader.

Although reading is the most common way to share literature, a number of other techniques engage children and help them to build understanding of literature: telling a story without a book or using a prop such as a puppet or flannelboard, having children act out stories, and listening to recordings of stories and poems. **Literature extensions**—such as cooking oatmeal and waiting for it to cool after reading *Goldilocks and the Three Bears*—help children understand a story.

Although children's literature can be expanded into many other areas of classroom life, it is important not to turn literature into reading texts or use it as a basis for worksheets and tests. When children's literature is "basalized" in this way, children's inherent love of books is in danger of being squelched.

Figure 10.10 lists some books and Internet resources that will help you learn about the communication curriculum.

Golden Rules

for Reading a Story to a Group

1. Practice so you know the story well and can pronounce all the words.
2. Sit close to children on a low stool or chair so children can see the book.
3. Focus the group with a song or finger play or by showing the cover of the book and talking about it.
4. Have an alternative activity for young children or children with disabilities so they can leave if they get restless.
5. Use a natural voice and speak clearly and loud enough for the group to hear.
6. Be expressive—match your voice, volume, tempo, facial expression, pauses, and gestures to the content of the story.
7. Stick to the story—avoid asking many questions or interrupting with too many comments.
8. Pay attention to the children (make eye contact with them and notice their faces and bodies) and have children move if they are restless, then continue reading.
9. Leave them wanting more—quit before children are tired, bored, and restless.

Figure 10.10 Books and Internet Resources for the Communication Curriculum

BOOKS

Language

Learning Language and Loving It, by E. Weitzman & J. Greenberg (Hanen Centre)

Learning to Listen and Listening to Learn, by M. Jalongo (NAEYC)

One Child, Two Languages: A Guide for Early Childhood Educators of Children Learning English as a Second Language, by P. O. Tabors (Brookes)

Basics of Supporting Dual Language Learners, by K. Nemeth (NAEYC)

Literacy

Let's Begin Reading Right: A Developmental Approach to Emergent Literacy, by M. V. Fields, L. Groth, & Katherine L. Spangler (Merrill/ Prentice Hall)

Literacy and the Youngest Learner: Best Practices for Educators of Children from Birth to Five, by Bennet-Armistead et al. (Scholastic)

The Living Classroom: Writing, Reading, and Beyond, by D. Armington (NAEYC)

Much More Than the ABC's, by J. Schickedanz (NAEYC)

Writing in Preschool: Learning to Orchestrate Meaning and Marks, by J. Schickedanz (NAEYC)

Learning to Read and Write: Developmentally Appropriate Practices for Young Children, by S. B. Neuman, C. Copple, & S. Bredekamp (NAEYC)

Literature

The Important Books: Children's Picture Books as Art and Literature, by J. Stanton (Scarecrow Press)

The Read Aloud Handbook, by J. Trelease (Penguin Books)

Reading Magic: Why Reading Aloud to Our Children Will Change Their Lives Forever, by M. Fox (Mariner books)

Story Stretchers (3 Versions: Infants and Toddlers, Preschoolers, and Primary); also *More Story Stretchers*, by S. Raines & R. J. Canaday (Gryphon House)

Using Caldecotts Across the Curriculum, by J. Novelli (Scholastic)

Young Children and Picture Books, by M. R. Jalongo (NAEYC)

INTERNET RESOURCES

ReadWriteThink *(ideas for teachers in K–3 settings)*

The International Reading Association

Children's Literature Network

Children's Literature Web Guide

Guide to Research in Children's and Young Adult Literature

Vandergrift's Children's Literature Page

National Children's Literacy Website

A Quick Check 10.3

Gauge your understanding of the concepts in this section.

The Creative Arts Curriculum

The arts are vital in the development of children who can feel as well as think and who are sensitive and creative. Art, music, and creative movement help children express their feelings, communicate ideas in new forms, and develop their senses. Creativity is not restricted to artists. All people are creative as they put together what they know to produce something that is new to them. Creativity occurs in activities such as building with blocks and dramatic play and as children engage with the arts. Through arts experiences, children come to:

- feel good about themselves as individuals;
- observe and respond sensitively;
- express feelings and ideas;
- develop creativity;
- learn art, music, and movement skills;
- develop beginning understanding of arts disciplines;
- appreciate music, art, and dance from diverse cultures, times, and places;
- construct understanding;
- communicate what they know.

You can provide satisfying experiences with the arts when you understand what you can reasonably expect of children and when you provide activities that match their needs and abilities.

Three-year-old Katie comes to the children's center with her mom for the first time. She is attracted to the easel and the brilliant colors of paint. Katie takes a brush full of magenta and paints a large blotch of color. A brush full of deep blue follows, then one of yellow and another of black. The dripping colors glisten wet and intense on the paper. Katie steps back, turns, then grins at her mom.

For very young children like Katie, the most important aspects of the arts are the development of awareness, new skills, and feelings of self-worth. Your role is to provide an environment, materials, and experiences that support creative development and **aesthetic appreciation**. A classroom that provides for all of these needs has a creative climate that supports creativity, imagination, and self-expression.

It is not necessary to be an artist, a dancer, or a musician yourself to teach the arts to young children. It is necessary, however, to believe that experiences with and participation in the arts is valuable. It is also important to have a basic understanding of arts disciplines—to understand the elements that make up each of the arts and to have a beginning understanding of the techniques that young children can learn.

Creative expression is stimulated by rich life experiences as well as exposure to the arts. When children have diverse real-life experiences and opportunities to view artwork, listen to music, and see dance and drama, they begin to understand the purpose and power of the arts.

Reflect On

Your Experiences with the Arts in School

Remember an experience with the arts that you had in school. How did your teacher support or discourage your creativity and individuality? How did this influence your feelings about yourself as an artist, a musician, or a dancer?

Through their artwork, children can disclose their ways of perceiving. They can risk this expression only if they feel safe and are encouraged. You support creativity by accepting all of the feelings and ideas that children create, whether or not they are "nice" or "pretty" by adult standards. Things that move children and adults are not always the most pleasant aspects of their lives. Nevertheless, if they have the power to evoke strong feelings, they are important parts of life and a part of their creative expression (see Figure 10.10).

To understand how arts curriculum is addressed in standards, check out your state's early learning guidelines or the Consortium of National Arts Education Associations Content Standards.

Visual Art Curriculum

Visual art curriculum is designed to help children gain a sense of themselves as artists and art appreciators. Art media give children a way to express feelings and understanding and provide opportunities for children to explore and manipulate. Creating art is a way of learning and a way of communicating. For very young children it is a form of sensory play. As they mature, children use art to express ideas, but they continue to enjoy the satisfaction of "messing about" with materials. For very young children, *process* is the whole of the art experience, *product* is not important. Toddlers are unconcerned with their finished artwork. As children grow older, they use art to create meaning and to express what they know and feel. They may begin to be self-critical and destroy work that does not meet their standards.

SOURCE: Jeff Reese

As children use art media, they reap educational benefits. They develop motor control and perceptual discrimination. They use language and learn new vocabulary. They learn about materials and develop problem-solving strategies. Art is also a primary way to construct and communicate understanding (see Figure 10.11). Developing aesthetic awareness and appreciation are important benefits of art experiences. (see Figure 10.12).

Figure 10.11 Caterpillar on a Crown Flower Leaf

SOURCE: Reprinted with permission from Kapua Kawelo.

Figure 10.12 My Mommy Is Mad at Me (drawing by a 4-year-old)

Figure 10.13 Drawing of a Cockatiel

SOURCE: Reprinted by permission from Robyn S. B. Chun.

One day at school, a new pet arrives—Kea, a gray and white cockatiel. The children crowd around the new addition to their classroom. They watch it as it hops from perch to perch in the large birdcage. Five-year-old Jonah asks the teacher for a piece of brown paper. He takes black and white crayons from the shelf. He sits down, studies, and painstakingly draws the cockatiel. Looking up every few seconds as he draws, gray and white feathers, a crest, pink three-toed feet, a long tail, and a pointy beak emerge. He draws a pattern of crisscross black lines above and below the bird. The teacher says, "Tell me about your drawing." And Jonah explains that he has drawn Kea. "Tell me about this part," the teacher says, indicating the black lines. "Those are the wires," Jonah explains, pointing to the mesh of the cage. You can see Jonah's drawing of a cockatiel in Figure 10.13.

Three approaches to teaching art to young children have developed over time: child centered, teacher centered, and art centered (Dixon & Tarr, 1988).

A child-centered approach reflects the view that art for young children should be open ended and process oriented. Children are given free access to art materials and little instruction. Adult instruction and intervention is avoided because it is viewed as stifling artistic development. The goal is to give children maximum freedom to create. Until recently, this viewpoint has been predominant in early childhood education.

In a teacher-centered approach, there is a focus on pattern art (often called craft). In this approach, children copy an adult-made model or cut out or color templates created by adults. The goal is to produce a uniform product and teach children to follow directions rather than create. This approach has been predominant in some preschools and many primary schools.

An art-centered approach focuses on art production and art appreciation (Dixon & Tarr, 1988). The teacher provides some instruction and modeling of techniques and also helps children learn about art by viewing and discussing fine artwork. The goal is to nurture children's creativity and aesthetic development. The teacher's job is to support children in developing the ability to express ideas and feelings, not dictate what they draw, paint, or sculpt. We advocate this approach because it supports artistic development, exposes children to beauty, and allows them to explore the world through art.

Art for young children includes five basic processes: drawing (sometimes referred to as graphic art), painting, printmaking (making an image by stamping or burnishing), collage and construction (creating a work of art by affixing materials to one another), and modeling and sculpting (fashioning three-dimensional art out of a malleable material, such as clay, or carving a hard material, with a tool).

Every work of art is composed of visual, graphic, and other sensory art elements: line, color, shape, space, and design. Much of the creative process of art for young children is exploration of the elements of art. You will help children think about art by talking with them about these elements. Table 10.1 describes some aspects of the art elements.

Reflect On

Talking with Children about Art Elements

Look at the artwork in Figure 10.14. How do you respond to it? What do you think you might say to a child about it? Now notice the way the child used color, shape, space, and design in the work. Think of some other things you might say to encourage the child and develop awareness of art elements.

Table 10.1 The Elements of Art

Art Element		Words to Use in Talking About the Art Element
Line	That line is . . .	straight, curved, heavy, light, wide, thin, wandering, wiggling, jagged, broken, zigzag, long, short
	It goes . . .	up and down, diagonally, from side to side
	Those are . . .	crossed, separate, parallel lines
Color	You used . . .	pure or primary colors (red, yellow, blue), mixed or secondary colors (orange, green, purple), or tertiary colors (magenta, turquoise, chartreuse)
	The color is . . .	cool (blue end of the spectrum), warm (red end of the spectrum)
	The colors are . . .	intense, saturated, luminous, bright, dusky, shadowy light, dark
Shape	Those shapes are . . .	open, closed, irregular, regular (rectangle, circle, triangle, trapezoid, hexagon, octagon, oval, square, and so on), filled, empty, connected, overlapping, enclosed
	That shape is . . .	
Space	You used the . . .	center, top, bottom, side, corner, inside, near, far part of the paper
	It is . . .	crowded, full, sparse, empty, balanced/unbalanced, included/excluded
Design	I see how you . . .	organized, repeated, made some texture, used the idea of . . ., varied the . . ., made it symmetrical, balanced the . . ., alternated the . . .

Young children need time, space, and materials to become artists but do not become artists simply because art media are available. They need the support of adults. Much of the creative process of art for young children is exploration rather than an attempt to represent something. Realizing this can help you appreciate children's early artwork. Your most critical task is to understand and value the art of young children. It has worth in and of itself—not for what it may become when children gain more skill but for what it is now.

The way you talk to young children can support their artistic development. As they work, it is best, at first, to offer only minimal input. Avoid asking what they have created. They may have had nothing particular in mind, and the question implies that they should have. Instead, ask them if they wish to tell you about what they have done and accept it if they do not. You can comment on aspects such as the following:

- **Effort.** "You worked on your clay for a long time today."
- **Innovation.** "When you used the side of the crayon, it made a different kind of mark than drawing with the tip."
- **Technique.** "There are lots and lots of dots on your painting."

You can also comment on children's use of art elements:

- **Color.** "The green looks really vibrant next to the red."
- **Line.** "You used thick and thin lines in your painting."
- **Shape.** "What a lot of circular objects you chose for your collage."
- **Space.** "Your box collage is almost as tall as the top of the shelf."
- **Design.** "The top of your paper has lots of little prints and the bottom has lots of big prints."

Some children may not seem interested in art. For some a period of disinterest or observation precedes participation. Other children are more interested in other activities or ways of being creative. Still others do not want to attempt art because they fear they cannot measure up to teacher's or parents' expectations. Some children fear being scolded for getting messy. Easily accessible, plentiful supplies, encouragement without pressure, and acceptance and appreciation for the child's work can give children confidence to try in art activities.

Children's artistic development is closely related to the culture in which they live. Studying the way art is taught in other cultures is leading to a growing

Video Example 10.5: The Development of Art Skills in an Integrated Study

Watch this video to see Jonah drawing the cockatiel and other children creating images of birds. What surprised you about the way in which these children worked? What do you think contributed to their focus and artistic ability?

understanding that teachers can support young children's artistic abilities by providing frequent opportunities to be involved in art, giving careful attention to the quality and presentation of art materials, providing appropriate tasks, talking with children about their intent and efforts, instructing children in technique, providing lots of time to explore and revisit methods, and carefully displaying children's work. The children's art that you see in this book (Figures 10.3, 10.11, 10.12, 10.13, 10.14, 10.15, 10.18, 10.20, 10.21, and 10.22) are examples of work produced by children who were given this kind of support and whose work was truly valued and respected by their teachers.

Figure 10.14 Child's Painting: Hala Seed Growing in a Pot

SOURCE: Reprinted with permission from Kapua Kawelo.

At times, teachers will make a distinction between work they call "craft" and other work they call "art." Often the "craft" activities consist of look-alike coloring patterns. What is craft? The dictionary defines "craft" as something such as pottery produced skillfully by hand, especially in a traditional manner. The handwork that we give children to do—claywork, woodwork, stitchery, paper folding, and cutting—is craft and worthwhile for young children—especially primary-age children who have the required fine motor coordination. True craft is a far cry from look-alike coloring books or identical snowmen made with cotton balls. Creative expression should be a reflection of the child's ideas and abilities—not patterns from a teacher's magazine or book. Coloring books and prepared patterns to be copied by children have nothing to do with the development of creativity—in fact, they can be destructive to children's feelings of competence and self-worth. These activities take up valuable time that children should be using to develop other skills and ideas. They are not used in good early childhood programs.

Music Curriculum

Music is pervasive and has been called a universal language. In the heart of a city, we experience the "song" of traffic, footsteps, and voices. In the solitude of the country, we listen to the harmony of birds, wind, and water. Even before we are born, we experience the music of a heartbeat. Music can make us happy or sad or calm or excited and can evoke feelings of patriotism, nostalgia, sanctity, love, or empathy.

All young children need music. The most important reasons to provide music to children are that listening to and making music brings pleasure, it provides a powerful and direct link to emotions, and because sharing music with others is an important way to be a part of your culture. Of course, it is also the way children begin to learn about music as a subject, start to develop the skills of a musician, and build the ability to listen. Music can also be a path to many other kinds of learning. It can be a vehicle for language ("The song says that Aiken Drum played upon a ladle—have you ever seen a ladle?"), and it helps build literacy skills related to phonemic awareness ("Willowby wallaby woo") and even for remembering facts that might not otherwise be easy to recall (e.g., singing the "ABC" song to remember whether "Q" comes before "R"). There is research that demonstrates that listening to music has a positive impact on learning (Campbell, 2000) and that children's musical skills (e.g., being able to keep the beat in a song) are linked to school success (Weikart, 2003).

Musical elements (rhythm, tone, and form) are the raw materials out of which every piece of music is made. The organization of these elements is what distinguishes music from noise. As children engage in music, they experience these elements. Table 10.2 explains these music elements and describes some aspects of them that you can help children to notice.

The music curriculum you provide should help children acquire music skills to the degree appropriate for their age: singing, playing instruments, composing and improvising, listening to and appreciating music, and performing.

Singing offers opportunities for children to experience music and to develop music skills. Children have an easier time learning songs that are relatively short and simple and have a distinct rhythm. All early childhood educators need a repertoire of singable songs with different moods, subjects, tempos, and styles.

Figure 10.15 Tissue Paper Collage: Yellow Sunflower

SOURCE: Reprinted with permission from Kapua Kawelo.

Table 10.2 The Elements of Music

Music Element	Some Aspects to Help Children Notice
Rhythm (characteristics of music that relate to movement and time)	Beat: the musical pulse
	Melodic rhythm: the rhythm of the melody or words
	Tempo: the speed of the music
	Rests: the silences in music
Tone (characteristics of the notes)	Pitch: high or low
	Melody or tune: the arrangement of notes in a singable sequence
	Tone color of timbre: the characteristic sound of an instrument
	Dynamics: loudness or softness
Form (structure of a piece of music)	Phrase: short but complete musical ideas in a piece of music
	Repetition: when identical phrases recur in a piece of music
	Variation: when similar phrases occur in a piece of music
	Contrast: when very different phrases occur in a piece of music

Playing instruments helps young children acquire music skills. Simple rhythm instruments provide excellent first experiences.

Composing and improvising represent the creative use of music skills. Young children who have had many music experiences spontaneously improvise songs to accompany their play. You help children to improvise when you ask them to think of new words for a song. Composing requires creating and preserving a composition.

Listening to and appreciating music made by others is an important part of music education. Recordings can provide experiences with diverse styles of music and music from different cultures. When adults play instruments and sing in the classroom, you help children understand that music is made by people.

Performing for others is another music skill. Because the goal of music education is to help children to become comfortable with musical expression, performance is the least important part of the music curriculum for young children. The National Association for Music Educators (1991) position statement asserts, "[Young] children should not be encumbered with the need to meet performance goals.*"

Every young child's day should include music in the daily schedule, and in your interactions with children. When music making is a part of their lives, children become spontaneous music makers. You can help children be comfortable with music by bringing it informally into the classroom and by formal planned music experiences during a special time each day.

Show you like music by clapping, tapping your feet, and dancing as you sing or listen to music. Sing with children every day—individually in spontaneous activities, during transitions, and during group times. Choose simple songs with singable melodies

Video Example 10.6: Including Song in the Classroom

Watch this video to see a teacher singing with preschool children. What do you notice about the way the children participate? How did the use of props help or hinder the activity?

Video

---

* From MENC's Position Statement on Early Childhood Education, adopted by the MENC National Executive Board in July 1991, National Association for Music Education (formerly MENC).

and lyrics. Sing in a comfortable range for children (approximately middle C to E an octave above). Sing about the children and their activities and interests. Add movement to music to enhance children's interest. Regularly use simple rhythm instruments in guided activity. Take good care of these instruments and avoid leaving them out to be damaged or turned into noisemakers. Learn to play a simple chorded instrument (e.g., guitar, autoharp, ukulele, or omnichord) to accompany music activities. Include diverse styles of music from many cultures.

Creative Movement Curriculum

Another way that children express themselves is through creative movement. When is movement creative? When ideas and feelings are expressed in imaginative ways through movement. It is different from and not a substitute for games or large muscle activities on the playground. It is the forerunner of dance and theater but differs from them. Dance and theater are more formal and prescribed than creative movement.

In creative movement, children interpret and follow suggestions and are encouraged to find their own innovative ways of moving. They express ideas with their bodies and develop a repertoire of movement possibilities. Creative movement offers challenges and new ways to practice developing physical skills. As children participate in creative movement, they experience the elements of movement: body awareness and control, space, time, and form. Table 10.3 discusses these elements and gives some examples of how you might use them in movement activities with young children.

Successful creative movement activities take thoughtful planning. Basic rules for safety (no pushing or bumping and so on) and an attitude of respect for individual interpretations and skill levels need to be established. We find it useful to have a written plan to use as a "map" to guide us as we lead children in creative movement activities. With a group of very young children, creative movement might be as simple as jumping and stomping to the beat of a drum. As children become more experienced, they can be given more complex movement tasks, such as moving a single body part in isolation ("Show you're happy with your foot!") or representing something ("As I play my drum, slowly grow toward the sun and blossom like a flower."). Older preschoolers and primary-age children enjoy choreographing a song or story.

Table 10.3 The Elements of Creative Movement

Movement Element	Aspects of the Element	Examples of Using the Element
Body awareness (awareness and control of body)	Location: where you are in space	"Look at who's in front of you, who's behind you, what's above you."
	Locomotor movement (actions): the ways you can move from one place to another	"Walk, jump, hop, run, skip."
	Nonlocomotor movement: the ways you can move while staying in one place	"Keep your feet planted on the ground and make your arms stretch."
	Body isolation: moving part of the body without moving the rest	"Wave good-bye with your elbow."
Space (how area is used)	Personal space (occupied just by you) versus general space (used by the whole group)	"Imagine yourself inside a bubble."
	Level: high/low/middle	"Make your head float to the sky."
	Boundaries: inside/outside	"Put one body part inside the hoop."
Time (tempo or speed)	Slow or fast	"Flap your eagle wings slowly, then soar across the sky."
	Steady or changing	"March, march, march to the drumbeat."
Force (energy)	Heavy or light	"Tromp like an elephant across the room."
	Relaxed or tense	"Float like a butterfly."
	Smooth or jerky	"Pretend your legs are made of boards and can't bend."
		"Walk like a machine."

Golden Rules

for Creative Movement with Young Children

1. Begin movement sessions sitting down or standing still before inviting children to move freely around the room.
2. Establish a signal (like a hard drumbeat) to tell the children to freeze. Practice stopping to this signal as a game until they understand it as an integral part of every movement activity.
3. Include all children. If children are not yet comfortable enough to participate, ask them to be the audience and watch and clap at the end.
4. Alternate vigorous and quiet movement. Start low, small, slow, and light; gradually build to high, big, heavy, and quick—then slowly work down to slow and small again.
5. Quit while you're ahead—when it's going well and you have reached a natural ending place.
6. End with movement in a way that provides a transition to the next activity: "Tiptoe to the playground when I touch you on the shoulder."

As children develop confidence and movement skills, they will become able to express their ideas with little direction. In the beginning, however, you will need to provide guidance. (See the accompanying "Golden Rules for Creative Movement with Young Children.") Most children are delighted to participate in creative movement, but a few will hesitate. Children should never be forced to participate in these activities or be criticized for the way they move.

Aesthetics Curriculum

Aesthetics refers to the love of beauty, to the cultural criteria for judging beauty, and to individual taste. It involves responding to the singular quality of things and rejecting stereotypes (Ross, 1981). You can support young children's aesthetic development. First of all, be aware of beauty in your environment and talk about it with children. Secondly, add beauty to your classroom by including beautiful natural objects, flowers, sculpture, and representations of the work of fine artists (available in museum and gallery shops). Play beautiful music before activities and routines. Make games in which children sort and classify artwork by subject matter, technique, color, or personal preference.

When introducing children to fine art, guide them in a way that is personally meaningful. For example, you might ask children to talk about what they see in the different parts of the picture and what the artist might have been thinking and feeling when he or she created the work. Beautifully illustrated children's literature can be used to discuss aesthetic impact and preferences in art.

Help children reflect on colors, patterns, and textures found in nature as you go on walks and other trips into the natural world. Take trips to view works of art in your community (e.g., to see a sculpture that adorns a public building). The early years may be the optimal time to lay the foundation for a lifetime of pleasure and enjoyment. The national arts content standards incorporate aesthetic appreciation as a part of each arts area.

You have many gifts to give children. Being able to create and appreciate art, music, and dance and to express ideas and feelings through the arts is a gift. Figure 10.16 lists some books and websites that can help you learn more about the creative arts and aesthetic curriculum.

Figure 10.16 Books and Internet Resources on Creative Arts and Aesthetic Curriculum

BOOKS

Art

Don't Move the Muffin Tins: A Hands-Off Guide to Art for the Young Child, by B. Bos (Turn the Page Press)

In the Spirit of the Studio: Learning from the Atelier of Reggio Emilia, by L. Gandini, L. T. Hill, L. B. Cadwell, & C. Schwall (NAEYC)

The Art of Teaching Art to Children: In School and at Home, by N. Beal (Farrar, Straus & Giroux)

Art: Basic for Young Children, by L. Lasky & R. Mukerji-Bergeson (NAEYC)

Experience and Art: Teaching Children to Paint (2nd ed.), by N. Smith, C. Fucigna, M. Kennedy, & L. Lord (Teachers College Press)

The Language of Art: Inquiry-Based Studio Practices in Early Childhood Settings, by A. Pelo (Redleaf Press)

Young at Art: Teaching Toddlers Self-Expression, Problem-Solving Skills, and an Appreciation for Art, by S. Striker (Henry Holt and Company)

Music

First Steps in Music for Preschool and Beyond, by J. M. Feierabend (GIA Publications, Inc.)

Music and Movement: A Way of Life for the Young Child, by L. C. Edwards, K. M. Bayless, & M. E. Ramsey (Pearson Education)

Music in Our Lives: The Early Years, by D. T. McDonald (NAEYC)

TIPS: Music Activities in Early Childhood, by J. M. Feierabend (Rowman & Littlefield Education)

Creative Movement

A Moving Experience: Dance for Lovers of Children and the Child Within, by T. Benzwie (Zephyr Press)

Creative Experience for Young Children, by M. B. Chenfeld (Heinneman)

Experiences in Music & Movement: Birth to Age 8, by R. Pica (Wadsworth Publishing)

Hello Toes: Movement Games for Children, Ages 1–5, by A. L. Barlin & N. Kalev (Princeton Book Company Publishers)

Feeling Strong, Feeling Free: Movement Exploration for Young Children, by M. Sullivan (NAEYC)

Teaching Children Dance, by T. Purcell & S. Cole (Human Kinetics)

Aesthetics

The Arts in Children's Lives: Aesthetic Education in Early Childhood, by M. R. Jalongo & L. N. Stamp (Pearson)

Aesthetics for Young People, by R. Moore (ed.) (National Art Education Association)

Designs for Living and Learning: Transforming Early Childhood Environments, by D. Curtis & M. Carter (Redleaf Press)

INTERNET RESOURCES

ArtsEdge—the National Arts and Education Network

Children's Music Network

Children's Music Web

National Dance Education Organization (NDEO)

National Art Education Association

National Association for Music Education

 A Quick Check 10.4

Gauge your understanding of the concepts in this section.

The Inquiry Curriculum

Young children have a compelling curiosity to figure out why and how the world works. They learn by doing. They observe, discover relationships, search for answers, and communicate their discoveries. They construct understanding as they explore and act on their environment. Children inquire (seek information) and develop concepts as they play and as they participate in curriculum activities. Experiences in mathematics,

Figure 10.17 Inquiry Processes That Best Apply to Young Children

Exploring: Using the senses to observe, investigate, and manipulate

Identifying: Naming and describing what is experienced

Classifying: Grouping objects or experiences by their common characteristics

Comparing and contrasting: Observing similarities and differences between objects or experiences

Hypothesizing: Using the data from experiences to make guesses (hypotheses) about what might happen

Generalizing: Applying previous experience to new events

science, and social studies are uniquely suited to the development of thinking and problem solving and are the areas of the curriculum in which inquiry is a primary emphasis.

If you remember math, science, and social studies as memorizing facts to recall for a test, you may question whether these subjects are appropriate for young children. If so, you will be pleased to know that learning "facts" is not the purpose of the **inquiry curriculum** in early childhood education. Instead, the goals are to support children's natural curiosity and sense of wonder, to help them learn to think flexibly, inquire and solve problems, and gain greater understanding of the world. Giving children information is not your primary role in the inquiry curriculum. Instead, you help children construct understanding by providing time, space, equipment, and experiences.

Inquiry means to ask, to find out, to think, to take risks, to make mistakes, and to learn from them. Facts pronounced by adults deprive children of the opportunity to learn through inquiry and develop higher-level thinking skills. Children need to understand that it is desirable to think creatively about problems, acceptable not to have an answer, and okay to give the "wrong" answers.

The processes a child uses to learn about the world and construct concepts are called inquiry processes. Inquiry for a young child involves the organization of experiences through exploration. An inquiring child uses the senses to gain information that will contribute to the development of concepts. Figure 10.17 provides a list of inquiry processes that best apply to young children. Figure 10.18 shows an example of a child's work that demonstrates his development of a concept.

Talking with children as they explore is one of the most important things you will do to help them learn to think. Supportive comments encourage inquiry and model an inquiring mind. They help children form concepts but do not hand them preformed ideas. Children are encouraged to think when they are asked open-ended questions (questions that can be answered in a number of ways and have more than one answer, see Figure 10.19). Closed questions (those that have only one answer—for example, "What color is it?") do not stimulate inquiry, but can help you understand what children know. For this reason, in most classrooms, educators use a mixture of open and closed questions.

Figure 10.18 Drawing of Sunflower with Roots (annotated work sample)

Annotation: After transplanting flowers in the garden during outside time, Alex went to the art area. He drew a flower with a marker then painted over his drawing with liquid water color. Afterward he said to the teacher, *These are the roots for the flower to drink water*.

Comment: Alex observes, makes inferences, and demonstrates knowledge—he drew and painted to express what he knows about plants.

SOURCE: Reprinted with permission from Erin Baum.

Figure 10.19 Asking Open-Ended Questions

Open questions can be answered in a number of different ways and have more than one correct answer. If you wish to stimulate children to inquire, you will ask many open-ended questions and allow children time to think and answer.

Ask questions and make statements that help children to:

- **Reason:** "What do you suppose?" "How do you know?" "What would happen if?" "How could we find out?"
- **Notice details:** "What do you see (hear, feel, smell)?" "I wonder why clouds are moving so quickly?" "The baskets all nest together, the little ones inside the big ones." "I can feel the rabbit's heart is beating quickly and hard."
- **Make comparisons:** "How are they the same (different)?" "Look how different each shell is."
- **Come to conclusions:** "What would happen if . . .?" "Why do you suppose that's happening?"

Math Curriculum

Mathematics is about quantitative, logical, and spatial relationships. Young children are genuinely curious and unafraid of mathematical processes. In the same way that young children will pretend to write and read, they will label distance and ages with numbers: "My doll is twenteen" or "It's thirty-fifty miles."

The conceptual underpinnings of math are based on concrete experiences that may not seem to relate to mathematics. You may be surprised that math curriculum for young children is far more than numbers, equations, counting, and measuring. In fact, although numbers are useful, much of math is not about numbers. It includes concepts such as more and fewer, far and near, same and different, short and tall, now and later, first and last, and over and under. These concepts provide the foundation of science and social studies as well as mathematics and form the math curriculum for young children (see Table 10.4).

Math is learned in play. A child comparing and arranging dishes and setting the table in the dramatic play area is using ideas of one-to-one correspondence, classification, and quantity. A child building a block tower is using concepts of proportion (the sizes of blocks) and symmetry (the arrangement of blocks so that the sides of the tower match), shape, and proximity. Based on your observations of children, you can add activities and ask questions that will help them to learn math concepts.

Questions can encourage mathematical thinking: "What shall we put next in our pattern?" or "How could we find out who's tallest?"—but be prepared to forgo questions when children do not appear interested. Provide children with many opportunities to manipulate objects—including those made as math teaching equipment (like Unifix cubes or Cuisenaire rods) and other materials (like blocks and button collections). Children learn about math in the routines of the day. When each child has one cracker and rests on one mat, one-to-one correspondence is experienced. As they learn the sequence of the day, learn to pour half a glass of milk, or cut apple slices in two parts, they are using math.

Many teachers of young children have "math anxiety" (a fear of math similar to stage fright), and are afraid to teach math. If you have math anxiety, remember all the ways you use pattern, measurement, reasoning, estimation, classification, and order in your life. As you do, you will realize that you are much better at math than you think. You can teach math. Here are six ways to teach math in early childhood that don't seem like math:

1. Sing songs with mathematical ideas, such as "Eency Weency Spider" (geometry and spatial awareness), "Old MacDonald Had a Farm" (pattern), and "Five Little Monkeys Jumping on the Bed" (number and operations).

Table 10.4 Math Concepts Learned by Young Children

Concept	What It Is	What a Child Might Do That Demonstrates Understanding
Matching	The foundational skill for understanding one-to-one correspondence. There are several kinds of matching tasks—matching identical items, different items, and matching groups or "sets" of identical items.	Put together matched pairs of shoes. Place one napkin at each place at the table. Place a cup on each saucer.
Sorting and classifying	Sorting or grouping by shared characteristics.	Put all the beads in a basket and all the buttons in a box.
Ordering and seriation	Sequencing based on a difference in the degree of some quality such as size, weight, texture, or shading.	Arrange balls from smallest to largest.
Number: • One-to-one correspondence • Quantity or cardinal number • Order or ordinal number • Numerals	Quantity and order: • Matching objects one for one • "Many-ness"—the amount or number of different objects • The order of objects—first, second, third • Symbols that stand for certain quantities or order (i.e., 1-2-3)	Pass out one bell to each child (see matching). Note that there are three bears and three chairs. Note who arrives first at school and who is second. Place three items by the numeral 3.
Operations • Counting • Part–part–whole relationships	Actions or procedures that produce a number value: • Adding one more to a series—a sequence of number names always used in the same order • Understanding that a number of objects includes smaller groups of objects	Count three to five objects. Say, "I have two red beads and three green beads" or "I have five beads."
Patterns	Ordering based on repetition.	Create a bead necklace with alternating colors; sing the chorus after every verse of a song.
Measurement	Comparing size, volume, weight, or quantity to a standard.	Find out how many blocks cover the table top; compare the heights of friends.
Geometry and spatial sense	Properties of objects and the way objects relate to one another based on position, direction, proximity, arrangement, and distance.	Place the long blocks on the bottom shelf and the short blocks on the shelf above; drive a tricycle forward and then backward; kick a ball to a child who is near.
Shape	Two- and three-dimensional objects and their properties. Regularity and irregularity, whether open or closed, how appearance changes based on position, and how shapes can be manipulated while retaining their characteristics.	Hold and show objects from different angles. Flatten a ball of dough into a circle.
Data analysis	The collection, organization, and representation of information (e.g., a chart comparing who has a cat and who does not have a cat—you are collecting, organizing, and representing data; a graph of how many pockets are in our clothes).	Create a picture showing how many are needed.
Probability	How likely it is that an event will occur.	Talk about likely and unlikely events—"Maybe it will rain" or "It probably won't be a tornado."

2. Read books that showcase math, such as *The Doorbell Rang* by Pat Hutchins and *Ten, Nine, Eight* by Molly Bang (number and operations), *Guess How Much I Love You* by Sam McBratney (measurement), *The Secret Birthday Message* by Eric Carle (space), *The Three Bears* by Paul Galdone (seriation), *The Very Hungry Caterpillar* by Eric Carle (pattern, number, and operations), and *Bread Bread Bread* by Ann Morris (displaying and analyzing data).

3. Build with blocks with children and use words like *half unit*, *unit*, *quadruple unit*, *big*, *little*, *tall*, *short*, and *wide* (geometry and spatial awareness, number and operations, seriation, pattern, and measurement).

4. Play with sand and water. Provide scoops and containers of different sizes (number and operations, geometry and spatial awareness, and measurement).

5. Cook good things to eat. Follow recipes that are written out and visible to children (number and operations, measurement, time, geometry and spatial awareness, and seriation).

6. Use routines. Have children set the table (number and operations), clean up (classification, geometry, and spatial awareness), take roll (number and operations), feed pets (measurement), or vote for activities/names (number and operations and displaying and analyzing data).

Reflect On

Your Feelings about Math

How do you feel when you think about teaching math? What experiences in your life contribute to your feeling positive or negative about it? How might you communicate your feelings to children? What do you want to communicate?

To understand how math curriculum is addressed in standards, check out your state's early learning guidelines or the Common Core State Standards for kindergarten through grade 12. You may find it useful to look at the Head Start Early Learning Outcomes Framework for Mathematics Knowledge and Skill. It provides guidelines for curriculum planning and assessment that align with most states' early learning and development standards.

Science Curriculum

Young children are born scientists. You can see this in an infant learning about physiology as he or she first discovers his or her toes and about physics as he or she drops a bottle from a high chair. It is also true for a preschooler who is carefully observing and drawing a cricket (see Figure 10.20).

Some adults think of science as a collection of memorized facts and concepts taught by a teacher or a textbook. Others think it is information taught to children. Some teachers believe "playing around" is sufficient science curriculum in the early years. We know today that science education for young children must be not only "hands-on" but also "minds-on"—in other words, intentional. You can see by the drawings and paintings done by 3-, 4-, and 5-year-olds included in this chapter (see Figures 10.3, 10.12, 10.13, 10.14, 10.15, 10.18, 10.20, 10.21, and 10.22) that young children can be careful observers of the world. Scientists—and educators who have maintained their own playfulness and enthusiasm for science—view it as a process of exploration and experimentation through which they find out about the world. It is this view that we want to share with children.

What do you teach young children about science? The most important thing you teach is ability and disposition to inquire. The first of the National Science Education Standards for young children is that all children should develop abilities to do scientific inquiry. Doing science depends on sensory input—hearing, smelling, seeing, touching, moving, and tasting. Therefore, sensory experience should be at the core of the early childhood science curriculum. To do scientific inquiry, children need to be able to do the following:

- Ask questions about objects, organisms, and events in the environment.
- Plan and conduct a simple investigation.
- Employ simple equipment and tools to gather data and extend the senses.
- Use data to construct a reasonable explanation.
- Communicate investigations and explanations (National Research Council, 1996).

Figure 10.20 Annotated Drawing of a Cricket

Annotation: Tyler observed the crickets in the bug box for about 3 minutes before picking up markers and drawing the cricket. He looked up frequently as he drew. He took a magnifying glass and looked at the cricket, then added hair to the legs.

Comment: Tyler demonstrates inquiry skills—he observes to gain information and records data in meaningful ways.

SOURCE: Reprinted with permission from Lani Davan.

and use power to make and enforce decisions), *geography* (the earth, its features, and the effects of human activity), and *history* (the events of the past).

Young children are interested in other people. They study the behavior, customs, interactions, power, and work of the people who share their homes, schools, and communities. They experience the geography of their homes. They do not wait to learn social studies until they are old enough to read a textbook about it. When appropriately taught to young children, social studies has important content that is worth knowing. It can help them to:

- Appreciate and respect themselves, other people, their culture, and their environment.

- Deal with important issues in their lives.

- Develop a sense of belonging to and responsibility for their family, community, and environment.

- Recognize some of the significant patterns that shape people's lives and the world.

- Explore, understand, and experience aspects of the world that lay the foundation for later comprehension of the social sciences.

- Develop skills in a range of subject areas.

Virtually any curriculum area can be geared to social studies learning. Art, music, cooking, graphing, stories, and creative dramatics can be integrated with social studies. Because social studies is so broad, it can be approached in many different ways. Food preparation, visits from resource people, songs, dances, artifacts (from a family, culture, or place), books, and trips related to a topic all contribute to concept development in the social sciences (see Figure 10.23). Follow-up activities can occur in every area of the curriculum. Children gain deeper understanding when they re-create and re-experience concepts in blocks, dramatic play, art work, graphs, child-authored books, songs, and games.

Some (but not all) states have preschool social studies standards. To understand how social studies curriculum is addressed in your state's preschool programs, look at the early learning guidelines. The National Council for the Social Studies has identified 10 themes that belong in education for children from kindergarten on. You can find these at their website. It provides guidelines for curriculum planning and assessment that align with most states' early learning and development standards. To understand how social studies curriculum is addressed in standards, check out your state's early learning guidelines.

Figure 10.24 lists some books and Internet resources that can help you learn more about the inquiry curriculum.

Figure 10.23 Five Activities That Are Primarily Social Studies

Learning Trips are "field work" (the most important social studies activity); children are social scientists going into the community to learn.

Using and Making Maps (representations from a bird's eye perspective) are valuable when they are concrete and of high interest, such as body-tracing (a life-size map), mapping with blocks, and mapping a familiar place like the playground.

Resource Visitors serve as a subject to be learned about (a pregnant mom who allows children to feel the baby kick), to demonstrate a skill or artifact (a cultural representative who teaches a song and demonstrates making a special food), or to share information (a trainer with an assistance dog).

Block Building enables children to recreate their experiences and build social studies concepts.

Dramatic Play like block building, enables recreating experiences and building concepts.

Figure 10.24 Books and Internet Resources on Inquiry Curriculum

BOOKS

Math

Active Experiences for Active Children: Mathematics, by C. Seefeldt & A. Galper (Prentice Hall)

Mathematics in the Early Years, and the Young Child and Mathematics, by J. V. Copley (NAEYC)

Spotlight on Young Children and Math, by D. G. Koralek (NAEYC)

Early Childhood Mathematics, by S. Smith (Pearson)

Young Mathematicians at Work: Constructing Number Sense, Addition, and Subtraction, by C. T. Fosnot (Heinemann)

Science

Discovering Nature with Young Children, by I. Chaulfour & K. Worth (Redleaf Press)

Science with Young Children, by B. Holt (NAEYC)

Science Experiences for the Early Childhood Years: An Integrated Approach, by J. D. Harlan & M. S. Rivkin (Merrill/Prentice Hall)

Active Experiences for Active Children: Science, by C. Seefeldt & A. Galper (Merrill/Prentice Hall)

Worms, Shadows, and Whirlpools: Science in the Early Childhood Classroom, by K. Worth & S. Grollman (Redleaf Press)

Social Studies

Active Experiences for Active Children: Social Studies, by C. Seefeldt & A. Galper (Merrill/Prentice Hall)

Alike and Different: Exploring Our Humanity with Young Children, by B. Neugebauer (Exchange Press)

Explorations with Young Children, by A. Mitchell & J. David (Gryphon House)

Roots and Wings: Affirming Culture in Early Childhood Programs, by S. York (Redleaf Press)

INTERNET REOURCES

National Council of Teachers of Mathematics

National Science Teachers Association

National Council for the Social Studies

Montessori Mathematics Introduction

NAEYC Position Statement on Early Childhood Mathematics: Promoting Good Beginnings

 # Application Exercise 10.1

Watch and Write About Identifying Curriculum When Children Play

A Quick Check 10.5
Gauge your understanding of the concepts in this section.

Final Thoughts

Young children learn by doing, observing, and interacting. They construct and order knowledge through play. You will guide them on this voyage of discovery and help them understand the world in which they live. As you do so, you support their natural curiosity, develop their love of learning, and help them be the thinkers and problem solvers of the future.

There are many ways to organize curriculum to ensure that you provide a full range of appropriate activities for the children in your program. No single "right way" prescribes how to think about or teach a particular subject to young children (though some ways are "wrong" because they do not reflect what we know about how children learn).

As you grow as an early childhood educator, you will have opportunities to learn much more about curriculum. In creating this chapter, we wanted to give you an overview of the kinds of learning experiences that are developmentally appropriate and meaningful to young children—a framework onto which you can add the practical details you will need to actually teach. We applaud you as you begin this adventure.

Application Exercise 10.2 Final Reflection

To Learn More

Read

Developmentally Appropriate Practice in Early Childhood Programs (3rd. ed.),
S. Bredekamp & C. Copple (2010).
Enthusiastic and Engaged Learners, Approaches to Learning in the Early Childhood Classroom, M. Hyson (2008).
Explorations with Young Children, A. Mitchell & J. David (Eds.) (1992).
Learning Together with Young Children: A Curriculum Framework for Reflective Teachers,
D. Curtis & M. Carter (2007).
Meaningful Curriculum for Young Children, E. Moravcik & S. Nolte (2018).
The Intentional Teacher: Choosing the Best Strategies for Young Children's Learning, A. S.
Epstein (2014).

Visit a Website

The following agencies and organizations have websites related to curriculum:
Association for Childhood Education International
Association for Early Childhood Educators (Singapore)
British Association for Early Childhood Education
Canadian Child Care Federation
Early Childhood Australia
European Early Childhood Education Research Association (EECERA)
Learning and Teaching Scotland
National Association for the Education of Young Children
Southern Early Childhood Association
Te Tari Puna Ora o Aotearoa (New Zealand Child Care Association)

Document Your Skill & Knowledge About Curriculum in Your Professional Portfolio

Include some or all of the following:

- An explanation of what curriculum is in early childhood programs and how and why it is different from curriculum for older children

- A computer slide presentation or video comparing Classrooms for Two Ages showing how curriculum in each enhances children's development

- A report on one of the areas of curriculum (physical development, communication, creative arts, or inquiry). Describe how to support children's development in this area.

Shared Writing 10.1 Your Experiences with Curriculum

Curriculum Planning

SOURCE: Jeff Reese

Awareness of alternatives and the bases of choices distinguishes the competent teacher from the merely intuitive one.

ELIZABETH BRADY

 ## Chapter Learning Outcomes:

11.1 Explain the purpose of planning.

11.2 Identify influences on planning.

11.3 Describe the process of planning.

11.4 Write plans to guide teaching.

11.5 Recognize and describe an effective integrated study.

NAEYC Professional Preparation Standards

The NAEYC Professional Preparation Standards that apply to this chapter:

Standard 4: Using Developmentally Effective Approaches to Connect with Children and Families (NAEYC, 2009)

Key elements:

4b: Knowing and understanding effective strategies and tools for early education

4c: Using a broad repertoire of developmentally appropriate teaching/learning approaches

Standard 5: Using Content Knowledge to Build Meaningful Curriculum

Key elements:

5a: Understanding content knowledge and resources in academic disciplines

5b: Knowing and using the central concepts, inquiry tools, and structures of content areas or academic disciplines

5c: Using their own knowledge, appropriate early learning standards, and other resources to design, implement, and evaluate meaningful, challenging curricula for each child

The Purpose of Planning

Worthwhile curriculum contributes to all aspects of development and provides opportunities for children to learn. Curriculum is the intentional learning experiences designed by teachers in response to what they know and observe about children as well as program goals and standards. **Intentional teaching** means using knowledge, judgment, and expertise to organize learning experiences purposefully and to respond to unexpected situations as teaching opportunities. Keeping specific goals in mind enables you to integrate and promote meaningful learning in all domains of development.

As an early childhood teacher, one of your tasks will be to plan challenging and engaging curriculum that will help children understand the world, develop skills, and acquire attitudes that will lead them to become caring and productive human beings. Meaningful curriculum includes three interconnected elements: the learner (who), the *content* or subject matter (what), and the process or planned learning opportunities (how). Your study of child development teaches you about the who. Classes on curriculum teach you about the what. In this chapter we explore the how—the selection and organization of curriculum.

Why do you plan? In everyday life when you make a list of what to buy at the grocery store, register for a class, or agree to meet a friend for coffee, you are making a plan. Whether you write your plans down or keep them in your head, planning is a part of your life as a competent adult. You plan in order to make sure you can do the things you want and need to do in order to accomplish your goals, both big (get a degree) and small (meet Robyn for coffee).

Reflect On

Something You Planned

Think of a time when you planned something for yourself, your family, or your community—a trip, a party, a project. Reflect on what you did and how you went about organizing the event or activity. What did you do? How did you know that you had succeeded? How did planning or lack of planning impact how it turned out?

Teachers of young children plan for some of the same reasons you plan in your day-to-day life. They plan in order to make sure they know what they're doing and that they have everything they need. They plan because they want a good result! But when teachers talk about a **plan**, they mean something more than a list of supplies or a schedule of activities. They mean a written, detailed guide for teaching.

Virtually all teachers create some form of written plans. Why do teachers write plans? They write plans to make sure learning experiences are appropriate for children as individuals and as a group. They write plans to meet their obligations to address standards and program expectations. They write plans to share with families and colleagues about what they are teaching and why.

Because you are learning to be a teacher, you learn to write plans. At first, for your college instructor, later for your employer, co-workers, or children's families. When you plan well, it enhances your ability as a teacher and adds to your satisfaction in your work. Then you are planning for the children and for yourself.

> ✓ **A Quick Check 11.1**
> Gauge your understanding of the concepts in this section.

Influences on Planning

When you plan curriculum, you will choose *what* to teach. You will choose how to *organize* the curriculum. You will also choose *how to teach*—the *methods* you will use. The many decisions you have to make in planning will be influenced by your values and beliefs, your knowledge of curriculum and children, and the community and setting in which you teach.

What You Teach

What you teach (the content) will be based on your values and beliefs about children and education (and those of the program in which you teach); your assessment of children and knowledge of their families, cultures, and community; and your appraisal of whether the content is worthwhile for young children to learn.

VALUES AND BELIEFS Your choices about teaching are the way you touch the future. Barbara Biber of Bank Street College has pointed out that programs for young children are a powerful force in influencing the intellect and more:

> *The school is a mighty force not only [for] the excellence of intellect but in shaping the feelings, the attitudes, the values, the sense of self and the dreaming of what is to be, the images of good and evil in the world about and the visions of what the life of man with man might be (Biber, 1969, p. 8).*

Reflect On

The Role of Education in Shaping the Future

What do you want the world to be like in the future? What would people need to be like in order for the world you envision to exist? What do children need to learn and experience in school in order to become these people?

Your teaching reflects your values for society. The children you teach today are potential doctors, politicians, caregivers, artists, teachers, and parents—people who will one day make the decisions and do the work that will affect the lives of others (including your own). What do you want the people of the future to be like? What knowledge and skills will the children you teach need to have to be productive citizens in society as it exists now and as it will exist tomorrow? Your answers to these questions will help you determine your *aims* as an educator.

What do you believe about how children learn and what they should be learning? Do you believe children are self-motivated and self-directed learners who naturally choose what they need to learn? Do you believe that selecting what

SOURCE: Jeff Reese

children will be taught is the responsibility of adults who have more experience and knowledge? Your beliefs about children's motivation and ability to choose worthwhile learning will influence what you teach.

Teachers' beliefs about how children learn and what they should be learning fall along a continuum that ranges from the belief that children are capable of making choices that will help them acquire needed knowledge and skills (i.e., the process of learning is more important than the specific content) to a belief that young children will not naturally learn without direction (i.e., the content—the acquisition of specific knowledge and skills—is more important than the process). Most teachers' beliefs fall somewhere in the middle. Early childhood educators have typically believed in children's inherent ability to learn and in the importance of process. We, the authors, believe all areas of children's development are important; we trust children to create many opportunities for their own learning; and we believe play, child choice, and cooperative relationships are essential parts of a child's educational experience. We value the individuality and dignity of children and families and appreciate that they are part of a culture and community. We also believe adults have a responsibility to select rich and diverse educational experiences for children. Our beliefs fall in the middle of the continuum but nearer to the end that addresses process. In this chapter, we describe ways of planning curriculum that are consistent with this philosophy.

Programs are founded on values and a view of children and learning that will influence your curriculum choices. Many early childhood programs are based on a view of children as capable learners and have a mission to foster the development of the whole child and create lifelong learners. Others are designed to impart the values of a religious or cultural group. Some are founded on the belief that the primary goal of education is the acquisition of academic skills and knowledge.

KNOWLEDGE OF CHILDREN   Early childhood teaching practice is based on knowledge of children. Early childhood teachers plan curriculum appropriate to children's age and individual needs, backgrounds, and interests. This is called **developmentally appropriate practice**. According to the National Association for the Education of Young Children's Developmentally Appropriate Practice in Early Childhood Programs (Copple & Bredekamp, 2009), two core considerations of developmentally appropriate practice are:

- Anticipating and responding to the age/developmental characteristics of children
- Making curriculum choices to provide optimal learning experiences for a particular child.

Your knowledge of children's developmental characteristics provides a framework from which you will prepare the learning environment, select teaching practices, and plan experiences to benefit children of a particular age and stage of development. Your knowledge of the strengths, interests, and needs of each individual child helps you to respond to each individual's pattern and timing of growth as well as his or her unique personality, interests, and learning style. Both the curriculum and your interactions with children should be responsive to individual differences.

Just as educational experiences for *individual* children within a group differ, planning for the range of age-groups is markedly different. The younger the children, the more child-centered and family-sensitive the curriculum. For infants and young toddlers, you develop broad goals applicable to all children in this stage. Their basic needs are intense and must be met quickly. They need warm physical contact with a few affectionate adults. They are developing a sense of themselves. They are growing and developing skills with amazing speed. They are embedded in families with child-rearing practices that must be taken into consideration. The curriculum for infants and toddlers consists of opportunities for spontaneous exploration, with individualized activities for particular children. Planning is flexible and done on a short-term basis.

Curriculum is more elaborate for preschoolers and kindergartners. Three- to five-year-olds learn by doing and by actively exploring. They are beginning to use language effectively. They enjoy playing with one another but have some difficulty working as a group. They seek new stimulation and have a low tolerance for inactivity. They benefit from planned learning experiences that supplement their play and exploration. You plan for short-term activities and also further in advance to make sure that more complex activities (such as trips and projects) can occur.

For primary-age children, curriculum can be more subject-related, project-oriented, and structured. School-age young children are able to think more abstractly than pre-schoolers, but, like pre-schoolers, learn best through active, hands-on experiences. They are increasingly able to read and write about what they are learning so teachers can take advantage of these abilities by pairing hands-on experiences with opportunities to read and write about what they have learned.

If you teach in a primary school, especially in the public sector, you will be tasked with addressing academic standards and readying children for standardized tests. These mandates should not prevent you from providing developmentally appropriate meaningful learning experiences.

FAMILY, CULTURE, AND COMMUNITY   Young children live in families with the characteristics and values of their culture and community. Developmentally appropriate practice means considering what will make sense to a child given his or her background, family, and community. As you plan, ask yourself, "What do these families believe is important for children to learn? Are there subjects or activities with which members of the family or community might be uncomfortable? How can families and community serve as resources for curriculum?" This will help you plan learning experiences that are meaningful, relevant, and respectful.

Events in the families and community will influence your planning. What curriculum might you plan if several families in your class are having new babies? What if a cultural celebration is taking place or the city is installing wheelchair ramps at the street corners? What if a nearby field or garden is ready for harvest, or if heavy rains caused a flood. Skillful teachers use these events as opportunities for discovery because they know that real events can lead to powerful learning.

WHAT'S WORTH KNOWING   What's worth knowing when you are a young child? Curriculum has little value if the content isn't worthwhile to the learner. Children want to know many things about the world in which they live. They want to know about themselves, about how to get along with others and care for their own needs, about their families and communities, and about the natural and physical aspects of their world. You can see this as you observe a 1-year-old's fascination with water, a 2-year-old's triumphant "Me do it!," a 4-year-old's passion for firefighters, or a 6-year-old's enthrallment with horses.

We find ourselves fascinated when we listen to young children's questions and conversations. They show observation skills, curiosity, and intellectual engagement, as these quotes from 4-year-olds demonstrate:

"There's two caterpillars, that's why they have antenna on both sides."

"The little pickle is light green and the big cucumber is dark green."

"Me and my dad moved the sofa lasternight."

"There are eleventeen-hundred-thousand and thirty-one kids in the whole wide world."

"Not everything on TV is true. I watch TV and not everything on TV is true."

"Do you know how much is in here? [shaking a container] Ten! That's why it sounds so many."

"God made a big boom that started the world turning—but that was a long time ago."

"Bees like this kind of flower. They get honey from it."

"Oh, look, the moon! The moon is out. It's half a moon."

"Where's the praying mantis to sit on the praying mantis egg?"

"This is my computer to see where Megan's blood goes. See, here is where it goes."

"There's two helicopters! I think they're finding the airport!"

Reflect On

Something You Wanted to Know When You Were a Child

Remember a time in your childhood when you were intensely interested in learning something. What did you want to know about? Why was it important to you? What did you do to find out? What did you learn? How was this similar to or different from what you did in school?

When we ask our students to reflect on what they wanted to know when they were young children, their memories are rich and sometimes surprising. They wanted to know about birth and death, the moon and the stars, the nature of God and the nature of sand, divorce and conflict, power and authority, the workings of the plumbing, the workings of the mind, the structure of their bodies, and the structure of a worm. With few exceptions, they sought the answers outside of school.

Children want and need to know complex things about complex topics. But schools often limit curriculum for young children to simple facts to recite: shapes, colors, the alphabet, and numbers. We maintain that for curriculum to be of worth to young children, it must be based on the genuine investigation of a topic that has intellectual meaning—in other words, something that is real and requires genuine investigation and thought. In this chapter, we give you an example of one such investigation: a study of birds.

What about shapes, colors, numbers, the alphabet, and so on? There is certainly value in knowing about these things. It is our responsibility to help children learn about them. However, these things can be learned as children pursue tasks and learn about things that are interesting and meaningful to them rather than as isolated fragments divorced from context and meaning.

CONTENT STANDARDS Teachers today are required to be accountable for their teaching. That means they need to know what they are supposed to be teaching and

Video Example 11.1: Planning a Study of Birds

Watch this video to see how a group of teachers started to plan an integrated study of birds. What initiated the study? What did the teachers consider in choosing the topic?

must teach those things. As an early childhood educator in the 21st century, you need to know about *early learning guidelines or standards*, also known as **outcomes** or *content standards*, which describe either (1) what young children need to know, understand, and be able to do in a variety of learning domains or (2) the learning opportunities that should be provided in early care and education programs. States and professional associations have written K–12 standards for most curriculum areas. Head Start and almost all states have early learning guidelines for many curriculum areas. You can find guidelines for almost every state online. The Early Childhood Technical Assistance Center has links to all state early learning guidelines (search for State Early Learning Standards/Guidelines). Other countries (including United Kingdom, Sweden, Singapore, Finland, New Zealand, Australia and Canada) also have national early learning standards you can view online. Your program's goals may be based on your state's standards, or they may have been developed independently. These standards help you know broad expectations for what children should learn and how you should teach.

When early learning guidelines are written with knowledge of how young children learn, they help you identify how to help children acquire skills, knowledge, and **dispositions**. They help you design curriculum. Content standards are not a substitute for thoughtfully considering what is "worth knowing" for a group of children. Good early childhood practices, such as creating a rich play environment and providing appropriate teacher-led activities, help you meet standards.

Accountability does not come about simply because you are following good practice. It involves demonstrating how the curriculum you plan addresses the required standards. One way to do this is to identify relevant standards in your plans—so keep a copy of your state or program standards close at hand.

How Curriculum Is Organized

There are three basic approaches to organizing curriculum: learner-centered, integrated, and subject-centered. These approaches are not mutually exclusive. You may find elements of more than one in any program.

LEARNER-CENTERED CURRICULUM ORGANIZATION When curriculum organization is based on the developmental stage, needs, and interests of children, it is called learner centered. In a learner-centered curriculum design, teachers provide few planned activities and instead ensure that children have large blocks of time to play and explore in a planned environment. They make changes in the environment in response to their observations of children. Many advocates of this approach believe all planned learning experiences should emerge from observations of children and be based on children's interests. They feel that imposing activities from outside sources is counterproductive because children will fail to engage with the content. For this reason, this approach is often called emergent curriculum.

A **learner-centered organization** is the best way to plan for infants, toddlers, and young preschoolers. It can also be used with older preschoolers, kindergartners, and primary-age children. But because it is limited by what children bring to the educational experience, it may not be sufficient to provide intellectual challenge and stimulation as children get older.

INTEGRATED CURRICULUM **Integrated curriculum** refers to an educational approach in which a topic of study provides a focus for the curriculum. The topic serves as an umbrella under which different developmental and subject areas are integrated. In an integrated study, children investigate a topic in depth over a period of time. The topic forms the hub for curriculum in many different subject areas. Children's interests or the teacher's ideas about what children would enjoy or benefit from can be sources of the topic. You have experienced integrated curriculum formally and informally in your life. You experienced integrated curriculum if you studied a country in school and made traditional food (math, science, nutrition), learned a traditional dance (physical education, music), read their folklore (reading, language, literature), and made maps of the country (geography). That was a *social studies* integrated study. You experienced an *informal* integrated study if you went on a trip and experienced the climate and landscape of a new place (social studies), saw the plants and animals that lived there (science), learned phrases local people used (language), bought a souvenir and calculated how much you had to spend on it (math), visited a gallery (art), and listened to the local radio station (music).

An integrated approach reflects that children learn *holistically*. It is mindful of the idea of multiple intelligences—that is, individuals learn best through their particular strengths or intelligences. Good integrated curriculum provides many different avenues for learning about a topic. A study can be tailored to fit the learning styles of a group of children and of individual children in the group.

Advocates of integrated curriculum believe that it is appropriate and effective, especially for children 4 years and older. We have seen it used effectively with much younger children when the topic was carefully selected, with activities matched to their stage of development. For example, in a toddler classroom we know, the children's activities for several weeks were focused on water. Children experienced water in many forms—for washing, playing, and drinking. It was an appropriate exploration of the nature of water, quite different from a study of water in a kindergarten or 4-year-old class.

An integrated study of a topic contributes to children's growing awareness, skill, and understanding in many areas. It provides opportunities for children to learn by doing through direct experiences with the world. Used well and thoughtfully, it helps children understand that learning is connected to life. For these reasons, we think integrated planning is the most effective curriculum for older preschool, kindergarten, and primary school children. In our experience, it also makes teaching more interesting and satisfying.

SUBJECT-CENTERED CURRICULUM ORGANIZATION **Subject-centered organization** (curriculum organized by subject areas also known as **direct instruction**), reflects the view that education is about the attainment of knowledge. Programs using this organization set aside blocks of time to address different subject areas (e.g., reading 9:00 to 9:45 and math 10:00 to 10:30). Sometimes two or more disciplines—for example, math and science—are combined for instruction. This approach is common in schools for older children, adolescents, and adults. It is rarely used in programs for young children.

Why is it rarely used with young children? Although organization by subjects ensures that content areas are given attention, it does not help children understand relationships between subjects. It fails to take into account that young children learn **holistically**, through their senses, body, and mind working together. Therefore, it is not appropriate for young children.

A Quick Check 11.2

Gauge your understanding of the concepts in this section.

The Process of Planning

Whether you are planning a 15 minute activity or a 3 month study all plans are designed to accomplish a purpose. The process of planning involves identifying your purpose and choosing appropriate actions to achieve that purpose. In teaching, purpose relates to values and beliefs, the characteristics of children and families, and curriculum standards. Every well-written teaching plan includes the same essential components. These are a statement of purpose, content, appropriate methods, and meaningful assessment.

Statements of purpose go by a number of different names. They can be called objectives, goals, intended learning outcomes, or aims. Although you may see these used interchangeably, a distinction can be made between them. **Aims** are ideals based on philosophy and values that frame the program as a whole (e.g., the aim of our program is to help children become active learners). **Goals** are broad statements of desired ends toward which teaching is directed (e.g., a goal of this study of birds is to help children gain knowledge and develop respect for, interest in, and curiosity about life in general and "birds" in particular). **Objectives** or **intended learning outcomes** are statements outlining the intended result that a particular activity is designed to accomplish (e.g., by participating in this activity, children will learn that birds have feathers).

Content is what you teach; in other words, the curriculum. When we use the word content, we are referring to subject area (e.g., math), knowledge and skills (e.g., counting), and any larger topic (e.g., birds) about which children are learning while applying the knowledge and skills (e.g., counting birds). Young children have little knowledge and few skills, play a great deal, and require much care. So it seems to many non-educators that the content of the early childhood curriculum must be extraordinarily simple. However, as you will discover, it is complex. Understanding the content of early childhood curriculum requires your intellect and attention.

Many **strategies** or **methods** can be used to teach. One of the pleasures of being an early childhood educator is that there are many ways to teach. For example, to teach children about birds, you might take a trip to the zoo to see different kinds of birds, read books about birds, sing songs about birds, paint with feathers, play a matching game with birds and feathers, set up a bird feeder, or hatch eggs in an incubator. One of your teaching challenges will be to select methods that both engage children and help them learn things that are meaningful.

How do you know whether you have accomplished your purpose—whether children have learned what you intended to teach? Assessing what children have learned is a part of planning. In early childhood settings, this is most often done by observing what children do that demonstrates concepts and skills they have learned and documenting what you observe in written records, photographs, videos, or work samples.

Purpose, content, methods, and *assessment* relate to one another. To achieve a purpose (e.g., to help children understand distinguishing feature of birds), you select content (birds have feathers) and use methods (observing and drawing a live bird). The methods will determine how you assess (analyze the children's drawings). What you assess depends on your purpose (do the drawings include birds with feathers?).

Basing Plans on What You Observe

In programs for children 5 and younger, the purpose should reflect what you have observed about the children. As an early childhood student, you are developing observation skills. Observation helps you be a more intentional planner. You use what you learn from observation to help you plan. When you base plans on what you observe, you are much more likely to plan appropriate, successful activities.

OBSERVE INDIVIDUALS

Zoe, Tyler, Aidan, and Kaitlin (all 4-year-olds) are playing in the dramatic play area. Zoe wears an apron and directs Kaitlin and Aidan, "You be the mom. You be the baby. Have dinner at the Spaghetti House." Tyler gives them a piece of paper and asks, "What do you want to eat?" Kaitlin looks at the paper and then says, "Peanut butter." Tyler explains, "It's a spaghetti restaurant; you have to have spaghetti." He scribbles on a pad of paper, picks up a phone, and says to Zoe, "Make spaghetti for the mom and milk for the baby." Aidan sits quietly and watches the others.

Intentional teachers observe children all the time. They are looking for a number of things so they can consciously support children's development through curriculum. You will observe children to learn about the following:

- *Their strengths.* What a child is able to do well gives you ideas for what and how to teach. New knowledge and skills can be built on the foundation of each child's abilities.

- *Their interests.* Children learn best doing the things they like to do. Let their interests guide you so that a child will want to learn.

- *Their needs.* All children have strengths; all children have needs. While it is important to consider children's needs, avoid basing plans on what a child cannot do or does not know. It is far more engaging to start with interests and abilities as a base from which to learn new things.

If you happened to observe the restaurant dramatic play described above, you might decide to create a literacy activity that would build on Tyler's obvious understanding of the purposes of reading and writing. You might plan a cooking activity to support Zoe's interest in food, and you might add some props that encourage cooperative interactions (e.g., another small table and chair) to invite Aidan to engage as another customer in the restaurant.

OBSERVE THE GROUP
Good teachers see their children not only as individuals but also as members of a community. Every class has a group identity and a group personality with friendships, relationships, and rivalries. Sometimes, a group is mature with many life experiences and skills. At other times, the group will seem much younger and be less experienced. The curriculum you plan will be different for each.

For example, if you observed the restaurant play described above, you would have noticed children's interest in restaurants. You might have noticed that Tyler and Zoe directed the others. You would have seen that Kaitlin and Aidan did not seem to know as much. As a result, you might read a book about a restaurant to build on these interests and to give all of the children some background knowledge.

SOURCE: Jeff Reese

OBSERVE WITH A FOCUS In order to *plan* intentionally, you must also *observe* intentionally. For example, if you wanted to plan for social studies, then you would observe the dramatic play episode just described with a social studies focus. You might ask yourself, "What do these children understand about how people in communities work to meet one another's needs?" You might use their interest as a springboard for an integrated study of your local community and the different ways people make, buy, and sell food.

Teaching Methods or Strategies

Young children are learning all the time, from all of their experiences. Much of what they learn comes through the routines, relationships, and encounters with people, places, and objects. They learn through their own self-directed play. For infants and young toddlers, these are the only ways that they learn; routines, learning environments, and relationships are the curriculum. In fact, routines, learning environments, and relationships are the foundation of curriculum for all young children. Whatever the planned curriculum, it is the life of the classroom that is most important—the snack, play time, the teacher, friends, and toys.

Routines, relationships, and spontaneous play remain important curriculum activities throughout the early childhood years. As children get older, teachers also plan a variety of activities to present curriculum content. The art of planning involves selecting content right for children's particular interests, cultures, and abilities and strategies suited to the information or skill being taught. Four categories of teaching strategies form the foundation of early childhood pedagogy (see Table 11.1). These can be thought of as existing on a continuum from most child initiated (i.e., activities that are selected and directed by a child) to most teacher directed (i.e., selected and guided by the teacher).

 Application Exercise 11.1

Watch and Write About Children's Interests, Knowledge, and Strengths

Table 11.1 Categories of Teaching Strategies

| | Child-Directed Activities | | Teacher-Guided Activities | |
	Play	Scaffolded Activities	Small-Group Activities	Large-Group Activities
How many children	1 child alone or with 2–4 peers	1 to 3 children with a teacher	3 to 10 children	Whole class—10 or more children
Who controls and initiates	Almost completely child-selected, initiated, and directed	Primarily child-selected and directed but may be teacher planned. Either may initiate	Primarily teacher selected, directed and initiated	Almost completely teacher initiated, selected and directed
What they do	Play and explore independently in an age-appropriate environment designed for play and learning	Engage in an individually appropriate play/learning dialogue	Engage in a purposeful age-appropriate activity which teacher leads but involves children in shaping its pace and direction	Engage in a purposeful age-appropriate activity which teacher leads with awareness of children's interests and responses
Role of the teacher	Teacher purposefully arranges environment specific to the characteristics of the children to stimulate exploration, then supervises to support play and learning	Teacher purposefully arranges environment specific to the characteristics of the children then responds to the child. May shape the activity	Teacher purposefully plans and directs an age-appropriate activity and responds flexibly to children, inviting their input	Teacher plans and directs age-appropriate activity giving children guidance for order and positive learning. Less responsive to individuals

 Application Exercise 11.2 Table 11.1: Observation of Teaching Strategies

PLAY   Early childhood teachers have historically placed play above all other teaching strategies. Through self-initiated play in a planned learning environment, children develop skills and knowledge of many kinds. In play, they enjoy themselves and become motivated to keep exploring and learning.

Young children need many opportunities for play each day. How and when do you plan for play? When you purposefully provide play opportunities that support the curriculum you have chosen, you are planning for play. For example, to support one child's fine motor development, you might plan to provide opportunities for all the children to play with clay, play dough, or stringing beads. To support the development of the understanding of concepts of volume and measurement, you might plan for open-ended play activities with water, sand, and containers of different sizes. To develop understanding of people, you plan to ensure that children have lots of time to play with one another. And while children are playing, you can be teaching (see Figure 11.1).

Figure 11.1 Some Strategies for Teaching While Children Play

Intentionally wait. Allow children time for purposeful play, mindful struggle, and independent discovery.

Observe and make notes while children are playing to inform your planning.

Play with children to build relationships and help them develop play skills. Model how to play (how to use toys, take on roles, support other players). Sensitively join the play without taking it over or interfering.

Acknowledge and encourage children who are working on a skill. Physically or verbally acknowledge them and encourage them to persevere.

Scaffold (support) children as they develop a skill or concept during play by physically or verbally helping them only as much as they need. As a child acquires a skill or concept, gradually withdraw assistance until the child is able to be independent.

Adjust the challenge. Be alert to the signs that a child needs a different (harder or easier) challenge. If a toy is misused, if children destroy or walk away from their work, or if a child finishes a project without thought or attention, it may be that the level is wrong.

SOURCE: Based on information from E. Moravcik, & S. Nolte, Meaningful Curriculum for Young Children, 2nd edition 2018.

SOURCE: Jeff Reese

Play is the most appropriate learning medium when you want children to explore and discover for themselves. You can also plan for play while using an integrated curriculum study. For example, in the study of birds that we use as an example in this chapter, teachers planned for play by adding bird puppets, toy birds, and cloth hoods colored and shaped like the crests of birds to the dramatic play and block areas to encourage children to reenact their developing understanding of birds.

SCAFFOLDED ACTIVITIES   Do you remember learning to drive a car? It's unlikely you would have developed driving skill by playing with a car. You also probably would not have learned if you had attended a lecture class on driving. Instead, you learned when you were ready and interested with the guidance from someone more competent than yourself. New abilities are first developed in collaboration with an adult or more competent peer in what Vygotsky called the zone of proximal development (Berk & Winsler, 1995).

When you want to help a child acquire a concept or skill, you may want to plan a scaffolded activity with that child. This kind of planned activity enables you to concentrate on a particular child's learning process in a learning dialogue. As you work together, you observe and assess a child's knowledge and skill and modify what you do based on the child's response. You can plan to support the development of skills and concepts for an individual child, skills and concepts that you want all the children to develop, or support the development of the major understandings of a topic of study. For example, in the study of birds that we describe in this chapter, the teachers prepared several workjobs (simple teacher-made games that help children learn concepts and develop skills) that were introduced to children individually: one involved counting birds in fine art postcards, another involved matching photographs of different birds that inhabited the playground, and another involved sequencing the stages of a bird's development from hatching to fledgling.

Group size, teacher–child ratio, and the way you organize both time and the physical environment will influence the extent to which you can engage in teacher–child activities. The smaller the group and the more that self-selected independent activities are supported, the more you will be able to engage in one-on-one activities with children. This is why low teacher–child ratios and smaller group sizes are hallmarks of quality in early childhood settings (Phillips, Mekos, Scarr, McCartney, & Abbott-Shim, 2000).

GROUP ACTIVITIES   **Small-Group Activities.** When you work with a few children at a time, it is called a small group. The size of a small group varies with the age of the children. For toddlers, a small group is 2 to 4 children. With preschoolers, a small group may be 5 to 10 children, though fewer is better, especially for 3-year-olds. And with kindergarten and primary school children, 8 to 12 children is a small group—though, again, fewer is better.

A small group size helps you present concepts, facilitate conversations between children, and have meaningful personal contact with each child. It is probably the most effective teaching strategy for preschool and primary children. This approach reduces waiting time and allows for activities that involve turn taking, guided peer interaction, manipulation of materials, and quite a lot of teacher assistance.

In a small group, you are able to attend to the way children respond and can evaluate and modify what you do. When you have children with diverse developmental

Video Example 11.2: Scaffolding Using an Eye-Dropper

Watch this video to see a teacher scaffolding a child who is learning to use an eyedropper. What do you notice about what the teacher does? Why do you think she stopped instructing the child?

needs (as you do in any mixed-age classroom), you can tailor the length of the small-group time and the kind of activity to match the children. For example, a planned process for naming groups in a class of children aged 2½ through 5 took place in two small groups divided by age. The younger group spent 10 minutes thinking of and naming their group (the Flowers). The older group spent three 15-minute group times on subsequent days brainstorming, negotiating, and voting for their small-group name (the Cloud-Airplanes).

If you need to discuss an activity with the children while it is happening, then a small group is the best choice. Activities such as *I Spy*, discussions, acting out stories, creative movement, cooking, and walks work best in small groups.

Small groups that meet together on a regular basis develop an identity of their own. They help children develop some important skills, including the ability to listen and converse in a group, solve problems and make decisions democratically, take leader and follower roles, and accept responsibility for the outcomes of their decisions.

Large-Group Activities. Large-group activities (planned for a group of more than 10 children) are generally the least effective for teaching and the hardest for teachers to implement successfully. This may account for the fact that they are often named by children as their least favorite activities in school (Wiltz & Klein, 2001).

In most classrooms, children gather together at least once a day for a large group meeting, often called circle time. These gatherings can be valuable when they allow children to share a common experience and build a sense of community. In preschool, they are appropriate only when all children can be active (e.g., singing and creative movement). Older children can benefit from appropriate large-group activities that do not require a great deal of passive listening (e.g., show-and-tell) or when children must wait a long time for a short turn (e.g., in cooking). They can be effective for story time, singing, and group games. In general, the younger the children the fewer large-group experiences you plan.

Video Example 11.3: Small-Group Activities in a Study of Birds

Watch this video to see several examples of small group activities in the study of birds. What does the small group format allow the teacher to do? How does the teacher demonstrate interest in the learning?

Video Example 11.4: Large-Group Activities as Part of a Study of Pets

Watch this video to see an example of a large-group activity. What differences do you notice between the large group and the small group experience for children? Which do you feel is a more effective learning experience? Why?

SELECTING A TEACHING METHOD There are many hundreds of different kinds of activities that can deliver early childhood curriculum. You will select those that best match your children, that meaningfully address the content, and that you can present effectively in your setting. The relative balance of child-directed activities and teacher-guided activities will vary based on the characteristics of the children as well as on the characteristics of the program. Both processes have advantages and disadvantages and are most appropriate for different kinds of content. For example, it is unlikely that a 5-year-old would spontaneously learn to read a clock or tie shoelaces without individual help from a teacher. Similarly, it is unlikely that any amount of planned activity would teach that same 5-year-old to climb a rope, although he or she might learn to do so in focused, self-initiated play.

Infants, toddlers, and pre-schoolers learn little through direct instruction. Both you and the children will feel frustrated if you try to tell children what you want them to learn. As they get older, children will learn from guided teaching if they are interested and motivated. Every educator will seek an optimal balance between child-directed and teacher-guided activity. As you plan, you need to ask yourself which approach best meets the developmental characteristics of the children and your educational purposes. The answer to this question will help you find the right balance.

Choosing Appropriate Methods and Avoiding Inappropriate Methods We know that young children learn at varying rates, are active learners, learn through play, and need many opportunities to practice skills as they are acquired (Copple & Bredekamp, 2009). They learn through active engagement and concrete experiences. Because we know these things, we also know they do not benefit from abstract methods of teaching, such as worksheets, lectures, and drill on isolated skills. These methods of teaching are inappropriate.

Observe a young child who is required to sit still and listen to an adult try to teach a fact out of context. Chances are good that you will see a child who is inattentive or disruptive. In addition to knowing what methods are *appropriate* for young children, you also need to be able to identify and avoid *inappropriate* methods. Inappropriate teaching methods do not build understanding and, because they are often aversive, can lead to negative feelings toward schooling. They do not belong in programs for preschool and kindergarten children. They have limited utility in programs for primary school children. When you observe a child who is actively engaged in a hands-on learning experience relating to a topic of interest it is different! When children are focused and joyful, the teaching you are observing is appropriate.

Figure 11.2 The Planning Process

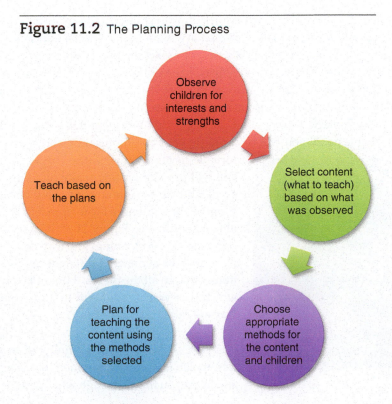

Reflect On

Curriculum You Have Observed

Think of an early childhood program you know. What did you see children doing? How could you tell the children were learning? During what kinds of activities did you sense the children were most engaged?

A Quick Check 11.3

Gauge your understanding of the concepts in this section.

Writing Plans to Guide Teaching

When early childhood teachers use the word plan they can mean different things. Sometimes, they mean a detailed outline for a learning activity, called an activity plan or **lesson plan**. At other times, they mean a calendar of activities for the week, sometimes called a **weekly plan**. They may also mean a plan for several weeks of activities, addressing many different subject areas, based on a topic, called an **integrated plan**.

Teachers of infants and young toddlers usually write plans for individual children and for ways to modify the environment. Preschool and primary teachers usually write a weekly calendar to share with others and keep track of what happens next. In some preschools and most kindergartens and primary schools, teachers write short complete activity or lesson plans with objectives for many of the activities in a day or a week. If the group includes children with disabilities or other special needs, special education teachers write lesson plans just for each of these children.

Activity or Lesson Plans

A detailed written design for a single curriculum event is usually called an **activity plan** in preschools and a lesson plan in elementary schools and special education settings. These specify objectives, list materials, describe teaching procedures, and outline ways to assess success in achieving the objectives. To be useful, an activity or lesson plan must be brief, specific, and complete. You can think of such a plan as a recipe for teaching. Like a recipe, it outlines each essential step but assumes that you know the basics.

Carefully thinking through and writing an activity plan helps you teach. When your planning is good, you will be clearer in your communication and feel more comfortable in teaching. Because this is so valuable, you will practice writing many plans during your preparation to become an early childhood educator. We give our students a basic format to use in planning activities (see Figure 11.3). It includes a typical sequence for planning. The way you write your plans may be somewhat different. As long as you think through all the pieces, it doesn't really matter which part you write down first or what exactly they are called.

WHAT AND WHY The beginning of an activity/lesson plan is a brief explanation that sets the stage and helps you think through what you are going to

SOURCE: Jeff Reese

Figure 11.3 Format for a Detailed Activity Plan

Activity name & description

Primary curriculum area

Who it's for

Rationale (why you have chosen this activity for these children at this time)

Objectives By participating in this activity the children will . . .

Standard(s) (state or national)

What You Need

Materials/equipment	Space/time	Preparation/setup

Teaching

Introduction: (how to begin so children will be interested and know what to do)

Teaching steps: (what to do and say step-by-step to provide the experiences that will teach children the concepts, develop the skills, build the attitudes or dispositions that are described in the objectives)

Closure: (what you will do or say to reinforce/support what children have learned and help them make a transition to another activity)

Plan for assessment (what to look for to identify if the objectives were met and how to document)

Objective	If the objective is met children might . . .	How to document
objectives from the first part of the plan	things a child might do or say during the activity if objectives were met things a child might do or say later during play, routines, or other activities if objectives were met	Observations, work samples, photographs, etc.

do with children and why. The first thing you have to do is decide what you are going to plan. To do that, you need to think about your particular circumstances—what you have observed about individual children and the group, the resources and limitations of the setting, the families, and the standards and expectations of the program:

Activity name and description.   Every teaching activity has a name you use to talk about it. It can be classified by type (e.g., a game, a discussion, or a book). If you are writing plans to share with others (colleagues, families, or your college professor), give your activity a name that communicates what you are going to do and briefly describe it.

Primary curriculum area.   Good early childhood teaching activities address a number of curriculum areas. Identifying the curriculum area that is going to be the primary focus is helpful for a number of reasons when you are learning to plan. When you are clear about the curriculum area you are more likely to accomplish your purpose. For example, children engaged in a finger-painting activity are developing sensory awareness and fine motor control (physical development), learning about how colors change (science), expressing feelings with paint (art), and having conversations as you talk with them about the experience (language). If your primary curriculum area and purpose is to help children express feelings using art media, you will call this an art activity. And you will want to use good-quality paint and paper in order to preserve children's efforts. You will focus your teaching and comments on children's awareness of how their work expresses a feeling or idea ("Your swirls of gray remind me of a stormy cloud"). If your primary curriculum area and purpose is to enhance children's awareness of texture, you will call this a sensory activity. You might use colored shaving cream on a tray that can be easily hosed off and that leaves no lasting documentation. Again, your comments and teaching will be targeted: "How does the paint feel against your fingers? Is it slick or sticky? Sniff it. What does it remind you of?"

Who it's for: the children.   You are planning for specific children at a specific time in a specific place. When you write a plan, it is valuable to note on the plan the individuals you are planning for, the name of the group, and the age and number of children for whom you are planning.

Rationale.   What you observed provides the rationale, or reason, for your plan. We believe that writing a statement of rationale is one of the most useful things you can do to help yourself become an intentional teacher. We ask our college students to write a rationale statement that answers the question: "Why have you chosen this activity for this child/these children at this time?" This is different from a statement of objectives. Your answer ("I have chosen this activity for the Elephant Groovers because I observed that they enjoy and are interested in sensory activities.") helps you make sure that what you are doing has some meaningful connection to the children.

Objectives.   Every written activity has objectives: attitudes, skills, concepts, and experiences you want to help children acquire. An important part of your professional role is articulating the area of learning and the purpose of the activities you do with children (whether or not you have written a plan for it). Being able to do so distinguishes you as a professional teacher. It is rare for a single activity to "teach" a skill, understanding, or attitude for all time. Instead, think of objectives as drops of rain contributing to filling a pool.

Another category of objective for which we plan is the acquisition of "dispositions," what Lilian Katz (1993) calls "habits of mind." Curiosity is an example of a disposition that we want children to acquire. There are many other dispositions that we wish to encourage—a disposition to read, a disposition to be kind, and a disposition to be resourceful or to ask questions. When you plan curriculum activities for children, it is valuable to remember that these dispositions are important objectives.

The objectives describe a plan's intended outcomes in terms of the abilities, knowledge, experiences, and dispositions that you want children to gain. For example, for a music activity, you might write any of the following objectives—though you are likely to only choose one or two:

By participating in this activity, children will:

- Learn the term tempo and understand that tempo means the speed at which a song is played or sung
- Develop beginning ability to play simple rhythm instruments with care
- Hear and begin to appreciate music from another culture
- Understand music can express feelings and develop a disposition to express feelings through music.

The age-group of children and the program in which you work will determine the kinds of objectives you choose. Objectives for pre-schoolers may be broader than those for elementary age children and may include involvement, awareness, and appreciation as well as concepts, understandings, and skills to be acquired. The objectives should relate to the rationale. They should be achievable by doing the activity. It is reasonable for a music activity to help children to hear and begin to appreciate music from another culture. It is not reasonable to expect that same music activity to help children to be accepting of people who are different from themselves.

Objectives can be thought of as progressing from simple to complex (see Table 11.2). Simple objectives involve recalling and identifying. More complex objectives involve

Table 11.2 Bloom's Taxonomy of Educational Objectives

Level	What It Is
Recall	The ability to repeat or recognize a concept or skill
Comprehension	Understanding and the ability to explain what is known
Application	The ability to use what is known
Analysis	The ability to make connections, see patterns, or understand interrelationships
Synthesis	The ability to integrate and recombine
Evaluation	The ability to assess, critique, or appraise based on specific criteria

(Left axis: Most complex → Least complex)

SOURCE: Based on Bloom et al. (1964).

making connections, understanding relationships, solving problems by combining what is known, and evaluating (Bloom, Mesia, & Krathwohl, 1964). As you write objectives, it is useful to consider whether your objectives and your activities are helping children acquire more complex skills. For example, in the objectives for the music activity just described, the first objective (learn the term tempo) is a simple objective—recall; the second objective involves application (beginning ability to play simple rhythm instruments with care); and the fourth (understand music can express feelings and develop a disposition to express feelings through music) is more complex and involves evaluation.

When you begin to write plans, you may find that writing objectives is not easy. There are many things to consider. Our college students find it helpful to look at a number of beginnings to objectives to get started (see Table 11.3).

Objectives that precisely describe a behavior are called measurable or **behavioral objectives**. They describe specific behaviors, the conditions under which they take place, and the criteria for success ("When presented with five sheets of paper with lines drawn down the center, the child will cut at least one sheet of paper along the line."). There are different points of view regarding how specific and measurable objectives ought to be. For example, we think it is reasonable for a music activity to help children begin to develop a disposition to use music to express feelings. However, because this disposition is not measurable, some educators reject this objective.

Behavioral objectives leave little room for individual choice, require all children to be at the same place at the end of a lesson, and do not allow for spontaneity or creativity. They are frequently used in special education, where teaching is often quite prescriptive. They are not consistent with the belief that children must construct knowledge from their own active involvement with materials and experiences. Because they

Table 11.3 Examples of Beginnings for Objectives

Knowledge/Concepts	Skill	Attitude	Experience
Learn about . . .	Practice . . .	Develop awareness of . . .	Try . . .
Understand . . .	Develop the ability to . . .	Develop a disposition to . . .	Explore . . .
Describe . . .	Begin to . . .	Be sensitive to . . .	Examine . . .
			Perceive . . .
			Hear
Recognize . . .	Become proficient at . . .	Be respectful of . . .	See
			Taste
			Smell
			Touch
Identify . . .	Compare/Contrast . . .	Appreciate . . .	

sometimes focus on trivial though achievable goals, they can lead teachers to emphasize less important aspects of activities and lose track of important learning that isn't observable or measurable.

Measurable objectives can help you demonstrate that your teaching has had an effect. When you are required to write them, it is important to learn how to do so in ways that have integrity.

Standards.   To show how you are teaching to meet your state or program's guidelines, we recommend identifying the relevant standards for activity/lesson plans along with the objectives. Many teachers find it helpful to have a copy of their state early learning guidelines or program standards close at hand as they write plans. Because most of these are available online, this can simplify the process of writing plans. Even if you are not required to use standards in your written plans, you may find it helpful to use them as a guide for wording.

WHAT YOU NEED   Once you have selected what you are going to do and identified objectives, the next step is to begin to think through what you will need for your activity. As with a recipe, you need all the ingredients to make your plan work. Make a list of the materials that you need to have at hand. Think about the space and equipment you need, the best time for the activity, and how much time to allow. Consider what you need to prepare. Does anyone need to be alerted? Do you need to cut paper? Plan for it.

As you think through the steps of the activity and write down the procedures, you may discover that there are additional things you need. You will go back and add these.

THE TEACHING PROCEDURES   Teaching procedures spell out what you will do and say and in what order. They are the heart of a plan for teaching. Procedures generally include three parts—an introduction, steps to teach the objectives, and closure.

The *introduction* describes how you will get children's attention, engage their interest, and let them know what to do. For many activities, the introduction can be very simple: "I brought a new game to share with you today. It's this box. There is something soft inside. You can put your hand in here and guess what it is."

If the activity involves an unfamiliar word, concept, or skill, you may need to introduce it. If the activity involves an item that is new or highly attractive, plan a way for children to get acquainted with it (e.g., "Each person will get a turn to pat the puppet before I tell you the puppet story."). Skilled teachers know that it is important to give children lots of time for a new experience. In fact, simply introducing an item may be an entire activity. One of the most common mistakes of novice teachers is to introduce many intriguing objects at one time. They are then surprised when children focus on the "things" rather than the content they tried to teach.

Teaching steps describe what you will do and say to accomplish your objectives. The steps should match the objectives you wrote and should be appropriate for the children. The amount of detail you write in a plan will vary. You need an outline of the basic steps, with enough information so that you (or a colleague) will be able to follow it. Beginning teachers and anyone planning a complex activity should map out what to say to support the objectives. A common mistake of novice teachers is to plan an elaborate introduction without planning how to help children acquire the concepts, skills, or dispositions. As you gain experience, you will not need to plan as much detail. But while you are learning, detailed planning is more than a class assignment—it will help you learn to think like a teacher.

Closure ends the activity, sums up the learning, and helps children to make a transition. It should make sense for children. It may include a statement ("You really knew a lot about birds."), or a way for children to show something that they know ("Think of a bird and fly like your bird to the playground."). A well-thought-out closure and a smooth transition help you focus children on what they know and are able to do (see Figure 11.4).

Figure 11.4 Detailed Activity/Lesson Plan Example

Activity name & description	***The Names of the Birds Workjob***: A table game in which children match photographs of birds with printed names
Primary curriculum area.	Literacy
Who it's for	4- to 5-year-olds in the Lion Dancers Group (esp. Megan, Jonah, Janae, and Edwin)—introduce to group of 9 children, and work with 2–3 at a time
Rationale	The children are highly aware of the different birds in the yard and what they are called. Megan, Jonah, Janae, and Edwin are particularly intrigued by letters and words.
Objectives	*By participating in this activity the children will . . .* 1. understand print has meaning 2. begin to connect sounds to letters 3. build vocabulary (beak, crest, tail, whiskered, wings, cardinal, dove, egret, finch, mejiro, northern, plover, sparrow)
Standard(s) head start and early learning outcomes framework	Domain: Literacy **Goal P-LIT 2.** Child demonstrates an understanding of how print is used (functions of print) and the rules that govern how print works (conventions of print). Domain: Language and Communication **Goal P-LC 5.** Child expresses self in increasingly long, detailed, and sophisticated ways.

What you need			
	Materials/equipment	***Space/time***	***Preparation/setup***
	Workjob in a box Table with chairs	Table Games area Introduce at small group and teach during activity time	Download photos of yard birds size picture (2.5″ × 2.5″). Print 2 copies of each one with name of bird underneath. Laminate. Print names separately. Laminate. Decorate box with picture/title.

Teaching

Introduction:	At small group time show the game. Spread out cards. Pick a card with familiar bird. Invite children to name bird. Point out the name written underneath. Explain: There is a matching picture for this bird. Ask: Can you find it? When found say: There's something even trickier. There's a word that matches. Can you find it? Once word has been found, explain the game will be available to play with during activity time. Say: You can play this on your own or with a friend.
Teaching steps:	During activity time as children play the game, observe, scaffold, and individualize by saying things like: That one says RED CRESTED CARDINAL. Can you find another with RED in its name? That one is a Mmmmmmejiro—I wonder what its name starts with. Encourage more able children to help those who have difficulty: I saw Megan find the Northern Cardinal's name. Ask her if she can help you. If a child has difficulty, suggest the child just match the pictures. If a child is having an easy time, invite the child to match the word to the word.
Closure:	End the activity: Tailored to ability, play a putting-away game, something like: You tell me one to put away and then I'll tell you one to put away. Acknowledge the learning: You know which one is the Northern Cardinal. I wonder if I'll be able to get the next one. Or: You know 10 different birds! Facilitate a transition: Tell me where you will play next.

Plan for assessment

Objective	*If the objective is met children might . . .*	How to document
1. Understand print has meaning	match words and pictures draw birds and ask teacher to write about the birds on their work	Anecdotal records Work samples
2. Connect sounds to letters	attempt to write bird name while saying name	
3. Build vocabulary	Say things like the cardinal and the red-crested cardinal have crests	

THE ASSESSMENT PLAN   What children do and say during and following an activity gives evidence of what they have learned. The last part of a plan describes what you will look for that shows children have gained the knowledge, skills, or attitudes in the objectives.

In our earlier example, we looked for whether children were attentive to the music and asked questions about it or asked to have it repeated, whether they moved to the music, whether they played the instruments in ways that made sound and were rhythmic, and whether they began to recognize and use the names of the instruments. This growth could be documented through anecdotal records, through video or audio recordings, or even through work samples— children's drawings and journals. We like to use an anecdotal record form like the sample included in Figure 11.5 to record children's responses.

IMPLEMENTING, ASSESSING, AND EVALUATION   Although a good plan helps you teach in the same way that a good recipe helps you cook, children are not as predictable as flour and salt. The best planned activity can fail miserably if you are not responsive to children. If you went to a lot of trouble to write a plan, you may feel committed to using it the way it's written. Just as a cook must adjust to the diners, the ingredients, and the equipment, a teacher must adjust to the children and the circumstances. Experienced teachers know they need to make modifications. Their teaching resembles a dance in which children are their partners. They observe and respond to the children—and the children respond to them.

Inexperienced teachers often find it difficult to be flexible. For example, we observed a student teacher attempting to lead a group of 4-year-olds in a movement

Figure 11.5 Anecdotal Records

Activity: *The Names of the Birds Workjob*

Child: *Megan*

Played game first. Matched all pictures, then matched half the words. Said words as she worked: myna, mejiro, cardinal. Later went to writing table and drew a Brazilian cardinal and wrote letter B and K (see work sample).

Objective demonstrated: OB 1, 2, & 3
Comment: *First inventive spelling?*

Child: *Jonah*

Wanted teacher to play with him. When teacher had "difficulty" finding pieces J laughed aloud—found pieces, said name of bird, said: I am very good at this.

Objective demonstrated: OB 1
Comment: *Seems confident; likes the idea of reading.*

Child: *Janae*

Did about half the game matching pictures and words. Asked: Which one is the mommy bird, how does she lay her eggs? Then went to writing center and drew a picture of mother bird with eggs and asked the teacher to write explanation (see work sample).

Objective demonstrated: OB 1, 2, & 3
Comment: *Ready to use reference materials?*

Child: *Keila*

Looked and matched the cardinal pictures then left—did not put pieces away.

Objective demonstrated: OB 1
Comment: *Didn't seem very interested.*

Child: *Edwin*

Took out each set (pictures and words, pictures only, words only) and lined up. Matched all. Did not interact with other child during activity. Wrote bird names in writing center using cards as model (see work sample).

Objective demonstrated: OB 1 & 2
Comment: *Very serious!*

Child: *Brandy*

Smiled a lot during intro. Made several comments—egret does not come to bird feeder, there are two kinds of sparrows—Did not try the game.

Objective demonstrated: OB 3
Comment: *Does not yet show much interest in print.*

activity (walking as a group like a centipede with many legs). The children had many things to say about centipedes and did not attend to the planned activity. The novice teacher became flustered and was unable to find a way to use their ideas in the activity. With more confidence and attention to the children, their ideas could have contributed to the activity instead of detracting from it.

Assessing Children   The measure of your success as a planner is whether children learned what you intended to teach. If you observe children carefully, you will see evidence of whether they have or have not gained the knowledge, skill, or attitudes that were your objectives. In the example in Figure 11.4, the teacher would watch to see if children matched words and pictures in the game, created images of birds using art media, and asked the teacher to write about their work or if the children used bird-related vocabulary. This growth could be documented through anecdotal records like those in Figure 11.5 or work samples that could be annotated (see Figure 11.6) to provide documentation of children's learning.

While it is valuable to document children's learning, it is important to make sure that the documentation authentically shows what children have actually learned. A photograph of a child posing for the camera rarely provides evidence of learning.

Evaluate the Plan: What Worked and What Didn't Work   Whether you plan an activity with children or a party for your friends, you evaluate your plan. Did it go well? Could it have gone better? Is it worth doing again? Did it accomplish what I intended? After you have written and implemented a plan, take a few moments (that's probably all you'll have!) to reflect on what you did and how children responded. This ensures that the experience you planned for children also is a learning experience for you.

Figure 11.6 Annotated Work Sample

The Mama bird makes eggs with baby birds inside.
They come out right there under her tail.

Child: Janae

Following playing the "Name of the Birds Workjob," Janae went to the writing center and drew the above picture. She asked the teacher to write her words: *The Mama bird makes eggs with baby birds inside. They come out right there under her butt.* When the teacher read the words back to her Janae asked the teacher to change it: *The Mama bird makes eggs with baby birds inside. They come out right there under her tail.*

Objective demonstrated: OB 1, 2, & 3

Comment: Janae demonstrated growing understanding of both science and literacy.

SOURCE: Reprinted with permission from Leah Schnabel.

Figure 11.7 Evaluation

> ***Evaluation, comments, what to do next:***
>
> The activity went fairly well. It was interesting to most kids. Too many pictures, too small—next time limit the number of pictures when introducing game, and add a set of pet bird pictures and words.

Evaluating your planning is different from assessing whether the children acquired the objectives for the activity, as you can see in Figure 11.7.

Sometimes, a teaching disaster may be the result of the wrong materials, timing mistakes (not allowing enough time for children to explore materials or asking them to wait and listen when they need to move and do), poor room arrangement, insufficient opportunities for physical activity, or expectations that are too challenging or not challenging enough for the children. Modified and tried again, the plan may prove sound. But if you don't reflect on what happened, you will never be able to figure out what went wrong and make changes.

It may be even harder to evaluate a success. Were the children engaged in the activity because the materials were interesting, because you were responsive to the children, or because Jon was absent today? Evaluate your successes as well as your failures.

It is worthwhile to make a note of anything you would add or do differently on the plan. When you go back to your plans, you will remember what happened last time. Reflecting and evaluating and planning what to do next closes the planning circle.

Reflect On

Planning for Children

Think about a time when you planned an activity to do with children. What happened? How did having a plan help you? What happened that surprised you? Would you use your plan again? What would you do differently?

WRITING ACTIVITY/LESSON PLANS IN THE REAL WORLD   When you become a teacher, will you write plans for every activity? It would be impossible and a little silly to spend hours writing plans for everything you do with children. Written plans are useful and necessary when clarity and sequence are crucial or where procedure or content is complex or unfamiliar. An activity such as reading a simple, familiar story will be included in a weekly plan but generally does not call for a detailed written plan. Locating the book, reviewing it, and spending a few moments thinking about questions to ask and how to structure discussion may be enough preparation. However, you should be *able* to write a clear plan for even a simple activity.

Experienced teachers use a simplified format, such as the one in Figure 11.8, for activity plans. We like to keep these so that they can be easily retrieved and used again—in a digital file, in a notebook, or on 5-by-8 cards in file boxes or on metal rings. Digital storage allows you to easily retrieve and revise plans, but because technology changes, you may find digital versions unreadable in a few years, so it is wise to also keep a hard copy.

Weekly Plans

Experienced teachers almost always plan for each week by writing down the names of the activities, identifying when they will be implemented, and noting what will be needed (see the example in Figure 11.9). They identify objectives for the activities,

Figure 11.8 Simple Format Activity Plan

Activity: Names of Birds Workjob

Curriculum Area: Literacy

Objectives: To help children . . .

1. Understand print has meaning

2. Connect sounds to letters

3. Build vocabulary.

Standards: Head Start Child Development and Early Learning Framework Literacy Knowledge & Skills print concepts & conventions and Language Development receptive & expressive

What you need: Workjob in a box

How to teach:

1. Show/Explain game at small group. Invite children to play in game center.

2. At center extend learning. Encourage more able children to help those who have difficulty.

3. Play a putting-away game.

How to assess: Children match words to pictures, create pictures/write about birds, or use bird vocabulary.

Figure 11.9 Preschool Weekly Plan

A Study of Birds • Week 4

Objectives for the week: To help children to . . . build understanding of the habits, needs, and habitats of birds; build skill in representing ideas and feelings symbolically; acquire greater ability to cooperate as members of a community

	Monday	Tuesday	Wednesday	Thursday	Friday
Story 8:50	*One Crow*—Aylesworth	*What Makes a Bird a Bird?*—Garelick	*Do Like a Duck Does*–Hindley and Bates	Learning Trip to Audubon Nature Park	*Tough Boris*—Mem Fox
Outdoor Activity 9:00–10:00 *Activity purposes: to help children to . . .*	**Parachute Play**	**Build a Waffle Blocks Structure**	**Woodworking: Making a Brooder House**	*Trip Purpose—to give children experience with diverse birds and help them understand birds' needs, habits, and habitats*	**Bubbles in the Water Table**
	develop large motor coordination *work cooperatively with others*	*build large motor coordination* *work together cooperatively*	*use measurement tools* *acquire concepts of shape and space*	*Reminders:* • Bring a sack lunch that does not require refrigeration. • Wear secure shoes.	*develop sensory awareness* *learn about cause and effect*
Small Group (4–5 year-olds) 10:00–10:20 *Activity purposes: to help children to . . .*	**Bird Clay Sculpture**	**Clay Sculpture**	**Trip Prediction**—*What Might We See at the Nature Park?*	• Apply bug repellent before school, if desired. • Be here by 8:00—the bus will leave at 8:15. • Families are welcome to come on this trip. • We will be back by 1:30.	**Make a Book About the Trip**
	learn art techniques (modeling and sculpting) *explore shapes and gain awareness of birds' bodies*	*practice art techniques (modeling and sculpting)* *explore shape and space*	*prepare for field trip* *develop the ability to hypothesize*		*understand the purpose of print* *reconstruct understanding of birds' needs, habits, and habitats*

(continued)

Figure 11.9 Continued

	Monday	Tuesday	Wednesday	Thursday	Friday
Small Group (3–4 year-olds) 10:00–10:10 *Activity purposes: to help children to . . .*	**Move Like a Bird**	**Move Like a Bird**	**Trip Discussion—** *What Might We See at the Nature Park?*		**Look at Pictures of the Trip**
	express ideas through movement *develop awareness of birds* *increase large motor coordination*	*express ideas through movement* *develop awareness of birds* *increase large motor coordination*	*prepare for field trip* *develop the ability to hypothesize*		*develop understanding of birds' needs, habits, and habitats*
Indoor Activity 10:20–11:30 *Activity purposes: to help children to . . .*	**Clay Sculpture Using Tools**	**Clay Sculpture Using Tools**	**Feather Collage (also clay for two)**		**Play Dough Collage**
	practice art techniques (modeling and sculpting) *explore shape and space*	*practice art techniques (modeling and sculpting)* *explore shape and space*	*learn about art elements of color, texture, and design* *create and express ideas using a variety of art media*		*build fine motor control* *use art elements of color and design*
Circle Time 11:30–11:45 *Activity purposes: to help children to . . .*	**Manu Lai Titi (Pretty Little Birdie) Song and Movement**	**Manu Lai Titi (Pretty Little Birdie) Song and Movement**	**Los Pollitos (Baby Chicks) Song and Movement**		**Los Pollitos (Baby Chicks) Song and Movement**
	express ideas through music / movement *develop awareness of birds, develop awareness of language and cultural diversity*	*express ideas through music / movement* *develop awareness of birds, develop awareness of language and cultural diversity*	*express ideas through music and movement* *develop awareness of birds, develop awareness of language and cultural diversity*		*express ideas through music / movement* *develop awareness of birds, develop awareness of language and cultural diversity*
Learning Centers	**Block area**—add bird figures, tree blocks.	**Pretend area**—add bird hoods and bird puppets.	**Manipulatives area**—add new bird puzzle.	**Writing area**—bird word cards.	**Discovery area**—visiting birds: zebra finches.
Outdoor Zones	**Social-dramatic** zone—add boots and hats.	**Active play** zone—add rickshaw trikes.	**Natural elements** zone—sand in the sensory table.	**Manipulative creative** zone—palette painting at the easel.	

To Do Bring in supplies for the brooder house: recycled wood and plexiglass, have Jonah's dad cut wood and plexiglass for brooder house—he has the plan, put up poster (Monday) and e-mail reminder to parents (Wednesday) about learning trip

How It Went—What We Changed: Clay sculpture was surprisingly successful. Children consulted pictures of birds as well as the visiting finches as models. The trip was wonderful! Following the trip we added a new suet feeder to the yard.
Assessment of Objectives: Children talked about the birds and what they needed and showed their understanding in the book.

though not all teachers write these down. These few notes may guide them through most activities. More important, mapping out the week helps them to sequence learning for children. It helps them to ensure that there is balance and continuity in the program.

Writing a weekly plan helps you think through what you will do and stay organized. It also helps to keep the teaching team on track. Many teachers post their weekly plans in the classroom and send copies or e-mail them to families so that they know what's coming up and can participate in the program.

For most preschool teachers and many kindergarten teachers, the schedule of regular daily activities (e.g., story, small group, circle, and outdoor play) and special weekly events (e.g., cooking and field trips) provides a structure for weekly plans. Many also include the ways they will modify learning centers each week.

As you plan for a week, keep in mind the skills and concepts you want all the children to develop as well as plans for specific children. Include routines that are a feature of the week (e.g., cooking or a weekly visit from an adopted grandparent) and activities related to a curriculum focus (e.g., trips or visitors). Consider the impact of events in the school, among families, or in the community (e.g., holidays, elections, seasonal activities, bake sales, or open house). In addition to planning the activities, write a short statement of objectives for the week.

Teachers vary in the amount of detail they include in weekly plans. Some include an objective or purpose statement for each activity. Some include a list of materials to prepare or things to do. When the week is over, a brief assessment can be written directly on it and kept for future reference.

Connecting with Families

Using Weekly Plans

Families want to know what their children do each day, and they want to know why you teach the way you do. You can let them know and help them be more involved by sharing your weekly calendar. Doing this encourages families to talk with their children about school! There are several ways to do this:

1. Post the weekly plan by the entrance so that families can read it when they drop off and pick up their children.

2. Send a copy of the plan home each week so that families can post and refer to it.

3. E-mail a copy to families each week.

A Quick Check 11.4

Gauge your understanding of the concepts in this section.

Integrated Curriculum Planning

As we have said, we believe that the most effective way to organize curriculum for older preschool, kindergarten, or primary school children is through integrated studies. In addition, it is an interesting and satisfying way for teachers to plan.

In a well-designed integrated study, children have many real experiences with a topic. These experiences are the foundation of the study and are critical. They provide content for children to reflect on, represent, read about, and re-create through dramatic play, block building, discussions, writing, drawing, art, music, movement, measuring, graphing, and mapping. This is how children learn concepts and develop skills.

An effective integrated study starts with the investigation of something tangible that is meaningful to young children. Because the study will last several weeks to several months it needs to be interesting and complex enough to engage both children and adults. A good integrated study helps children investigate meaningful ideas. It is appropriate to the individuals and group, flexible, and meaningful.

There are different approaches to integrated curriculum (see Figure 11.10). However, all are created in a dynamic process that involves initial planning, providing

Figure 11.10 Comparison of Approaches to Integrated Curriculum

1. **Appropriate Approaches to Integrated Curriculum**

   Developmental Interaction Approach—Curriculum is integrated around a social studies topic selected by the teacher based on knowledge of children and the learning potential of the topic. The topic is investigated in depth over several weeks through learning trips and follow-up through play and planned activities (blocks, dramatic play, writing, art, etc.). The community of the classroom is emphasized. A culminating activity ends the study.

   Reggio Approach—The teacher and children select an in-depth project. Many modes or "languages" are used for children to express their growing knowledge. Strong emphasis is placed on the arts and the learning environment. Less emphasis is placed on ensuring that every area of curriculum is addressed. Teachers collect and prepare documentation of children's projects to share with families and the community.

   Project Approach—The teacher and children select a project that is of high interest to the particular group. Research is conducted to answer questions posed by the children and/or teacher. The project has three distinct phases: (1) introduction/initial assessment of knowledge, (2) research and representation of learning, and (3) culmination and sharing.

   Emergent Curriculum—A child or group of children with their teacher explores a topic of particular interest. It may be quite small (e.g., Band-Aids) and fleeting (a day, a week), but more typically lasts for several weeks. The teacher webs ideas for activities, and then designs experiences to expand on children's interest.

   "Deep" Unit/Theme—A study is selected by the teacher based on knowledge of the children and the learning potential of the topic. The topic is investigated over 1–3 months through learning trips and follow-up activities. The process for creating the study is not established, but plans are created by the teacher.

2. **Inppropriate Approach to Integrated Curriculum**

   "Shallow" Unit/Theme—In a shallow unit or theme a topic is selected by the teacher or program administrator based on the calendar, tradition, or whim. In a shallow unit the topic is an organizing motif for a brief 1- to 2-week period during which few (if any) real experiences are provided. Because the activities are often abstract and unconnected activities (e.g., worksheets, songs, games) shallow units/themes do not serve children, teachers, or our field well and bring integrated curriculum under fire for lacking intellectual integrity.

SOURCE: Based on information from E. Moravcik, and S. Nolte, *Meaningful Curriculum for Young Children*, 2nd ed. (2018).

experiences, observing children, and then planning additional opportunities for learning. In this chapter we introduce you to the basics of designing an integrated study.

Choose a Topic

Meaningful integrated curriculum based on a well-chosen topic helps children make connections. Some topics are better than others for the purpose of integrating curriculum. When the topic has been chosen well, there is an almost magical quality to the curriculum. Children are focused, energized, and intensely engaged in the business of learning. Teachers are excited and creative. Families are engaged and participate. In order for this to happen, the topic must meet several criteria:

1. **Interest.** The topic must be of interest to children, teachers, and families. For example, when the teacher and several mothers of children in a 4-year-old class became pregnant, a curriculum study of babies and birth was a natural focus. The teacher brought in many books, made a sequencing game of fetal development, helped children compose a simple lullaby, had babies and puppies visit, and took the children

on a trip to the local hospital to view the nursery. The children built a hospital in the block area, created a nursery in the dramatic play area, and painted and drew many pictures and wrote many stories about babies.

2. **Accessibility.** The topic of study must be accessible—you must be able to give children direct and frequent hands-on experience with the topic. If real experience is not available, the topic—no matter how interesting—will not lead to genuine understanding.

3. **Importance.** A topic needs to be worth knowing about, worthy of study. A good integrated study requires time, effort, and intellectual engagement on the part of children and teachers. It's not worth your time or that of the children to study something that is trivial and not worthy of intellectual engagement. What's important? The topic should be something that has an impact on children's lives. This can be something quite small such as the bugs on the playground or something quite large like the water on which we all depend. If it is worth learning about for children it is also a topic worthy of study by adults.

4. **Size.** Finally, you should consider whether the topic of study you choose is the right size for children's age and stage of development: simple enough to be understood but complex and interesting enough to be explored in some depth. It should involve concepts and skills that provide the right level of challenge. We call this the "three bears" principle (not too easy, not too hard, but "just right"). We have found that topics that are too broad (e.g., "animals," "nature," "change") don't provide enough focus. Topics that are too small (e.g., "pasta") don't sustain interest or provide enough to learn about.

Many topics are interesting, accessible, worth knowing, and the right size and can be used for successful integration of subject areas. We have seen teachers of preschoolers plan successful integrated studies of topics such as water, food, trees, animals, insects, family, self, rain, flowers, seeds, butterflies, vehicles, vegetables, stores, babies, bread, birds, gardens, and farms. Each study gave teachers, children, and families a greater understanding of and appreciation for critical elements of their lives. The artwork throughout this text grew out of preschoolers' integrated curriculum studies. We have seen teachers of older children investigate these same topics with more depth and also more complex topics, such as life cycles, the ocean, harbors, grocery stores, hospitals, and bakeries. The accompanying "Golden Rules for Selecting a Topic for an Integrated Curriculum Study" box provides you with some criteria to help you choose a topic of integrated study.

Golden Rules

for Selecting a Topic for an Integrated Curriculum Study

1. Choose a topic that is interesting—to the children and to the teachers.
2. Choose a topic that is accessible—you can provide real, frequent, hands-on experience.
3. Choose a topic that is important—worth knowing about to a young child.
4. Choose a topic that is the right size—not too big and complex, not too small and trivial.
5. Choose a topic that is consistent with program philosophy and goals.
6. Choose a topic that can be taught through direct experiences.
7. Choose a topic that builds understanding and appreciation—of self, others, and the world.
8. Choose a topic that can integrate—experience, subjects, and development.
9. Choose a topic that is realistic—in terms of resources available.
10. Choose a topic that can have lots of ways to involve families and encourage family input and participation.

SOURCE: Jeff Reese

Not all topics are effective for generating meaningful learning experiences. A topic can give a surface appearance of connecting ideas but do nothing to enhance children's understanding. We once observed 3-year-olds "studying" the letter M by making magazine collages, baking muffins, and coloring a picture of a monkey. When we asked the children what they had been learning, they responded that they had been gluing, cooking, and coloring. Their teacher corrected them, saying that they had been studying M. This approach failed to integrate children's learning because it focused on an abstract symbol that was not of real interest to an inquisitive group of 3-year-olds. It is an example of a "shallow" unit/theme that we describe in Figure 11.10 as inappropriate.

Similarly, just because children "like" or are fascinated by something does not necessarily make it a good topic. For example, after viewing a movie about pirates, children may seem to like and be interested in pirates. It might even have historical relevance if your program is located near a coastline where piracy frequently occurred. However, the reality of piracy, a serious crime at any time in history, is quite chilling and has little to do with the swashbuckling fiction seen in movies and on television. It would be impossible to provide curriculum on pirates that had integrity (honesty) and that was appropriate for young children.

Often, holidays are used as the basis for integrated curriculum. Holidays that have an impact on children's lives can be studied in terms of culture, the joys of family celebrations, and their impact on children. Others have little or no appropriate content for young children. Even meaningful holidays used as topics are often made trivial and inappropriate when they are reduced to look-alike crafts and commercial symbols. The study of holidays that are based on religious content in public schools is likely to have little real meaning because the religious content has to be excised based on the necessity of separating church and state.

An integrated study should be a source of genuine learning and not a way to sugarcoat academic activities. Worksheets covered with dinosaurs or bees used as part of a "theme" are not even distantly related to meaningful learning or good integrated planning. When we encounter colleagues who dismiss thematic planning or unit planning as superficial or inappropriate, we are quite sure that this is the kind of plan they have in mind.

Reflect On

An Integrated Study in Your Childhood

Remember a time when you experienced an integrated study in school. What did you learn about? What do you remember most about the study? How was it different from other ways of learning? What did you enjoy? Is there anything you wish your teachers had done differently?

In this chapter, we are using a study of birds as an example of integrated curriculum. The teachers of the 3- and 4-year-olds at the Leeward Community College Children's Center, along with Eva and her college students, selected this topic for the following reasons (*the rationale*):

- They had observed children's interest in the abundant bird life that visited the school playground and the surrounding community.

- A nest of baby birds had fallen into their yard, and the class was caring for them.
- They had pet chickens, which were an ongoing source of interest to the children.
- The staff themselves were interested in birds, and both teachers had pet birds.
- Four families in the class raised birds or had birds as pets.

Their goals for this study were:

- To help children develop an increased knowledge of birds, their characteristics, and habits;
- To help children develop a disposition to be curious and inquiring about the birds in their environment;
- To help children develop an attitude of respect for and disposition to be kind and humane to birds and other living creatures;
- To help children develop skills in language, literacy, inquiry, physical coordination, and creative expression.

When you conduct an integrated study it is useful to write down *your* reasons for your topic choice and *your* goals to help you communicate with families and colleagues, and to help you stay focused on your purpose.

Video Example 11.5: Meeting the Criteria for an Integrated Curriculum Topic

Watch this video to hear a teacher explain how the study of birds met the criteria for a good integrated curriculum topic. How does what the teacher says compare with or add to the Golden Rules for Selecting a Topic for an Integrated Curriculum Study boxed feature that you read?

Learn about the Topic

The first thing to do once you have selected a topic is to learn about it. This is a critical part of the planning process. Teachers often assume that they already know enough to teach any subject to young children. While you do not need to know everything about a topic, it is necessary to learn something, particularly if the topic is outside your areas of expertise. Even if the topic is something "simple," such as studying "me," you will need to gather information on the children and their families. In our own work we make use of the information readily available on the Internet. Online encyclopedias, such as Wikipedia, provide instant access to basic facts and help us identify sources for finding out more. The public library and your school library are other important resources.

Write the Big Ideas

Once you have acquired some basic information, you can identify the important understandings or "big ideas" that you want children to acquire. These will give you a guide for planning and will help you decide if the activities are contributing to children's understanding of the topic. We brainstorm words related to the topic, write each on a slip of paper, and then sort them to identify the major understandings for an integrated study.

For example after researching birds the teachers and college students at the Children's Center wrote down all the words they could think of about birds. They sorted the words into five piles and assigned a category to each pile. The papers were sorted several different ways, and the content was considered. These were the results:

- Different kinds of birds: chickens, egrets, parakeets, parrots, conures, peacocks, endangered birds, ducks, swans, mainland birds, Hawaii birds, cardinals, nene goose, mynah birds
- Special things about birds: flying, feathers, eggs, colors, nests, baby birds, incubators, crowing, singing
- Where birds live: seabirds, cliffs, homes, aviaries, trees, farms, playground, by the freeway
- How birds move: flying, hopping, swimming, walking, migrating
- Birds contributions to our lives: pets, Thanksgiving turkey, feathers, guano, omelets, bird feeders, egg farm, state bird

After they identified the categories, they thought about what they wanted children to know about each category and wrote a statement of major understandings:
"Big Ideas" for a Curriculum Study of Birds

- There are lots of different birds with many colors, sizes, and shapes.
- All birds have feathers and lay eggs to create baby birds.
- Birds move in different ways—most fly, some hop, some walk, and some swim.
- Birds are part of people's lives—some can be pets, some give us food and feathers, and some help the plants to grow.
- Birds live in different places where they can find food, be safe, and raise their young.

We write "big ideas" in simple language such as a child might use or understand. The point of this activity is to help you to identify understanding that children will construct for themselves.

Generate Ideas for Activities

The next step is to generate ideas for activities that will help children acquire the major understandings. For many years, we have used a system called **mind mapping** to begin our planning. In a mind map, you place a topic in a circle in the center of a piece of chart paper off of which numerous lines are drawn to map ideas related to the topic. You will see similar charts referred to as **curriculum webs** or maps. The process of mind mapping or webbing is useful because it allows you to add ideas as they arise without being concerned about their order or organization. When the map is completed, you can examine each item to see how it fits in the whole plan.

In our planning we begin by selecting trips and resource visitors because these may determine other experiences we will offer. Ideas for other activities that support the major understandings are then webbed. This is also a time to make a list of some of the new vocabulary, especially "rare words" that will be introduced and used during the study.

The value of activities should be assessed with consideration of the goals, the extent to which the activities support the major understandings, and the resources and time required. If you find there is a big idea for which you can think of no age-appropriate activities or if you think of good activities that do not seem to fit within your big ideas, it means you need to go back and add or omit big ideas.

The initial web is the starting place. As you learn with children about the topic, you will get ideas for additional activities and some of the activities generated at the beginning may be dropped.

Enrich the Environment

Following initial planning, you will gather and create resources to teach. A good curriculum study will be visible in almost every classroom center. You will assess pictures, puppets, dramatic play and block props, games, puzzles, and toys that will help children learn about the topic. You will go to the library to borrow children's literature. Be sure to ask a librarian to help you find good books. Tell families about the study and invite them to participate by sharing resources. Your local museum or art gallery may have prints, posters, or artifacts that can be borrowed.

Figure 11.11 Initial Curriculum Activity Brainstorming Web

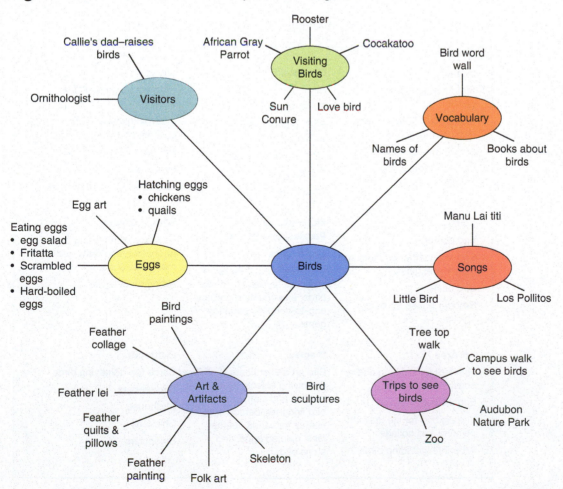

Video Example 11.6: Enriching an Environment for a Study of Birds

A good curriculum study will be visible in almost every classroom center. For example, in the bird curriculum, the teachers added the items in Figure 11.12 to the environment. Read through the items listed in Figure 11.12 and then watch the video to see these enrichments.

Figure 11.12 Environment Additions for a Curriculum on Birds

Blocks

Bird figures (wooden and plastic)

Stuffed bird toys (shared with dramatic play)

Art prints of birds in a nest

Wooden flying goose mobile

Science Center

Egg poster

Egg and feather artifacts and magnifying glass

Bird nests

Brooder house for baby chicks

Art Area

Feathers for painting and collage

Eggshells for collage

Visiting bird for life drawing/ painting and collage

Art prints including birds

Dramatic Play

Bird hoods

Bird puppets

Stuffed bird toys (shared with blocks)

Mobile with origami cranes

Plastic eggs

Art prints of birds

Manipulative Toys, Puzzles, and Games

Bird puzzles

Workjobs: 1, 2, 3 Birds art postcard games; words for birds; egg counting game; egg-to-fledgling seriation game

Display

Bird art and artifacts shelf for displaying objects brought by families and staff, including bird figurines, ostrich egg, feather hatbands, feather fans, painted eggs, and stone eggs

Library

Storybooks on birds (see book list)

Informational books for children on birds and eggs

Nature guides on birds

Poster: bird book

Pillows with bird print fabric

Writing Center

Birdcage with visiting birds to observe and draw and make books about

Art prints of birds

Outdoors

Cards for identifying birds

Bird feeders

Birdhouse

Chickens

Binoculars

Plan

Once you have goals, major understandings, and a list of activities you have generated, you are ready to plan for teaching. Think about ways to bring real experience into the study right away (a trip, a visit from a resource person, making or cooking something, or bringing in real animals, plants, or other artifacts).

Think about an activity that will make a good beginning to introduce the topic to children and families. Think about activities that will help children build understanding to use in the middle of the study. Consider which activities will help children express and generalize their understanding at the end. Plan ways to involve families throughout the study. Schedule trips and resource people and begin to plot activities for the first weekly plans. We make contact with the sites/visitors and set up the trip(s)/visits right away and always plan an initial trip early in the study so that children have meaningful real experiences right from the start.

Because creating an integrated study plan is a big job, it's a good idea to begin to create a simple guide to refer to as you work. The outline for an integrated study plan in Figure 11.13 suggests some things to include. Remember that you will continue to observe children and plan for each week and day as you go along. The children's responses, teacher's new insights, families' input, and the serendipitous opportunities that you discover will be added to the integrated plan. You will not finish writing your **integrated plan** until close to the end—when you do, it may look something like the plan in Figure 11.13.

Implement the Study

Once the initial plans are in place and you have begun to bring the topic into the learning environment, you will start to implement activities. The first activities provide an introduction to the topic. Introductory activities give children awareness of the topic

---

Figure 11.13 Outline for an Integrated Thematic Study

1. **Topic:** focus of the study

2. **Children:** age and characteristics for whom you are planning

3. **Rationale:** why this topic was chosen for these children at this time

4. **Goals:** 3–6 broad statements of desired ends—the attitudes, skills, abilities, and experiences that children are intended to gain by participating in this study

5. **Major understandings:** 4–6 important ideas you intend children to construct by participating in this study, worded as children might understand them, not as objectives

6. **Resources:** books, articles, and other resources that you used to guide your development of the study

7. **Environment additions:** a list of materials to add to each learning center to support awareness of the topic and the development of the big ideas

8. **Trips:** a list of learning trips to give children real experience

9. **Brainstormed activities:**
   a. Introductory activities: to introduce the study to children and build awareness of the topic
   b. Activities to build understanding: to encourage exploration, support the major understanding, and build skills
   c. Culminating activities: to help children express and generalize what they have learned, and how you will end the study
   d. Assessment activities: to demonstrate understanding and serve as documentation (observation, photos, work samples)

Connecting with Families

Through Integrated Curriculum

An integrated curriculum study is better when you involve children's families. Families can make many contributions, and many welcome the opportunity to do so. Ask them to:

1. Give input—share ideas for the study.
2. Find community resources.
3. Share expertise with teachers and/or children.
4. Loan and donate materials.
5. Come on trips.
6. Help enrich the environment by making games and props or rearranging the furniture or outdoor space on a work day.

Remember that when you ask for involvement it is important to use family offers!

through real experience and books. They provide the raw material for the children's developing understanding of the topic.

Some teachers begin the curriculum by interviewing the children, asking them questions such as "What do you know about the topic? What would you like to learn?" This activity is also often used as a culminating activity for an integrated study (called K/W/L, which stands for "What do you KNOW? What do you WANT to learn? What have you LEARNED?").

Teachers in elementary schools often use this process to guide the design of a study. Although it is a good starting place for planning, it must be supplemented with observation of children, reflection, and research. As you can see from the example in Table 11.4, preschoolers are more able to identify what they know than to identify questions for investigation. Inquiry questions will emerge as they investigate a topic.

In preschool, we usually select a more hands-on introduction to a topic. In the study of birds we have been describing, teachers introduced the study by bringing pet birds into the classroom and by asking the children what they knew about birds and what they wanted to learn about birds. They took a walk to look for birds in the trees and lawns around the school. During the first weeks, they enriched the environment with fine art prints that included birds, puzzles and games featuring birds, bird toys

Table 11.4 Example of a K/W/L Chart Made with 4- and 5-Year-Olds

What Do You KNOW About Birds?	What Do You WANT to Learn About Birds?	What Have You LEARNED About Birds?
Hummingbirds fly really fast and eat from flowers. Some birds have sharp claws that scratch your arm.	How do peacocks eat?	Peacocks can fly up into the trees.
Birds peck branches.	What do peacocks look like?	Hornbills eat mice.
Birds drink water.	How do birds lay eggs? How do eggs become baby birds?	Chickens eat chicken scratch and bread.
Birds use their beaks to eat. Cardinals use the tips of their beaks to eat.		Baby birds have pink skin.
Lovebirds sometimes bite you.		Birds have sharp claws to hold onto branches.
A little bird is called a chick.		Peacocks make their tails big.
Baby birds can't fly, but they can when they're older.		Some birds can swim.
Mama birds and daddy birds make nests with hay and sticks—they sit on the eggs to keep them warm.		Baby birds have to peck on the eggs to get out.
Some birds chase tractors—they like the bugs.		Big birds have big nests, and little birds have little nests.
		Cardinals eat papayas.
		Baby birds get real hungry. Their mamas bring them food.
		Some people have pet birds.

and puppets for the dramatic play and block areas, and many books about birds. They constructed and put up bird feeders in the yard and added bird feeding (wild and pet) to the jobs that children did each day. During the third week, they went on a trip to the local zoo, which had an extensive bird collection.

After the initial input, activities to help children build and demonstrate their understanding are implemented. Blocks, art media, dramatic play, music, and bookmaking are all excellent ways for children to demonstrate what they are learning. This is a good time for children to discuss their ideas about the topic.

While you are implementing a plan, it is important to remain open to changes in children's interests and to fortuitous events. For example, the interest that the children showed in birds laying eggs and nesting (see the annotated work sample in Figure 11.6) convinced the teachers to begin a project that involved incubating and raising quails.

The activities in a good integrated study can address every (or most) curriculum areas and help you teach many content standards. However, they are not the only thing that happens in your classroom. Children will continue to read books, sing songs, create art, engage in physical activities, and learn about many things other than your subject. As you can see from the week's plan in Figure 11.9, not all the planned activities during the bird study were about birds. Trying to fit every activity into a study topic is unnecessary.

Early in the study, the teachers invited families to participate. Over the 3-month course of the study, families brought in pet birds, sewed bird hoods for dramatic play, went on trips to the zoo and a nature preserve, donated a pet cockatiel, made bird feeders with the children, came in to read stories, and loaned artifacts from their cultures, including Japanese origami cranes, a German toy goose, Samoan feather fans, an Italian rooster-shaped pitcher, a Hawaiian feather lei, a French porcelain Chanticleer (a rooster), a Chinese platter depicting a peacock, a Haida (Northwest Coast tribe) raven, and a Czech turkey toothpick holder.

An integrated study has a life span of its own. You may find that children's interest in the topic deepens, as we saw in the study of birds that we are using as an example. The initial plan for 8 weeks of study extended to the end of the school year—3 months. You may find that the study links to another topic, as we saw when a study of water led to a study of the ocean.

Eventually, you will draw your study to a close. When you are ready to move on to a new topic, it is important to plan closure for the children, families, and the teachers. A class book or newsletter explaining what was learned, a documentation panel, a scrapbook or video that shows the outcome of the study, or a social event during which children's work and learning are shared with others are good ways to both assess the study and bring it to an end. The study of birds was brought to an end by inviting families to the school for an evening walk to see the birds settling down for the evening, followed by a potluck, a reading of class-made books about birds, and a sing-along of all the songs learned about birds during the study. During the evening, children's work and documentation panels of the study were displayed, and videos of the children engaged in the many activities were shown.

For our own documentation when we are teaching children, we create a sunburst, a graphic expansion of the original mind map to show everything that was planned during the unit (see Figure 11.14), and put together all the plans, songs, finger plays, newsletters, and so on that we created during the study. We make this an assignment for students in our college classes in which they are studying integrated curriculum. Students then share these with one another as valuable resources for their future teaching.

Evaluate the Integrated Study

As you implement, remember to assess children's learning and evaluate the study. To evaluate whether children have acquired the major understandings you have targeted, you can observe their play as it pertains to the study or have children discuss the topic,

Video Example 11.7: Analyzing an Integrated Study of Birds

Watch either the first video on a study of birds or watch both videos to see the study in its entirety. If you watch the individual segments of the bird study video, reflect on what you have seen. Or, if you view both videos, evaluate them as a study. Is there evidence that the goals of the study were met (the goals were: to help children develop an increased **knowledge** of birds, their characteristics, and habits; *a disposition to be curious and inquiring* about the birds in their environment; an **attitude of respect for and disposition to be kind and humane to birds** and other living creatures; and **skills** in all curriculum areas: language, literacy, inquiry, physical coordination, and creative expression)?

dictate stories, or write in their journals. Children who make representational drawings may spontaneously or on request draw pictures that demonstrate their understanding. For example, during the study of birds, the 3- to 5-year-old children were provided with many different kinds of art media. Their drawings, sculptures, and collages provided visible proof of the internalization of concepts relating to birds (see Figure 11.15).

Photographs and video of the children engaged in learning activities also provide valuable evidence of the learning that is occurring. Photographs, work samples, and

Figure 11.14 Bird Sunburst

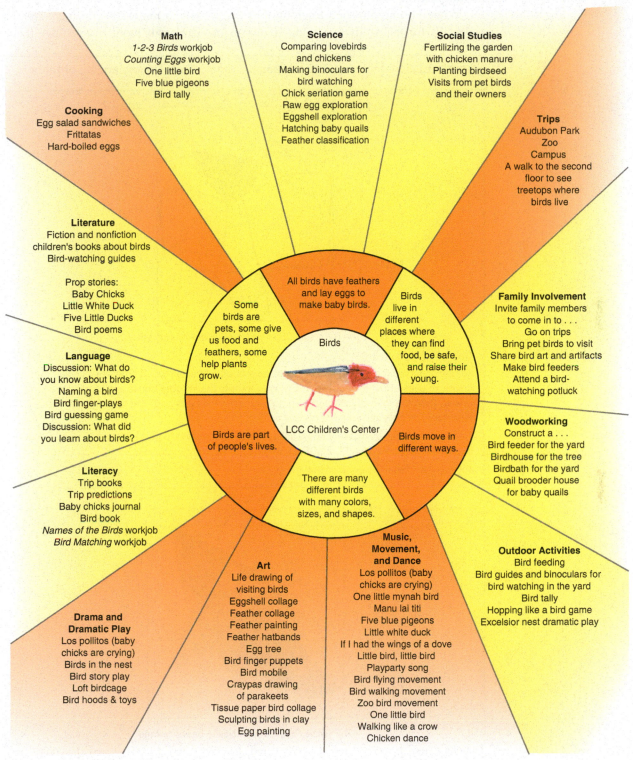

Math
1-2-3 Birds workjob
Counting Eggs workjob
One little bird
Five blue pigeons
Bird tally

Science
Comparing lovebirds
and chickens
Making binoculars for
bird watching
Chick seriation game
Raw egg exploration
Eggshell exploration
Hatching baby quails
Feather classification

Social Studies
Fertilizing the garden
with chicken manure
Planting birdseed
Visits from pet birds
and their owners

Cooking
Egg salad sandwiches
Frittatas
Hard-boiled eggs

Trips
Audubon Park
Zoo
Campus
A walk to the second
floor to see
treetops where
birds live

Literature
Fiction and nonfiction
children's books about birds
Bird-watching guides

Prop stories:
Baby Chicks
Little White Duck
Five Little Ducks
Bird poems

Family Involvement
Invite family members
to come in to . . .
Go on trips
Bring pet birds to visit
Share bird art and artifacts
Make bird feeders
Attend a bird-
watching potluck

Language
Discussion: What do
you know about birds?
Naming a bird
Bird finger-plays
Bird guessing game
Discussion: What did
you learn about birds?

Woodworking
Construct a . . .
Bird feeder for the yard
Birdhouse for the tree
Birdbath for the yard
Quail brooder house
for baby quails

Literacy
Trip books
Trip predictions
Baby chicks journal
Bird book
Names of the Birds workjob
Bird Matching workjob

Outdoor Activities
Bird feeding
Bird guides and binoculars for
bird watching in the yard
Bird tally
Hopping like a bird game
Excelsior nest dramatic play

**Drama and
Dramatic Play**
Los pollitos (baby
chicks are crying)
Birds in the nest
Bird story play
Loft birdcage
Bird hoods & toys

Art
Life drawing of
visiting birds
Eggshell collage
Feather collage
Feather painting
Feather hatbands
Egg tree
Bird finger puppets
Bird mobile
Craypas drawing
of parakeets
Tissue paper bird collage
Sculpting birds in clay
Egg painting

**Music,
Movement,
and Dance**
Los pollitos (baby
chicks are crying)
One little mynah bird
Manu lai titi
Five blue pigeons
Little white duck
If I had the wings of a dove
Little bird, little bird
Playparty song
Bird flying movement
Bird walking movement
Zoo bird movement
One little bird
Walking like a crow
Chicken dance

Center circle text:
Some birds are pets, some give us food and feathers, some help plants grow.

All birds have feathers and lay eggs to make baby birds.

Birds live in different places where they can find food, be safe, and raise their young.

Birds
LCC Children's Center

Birds are part of people's lives.

Birds move in different ways.

There are many different birds with many colors, sizes, and shapes.

SOURCE: Art reprinted with permission from Robyn S. B. Chun.

observations can be put together into documentation panels (posters with photos and work samples). These document children's learning and make it visible to families and community members.

When you are finished teaching, put the plans and materials you have created especially for this study in a resource box so you can easily store and retrieve them.

Figure 11.15 Children's Artwork Demonstrating Their Understanding of Birds

The Baby Quail Shakes His Wings—Journal entry

Child: Megan

Megan observed the baby quails in the brooder house. At small group time when invited to create an entry about the baby quails, Megan went to the brooder house and studied the baby quails. Then she took a black pencil crayon and drew the baby bird. The teacher took her dictation: *The baby quail shakes his wings.*

Comment: Megan demonstrates the ability to use observation to gain information and illustration to record data. SCIENCE, LITERACY

SOURCE: Reprinted with permission Robyn S. B. Chun.

The Birdie Flies Away!—Tissue paper collage

Child: Emily

Today after the rescued birds were released, Emily made this collage. Varied shapes of pieces were made available, and Emily carefully chose and arranged the pieces then brushed them with dilute glue. The teacher asked if she wanted words to go with her collage, and Emily said, *The birdie flies away!*

Comment: Emily uses art materials with skill to express ideas. Fine motor control well-developed. ART, FINE MOTOR, LANGUAGE

SOURCE: Reprinted with permission from Amy Garma.

A Red Parrot—Felt marker drawing

Child: Jonah

After Kaitlin's father brought in red and gray parrots, Jonah used felt markers to draw the red parrot. He explained that the feet had claws to hold on tight to Kaitlin's daddy's arm.

Comment: Jonah was able to accurately capture details of the parrot, including the black beak and eye ring, the yellow 3-toed feet, and the blue feather on the wing. Clearly observing a great deal of detail. SCIENCE, ART

SOURCE: Reprinted with permission from Steve Bobilin.

Cardboard banker's boxes or lidded plastic storage boxes work well for this purpose. It may be some time before you use the resource box again, but when you do, the materials will be there. If and when you decide to revisit the topic, you will make changes based on new ideas, interests, materials, children, and families, but you will not have to start over from scratch.

A Quick Check 11.5

Gauge your understanding of the concepts in this section.

 Final Thoughts

The curriculum you plan should reflect your vision for children, for society, and for the future. It should be intellectually engaging for children and for teachers. The choices you make as you select what to teach and how you will teach it impact children's lives, your own life, and possibly the larger world. If you take this responsibility seriously, you will be thoughtful and thorough in your planning. Your plans will help you support all areas of children's development. They will increase children's understanding of the world, build their love of learning, and help them be curious, creative, active problem solvers. It will help them become the kind of adults that our society needs.

 Application Exercise 11.3 Final Reflection

 # To Learn More

Read

Eight Essential Techniques for Teaching with Intention: What Makes Reggio and Other Inspired Approaches Effective, A. Lewin-Benham (2015).

Explorations with Young Children, A. Mitchell & J. David (1992).

Learning Together with Young Children: A Curriculum Framework for Reflective Teachers, D. Curtis, & M. Carter (2007).

Meaningful Curriculum for Young Children 2nd ed., E. Moravcik, & S. Nolte (2018).

Powerful Interactions: How to Connect with Children to Extend Their Learning, A. Dombro, J. Jablon, & C. Stetson (2011).

Reflecting Children's Lives: A Handbook for Planning Your Child-Centered Curriculum, 2nd ed., D. Curtis, & M. Carter (2011).

The Hundred Languages of Children, C. Edwards, L. Gandini, & G. Forman (2011).

The Intentional Teacher, A. Epstein (2014).

Twelve Best Practices for Early Childhood Education: Integrating Reggio and Other Inspired Approaches, by A. Lewin-Benham (2011).

Young Investigators: The Project Approach in the Early Years, 3rd ed., by J. Harris Helm, & L. G. Katz (2016).

Visit a Website

ARTSEDGE (the National Arts and Education Network)—free, standards-based teaching materials, professional development resources, student materials, and guidelines for arts-based instruction and assessment

Bank Street: theory & practice (to learn about the Developmental-Interaction Approach to Integrated Curriculum)

The Progressive Education Network (to learn about the Developmental-Interaction Approach to Integrated Curriculum)

Reggio Children (to learn about the Reggio Emilia Approach to Integrated Curriculum)

NAREA—the North American Reggio Emilia Alliance (to learn about the Reggio Emilia Approach to Integrated Curriculum)

The Project Approach (to learn about the Project Approach to Integrated Curriculum)

Illinois Projects in Practice (to learn about the Project Approach to Integrated Curriculum)

Document Your Skill & Knowledge About Curriculum Planning in Your Professional Portfolio

Include some or all of the following:

- **Curriculum Planning Philosophy.** Write a one-page statement. Ask yourself, "As an educator, what am I trying to accomplish—for children and for society? What does that mean for the the curriculum I want to teach and how I want to present it?"

- **An Activity Plan.** Write a plan for an activity for children using the planning format found in this chapter. Implement your plan with children. Write anecdotal records on children's responses, reflect on what happened and what you learned, and evaluate your work. Put the plan and records in your portfolio to document your competence as a planner.

- **A Week's Plan.** Write a plan for a week of activity for children using the planning form found in this chapter. Implement your plan with children. Reflect on what happened and what you learned and evaluate your work. Put the plan in your portfolio to document your competence as a planner.

- **An Integrated Plan.** Develop an integrated plan using the guidelines found in this chapter. Create a sunburst for the plan. Implement part or all of it and document children's learning with work samples, anecdotal records, and photographs. Put the sunburst and a select sampling of the documentation in your portfolio.

 Shared Writing 11.1 Your Ethical Responsibilities Planning Curriculum

Including All Children

We all have different gifts, so we all have different ways of saying to the world who we are.

FRED ROGERS

Chapter Learning Outcomes:

12.1 Discuss what research tells us about dual language learning and describe some strategies that can be used to work effectively with children who do not speak English as their first language.

12.2 Discuss preferred terminology for talking about people with disabilities, laws governing programs and services, the kinds of programs that are available for children who have disabilities, and the benefits of inclusion of children with disabilities in regular education programs.

12.3   Identify some disabilities that you might encounter in an early childhood program, describe characteristics of young children with these disabilities, and discuss some strategies for working effectively with each one. Explain some reasons that inclusion is a desirable approach for working with children with disabilities.

12.4   Identify special needs in addition to disabilities you are likely to encounter in an early childhood program, describe characteristics of young children with these special needs, and discuss some strategies for working effectively with them.

12.5   Identify some issues faced by families who have children with disabilities and other special needs and discuss some ways that you can work with them effectively.

NAEYC Professional Preparation Standards

The NAEYC Professional Preparation Standards that apply to this chapter:

Standard 1: Promoting Child Development and Learning (NAEYC, 2011)

Key elements:

1a: Knowing and understanding young children's characteristics and needs, from birth through age 8

1c: Using developmental knowledge to create healthy, respectful, supportive, and challenging learning environments for young children

Standard 2: Building Family and Community Relationships

Key elements:

2c: Involving families and communities in their children's development and learning

Standard 4: Using Developmentally Effective Approaches to Connect with Children and Families

Key elements:

4a: Understanding positive relationships and supportive interactions as the foundation of their work with young children

4c: Using a broad repertoire of developmentally appropriate teaching/learning approaches

As a teacher who will be working with young children in the 21st century, you are certain to encounter great diversity in those you teach. Some children will live in poverty, and others will come from wealthy families. Children may come from a wide range of cultural and ethnic backgrounds. Some will speak a language other than English. Some will be recent immigrants. Some will learn differently—more quickly or more slowly—than most other children. A few will have health issues limiting their ability to learn. Some will have experienced abuse or neglect. As an early childhood educator, you have a responsibility to support the development and promote a sense of belonging for all of these children in your classroom.

Early childhood educators entering the field today need to be aware of the growth of diversity in our society and consider the implications of this diversity for meeting the educational needs of all children. We hope you will come to see that diversity is something to be embraced. Because building relationships is such an important developmental task of childhood, it is worthwhile for all children to experience playmates from a range of different kinds of backgrounds. All children benefit when those with diverse abilities and backgrounds have the opportunity to play and learn together. However, working with children from diverse backgrounds and with different ability levels has some distinct challenges. It will require you to have an open mind and heart and a willingness to grow and learn as a teacher.

Remember that knowing how to implement good early education practice provides a strong foundation. Knowledge of child development, the ability to reflect on your own feelings, and skill in guiding behavior, designing learning environments, planning curriculum, and relating to families are basics for working with *all* children. Specialized knowledge about the characteristics of children who come from a variety of backgrounds and who have diverse abilities will help you work more effectively with every child who enters your classroom. The Division of Early Childhood (DEC) encourages teachers to celebrate diverse backgrounds and use culturally responsive practices that support the full participation of children and families who are **culturally, linguistically, and ability diverse (CLAD)** (2010).

 # Dual Language Learners

In most classrooms today, you will find children whose first language is not English. Children who are learning two languages come from a variety of different backgrounds and circumstances; what they have in common is that English is not their home language. Some of them will be recent immigrants, and others will be temporary residents. Because they are learning two languages at the same time, we refer to them as **dual language learners** (they are sometimes called English language learners). The growing number and diversity of immigrant families in the United States today means that it is very likely that you will have the opportunity to work with children whose families have a wide range of values, beliefs, and goals for their children's early education. Children whose families do not speak English have the potential to be **bilingual**—fluent or nearly fluent in two languages.

Being bilingual is an asset to be encouraged and celebrated, not a deficit to be remedied or a "problem" to be solved. Understanding, speaking, reading, and writing in two or more languages is a valuable skill that is very much needed in today's world. Bilingualism gives children additional linguistic, cognitive, social, and cultural resources with which to navigate increasingly complex demands on people in our society. Bilingual and bicultural individuals are in high demand in the workplace today in many fields. In order to become and remain bilingual, however, children need to have ample opportunities to hear and use both of their languages—not just English. It is our responsibility as early childhood educators to nurture and encourage bilingualism in children in our care—even if we can speak only one language. Children do not have to lose their home language in order to acquire English (subtractive bilingualism)! They can become bilingual in their home language and English (additive bilingualism) instead of only English proficient.

A review of the research (Center for Early Care and Education Research—Dual Language Learners, 2014) concluded that young children who are still developing oral and literacy skills in their home languages benefit most in early childhood programs that expose them to both languages. The study emphasizes that dual language learners develop language and literacy skills differently than children who are learning only one language. Children learning two languages learn both more slowly than monolingual children, but with proper support, they can become fluent in two languages. This is a normal phenomenon and does not indicate a potential language delay. English Language Learners (ELL) go through a progression as they acquire a second-language. When children are exposed to a second language they generally focus first on listening and comprehension. These children are likely to be very quiet, speaking little as they focus on understanding the new language. A *silent period* is common at first. The younger the child, the longer the silent period tends to last. Older children may remain in the silent period for a few weeks or months, whereas preschoolers may be relatively silent for a year or more. *Interference* or *transfer* from their first language (L1) to English (L2) is also common. This means that a child may make an English error due to the direct influence of an L1 structure. *Codeswitching* involves changing languages over phrases or sentences using both languages at once. Over time, children become increasingly skilled at both comprehension and production of language, progressing from demonstrating proficiency in situations that are at first structured, then semi-structured, and finally spontaneous.

Working with Dual Language Learners

All good early childhood education programs support the development of language and literacy. But the language teaching strategies that you use for dual language learners will be somewhat different than those used for children whose first language is English. What can you do? This will depend on your language background, how many children in your classroom are English language learners, and whether all children in your classroom speak the same or different home languages. If you found yourself in a place where you could not communicate in the language that was being spoken, the first thing that you would be likely to want would be for the people around you to be kind and supportive.

Because teaching and learning occur in the context of trusting relationships, you will begin by building strong relationships with dual language learners and with their families. Create opportunities to share experiences that do not involve words, such as making a classroom snack or pretending to feed a doll. Such shared moments help establish feelings of commonality and trust. If you can, use the child's first language. If you can't speak the child's language, learn a few words. Family members are often willing to help you learn some basic words and phrases that will allow you to communicate with their children. "Feeling words" are especially useful for providing comfort and support. If you do not speak a child's home language, utilize others (staff, volunteers, family members, or other children) who do. Hearing the first language spoken at school helps children realize that both languages are valued. Relationships will be supported if you create a learning environment that welcomes families by reflecting their backgrounds in books, materials, and displays on classroom walls.

Building relationships also involves getting to know the family. Find out all you can about the family, their culture, and the languages they use at home. Ask family members to share information over time about their children's interests (you will also learn this from the child's activities in the classroom). Find out the family's feelings and attitudes about maintaining its home language and acquiring English. You can share that the value of learning two languages is well supported by research if you learn that the family has a preference for maintaining the home language. This can help them make a decision informed by data. You may need to find a colleague or volunteer who can assist with translations. You will also want to provide opportunities for families and members of their community to share stories and information in their home language with the school. While learning English is important for dual language learners, it is also important to help children maintain and increase skill in their first language and culture. You may need to encourage families to continue to support the primary language at home as they may feel their children will learn English faster if they hear and speak only English.

Programs can develop policies that endorse the continued development of children's home languages. It is also advisable for them to provide staff with opportunities to learn about first and second language acquisition and culturally and linguistically responsive practices.

Figure 12.1 lists some teaching strategies that have been shown to be effective for supporting the development of young dual language learners. These strategies can supplement what

SOURCE: Jeff Reese

Figure 12.1 Strategies for Supporting Dual Language Learners

- Use slower, expanded, simplified, and repetitive speech.
- Use gestures, body language, and expressive communication.
- Stop to check that the child has understood a direction.
- Provide repetition through routines, such as a welcome and greeting song to begin each day.
- Give simple one-step directions.
- Use visual clues such as pointing and picture cards with directions.
- Create charts with pictures for songs, poems, and instructions.
- Allow longer wait times to allow child to process.
- Present new vocabulary in context, such as names of foods at snack time.
- Present new concepts and ideas in the child's first language.
- Print words and displays in the primary language.
- Read children's literature that authentically depicts the cultures present.
- Use words in the primary language to hold conversations and build relationships.

you are already doing in your classroom and should be presented through play, activities, and daily routines. Remember that dual language learners are individuals from very different backgrounds—no one strategy will work for every one of them.

A Quick Check 12.1

Gauge your understanding of the concepts in this section.

Children with Disabilities

In addition to programs for children who are typically developing, there are early childhood programs and services dedicated to serving children who do not develop according to typical patterns. Children with disabilities and those who are gifted and talented are not regarded as typically developing and may be served by specialized programs.

Regardless of the setting in which you work it is very likely that you will find yourself teaching young children who have **special needs** (these may include children with physical, sensory, or cognitive impairments, as well as those with health care needs such as asthma and emotional health issues). The more specific term **disabilities** refers to physical or mental impairments that limit a child's movements, senses, or activities. Children with disabilities are characterized by development outside the expected range and they may exhibit a wide range of developmental differences. The Centers for Disease Control and Prevention (n.d.) reported that families of one in six children had been told that their child had some kind of developmental disorder. Boys had a higher prevalence compared with girls, and children from families with low-incomes had a higher prevalence of many disabilities (Boyle, Boulet, Schieve, Cohen, Blumberg, Yeargin-Allsop, et al., 2011).

Children are considered to have a **developmental delay** when it has been determined that they do not meet developmental milestones in one or more domains—physical, cognitive, language, social, or emotional. This term describes children who are at risk for the development of disabilities—though the disability may not have been identified. Children with developmental delays may be eligible for special services. The delay or disability will often be identified first when the child enters a preschool or kindergarten program for typically developing children.

Terminology

Throughout this chapter, we will use the term *children with disabilities* or *children with special needs* rather than calling them *disabled children*. There is a reason for this. It is important to recognize that individuals with disabilities are people first. One of their many characteristics is that they have a disability. In order to acknowledge that the child is more important than the disability, educators recommend the use of **people-first language** (e.g., saying "a child with autism" rather than "an autistic child"). This view of the appropriate language underlines that it is important to see the whole child, including areas of strength and abilities. Refer to a child by his or her name and mention the disability only when that information is relevant in a particular situation. Defining people by their limitations promotes stereotypes that devalue children with special needs as individuals.

The terms *children with disabilities* and *children with special needs* are often used interchangeably, although a child with a disability may be described as having special needs, while a child with special needs may have a condition that is not included in the definition of disability.

Laws Governing Services to Children with Disabilities

Before 1975, the majority of children with disabilities were segregated into special education classrooms or facilities and denied participation in the public education programs attended by typically developing children. In order to better meet the needs of children with disabilities, in 1975 the U.S. Congress enacted the Education for All Handicapped Children Act, which governed how states and public agencies should provide early intervention, special education, and related services to children with disabilities.

In 1990, the original act was replaced by the Individuals with Disabilities Education Act (IDEA), which was created to ensure that all children with disabilities had access to a free, appropriate public education (FAPE). Services were also mandated under the Americans with Disabilities Act, which requires access to public accommodations for all individuals regardless of disability. In 1997, it was expanded to include developmentally delayed children.

In 2004, IDEA became the **Individuals with Disabilities Education Improvement Act (IDEIA)**, and requirements for evaluating children with learning disabilities were revised. The goal of IDEIA was to ensure that children with disabilities would have access to the same educational opportunities as other children. The six major principles of IDEIA are:

1. Schools must educate *all* children with disabilities.

2. A full evaluation should be conducted to determine whether a child has a disability and requires special education services. The evaluation must draw on a variety of sources and be administered in an unbiased manner.

3. All children with disabilities should have access to **free appropriate public education** in the same environments as their typically developing peers. This involves the development of an **individualized education plan (IEP)** designed to meet the needs of each individual with a disability.

4. Children with disabilities must be served to the greatest extent possible in the **least restrictive environment**, meaning that children should have opportunities to participate in regular education classrooms with their peers who do not have disabilities and experience the same curriculum that is provided for all children. Children with disabilities should be served in separate classes or schools only when the nature or severity of their disabilities makes it impossible for them to receive an appropriate education in a general education classroom with supplementary aids and services.

5. Schools must protect the rights of children with disabilities and their parents and provide family members with enough information to participate in educational decisions.

6. Schools must collaborate with parents of students with disabilities in the design and implementation of special education services.

The IDEIA legislation calls for children with disabilities to have access to natural environments—the places where children learn naturally, such as preschools, playgrounds, and parks—and that they be educated in the same learning environments as their peers—a practice called **inclusion**. The provision of inclusive services is based on the belief that all children benefit when those with a range of abilities learn together in the same classroom. The Division for Early Childhood (DEC) and the National Association for the Education of Young Children (NAEYC) (2009) have developed a joint position statement on early childhood inclusion that affirms that young children with disabilities and their families are full members of the community, that the children should learn and develop with their typically developing peers, and that every child deserves to have a sense of belonging. *Access, participation*, and *supports* are the three key components of high quality inclusion according to the DEC/NAEYC statement. Access allows each child a wide range of learning activities and environments by removing barriers and providing multiple ways to join in. Participation affords every child a sense of belonging and engagement in play and learning by using a broad range of instructional strategies and approaches that meet individual needs. Supports are the many ways that systems can ensure the adults involved with children and families have the skills, knowledge, and disposition for providing inclusive practices, including professional development.

Programs for Children from Birth Through Age 2

Infants and toddlers (birth through age 2) and their families may receive services under Part C of IDEIA. This legislation makes funding available to states to provide early intervention services for children who have or who are at risk of developing disabilities. Services are designed to minimize the potential for developmental delays, reduce the need for special education services when the child reaches preschool, and enhance the family's capacity to meet the child's needs. These services are usually provided in the child's natural environment, typically his or her home or child care setting. There is a lead government agency in each state (usually a department of health and human services or an office of families and children) responsible for assessment and coordination of services for infants and toddlers who are eligible for early intervention.

Eligible children are required to have an **individualized family services plan (IFSP)** to guide the provision of early intervention. The IFSP is a written plan that includes outcomes for the family as well as the child. Family members and service providers work as a team to plan and evaluate services that will suit the needs of the child and family. Services often include speech-language therapy, occupational therapy, and/or physical therapy. An IFSP emphasizes the provision of services in natural settings. Services are provided to the family through a coaching or consulting model rather than to the child directly. This family centered approach supports the adults in the family in helping their child engage in daily routines and activities rather than limiting intervention only to when a professional is present. A service coordinator is designated to manage the services, and the plan is reviewed regularly by the service team and the family to ensure that it effectively supports the child's development. If you work as a teacher of infants or toddlers with disabilities, it is very likely that you will help develop and carry out some of the recommendations in the child's IFSP. See Figure 12.2 for an example of items that are typically included in the IFSP.

Figure 12.2 Example of Items Typically Included in an Individualized Family Service Plan (IFSP)

Child and family information: This includes contact information, the family's preferred language, typical routines and community activities.

Service coordination: Person and agency responsible for coordinating services to the child and family.

IFSP team members: The team will include family members, teachers (regular and special education), and others who will provide education and specialized services to the child, such as a speech pathologist, occupational therapist, and physical therapist.

Statements of family strengths and resources: To best support families, it is important to determine their strengths and existing resources, which help guide interventions.

Statements of family concerns and priorities: Families can identify the areas they would like to see addressed and prioritize the things they want to work on.

The child's present level of development and abilities (including strengths):   Curriculum-based developmental assessments and observations of the child in natural settings are used to gather these data. These assessments address developmental domains, including language (expressive and receptive), cognitive development (concept development, problem solving), motor development (large and small muscles), social–emotional development, and adaptive (self-help) skills such as eating, dressing, grooming.

Desired outcomes for early intervention: This section includes a list of desired outcomes and short-term objectives for achieving and measuring each outcome. There may be objectives for families as well as for children. Families' priorities for kinds of intervention and services provided are of primary importance in developing the outcomes.

Strategies/activities: How outcomes will be achieved, beginning and ending dates, frequency, and location of the services. Ideally, services will be provided in the same natural settings as those used by children who do not have disabilities.

Transition plans: Provision for helping the child move from IDEIA Plan C services to Plan B services or another kind of program. This might involve meetings with the family to prepare them for the change and visits to the child's next classroom.

Programs for Children 3 to 5 Years of Age

Children and youth ages 3 through 21 receive special education and related services under Part B of IDEIA, which is designed to provide children with disabilities opportunities to learn with their typically developing peers. A child may transition from IDEIA Part C to Part B at the age of 36 months. At this time, an assessment is made by members of a trained team (usually coordinated by a department of education) in order to determine if the child meets the criteria for one of the categories of disability identified by IDEIA.

If the assessment indicates that the child needs special education services in order to achieve his or her educational potential, a team is convened to develop an IEP. The purpose of the IEP is to lay out a series of specific actions and steps through which the child's stated goals may be reached. The IEP is a written plan developed with participation from family members, teachers, school administrators, educational specialists, and others with relevant expertise.

The IEP specifies who will be responsible for each goal or accommodation and the frequency of the intervention. For example, an IEP might say that a child will meet with a speech therapist twice a week to increase expressive language and that the classroom teacher will make daily attempts to teach the use of appropriate communication, or an occupational therapist will come to the classroom weekly to assist the child in learning to button and zip his or her clothing. Each person on the team will make regular assessments of the child's progress, and the members will meet at least once a year to discuss, update, and revise the IEP. Figure 12.3 provides an example of items that are typically included in an IEP.

Whatever program children attend, it is very important that there is careful planning to guide the

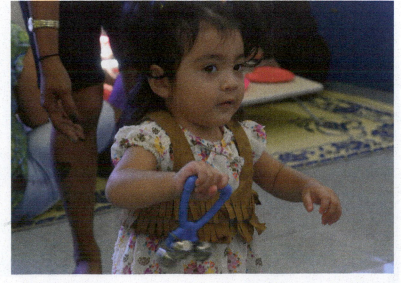

SOURCE: Jeff Reese

Figure 12.3 Example of Items Typically Included in an Individualized Education Program (IEP)

Information about the child: Name, date of birth, age, and grade.

IEP team members: These will include the child's parents, regular education and special education teachers, a person who can interpret evaluation results, a person representing the school system, providers of specialized services (e.g., speech-language and occupational therapists).

The child's current performance: How the child is functioning academically in all subject areas as determined by classroom tests and assignments and standardized assessments. The curriculum-based assessments used in the IFSP may also be administered as part of the IEP process.

Measurable annual goals: List of goals a child can reasonably be expected to accomplish in a year and how progress will be measured.

Short-term objectives/benchmarks: List of short-term objectives that will lead to achievement of the annual goals and specific benchmarks.

A description of how progress toward achieving the goals will be measured   and when families will be informed about the child's progress.

Description of the services and modifications to be made: List of services to be provided, modifications to be made (may include taped instructions, assignments given to the family so they can help the child to prepare, additional time for quizzes and tests, modifications of assessment procedures), frequency, location (may include general education classroom, resource room, special classes, home-based services), dates, duration, and who is responsible for the provision of services.

transition from early intervention to the next educational experience. In order to participate in the least restrictive environment, it is preferable for preschool age children to attend programs that serve typically developing children. They can be included in private community preschools, Head Start programs, and state-funded pre-K classrooms. Some states have self-contained public school preschool programs that serve only children who have been identified as having disabilities. These programs are a holdover from a time when children and adults with disabilities were segregated from their peers, and this approach is not desirable because children are not learning in the least restrictive environment.

Video Example 12.1: Early Intervention

Watch this video that shows a parent discussing the impact of early intervention on her child. What did you learn about how early intervention serves a child and family, and why it is worthwhile?

Programs for Children 5 to 8 Years of Age

Children 5 to 8 years of age who have disabilities are almost always served in public school kindergarten and primary-grade classrooms. Public schools are increasingly adopting inclusion programs that place children with disabilities in classrooms with typically developing peers. If you take a job as a K–3rd grade teacher in an elementary school, it is quite likely that you will have a child (or several children) with disabilities placed in your classroom.

As with the transition from early intervention to preschool, it is important to carefully consider how to support a child in making a smooth transition from preschool to kindergarten. It is very helpful for the kindergarten teacher to reach out to the preschool teacher who can provide information about the child's development and how he or she might best be served in the kindergarten program.

Kindergarten and primary-age children also receive an IEP to guide the provision of services. They are provided with necessary specialized assistance to support their participation to the greatest extent possible in the regular classroom program.

RESPONSE TO INTERVENTION   **Response to Intervention (RTI)** is an educational approach that provides support for kindergarten and primary-grade children who are having difficulty with school expectations and who might be candidates for special education services. The intent of RTI is to promote early identification of problems and to provide instructional support for children who need additional help. RTI includes frequent measurement of progress to determine the effectiveness of instruction and adjustment and modification of teaching strategies for a child who is having trouble mastering what is taught. Teachers who implement RTI gather data and analyze progress in order to design more effective instruction (Buysse & Wesley, 2006; McInerney & Elledge, 2013).

A three-tier process is used to guide the provision of RTI. The first tier is to deliver core academic instruction to *all* of the students in a grade level. Tier 2 involves assessing learning and providing supplemental instruction for *small groups* of students who are identified as needing more targeted assistance. Students who receive Tier 2 services are evaluated again, and those who have still not mastered the prescribed content receive Tier 3 services—*individual* instruction. Only when all of these supports are determined to be ineffective is a child referred for evaluation for special education services (McInerney & Elledge, 2013).

Although RTI is a general education program, it often receives special education funding. The ideal situation is a partnership between special education and general education teachers. Most states currently implement some form of RTI. Research indicates that it is effective for reducing the prevalence of learning disabilities and special education placements in young children (Allington, 2009).

A preschool version of RTI called **Recognition and Response (RTI Pre-K)** employs a similar framework for providing intervention tailored to the needs of 3- to 5-year-olds (Coleman, Buysse, & Neitzel, 2006). This approach is designed to improve the quality of instruction for all children as well as provide support for children who need additional assistance to be successful in school. Researchers at the Frank Porter Graham Child Development Institute in North Carolina assessed children using a screening instrument and then delivered small-group intervention to those who needed help with language and literacy skills. Small-group intervention was based on a shared storybook reading approach. Children who received the intervention showed gains in print knowledge, phonological awareness, and language comprehension (Buysse et al., 2013).

UNIVERSAL DESIGN FOR LEARNING   Each child has unique ways he or she is able to acquire new information, show understanding, and demonstrate engagement in learning. The framework of **Universal Design for Learning (UDL)** offers teachers guidance on creating curriculum and environments that engage all students, that remove barriers, and that create greater equality for students' cultural, linguistic, and ability diversity. Using UDL, teachers design learning experiences for the broadest range of children so that it is unnecessary to modify the experience for every child. This is best achieved by providing all children with a variety of different opportunities to take in and process information, demonstrate what they know, and engage in learning experiences.

The Center for Applied Special Technology (CAST) offers guidelines on how teachers can support children using the three UDL principles (CAST, 2011). The authors of *The Universal Design of Early Education: Moving Forward for All Children* (Conn-Powers, Cross, Traub, & Hutter-Pishgahi, 2006) elaborate on how this approach can be applied to young learners.

1. Provide multiple means of representation that give learners a variety of ways to gain information (present curriculum through pictures, words and sensory experiences).

2. Provide multiple means of action and expression to enable children to demonstrate what they know (allow children to respond verbally and physically (through actions, singing, and using construction materials).

3. Provide multiple means of engagement to encourage children's interests and increase motivation (offer a variety of instructional methods, offer choices and opportunities for children to work independently, allow children to respond and reflect in personal ways, and foster collaboration and community).

Every child can make progress when curriculum supports his or her own style of learning. When teachers are thoughtful about how they can support each child's uniqueness by creating accessible environments from the beginning of their planning they help ALL children learn.

Identification of Disabilities

Some children enter school with disabilities that have not yet been identified and that are first detected when they enter a preschool or kindergarten. As a teacher, you will be in a good position to notice that a child is having problems learning and adjusting to school and might benefit from evaluation and the provision of special education services.

> *Fifteen eager 4-year-olds are eating their morning snack. It is the middle of the school year, and they have all learned how to cooperate to make snack time pleasant—except Jeremy. He cruises the edges of the room, stopping briefly to dump a puzzle from a shelf and run his hands through the pieces, only to be distracted by the morning's paintings drying nearby. As he passes a table of children, his attention is again deflected. He tries to squeeze his body onto a chair occupied by another child.*

Jeremy's behavior consistently precipitates conflicts with the other children and adults. He is unable to engage for any length of time in meaningful activity. Many 4-year-olds are easily distracted, but Jeremy's behavior appears to be extreme. The first thing you should do when you encounter a child like Jeremy is to check in with his family to find out how they view his behavior, how he behaves at home, and what they think might be triggering his behavior. Remember that family members know a child best—they have known Jeremy since he was an infant and they see him in all of his activities throughout the day. Their insight into Jeremy's actions at school is invaluable. Next, you can try to modify the learning environment, schedule, and curriculum of your classroom to see if any of these things help Jeremy to control his behavior. If these changes are not effective, you might conclude that Jeremy needs additional help to cope with the school requirements.

If your first teaching position is in a setting with typically developing children, a situation like this one may be your first encounter with a child who has a disability. When you have concerns about a child, the first thing you will do is to talk with the family. Be sure to think through in advance about what you will say. Use this conversation to learn about family beliefs and perceptions about their child and things they have noticed about the child. Next, you will observe in a variety of situations and note the ways that the child is functioning appropriately and the things that seem atypical or are a cause for concern. Write careful anecdotal records, being careful to make objective statements about what you observe the child doing. Consider whether there might be a cultural or language difference that is related to the problem. You might ask an experienced colleague to make an independent observation of the child to see if he or she corroborates your impressions. Once you have documented the child's behavior and reviewed your observations, you can decide on the next step. Be careful not to come to conclusions too quickly or to label or blame the child. At this time, it is likely that you will wish to have a conference with the family. Remember that it is possible that you are the first person outside of the family who has mentioned a concern and that this conversation may be difficult for the family. Be sure to share observations—"I notice that it is hard for Jeremy to sit still during circle time"—rather than your perceived diagnosis—"I think he might have attention-deficit/hyperactivity disorder." Your role is *not* to diagnose or to label but to assist the family in supporting the child's learning and to help them connect with needed resources and supports. For a variety of reasons, that may include disbelief or sadness, a parent may be hesitant to accept that there is a problem or may need to go through a period of grief before they are willing to access services. Early intervention services for infants and toddlers are family centered. If eligible for services, the consulting professional can support the parent with their emotional needs, along with developing an individualized family service plan that addresses the child's special needs.

Occasionally, despite your best efforts and ongoing communication with a family, you may be convinced that a child needs assistance beyond what you are able to provide. At this point, it may be a good idea to discuss your concern with a program administrator who knows community resources and procedures for getting children evaluated for special education services. You or the administrator may ask the family for their consent to a referral for an evaluation that will further explore the issue and provide appropriate assistance for the child if it is needed. If you are working in a public school, your district will probably have specialists on the staff whose job it is to help teachers evaluate children who need special education services. If the child is eligible for early childhood special education supports, service coordinators or other team members may consult with teachers to offer valuable coaching and recommendations to help the child to participate successfully in the classroom.

Knowledge of child development; awareness of the signs of physical, emotional, and cognitive difficulties; and good observation skills will help you recognize a child whose development differs significantly from other children in your group. Early identification, coupled with appropriate intervention, can often help avoid developmental problems that are more difficult to remediate when a child gets older.

Because development varies so greatly between individuals, in the early years the distinction between a child who has a disability and one who is typically developing is often not very clear. You already know that you are likely to have children with a wide range of developmental levels in every group. Take a good look at your expectations to make sure that they are developmentally appropriate. We have met teachers who were surprised when they encountered a 2-year-old who didn't speak clearly or a 5-year-old who did not follow directions well (both of which are within the range of normal at this age). Some worrisome behaviors are also the function of the child's temperament, maturity, and life experiences and do not indicate a disability.

Reflect On

Your Own Abilities and Challenges

Think about your own abilities and challenges. What things were most difficult for you when you were a child? How did these difficulties influence your childhood experiences? Do they still affect your life today? What do you wish your teachers had known? What are the implications of these experiences for your work with young children?

SOURCE: Jeff Reese

Inclusion

There are two ways that a child with disabilities or other special needs might be included in your classroom. You may have initiated an evaluation for a child whom you think needs additional support and are waiting for a decision, or you may have a child who has been identified as having a disability placed in your classroom. You do not need to become an expert on the causes, symptoms, and nature of a disability to be effective in working with all young children. But you may need specialized information or training to guide you in providing appropriate experiences for some of them. Sometimes, this will be fairly simple, like learning what to do for a child who has seizures. Sometimes, it may require specialized training, like learning some sign language to communicate with a child with a hearing disorder.

Inclusion, the process of providing opportunities for children with disabilities to participate in the same programs and activities as their typically developing peers, means that the child will participate in "natural settings"—those the child would be in if he or she did not have a disability.

Inclusion is not just about a place. It is about children being valued and having choices. It is about acceptance and appreciation of human diversity. And it is about providing necessary support for children, teachers, schools, and families so that all children and their families can participate in the programs of their choice. As described in Figure 12.4, "Benefits of Inclusion," everyone involved is positively influenced when children with disabilities and their typically developing peers play and learn together in the same classroom.

The goal in early childhood education is to create inclusive environments that acknowledge individual differences within a welcoming and supportive community of learners.

Figure 12.4 Benefits of Inclusion

When Children with Disabilities Attend School with Their Typically Developing Peers

- **Children with disabilities benefit.** They develop friendships and are able to observe and learn from their peers who are typically developing. They learn to cope with everyday expectations and problems, and they practice new skills in the real world of the classroom.

- **Children without disabilities benefit.** They learn that children who look different or learn differently are like them in many ways, can be their friends, and can make worthwhile contributions to the classroom. They witness perseverance and the value of struggling to accomplish something. They have the opportunity to be a coach, a helper, or a tutor to another child. The caring relationships developed among children is one of the most positive outcomes of inclusion.

- **Teachers benefit.** They broaden their professional understanding and gain a sense of satisfaction as the child with disabilities or other special needs successfully learns and functions in the classroom. It also gives them a valuable opportunity to teach things they could not teach or would teach in different ways if the child with disabilities or special needs was not a part of the group.

- **Families benefit.** Families of children with disabilities feel their children are accepted, and they feel part of a community of families and children. They gain support that helps them to better meet their child's needs.

Video Example 12.2: Benefits of Inclusion

Watch the video in which teachers discuss the benefits of inclusion. Do you think you would enjoy working in an inclusive classroom? What preparation would be helpful?

GETTING STARTED   You might be concerned about having a child with a disability in your classroom because you didn't choose to be a special education teacher and you are unsure of your ability to handle the responsibilities. It may help to remember that including a child with special needs is consistent with what you have already learned about early childhood education—viewing each child as an individual, reflecting on your own feelings, observing, welcoming children and families, and nurturing the development of every child. Children with disabilities need teachers who can do these things and who value acceptance and equality.

If a child has already been identified as having a disability, training and consultation are likely to be available to you. Your program may provide you with professional development opportunities, or you may find training related to working with children with disabilities in your community. The Office of Head Start has resources available online that are intended to support their long-standing commitment to inclusion. The Head Start Center for Inclusion has materials designed to address barriers to inclusion and to support teachers in becoming more skilled in working with children with special needs.

While young children tend to be accepting of differences, you will want to consider some things you can do to help the other children in your group understand and accept a new child who has a special need. Think about the words you will use if children ask questions or want more information about the child. A simple explanation of the condition with some personally meaningful examples is a good approach. For example, for a child who has difficulty with expressive language, you might say, "Mark has trouble saying what he wants to say sometimes. Do you ever want to tell someone something and the words come out all mixed up?"

Answer children's questions as honestly and directly as you can. Help them understand any differences they notice. You could say, "Rose wears a hearing aid so that she can understand us when we talk to her." If they seem interested, you might find a way to bring in some hearing aids for children to try and to learn about how they work.

You may need to assure other children that a disability isn't "catching." Some children (especially those of elementary age) may initially laugh at or ridicule a child who looks or learns differently. Remember that this response is probably fueled by embarrassment. This situation provides you with an opportunity to talk about the wide range of human differences and the value of respectful relationships. Your accepting attitude will provide a powerful example.

You can help the children in your class understand that no one can do everything equally well and that all of us have strengths and weaknesses. You may also help them find specific ways to include a child with a disability in their activities. For example, you might show them how to help a child with a visual impairment feel the shape of a block structure and then give verbal guidance so that the child can be successful in placing a block in the structure.

IMPLEMENTING INCLUSION   Implementing inclusion involves learning about the needs of the individual child, the nature of the disability, program modifications, and teaching strategies that will support development and learning. The most valuable source of information about any child is his or her family. You will also gather information from careful observation of the child. When you get to know a child with a disability as a person, you will be better able to meet his or her needs in your program. Pediatricians, therapists, special education teachers, early intervention specialists, workshops, and classes can also help you learn more about the child who has a disability.

Remember that knowledge about a disability may help relieve your anxiety, but it will not help you know the individual child. A disability is only one characteristic of a person. When a child who has a brace or walking splint on his or her leg works a puzzle or paints at an easel, your first response will be to acknowledge what the child has done. When he or she is on the playground and cannot run or climb like the other children, you may need to provide physical assistance or help the child find alternative activities. Be sure to focus on the ways that children with disabilities are like other children instead of concentrating on the remediation of deficits and delays.

Your knowledge of developmentally appropriate practice will help you to decide on the materials and teaching strategies to use. You will begin with observations of the child's strengths, interests, and preferences. Just as you do with all children, you will model desired behavior, demonstrate the sequence in an activity, and interact with the child. Remember to let the child take the lead when possible, provide encouragement, and stay nearby so you can offer necessary support. Be sure to give the child the opportunity to participate as fully as possible in the daily events of the classroom in order to support his or her developing sense of competence. Avoid protecting the child too much—this might single out the child as less competent. Other children may then become overprotective or may exclude the child. Figure 12.5 provides some suggestions for including a child with disabilities or other special needs in your classroom.

Successful inclusion means that children with disabilities enjoy full participation in activities with their peers and have the supports they need to be successful. Providing access includes removing physical barriers, providing a wide range of activities, and offering many opportunities for children to learn and to interact with peers. The Division for Early Childhood (DEC, 2014) offers an updated set of recommended practices to guide families and professionals about the most effective strategies to support children birth through age 5, who have or are at risk for developmental delays or disabilities. These practices include eight domains: leadership, assessment, environment, family, instruction, interaction, teaming and collaboration, and transition.

You can make your classroom a good place for a child who has a disability by making some fairly simple and often inexpensive adaptations to the learning environment, curriculum, and materials. The general goals you have for children with disabilities will be the same as those you have for other children. Keep in mind that, like all children,

Figure 12.5 Including a Child with Disabilities or Other Special Needs

- Learn about the child by talking with his or her family members. They will be your best source of information about the child's strengths, needs, and challenges. Be sure to listen carefully to family members and others who know the child.

- Consult with the child's doctor, therapists, and former teachers for additional information. Find out whether the child is taking medication and any side effects that might be an issue. Ask what special classes or therapy services the child participates in and find out any precautions, limitations, or requirements you should know about.

- Maintain regular communication with the family and other specialists who are working with the child.

- Find out what services will be available to support your work with the child.

- Brainstorm with the experts on how you can best support the child's development.

- Be careful not to make judgments based on first impressions. Get to know the child and be sure to look for strengths and abilities.

- Ask yourself: "How can I make classroom routines and activities relevant to this child and also meet the needs of the other children?"

- Be patient—some children may need to be told or shown several times.

- Be flexible and open to learning new things about children and about yourself.

those with disabilities need to have opportunities to develop confidence through exploring, communicating, practicing self-control, and developing relationships.

The fewer modifications and changes you make, the better. The activities you provide for children with disabilities may have a slightly different focus but should be as close as possible to the activity that other children are engaged in. For example, when the typically developing children are identifying the shapes and colors of the table blocks, a child who learns more slowly may be stacking the blocks. You can tailor learning activities to the needs of each child, those with learning disabilities, those who qualify as gifted, and all of the others.

Adapt the Environment and Instruction   Sandall and Schwartz (2002) present six types of curriculum modifications that can be used to support learning in children with disabilities. These provide a useful framework for adapting your classroom to serve a wide range of children:

1. *Environmental support*   involves modifying parts of the environment (including the routines and schedules) to make it more responsive to a child with special needs. If a child has trouble with mobility, you may need to widen pathways between areas. If a child has a verbal processing problem, you can provide a picture of the activity or area he or she is to go to next. If a child is having trouble attending in a group, it might be helpful to shorten the amount of time devoted to group activities. You may also want to be sure that your classroom has barriers in place to keep a very active child from running.

2. You can *modify materials*. For example, it will be easier for a child with motor difficulties to participate if you wrap tape or yarn around the handles of brushes, sew handles on stuffed animals, provide short-handled eating utensils, lower the easel, tape pieces of wood to the pedals of the bike, and use nonslip materials to keep toys from sliding. An occupational or physical therapist can help you figure out simple modifications that can make a big difference.

3. *Simplify activities*   for children who are having difficulties with tasks. Breaking down a complex task into its component parts and teaching them separately as a series of subskills (called **task analysis**) is a useful tool. Tasks such as putting on clothes and brushing teeth can be practiced in small chunks as preparation for

carrying out the whole task. If you have ever taught a toddler to pull up his or her pants, you have some practical experience with this process.

4. *Adaptive devices* (specially designed furniture and equipment) can be employed to assist a child's involvement in activities. Specialists can help you arrange for furniture and materials, such as a special table to help a child in a wheelchair get near an activity, adaptive scissors to assist a child who has fine motor difficulties, and footrests and back props on a chair for a child who has difficulty sitting up. Assistive technology, such as touch screens, is also available to help a child to communicate.

5. *Peer support* involves pairing the child who has special needs with one who knows the activities and routines and who will be supportive and a good role model.

6. *Invisible support* involves arranging activities in ways that are not obvious to support a child's participation. This might include making sure that the child with special needs has a chance to see how other children are doing an activity, letting the child pour last so the pitcher isn't too full, or having the child go first to ensure that he or she has enough time to complete an activity.

Reflect On

Your Experiences with Children with Special Needs

Think about the ways in which children with disabilities were or were not a part of your early school experiences. If children with disabilities were in your school or classroom, how do you think teachers and children felt about them? What implications do these reflections have for you as a future teacher?

Provide Opportunities for Children to Play Providing a good inclusive classroom for children with a range of needs and abilities will draw on your skill in implementing developmentally appropriate learning experiences. Children with disabilities, like all children, need opportunities to engage with a wide variety of experiences, including play.

It is important that teachers who work with children who have disabilities and other special needs do not become so concerned with remediation that they forget that all children need opportunities to play. Play is particularly important for children with disabilities because its open-ended nature offers opportunities for them to experience feelings of competence that are so crucial in the development of positive self-esteem.

Providing guidance can be particularly important for supporting the play of children with disabilities. You may need to take an active role in helping a child learn to play and do some direct teaching of play skills if the child has not yet learned them.

COLLABORATION When you have children with disabilities and other special needs in your classroom, it will be necessary to collaborate regularly with other professionals. This may involve working with special education teachers, consultants, professionals from different disciplines, and paraeducators or assistant teachers who may spend time with them during the day. In the past, specialists in different areas tended to work in isolation. For example, when a child attended speech therapy outside of school, the teacher and speech therapist might not have communicated with each other. Today, educators and specialists work together to address the needs of children and families in a more integrated and systematic way. This collaborative approach can be beneficial to you because professionals who have specialized knowledge about disabilities are available to provide resources and support. In

SOURCE: Jeff Reese

turn, you can share the natural ways that you embed learning opportunities into the daily program and continue to take responsibility for the children supported by an IEP in the classroom.

Collaborating with others to provide the best possible experience for a child with a disability can be gratifying. It can also be challenging because working with a team involves crossing discipline boundaries. In order to serve children effectively, team members need to work on building trust, respecting each other's contributions, and communicating effectively. Good collaboration enables a team of educators, specialists, and family members to share their resources to help children and address any issues that arise.

> **A Quick Check 12.2**
>
> Gauge your understanding of the concepts in this section.

Characteristics of Young Children with Disabilities

IDEIA defines more than a dozen categories of disabilities—conditions that significantly interfere with a child's learning and development. The pages that follow contain brief descriptions of some disabilities that you may encounter in early childhood programs and suggestions for how you might work effectively with children who have them. Keep in mind that a label does not give you a full picture of a child. Characteristics observed in children with one disability are often similar to those of other children with different disabilities. Children who have been determined to have the same disability are likely to differ from each other as much as they differ from other children.

You will not encounter children with all of these disabilities in any classroom and may not encounter all of them in your whole career. The information that follows will be most helpful when you encounter a child who seems quite different from his or her peers. After observing for a while, you might consider referring a child for evaluation or try some of the strategies suggested here.

Children with Orthopedic Impairments

Children who have orthopedic impairments have difficulty controlling or moving their bodies. It may be helpful to talk to the child's family and therapists to learn about activities the child enjoys that can be used with the whole group. For example, body awareness activities will be helpful in improving all children's ability to move and learn to control their bodies.

Young children are often fascinated by special equipment, like walkers or wheelchairs. Check with the family—they may be willing to let other children try out the equipment. You might also invite an adult with an orthopedic impairment to visit with the children and answer their questions. Figure 12.6 offers suggestions that will help you to work effectively with children with orthopedic impairments.

Figure 12.6 Suggestions for Working with Children with Orthopedic Impairments

- Rearrange furniture to make it easier for the child to move from one area to another.
- Adjust table and easel heights.
- Relocate supplies and toys to make them more accessible.
- Adapt standard equipment, like tricycles.
- Let the child discover his or her own abilities and limitations by trying activities.
- Encourage independence by teaching self-help skills, like dressing and eating.

Children with Cognitive Delays

Although all children learn at different rates, some learn significantly more slowly than their peers. Cognitive delays can arise before, during, or after birth. One of the leading causes of cognitive delay is a genetic abnormality called Down syndrome. During the preschool years, children with cognitive delays appear much younger than their chronological age and may have difficulty learning skills and concepts, remembering things or using information to solve problems. They may also have trouble using language or may encounter difficulties initiating activities or interactions, or learning to function independently.

Children who have mild cognitive delays may not seem much different from the youngest children in a group. Children who have moderate cognitive deficits will have greater difficulties in self-help skills, motor development, social skills, and language development. Children with significant cognitive delays will have trouble functioning in most areas of development. See Figure 12.7 for suggestions for working with children with cognitive delays.

Figure 12.7 Suggestions for Working with Children with Cognitive Delays

- Break down directions, giving them more slowly.
- Provide many opportunities for the child to successfully practice a new skill.
- Simplify routines, and allow more time for transitions.
- Do not assume what the child can do and can't do. Encourage the child to try.
- Use shorter sentences and a simpler vocabulary than you might with the other children.
- Spend more time and use a multisensory approach when you teach a new activity.
- Focus on contrast and give lots of real-life examples when helping the child learn a concept.

Children with Learning Disabilities

The term **learning disability** refers to a variety of problems exhibited by children with normal intelligence but below-age-level academic functioning. Children with learning disabilities can be extremely uneven in their development. For example, a child may have advanced verbal abilities and find it very difficult to learn how to read. When you work with a child with learning disabilities, be sure to focus on strengths and provide lots of encouragement for successes.

Learning disabilities are diagnosed infrequently in preschool children because they do not have much impact on daily functioning. This condition is most often noticed when a child enters kindergarten. In school-age children, the inconsistency between ability in one area of development and disability in another often leads to children being blamed for not trying hard enough or for being lazy. Figure 12.8 presents suggestions for assisting children with learning disabilities.

Figure 12.8 Suggestions for Assisting Children with Learning Disabilities

- Use several sensory modalities so that the child can learn in the way that suits him or her best.
- Allow the child to touch and manipulate materials.
- Be well organized and keep activities short.
- Plan activities for the child to do when a task is completed.
- Keep transitions and large-group times short to avoid situations where the child is waiting with nothing to do.
- Allow adequate time and opportunities for the child to practice new concepts and skills.

Children with Communication Disorders

It is typical for young children to have problems with language and communication. Lack of fluency is part of normal speech development; so are errors in articulation. You should be concerned about a child's language development if he or she does not talk by age 2, is not speaking in two- or three-word sentences by age 3, is very difficult to understand after age 3, or uses poor sentence structure or stutters after age 5. Preschool children exhibit many normal articulation errors, such as saying "wif" for "with." When these differences persist beyond the age of 5 or if unusual pitch, volume, or voice quality characterizes a child's speech, an evaluation by a speech therapist is in order.

Children with receptive language problems have difficulty understanding the meaning of words or the way words are put together. Children with auditory processing problems may be unable to tell the difference between speech sounds (auditory discrimination) and may be unable to isolate the sounds from a noisy background. Children with speech problems are often difficult to understand. When children have expressive language problems, they have difficulty verbalizing ideas, selecting appropriate words, or using correct grammatical structures. When children cannot communicate, they have difficulty learning, and social interactions are hindered when it is difficult for others to understand them. Figure 12.9 contains suggestions for assisting children who have communication disorders.

Figure 12.9 Suggestions for Assisting Children with Communication Disorders

- Converse with the child regularly and encourage conversation among all the children.
- Be careful not to interrupt, rush, or pressure the child.
- Model correct language and expand the child's own comments.
- Use simple constructions and vocabulary.
- Provide many opportunities for all children to enjoy language in activities.
- Incorporate songs, rhymes, and chants into daily routines.
- Use picture cards to help the child express feelings during times of stress, frustration, or excitement.
- Redirect the communication to another child: "Could you tell Willie what you just told me?"

Children with Sensory Impairments—Visual

A child whose inability to see interferes with participation in daily activities is considered visually impaired. A child with partial sight may have a visual acuity problem that is correctable with glasses. Few children are completely unable to see. Many can see light and dark areas or broad shapes but not details or have peripheral (side) rather than frontal vision.

The development of children whose visual impairment occurred after birth generally resembles that of other children, but the development of children who were blind at birth tends to be much slower. Because they may not be able to see well enough to imitate the actions of peers and because movement may be perceived as dangerous and therefore curtailed, children with visual impairments may be somewhat slower in physical development than their peers. Social development may also lag behind because they may not see facial expressions that provide social cues that are a necessary part of social interaction. Figure 12.10 includes suggestions for assisting children who have visual impairments

---

Figure 12.10 Suggestions for Assisting Children with Visual Impairments

- Provide good overall lighting. Avoid glare or deep contrasts between light and shade.
- Keep the room arrangement and traffic patterns simple and uncluttered—and when a change is needed, have the child with the visual impairment participate in making the change.
- Use detailed description to accompany your actions when you introduce an activity or game.
- Keep a child with visual impairment close to you for group activities so that you can provide physical cues for participation.
- Provide larger toys and add different textures or sounds to materials when possible.
- Remind the child to look in the direction of the person speaking.

Children with Sensory Impairments—Hearing

A child who is hearing impaired finds it difficult to hear and discriminate among sounds. A hearing impairment may involve volume or clarity of sound. When children cannot hear, even with the use of a hearing aid, they are said to be deaf. Those who have a permanent but less severe hearing loss may be assisted by the use of a hearing aid. Individuals with severe hearing loss may use a cochlear implant—a device implanted into the skull that sends electrical signals to the brain, enhancing sounds, particularly speech. Figure 12.11 suggests some ways that you can assist children whose hearing is impaired.

When children cannot hear well, they do not have access to the vocabulary words, directions, jokes, explanations, and questions found in early childhood classrooms. Social interactions may be hindered when it is difficult for others to understand them or when they do not respond to verbalizations from peers. Cognitive skills may be slower to develop. Teachers need to be patient and refrain from concluding that the child "won't pay attention" or "ignores me and just does what he pleases."

If a child has trouble paying attention (especially in group activities), doesn't answer when called, seems confused by directions or questions, or often gives the wrong answer, you might suspect a hearing problem. Other signals you might observe include frequent touching or tugging at the ear. Children who strain to decode verbal signals are often easily tired.

Figure 12.11 Suggestions for Assisting Children with Hearing Impairments

- When speaking to the child, place yourself at the child's eye-level and in a well-lit place.
- In a group activity, have children sit in a circle, so all faces are visible. Seat the child next to you so that you can touch him or her and signal that you want him or her to watch your face.
- If the child uses a hearing aid, ask the family to teach you how it works and how to care for it. Hearing aids are very expensive and can easily be tugged out when a jacket or T-shirt comes off. Ask the parent for suggestions for keeping it in place.
- If the child seems not to understand, rephrase your sentence instead of simply repeating it.
- Use visual clues and gestures to aid understanding. If the family is teaching the child sign language ask them to teach you the sign language gestures for simple requests or phrases they use at home.
- Encourage participation in activities like dramatic play that involve lots of language.
- Invite the child's early intervention provider to visit your classroom and talk with you about how your program might better support the child's goals.
- Hearing impairment can be isolating and undermine self-confidence. Verbal cues may be lost, but thumbs up, high fives, winks, and bright smiles can go a long way toward ensuring that this child feels appreciated and included.

Otitis media, or middle ear infection, is common in young children and can cause not only temporary hearing loss but pain as well. Frequent infections can lead to permanent hearing loss. For this reason, it is important to communicate with families about your observations and concerns and learn if the child has seen a physician. If the situation persists, talk it over with your administrator and learn how to refer the family for free or low-cost screening.

The advent of universal newborn hearing screening, which is now administered in hospitals in most states, allows early identification and treatment for children with hearing impairment. This screening identifies infants so their development plans can begin early, increasing the effectiveness of early intervention services. It also reduces the number of children being identified after age 36 months—the critical period for speech and language development.

The recent emphasis on developmental screening in early childhood programs is also beneficial to hearing impaired children. Screening makes it possible to monitor a child's development across time. Reliable developmental screening systems can alert a family or a teacher to a change in developmental status in the communication domain, including hearing.

Children with Sensory Impairments—Sensory Processing Disorder

Sensory integration is the process by which the brain assembles a picture of the environment using information from the senses. The importance of this process was highlighted in the 1960s by occupational therapist Jean Ayres. In most children, sensory integration occurs naturally, but in others, the brain isn't able to effectively integrate information from one or more of the senses. Sensory integration disorder was the term used to describe difficulty organizing and interpreting sensory information that makes it difficult for the child to focus. One of the first signs of a sensory integration issue is that a child may have a strong reaction to the taste, temperature, or texture of food.

The term sensory integration disorder is still in use, but a new term, **sensory processing disorder**, has been created to describe this condition in an effort to get it recognized as a medical diagnosis eligible to receive insurance coverage for evaluation and treatment.

Ayres and others have developed approaches to intervention that involve a wide variety of sensory experiences. The primary goal of these activities is to help children improve their ability to regulate motor and behavioral responses to sensory stimuli. Desired outcomes include increasing appropriate attention to people and activities, and developing modified responses to sensory input and the ability to complete daily tasks, such as dressing, eating, and communicating with others. See Figure 12.12 for some ideas about how you can assist children who have sensory integration disorders.

Figure 12.12 Suggestions for Assisting Children with Sensory Integration Disorders

- Provide children with many opportunities to touch and play with a variety of textures. Messy activities like playdough and shaving cream may be soothing, though some children may be reluctant to engage them.

- Provide "heavy work" activities that stimulate these neurological systems. These may include using weights, jumping, bouncing, rocking, pushing, pulling, and swinging.

- Provide opportunities for the child to get tactile input from materials like sand and water.

- Provide opportunities for **vestibular** (the system that contributes to balance and spatial orientation) movement. These may include trampolines, swings, rocking toys including glider rockers, and therapy balls to bounce or lie on.

- Massage and vibrating toys can be useful for calming or stimulating children, though it may take a long time before a child is able to tolerate vibration.

SOURCE: Jeff Reese

Children with Attention-Deficit/Hyperactivity Disorder

Children who show an inability to focus and stay on task may have **attention deficit disorder**. When they also exhibit impulsive, out-of-control behavior and hyperactivity beyond what is appropriate for their age-group, it is called **attention-deficit/hyperactivity disorder (ADHD)**. Children with ADHD may be easily excitable and have trouble waiting for explanations or taking turns and can seldom pause long enough to relax, watch, or listen. Jeremy, the child in the example earlier in this chapter, may exhibit this disorder. Children with ADHD often struggle to learn because they have difficulty focusing. Their impulsive behavior also makes it difficult for them to develop social skills.

Children with ADHD often exhibit extremes of behavior. Symptoms include impulsiveness, short attention span, distractibility, inability to focus on a task, constant motion, and difficulty following directions. Drugs like Ritalin can be helpful for calming down children with ADHD, but they need to be prescribed by a medical doctor based on careful evaluation. A diagnosis of ADHD is made only for children who are between 6 and 12 years of age and who exhibit symptoms for more than 6 months.

A highly active child who is consistently presenting the behaviors identified above may be ADHD. But be careful to resist the temptation to label every very active child as hyperactive; a high activity level may simply be a characteristic of a child's temperament. After careful observation, if you think the child might really have ADHD, suggest an evaluation. Because this behavior can be disruptive, a consultation with a pediatrician or other medical professional specializing in ADHD can help you develop effective classroom strategies. Figure 12.13 provides suggestions for assisting children who have ADHD.

Figure 12.13 Suggestions for Assisting Children with ADHD

- Simplify surroundings and reduce visual/auditory stimulation to help the child focus.
- Clearly define the child's work or play area.
- Position yourself near the child so you can offer assistance or encouragement.
- Acknowledge constructive and appropriate behavior.

Children with Emotional Disorders

Children with emotional disorders may be more aggressive, unhappy, anxious, or withdrawn than their peers. They can be extreme in their reactions and may require specialized care. They may also exhibit unusual behaviors, such as self-mutilation, rocking, running with arms flapping, extreme fearfulness, withdrawal, or total loss of self-control. Emotional disorders interfere with relationships, with learning, and with the development of a positive sense of self. See Figure 12.14 for suggestions about how you can assist children who have emotional disorders.

A child with emotional disorders may be challenging for you to handle not only because the child is intense but also because even the experts disagree about the causes, classification, and treatment of these conditions. You may want to consult with a mental health professional to help you understand and work with a child you think might have an emotional problem. You may also need to be persistent in seeking appropriate assistance for the child and family.

Figure 12.14 Suggestions for Assisting Children with Emotional Disorders

- Provide consistent and predictable schedules and routines in order not to trigger anxiety.
- Alert the child well in advance if there are going to be changes in the schedule or routines.
- Make classroom expectations very clear and consistent.
- Use a variety of strategies in teaching including demonstration, visual cues, and consistent directions.
- Limit extraneous stimulation by providing the child with a quiet and protected place to work.

Children with Autism Spectrum Disorders

Autism is a developmental disorder that affects communication skills and social relationships. At present, our best understanding is that it is a medical condition that results from some abnormality in brain development. A pediatrician or another professional who specializes in working with children with autism usually diagnoses it. The term used today is **autism spectrum disorder** because individuals vary in the degree of severity of their symptoms and the characteristic ways they behave, develop, and learn.

Autism is typically identified in the first 3 years of life and is four times more common in boys than in girls. There has been a tremendous increase in the number of children with autism spectrum disorders (ASD) in the past 20 years. The Centers for Disease Control and Prevention reports that, "About 1 in 68 or 1.5% of children were identified with ASD based on tracking in 11 communities across the United States in 2012." They also state that "It is too soon to tell if the percentage of children identified with ASD is still increasing or has stabilized." (Retrieved from: https://www.cdc.gov/features/new-autism-data/index.html)

There is also a growing body of information about the disorder from people who have autism, from parents of children with autism, and from researchers who study it. Temple Grandin, a writer who has eloquently described her experiences as a child with autism, explains that she was almost unbearably sensitive to things like the rubbing of new clothing on her body and that she was unable to modulate noise. She says that if she didn't try to shut out the stimulation and withdraw, it would all come rushing in (Turnbull, Turnbull, Shank, & Smith, 2004).

Reflect On

Working with Children with Disabilities

Think about working with children with disabilities. Does the idea make you feel interested and enthusiastic or anxious and uncomfortable? Why do you think you react this way? What might help you prepare for this challenge?

Children are considered to have an autism spectrum disorder when they exhibit some or all of the following characteristics:

- Significant delay in social interaction in areas such as eye contact, development of peer relationships, sharing with others, and social reciprocity.
- Impairments in communication, such as delay in or lack of spoken language, difficulty in conversing with another person, repetitive use of language, or inability to engage in make-believe play appropriate to the child's developmental level.
- Strong negative reactions to sensory stimuli.
- Restricted, repetitive, and stereotyped patterns of behavior. For example, rigid following of nonfunctional routines or rituals, as well as motor mannerisms like hand or finger flapping (Hall, 2009).

Asperger syndrome is a disorder that is part of the autism spectrum. It can range from mild to severe in its symptoms and is characterized by tendencies toward social isolation, communication difficulties, and eccentric behavior. Individuals who have Asperger syndrome fall within the normal intelligence range, do not have delays in language, and can communicate normally. They often exhibit exceptional skill or talent in a specific area (Dunlap, 2009).

There are still many questions about best approaches for working with children who have autism spectrum disorders, but there is growing consensus today that early intervention can make a significant difference in how a child can learn to interact with others and function in educational and other social settings. Figure 12.15 offers suggestions for assisting children who have autism spectrum disorders.

Figure 12.15 Suggestions for Working with Children Who Have Autism Spectrum Disorders

- Make sure that daily routines are well-known, consistent, and predictable.
- Clearly define the areas of the learning environment and make sure it will not overwhelm a child's senses.
- If needed, provide a quiet place where a child can go to reduce the sensory input they receive.
- Provide verbal reminders of what will happen next.
- Provide picture schedules to let children know what to expect.
- Give children choices and opportunities to direct their own learning.
- Support communication with peers by creating cards with pictures and symbols that a child can use to introduce him or herself and communicate needs and feelings.
- Give the child many opportunities to practice social behaviors.
- Provide soothing activities like water play.
- Be sensitive in comforting the child—one child may respond positively to being hugged while another may shrink away from physical contact.
- Find an activity or interest that you can talk about with the child and, if possible, incorporate it into daily activities.

Video Example 12.3: A Discussion on Autism

Watch the video of two teachers discussing their experiences of working with children with autism. What are your thoughts on working with autistic children?

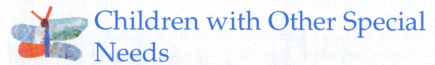

Children with Other Special Needs

You will also need some specialized information and skills to work effectively with children who have special needs that are not identified disabilities. These special needs can take a variety of forms. Some children may be gifted and talented, some may have been abused or neglected, and others may have a variety of chronic health problems and other conditions that require special attention.

Children with Special Gifts and Talents

Children who have unusual strengths, abilities, or talents are called **gifted**. In the past, giftedness was determined by a single test of intelligence. Today, it is considered to include several traits, and there is no single measure used to identify it. Children who are gifted may exhibit one or more of these characteristics: intense curiosity; passionate interest in a particular topic (or topics); capacity for abstract thinking and the use of symbol systems at an early age; independent learning; unusually perceptive; extraordinary memory; great persistence in self-chosen tasks; advanced language, science, or mathematical ability; exceptional creativity; the ability to use and appreciate verbal humor. Some children may have both a "gift" and a disability, as did the son of a friend of ours who had unusual verbal and artistic ability and a learning disability in reading.

Although children who are gifted and talented are not included in IDEIA, they have unique needs and require some specialized opportunities in the classroom in order to reach their full potential. If the special characteristics of children who are gifted and talented are ignored when they are young, they may become bored in school because the regular curriculum does not challenge them or address their interests. When this happens, they can become disengaged or disruptive.

Gifted and talented children, like all children, need to be given learning experiences that challenge them in order to develop their potential. If you have a child in your program who appears to be unusually advanced in one or more areas of development, you can provide encouragement by offering many opportunities for the child to develop and extend his or her interests. Gifted and talented children generally benefit from learning materials that are open ended and from self-directed activities that require active involvement and problem solving. Find out what the child wants to know and do and then find the materials that will support these desires. You may have to find materials designed for children who are older than those in your group. The child who is gifted may require less structure than most other children and may be able to work quite independently. Large blocks of time for exploration will give the child the opportunity to concentrate and to do in-depth work. You can support gifted children's learning by providing them with a variety of books and materials, by taking their interests seriously, and by helping them explore the things they are passionate about.

SOURCE: Jeff Reese

In the past, the primary strategy for addressing the needs of gifted children was acceleration—moving them through the curriculum at a faster pace than other children. This meant having them skip grades in order to place them in classrooms that were a better match for their intellectual abilities. This strategy is still used, but it is controversial. Proponents claim that students need acceleration to maintain their interest in school, while others maintain that it is harmful for their social-emotional development to be placed in settings with older children.

Today, the value of teaching children who are gifted and talented in regular classrooms with their same-age peers is recognized. Their interest and enthusiasm can influence other children, and the child who is gifted can experience the range of abilities they will encounter in the real world and learn valuable lessons from assisting other children. When you provide intellectual challenges to children who are gifted, make sure that you meet their social and emotional needs and provide them with meaningful curriculum, and these children will thrive in school and the other children (and the teacher) will benefit from their special abilities.

Children Who Have Been Abused or Neglected

Like all children with special needs, those who have been abused or neglected can benefit from relationships with caring adults in a thoughtfully planned program. Children who have experienced trauma from an adult may be emotionally fragile and have problems with relationships with other children and adults. Their behavior may be an indication of the high levels of stress they are experiencing, which can include acting out by hurting others or closing down and being fearful. To rebuild a healthy self-concept and the ability to trust adults, the child may need extra time and attention. If possible, one person on a teaching team should be designated as the child's primary contact, responsible for being physically and emotionally available to meet needs for attention, care, comfort, and positive discipline. The consistency of loving firmness can help the child realize that adults can be trustworthy, predictable in their reactions, and in control of themselves and the environment. It will also be helpful if you structure a safe, consistent, and comforting environment; keep the child physically safe; and ensure predictable routines to provide a sense of security.

The child's experience should be structured to promote feelings of mastery, safety, and control. A caring adult can participate with the child in sensory activities, such as play dough and water play—first as a way to foster a nurturing relationship and then as a bridge to encourage normal interest in play activities and relationships with children and adults. It is also important that teachers refrain from criticizing the child's family or otherwise expressing disapproval of them.

Children with Acute or Chronic Health Conditions

Children with acute or chronic health conditions may have any of a wide variety of ailments, including respiratory conditions, diabetes, severe allergies, asthma, cancer, and other health issues. Children who experience these conditions can thrive in a regular classroom, but require special assistance.

Health problems may have an impact on the child's ability to function in a school setting. Children who have been ill may lag in the development of motor skills. They may tire easily and need extra time or support for participation in class activities. Some may be more dependent on adults than is typical of children their age. In dealing with chronic health problems, as in all of the other situations we discuss in this chapter, you will need to know the child, and you will make every effort to provide support and encouragement that will let the child function as much as possible like others in the group.

A child's need for support from the teacher and program will vary with the nature and seriousness of the health condition. A child with a serious allergy, for example, might need only protection from the allergen and a teacher trained to administer emergency first aid, while a child with epilepsy or a feeding tube may need regular assistance.

The family, pediatrician, and the health department in your state will be able to help you plan for inclusion of a child with health problems. When a child who has a severe chronic health condition enters your program, you will need to be involved in planning and collaboration with health professionals. A team including school personnel, a nurse from the school or a community agency, the child's family members, and others can be convened to develop an **individualized health care plan**. This plan will address routine health care procedures, identify who is responsible for addressing needs, and establish communication networks among the members of the team. Health care specialists will handle many of the provisions of the plan, but the teacher may be trained to deal with some procedures, such as giving the child medication (French, 2004).

✓ **A Quick Check 12.4**

Gauge your understanding of the concepts in this section.

Working with Families of Children with Disabilities

When working with children with disabilities and other special needs, it is imperative for you to engage family members as partners and communicate with them frequently. Disabilities impact the family in profound and lasting ways. Your communication and support can go a long way toward making life a little easier.

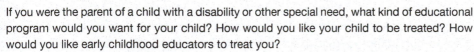

Reflect On

How You Might Feel as the Parent of a Child Who Has a Disability or Other Special Need

If you were the parent of a child with a disability or other special need, what kind of educational program would you want for your child? How would you like your child to be treated? How would you like early childhood educators to treat you?

Soon after you have collected observational data about a child like Jeremy, who was described earlier in this chapter, you will schedule a conference with the family. We do not advise approaching the family by saying, "Jeremy has a problem I want to discuss with you." This kind of statement may arouse their anxiety to such a degree that good communication becomes difficult if not impossible. Instead, make a simple statement about the problem: "I'd like to talk with you about what we're trying at school to help Jeremy get involved in play activities. Can we get together some afternoon this week to talk about it?"

When you meet with a family to discuss a concern, begin on a positive note. Parents appreciate hearing what you especially enjoy about their child, so begin with positive comments. Tell them what you see as their child's strengths and capabilities. Then share the recorded observations that caused your concern. Work to build an alliance with the family by asking them if they have observed similar behavior and how they handled it. Offer to work with them to clarify the problem and seek assistance for the child. If they need some time to think over what you have talked about, you might want to schedule a second meeting to discuss it further.

Often, family members have concerns about their child but may not know where to turn for help. They may be relieved to learn that you are committed to supporting them and working together to find answers to your mutual concerns. The information and insight you offer may prompt them to arrange a referral for evaluation of the child, or they may ask the school to arrange for the referral. On the other hand, if you are the first professional who has suggested that there might be a problem, the family may react defensively and reject the possibility that something could be "wrong" with their child. They might prefer to believe it is something the child will outgrow. When family members do not want to participate in getting help for the child, you will need to explore other avenues. You might talk to your program administrator about other ways to approach the family.

In some cases, it might be helpful for you to encourage family members to come into the classroom to observe the child or ask them to discuss the concerns with their pediatrician or early intervention/early childhood special education agency in your area. A screening instrument such as the parent completed child monitoring tool Ages and Stages Questionnaire 3rd Edition (ASQ-3) (Squires & Bricker, 2009), or another developmental checklist can help identify red flags that may support the parent seeking further assessment and evaluation. During this process, it is important that you continue to do everything you can to meet the child's needs in your classroom and to maintain good communication with the family. All families need to be reassured that a concern about a child does not mean that you or your program will reject the child and family. This can be challenging for a beginning teacher, and you may want to get some help from an experienced colleague or administrator when this situation occurs.

The family of a child with disabilities faces some difficult challenges: accepting the fact that their child has a disability, finding help for the child, providing special care, and interacting with professionals who are working with them and the child. Like all families, they need your respect and support. Keep in mind that they have their own culture and unique set of strengths, values, skills, expectations, and needs. They need acceptance, open communication, and to be treated as part of a team working on behalf of the child.

The family has both the right and the responsibility to play a primary role in determining the nature and extent of services provided for their child. They should always be involved in decisions and must give their consent to any services their child receives in addition to those provided for all children in your program. You can help by being a bridge between the family and others who are interacting with the child and working to ensure that communication is clear between home, school, and professionals.

If you teach in a public school, there will be procedures in place for evaluating children and providing specialized services. If you teach in a preschool, you will probably need to refer the child to the local school system for an evaluation. You will continue to work with the child and family while the evaluation is conducted, and if the child is not determined to have a disability, he or she will remain in your classroom, and you will need to find help in meeting his or her needs. Sometimes, after making a concerted effort, you may conclude that you do not have the specialized training you need to work effectively with the child and that your program is not an appropriate place to meet the needs of the child and family. This is a difficult decision and should be carefully considered. Principle 1.7 in the NAEYC Code of Ethical Conduct (2005/11) offers guidance on how a teacher can approach this decision in an ethical manner.

Confidentiality is an important issue. How much is appropriate to reveal to others? If you have a child with a disability in your class, it would be a good idea to ask the family what they would like you to share with other families and the children in your group about the disability. If parents of other children in the group ask, tell them that you have an ethical obligation to not share confidential information about any child and therefore you are not able to give them details about this child's condition. (You can cite Principle 2.13 of the NAEYC Code of Ethical Conduct.) It may be helpful to assure them, without violating confidentiality, that the child's condition is not "catching." They need to know that children rarely adopt any developmentally inappropriate behavior displayed by a child with a disability. You can offer general reassurance, emphasizing the benefits of children learning to accept differences and becoming compassionate, caring members of a community. Encourage families to get to know one another. This may alleviate some of the social isolation that accompanies having a child with a disability. Your own attitude can provide a positive example.

Reflect On

Your Ethical Responsibilities

A parent volunteer in your class often asks questions about which children have disabilities, the kinds of disabilities they have, and how they are being treated. Using the "Guidelines for Ethical Reflection" on page 24 reflect on your ethical responsibilities in this situation and think about an ethical response that you might make.

A Quick Check 12.5

Gauge your understanding of the concepts in this section.

Final Thoughts

Making room for everyone is one of the early childhood educator's most important responsibilities. The message we want to convey in this chapter is that as a teacher of young children, you can embrace the diversity found in your classroom and help every child reach his or her full potential. You can do this by approaching every child as an individual who has unique strengths and abilities, by understanding typical and atypical development, and by knowing effective strategies for supporting the growth of children who have a range of needs and abilities.

The current commitment in the early childhood field to providing inclusive opportunities for children with disabilities and other special needs is a positive movement that marks the recognition of the common humanity in all people. Working with a dual language learner or with a child who has a disability or a special need has the potential to be an unparalleled learning experience in your own development as a teacher. You will learn about the child and the family, you will develop skills, and you will see the child benefiting from your efforts. You will also be learning to appreciate the wide spectrum of human differences.

Application Exercise 12.1 Final Reflection

To Learn More

Visit a Website

The following agencies and organizations have websites related to children with
disabilities:

American Speech-Language-Hearing Association (ASHA)

Autism Society of America

Center for Applied Special Technology (CAST)

Center on the Social and Emotional Foundations for Early Learning (CSEFEL)

Children and Adults with Attention Deficit/Hyperactivity Disorder (CHADD)

Division for Early Childhood of the Council for Exceptional Children (DEC)

Head Start Center for Inclusion

National Center for Universal Design

National Center on Cultural and Linguistic Responsiveness

National Dissemination Center for Children with Disabilities

National Early Childhood Technical Assistance Center (NECTAC)

Sensory Processing Disorder (SPD)

United Cerebral Palsy

U.S. Department of Education, Office of Special Education and Rehabilitative
Services (OSERS)

Document Your Skill & Knowledge About Including All Children in Your Professional Portfolio

Include some or all of the following:

- Research and write a pamphlet on resources that are available in your community
  for families of children with disabilities or with another special need. Include a brief
  description of the resources, who provides them, who is eligible, phone numbers,
  and names of contact persons.

- Write an observation of an early childhood program that includes a child who is
  a dual language learner or who has a disability or other special need. Report on
  how the staff works to meet the child's needs. How do they appear to feel about the
  child? Reflect and then comment on the effect that this child has on children and
  staff in the program. What did you learn from this observation, and how might it
  influence how you would work with this kind of child in the future?

Shared Writing 12.1 Your Ethical Responsibilities to Children

Chapter 13
Partnerships with Families

SOURCE: Jeff Reese

Parents are like shuttles on a loom. They join the threads of the past with the threads of the future and leave their own bright patterns as they go, providing continuity to succeeding ages.

FRED ROGERS

 ## Chapter Learning Outcomes:

13.1 Describe the characteristics of contemporary families.

13.2 Build effective relationships with families.

13.3 Promote family engagement.

13.4 Support families during difficult situations.

NAEYC Professional Preparation Standards

The NAEYC Professional Preparation Standard that applies to this chapter:

Standard 2: Building Family and Community Relationships (NAEYC, 2011)

> Key elements:
>
> 2a: Knowing about and understanding diverse family and community characteristics
>
> 2b: Supporting and engaging families and communities through respectful, reciprocal relationships
>
> 2c: Involving families and communities in their children's development and learning

Each child is a part of a unique family and comes to school wrapped in the family's values, attitudes, and behaviors. Family members play a critical role in young children's lives and are children's first and most important teachers. Therefore, your relationships with families are of the utmost importance. This chapter is about the ways you build effective partnerships with families and encourage their engagement in their children's early education program.

You probably entered the field of early childhood because you wanted to work with young children and you may not have realized that working with families is an important aspect of the work of an early childhood educator. Creating family-school partnerships is a rewarding part of your work. It offers you an opportunity to be part of a family's journey and to work with them as they raise their children. Because it is a significant part of your role, you need to understand families and have skills for working with them.

Understanding Families

All families are concerned with the welfare of their children and want the best for them. As a teacher, you share this wish along with a joint commitment to supporting their children's development. This mutual concern is the basis for your relationship. While individual families have particular needs, interests, and knowledge, they share many similarities. Knowing about common characteristics of many families and taking steps to create meaningful relationships with individuals helps you teach young children effectively.

Families take a variety of forms and often include adults other than parents. Stepparents, siblings, grandparents and other relatives, foster parents, or friends may assume parental roles. To simplify the wording of this chapter, we will often use the term *family* instead of *parents*, and in doing so we are speaking of the entire cast of adults who play a significant role in a child's life. When we speak of *parenting*, we are discussing the nurturing done by all of the important adults who take on a parental role.

Parenting young children is both a delight and a challenge. It comes with moments of great tenderness and humor and with times of anxiety and exasperation. The stresses may sometimes seem to overshadow the pleasures. Yet, many parents say that their years of raising young children were among the happiest and most rewarding periods of their lives.

As an early childhood teacher, increasing your awareness of the many aspects of parenting—the responsibilities, the joys, and the struggles—will help you relate to families effectively. This understanding will allow you to be supportive and sympathetic. It is also important that you understand the particular circumstances of each family's life that influence their ability to nurture and care for their children. The information that follows can help you appreciate

SOURCE: Jeff Reese

individual families and know about the dynamics that influence their relationships with their children and with you, their child's teacher.

Responsibilities of Today's Families

During the past century, the primary responsibilities of the family have increased from ensuring children's physical well-being (food, shelter, clothing, health, and safety) to providing psychological security along with the skills needed for dealing with an increasingly complicated world. Families may be unsure of what abilities and knowledge will be important for their children to master in today's rapidly changing society. With torrents of information and opinions available from all types of media, families may feel bombarded, confused, and concerned about what parenting strategies to use or what types of education will best serve their children in the future.

Additionally, many families are increasingly aware of the importance of the early years in children's development and learning. Some feel they must hurry their children into activities that are supposed to ensure success—academic tutoring; lessons in music, dance, art and athletics; and team sports. They may worry about enrolling their children in the "best" preschool to ensure access to the best primary school, high school, and even college. The current trend toward high-stakes testing and the recurring pressure to meet academic standards may contribute to family pressure on schools and teachers to focus on academics at the expense of other activities.

In a technology-saturated era, families often wonder about their responsibilities related to providing their children access to the broad array of programs, applications, and devices that are available. Commercial information abounds about the benefits children can gain from a game or an app. Competing information from some "parenting experts" may warn families to limit screen time; others may suggest the importance of exposing children early to these powerful tools. The amount and accessibility of information available to families may increase their sense of confusion and concern about meeting their young children's needs appropriately. And in some families, the challenges of daily living—earning a living, dealing with stressful environments, handling ongoing responsibilities—may consume all the energy and time that is available for the adults in the family.

Becoming a parent requires that people learn to balance many competing responsibilities; care and nurturance of young children must be handled in tandem with other important duties, such as relationships with partners, work responsibilities, home tasks, attention to other family members, and social relationships. Ellen Galinsky (1981) described the early childhood years as the time when parents learn to be nurturers and to define themselves as authority figures in the family. Assuming this role while balancing their many competing responsibilities can be stressful. Families appreciate it when teachers understand the challenges inherent during this stage of parenting. When you take a moment to acknowledge their efforts and are sympathetic on the occasions when they are late or seem disinterested, you are letting them know that you understand that they mean well and are handling their many obligations to the best of their ability.

Diverse Families

Families come into your program from a wide variety of backgrounds and circumstances. Their experiences, along with their values and beliefs about children and education, may be quite different both from one another and from those of your family and culture.

> *Sasha, a teacher in a 3-year-old class, welcomes the children and families as they enter. In the first half hour, she greets Leah and her grandma, Carol; Maré and her mother, Selina, and baby brother, Sol; Braylon and his stepdad, Jamal; Kalia and her "nang-nang" (great-grandmother); Emma and her half-brother, Suli; and Noah and his dads, Sam and Martin.*

There is great diversity in family structure in the United States, and this has been true for many years. According to the Pew Research Center's American Community Survey (ACS) and Decennial Census data (2017), 46% of children in the United States live in homes with two married heterosexual parents in their first marriage. Many live in families with single parents (34%), stepparents (6%), or foster parents. Some live

Child-Rearing Practices Influenced by Culture

- **Toileting**—the age at which families expect children to be toilet trained, and the process they use to teach children how to use the toilet

- **Food and feeding**—when different foods are introduced, what foods are considered appropriate and inappropriate, how much food children are expected to eat, who feeds children and until what age, where and with whom the child should eat, table manners, and when children should be fed

- **Nursing, bottles, and pacifiers**—whether children should be nursed and until what age and in what circumstances, whether infants are fed on demand or on a schedule, at what age bottle-fed babies are expected to give up the bottle, and whether pacifiers are given and when they should no longer be offered

- **Sleeping arrangements**—with whom the child sleeps; when, where, and how the child is put to sleep; whether the child takes regular naps and, if so, for how long

- **Bathing and grooming**—how often the child is bathed; time and attention given to creating and maintaining neat hair, nails, and clean teeth; and the extent to which children are expected/allowed to get messy

- **Personal care and independence**—when children should be expected to complete self-help tasks independently, whether children should be carried after they can walk, and how much assistance children should be offered when completing tasks

- **Respectful behavior**—whether children are expected to make eye contact as a sign of respect; whether children are expected to ask adults questions, engage in dialogue, or make jokes with adults; and the names adults are called by children (i.e., are respected adults called by first name, Miss/Mr., Auntie/Uncle, Ma'am/Sir)

- **Role of the child in the family**—whether children or adults are central in the household and family, the extent to which children's activities influence the household and where children's belongings are located in the home, and whether children are included or excluded from important family events, such as weddings and funerals

- **Responsibilities of children**—whether children are expected to perform household tasks and the age at which serious responsibility such as caring for younger siblings is given to children

- **Relative value placed on play and academics**—whether play is viewed as an important task or a distraction and whether academics are viewed as the most significant type of learning; the value placed on academic success by the significant adults in the family

- **Definitions of safe and healthy**—whether children should be protected from health and safety risks, such as getting cold or climbing high, or whether they should be exposed to risks to build strength and skill

- **Appropriate dress for school and other situations**—whether the child is dressed in specially purchased school clothes that the child is expected to keep clean or is sent to school in play clothes that can get dirty

- **Gender roles**—whether the child is expected to play and behave in ways designated by gender (e.g., playing with dolls versus roughhousing) and whether adults are expected to adhere to traditional gender roles

- **Modesty**—what body parts should be covered; what types of clothing and adornment are considered appropriate/ inappropriate for young children and adults

- **Personal possessions and privacy**—whether family members consider all items to be jointly owned and shared by all members or each member has possessions that are seen as exclusively theirs; how space is allocated; whether children have their own rooms and beds and other furnishings; expectations for dressing, toileting, and other activities as private or okay to be done in the presence of other family or non-family members

- **Appropriate knowledge for children**—whether and at what age children are exposed to such things as the proper names of body parts, sexuality, birth, illness, disability, death, and violence

- **Attitudes toward emerging sexuality**—whether children are expected to be innocent and ignorant of sexuality and whether adults think some exploration of sexuality is appropriate in "blended" families that include children of parents' current and former relationships. Some children have parents who are gay, lesbian, or transgendered. Some live in extended families with grandparents and other related and unrelated adults. In some families, parents are not present and grandparents or other family members serve as parents. All of these configurations can and do provide loving, healthy, and secure relationships for children.

A 2014 census report shows a growing diversity in the US population and this trend is projected to continue. More than 5 million children under the age of 5 from immigrant families lived in the United States in 2014; 25% of the total population of children in this age group (Migration Policy Institute, 2015). This means that you will work with children whose families are from a variety of races and ethnicities. They will bring parenting practices and values about child rearing that are influenced by their cultures and families. Some of these will feel familiar and comfortable to you; others will be different from what you know about and may even seem inappropriate. It is important for you to keep in mind that families' knowledge and beliefs about the best ways to raise their children have been significantly influenced by their own past experiences, particularly by their culture. In fact, it is the role of a culture to teach its rules and beliefs to future generations. Differences may be reflected not only in language, religion, and country of origin. Cultural differences may be found between families that are racially similar but come from different socioeconomic backgrounds, between individuals with the same ethnic backgrounds whose families immigrated in different generations, and between those who came from different parts of the same country, including our own.

It is beyond the scope of this book to provide you with information on the multitude of ways that culture can influence families and their views of children and education. The accompanying box, "Child-Rearing Practices Influenced by Culture," describes some common differences you are likely to encounter.

Remember that all families need your respect. It is important that you recognize that they rely on teachers to assist them in preserving the cultural values of their families. Learn about their preferences and welcome their differences into your early learning program.

Family Systems Theory

Family systems theory looks at the interconnectedness of family members and describes how they influence one another in predictable and recurring ways. It focuses on roles and patterns of behavior of family members and how these effect adults' and children's relationships, both with one another and with people outside of the family.

Family systems theory is most often used by family counselors and therapists. However, many of its principles help teachers understand the diverse needs of families. Six dimensions of family systems theory are particularly relevant to those who work with young children. It is important to use these dimensions as a tool to understand, not judge, families:

1. **Boundaries.** *Expectations for togetherness or separateness and understanding about who is in or out of the family.* Families' boundaries fall along a continuum. Families who value separateness and independence (called low boundary) are at one end, while those who emphasize togetherness, conformity, and family control (called high or strong boundary) fall on the opposite side. Strong family boundaries may mean that decisions about discipline, self-help skills, and children's social connections are determined by the family and input from others is considered intrusive. In families with very strong boundaries, a low score on a reading test or misbehavior at circle time may be viewed as a negative reflection on the entire family. Families with strong boundaries are likely to attend school events en masse, so

teachers must be prepared and welcoming. Low-boundary families value independence and openness to ideas of others who are not in the family unit. They may seem disconnected from children's school experiences or may let children make many decisions. Their focus on autonomy may appear to be disinterest. Remember that neither of these is better or worse than the other—just a different family dynamic.

2. *Roles.* *The parts individual family members play in their relationship to others.* In all families, each member, children as well as adults, has one or more roles. One may be the peacemaker, expected to always assist with resolving conflicts. Another may be the clown; another the victim, the problem solver, or the caretaker. These roles carry over into the school setting, influencing how children and their grown-ups behave. Your awareness of roles will help you understand children better and communicate more effectively with their families.

3. *Rules.* *The standards and procedures for how to behave and relate to others.* All families have rules, both spoken and unspoken, about how to act in particular situations and with particular individuals. Some families have many and very stringent rules; others have fewer rules and/or are more relaxed about applying them. Many rules are culturally determined. In some cases, family rules may be different from school rules. For instance, some families require that children "stand up for themselves" and behave aggressively when they feel threatened. Certain school experiences, such as both boys and girls playing dress-up, may be counter to family rules about gender behavior and expectations. As you interact with families and get to know them, you will become aware of their family's "rules." This knowledge can assist you in helping children negotiate these differences, to anticipate problems, and to discuss them sensitively and respectfully with families.

4. *Hierarchy.* *Which members have decision-making power within the family.* In some families, decision making is shared by all parental adults, while in others only one holds this role. In other families a respected elder makes the significant decisions. Understanding a family's hierarchy will help you understand how family members communicate and relate to one another, to their children, and to you. Hierarchy may be determined by age, gender, or status within the family. It is important to address concerns and questions to the members of the family who have the role of decision makers without leaving out other family members. You can learn about a family's hierarchy by talking with family members and listening carefully as children share stories about what happens in their family.

5. *Climate.* *The emotional and physical environment of the family.* This dimension includes the extent to which families are warm and supportive or distant and detached. Families can provide warm and supportive relationships in a variety of circumstances, even those where fiscal resources are limited or the surrounding physical environment is harsh or threatening. Conversely, affluent families can fail to offer emotional support to individual members despite a physical environment that appears comfortable and nurturing. It is important to create supportive classroom climates for all children, particularly those from families with challenging emotional or physical environments.

6. *Equilibrium.* *The stability or consistency offered by the family.* Families on one end of this continuum experience a great deal of stability and there is little change in their day-to-day circumstances; families on the other end experience a great deal of inconsistency and imbalance. Most families fall somewhere in the middle. Illness, unemployment, death, or mental illness decrease equilibrium, as do positive changes such as a move, a new baby, or a job promotion. Understanding individual family equilibrium will increase your understanding of their relationships and how these affect the child. When you provide a consistent school setting, you help children deal with disequilibrium at home.

Understanding Yourself

DIFFERENCES BETWEEN BEING A TEACHER AND BEING A PARENT   As you begin to work with families, it is helpful to recognize some of the differences between the role of a teacher and that of a parent. We have found the distinctions described by Lilian Katz (1980) to be very helpful for beginning teachers. Katz explains that while there are similarities between the roles of families and of teachers, there are also important differences. The role of the parent is to be their children's most passionate advocate and fan. They will care about their children for a lifetime. A teacher's role is to appreciate children realistically; to observe and evaluate them objectively and to balance the requirements of each individual with the overall welfare of the group. While you will care about children who are in your class, will remember them with fondness when they are grown, and will want to know what they do in life, your immediate concern is for the time that they are in your program. Do not expect families to have your perspective—their job is to be their child's champion. And, though you are committed to each child's learning, your commitment to the child is time limited—much different from that of their family.

YOUR DEVELOPMENT IN RELATING TO FAMILIES   Just as children and parents go through developmental stages, teachers typically go through stages in relating to families (Gonzalez-Mena & Eyer, 2015; Keyser, 2006). Knowing about these stages can help you understand yourself, your feelings, and your reactions to families.

Stage 1: Savior.   When you first begin teaching, you may find yourself wishing to be a savior to children. You may see your role as rescuing children from their family. In this stage, teachers feel that their knowledge makes them more capable of child rearing than children's families. If you find yourself thinking you would like to take all the children home with you and that you would make their lives better, you are probably in this initial stage.

Stage 2: Fixer.   In this stage, you may find yourself wanting to change and to "fix" families to make them better for their children. You understand that families are the predominant force in children's lives, the ones who have the most influence on them, but you wish you could help them be better at their jobs. If you find yourself wishing you could give a family more skills and knowledge for interacting with their children, you are most likely in this stage.

Stage 3: Partner.   When you fully accept that each child is with you for a relatively brief period and understand that your role is to support the family in their permanent relationship with their child, you are in the final stage. In this stage, you are able to honor families' expertise and share your own to form real partnerships with families—a truly satisfying part of your role.

YOUR VALUES AND BELIEFS RELATED TO CHILD REARING   Throughout this book, we have encouraged you to examine your values and attitudes about working with children. You also need to be aware of your values and beliefs about parenting. You will work with families who have a variety of approaches to child rearing and a range of views about education. Some of their views and beliefs will be congruent with yours; others will be quite different. Consider these two parents:

> Four-year-old Miana comes to school dressed in shiny white shoes and a crisply ironed dress, with her hair carefully combed, braided, and decorated with barrettes. Her friend Tani arrives in sneakers, old shorts, a clean T-shirt, and disheveled hair. By the end of the day, Miana's shoes are scuffed, her dress is painted, and her barrettes are missing. Her mother scolds her, "You wrecked your new dress! I can't afford to buy you new clothes every week!"
>
> When Tani's dad comes at the end of the day, her shirt is covered with paint, and she has torn her shorts. Her dad says, "Looks like you had fun today!" and gives her a hug.

Which parent's viewpoint was closest to yours? Did you react strongly to either child's dress or either parent's behavior? Which is more consistent with how you were raised? It is typical for people to view differences as "wrong" rather than different. By becoming an early childhood educator, you are making a commitment to learning about and being open to the range of families you will encounter and the ways they care for and raise their children. When you find that you are reacting intensely to a family's child-rearing beliefs or practices, it is a sign that you need to look more deeply at your own values and beliefs.

It is useful to be aware that when you encounter differences in ideas about how children "should" be cared for, what you may be experiencing is a cultural difference. Review the box "Child-Rearing Practices Influenced by Culture" for specific examples of these. Some of the biggest areas of miscommunication between teachers and families concern the things each may take for granted because of their cultures. With this insight, you may find yourself more willing to accept and appreciate all families. In order for this to happen, you must be aware that your views of what constitutes good parenting come from your own culture and experience.

Reflect On

Your Ideas About Child-Rearing Practices

Choose two or three of the practices described in the box "Child-Rearing Practices Influenced by Culture." Think about how these were handled in your home when you were a child. Do you have some strong views about how they should be done? How might your feelings about these practices impact your relationship with families of children with whom you will work?

A Quick Check 13.1

Gauge your understanding of the concepts in this section.

 # Building Relationships with Families

The most effective programs for young children are ones in which teachers and administrators genuinely value families, work hard to build meaningful relationships with them, and include them in classroom and program decision making. This takes both practice and intention—you must decide that building relationships with families is important and worth the time and effort it takes. You may need to switch from focusing exclusively on children to enlarging your focus to include families as well as children (Keyser, 2006).

The things that you do to build good relationships with the families in your program are often small and easy to overlook. They can be as simple as common courtesy and as complex as written policies. Planning carefully for initial enrollment and first meetings, intentional use of welcoming communication strategies, and regular family events, meetings and conferences can go a long way towards ensuring that families engage in the program in ways that are appropriate for them and supportive of their children. Don't forget that a warm greeting—"*Hi Mrs. Gonzalez; How was traffic this morning?*"; a few moments of conversation—"*Did you pick the color for the baby's nursery yet?*"; and brief sharing at the end of the day –"*Lila was so excited when she climbed to the top of the climber this morning!*" go a long way in laying the foundation for strong relationships. The following sections discuss strategies that can help you build meaningful relationships with families.

Strong Beginnings

From the moment a child first joins your classroom, you have opportunities to build a partnership with his or her family and to encourage their engagement in your classroom. It is important for you to talk with family members to learn about their child's growth and development, to listen to their perspective on their child as a person, and to get insight into their methods of child rearing. If possible, try to schedule an initial meeting, so that you can engage the family in dialogue to learn about their goals for their child and their expectations of the program. This is a good time to ask them how they would like to be involved in the program. You may also ask the family to complete a written questionnaire that provides information about their child's habits, preferences, needs, strengths, and skills. It is helpful to include questions that invite family members to share both their perceptions about their children and their goals, wishes, hopes, and dreams for them. We like to use both a written form and an initial meeting to begin our relationship with new families in our programs.

To build truly respectful relationships, take time to get to know family members as individuals and avoid making assumptions. Remember that families do not all celebrate the same holidays, eat the same foods, see the role of child and parent in the same way, or have the same ways of caring for children. To avoid making assumptions, ask families to help you support their child by explaining their perspectives, values, and beliefs. One way to begin this kind of dialogue is to ask families to tell you about if and how they celebrate holidays and birthdays (see Figure 13.1).

Many programs also invite all families to participate in an orientation or welcome meeting at the beginning of the school or program year. At this meeting, goals and policies of the program are introduced and families are encouraged to ask questions and to meet one another. This sets the stage for building a strong family-school community where parents know one another and work together to support the program.

Home Visits

Some programs, particularly Head Start and programs for infants and toddlers, use home visits as a way for families, children, and teachers to become acquainted and comfortable with each other. Teachers set up a convenient time for a 30 to 45 minute visit at each child's home prior to or soon after the beginning of a new school year. In Head Start programs, home visits may be scheduled more frequently. Some children will be very excited to show their special toys or pets to their new teacher; others will feel shy. Some families and teachers welcome these opportunities to get to know one another in a home-setting; others find them unpleasant and awkward.

Research on home visits indicates a variety of positive outcomes for children, including higher math, literacy, and classroom adaptation scores (Halgunseth & Peterson, 2009). In addition, many teachers and families feel that home visits are a valuable tool for fostering positive communication. Be aware, however, that they can be stressful for families. Some feel uncomfortable about the appearance of their homes and worry about being negatively judged. Others feel that their personal space has been invaded. They may think of it as an inspection of their parenting. Immigrant families who fear deportation may associate a home visit from early childhood staff with contacts with immigration authorities and therefore be especially anxious. If you do home visits, it is essential that you tell families of the purpose of a home visit—to encourage families, children, and teachers to get to know each other and to help children know that their families and teachers trust one another—and to offer them the choice of whether or not they wish to have a teacher visit them at home.

Communication

All relationships involve communication. To a large extent, your success at building strong relationships with families will be a result of your ability to communicate

Figure 13.1 Celebration Survey

CELEBRATION SURVEY

Most people have special days they celebrate that are part of their cultural and family traditions. We believe in including all families' celebrations in our program and would like to include yours in an appropriate way. Please help us do this by sharing some information with us. If, for religious or philosophical reasons, you prefer that your children not participate in celebrations or activities, we want to know that, too. We're beginning with the fall celebrations that are coming up and would like to know about all celebrations or holidays that are important in your family. Thanks for your help.

Family name: _____

Are there any holidays, celebrations, or celebration activities that you prefer we avoid while your child is enrolled? Please describe:

Please tell us about what you celebrate in your family and how you celebrate.

Holiday	How you celebrate it in your family	Would you like to share your celebration at school in some way? How?
Birthdays		
Fall		
Halloween		
Day of the Dead		
Rosh Hashanah		
Other fall celebrations		
Winter		
Christmas		
Kwanzaa		
Hanukkah		
New Year's Day		
Valentine's Day		
Lunar (Chinese) New Year		
Other winter celebrations		
Spring		
Ramadan		
Girls' Day		
St. Patrick's Day		
Mother's Day		
Other spring celebrations		
Summer		
Father's Day		
4th of July		
Other summer celebrations		

effectively with each person. When you do, you create a sense of rapport and mutual trust. This allows each of you to share important information with one another. Families have knowledge about their child as an individual, and you bring your knowledge of children in general and awareness of current best practices in working with young children. Both types of information are vital if you are to create the optimal experience for each child.

Every day you will engage in communication with families. Some communications will be easy and comfortable; others will be confusing and perhaps involve hurt feelings or missed opportunities to share information.

Jamari's mom, Rhea, arrives at 5:29 P.M. to pick him up. The center closes at 5:30. The teacher, Eliza, is busy putting away toys and tidying up the classroom. Eliza needs to leave right at 5:30 to get her daughter to a music audition. Rhea notices a band-aid on Jamari's arm and says loudly, "What! You got hurt again!" "There's a note in his cubby about it," Eliza tells Rhea. "It explains what happened. See you tomorrow." Rhea grabs the note and without another word takes Jamari's hand and goes out the door.

In the situation above, Eliza was unaware that the way she chose to tell Rhea about Jamari's scratch could be upsetting or even offensive to her. Learning effective communication skills can serve you well in your efforts to engage with families of the children in your program.

MAKING FAMILIES FEEL WELCOME   Whether it is the first or the 40th time they enter your classroom, it is important always to make family members feel that they are welcome in your program.

> *It is the middle of the morning during the first month of school. Jackie, the 3-year-olds' teacher, is making cinnamon toast with the children. Hui Zhong's mom comes through the door. "Hi, Lan!!" Jackie says, looking up and smiling. "Would you like to join us?"*
>
> *In the 4-year-old classroom across the hall, Matt's mom, Kelsey, enters. Wendy, Matt's teacher, is reading a story. Wendy looks up, her brows knit, and frowns. Kelsey stands by the classroom door for about 10 minutes without acknowledgment from Wendy or her assistant. Finally, Kelsey sighs, calls to Matt gruffly, "Let's go!" and leaves without having talked to a teacher.*

The ways that these family members were treated gave very different messages about whether they were welcome in the classroom. What makes a person feel welcome? It is welcoming when teachers greet family members by name and use the form of address that they prefer. Some adults prefer to be called by their first names; it feels friendly to them. Others prefer to be called by a formal title (e.g., Mr. or Mrs.) and see this as a sign of respect. You can include a question on your initial questionnaire to invite families to tell you their preferred form of address. Learn their names as soon as you can and use them often during conversations.

Most early childhood programs have an **open door policy**—meaning that family members can come into the classroom at any time. Such policies are often mandated both by program requirements and state regulations. It is welcoming to families when you embrace this practice, greet them warmly whenever they arrive, and treat them like valued guests, not intruders. Even if you are busy, take a moment to say hello and ask how they are doing. Remember what they tell you about their child and family. Invite them to come into the classroom and be understanding when they don't have time to stay. If possible, make time to answer their questions. It may take some practice and added effort at first, but these simple strategies will help you build relationships that will support the family, the child, and the program.

Another way to make families feel welcome and included is to have a **family corner.** If your classroom has space, you can set up an area with a comfortable adult chair or a couch, some reading materials about children's growth and learning, and photos of children at work and play. Some schools have separate rooms that also offer access to coffee or tea, a lending library and sometimes simple video presentations about the program or of the children engaging in a variety of activities. Family members may enjoy talking to one another in this area, and bonds between families can be

SOURCE: Jeff Reese

promoted. In infant programs, a comfortable, private space for a nursing mother supports mother–child attachment and healthy infant nutrition and lets the family know that you value their special relationship with their babies.

TOOLS FOR COMMUNICATING   You can apply the communication tools you are learning as you study child guidance to communication with adults. Active listening and I-messages are useful when interacting with people of all ages. Active listening means paying attention not only to family members' words but to their nonverbal cues. Let them know you are listening by checking back on what you believe you hear. *"It sounds like you are concerned that Grace is not getting the skills she will need to be successful in kindergarten"* or *"I think you are telling me that you are worried that Carlyle will catch cold if he plays in the water table."* Active listening helps families feel that you are attentive to their concerns.

Practice sharing your ideas clearly with respect: *"Sam just loves the new tweezers and bead game—I know you've been worried about his writing, and I wanted you to know that this will help build strength in his hands for writing"* or *"Becca doesn't seem to want to paint—do you think she might try if I let her change into an old T-shirt for painting so she wouldn't get her beautiful dresses dirty?"* These types of statements describe your thoughts accurately but in a non-confrontational manner.

Learn to explain your knowledge of child development and early childhood education in ways that are meaningful so that families understand your goals and how the program contributes to their child's growth and learning. This means translating professional jargon into language that is clear to families. For example, saying that you *"provide opportunities for motor development"* is not as valuable as letting a family know that *"swinging, sliding, trike riding, and climbing help your child develop strength and coordination."* And it may not be nearly as meaningful as letting them know that *"Jordon is building so many physical skills and becoming more confident in many ways. This will help him to be successful both socially and academically in elementary school and beyond."*

Remember that both you and the family have worthwhile ideas and that neither of you is infallible. Be sure to share information in a dialogue, not a lecture. While you must be respectful of families, you also need to act on your best professional judgment. If a family's requests violate what you know to be best for children, you have an ethical responsibility to do what is right for children—but you will need to consider carefully and explain the reasons clearly and with courtesy.

DAILY COMMUNICATION   In most early childhood programs, families come in each day to drop off and pick up their children. This can be a great time for communication; however, it requires flexibility and planning. This means thinking about how staffing can be arranged so that someone is available to talk with families and to supervise and care for children. If you schedule these times carefully, you will have daily opportunities to share important information with families.

> *"Sidney worked very hard on math today. He was persistent and figured out how to group math cubes into different sets. He was so excited when he explained to me the different ways he had organized his groups."*
>
> *"Courtney had some sad moments today. She was unhappy when LeShan wouldn't play with her. Then her bunny got buried in the sand, and we couldn't find it at nap time, and she couldn't sleep for a long time. She finally slept a little and felt better this afternoon, especially after we found Bunny."*
>
> *"Lila spent 20 minutes today going up and down the steps. She's so intent on mastering that skill!"*

Almost every parent wants to know about important moments missed while away from his or her child and is happy to hear stories about happenings in their child's school day. This type of daily communication helps families feel comfortable with the program and provides ways for them to talk with children about their school experiences.

Informal daily conversations are also a great time to acknowledge events and transitions in the child's school life and in the family's life at home. When you take a moment to recognize and share a family's joys and sorrows—"*It would be wonderful if you could bring Ira's new baby sister in and introduce her to the class; Ira would be so excited, and we'd love to meet her!*" or "*I was very sad to here that Alexis' grandmother has been ill*"—it goes a long way towards building strong bonds between teachers and families.

It is also appropriate to let families get to know you as a person with particular enthusiasms and skills—"*I made that great lasagna from the school cookbook last night; my family really loved it!*"—though it is *not* appropriate to share your personal problems. Remember to be scrupulous about maintaining confidentiality, even in casual conversation. Nothing destroys trust faster than idle gossip and broken confidences.

Daily contact should always include positive points and anecdotes about what the child did well and enjoyed. When a child has difficulties, it is important that you find ways to share this information with the family as well. However, avoid having this be the sole or even the main focus of your daily interactions. We sadly recall a mom sharing with us that she dreaded picking up her child because of the litany of "bad behavior" stories she knew she would hear. When you share information about concerns, be certain to do so in a tactful manner. If you have ongoing concerns, schedule a time to sit and talk with the parent privately.

Remember that the many commitments of daily life—dinner to be prepared, appointments to be kept, partners who are waiting, and work responsibilities—may prevent families from having time each day to chat. When pick-up and drop-off times always seem too rushed for conversation, choose another method for communicating with the family.

WRITTEN COMMUNICATION Learning to prepare written materials for families is an important skill for all teachers to develop. Whether you share information through bulletin boards, notes, texts-messages, newsletters, e-mail or online communication apps, regular written communication is an important method of staying connected with families. If there are families in your program who do not read English, it is important to locate resources for translating written materials into the families' home language. Sometimes a member of a family who is fluent in both languages may be willing to assist with translations. Other staff may also be a resource for translations. In some communities, a nearby church, synagogue, temple, or other faith-based organization may be willing to provide translation services.

In many infant–toddler programs, a written daily report is given to families each day. This provides families with important information, such as what and when the child ate, slept, and had a diaper change. A brief description of something special about the day helps families feel included. Many schools also ask families to provide home information at drop-off time to help ensure that the child's needs are met by the staff. Figure 13.2 offers two types of forms; the first uses written language exclusively; the second requires very little written language and still communicates important information.

A family communication center—a place where families can get a quick written update on what's happening in their child's classroom—is an important feature to include in classrooms that families come into regularly. It is a good idea to have a mailbox or message pocket for each family near the sign-in sheet. A bulletin board or dry-erase board can be used to post announcements about upcoming events, happenings of the day, and other brief messages you wish to share. Hang the week's plan near the communication center so that families can be informed of each week's activities and your goals for children's learning.

In programs that run longer than eight hours or when families do not come into the classroom regularly, you may not get to talk with families every day. In these cases, we have found it effective to keep a communication log (in a notebook or folder) for each family to serve as a substitute for face-to-face communication. Staff and family members

Figure 13.2 Daily Information Form for Infants or Toddlers

Written Daily Information Form

Date: _____   Child's Name: _____

Family Section:

When you check in, please give us some information to help us meet your child's needs today.

Feedings: _____

Sleep: _____

Diapers/toileting: _____

What else do you want to share with us today? _____
_____
_____

School Section:

Dear Family: Here's some information about your child's day. Please talk with us for more information.

Feeding/eating: _____

Sleeping: _____

Diapers/toileting: _____

Other information about today: _____

Emoji Daily Information Form

Date: _____

Child's Name: _____

Family Section:

While I was at home, I....

	Feeding/eating:		
	Sleeping:		
	Diapering:	x_____	x_____

School Section:

While I was at school, I...

	Feeding/eating:		
	Sleeping:		
	Diapering:	x_____	x_____

read and write in it frequently to share information about the child. A weekly newsletter or short, frequent text messages or e-mails can also help you maintain communication. Some teachers communicate via an e-mail listserv or a regularly updated class blog. Some schools are using commercially available parent-communication apps specifically designed to allow teachers to send information and photos online to families.

SOURCE: Jeff Reese

School or class web pages and newsletters offer opportunities to provide information of general interest, to explain aspects of the program in greater detail, to solicit input and assistance from families, and to provide information about child development and other topics of interest. These are most successful when they are attractive, short, and easy to read.

Written communications must be available to and understandable by all family members who care for the child. Regardless of their age, when children live in two families, it is important to find ways to share written materials with both households. And of course, all written materials, whether a note or an end-of-term progress summary, need to be correct in terms of grammar, spelling, and punctuation. If this is a challenge for you, ask a colleague to proofread your writing before sending it to families.

FAMILY CONFERENCES   Conferences with family members will be a regular feature of your life as a teacher. A conference provides time for teachers and families to share information and insights. It allows for an in-depth and personal exchange of information that is not possible in other ways.

A central purpose of a conference is to form an alliance with the family to support their child's development. Regular conferences help you build relationships with families. If conferences are held only in the event of a problem, they will be stressful and less helpful both for you and for the family.

Family members may be apprehensive about attending a conference. They may have unpleasant memories of their own school experiences and may associate a parent conference with the telling of bad news. Be certain to explain the conference's purpose when you invite families to attend and make a clear distinction between a regularly scheduled conference to share progress and information and one planned to discuss a particular concern. Some families may be concerned about their limited English proficiency and their ability to understand and participate in the conference. If possible, have a translator available and ensure that written materials are prepared in their home language.

Plan carefully to ensure that you have time and space for an unpressured and productive meeting. You may have to come in early or stay late to make sure to have enough time. Prepare by looking over anecdotal observations and other assessments, review records you have on the child, and gather photographs, videos, or samples of the child's work to illustrate the child's development and learning. Many teachers create a portfolio, write a developmental summary, or fill out a checklist to document the child's progress. Some teachers find it helpful to prepare a written conference plan using a format such as the one in Figure 13.3. This helps them feel more relaxed about the conference, knowing that they have organized their ideas and are less likely to forget important points they wish to share with the family. The written plan also serves as a reminder to encourage the family's contributions as an important part of the conference.

Most programs have regularly scheduled conference times, often twice per year. Begin a first conference by explaining that conferences are regularly scheduled times for

Figure 13.3 Family Conference Planning Form

Family Conference Form

Child: _____   Date: _____

Family member(s): _____

Teacher(s): _____

Topics to Discuss

Ideas for supporting the child's growth at school:

Ideas for supporting the child's growth at home:

Resources requested by family at the conference:

Questions or concerns raised at the conference:

Follow-up plan:

Family's plan for child's future (next school, etc.):

parents and teachers to share information and get to know one another better. Assure family members that you welcome their ideas and questions and that the conference is a collaborative process. Use the conference as an opportunity to set common goals for the child that you will revisit during subsequent meetings.

As you share your perceptions of the child in school, try to describe what the child *does* rather than saying what he or she *is*: "*Lucas usually watches the others use a new piece*

Video Example 13.1: A Conference with Kayla's Mom

Watch the video to see an example of a teacher preparing for a conference. What concerns did the teacher have when preparing for the conference? What strategies did she use to help her feel ready and confident?

of equipment before he tries it. He seems to like to have a quiet space and a long period of time." Do not say, *"Lucas is very shy."* It is best to discuss the child's strengths and skills and look at other aspects in terms of areas for growth. Invite parents to contrast what they know from their experience of the child to your observations and perceptions. Ask them to tell you about what they have observed and to share their suggestions for activities and strategies that will meet their child's needs.

In many elementary schools and some preschools, the child participates in the conference and takes the lead in describing classroom activities and sharing his or her work. Teachers who have done this kind of conference report that they are very pleased with how effectively it involves the family and communicates the child's school experience. While not appropriate for infants, toddlers, or younger preschoolers, this format can be useful with older 4-year-olds, kindergartners, and elementary school children.

When it is necessary to discuss a problem—for example, when you are working with a parent to identify ways to help a child find alternatives to hurting others—assume that family members have good intentions and that solutions can be found. You can use conference time to clarify the issues, agree on goals, develop a plan of action for home and for the program, and decide when you will meet again to evaluate what you have done. We recommend writing down what you agree on with families and providing a copy for each of you.

ADDRESSING QUESTIONS AND CONCERNS

When Jules's grandmother comes to pick him up, he is sitting alone at the snack table, finishing a cracker and the last sips of his milk. "Why do you leave him all alone like that?" she asks his teacher.

Because families are so deeply concerned about their children, it is inevitable that questions and concerns will arise regarding things that are happening in your program. It is valuable to remind yourself that it is not only a *right* of family members to ask questions but also their *responsibility*. Parents who are doing their job want to know what you are doing and why you are doing it. Such questioning can lead to an open exchange of

Video Example 13.2: A Successful Parent-Teacher Conference

Watch the video of a teacher and parent engaging in a successful family conference. What did the teacher do to help the mother feel comfortable? What concerns did the mother bring up? Do you think the teacher addressed these effectively? Why?

information that can help you better understand the family and their relationship to their children. You need to be prepared to respond to questions without being defensive and in ways that keep the lines of communication open. Families often ask about whether their children are receiving appropriate instruction that will prepare them for future academic success and why the program spends time in play-focused activity. They also often ask about whether children's possessions are being looked after carefully and whether children's health and safety is being attended to. These types of questions indicate their expectations for their children and may relate to their culture.

> Rose, the mother of 4-year-old Peter, came into her son's class one morning and said to Gary, the teacher, "I don't think you're offering Peter enough challenge. He will write his ABCs when I sit down with him at home. But all he does here is play with blocks and ride trikes. He's going to go to kindergarten in the fall, you know."

What should Gary say? If he answers defensively—"*We told you when Peter started here at our center that we had a play-based program because research tells us that children learn through play*"—he will not have demonstrated that he has understood or cared about what Rose said. Similarly, if Gary does not take responsibility—"*Well, a lot of the children are interested in letters, but Peter just doesn't seem to focus on them unless we force him*"—he will not have addressed her concern.

When families question you about the curriculum, your teaching practices, or the overall program, it is essential that you take their concerns seriously and not dismiss them. When they look at your program, they may not see activities that they associate with academic learning. They may have had little experience with the hands-on learning activities that are a feature of your program. As you talk with them, you can reassure them that you are committed to their children's future academic success. You can help them understand that young children learn in ways that are significantly different from adults and that the development of motor and perceptual skills form the base of later, more abstract learning. You can remind them of the things that they learned by doing—cooking, driving a car, bathing a baby, using a computer—and that *doing* is an important way of learning. Explain the sequence of development in concrete terms: *"Children first have to learn to tell the difference between more obvious things like round blue beads and square purple beads before they can tell the difference between less distinctive things like numbers and letters."* Specific examples will help adults see the purpose of the activities that you do with children.

Gary, in the previous example, might have a dialogue with Rose that sounds something like this:

> **Gary:** *Thank you for telling me about what you've been doing and what you're worrying about. I've noticed that Peter can write the alphabet. But it doesn't seem to be what he's most interested in at school. Does he enjoy writing the alphabet at home?*
>
> **Rose:** *Well, not unless I sit him down. But he knows he has to do his work.*
>
> **Gary:** *What I've noticed is that Peter loves to look at books and listen to stories. That's a really important first step in learning to love reading. Another thing I've noticed is that he likes playing with rhyming words. That's another important part of learning to read.*
>
> **Rose:** *What about teaching letters and words? I bought a workbook for him last week, and that's his homework—just like his big brother. Why aren't you teaching him anything like that?*
>
> **Gary:** *What I have been doing is to create a word bank for each of the children. Here's Peter's file of "special words." He has five words—all the members of his family. I've also been introducing more print into the room. You know, back at the beginning of the year I put up some labels on different things in the classroom, like the fish tank, and recently I've added some more labels as well as some signs. Peter has been noticing these recently. He has also been enjoying a "hunt the letter" game we've been playing. What seems to work best for him is when I make letter activities personal and active.*
>
> **Rose:** *Yeah, he really does like to move.*
>
> **Gary:** *I want him to keep on liking school, so I want to make learning about reading fun and meaningful. His whole group is going to kindergarten in the fall and we are planning more letter activities for the rest of the year. I'll be sure to let you know how Peter responds to them. Does that sound good to you?*

Another issue that concerns families is cleanliness and the condition of their children's clothing. Many a parent is distressed to return at the end of a long workday and find that the clean clothes they helped the child put on in the morning are dirty or stained. The messes inherent in the sensory activities, art, and science curricula are frequent topics of concern. Sometimes families feel better about this once they understand the purpose of these activities. Some families are willing to send their children to school in clothes that can get dirty. For others, this is not comfortable—they want their child to look good, and they want people to know they take good care of the child. Some families prefer to keep play clothes at school and have their child change into clean clothes before going home at the end of the day. Others may agree to having their children wear aprons or smocks when engaging in messy play. Whatever their preference, it is important to continue a dialogue with them about this and to reach a solution that you both can agree to.

Reflect On

Your Ethical Responsibilities and Family Communication

A mother has requested that her daughter stay indoors every time there is any suspicion of a slight illness beginning. This would require that a staff member remain indoors with the child, creating a much higher child-to-staff ratio on the playground than is safe.

Using the "Guidelines for Ethical Reflection" in the Personal Values and Morality section of Chapter 1, reflect on your ethical responsibilities in this situation.

A third issue that is frequently brought up by families has to do with the physical challenges children undertake in early childhood settings. These may astonish and alarm them. They may never have allowed their children to climb to the top of a climbing structure or to use functional saws, scissors, or knives. They may not understand why you do. They may not be aware of what young children can safely do with close supervision. We find it helpful to let family members know that we share their regard for safety and then go on to talk about the value of the activity and the safeguards that we take. You can let families know that you won't allow children to attempt activities that are beyond their capacities and then describe the ways that you safely provide opportunities for exploration that contribute to development.

Families whose children have disabilities may question how well you are helping their child to meet identified goals and milestones and/or whether their child is being accepted by others and given equal opportunities for participation. Take time to answer these concerns thoughtfully using specific examples. Often your explanations will help families to see the many ways that their child is similar to other children and to know that the child is experiencing daily successes and interactions with others.

In any situations where a family expresses concern, it is important to discuss it with them openly. Listen carefully to their ideas and suggestions. Work for a mutually acceptable solution and avoid judging families if their opinions are different from yours. Parents who feel heard are much more likely to be supportive of your program. They are also much more likely to hear your answers and explanations when they have concerns.

The "Golden Rules for Building Strong Relationships with Families" box offers a summary of some strategies for relating to families.

Confidentiality

Maintaining **confidentiality**—sharing information about families and their children only when there is legitimate need to do so and only with those who have a legitimate need to know—is an ethical obligation of every teacher and one whose importance we cannot stress strongly enough. Without it, effective relationships with families cannot be maintained. Even a "cute" story told to a friend that identifies a child in your classroom is a violation of confidentiality. The NAEYC Code of Ethical Conduct (see Appendix A) reminds us of this responsibility.

> P-2 13-We shall maintain confidentiality and shall respect the family's right to privacy, refraining from disclosure of confidential information and intrusion into family life.

A related legal responsibility has to do with children's records. Generally, the only individuals who legally may have access to a child's file (apart from the child's teachers

Golden Rules
for Building Strong Relationships with Families

1. Listen more than you talk.
2. Communicate with all families; use a variety of strategies.
3. Smile and greet families as they enter the classroom or playground.
4. Include positive points in every communication.
5. Help families identify and articulate their goals, hopes, and dreams for their children.
6. Keep all information about families strictly confidential.
7. Develop resources to assist with translation, both oral and written, into families' home languages.
8. Create comfortable places for families in classrooms.
9. Offer a wide variety of opportunities for families to be part of the program.
10. Encourage families to know and support one another.
11. Let families know that you enjoy and appreciate their child.

and program administrative staff) are parents or guardians and those professionals who have been identified in writing by the family as needing to have the information to serve the best interests of the child. The Family Education Rights and Privacy Act (FERPA) grants families the right to examine their child's official records and protects the privacy of the records. In most programs, official files are stored in a locked file cabinet.

✓ **A Quick Check 13.2**

Gauge your understanding of the concepts in this section.

 # Engaging Families in Your Program

Quality programs engage meaningfully with each family. Much of our discussion in this chapter has focused on practices that encourage authentic **family engagement**. Our understanding of family engagement has changed significantly over the past decade. In the past, early childhood programs offered opportunities for parents to participate in the program mostly by volunteering and by attending classes and workshops related

---

What Is Family Engagement?

Family engagement is a term used to define program practices that include families in all aspects of their children's learning and welcome their active participation in schools. Research about children's success in school indicates that when families are engaged in their children's early education programs, children tend to show more initial school readiness skills and experience long-term academic success (Halgunseth & Peterson, 2009; Henrich & Gadaire, 2008).

Programs that promote family engagement are characterized as follows:

- All families are invited to be participating members in decisions about the program; for example, teachers invite family input in determining learning outcomes for their children and provide opportunities for them to be members of policy-making committees.

- Families are encouraged to offer ideas and suggestions, no matter their background, skill set, or past experiences.

- Communication systems, such as those discussed earlier in this chapter, are developed to ensure that all families can communicate with program staff so that they can collaborate and share ideas in a reciprocal way.

- The enrollment process is streamlined in order to be accessible to immigrant and homeless families; this includes multiple ways to document children's ages, translated enrollment forms, enrollment assistance, and interpreter services (US Dept. of Education, 2017).

- Staff and families create an ongoing and comprehensive system for creating family engagement; teachers and administrators receive ongoing training in ways to engage families in leadership and decision-making roles.

- Programs work in partnership with families and community members to ensure that children are offered learning opportunities both at home and at school that are consistent with each families' beliefs and values and that extend the program's learning goals into the home and the community (Halgunseth & Peterson, 2009).

Because family engagement has been shown to be pivotal to student success in all age-groups (Harvard Family Research Project, 2016), the U.S. Department of Education has created a framework for family engagement. *The Dual Capacity Framework for School-Family Partnerships* provides a model that schools can use to build effective family and community engagement in programs for children of all ages. To learn more about this framework and how states are using it in their schools, visit the US Department of Education website and search for *Family and Community Engagement.* In addition, this department has developed a resource guide, *Building a Bright Future for All: Success in Early Learning Programs and Elementary School for Immigrant Families.* You can also access this guide from their website.

to parenting, child development, and/or other issues of interest to families. Today we know that while these activities can be useful, families must also be involved in deeper and more meaningful ways. True family engagement means that staff and families share responsibility for children's progress as well as for school practices and policies that involve families.

Building Partnerships

In order to build true family-school partnerships, early childhood staff must hold the belief that every family has strengths and that they play a pivotal, positive role in their child's development. This frame-of-mind ensures that families are offered a variety of ways to be participants in their children's education and learning. When programs focus on families' strengths and their shared commitment to children's overall growth and well-being, they are taking steps to create meaningful partnerships with families (National Center on Parent, Family and Community Engagement, n.d.). There are many ways to effectively build partnerships. All can be useful and it is important that programs strive to provide opportunities to include families in authentic partnerships.

In Figure 13.4, strategies for building partnerships appear in sequence from most-inclusive to least-inclusive. Examples of practices are offered for each type.

Figure 13.4 Building Family Partnerships

Most Inclusive

Partnership

- Families are included in all aspects of the program including goal setting, program planning and the creation of policy.
- Family members serve on committees or policy boards.

Engagement

- Families' preferences, interests and strengths are part of program and curriculum planning.
- Families are active in planning the program's family events.
- Family culture and home language are included in the program in relevant and respectful ways.

Involvement

- Families are invited to share ideas about their child's strength's, needs & interests and to help set goals for their child.
- Families' suggestions are considered by staff when making decisions about program and curriculum.

Participation

- Families are invited to special events.
- Families volunteer in the classroom or for field trips.
- Families are invited to information & education sessions planned by program staff.

Information-Sharing

- Families receive information about what their child is doing.
- Families share information about issues and routines such as allergies, fears, pick-up instructions.

Least Inclusive

We have found it most effective to offer a variety of ways that families can be engaged in the program and to invite their participation and partnership using a variety of strategies. This allows them to be included in whatever ways feel most comfortable to them.

As your relationships with them grow, they may be more willing to let you know how they wish to be a part of the program. Offering a Family Partnership Survey (see Figure 13.5) when families first enroll can provide you with important information and may help them to consider ways they wish to be a part of their child's early childhood program.

Classroom Participation

For many families, opportunities to participate and be included in the classroom are an important aspect of a school-family partnership. Families bring knowledge and

Figure 13.5 Family Partnership Survey

At our school, we view family members as partners with us in creating a program that supports each child's growth and learning. We welcome your involvement in all aspects of our school. Being a part of your child's early childhood program is a great way to share in your child's experiences. It shows your child you care about his or her education, helps the teachers, and it can be fun, too! There are lots of ways for you to be a part of our school, depending on your time and interests. We know that not everyone will want or be able to do everything. Please let us know how you want to be involved by filling out this survey.

Your name: _____   **Phone number:** _____   **E-mail:** _____

The Program for Children

_____ I'd like to come and have lunch with the children at school.

_____ I'd like to come on a field trip and assist.

_____ I'd like to help out in the classroom.

_____ I'd like to help plan an event for the children (a trip, a party, etc.).

_____ I'd like to bring in an activity to do with the children such as cook, share a story, work in the garden, teach a song. I'd like to:

Best days and times for me:

The Program for Families

_____ I'd like to attend a parent social event such as a potluck, campout, or a picnic.

_____ I'd like to meet with other parents for a parent support group.

_____ I'd like to attend a parent education event (about guidance or child development and learning, etc.). Topics that interest me are:

_____ I'd like to join the *Parents & Friends Club* and participate in their activities.

_____ I'd like to work with other parents on fund-raising or planning events for families and children. Specifically I'd like to help with:

Improving and Maintaining the Environment

_____ I'd like to send in plastic bags or other recyclables that we use (ask first please).

_____ I'd like to help out on a work day, on a weekend, or school break.

_____ I'd like to borrow/return library books, or do shopping.

_____ I'd like to make or mend something for the classroom (we have lots of projects for someone who's handy: make a new batch of play dough, sew or mend dress-up clothes, make pillows, put together a game or scrapbook). Specifically I'd like to:

Managing or Promoting the Program

_____ I'd like to sit on a committee/board to give input into how the school is run.

_____ I'd like to be part of a committee to give input about curriculum.

_____ I'd like to help plan family events.

_____ I'd like to be part of a hiring committee.

_____ I'd like to review the policy handbooks and make recommendations for changes.

_____ I'd like to help out in the office.

_____ I'd like to speak as a parent representative to legislators or community groups.

_____ I'd like to organize a display in the community to educate others about the program.

Other ideas that staff haven't thought of:

In addition, the staff and families must gather the required equipment and materials, arrange for food, and make sure that the jobs can be done in the designated time. Work days can include children but responsible adults must be selected to monitor their safety while staff and parents are working. Events such as hands-on workshops and family work days can contribute to creating a sense of community among families in your school. Many families of young children feel isolated from others. This may be particularly true for families who have recently moved to a new community and those whose children have disabilities. Opportunities to work alongside others will help them build support networks and share the joys and stresses of parenting young children.

Family members can also be included as members of advisory councils, policy boards, and hiring committees. When families are members of decision-making bodies, they become genuine collaborators with staff in creating programs that are family centered and that accurately reflect the values, interests, and needs of the families involved. Family members who participate in policymaking feel that the program truly belongs to them and their children. They are willing to expend more of their energy and resources because of their greater commitment. These parents become valuable advocates for your program.

All families are committed to their children's development and learning. Be sensitive to their different strengths and styles and offer a variety of ways to become involved. The "Connecting with Families About Program Involvement" box summarizes the strategies discussed above.

Family Education

Traditionally, programs for young children have included family education activities. Family education can focus on a broad range of topics: those related to children's development, parenting skills, and other interests of family members. You provide family education informally in your regular interactions with families and as you model positive interaction strategies in your classroom. When you find that a number of family members share areas of interest, you can offer more structured opportunities to provide them with appropriate information, such as a newsletter article, a family discussion night, a workshop, or a class. If a topic is beyond your skills and expertise, you can draw on others in your school and community.

Families and community members who have been involved in your program may have resources for a family education event. We have experienced topics as diverse as a workshop on allergies conducted by a pediatrician parent and a workshop on home

Connecting with Families

About Program Involvement

Families are encouraged to become involved when you offer them:

1. **Information.**   Share fliers, handouts, and articles about parenting, child development, child guidance, and ways to support children's growth and learning. Connect families with information about community resources.
2. **Opportunities to share information.**   Create ways for families to tell you about their dreams and hopes for their children and their expectations of the program.
3. **Suggestions for contributions.**   Let families know that you welcome both material contributions and ideas and suggestions about the program. Be sure to give them opportunities to participate in program decision making.
4. **Participation opportunities.**   Provide a variety of ways for families to volunteer their time and expertise both in and out of the classroom. Encourage family members to be part of decision-making committees.
5. **Strategies for encouraging children's learning.**   Share ideas about ways that families can provide activities and experiences at home or in the community that support children's learning.

gardening presented by a father and his sister who were skilled in creating and maintaining gardens. Family members who understand the values and goals of the program will often be willing to share their special skills and knowledge and even invite their friends to contribute.

Reflect On

Family Engagement You Have Seen

Think about a program that you have observed or worked in. What kinds of family engagement opportunities did you observe? What appeared to be the attitudes of the school staff toward families and towards their participation? How do you think families felt about what was done?

Like other aspects of the early childhood program, a family education program requires planning. It is valuable to survey the families to find out what they most wish to learn about and what times and settings will work best for them. Participation in family education events will increase if you provide child care and offer children and families a meal or hearty snack before, during, or after the presentation. In some settings, providing transportation for families increases their ability to attend. Lively, interactive sessions are usually the most effective, and families are most likely to be engaged in the presentation when the presenter is informed in advance about the knowledge level and learning style of the participants.

Another way to provide parenting education is to develop a library of books, magazines, and informational DVDs for families to borrow. A local business or foundation may be willing to make a contribution to fund this, or families might hold a fund-raiser to cover the costs. Sometimes, families will donate materials that they have found helpful. An attractive display space either in the classroom or near the office may entice parents to look at and borrow materials. You can also include brochures and pamphlets related to family topics. There are many websites that allow you to print these types

 ## Application Exercise 13.1

Watch and Write About Strategies for Engaging Families

of brochures. Visit the *Zero-to-Three* website and go to the "Resources for Parents" area to see examples. Many parents also appreciate having a list of reliable websites related to parenting. The American Academy of Pediatrics's *Healthy Children* website, Neumours's *Kids Health,* and The National Association for the Education of Young Children's (NAEYC) *for families* are examples of sites that families may find helpful.

A Quick Check 13.3

Gauge your understanding of the concepts in this section.

 # Supporting Families

All families must deal with a variety of situations and challenges that occur in the course of daily parenting. However, some families face circumstances that require particular support. One of your tasks will be to recognize these challenges and offer appropriate kinds of assistance.

Helping in Times of Stress

Everyone experiences stress. Some stress is relatively minor, the result of juggling the responsibilities of a busy life. Other stresses are more serious, such as when a family structure changes, as with a new baby, death, divorce, deployment, or remarriage, or when there is a loss of a job, a home, or a loved one. The trusting relationship that you initially establish with each family can help them feel comfortable letting you know when there is upset in their lives and allowing you to offer support when such situations occur.

Even though you are not a counselor, you will find it helpful to know about and have strategies for helping families during difficult times. There are several ways that you can do this. The first is by being there and doing your job. Children and families are supported when you are present, attentive, and professional. When you are not, it adds to their stress.

One of the simplest ways you can help is by being aware and keeping a child's school life as stable as possible during periods of upheaval. These are not times to move a child to a new group or make major changes in the schedule or room arrangement. A second way is to help families find needed assistance. To do this, you need to know how to access resources such as medical clinics, family counselling, legal aid, mental health services, family violence shelters, family mediation organizations, and fiscal support services, such as the Supplemental Nutritional Assistance Program (SNAP), formerly known as food stamps, and the Women, Infants, and Children program (WIC). We find it helpful to keep a resource list of program names and services, hours of operation, and contact information. Families will appreciate it if you can give them specific information that makes it simple for them to contact the appropriate agency or program.

It is almost inevitable that at some time you will be asked to play a supportive role for one or both parents in divorce or child custody conflicts. A clear statement explaining your program's policies and procedures in these situations (often found in the family handbook) can help the parents understand what you can and can't do and that your primary commitment is to the child's welfare. One way to offer support to families going through a divorce or separation is to communicate to families that such problems are by no means

SOURCE: Jeff Reese

unique or a sign of failure. When a divorce or custody battle does take place, it can be tempting to express your preference for one parent or the other. Keep in mind that you serve a child better by maintaining neutrality. In cases where family members are in conflict, the National Association for the Education of Young Children (NAEYC, 2005) *Code of Ethical Conduct* states, "In cases where family members are in conflict with one another, we shall work openly, sharing our observations of the child, to help all parties involved make informed decisions. We shall refrain from becoming an advocate for one party" (section P-2.14).

Reflect On

Your Strengths and Challenges in Supporting Families

What do you see as your potential strengths in communicating with families and supporting them when they are dealing with stressful situations? What might be challenging for you? What experiences, understandings, and skills do you have that may help you? What understandings and skills do you need to work on?

Preventing and Reporting Child Abuse and Neglect

Because of your important role in the lives of children and families, you can play a key part in preventing child abuse and neglect. Your work helps reduce children's risk of abuse and neglect by supporting and strengthening families (NAEYC, 2004). The Center for the Study of Social Policy (2014) has identified five factors that protect children from child abuse and neglect: (1) parental resilience, (2) family social connections, (3) parental knowledge of parenting and child development, (4) children's social and emotional competence, and (5) concrete family support in times of need.

When you put into place many of the strategies discussed in this chapter, you are promoting the development of these factors. By taking steps to help families acquire the knowledge and skills that they need to relate positively to their children, you promote the families' overall well-being and lessen the risk of abuse. NAEYC's *Supporting Teachers, Strengthening Families* initiative encourages teachers to learn about and use a family-strengthening approach in their early childhood programs. Figure 13.7 shows the framework for this approach.

Figure 13.7 The Family Strengthening Approach to Abuse Prevention

Early childhood teachers support and strengthen families and reduce the risk of child abuse and neglect when they:

1. Provide quality care and education through developmentally appropriate practices.

2. Develop reciprocal relationships with families.

3. Recognize situations that may place children at risk of abuse and provide families with appropriate support.

4. Recognize signs of abuse.

5. Understand, and help families to understand and handle, children's challenging behaviors.

6. Build on child and family strengths.

7. Inform themselves about their professional responsibilities.

SOURCE: Information from M. Olson, "Strengthening Families: Community Strategies That Work," *Young Children*, 62(2), 2007; NAEYC, *Building Circles, Breaking Cycles—Preventing Child Abuse and Neglect: The Early Childhood Education Role*, 2004.

You can request up to 50 free copies of NAEYC's brochure *Building Circles, Breaking Cycles—Preventing Child Abuse and Neglect: The Early Childhood Educator's Role* by visiting the NAEYC website. You can view a copy of this useful resource online by searching for "Building Circles Breaking Cycles."

Despite your efforts, sometime in your career you will be faced with a situation where you believe that a child in your care is being hurt or neglected by a family member or another adult. As an early childhood educator, you have an ethical and legal responsibility to report suspected cases of child abuse or neglect. Just like a doctor, you are a **mandated reporter**. Every state has its own laws and regulations pertaining to child abuse reporting in early childhood education programs. Compliance is often the obligation of program administrators; however, it is important for you to be aware of your specific responsibilities. You can learn more about legal mandates from the agency that regulates early childhood programs in your state. Families should be notified during initial enrollment that early childhood educators are "mandated reporters" and that the staff's goal is to work with family members to ensure that children are kept safe from physical and emotional harm.

Every program should have written policies that describe the staff's obligation to report child abuse and neglect and the procedures to follow if there is reason to suspect abuse has occurred. This information should be given to you as part of your orientation to a new job. Be sure to ask about this if it has not been made available to you. It is important that you become familiar with the reporting procedures of your program and your state so that you will know what to do when you suspect that a child is being hurt. Most schools and child care centers have a person, often the principal or director, who will provide guidance and help you in documenting your concerns and reporting cases of abuse. The Child Welfare Information Gateway at the U.S. Department of Health and Human Services website offers useful general information as well as state-specific resources for child welfare. Indicators of abuse and neglect are also described.

If you believe that abuse has occurred, you must report it, following the guidelines of your program and your state's child welfare agency. If you find yourself in this situation, make every effort to maintain a good relationship with the family and work with them as cooperatively as possible. Focus on positive aspects of the child in your discussions with the family and take care to notice and comment on the family's attempts to handle the child in a constructive way. Do all you can to suspend judgments about the family and let them know that your goal is to support them and help them cope. Avoid communications that might make the parent feel inadequate or incompetent and try to reassure them that they continue to have your respect. Neither child nor parent should be labelled as "abused" or "abuser," and confidentiality should be rigorously kept. Remember that families suspected of abuse or neglect are living in stressful circumstances and may need additional support and assistance in their efforts to nurture their children.

Supporting Families of Children with Disabilities

Families of children with disabilities should be a welcome part of your program. Make sure they have the same opportunities to participate as families of typically developing children. Invite them to help at a workday or provide field trip assistance just as you would with any other family. Help them to meet other families. For example, at a family event or when they drop off or pick up their child, you might say something like, *"Mrs. Brown, I'd like you to meet Mrs. Ortiz. Her daughter Lisa was Nicole's partner on our neighborhood walk today."* When planning family events, be sure the child care provided will meet the needs of all children.

Just like families of typically developing children, families of children with disabilities need regular communication and sharing of positive information. The anecdotal records you keep on the child can serve as the basis for a dialogue between you and family members. Make a special effort to collect data on children with disabilities because the more data you have, the easier it will be to see progress that you can share with the family.

Noburo, age 3, enters your program in the fall. In your initial interview with his family, they tell you that he is very, very smart and that they are enrolling him in school because they feel he needs more education than he is getting staying at home with his obaasan, his grandmother. You notice immediately that Noburo does not speak and does not appear to make eye contact with you or with other children. After several days, you speak with his mom, explaining that he is enjoying many of the small motor toys and games and asking if he speaks at home and if they speak Japanese or another language at home. Mom says, "Oh yes, he talks. And we only speak English at home, even his grandmother speaks only in English." For several weeks, you keep anecdotal records of Noburo, recording his ability to complete complex puzzles quickly, to recreate patterns with inch cubes and to build large structures with unit blocks. You also note his lack of response to any spoken language from you or from other children. You make time to talk with his mom every day when she comes, focusing on how skilled he is at working puzzles and creating patterns. She seems happy and excited to hear of these skills. After several months when you have heard no spoken language, you schedule a conference with Noburo's parents. You share with them how well he is doing in cognitive and motor tasks. You also point out that you believe that his lack of verbal skill is hindering his ability to form relationships with others and to achieve tasks related to language and communication. With some reluctance, they agree to take Noburo to a speech-language specialist for an assessment.

Because Noburo's teacher took time to get to know Noburo and to talk regularly with his mother, she was able to share her concerns in a way that helped his parents to see the need for further assessment. These strong relationships go a long way toward helping families trust that your recommendations are in the best interest of their child.

Video Example 13.3: Providing Support for Parents of Children with Disabilities

Watch this video of a parent of a child with attention deficient disorder explain her feelings about meeting with her daughter's teachers. What differences did she describe between her feelings at her daughter's former school and her feelings at her current school? To what did she attribute these different feelings? How could you apply your thoughts about what she said about meeting with her daughter's current teachers to your conversations with all families, both those whose children have disabilities and those who are typically developing?

If a family has been in your program for a while before their child is identified as having a disability, you may need to increase the frequency of communication to ensure that the child and family get needed services. Make a special effort to keep the family involved in ordinary events as well. Even if they can't participate much while they are adjusting to this new dimension of their lives, later they will appreciate being kept informed.

 A Quick Check 13.4

Gauge your understanding of the concepts in this section.

 # Final Thoughts

Families and teachers of young children can become partners who share a common goal—to educate and care for children in ways that support optimal development. Teachers know that when they care for children, they are also caring for and caring about families. As a member of this field, you will play an important role in the lives of many families. You will be part of the network of people who will lend support to the families' efforts to function in a complex society and provide their children with the protection and nurture they need. When you see family members as competent, caring people who are doing all they can to provide for their children, you will engage with them in a productive and mutually satisfying relationship that promotes the well-being of the child and of the family.

 Application Exercise 13.2 Final Reflection

 # To Learn More

Read

From Parents to Partners: Building a Family-Centered Early Childhood Program, J. Keyser (2006).

Parent Engagement in Early Learning: Strategies for Working with Families, J. Powers (2016)

Partnering with Families: Winning Ways for Early Childhood Professionals, D. Schweikert (2012).

The Essential Conversation: What Parents and Teachers Can Learn from Each Other, S. Lawrence-Lightfoot (2004).

Visit a Website

The following agencies and organizations have websites related to families:
Center for the Study of Social Policy: Strengthening Families
Families and Work Institute
Family Support America
NAEYC for Families
National Child Traumatic Stress Network
National Coalition for Parent Involvement in Education (NCPIE)
National Network of Partnership Schools (NNPS)
Parents as Teachers

Document Your Skill & Knowledge About Partnerships with Families in Your Professional Portfolio

Include some or all of the following:

- A newsletter article that you have written to help family members understand a specific aspect of children's development and learning.

- A description and photographs of how you have made a classroom more family-friendly—for example, the addition of an adult-size chair, a parent area, or a family bulletin board.

- A list of ways for family members to be involved in the classroom or program—consider meeting with several family members and a teacher to assist you with creating a meaningful list; include a reflection about how family members responded.

- A plan for, description of, and reflection about a family event that you have planned or participated in planning—include photos if you have them along with a discussion about whether or not the event was effective in involving families and what you learned from the experience.

- A Resource Directory for Families that you have created that lists contact information, referral procedures and a brief description of agencies in your community that provide services or offer resources to families with young children.

Shared Writing **13.1** Your Ethical Responsibilities Related to Building Partnerships with Families

Chapter 14
Becoming an Early Childhood Professional

SOURCE: Jeff Reese

*Those of us who are in this world to educate—to care for—
young children have a special calling: a calling that has
very little to do with the collection of expensive possessions
but has a lot to do with the worth inside of hearts and
heads. In fact, that's our domain: the heads and hearts of the
next generation, the thoughts and feelings of the future.*

FRED ROGERS

Chapter Learning Outcomes:

14.1 Describe some current realities in the field of early education of which a teacher of young children should be aware.

14.2 Discuss some things you need to know about the field and about yourself as you begin to work in the field of ECE.

14.3 Reflect on some of the commitments you will need to make as you become an early childhood professional.

NAEYC Professional Preparation Standards

The NAEYC Professional Preparation Standard that applies to this chapter:

Standard 6: Becoming a Professional (NAEYC, 2011)

Key elements:

6a: Identifying and involving oneself with the early childhood field

6b: Knowing about and upholding ethical standards and other early childhood professional guidelines

6c: Engaging in continuous, collaborative learning to inform practice

6d: Integrating knowledgeable, reflective, and critical perspectives on early education

6e: Engaging in informed advocacy for young children and the early childhood profession

Current Realities in Early Childhood Education

This chapter is intended to provide some guidance for your journey into the "real world" of teaching. In it, we discuss knowledge and skills needed by early childhood professionals; we provide information about some issues you are likely to encounter in programs, and we explore some of the commitments you will need to make as you begin your career. We want to give you a bit of a "heads-up" so that these things do not take you by surprise when you encounter them.

Our Society Is Changing

We begin with a brief look at the societal influences on families and children that early childhood educators are likely to face in the 21st century. As you move into your first position, you will have daily contact with a community of children, families, and colleagues. Much of what happens within any community is directly impacted by circumstances within the larger society.

When you understand some of these, particularly the demographics of families and the ways they are changing, you will be better prepared to teach children effectively. You will need to understand some of the challenges that families face. For example, practically all families of young children work and the great majority need child care. Many are poor, some face food insecurity, lack of adequate shelter, and have inadequate health care. Some will be concerned about their immigration status and fear being deported. Many have less access to computers and the other information technology than more affluent families. As we know from the work of Hart and Risley (1995), children from low income families often hear many fewer words than those from high-income families

SOURCE: Jeff Reese

and this directly influences their vocabulary development as well as their success in kindergarten and beyond. These and many other factors affect children and their families. Wherever you work, you will need to learn about and adapt to the children, family expectations, and the community.

Another trend influencing early education is the explosion of screen media in our society. It is routine for children today to experience this media as a constant background in homes, restaurants, and businesses. From an early age, children engage with games and entertainment from a variety of devices, including television, computers, tablets, phones, and game devices. Very young children are fascinated by a responsive screen, so it is increasingly common for families to give them a smartphone or tablet to entertain them while adults are engaged in other tasks. Children are increasingly "media savvy," and their experiences are frequently based on media exposure rather than experiences in the real world. Hence, they may come to school talking, drawing, and writing about media games and programs. This will affect how they learn, what they are interested in, and the ways you select learning experiences and curriculum content.

Continuing Issues

Many **issues**—subjects of ongoing discussion and debate—face our field today. Some of these issues have been the topic of lively discussion since we began to work as early childhood educators. It is likely that they will continue to be deliberated about for some time to come. Here we highlight five of these: views about curriculum and teaching; accountability; the nature of school readiness; balancing the needs of children, teachers, and families; and the role of government in the provision of programs for young children.

CURRICULUM AND TEACHING There are two widely implemented approaches to early childhood education today and there are strong proponents of each one. The choice of curriculum and teaching strategies in early childhood programs are closely related to the program's goals and values. In the past, most preschools focused on all areas of children's development. Many early childhood programs continue to embrace this view and implement what we refer to in this book as the education of the *whole child* or *developmentally appropriate practice*. This approach emphasizes supporting all aspects of development and building critical thinking skills, self-regulation, and creativity. Programs that support this view provide children with curriculum that involves hands-on learning and many opportunities to learn through play. Advocates of this approach believe that rich, meaningful learning experiences promote social-emotional and cognitive skills at the same time. They maintain that the most effective approach to assessment is "authentic"—based on observation of children's behavior and study of work they create within the natural environment of the classroom.

Other early childhood programs have a more academic approach to teaching young children. They generally believe that the primary goal of early education is the acquisition of knowledge and skills that prepare children for the expectations they will encounter in later grades. Educators in these programs focus on promoting academic achievement, particularly for those children who don't have the language and literacy skills that are considered important for school success. Teacher-led direct instruction may be a prevalent teaching strategy in these programs as teachers focus on the subject areas of literacy, science, and math. They often use standardized tests to evaluate how well children have mastered the learning objectives of the curriculum.

Reflect On

Curriculum and Teaching

What do you remember about the curriculum and teaching strategies that were implemented in early childhood programs that you attended? Do you think it reflected a whole-child focus or an academic focus? What were your feelings about it? What approaches to curriculum do you see in the programs you observe and work in today?

Discussions about approaches to and strategies for teaching young children are ongoing and are certainly something you will encounter when you begin teaching and throughout your career. Research regarding the impact of different approaches on children's development and learning is ongoing. Our advice to you is to stay current and to be a thoughtful consumer of research that is consistent with what you know is best for young children.

ACCOUNTABILITY   Over the past two decades there has been a call for greater oversight of government-funded early childhood programs in order to ensure that they are doing what they are intended to do. Accountability systems have been put in place to evaluate programs and to determine if they are to be rewarded and continue to receive funding based on their performance.

There are several ways accountability is implemented in early childhood programs. State licensing of programs for children 0–5 sets standards for safety and health and minimal levels of educational requirements that child care staff must obtain. Voluntary national accreditation systems, such as the National Association for the Education for Young Children and the National Association for Family Child Care, have higher standards for accountability that are more rigorous than licensing. In addition, many states have adopted Quality Rating and Improvement Systems (QRIS) that use standards, above and beyond licensing standards, to recognize and reward program quality.

Other sectors of the early childhood field have different accountability systems. Head Start programs are monitored to determine if they have met performance standards related to promoting children's health, family well-being, and children's learning. Some prekindergarten classrooms are part of the public school system and thus are required to meet standards related to teaching effectiveness and improvements in children's performance on standardized assessments. Programs designated for children who have special needs are required to meet different standards that are oriented largely around the development and use of children's individualized education plans.

Some accountability systems have been in place for decades. What has shifted is that programs are now being required to meet more rigorous and specific standards; for example, in Head Start and some other programs, assessment tools like the **Classroom Assessment Scoring System (CLASS)** (a tool for looking at classroom interactions) are being used to evaluate the effectiveness of teacher's instructional strategies. Programs are also being asked to assess and report children's progress toward meeting state early learning standards. Today there is greater pressure to perform that can be stressful for teachers and administrators

SOURCE: Jeff Reese

as well as for children. It can also lead to an emphasis on activities that can be readily measured, such as math computation and letter recognition, rather than on less measurable outcomes, such as creativity and critical thinking.

As a beginning teacher, you will almost certainly be called on to address one or more sets of standards in your work with children. It may help you be prepared if you realize that you will need to address standards and expectations related to accountability.

SCHOOL READINESS   **School readiness,** children's ability to be successful at their next level of education, is a topic of concern to families, teachers, administrators, and policymakers. As a teacher, you are likely to hear a great deal about the importance of preparing children for the next school or grade level and about whose responsibility it is to ensure that children are ready. We offer a brief overview of the history of the issue of school readiness in order to help you develop an informed position about this important topic.

Before 1980, discussions about readiness focused on the child. It was generally believed that children were ready for school when they had matured and developed the skills needed to function effectively in the school setting. During the 1980s academic expectations began to be pushed down to the lower elementary grades and to kindergarten. And as expectations grew, teachers and administrators began to notice that many children were falling behind. Across the nation there was increasing concern about children's lack of "readiness." School districts responded by raising the age of kindergarten entry, by using readiness tests to exclude children who were judged to be "unready," and by retaining more and more children in kindergarten because they were not adequately prepared for the expectations of the first grade.

Ongoing concern with children's readiness for kindergarten led to discussions of how readiness should be defined (Lewit & Baker, 1995). Most educators agreed that school readiness involved children's competencies at the time of school entry that are important for school success (Snow, 2006). Viewpoints differed regarding the type of skills, abilities, and knowledge needed as children enter formal schooling.

In the 1990s, a more comprehensive model of readiness emerged that shifted from a focus on the child alone to a broader view of the child within a social context. The new idea was that while the skills that each child brings to school are important, the support from family and community that a child has received before entering kindergarten and attendance in a high quality preschool—also play a role in readiness for school. This view, spelled out by the National Educational Goals Panel (NEGP, 1997), recommended three components: (1) readiness in the child, (2) schools' readiness for children, and (3) family and community supports that contribute to readiness. The panel promoted the view that schools' readiness for children was just as important as children's readiness for school (NEGP, 1998). This broader and more comprehensive definition is important because it acknowledges that readiness is a multifaceted process and a shared responsibility.

Understanding how the concept of readiness has evolved and knowing that it includes both children's skills and social contexts may help you to communicate with families, colleagues, and administrators in ways that encourage appropriate policies and programs that help all children to be successful in kindergarten and beyond.

BALANCING THE NEEDS OF CHILDREN, FAMILIES, AND TEACHERS   The tension between children's need for *quality* programs to support their development, teachers' need to receive adequate *compensation*, and families' need for programs that are *accessible* in both location and cost is an ongoing issue in our field.

Quality. Numerous studies over the past 20 years have established that children who attend high-quality early childhood programs gain skills they need to succeed in school and to be productive members of society. But what is *quality*? How do researchers, administrators, teachers, and students of early education determine what a *quality* program looks like? A substantial body of research has been developed over the past three decades that examines indicators of quality and how they relate to positive outcomes for children.

Researchers have identified six major components of program quality:

- Provisions ensure that children are kept *safe and well* (American Academy of Pediatrics, 2011).

- Teachers have received *education and training* specifically related to the care and education of young children (NIEER, 2006; Kelley & Camilli, 2007; National Research Council, 2000).

- *Group sizes and teacher–child ratios* are appropriate for the ages of the children (NIEER, 2004; Phillips, Mekos, Scarr, McCartney, & Abbott-Shim, 2000).

- There are *warm, nurturing, and language-rich interactions* between teachers and children (NIEER, 2006; Pianta, 1999).

- *Learning opportunities* are *appropriate* for the children and *comprehensive early learning standards* are used to assess children's progress (Barnett, Carolan, Squires, & Clarke Brown, 2013; Mashburn et al., 2008; National Institute for Early Education Research, 2006).

- Programs offer *comprehensive support services* including meals, opportunities for family engagement, access to vision and developmental screening programs, and referrals to health and family support services (Barnett, Carolan, Squires, & Clarke Brown, 2013).

Unfortunately, national studies reveal the fact that many programs today are not delivering high-quality care (National Institute for Early Education Research, 2014, Barnett et. al., 2013).

Compensation. Some teachers of young children do not receive enough income to meet their basic needs. Teacher salaries in private center-based programs for children under age 5 are almost always lower than those for comparable positions in publicly funded prekindergarten and elementary school programs because their source of funds is the tuition paid by families (Zaslow, Tout, Halle, Whittaker, & Lavelle, 2010). Low teacher salaries and inadequate benefits make it difficult to recruit and retain good teachers in many early childhood programs. This contributes to high staff turnover and the reluctance of men to enter the field. Frequent staff turnover undermines the stability of relationships which are so critical for young children's development and their ability to thrive in child care settings.

Because of the low wages and limited benefits, early childhood graduates tend to seek employment in state-funded preschool programs that offer better compensation. As a result, private programs that serve the youngest children and have limited fiscal resources are often left with teachers who are less trained and are less skilled than those in publicly funded programs.

Accessibility. The third part of this issue has to do with families' ability to find the kind of care they need in a convenient location and at a price they can afford. Finding quality child care is a challenge for all families, particularly for low-income working parents, for whom the cost of quality care is a real and daily problem.

Child care in the United States is expensive, and the costs are rising. According to a report by Child Care Aware (a membership organization primarily for child care resource and referral agencies), costs for child care can exceed those for housing and college tuition (Child Care Aware, 2016). The high cost of care results in low-income families being unable to afford child care at all or receiving the least expensive, poorest-quality care. Such care is very often unlicensed and unmonitored. This is especially problematic because these children are most at risk for school failure and could benefit most from high-quality early childhood programs.

RESPONSIBILITY FOR EARLY CHILDHOOD EDUCATION   Another continuing issue in early childhood education has to do with determining whose responsibility it is to help families provide early education for their children. Historically in the United

States, families were responsible for caring for their children until they entered public school. As a society, we have accepted that it is every child's birthright to have free public education beginning somewhere between 5 and 6 years of age. A well-defined legal structure outlines the authority and responsibility of federal, state, and local governments for the education of children from kindergarten through high school. In contrast, the years before age 5 have been regarded as a family concern, and have received much less attention and funding than programs for school-age children.

Today, the needs of working families, the push for school readiness, and the widespread recognition of the developmental benefits of high-quality programs have combined to raise national interest in the quality and availability of early childhood programs. This awareness led to a period of support for government-funded early childhood programs. Government's role and responsibility for funding these programs continues to spark debate. Recent political interest in the provision of government support for early childhood education may not continue in the face of an administration that is cutting funding for domestic programs. A major investment in early education has yet to be realized. You can expect that there will be more discussion about early childhood education as our society continues to grapple with this issue.

Reflect On

The Responsibility for Early Childhood Education

Who do you think should be responsible for early care and education? What do you think the role of government should be? What do you think policymakers should do to meet the needs of young children in your community, your state, and the nation?

 A Quick Check 14.1

Gauge your understanding of the concepts in this section.

 # Things You Need to Know About the Field and About Yourself

As a student of early childhood education, you are working towards becoming an **early childhood professional**. We use this term to describe an early childhood educator who has acquired the basic knowledge and skills that are necessary to work effectively with young children; who demonstrates professional behavior in the workplace; who has strong morality and behaves ethically in work with children, families, and colleagues; and who has personal qualities needed to nurture and care for the very young.

During the course of your studies, your understanding of what an early childhood teacher is and does may have changed. You have probably realized that teaching young children is complex and demanding work. In fact, as Fred Rogers says, it is a calling—an inwardly felt dedication. You may be thinking about what it would be like to be a teacher and wondering what you would need to do to be successful at this career. Perhaps you are also considering making a commitment to teaching young children and wondering what you should expect as you pursue this career choice.

Required Knowledge and Skill

Specialized knowledge and skill is an essential component of every profession—it is sometimes referred to as *technical competence*. Early childhood educators who strive

Figure 14.1 Nine Areas of Knowledge and Skill Identified in EC Professional
Preparation Standards

Nine areas of knowledge and skill that have been identified in professional preparation
standards for early childhood educators:

1. Knowledge of child development
2. Skill in observing and assessing children
3. Knowledge of health, safety, and nutrition
4. Skill in building relationships and guiding children
5. Ability to design a functional learning environment
6. Knowledge and skill in implementing meaningful and developmentally appropriate
   curriculum
7. Understanding of diverse children and families
8. Skill in partnering with families
9. Professional behavior

to be professionals must acquire the knowledge and skills needed to effectively
educate and care for young children, and they need specialized training to obtain
these. Because young children learn differently from older children, their teachers
need to base their work on child development research and use different approaches
to teaching and learning than those typically found in programs for older children.
Figure 14.1 lists nine areas of knowledge and skill that are included in most standards
for the professional development of early childhood educators. Your course work in
early childhood education and ongoing professional development classes and workshops will provide you with opportunities to learn about and develop skill in all of
these areas.

Reflect On

Your Knowledge Base

Which of the nine areas of knowledge and skill have you had course work and experience in?
In which do you feel most competent? Which do you think you need to work on more? What
do you want to learn before you enter the classroom? How will you gain this knowledge and
skill? Do you feel confident that you have a good grounding in the knowledge and skills needed
to be a teacher of young children?

Professional Behavior

It is also important that a professional early childhood educator adopt behaviors that
are desirable in the workplace. These include good communication skills, the ability
to develop positive relationships, skills in collaboration, a good work ethic including
doing the job to the best of your ability, a positive attitude, strong personal morality,
and adherence to professional ethical standards.

Early childhood education is a field built on relationships that involve responsive
caring and concern for children and their families. Like all good relationships, these
should be based on respect, honesty, empathy, trust, and warmth. These qualities are
also important for fostering relationships with colleagues, employers, and others with
whom early childhood educators interact.

Work ethic has to do with the ways a person meets the expectations of the workplace. When we hear complaints about a worker being "unprofessional," it usually

SOURCE: Jeff Reese

means that he or she violated an expectation regarding dress, attentiveness, or communication. Employees who are polite and conscientious are often described as being "professional"—something much appreciated by employers. We will discuss this more at the end of this chapter.

Personal Characteristics

When you teach and care for young children, the relationships you develop will influence the lives of children and their families in important ways. For this reason, your personal characteristics are an important part of who you are as a professional.

Unlike knowledge, skill, and professional behavior, personal qualities cannot be learned from a course or a book. They are deeply ingrained and are not easy to learn or change. It is important as a future teacher of young children that you are aware of your own personal characteristics and that you think about how these might impact your work. This will help you make choices in your career that are consistent with what you know about your personal and professional skills and talents.

Reflect On

Your Personal Characteristics

Consider your own personal characteristics. What words describe how you see yourself? Optimistic or pessimistic? Active or quiet? Friendly and outgoing or shy and reserved? Warm or cool? Flexible or rigid? Impulsive or cautious? Do you laugh easily, or are you serious most of the time? How do you think your personal characteristics might influence your work with children and families?

 A Quick Check 14.2

Gauge your understanding of the concepts in this section.

 Making a Commitment

Find Your Path

Feeling happy ultimately comes from being kind, not from all the stuff we collect in life. Everyone is looking for the something that is missing. Pledge to help children and remember what life is all about.

Fred Rogers

You have learned many important things and have begun to develop the skills that you need to be a caring and competent early childhood professional. Now (or in the near future), you will decide how you wish to apply this knowledge in your career.

The first question you need to ask yourself is "What age of children are you drawn to as a teacher?" Each stage in early childhood has its charms and teachers who love its particular joys and challenges. Some teachers are drawn to infants and toddlers, some to preschoolers, some to kindergartners, and others to primary-age children. Still others can find joy working with more than one of these ages or with adults (family members and teachers). Which one are you? You will be happier in your career choice—and children will be better off—if you select the right age-group. You do no service to yourself or children if you teach in inappropriate ways because you'd really prefer to work with children of a different age.

The next thing you need to consider is "What teaching role do you want as you begin your career?" Do you want to teach alone most of the time, or do you want to be part of a teaching team in which decisions are shared? Do you want to be "in charge," or would you prefer to start out assisting someone else who shoulders more of the responsibility? Sometimes, after they have completed a practicum placement and realized the scope of a teacher's work, our students decide that they would prefer to start out as assistant teachers.

Another thing to think about is how much autonomy you like to have and whether you want to work within the constraints and benefits of a school system. Everyone wants to make a decent salary, and everyone wants to be allowed the freedom to do what they believe is best. There is usually some trade-off, however, between having the greater freedom that can come with working in a small setting and having the stability, better salary, and benefits that accompany working in a larger system.

No job is perfect. But if you prefer working with younger children, like being part of a team, and would like to have a fair amount of freedom to choose how and what to teach, you probably will be happier working in a preschool or infant–toddler program. If you like to work with older children and are comfortable with curriculum and assessment specified by the school or district, you might prefer to teach in pre-K, kindergarten, or primary grades in a public or private elementary school. Reflecting on these questions can help you make choices about your educational path.

If you have not yet completed your teacher preparation program, another thing to think about is the kind of training that will best help you achieve your goals. Should you be in a program that prepares you to work with children younger than 5, one that will enable you to teach in elementary schools, or one that will allow you the flexibility to do either? It is important to be aware of the implications of this choice. We have had students who were surprised to discover that with an associate's degree, they would need several more years of school and another degree in order to teach in a public school. And we have colleagues who were shocked to discover that despite an elementary teaching credential and a master's degree, they had to go back to school to get the training required for working with infants and toddlers.

Reflect On

Becoming an Early Childhood Professional

What kind of setting and what kind of children would you like to work with as you begin your career? What would the perfect job for you in early childhood education be like? What training will you need to get this job?

Career decisions are not set in concrete and don't last forever. As you grow and change, so do your needs for professional fulfillment. The more experience you have in a variety of settings, the sooner it will become clear whether working with young children is the right choice for you, what age group you enjoy most, and what kinds of positions will suit you best. What is most important is to make a decision that will be good for you and for children and families.

Not everyone who gets a degree in early childhood education spends his or her entire career working with the same age group or working directly with young children.

Some move into other professional roles and find that their knowledge of child development and early learning provides a good foundation for these endeavors.

Video Example 14.1: Dolores' Career Path

Watch this video of an early childhood educator discussing her career path. What were your thoughts about the different positions that she had held? Do you think your future career path will include a number of different roles or do you envision just one?

Video

Take Care of Yourself

Throughout this book, we have asked you to reflect on yourself as a person because that is the foundation of who you will be as a teacher. *You* are the vital ingredient. *You* are the only real tool you have. And *you* are what you have to give—your caring, your energy, your knowledge and skills, and your commitment. So it is very important that you take care of yourself.

PAY ATTENTION TO YOUR HEALTH AND WELL-BEING   The first years of teaching can be stressful. You need to have energy and you need to be healthy, so take care of your body. Pay attention to nutrition, exercise, and relaxation. Doing so is not inconsequential, nor can it be put off. From the first day on the job, you will need to match the energy of young children. You will be exposed to a wide variety of ailments (colds, flu, head lice, and even pinworms!), so taking care of yourself is not an indulgence—it is a necessity. Find the exercise that brings you joy that you can do now and when you are too busy to exercise. Develop a habit of eating healthy foods and avoiding junk food. Make a good night's sleep a priority. We know these are the things your parents and your teachers told you. Now you need to tell it to yourself—for yourself and for the children you will teach.

Nurture your mind, so you stay excited and motivated as a learner. Teaching young children is a joy if you continue to find their growth and learning fascinating. If you think you know it all right now, you will soon be bored and discontented—so make the study of children and teaching your intellectual focus. There is plenty to learn.

It may be tempting to put all your energy into teaching (we hope it is!), but you will be a better teacher—and a happier one—if you are also a satisfied human being.

Nurture your spirit by taking time for quiet reflection, to listen to music, to enjoy beauty, to experience nature, and to pursue creative activities.

As a new teacher, you will be more content if you set realistic goals for yourself. Find your strengths and build on them; acknowledge your mistakes and learn from them. Don't expect to do everything perfectly in your first year or two of teaching (or even in your 20th!). You have many years to master the art of teaching.

CONNECT WITH COLLEAGUES   Your colleagues are the people who share your workplace and your commitments. If you are fortunate, they will share your philosophy and your passion, understand your joys and sorrows, and give you a sympathetic ear, a pat on the back, honest feedback, and words of encouragement.

Good working relationships with your coworkers will enhance the program for children and make your work easier and more enjoyable. People will regard you as a good colleague if you make every effort to be pleasant and fair and if you make sure that you do your share (and even a little more than your share) of the work. Be sensitive to and respectful of the cultural expectations, values, and ways of interacting of those with whom you work.

Video Example 14.2: Advice to Beginning Teachers

Watch this video of experienced teachers of young children giving advice to beginners. Is there anything in particular that they said that you would like to remember as you enter the teaching field?

Do Your Best for Children

What seems to matter most is intent. When your motive is to give the best, you grow into ways of giving it.

Fred Rogers

It is a privilege and a serious responsibility to work with young children. Your work should be grounded in the first, most important, and ultimate commitment as a professional early childhood educator—your allegiance to children. Doing your best for young children means having the values, knowledge, and commitment that will guide you in relating to them with care and respect, and teaching them with skill.

DEVELOP A PHILOSOPHY

I am persuaded that good teachers, first of all, must hold strong commitments and convictions from which their practices flow.

James Hymes Jr.

You came into the field of early care and education with some ideas about children and how they should be taught and some vision of who you wished to be in their lives. You have learned more. As you work in the field, these ideas will coalesce into an **educational philosophy**, an important part of your professional identity that will evolve and change throughout your career. Now is a good time to go back to the reflections you wrote as you read this book and consider what you believe, who you are, and who you want to be in the lives of children.

CONTINUE TO LEARN AND GROW Because you are committed to children, you will continue to learn about and appreciate them. One of your most powerful professional tools for learning about children is observation. Continue to practice this art and use what you learn to further your work with and appreciation for young children.

Because there is growing awareness of the importance of the early years, you will hear and read about new research and changing viewpoints about child development, curriculum, and guidance. Sometimes a new idea will resonate and you will respond with, "Yes! That makes sense. I really see that in the children I know." At other times, you may find yourself wondering if the writer or researcher ever spent time with children.

We encourage you to keep an open mind so that you can make use of new information. But don't blindly accept everything that "experts" tell you, particularly if they have something to sell. Use your experience and observations of children to help you distinguish between ideas that make sense and those that are inaccurate, poorly researched, inconsistent with what you know, or just a passing fad. Remember, some of today's accepted practices (e.g., putting up a poster of the alphabet) were once considered poor teaching. At the same time, now-discredited practices (e.g., lengthy group times for toddlers) were once considered perfectly fine. There are dangers both in blindly accepting new trends and in being stubbornly attached to old ways.

Once you have passed the initial "survival" stage of teaching, you are likely to want to gain additional knowledge. Many teachers find inspiration and renewal from reading, attending conferences and workshops, taking classes, and pursuing topics of interest. You can identify topics that seem interesting and fun and make decisions about what *you* want to do and to learn more about.

JOIN A PROFESSIONAL ORGANIZATION Organizations provide their members with a sense of common purpose and support. If you browse through the bibliographies in this book, you will notice that professional organizations publish books and journals and further the knowledge base of the field. Professional organizations do important work on behalf of children, practitioners, and the profession. They offer resources, create position statements, develop standards, advocate for children, and provide a collective voice for the field. Joining a professional organization gives you opportunities for learning and participating with your peers in conferences and at community events. Learning from and spending time with colleagues who share your interests and concerns is one of the great joys of being an early childhood educator.

Find an organization that is active in your area and get involved in it. A number of early childhood professional organizations are listed at the end of this chapter, and most have websites where you can learn about them and find out if they have chapters in your community.

Do What's Right

We live in a world in which we need to share responsibility. It is easy to say "It's not my child, not my community, not my world, not my problem." Then there are those who see the need and respond. I consider those people my heroes.

Fred Rogers

Because as an early childhood educator you will provide an important service to society, you need to be aware of the impact of your behavior. You will have the opportunity to do a great deal of good for young children and also the potential to do harm. Because of this, you have a particularly strong obligation to know about and to do what is right.

STAND FIRM EVERY DAY

Our job is to be a grain of sand in an oyster.

Fred Rogers

You have learned a lot about young children and the practices that serve them best. You know they learn through play, hands-on exploration, and interaction with a teacher who cares about them. You know you must consider each child in the context of family, culture, and community. When you teach according to what you know, you are doing what is right for children.

When you treat children with respect and insist others in your classroom do so, you are standing firm on what is right for children. When you suggest a change in the time your program schedules lunch because you have observed that children are hungry earlier than the scheduled meal time, you are doing what is right for children. When you question a curriculum recommendation that requires children to sit quietly for long periods of time, you are doing what is right for children.

At some points in your career, you may need to stand firm when you think decisions made by teachers, administrators, or school districts are not in the best interests of children. You may be asked to eliminate activities you believe are worthwhile for children (like art, or nap, or recess) in order to make more time for academics; you may be asked to teach children skills or content that are not appropriate to their age and ability; or you may be required to give tests that you don't believe are appropriate for the children's abilities or learning styles.

When these kinds of things occur, what can you do? If you don't want to ignore demands or run away, you could do what Mister Rogers suggests: "Be a grain of sand in an oyster." To be the grain of sand that forms the core of the pearl, you must learn the gentle art of using disagreement about educational practice to your advantage.

When pushed to focus on academic content, you can agree that the early years *are* a critical time for laying academic foundations. You can also point out that because the early years are so critical, it *is* crucial that we provide educational experiences that are appropriate for our youngest learners—those who are most vulnerable and have the most potential.

You will be better able to withstand pressures to follow practices that are not good for children if you are able to articulate your beliefs when others challenge your views. You must understand and be able to explain how play and other forms of appropriate instruction help children be academically prepared. You must do more than say, "Children learn through play." You must *know* what research tells us about how children learn. You must observe and document children's learning so that you can make it visible to their parents, to administrators, and to policymakers.

It may be difficult to do these things. It is not likely that one young teacher will be able to change policy. It will help to find and stay connected to other early childhood educators (join that professional association!) so that you have colleagues to help you express views about what is best for young children.

KNOW AND USE A CODE OF ETHICS   Understanding and using a code of ethics is an important part of your professional commitment to children and families. A code of ethics outlines your ethical responsibilities. It helps you stand firm and resist the temptation to do what is easy or what will make you popular at the expense of doing what is right.

The National Association for the Education of Young Children (NAEYC) Code of Ethical Conduct (as well as other applicable codes of ethics) also spells out your ethical responsibilities and gives you guidance on what to do when you encounter an *ethical dilemma* (a professional predicament for which there is more than one justifiable solution). In a dilemma, the good of one group or individual to whom you owe professional allegiance is in conflict with the good of another to whom you also have a professional responsibility. We have asked you to identify and address some ethical dilemmas in this book. Doing this takes practice and skill and will become easier as you gain more experience.

The Statement of Commitment that is included with the NAEYC Code of Ethical Conduct is an acknowledgment of willingness to accept the values and moral obligations of the field of early childhood education. We urge you to read it carefully and hope that you will embrace the commitments it describes (see Figure 14.2).

ADVOCATE   At some time in your career, you may want to do more for the welfare of young children than doing what is right in your classroom. As you learn more about the issues in our field and understand more about the policies and laws that affect children, you may decide that you want to publicly support policies that you believe in and actively work to change those you feel are not in the best interest of young children. This is called **advocacy**.

At first the idea of being involved in advocacy may be intimidating. Advocacy is often public and involves speaking out to policymakers, skills that are very different from the ones you use with children. However, there are other types of advocacy that are done in a less public arena and focus on communicating with colleagues, friends, and community members.

Figure 14.2 NAEYC Statement of Commitment

As an individual who works with young children, I commit myself to furthering the values of early childhood education as they are reflected in the ideals and principles of the NAEYC Code of Ethical Conduct. To the best of my ability I will:

- Never harm children.
- Ensure that programs for young children are based on current knowledge and research of child development and early childhood education.
- Respect and support families in their task of nurturing children.
- Respect colleagues in early childhood care and education and support them in maintaining the NAEYC Code of Ethical Conduct.
- Serve as an advocate for children, their families, and their teachers in community and society.
- Stay informed of and maintain high standards of professional conduct.
- Engage in an ongoing process of self-reflection, realizing that personal characteristics, biases, and beliefs have an impact on children and families.
- Be open to new ideas and be willing to learn from the suggestions of others.
- Continue to learn, grow, and contribute as a professional.
- Honor the ideals and principles of the NAEYC Code of Ethical Conduct.

SOURCE: From NAEYC Code of Ethical Conduct and Statement of Commitment, revised April 2005. Copyright © 2005 NAEYC®. Reprinted with permission.

Although you may not believe it now, you are an influential person. You are influential with your family and friends. They know and trust you, and what you tell them about the needs of young children may be more powerful than what they read online or see on television. You are influential in your community. The people on your street, in your place of worship, in your neighborhood, and in your town know you. You are *their* expert on early childhood education; they trust you. You are influential in your local government. You know the friends, families, and associates of the members of your local school board, your municipal council, and your state legislature. You represent the opinions and votes of those who elected them. You are as important—or more important—to them as is any expert.

As we grow as a profession, experienced early childhood educators are becoming increasingly committed to advocacy. We are becoming more sophisticated about the political process and are forming alliances with others who have similar concerns in order to heighten community awareness and influence public attitudes and legislation on behalf of young children and their families. You are doing what is right and furthering the goals of your profession when you become informed about the political process; when you stay informed about community, state, and national efforts to improve programs and services for children; and when you express your views and share your knowledge with members of your community, the media, and government leaders.

SOURCE: Jeff Reese

We urge you to stand up for children and make their well-being your primary concern. Speak out for what you know is right; say no when asked to do what is wrong. Choose to be true to high standards of professionalism. Say what you know to be true even when you risk making yourself unpopular and give others the support and courage to do the same. Support those who are champions for children—the ones who stand up for us all.

 A Quick Check 14.3

Gauge your understanding of the concepts in this section.

Final Thoughts

As you reach the end of your journey through this book, we want to encourage you to make a commitment to early childhood education. Young children, their families, and society need you. Today's children, the adults of tomorrow, will have many problems to solve. They need you to help them become problem solvers—knowledgeable, creative thinkers who can navigate the many challenges they are sure to encounter. They need your guidance so that as tomorrow's adults, they will appreciate and care for the fragile world in which we live. Today's young children need you to help them learn to cooperate so that tomorrow they will be peacemakers at home and in the world.

When you make a commitment to early childhood education, you are doing much more than taking the classes you need to get a degree and get a job. You are making a commitment to your profession, you are making a commitment to children, and you are making a commitment to the future.

Who will you be in the lives of children? Who will you be as an early childhood educator? Becoming an early childhood professional takes time and experience,

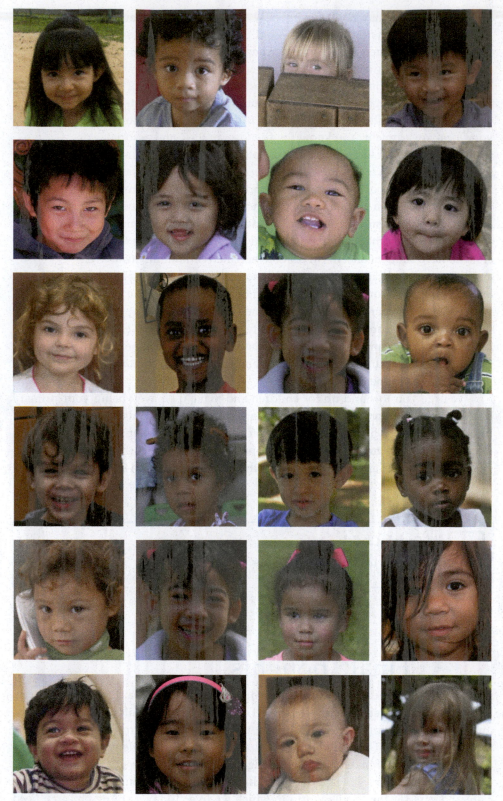

SOURCE: Jeff Reese

caring and dedication, and a willingness to keep on learning. It can be difficult and challenging, but it brings with it the joy and the satisfaction of being with young children and the knowledge that you are helping to shape the future. Finally, we want to let you know that the joys and the burdens you will carry on your journey will be shared by mentors and teachers who are traveling with you. As your colleagues, we welcome you.

Application Exercise 14.1 Final Reflection

 To Learn More

Read

Early Childhood Education for a New Era: Leading for Our Profession, S. Goffin (2013).
Ethics and the Early Childhood Educator: Using the NAEYC Code, 2nd ed., S. Feeney &
    N. Freeman (2012).
Professionalism in Early Childhood Education: Doing Our Best for Young Children,
    S. Feeney (2012).
Ready or Not: Leadership Choices in Early Care and Education, S. Goffin (2007).
Standing Up for Something Every Day: Ethics and Justice in Early Childhood Education,
    B. S. Fennimore (2014).

Investigate A Journal

Child Care Information Exchange
Childhood Education
Early Childhood Research and Practice
Early Childhood Research Quarterly
Journal of Early Intervention
Scholastic Early Childhood Today
Teaching Young Children
Young Children
Young Exceptional Children

Visit a Website

Canadian Coalition for the Rights of Children
The Future of Children
Child Care Aware
Child Rights Information Network
Child Welfare League of America
Children Now
Children's Defense Fund
Defending the Early Years
National Association for the Education of Young Children (NAEYC)
The Children's Foundation
Prevent Child Abuse America
Save the Children
Center for the Child Care Workforce

Document Your Skill & Knowledge About Becoming an Early Childhood Professional in Your Professional Portfolio

Include some or all of the following:

- Explore one of the continuing issues described in the chapter that is important in your community. Read about it to learn more. Interview some people who are involved in it in your community. What did you learn? Are opinions about it divided in your community or does there seem to be some consensus? Write about what you learned and the implications for you as a person entering the field of early childhood education.

- Consider your professional goals and create a 5-year plan for your career. Take it to a college counselor and find out what kind of financial resources might be available to help make your plan a reality. Document what you have done.

- Go back to the reflections you wrote as you read this book and reflect on what they say about what you believe, who you are, and who you want to be in the lives of children. Write an educational philosophy statement that describes your beliefs, guiding principles, and ideals that inform your professional practice. This can be the first draft of your "working educational philosophy", which can be updated over time to reflect changing ideas.

 Shared Writing 14.1 Advocacy

Appendix A
NAEYC Code of Ethical Conduct and Statement of Commitment

A Position Statement of the National Association for the Education of Young Children

Revised April 2005,
Reaffirmed and Updated May 2011

Endorsed by the Association for Childhood Education International

Adopted by the National Association for Family Child Care

Preamble

NAEYC recognizes that those who work with young children face many daily decisions that have moral and ethical implications. The **NAEYC Code of Ethical Conduct** offers guidelines for responsible behavior and sets forth a common basis for resolving the principal ethical dilemmas encountered in early childhood care and education. The **Statement of Commitment** is not part of the Code but is a personal acknowledgement of an individual's willingness to embrace the distinctive values and moral obligations of the field of early childhood care and education.

The primary focus of the Code is on daily practice with children and their families in programs for children from birth through 8 years of age, such as infant/toddler programs, preschool and prekindergarten programs, child care centers, hospital and child life settings, family child care homes, kindergartens, and primary classrooms. When the issues involve young children, then these provisions also apply to specialists who do not work directly with children, including program administrators, parent educators, early childhood adult educators, and officials with responsibility for program monitoring and licensing. (Note: See also the "Code of Ethical Conduct: Supplement for Early Childhood Adult Educators," online at www.naeyc.org/about/positions/pdf/ethics04.pdf and the "Code of Ethical Conduct: Supplement for Early Childhood Program Administrators," online at http://www.naeyc.org/files/naeyc/file/positions/PSETH05_supp.pdf.)

Core Values

Standards of ethical behavior in early childhood care and education are based on commitment to the following core values that are deeply rooted in the history of the field of early childhood care and education. We have made a commitment to:

- Appreciate childhood as a unique and valuable stage of the human life cycle
- Base our work on knowledge of how children develop and learn
- Appreciate and support the bond between the child and family
- Recognize that children are best understood and supported in the context of family, culture,* community, and society

---

* The term *culture* includes ethnicity, racial identity, economic level, family structure, language, and religious and political beliefs, which profoundly influence each child's development and relationship to the world.

Source: From NAEYC Code of Ethical Conduct and Statement of Commitment, National Association for the Education of Young Children (NAEYC). Copyright © 2011 NAEYC®. Reprinted with permission.

- Respect the dignity, worth, and uniqueness of each individual (child, family member, and colleague)
- Respect diversity in children, families, and colleagues
- Recognize that children and adults achieve their full potential in the context of relationships that are based on trust and respect

Conceptual Framework

The Code sets forth a framework of professional responsibilities in four sections. Each section addresses an area of professional relationships: (1) with children, (2) with families, (3) among colleagues, and (4) with the community and society. Each section includes an introduction to the primary responsibilities of the early childhood practitioner in that context. The introduction is followed by a set of ideals (I) that reflect exemplary professional practice and by a set of principles (P) describing practices that are required, prohibited, or permitted.

The **ideals** reflect the aspirations of practitioners. The **principles** guide conduct and assist practitioners in resolving ethical dilemmas.* Both ideals and principles are intended to direct practitioners to those questions which, when responsibly answered, can provide the basis for conscientious decision making. While the Code provides specific direction for addressing some ethical dilemmas, many others will require the practitioner to combine the guidance of the Code with professional judgment.

The ideals and principles in this Code present a shared framework of professional responsibility that affirms our commitment to the core values of our field. The Code publicly acknowledges the responsibilities that we in the field have assumed, and in so doing supports ethical behavior in our work. Practitioners who face situations with ethical dimensions are urged to seek guidance in the applicable parts of this Code and in the spirit that informs the whole.

Often "the right answer"—the best ethical course of action to take—is not obvious. There may be no readily apparent, positive way to handle a situation. When one important value contradicts another, we face an ethical dilemma. When we face a dilemma, it is our professional responsibility to consult the Code and all relevant parties to find the most ethical resolution.

SECTION I

ETHICAL RESPONSIBILITIES TO CHILDREN
Childhood is a unique and valuable stage in the human life cycle. Our paramount responsibility is to provide care and education in settings that are safe, healthy, nurturing, and responsive for each child. We are committed to supporting children's development and learning; respecting individual differences; and helping children learn to live, play, and work

cooperatively. We are also committed to promoting children's self-awareness, competence, self-worth, resiliency, and physical well-being.

Ideals

I-1.1-To be familiar with the knowledge base of early childhood care and education and to stay informed through continuing education and training.

I-1.2-To base program practices upon current knowledge and research in the field of early childhood education, child development, and related disciplines, as well as on particular knowledge of each child.

I-1.3-To recognize and respect the unique qualities, abilities, and potential of each child.

I-1.4-To appreciate the vulnerability of children and their dependence on adults.

I-1.5-To create and maintain safe and healthy settings that foster children's social, emotional, cognitive, and physical development and that respect their dignity and their contributions.

I-1.6-To use assessment instruments and strategies that are appropriate for the children to be assessed, that are used only for the purposes for which they were designed, and that have the potential to benefit children.

I-1.7-To use assessment information to understand and support children's development and learning, to support instruction, and to identify children who may need additional services.

I-1.8-To support the right of each child to play and learn in an inclusive environment that meets the needs of children with and without disabilities.

I-1.9-To advocate for and ensure that all children, including those with special needs, have access to the support services needed to be successful.

I-1.10-To ensure that each child's culture, language, ethnicity, and family structure are recognized and valued in the program.

I-1.11-To provide all children with experiences in a language that they know, as well as support children in maintaining the use of their home language and in learning English.

I-1.12-To work with families to provide a safe and smooth transition as children and families move from one program to the next.

Principles

P-1.1-**Above all, we shall not harm children. We shall not participate in practices that are emotionally damaging, physically harmful, disrespectful, degrading, dangerous, exploitative, or intimidating to children.**

---

* There is not necessarily a corresponding principle for each ideal.

This principle has precedence over all others in this Code.

P-1.2-We shall care for and educate children in positive emotional and social environments that are cognitively stimulating and that support each child's culture, language, ethnicity, and family structure.

P-1.3-We shall not participate in practices that discriminate against children by denying benefits, giving special advantages, or excluding them from programs or activities on the basis of their sex, race, national origin, immigration status, preferred home language, religious beliefs, medical condition, disability, or the marital status/family structure, sexual orientation, or religious beliefs or other affiliations of their families. (Aspects of this principle do not apply in programs that have a lawful mandate to provide services to a particular population of children.)

P-1.4-We shall use two-way communications to involve all those with relevant knowledge (including families and staff) in decisions concerning a child, as appropriate, ensuring confidentiality of sensitive information. (See also P-2.4.)

P-1.5-We shall use appropriate assessment systems, which include multiple sources of information, to provide information on children's learning and development.

P-1.6-We shall strive to ensure that decisions such as those related to enrollment, retention, or assignment to special education services, will be based on multiple sources of information and will never be based on a single assessment, such as a test score or a single observation.

P-1.7-We shall strive to build individual relationships with each child; make individualized adaptations in teaching strategies, learning environments, and curricula; and consult with the family so that each child benefits from the program. If after such efforts have been exhausted, the current placement does not meet a child's needs, or the child is seriously jeopardizing the ability of other children to benefit from the program, we shall collaborate with the child's family and appropriate specialists to determine the additional services needed and/or the placement option(s) most likely to ensure the child's success. (Aspects of this principle may not apply in programs that have a lawful mandate to provide services to a particular population of children.)

P-1.8-We shall be familiar with the risk factors for and symptoms of child abuse and neglect, including physical, sexual, verbal, and emotional abuse and physical, emotional, educational, and medical neglect. We shall know and follow state laws and community procedures that protect children against abuse and neglect.

P-1.9-When we have reasonable cause to suspect child abuse or neglect, we shall report it to the appropriate community agency and follow up to ensure that appropriate action has been taken. When appropriate, parents or guardians will be informed that the referral will be or has been made.

P-1.10-When another person tells us of his or her suspicion that a child is being abused or neglected, we shall assist that person in taking appropriate action in order to protect the child.

P-1.11-When we become aware of a practice or situation that endangers the health, safety, or well-being of children, we have an ethical responsibility to protect children or inform parents and/or others who can.

SECTION II
ETHICAL RESPONSIBILITIES TO FAMILIES

Families* are of primary importance in children's development. Because the family and the early childhood practitioner have a common interest in the child's well-being, we acknowledge a primary responsibility to bring about communication, cooperation, and collaboration between the home and early childhood program in ways that enhance the child's development.

Ideals

I-2.1-To be familiar with the knowledge base related to working effectively with families and to stay informed through continuing education and training.

I-2.2-To develop relationships of mutual trust and create partnerships with the families we serve.

I-2.3-To welcome all family members and encourage them to participate in the program, including involvement in shared decision making.

I-2.4-To listen to families, acknowledge and build upon their strengths and competencies, and learn from families as we support them in their task of nurturing children.

I-2.5-To respect the dignity and preferences of each family and to make an effort to learn about its structure, culture, language, customs, and beliefs to ensure a culturally consistent environment for all children and families.

I-2.6-To acknowledge families' childrearing values and their right to make decisions for their children.

I-2.7-To share information about each child's education and development with families and to help them understand and appreciate the current knowledge base of the early childhood profession.

I-2.8-To help family members enhance their understanding of their children, as staff are enhancing their

---

* The term *family* may include those adults, besides parents, with the responsibility of being involved in educating, nurturing, and advocating for the child.

understanding of each child through communications with families, and support family members in the continuing development of their skills as parents.

I-2.9-To foster families' efforts to build support net-works and, when needed, participate in building networks for families by providing them with opportunities to interact with program staff, other families, community resources, and professional services.

Principles

P-2.1-We shall not deny family members access to their child's classroom or program setting unless access is denied by court order or other legal restriction.

P-2.2-We shall inform families of program philosophy, policies, curriculum, assessment system, cultural practices, and personnel qualifications, and explain why we teach as we do—which should be in accordance with our ethical responsibilities to children (see Section I).

P-2.3-We shall inform families of and, when appropriate, involve them in policy decisions. (See also I-2.3.)

P-2.4-We shall ensure that the family is involved in significant decisions affecting their child. (See also P-1.4.)

P-2.5-We shall make every effort to communicate effectively with all families in a language that they understand. We shall use community resources for translation and interpretation when we do not have sufficient resources in our own programs.

P-2.6-As families share information with us about their children and families, we shall ensure that families' input is an important contribution to the planning and implementation of the program.

P-2.7-We shall inform families about the nature and purpose of the program's child assessments and how data about their child will be used.

P-2.8-We shall treat child assessment information confidentially and share this information only when there is a legitimate need for it.

P-2.9-We shall inform the family of injuries and incidents involving their child, of risks such as exposures to communicable diseases that might result in infection, and of occurrences that might result in emotional stress.

P-2.10-Families shall be fully informed of any proposed research projects involving their children and shall have the opportunity to give or withhold consent without penalty. We shall not permit or participate in research that could in any way hinder the education, development, or well-being of children.

P-2.11-We shall not engage in or support exploitation of families. We shall not use our relationship with a family for private advantage or personal gain, or enter into relationships with family members that might impair our effectiveness working with their children.

P-2.12-We shall develop written policies for the protection of confidentiality and the disclosure of children's records. These policy documents shall be made available to all program personnel and families. Disclosure of children's records beyond family members, program personnel, and consultants having an obligation of confidentiality shall require familial consent (except in cases of abuse or neglect).

P-2.13-We shall maintain confidentiality and shall respect the family's right to privacy, refraining from disclosure of confidential information and intrusion into family life. However, when we have reason to believe that a child's welfare is at risk, it is permissible to share confidential information with agencies, as well as with individuals who have legal responsibility for intervening in the child's interest.

P-2.14-In cases where family members are in conflict with one another, we shall work openly, sharing our observations of the child, to help all parties involved make informed decisions. We shall refrain from becoming an advocate for one party.

P-2.15-We shall be familiar with and appropriately refer families to community resources and professional support services. After a referral has been made, we shall follow up to ensure that services have been appropriately provided.

SECTION III
ETHICAL RESPONSIBILITIES TO COLLEAGUES   In a caring, cooperative workplace, human dignity is respected, professional satisfaction is promoted, and positive relationships are developed and sustained. Based upon our core values, our primary responsibility to colleagues is to establish and maintain settings and relationships that support productive work and meet professional needs. The same ideals that apply to children also apply as we interact with adults in the workplace. (Note: Section III includes responsibilities to co-workers and to employers. See the "Code of Ethical Conduct: Supplement for Early Childhood Program Administrators" for responsibilities to personnel (*employees* in the original 2005 Code revision), online at http://www.naeyc.org/files/naeyc/file/positions/PSETH05_supp.pdf.)

A—Responsibilities to Co-Workers
Ideals

I-3A.1-To establish and maintain relationships of respect, trust, confidentiality, collaboration, and cooperation with co-workers.

I-3A.2-To share resources with co-workers, collaborating to ensure that the best possible early childhood care and education program is provided.

I-3A.3-To support co-workers in meeting their professional needs and in their professional development.

I-3A.4-To accord co-workers due recognition of professional achievement.

Principles

P-3A.1-We shall recognize the contributions of colleagues to our program and not participate in practices that diminish their reputations or impair their effectiveness in working with children and families.

P-3A.2-When we have concerns about the professional behavior of a co-worker, we shall first let that person know of our concern in a way that shows respect for personal dignity and for the diversity to be found among staff members, and then attempt to resolve the matter collegially and in a confidential manner.

P-3A.3-We shall exercise care in expressing views regarding the personal attributes or professional conduct of co-workers. Statements should be based on firsthand knowledge, not hearsay, and relevant to the interests of children and programs.

P-3A.4-We shall not participate in practices that discriminate against a co-worker because of sex, race, national origin, religious beliefs or other affiliations, age, marital status/family structure, disability, or sexual orientation.

B—Responsibilities to Employers

Ideals

I-3B.1-To assist the program in providing the highest quality of service.

I-3B.2-To do nothing that diminishes the reputation of the program in which we work unless it is violating laws and regulations designed to protect children or is violating the provisions of this Code.

Principles

P-3B.1-We shall follow all program policies. When we do not agree with program policies, we shall attempt to effect change through constructive action within the organization.

P-3B.2-We shall speak or act on behalf of an organization only when authorized. We shall take care to acknowledge when we are speaking for the organization and when we are expressing a personal judgment.

P-3B.3-We shall not violate laws or regulations designed to protect children and shall take appropriate action consistent with this Code when aware of such violations.

P-3B.4-If we have concerns about a colleague's behavior, and children's well-being is not at risk, we may address the concern with that individual. If children are at risk or the situation does not improve after it has been brought to the colleague's attention, we shall report the colleague's unethical or incompetent behavior to an appropriate authority.

P-3B.5-When we have a concern about circumstances or conditions that impact the quality of care and education within the program, we shall inform the program's administration or, when necessary, other appropriate authorities.

SECTION IV
ETHICAL RESPONSIBILITIES TO COMMUNITY AND SOCIETY

Early childhood programs operate within the context of their immediate community made up of families and other institutions concerned with children's welfare. Our responsibilities to the community are to provide programs that meet the diverse needs of families, to cooperate with agencies and professions that share the responsibility for children, to assist families in gaining access to those agencies and allied professionals, and to assist in the development of community programs that are needed but not currently available.

As individuals, we acknowledge our responsibility to provide the best possible programs of care and education for children and to conduct ourselves with honesty and integrity. Because of our specialized expertise in early childhood development and education and because the larger society shares responsibility for the welfare and protection of young children, we acknowledge a collective obligation to advocate for the best interests of children within early childhood programs and in the larger community and to serve as a voice for young children everywhere.

The ideals and principles in this section are presented to distinguish between those that pertain to the work of the individual early childhood educator and those that more typically are engaged in collectively on behalf of the best interests of children—with the understanding that individual early childhood educators have a shared responsibility for addressing the ideals and principles that are identified as "collective."

Ideal (Individual)

1-4.1-To provide the community with high-quality early childhood care and education programs and services.

Ideals (Collective)

I-4.2-To promote cooperation among professionals and agencies and interdisciplinary collaboration among professions concerned with addressing issues in the health, education, and well-being of young children, their families, and their early childhood educators.

I-4.3-To work through education, research, and advocacy toward an environmentally safe world in which all children receive health care, food, and shelter; are nurtured; and live free from violence in their home and their communities.

I-4.4-To work through education, research, and advocacy toward a society in which all young children have access to high-quality early care and education programs.

I-4.5-To work to ensure that appropriate assessment systems, which include multiple sources of information, are used for purposes that benefit children.

I-4.6-To promote knowledge and understanding of young children and their needs. To work toward greater societal acknowledgment of children's rights and greater social acceptance of responsibility for the well-being of all children.

I-4.7-To support policies and laws that promote the well-being of children and families, and to work to change those that impair their well-being. To participate in developing policies and laws that are needed, and to cooperate with families and other individuals and groups in these efforts.

I-4.8-To further the professional development of the field of early childhood care and education and to strengthen its commitment to realizing its core values as reflected in this Code.

Principles (Individual)

P-4.1-We shall communicate openly and truthfully about the nature and extent of services that we provide.

P-4.2-We shall apply for, accept, and work in positions for which we are personally well-suited and professionally qualified. We shall not offer services that we do not have the competence, qualifications, or resources to provide.

P-4.3-We shall carefully check references and shall not hire or recommend for employment any person whose competence, qualifications, or character makes him or her unsuited for the position.

P-4.4-We shall be objective and accurate in reporting the knowledge upon which we base our program practices.

P-4.5-We shall be knowledgeable about the appropriate use of assessment strategies and instruments and interpret results accurately to families.

P-4.6-We shall be familiar with laws and regulations that serve to protect the children in our programs and be vigilant in ensuring that these laws and regulations are followed.

P-4.7-When we become aware of a practice or situation that endangers the health, safety, or well-being of children, we have an ethical responsibility to protect children or inform parents and/or others who can.

P-4.8-We shall not participate in practices that are in violation of laws and regulations that protect the children in our programs.

P-4.9-When we have evidence that an early childhood program is violating laws or regulations protecting children, we shall report the violation to appropriate authorities who can be expected to remedy the situation.

P-4.10-When a program violates or requires its employees to violate this Code, it is permissible, after fair assessment of the evidence, to disclose the identity of that program.

Principles (Collective)

P-4.11-When policies are enacted for purposes that do not benefit children, we have a collective responsibility to work to change these policies.

Statement of Commitment*

As an individual who works with young children, I commit myself to furthering the values of early childhood education as they are reflected in the ideals and principles of the NAEYC Code of Ethical Conduct. To the best of my ability I will:

Never harm children.

Ensure that programs for young children are based on current knowledge and research of child development and early childhood education.

Respect and support families in their task of nurturing children.

Respect colleagues in early childhood care and education and support them in maintaining the NAEYC Code of Ethical Conduct.

Serve as an advocate for children, their families, and their teachers in community and society.

Stay informed of and maintain high standards of professional conduct.

Engage in an ongoing process of self-reflection, realizing that personal characteristics, biases, and beliefs have an impact on children and families.

Be open to new ideas and be willing to learn from the suggestions of others.

Continue to learn, grow, and contribute as a professional.

Honor the ideals and principles of the NAEYC Code of Ethical Conduct.

---

* This Statement of Commitment is not part of the Code but is a personal acknowledgment of the individual's willingness to embrace the distinctive values and moral obligations of the field of early childhood care and education. It is recognition of the moral obligations that lead to an individual becoming part of the profession.

P-4.12-When we have evidence that an agency that provides services intended to ensure children's well-being is failing to meet its obligations, we acknowledge a collective ethical responsibility to report the problem to appropriate authorities or to the public. We shall be vigilant in our follow-up until the situation is resolved.

P-4.13-When a child protection agency fails to provide adequate protection for abused or neglected children, we acknowledge a collective ethical responsibility to work toward the improvement of these services.

GLOSSARY OF TERMS RELATED TO ETHICS

Code of Ethics — Defines the core values of the field and provides guidance for what professionals should do when they encounter conflicting obligations or responsibilities in their work.

Values — Qualities or principles that individuals believe to be desirable or worthwhile and that they prize for themselves, for others, and for the world in which they live.

Core Values — Commitments held by a profession that are consciously and knowingly embraced by its practitioners because they make a contribution to society. There is a difference between personal values and the core values of a profession.

Morality — Peoples' views of what is good, right, and proper; their beliefs about their obligations; and their ideas about how they should behave.

Ethics — The study of right and wrong, or duty and obligation, that involves critical reflection on morality and the ability to make choices between values and the examination of the moral dimensions of relationships.

Professional Ethics — The moral commitments of a profession that involve moral reflection that extends and enhances the personal morality practitioners bring to their work, that concern actions of right and wrong in the workplace, and that help individuals resolve moral dilemmas they encounter in their work.

Ethical Responsibilities — Behaviors that one must or must not engage in. Ethical responsibilities are clear-cut and are spelled out in the Code of Ethical Conduct (e.g., early childhood educators should never share confidential information about a child or family with a person who has no legitimate need for knowing).

Ethical Dilemma — A moral conflict that involves determining appropriate conduct when an individual faces conflicting professional values and responsibilities.

SOURCES FOR GLOSSARY TERMS AND DEFINITIONS

Feeney, S., & N. Freeman. 2005. *Ethics and the early childhood educator: Using the NAEYC code.* Washington, DC: NAEYC.

Kidder, R. M. 1995. *How good people make tough choices: Resolving the dilemmas of ethical living.* New York: Fireside.

Kipnis, K. 1987. How to discuss professional ethics. *Young Children* 42(4): 26–30.

Appendix B
Environment Checklists

Safety Checklist

This checklist can be used to evaluate the safety of an existing environment or to plan an environment for children.

Program/Classroom _____ **Date** _____

Number of staff _____ **Number of children** _____ **Age of children** _____

Use the following code as appropriate: ✓ = yes/adequate − = no/inadequate

General

____ Program is licensed or meets licensing standards.

____ Children are appropriately supervised at all times.

    ____ Infants and toddlers are never left unattended; they are always visible and within easy physical reach.

    ____ Preschoolers are never left unattended and are supervised by sight and sound.

    ____ School-age children may work independently for brief periods if supervised by sight or sound.

____ Building and equipment are structurally sound, free of rust, peeling paint, and splinters.

____ Bolts and rough edges on equipment and furniture are recessed or covered.

____ Entrances and yard are secure. Staff monitor anyone entering the facility.

____ Arrival and departure procedures ensure children are safe from traffic and from leaving with unauthorized persons.

____ Sign-in/out procedure is followed and well known to staff and families.

____ Inside and outside are free of debris and standing water.

____ Sharp tools and utensils, glass and breakable items, and bleach spray are out of children's reach.

____ Medicines, cleansers, pesticides, aerosol sprays, and other poisonous items are locked out of children's reach.

____ Stairs, ramps, lofts, decks, and platforms above 20" have stable guard railings.

____ Stairs, ramps, lofts, and platforms are kept free of toys and clutter.

____ Equipment is free of entrapment hazards (openings are less than 3.5" in width or more than 9").

____ Equipment and furniture are appropriately sized for the children enrolled.

____ Pathways between play areas (both indoors and outdoors) are kept clear of toys and equipment to prevent tripping.

____ Kitchen, storage closets, gardening sheds, adult bathrooms, and other areas with hazardous materials are secured from children.

____ A procedure for regularly surveying and maintaining program safety is in place.

____ Shooting or projectile toys are not permitted.

____ Plastic bags are kept out of children's reach; balloons are not allowed at any time.

Emergency Prevention and Preparation

____ A telephone is accessible with emergency numbers posted nearby; the address and phone number of the facility is posted.

____ A staff member with current training in pediatric first aid and CPR is always on-site when children are present.

____ There is a procedure for handling first aid emergencies and staff are familiar with it.

____ A first aid kit is adequately stocked, easily available, and marked for visibility.

____ A first aid kit is carried on trips.

____ A first aid handbook is available.

____ Injury reports are written and an injury log is kept.

____ A plan for handling medical emergencies is in place and is known to all staff.

____ Emergency exits are clearly marked and free of clutter.

____ An emergency evacuation plan is posted. The fire department has evaluated it.

____ Emergency evacuation procedures are practiced monthly.

____ Emergency procedures include a plan for children with disabilities.

____ A Disaster-Preparedness Plan exists and is known by staff and families.

____ Smoke detectors are installed and functional.

____ A fire extinguisher is available in each room, is tagged and tested annually; and staff know how to use it.

____ A plan exists for safe classroom coverage in case a child or teacher must be taken to the hospital.

____ When children are transported by the program they are appropriately, legally, and safely restrained in vehicles.

Inside

____ Environment is arranged so all areas can be easily supervised.

____ Furniture is stable.

____ AV equipment and equipment carts are secured so that they cannot be tipped over. They are put away when not in use.

____ Equipment is unbroken and in good working order.

____ Low windows, doors, and mirrors have safety glass or Plexiglas.

____ Glass doors and floor-level windows have stickers to ensure that people do not walk into them.

____ Heaters, radiators, pipes, and hot-water tanks are inaccessible to children.

____ Hot-water taps are turned off or are below 120°F so that hot water does not scald.

____ Stable, nonskid stools are provided if children must use high toilets, sinks, or water fountains.

____ Unused electric outlets are covered in programs for children under the age of 5.

____ Electric cords do not cross pathways or run under rugs.

____ Rugs are secured or backed with nonskid material and edges do not create a tripping hazard.

____ Floors where water is used and entrances have nonskid surfaces.

Outside

____ Outdoor play area is protected by fences and has child-proof gates.

____ No poisonous plants grow in the yard.

____ A well-stocked first aid kit is available in the outdoor area.

____ Permanent outdoor equipment is securely anchored and movable equipment is stable.

____ There is impact-reducing material beneath all climbing, swinging, and sliding equipment extending through fall zones.

____ Slides and climbing structures do not exceed safe height limitations (1 foot/year of age of the youngest user).

____ Swings are attached with closed fasteners, not open S hooks.

____ Swing seats are constructed of soft or lightweight material.

____ Swings are away from pathways, and barriers prevent children from walking into the path of a swing.

____ Swings have impact-reducing material on all sides; two times the height of the frame in front and back of the swing.

____ Metal slides are located so that they are shaded or facing away from the midday sun to prevent burns.

____ Equipment has no places where pinching or crushing of fingers can occur.

Special Precautions in Infant–Toddler Programs

____ Cribs and gates have slats less than $2\frac{3}{8}$" apart.

____ Cribs and child gates have locking devices that work.

____ Cribs meet 2011 CPSC Standards.

____ Infant walkers are not used.

____ Children are not placed in restrictive infant equipment such as swings, stationary activity centers, infant seats, bouncers, molded seats, etc. for more than 15 minutes twice per day.

____ Furniture that can be climbed is securely anchored.

____ Furniture has rounded edges or edges are cushioned.

____ Dangling strings do not hang from cribs, playpens, curtains, etc.

____ There are no dangling appliance cords.

____ Strollers and carriages are stable, have workable restraining straps, and have adequate brakes.

____ Toys are at least $1\frac{1}{2}$" in diameter.

____ Stairway gates are locked when children are present.

____ Separate space is set aside for nonmobile infants.

____ An adult keeps at least one hand on a child on a changing table at all times.

____ Infants and toddlers are visually supervised by adults when sleeping.

Infant–Toddler Learning Environment Checklist

Five principles of infant–toddler environments:

1. Home-like rather than school-like

2. Designed for comfort

3. Designed for function

4. Designed for flexibility—centered around an open, flexible activity zone/play area

5. Designed for movement

Use this checklist to plan an environment for a group of infants or toddlers or to evaluate an existing one. No program will have everything, but the * items are essential and are found in most high-quality programs.

Program/Classroom _____ Date _____

Number of staff _____ Number of children _____ Age of children _____

Use the following code as appropriate: ✓ = yes/adequate − = no/not adequate

Time

_____ Infants regulate their own schedule*

_____ Toddlers' schedules flexible with general times for predictable routines*

_____ Opportunity to play/be outside at least twice a day for all ages (weather permitting)*

Indoor Environment

Indoor Space

_____ Clearly defined "home" space separate from other groups/classes*

_____ 35 square feet per child*

_____ Arrangement of space allows one adult to see all of the children, all of the time*

_____ Room is orderly and attractive*

_____ Furniture is child-sized, clean, and unbroken

_____ Clutter minimized*

_____ Neutral color walls

_____ Drinking water, sinks, and toilets accessible*

_____ Sheltered from outside noise and stimulus*

_____ Ventilated and temperature controlled as needed*

_____ Well lit with natural light if possible*

_____ Obvious system and supplies for sanitizing mouthed toys*

_____ "Wet regions" (entrances, eating areas) have waterproof, easy-to-clean, uncarpeted floors

_____ "Dry regions" (e.g., sleeping and play areas) have clean (cleanable), comfortable floor coverings

_____ Access for individuals (family members, visitors, or staff) who use walkers or wheelchairs

_____ Arrival and departure area where families enter and exit*

_____ Flexible central play area/zone and interaction*

_____ Eating area* (with a food storage/preparation area nearby)

_____ Diapering area with running water away from eating and play area(s)*

_____ Sleeping area visually accessible to staff*

FOR INFANT ROOMS

_____ Protected area for nonmobile infants*

_____ Play areas for mobile children

_____ Low, stable chairs that offer back and side support

FOR TODDLERS AND TWOS ROOMS

_____ Accessible toilets*

_____ Toys area

_____ Table area

_____ Book area

_____ Pretending area

_____ Sensory play area

Indoor Areas

ARRIVAL AND DEPARTURE AREA

_____ (See safety checklist for special safety considerations for this area)

_____ Bulletin boards and mailboxes for communication between families and staff*

_____ Clock and sign-in*

____ Cubbies or shelves labeled with children's names and pictures*

____ Comfortable adult-sized chair or sofa

____ Good-bye window—place where children can watch family depart

DIAPERING/CHANGING/TOILETING AREA*

____ Sturdy adult-height counter or changing table* with stairs that roll in and out

____ Shelf above or beside changing table for easy organization for ointments, etc.*

____ Adult-height sinks, with warm water for hand washing*

____ Large/deep sink for bathing children

____ Paper towel dispenser that can be used with one hand

____ Labeled boxes or bins for each child's diapers and clothes*

____ Plastic bags for soiled diapers and clothes*

____ Lidded garbage can for soiled diapers*

____ Clipboard or notebook to record diapering/toileting*

____ Area clean and pleasant*

For Toddlers and Twos Rooms

____ Low toilets and sinks for toddlers or stable step stools to make toilets and sinks accessible*

____ Place for another child to sit/watch nearby

EATING/FOOD PREPARATION AREA*

____ Adult-height counter/table for preparing food*

____ Cabinets or shelves for equipment and supplies labeled to facilitate cleanup

____ Sink for washing hands and rinsing dishes* (dishwasher or triple sink if dishes washed)

____ Appliances (refrigerator, stove, or microwave)*

____ At least one child-safe locked cupboard

____ Clipboard or notebook to record eating

____ Dishes, pots, pans, etc.*

____ Cleanup equipment such as sponges, brooms, mops, etc.*

____ Child-sized tables and chairs*

____ Low chairs on which adults can sit with children at table*

For Infant Rooms

____ Adult seating for comfortably holding and feeding/ nursing children*

SLEEPING AREA*

____ Mirrors, pictures, mobiles, etc., where children can see them*

____ Labeled storage for shelves/bins for bedding and toys from home

____ Rocking chair*

____ Clipboard or notebook to record sleeping

For Infant Rooms

____ Cribs or other safe, culturally appropriate sleeping arrangements for infants*

____ Cribs with tight fitting sheets and empty of all other toys and equipment including bumper pads, blankets, stuffed toys, and any other items*

For Toddlers and Twos Rooms

____ Mats or cots

FLEXIBLE CENTRAL PLAY AREA*

____ Clean carpeted floors

____ Steps, stable sofas/chairs, cruise bars, platforms, or climbers*

____ Dumping containers (baskets, buckets)

____ Clean cages or aquariums for pets*

____ Plants/animals fed, watered, protected*

____ Unbreakable mirrors*

Toys are:

____ Large enough to be easily grasped with pieces too large to be swallowed

____ Light enough to be lifted

____ Soft enough not to hurt

____ Strong enough to be dropped, stepped on, or thrown

For Infant Rooms

____ Materials for play and exploration placed along the perimeter to bring into the larger space

____ Several play spaces for mobile children

____ Low barriers for protection for nonmobile infants if room includes both nonmobile and mobile infants

____ Couches or low tables that provide handholds

For Toddlers and Twos Rooms

____ Movable climber or platform

____ No high and unstable shelves

____ Shelves secured so they do not tip

SENSORY PLAY*

____ Table and chairs for messy play
____ Toddler-sized water table
____ Sand/water play with lots of containers*
____ Rhythm instruments
____ Clay and dough
____ Paint
____ Soap and goop

TOYS*

____ "Peek-a-boo" toys
____ Animal figures
____ Boxes with lids
____ Busy boxes
____ Complete puzzles with 1–8 pieces*
____ Homemade toys
____ Interlocking blocks like Duplos
____ Jack-in-the-box
____ Jumbo wooden beads with strings
____ Large snap beads
____ Music boxes
____ Nesting containers (plastic bowls, cups)
____ Pegboards and pegs (jumbo size)
____ Pop-up toys
____ Pull toys
____ Rattles and bells
____ Shape-sorting boxes
____ Simple one-piece knobbed puzzles
____ Simple-to-put-together toys
____ Squeeze toys
____ Stacking toys
____ No broken toys
____ Table blocks
____ Texture balls
____ Toys for sucking and teething
____ Toy vehicles
____ Low, open shelves for storage of materials*

BOOKS*

____ Cloth or board picture books*
____ No torn or scribbled-on books
____ Picture collections (mounted and covered)
____ A variety of styles of illustration*
____ Homemade books with photographs of the children and things they know*
____ New and classic books
____ Baskets or wall pockets to hold books
____ Simple stories with plots
____ Multiethnic and multiage nonstereotyped characters*

____ Not based on commercial products
____ Nursery rhymes
____ Wordless books and books with text
____ Mood and concept books*
____ Sturdy books that are not board books
____ Clean pillows and carpets
____ Soft, large chairs/couch for adults and children to sit together

ACTIVE PLAY*

____ Push and pull toys
____ Small climber with slide
____ Tunnel (purchased or homemade)
____ Large boxes to crawl through
____ Cars and trucks
____ Wagons and buggies to push and pull
____ Soft balls of various sizes
____ Soft pillows to climb on
____ Duplicates of toys and several choices (2–3) per child

Areas for Older Toddlers and Twos

These can be separate for older toddlers and twos or may be incorporated into the play zones as for younger toddlers.

Blocks

____ Posters or photographs of buildings
____ Low, open shelf where blocks can be stored*
____ Low napped carpet or clean floor*
____ Clean and unsplintered unit blocks (100 blocks in 5–10 shapes)
____ Large figures (animals/people) and vehicles
____ Table blocks
____ Large soft blocks
____ If space allows, 20 + light hollow blocks

Art

____ Painting surfaces—table, wall, or easel (toddler-sized)
____ Low tables and chairs*
____ Nontoxic, washable paints in at least primary colors (red, yellow, blue), black, and white*
____ Brushes in a variety of sizes: wide and narrow with short handles*
____ Base or paint for finger painting*
____ Dough boards and tools*

____ Large paper for easel painting*
____ White paper, clean on one side*
____ Recycled materials (card, Styrofoam, paper, ribbons, Fabric, plastic jars and lids)*
____ Large, nontoxic, unwrapped crayons and felt pens
____ Bowls, spoons, and measuring tools
____ Collection of textured materials (fabrics, etc.)
____ Yarn, string, ribbons
____ Smocks or old shirts (to protect clothing)*
____ Clay boards and clay tools*
____ Special papers (construction, tissue)
____ Trays and plastic cups or containers*
____ Potter's clay
____ Play dough*
____ White glue and paste*

Pretending

____ Child-sized table and chairs*
____ "Bed" or crib mattress for a child and dolls
____ Clean dolls and stuffed animals without missing limbs or features
____ Open shelf for storage*
____ Small open cupboard without doors
____ Full-length unbreakable mirror
____ Clothes and props that reflect children's families*, cultures, jobs, and fantasy roles*
____ Two telephones*
____ Pots and pans

____ Unbreakable dishes
____ Large wooden or plastic utensils
____ Pictures depicting family life and other scenes

Indoor Organization and Aesthetics

____ Orderly and attractive*
____ Neutral color walls
____ Shelves close to play areas*
____ Sets of toys stored separately, not jumbled*
____ Toys and books are in good condition*
____ Toys and books are neat and orderly*
____ Shelves labeled with pictures
____ Floor and table coverings available for messy activities
____ Clutter minimized*
____ Duplicates of items and several choices (2–3) per child
____ Extra materials stored and rotated
____ Patterns, colors, and storage coordinate
____ No promotional or media products or characters
____ Items of beauty such as flowers, plants, or sculpture
____ Pictures and displays at infant and toddler eye-level*
____ Wall hangings (textured and touchable)
____ Areas decorated with art prints, photographs, children's work, book covers, and displays
____ Pictures reflect culture and characteristics of children and families
____ Record/tape player and recordings* appropriate (e.g., soothing music for nap)

Outdoor Environment

OUTDOOR SPACE

____ Fenced for protection*
____ 75 square feet of outside play space for each child playing outside at any one time
____ No hazardous items (sharp stones, toxic plants)
____ Gates with child-safe locks*
____ Located near indoor environment
____ Access to toilets and sinks*
____ Natural features (e.g., boulders, hills, and trees)
____ Shelter from sun, wind, rain*
____ Hard surface for vehicles away from other play
____ Levels and textures to touch, crawl, climb on*
____ Comfortable places to sit and lie*
____ Access to water for drinking and play*
____ Shaded
____ Designated outdoor play space for toddlers separate from areas for older children

____ Designated outdoor play space for infants with separation for nonmobile children divided from areas for toddlers and older children*

OUTDOOR EQUIPMENT AND MATERIALS

____ Equipment scaled to size of children
____ Equipment for climbing, sliding, swinging with safe surfacing underneath
____ Large playground balls that bounce*
____ Water play toys (cups/spoons, basters, funnels, pitchers, tubing, water wheels, etc.)
____ Sand toys (cups/spoons, pots, cars, buckets, trowels, etc.)
____ Wading pool

For Infants

____ Blankets to lie on

____ Light catchers and wind chimes hung in trees

For Toddlers and Twos

____ Tables for outdoor table activities

____ Space for art

____ A line/rack to hang clothes and artwork

____ A covered sandbox or alternative

____ Toddler-height sand/water table or tub

____ Natural or manufactured balance beams

____ Mud toys (shovels, pots, pans, buckets, trowels)

____ Wagons and buggies to push and pull, and child-sized riding vehicles to propel by feet

OUTDOOR ORGANIZATION AND AESTHETICS

____ Toys set out each day and arranged in an orderly and attractive manner

____ Water, sand, mud toys separate from one another

____ Shed or other secure storage near where equipment is used

____ Nontoxic plants and stable items of beauty (e.g., brick pathways)

Preschool/Kindergarten Learning Environment Checklist

Five principles of good learning environments for preschool and kindergarten classrooms:

1. Use partial seclusion.
2. Provide extra space for centers children use in groups.
3. Include areas to be together and places to be alone.
4. Separate noisy areas from quiet areas.
5. No corridors or racetracks.

Use this checklist to plan an environment for a group of preschoolers or kindergartners or to evaluate an existing one. No program will have everything, but the * items are essential and are found in most high-quality programs.

Preschool and Kindergarten Programs

Program/Classroom _____ Date _____

Number of staff _____ Number of children _____ Age of children _____

Use the following code as appropriate: ✓ = yes/adequate − = no/not adequate

Indoor Environment

Indoor Space

____ Clearly defined "home" space*
____ 35 square feet per child*
____ Arranged in learning centers* using partial seclusion with shelves and dividers
____ Arranged for safe supervision (one adult can supervise children by sight and sound)*
____ Noisy and quiet areas are separate
____ Paths do not lead through centers*
____ Extra space for centers that children use in groups—blocks, dramatic play, manipulative toys
____ All areas useful (no "dead" space)*
____ Sheltered from outside noise and stimulus
____ Well lit* with natural light if possible
____ Ventilated* and temperature controlled
____ Drinking water, sinks, and toilets accessible*
____ No corridors (long and narrow paths) or racetracks (circular paths around shelves or tables)
____ "Wet regions" (entrances, art, eating) have waterproof, easy-to-clean, uncarpeted floors
____ "Dry regions" (e.g., blocks, dramatic play) have clean, comfortable floor coverings
____ Access for individuals (children, family members, visitors, or staff) who use walkers or wheelchairs

INDOOR LEARNING CENTERS/AREAS
____ Arrival/departure
____ Unit blocks*
____ Hollow blocks
____ Library*
____ Dramatic play*
____ Toys and games*
____ Art*
____ Writing*
____ Discovery (science, math, social studies)
____ Woodworking (may be outdoors)
____ Private area for children
____ Outside play environment*
____ Space for large group gathering*
____ Space for small group gathering*
____ Space for eating snacks/meals*
____ Space for resting (in full-day programs)*
____ Shelf tops uncluttered

WHERE CLIMATE DICTATES DAYS SPENT INDOORS
____ Indoor space for messy activities in the classroom
____ Separate indoor space for active play away from the classroom

Indoor Organization and Aesthetics

____ Room is orderly and attractive*
____ Furniture is clean and unbroken
____ Clutter minimized*
____ Neutral color walls
____ Patterns, colors, and storage coordinate
____ There are plants that are cared for*
____ Shelves, floors, and carpeting are clean
____ There is high or closed secure storage for staff personal items* and locked cabinet for hazardous materials*
____ Toys and books appear neat and orderly*

_____ There are items of beauty such as flowers, plants, sculpture, art prints, photographs, children's work, book covers, and displays

_____ Some pictures reflect culture and characteristics of children and families

_____ Most pictures and displays at child's eye-level*

_____ There is appropriate music used at appropriate times (e.g., soothing music for naps)

_____ No promotional or media products or characters

_____ Extra materials stored and rotated

Time

_____ Daily opportunity to play outside (weather permitting) at least 1 hour in morning and afternoon*

_____ Large blocks of time for child-selected activity indoors and outside (at least 1 hour in morning and afternoon)*

_____ Quiet, sedentary activities alternated with active play

_____ Structured group times are short (10–20 minutes based on age and ability of the group)*

_____ Times for nourishment, rest, and personal care scheduled*

_____ Children govern their own use of time (how long to work, play, eat, nap, etc.) as much as possible

_____ There are daily rituals* (e.g., a morning song, a nap-time story)

Indoor Equipment and Materials

ARRIVAL AND DEPARTURE AREA

_____ Child-safe gates/doors*

_____ Bulletin boards and mailboxes for communication between families and staff*

_____ Clock and sign-in

_____ Cubby shelf for children's things labeled with names and pictures*

_____ Adult-sized chair or sofa nearby

UNIT BLOCK AREA*

_____ Space for at least 4 children to build*

_____ 100–150 clean and unsplintered hardwood unit blocks* for 3- to 4-year-olds; 200–700 for 5- to 6-year-olds

_____ 14–25 block shapes

_____ Low, open shelves for storage of blocks*

_____ Low-napped carpet or clean floor*

_____ Blocks stored so that each type of block has its own individual place* clearly marked with an outline

_____ Blocks with similar qualities stored near each other, placed so the ways blocks differ is easily seen

_____ Posters or photographs and books about buildings

_____ Toy vehicles, street signs, dollhouses, small human and animal figures, tree blocks, and other props

_____ Special storage baskets and separate labeled space on the shelves for props*

_____ Blocks are not used as doorstops

HOLLOW BLOCK AREA

_____ At least 17 clean and unsplintered hollow blocks* and 6 planks

_____ Space for at least 4 children to build inside, on a covered porch, or outside in a sheltered location

_____ Located near dramatic play area if inside

_____ Low-napped carpet or soft surfacing to limit noise and prevent damage to the blocks*

_____ Stacking space for all blocks* on the floor or on shelves

_____ Hats, sheets, and lengths of fabric as props*

_____ Hollow blocks are not used as step stools

DRAMATIC PLAY AREA*

_____ Located near hollow block area if possible

_____ Child-sized table and 2–4 chairs*

_____ Small cupboard with doors

_____ Pretend stove/sink unit or alternative that can serve different functions*

_____ Open shelves with bins or baskets, or hooks to hang clothes on the wall

_____ Storage labeled with words and pictures

_____ Full-length unbreakable mirror

_____ Clean, untorn dress-up clothes for both boys and girls* that are easy to put on and reflect families, cultures, community, and locale

_____ Common objects of daily life such as tote bags, kitchenware, books, furnishings, and tools

_____ 2 telephones*

_____ Multiracial dolls

_____ Sturdy "bed" to hold a child and dolls

_____ Pictures depicting family life and other scenes

_____ Extra props and pictures rotated with children's interests and topics of study (e.g., uniforms, clothes, and props reflecting families, cultures, jobs, and fantasy roles)*

_____ Extra props and pictures stored in sturdy, attractive, lidded boxes organized by topic, occupation, situation, or role

MANIPULATIVE TOYS AND GAMES AREA*

____ Space for at least 4 children to play

____ Comfortable carpet or low tables and chairs*

____ Trays, mats, or table space for work

____ Low, open shelves for storage close to work space*

____ Building toys separate from table games if possible

____ Several sets of building toys, such as LEGO or Bristle blocks—sets stored separately, not jumbled*

____ Toys are in good condition*

____ Math manipulatives like parquetry blocks, Cuisenaire rods, and interlocking cubes—sets stored separately

____ Complete puzzles with 8–25 pieces*

____ Collection such as buttons or caps

____ Table games or teacher-made workjobs

____ No battery-operated toys of any kind

____ Containers/shelves labeled with words and pictures

____ Trays or space where children can save and display completed work

ART AREA*

____ Closed or covered storage for materials available to adults

____ Shelves for materials available to children

____ An easel adjusted so the smallest child can reach the top of one side*

____ Low tables and chairs* that may be dirtied and are easily cleaned

____ Brushes in a variety of sizes*

____ Scissors that can be easily used by children in either hand*

____ Dough boards and tools

____ Smocks or old shirts (to protect clothing)

____ Floor/table coverings available

____ Bowls, spoons, and measuring tools

Art Supplies

____ Liquid or powdered easel paints in at least primary colors, black, and white*

____ Liquid and cake watercolors

____ Finger paint base or paint for finger painting*

____ Food color

____ Potter's clay*

____ White glue and paste*

____ White paper, clean on one side*

____ Trays and plastic cups or containers*

____ Special papers (construction, tissue)

____ Recycled materials (cardboard, Styrofoam, wrapping paper, fabric, plastic jars and lids)*

____ Collections of textured materials and fabric

____ Yarn, string, ribbons

____ Wide-weave fabric

____ Clay boards and clay tools

____ Nontoxic felt pens*

____ Unwrapped nontoxic crayons*

____ Chalk

____ Play dough

____ Large paper for easel painting*

____ Broken toys, puzzle pieces are not used as art materials

LIBRARY*

____ Separate, quiet area*

____ Comfortable, clean pillows and carpets or chairs where children can sit and read*

____ Low bookshelf that displays covers*

____ Big, comfortable chair or couch where an adult can sit with a child and read

____ Even lighting*

____ All books in good condition* with all tears repaired (none are torn or scribbled on)

____ Many books appropriate for developmental stage* with some very easy and some a little challenging books* include:

    ____ A variety of styles of illustration*

    ____ Multiethnic and multiage characters in nonstereotyped roles*

    ____ Females and males in various roles*

    ____ Not based on commercial products

    ____ Fiction (realistic and fantasy)*

    ____ Informational books*

    ____ Mood and concept books*

    ____ Poetry*

    ____ New and classic books*

    ____ Child-authored books

____ Listening center with book-recording sets

____ Big books and a big-book shelf

____ Decorated with book jackets/posters and reading-related art prints

____ Puppets, props, and flannelboard for storytelling

WRITING CENTER*

____ Even lighting*

____ Child-sized table and chairs*

____ Storage shelf close to table*

____ Peeled crayons*

____ Nontoxic felt marking pens*

____ Hole punches (single and double)

____ Rulers, protractors

____ Sharpened primary pencils*

____ Paper cut in uniform sizes*

____ Yarn

____ Recycled envelopes and cards

____ Baskets, jars, cans for pens, crayons, etc.*

DISCOVERY/SCIENCE CENTER*

____ Low table or counter*

____ Located near window*

____ Located near sink

____ Located near electrical outlet

____ Photographs and posters to illustrate concepts

____ Aquariums and animal cages

____ Animals are fed, have water, and are protected in clean cages or aquariums*

Discovery Equipment That Should Be Available as Needed

____ Plastic tubs and pitchers*

____ Measuring cups/spoons

____ Balance and scale

____ Magnifying glass*

____ Trays*

____ Airtight containers for storage

____ Probes

Discovery Materials That May Be Found in Other Centers or Outside

____ Water/sand table*

____ Information books*

____ Sorting collections (buttons, rocks, etc.)

____ Math manipulatives (attribute beads or blocks, Cuisenaire rods, colored cubes, etc.)

____ Concept games and puzzles

____ Materials with sequence and proportion

____ Globes and maps

SENSORY PLAY AREA*

____ Located near sink or outside*

____ Low, open shelves for storage of materials*

____ Sand/water table

____ Table and chairs

____ Light table

____ Aprons or waterproof smocks*

____ Dropcloths (tarps, plastic tablecloths or shower curtains

____ Basins or tubs)*

____ Bowls, cups, and buckets

____ Ladles, measuring cups, and pitchers

____ Funnels, basters, whisks, and eggbeaters

____ Eyedroppers and translucent ice-cube trays

____ Clear colored toys for light table

____ Tablemats or trays for modeling work

____ Food color (available to teachers)

____ Dishwashing liquid (available to teachers)

A variety of sensory materials including:

____ Natural materials: water*, ice, sand, dirt, mud*

____ Modeling materials: (dough, clay)

____ Dry materials (sawdust and aquarium gravel if age appropriate; rice, beans, macaroni, oatmeal if allowed)

____ Teacher-made mixtures ("goop," "super sand," and "flubber")

WOODWORKING AREA

____ Sturdy workbench and platform for shorter children to stand on*

____ Sawing table children can kneel on

____ Storage for tools close to table,* with tools arranged in an orderly manner (e.g., a storage rack labeled with pictures and words)*

Woodworking Equipment That Should Be Available as Needed

____ Safety glasses* (for teacher and children) with adjustable nonelastic strap

____ C clamps or small bar clamp

____ Lightweight hammers

____ Regular adult hammer*

____ Hacksaw and extra blades

____ Small crosscut saw

____ Bit braces and drill bits, auger bits, and Phillips bits

____ Flat-head screwdriver

____ Phillips screwdrivers

____ Rasp and file

____ Tape measure

____ Speed square

Supplies

____ Screws, nails, and glue
____ Sandpaper
____ Pencils
____ Soft untreated wood such as pine or fir (not particle board)*
____ Storage for wood pieces*

Outdoor Environment

Outdoor Space

____ Fenced for protection*
____ 75 square feet of outside play space for each child playing outside at any one time
____ Gates with child-safe locks*
____ Located near indoor environment
____ Access to toilets and sinks*
____ Large grassy areas for running
____ Natural features (e.g., plants, grass, dirt, bugs, boulders, hills, and trees)
____ Shelter from sun, wind, rain*
____ Hard surface for vehicles away from other play
____ Levels and textures to touch, crawl, climb on*
____ Comfortable places to sit and lie*
____ Access to water for drinking and play*
____ There are visual boundaries to keep children from interrupting play or endangering themselves

ZONES/AREAS INCLUDE . . .

____ Transition*
____ Manipulative-creative
____ Physical/active play*
____ Natural elements*
____ Social-dramatic

Outdoor Organization and Aesthetics

____ Yard is orderly and attractive*
____ Clutter minimized*
____ Equipment/materials complete, working, and in good condition
____ Animals are fed, have water, and are protected in clean cages or aquariums*
____ Plants are cared for*
____ Locked storage for hazardous materials*
____ Storage labeled with words for staff or pictures for children
____ Toys stored in an organized manner*
____ Toys in good condition*
____ Items of beauty such as flowers, plants, or sculpture
____ No promotional or media products or characters

Outdoor Equipment and Materials

TRANSITION ZONE

____ Benches, tires, steps, or the edge of a wall for children to wait, gather, or see what is available and make choices*
____ Parking area for trikes, scooters, and wagons; vehicles near the entrance to the riding area
____ Storage for trikes and wagons*

MANIPULATIVE-CREATIVE ZONE

____ Tables and chairs for outdoor table activities*
____ Easels*
____ Woodworking table
____ A line/rack to hang clothes and artwork*
____ Art supplies available as described in Art Area and Writing Center in Indoor Environment

PHYSICAL/ACTIVE PLAY ZONE

____ Climbing or "super-structure"* for climbing, sliding
____ Swings
____ Surfacing underneath and to 6″ beyond structures (10″ sand, wood chips, etc., or 2″ rubber matting)*
____ Portable equipment for building and climbing
____ Natural or manufactured balance beams*
____ Materials to encourage active play: hoops, parachutes, rope
____ Trikes, 3-wheel scooters, and wagons sized for the children*
____ Varied sizes of balls that bounce*
____ Baskets and bags or other containers for ball play and storage

NATURAL ELEMENTS ZONE

____ Logs, smooth boulders
____ Bench or other place to sit
____ A covered sandbox or appropriate alternative*
____ Sand/water table or large tub*
____ Clean sand in plentiful supply*
____ Clean water in plentiful supply*
____ Dirt/mud for digging*
____ A place to garden

_____ A bird feeder, bird bath

_____ Pets—if weather permits

_____ Sand toys (cups/spoons, pots, cars, buckets, trowels, etc.)*

_____ Water play toys (cups/spoons, basters, funnels, pitchers, tubing, water wheels, etc.)*

_____ Mud toys (shovels, pots and pans, buckets, trowels)

_____ Water, sand, mud toys kept separate from one another

_____ Hoses and big buckets*

_____ Toys for bubble play

SOCIAL-DRAMATIC PLAY ZONE

_____ Playhouse or alternative

_____ Dress-up clothes and props

_____ "Loose parts" (hollow blocks, sheets, small tires, planks, and other movable items)

_____ A vehicle path

Primary Grades Learning Environment Differences/Additions

Primary grade classrooms can be quite similar to the preschool and kindergarten environments. There are some differences and some additions. In an after-school program for primary children, you may need to set up a temporary environment each day in a gym or all-purpose room. Use the preschool/kindergarten checklist, add the items on this checklist, and note where an item is different for primary grades. No program will have everything, but the * items are essential and are found in most primary grade programs.

Program/Classroom _____ **Date** _____

Number of staff _____ **Number of children** _____ **Age of children** _____

Use the following code as appropriate: ✓ = yes/adequate − = no/not adequate

Classroom Differences/Additions

_____ Teacher can supervise children by sight or sound most of the time (children may walk to cafeteria, bathroom, office, water fountain unescorted)

_____ Children and teacher have dedicated work space and storage for personal work supplies (e.g., desks or work tables)

_____ Technology/computer center where 2 + children can work

_____ There is flexible space for children to work on and display projects

Time Differences/Additions

_____ Daily opportunities to play outside (weather permitting) include formal physical education as well as regular recesses of 20–30 min at least 3 times a day*

_____ 20–30 minute blocks of child-selected activity indoors at least twice a day

_____ Daily opportunities to play outside (weather permitting) include formal physical education as well as regular recesses of 20–30 min at least 3 times a day*

_____ Structured teaching times vary in length based on topic and ability of the group

_____ Times for nourishment scheduled*

_____ Children govern their own rest and personal care as much as possible

Classroom Area Differences/Additions

BLOCK AREA DIFFERENCES/ADDITIONS

_____ Shelves labeled with pictures and words

_____ Paper and pens for writing signs available nearby

_____ Diverse blocks (e.g., turrets, tunnels, crenellated towers, tree blocks)

_____ Recycled materials such as cardboard tubes to construct roadways and pathways with marbles and balls

DRAMATIC PLAY AREA DIFFERENCES/ADDITIONS

_____ Prop boxes accessible to children

_____ More elaborate prop sets

_____ Shelves and racks labeled with pictures and words

_____ Boxes, platforms, etc., for children to create stage sets

MANIPULATIVE TOY/GAME AREA DIFFERENCES/ADDITIONS

_____ Jigsaw puzzles with 25–100 pieces

_____ Large sets of construction toys with wheels, gears, etc.

_____ Directions and patterns to use with construction toys

_____ Simple board games (e.g., Candyland, Chutes and Ladders, Monopoly Junior, Don't Break the Ice)

_____ Simple card games (e.g., Go Fish, Old Maid, Uno)

DISCOVERY/SCIENCE AREA DIFFERENCES/ADDITIONS

_____ Measuring tools

_____ Waterwheels

_____ Tubing/pipes

____ Space for ongoing experimentation and documentation

____ Tools like knives and scissors

____ Artifact collections

____ Globes and maps

____ Children's encyclopedia and other library resources (e.g., atlas)

____ Computer with Internet connection

ART AREA DIFFERENCES/ADDITIONS

____ Pencil crayons

____ Brushes clean and stored upright

____ Containers and shelves labeled

____ Oil-base modeling clay

____ Oil pastels

____ Clay tools

____ Space for ongoing projects

WRITING CENTER DIFFERENCES/ADDITIONS

____ Pencil and thin wax crayons

____ Dictionary or word file

____ Lined paper

____ Staplers

____ Computer and printer with simple word processing/page processing/drawing programs

Outdoor Environment Differences/Additions

OUTDOOR SPACE

____ Gates may be omitted

____ May be located a short walk from the classroom and bathroom

____ Hard surfaces for hopscotch, jump rope, etc.

OUTDOOR ORGANIZATION AND AESTHETICS

____ Storage may be located a short walk from the outdoor area

OUTDOOR ENVIRONMENT DIFFERENCES/ADDITIONS

____ Cargo nets and ropes

____ Bikes and 2-wheel scooters

____ Balls, bats, hoops, and other equipment for organized games

Glossary

Chapter 1

Attribute   Quality or characteristic inherent in or ascribed to a person

Before and after-school programs   Programs which provide care and education for young school age children prior to and after the regular school day

Bias   A preference or inclination to favor one person or thing over another

Calling   Work that involves a sense of purpose, strong values, and a deep sense of mission (what one wants to contribute to the world)

Child care centers   Settings providing education and care with a focus on providing care for working families with an educational focus

Child development associate (CDA)   A nationally awarded early childhood credential that requires 120 clock-hours of approved training

Child development centers   Settings providing education and care with an educational focus with the goal of promoting positive development and learning

Code of ethics   A document that spells out the ethical commitments of a profession and responsible professional practice

Confidentiality   The ethical responsibility that requires that information shared in a professional setting not be shared with others who do not have the need for it. Confidentiality is a hallmark of every profession.

Core values   Agreed on professional values that express members of a profession's central beliefs, commitment to society, and common purpose

Culture   The way a group of people lives as well as their shared, learned system of values, beliefs, and attitudes

Developmentally appropriate practice (DAP)   A research-based teaching approach to early education that focuses on growth and learning in all domains of development. It involves providing learning experiences based on children's age, individual circumstances, abilities, and culture

Dispositions   Tendencies to respond to experiences in certain ways

Early childhood   The period in the life span that includes birth through age 8

Early childhood education (ECE)   Education and care provided in all settings for children between birth and age 8

Early learning standards   Specify developmental expectations for children from birth through entrance to first grade in all domains of development

Ethical dilemma   A workplace predicament that involves competing professional responsibilities and has more than one defensible resolution

Ethical responsibility   Behaviors that early childhood educators are obligated to do or not to do. For example, "Above all, we shall not harm children." (P-1.1 NAEYC Code of Ethics)

Ethics   The study of right and wrong, duties and obligations

Family–child interaction program   Programs in which young children and their parents come together to play and learn

Home-visitor program   Programs in which an educator goes to a family home to provide education for both young children and their families

Ideals   Items in a code of ethics that describe exemplary professional practice

Intelligence   The ability to think and learn, culturally defined, based on what is needed and valued within a society

Intentional teacher   An early childhood educator who has a purpose for every decision and skill in articulating the reasons for actions

Kindergarten   Program for 5- and 6-year-olds, the first year of formal schooling

Morality   A person's views of what is good, right, or proper; their beliefs about their obligations; and ideas about how people should behave

Pedagogy   The art and science and of teaching

Preschools   Settings providing education and care with an educational focus with the goal of promoting positive development and learning.

Prejudice   A preconceived opinion (prejudgment) that is not based on reason or direct experience

Prekindergartens   Programs for children under 5 that are housed in public schools

Primary grades   Grades 1 through 3 (kindergarten may be included)

Principles   Items in a code of ethics that describe professional practices that are required, prohibited, and permitted

Profession   An occupation that provides an essential service to society and requires its practitioners to receive specialized training

Professional   An individual who has received training and who uses skills and abilities to serve society

Professional ethics   The moral commitments of a group, extending and enhancing personal values and morality through shared, critical reflection about right and wrong actions in the workplace

Professional portfolio   Material gathered by an individual to document professional skills, knowledge, and training

Stereotype   An oversimplified image or idea about a particular group of people, the belief that all people with a particular characteristic are the same

Teacher (used interchangeably with the terms caregiver, provider, practitioner, and early childhood educator)   A person with specialized training who works with young children in a variety of education and care settings

Temperament   An individual's behavioral style and characteristic ways of responding

Values   Principles or standards that a person believes to be important, desirable, or worthwhile and that are prized for themselves (e.g., truth, integrity, beauty, love, honesty, wisdom, loyalty, justice, respect)

Whole child   Concern with all areas of children's development—social, emotional, intellectual, and physical

Chapter 2

Accreditation (of programs for children)   A voluntary process that enables programs for children (from birth to 5 years of age) to measure themselves against a national set of standards used to define high quality practice in early education

Accreditation (of teacher education programs)   A process of peer review of teacher education programs designed to determine if they meet national standards for teacher preparation

Center-based education and care   Care and education provided in facilities that are specifically designed for groups of young children

Charter school   Independently operated, publicly funded programs that have greater flexibility than other public schools in meeting regulations

Child care   Provision of care and education for young children whose family members work or are in school or training programs; also called *day care*

Common Core Standards   Nationally agreed on literacy and mathematics curriculum standards intended to prepare students from kindergarten through grade 12 to be college and career ready

Content standards   The goals and objectives that are determined by each state to be important for every subject area for each grade

Early childhood   The period in the life cycle that includes birth through age 8

Early childhood education (ECE)   Education and care provided in all settings for children between birth and age 8

Early childhood family education   Programs that support families in their role as the child's first teacher—they can include home visiting programs and family–child interaction programs

Early Head Start   A downward extension of Head Start for low-income pregnant women and families with infants and toddlers—designed to enhance all areas of children's development and promote school readiness

Early intervention   Federally mandated programs and services for infants and toddlers with disabilities

Early learning standards   Outlines, described by state governments, of what young children should know and be able to do at different stages of their development; also called *early learning and development guidelines* and *early learning guidelines*

Family–child interaction programs   Programs that provide opportunities for families and children to play and learn together—based on the assumptions that parents are the child's first and most important teachers

Head Start   A federally funded child development program designed to ameliorate the effects of poverty on young children—provides comprehensive services, including an educational program, and health, nutritional, and social services

Home-based education and care   Care and education of young children provided in their own homes or the home of a caregiver

Homeschooling   Educating children at home rather than in public or private schools

Home visiting programs   An approach to early childhood education that provides pregnant women and families with young children with direct services in their homes

Individualized education plan (IEP)   A plan developed by a team for a child who meets state disability requirements and is identified as needing special services—it has individualized objectives that are reviewed and revised regularly

Individualized family services plan (IFSP)   A written plan developed by a team to guide the provision of early intervention services to children under the age of 3 and their families

Kindergarten   Originally a program for 4- to 6-year-olds developed in Germany by Friedrich Froebel. Today in the United States, the term refers to the first year of formal schooling for 5-year-olds. In many parts of the world, it is used to describe all programs for young children.

Laboratory school   Educational programs operated in association with a university, college, or other teacher education institution that provides opportunities for those learning to teach to observe children and acquire teaching experience

Licensing regulations   Requirements put in place by states to protect the health, safety, and well-being of children in early care and education programs

Nursery school   Originally, part day programs designed to give children opportunities to socialize and engage in creative activities. The nursery schools of the past evolved into what is called preschool today.

Parent cooperative   Early childhood programs that are organized and run by family members who are expected to actively participate in the program

Performance standards   Assessments, often in the form of tests, used by states to determine the extent to which children have mastered the content prescribed in the standards; also called *achievement standards*

Prekindergarten (pre-K) programs   Educational programs for children under age 5 designed to prepare them for the academic expectations they will encounter in kindergarten

Preschool   Programs for children under age 5 designed to support their development through the provision of education and care

Primary grades   First through third grades, kindergarten is sometimes included

Quality rating and improvement systems (QRIS)   State-developed systems that evaluate and rate the quality of child care programs (beyond licensing requirements)

School readiness   Children's preparation to engage successfully with school learning experiences and meet school expectations

Standards   Written descriptions of the knowledge and skills that children should possess at specific stages of their education

Teaching license   Recognition that an individual teacher has successfully completed a teacher preparation program, usually a bachelor's degree in education; also called *certification*

Chapter 3

Child-centered approach   The application of humanistic ideals to programs for young children in which the developmental stage, needs, and interests of young children are the central consideration for teachers

Developmental-Interaction Approach (DIA)   An approach to progressive education developed at Bank Street College in New York City. The child's direct experiences in the world, with an emphasis on learning trips, form the core of the curriculum.

Developmentally appropriate practice (DAP)   A research-based framework of principles and guidelines for early childhood practice that engages children and adapts for their development, strengths, interests, and needs and that considers the social and cultural contexts in which they live

Didactic materials   Specially designed instructional materials invented by Dr. Maria Montessori and used in Montessori classrooms to help children develop their senses and learn concepts

Gifts   Educational materials created by Froebel that included yarn balls, blocks, wooden tables, geometric shapes, and natural objects

Head Start   A federally funded program designed to ameliorate the effects of poverty on young children; it provides a comprehensive child development program

High/Scope   A well researched early childhood education approach developed in Ypsilanti, Michigan, in the l960s as a model for ameliorating poverty. The focus is on developmental tasks from Piaget's theory of cognitive development.

Humanism   A system of thought that focuses on human needs and values rather than on religious authority. Humanist beliefs stress the value and goodness of human beings and highlight respect for human dignity, and the right of people to shape their own lives.

Infant school   Nurturing schools for children 3 to 10 years of age originally established in England by Robert Owen. Today, the term is primarily used in England to describe schools for children between the ages of 4 and 7 years.

Kindergarten   Originally a program for 4- to 6-year-olds developed in Germany by Friedrich Froebel. Today, in the United States, the term refers to the first year of formal schooling for 5-year-olds. In many parts of the world, it is used to describe all programs for young children.

Laboratory preschools   Early childhood programs established in the 1920s and 1930s (and continuing) to serve as observation and practicum sites for those learning to teach young children and for child development research

Montessori method   An educational approach developed by Dr. Maria Montessori. It involves the provision of a child-sized learning environment and carefully designed and sequenced learning materials.

National Association for the Education of Young Children (NAEYC)   A large and influential American association for early childhood educators

Nursery school   A program created by Rachel and Margaret MacMillan in 1911 to alleviate health problems in children in poor communities. It evolved into half-day programs focused on social and emotional development. This name has been replaced with the term *preschool*.

Occupations   Handwork activities created by Froebel that include molding, cutting, folding, bead stringing, and embroidery

Parent cooperative nursery schools   Nursery school programs begun in 1916 (and continuing) that were cooperatively run by a teacher and parents who were required to assist in running the school and in conducting the daily program

Progressive education   Programs that evolved from the 19th century progressive political movement in the United States that sought to use science and reason to improve mankind. Today, progressive education programs emphasize learning by doing, integrated curriculum, problem solving and critical thinking, group work and development of social skills as opposed to rote knowledge.

Reggio Emilia approach   An educational approach developed in Italy inspired by the work of Loris Malaguzzi. It emphasized the child's strengths and representation of ideas through creative materials.

Tabula rasa   The idea promulgated by John Locke that a child comes into the world with a mind like a blank slate and that knowledge is received through the senses and converted to understanding by the application of reason

Unit blocks   Hardwood building blocks developed by Carolyn Pratt in the early 1900s. Each block is a fraction or multiple of a standard "unit" block 5.5 inches long, 2.75 inches wide, and 1.375 inches thick.

Universal education   Education for all rather than only for boys and for the rich

Waldorf education   Educational approach developed in Germany by Rudolf Steiner. It emphasizes stages and development of the child's body, mind, and spirit.

Whole-child approach   Focus of early childhood education on children's social, emotional, physical, and cognitive development

Chapter 4

Accomodation   Creating new mental frameworks to include new information

Altruism   Caring for others with no expectation of compensation or personal gain

Assimilation   Including new information into existing mental frameworks

Attachment   A close emotional bond between two people, specifically between a child and an adult

Behaviorism   Learning theory that behavior is changed based on the positive or negative consequences that immediately follow the behavior. The theory that behavior can be explained in terms of conditioning; behaviors that are rewarded will be repeated, and those not rewarded or punished will be extinguished.

Cephalocaudal pattern of development   The pattern of prenatal and infant physical development in which growth begins at the head and moves down the body

Chronological age   A child's age in years and months; often expressed as a decimal number (e.g., 4.10 to mean 4 years and 10 months)

Cognitive domain   The area of child development related to thinking, intellect, and language

Concrete operations stage   In Piaget's theory of cognitive development, the period between ages 7 and 11 when children develop the ability to use logical thought to solve concrete problems

Conservation   In Piaget's theory, the realization that the amount or quantity of a substance stays the same even when its shape or location changes

Constructivist theory   Theories of development that propose that humans generate knowledge and meaning from an interaction between their experiences and their ideas

Developmental milestones   Skills or tasks that most children can do at a certain age

Developmental norms   Typical characteristics, behaviors, or patterns of development at a given age

Domains   Areas of human development, including physical, emotional, social, and cognitive

Ecological theory   Urie Bronfenbrenner's theory that describes systems of social and cultural contexts that influence development

Egocentric   Being able to see things only from one's own perspective

Executive functions   Mental processes that allow people to manage their attention, emotions, and behavior and help them connect past experiences with present actions

Experience   An individual's interactions with people, places, and things

Goodness of fit   Term used by Chess and Thomas in their study of temperament to describe the interaction between children's characteristics and the expectations of the adults who live and work with them

Hand dominance   The preferential use of one hand to do many tasks, such as eating and writing; sometimes referred to as "handedness" (e.g., "left-handed")

Heredity   Characteristics and traits that are inborn and genetically determined based on an individual's ancestors

Maturation   The unfolding of genetically determined potential that occurs as the child grows older

Maturationist theory   A theory supported by the work of Arnold Gesell that postulates that development is controlled by each individual's genetic makeup

Moral development   The acquisition and application of a set of standards about what is right and wrong

Motor   Muscle activity and body movement; used to define skills acquired with the large muscles of the body (gross, or large, motor skills) and the small muscles of the body (fine, or small, motor skills)

Multiple intelligences theory   A theory proposed by Howard Gardner that suggests each person's intellect consists of different types of intellectual ability or "intelligences." Eight intelligences have been identified, and more are being researched.

Nature–nurture controversy   A long-standing debate regarding the relative influences of genetics versus the environment in human development

Neurons   Nerve cells in the brain

Object permanence   The understanding that objects still exist when they are out of sight

Operant conditioning   Consciously applying pleasant or unpleasant consequences to change behaviors

Perceptually bound thinking   Understanding based only on sensory information, such as seeing or hearing, not on logic or abstract thought

Physiological   Processes and activities that keep living things alive and that support their normal healthy functioning

Practice   An established way of doing something, especially one that has developed through experience and knowledge

Preoperational stage   In Piaget's theory of cognitive development, the period between ages 2 and 7 when children do not yet understand concrete logic, cannot mentally manipulate information, and have trouble seeing things from different points of view

Primary caregiving system   A child care staffing plan where a very small group of infants and/or toddlers are assigned to one adult who handles the majority of their care

Private speech   Words said aloud by children 2 to 7 years of age; spoken for self-understanding, self-guidance, and self-regulation of behavior, not for communication with others

Proximodistal pattern of development   The pattern of infant physical development in which growth and skill mastery begin at the center of the body and move outward to the extremities

Psychosocial theory   Erik Erikson's theory of personality that includes eight stages of development from infancy to late adulthood

Resiliency   The ability to recover quickly from misfortune or trauma; to "bounce back" from adversity and handle life situations with competence

Scaffolding   Providing an optimal amount of assistance, guidance, or direction to a child to enable him or her to accomplish a task or learn a skill that is just outside of his or her current ability

Schemata   A mental framework that individuals use to organize information gained from past experiences.

Self-actualization   The highest level on Maslow's hierarchy of human needs, it is the ability to focus on giving and receiving love, the pursuit of an understanding of the world, and self-knowledge

Sensitive periods   Times when an individual can most easily learn a particular skill or mental function

Sensorimotor stage   In Piaget's theory of cognitive development, the period between birth and age 2 when children learn through sensory perceptions and motor activities

Social cognition   Thoughts and understanding about social behaviors and relationships

Social context   In Lev Vygotsky's sociocultural theory, the circumstances of the family, the values of the school, and the geographic location of the community that influence the content and structure of thought

Sociocultural theory   Lev Vygotsky's theory that suggests that children's thoughts and behaviors are shaped by their social interactions, which are culturally influenced

Stage of development   A clearly distinguishable period in children's development that includes predictable behaviors (e.g., the toddler stage)

Synapse   A junction between two nerve cells, consisting of a minute gap across which impulses pass

Temperament   An individual's characteristic way of experiencing, responding to, and interacting with the world; an observable, biologically based pattern of behavior and emotions

Teratogens   Environmental substances that cause prenatal damage

Theory   An idea or set of ideas intended to explain facts or events; general principles related to a specific subject

Whole child   The view that all domains of development interact with one another in children's growth and learning and that all must be considered when planning appropriate care and education for each child

Zone of proximal development (ZPD)   The range of behaviors between what a child can accomplish independently and what the child can do with help

Chapter 5

Achievement tests   Standardized tests that measure what a child has learned

Anecdotal record   A brief open-ended, detailed narrative observation written after the fact using the past tense

Annotated photograph   A photograph that is accompanied by an anecdotal record

Assessment   A multipart process for the purpose of appraising development and learning

Assessment instrument   A systematic means of collecting and recording information; also called an *assessment tool*

Authentic assessment   Evaluation of a child's development or performance based on what the child does while engaged in everyday activities

Checklist   A list of traits, behaviors, concepts, and skills on which an observer puts dates or check marks when observed

Classroom portfolio   Organized assemblages of plans, documents, and records that provide evidence of implementation of accreditation criteria specific to a particular classroom

Confidentiality   The ethical principle of respecting a family's right to privacy by refraining from disclosing information to third parties

Core items   portfolio items collected at the same time from all children

Criterion-referenced tests   Tests that relate performance to a standard of achievement that do not compare the individual to a reference group

Developmental assessment   Criterion referenced assessment created for appraising children's skills and abilities in developmental domains

Developmental portfolio   A term used to distinguish portfolios organized by developmental domain from those organized by subject areas

Diagnostic tests   In-depth evaluations used to assess what children can and cannot do in specific areas of development

Digital portfolios   Portfolios without physical materials using photos, observations, video and audio clips, and work samples entered or scanned into a computer and assembled into a document that can be shared electronically; also called *electronic portfolios* or *e-portfolios*

Digital record   A video or audio record of a child engaged in school

Documentation (noun)   Tangible evidence of work, learning, and activity collected by teachers

Documentation (verb)   The process of making a record of what has been observed.

Documentation panel   Posters in which photographs, children's work, observations, and teacher-authored text are put together to document curriculum; a term associated with the schools of Reggio Emilia

Documentation presentation   A slideshow using a presentation (e.g., Powerpoint) or a photographic (e.g., Photoshop) application in which photographs, children's work, observations, and teacher-authored text are put together to present curriculum

Electronic portfolios or e-portfolios   Portfolios without physical materials using photos, observations, video and audio clips, and work samples entered or scanned into a computer and assembled into a document that can be shared electronically; also called *digital portfolios*

Event sample   A structured observation method which records what preceded a behavior or interaction (the event), what happens during the event, and what happens after the event (the consequence)

Facsimile   A re-creation of work created in the classroom, for example a rewritten chart on letter-size paper or a photograph of the chart

Formative assessment   Assessment carried out while teaching to inform and improve instruction

Frequency count   A structured observation method for tracking behaviors that occur at regular intervals in rapid succession using a grid to tally; also known as a *time sample*

High-stakes tests   Tests, used to make decisions for children, that have long-term consequences such as rejecting, retaining, or tracking

Interpretation   A reflection on what an observation might mean; sometimes called *conclusion, inference,* or *comment*

Interview   A structured observation technique in which the teacher selects a focus (a skill or concept) and then asks questions of all the children to determine their skill or understanding

Narrative observation   Open-ended written observations that describe children and provide details and a vivid picture

Norm-referenced tests   Tests that compare individual performance with an external norm established by administering the test to a large sample

Objective (adjective)   Observable, free of bias

Observation   Purposefully and systematically watching children and noting what they do; the first and most important form of authentic assessment

Portfolio   A meaningfully organized collection of observations, work samples, photographs, and other documents that authentically shows a child's characteristics and abilities; sometimes called a *portfolio assessment*

Portfolio assessment   An assessment based on a portfolio that contains evidence to evaluate whether and to what degree a child has acquired skills, knowledge, and dispositions; an alternative to tests, report cards, and letter grades

Portfolio systems   Products designed to systematize and guide teachers in observing, organizing, and interpreting children's work

Professional portfolio   Professional documentation gathered by an individual to represent that person's training and ability

Program portfolio   Organized assemblages of plans, documents, and records that provide evidence of implementation of accreditation criteria for an entire program

Rating scale   A structured observation method which indicates the degree to which a behavior or characteristic on a preexisting list is present

Readiness tests   Standardized tests that predict if children will succeed in particular grades or programs

Recording   Making a record, in writing or electronically, of what has been observed

Reliability   How often identical results can be obtained with the same test

Rubric   A structured observation method that indicates the extent to which predetermined skills have been demonstrated and that uses very specific criteria for different levels of ability

Running record   Lengthy, open-ended, detailed narrative accounts of a child's behavior written while it is happening, using the present tense; also called a *specimen record*

Screening test   Test designed to identify children who may need specialized services

Standardized assessment   Measuring and quantifying children's development and learning using standardized instruments

Standardized test   A systematic procedure for sampling a child's behavior and knowledge that summarizes the child's performance with a score

Structured observation   Forms of structured data gathering designed to reveal trends and patterns in behavior

Subjective   Biased, based on opinion, not substantiated

Summative assessment   Assessment that evaluates a child's acquisition of knowledge or skills after teaching is completed

Test   A systematic procedure for sampling a child's behavior and knowledge usually summarizing performance with a score

Time sample   A structured observation method for tracking behaviors that occur at regular intervals in rapid succession using a grid to tally; also known as a *frequency count*

Validity   The degree to which a test measures what it claims to measure

Video and audio records   Documentation of a child's skill and knowledge in video or audio format

Work sample   An example of a child's work that provides authentic evidence of understanding and ability

Chapter 6

Active listening   A term developed by Thomas Gordon that means responding to both verbal and nonverbal communication by describing the message understood by the listener

Altruism   Caring for others with no expectation of compensation or personal gain

Behaviorism   Learning theory that behavior is changed based on the positive or negative consequences that immediately follow the behavior; the theory that behavior can be explained in terms of conditioning; behaviors that are rewarded will be repeated, and those not rewarded or punished will be extinguished

Bullying   A set of hurtful behaviors that are done with the intent to harm or intimidate a person, particularly one who is perceived as weaker than the perpetrator

Challenging behaviors   Persistent behaviors that prevent children from being able to function in a group

Child guidance   The techniques and practices that adults use to help children learn about acceptable behavior and problem solving, as well as about the feelings of others and of themselves

Cooperation   The ability to work with others to achieve a common goal

Emotional intelligence   Understanding one's own feelings and the feelings of others and the ability to use this information to make decisions

Empathy   The ability to understand and share the feelings of others

Guidelines   Positively stated expectations that guide children's behavior

I-message   A communication pattern that describes a behavior, the speakers' feelings about the behavior, and how that behavior affects the speaker

Logical consequences   Outcomes that do not naturally occur as a result of behavior but are intentionally planned by a teacher or other adult

Mistaken behavior   A term developed by Dan Gartrell to describe children's inappropriate actions as mistakes that offer opportunities for learning

Natural consequences   Outcomes that happen as a result of behavior and that are not planned or controlled

Prosocial behavior   Behavior that benefits society and shows concern for the rights and needs of others

Punishment   A penalty given as retribution for an offense; pain, loss, or confinement given as a penalty

Reflective and responsive (R & R) statements   Verbal responses to children's actions that describe what teachers see them doing; "say-what-you-see" statements

Resiliency   The ability to effectively deal with difficulty and to bounce back from challenging situations

Self-concept   Beliefs about oneself based on perceptions of physical, social, and cognitive qualities

Self-esteem   A positive sense of self-worth that includes a realistic understanding of strengths and weaknesses

Self-identity   The way people define themselves and how they feel about their view of themselves

Self-regulation   The ability to control one's actions despite feelings or desires

Social intelligence   The ability to understand what others are doing, thinking, and feeling and to respond in a socially effective way

Transitions   Times in a school day when children move from one type of activity to another, such as from outdoor play to circle time

Chapter 7

Clean   Free of dirt and debris

Disinfected   Treated with a solution that destroys or inactivates germs

Epi-Pen   A spring-loaded hypodermic prefilled with the correct dosage of epinephrine; this prescription medication is administered when a person with allergies shows signs of anaphylactic shock

Hazard   A danger that one cannot anticipate or see and therefore cannot evaluate

Health   A state of overall well-being—physical, mental, and social; a state of holistic wellness

Health care consultant   A licensed pediatric health professional or health professional with specific training in health consultation for early childhood programs

Pathogens   Bacteria, viruses, or parasites that cause infection or disease

Risk   Exposure to the chance of injury or loss

Sanitized   Treated with a product that reduces germs on inanimate surfaces to levels considered safe by public health regulations

Sudden infant death syndrome (SIDS)   The unexplained death, usually during sleep, of a seemingly healthy baby

Well-being   A state of wellness of the body, mind, and spirit

Chapter 8

Active play zone   Outdoor space to run, jump, climb, skip, roll hoops, throw balls, and ride and pull wheeled vehicles

Atelier   The French word for "workshop," which has come to mean an artist's studio. In early childhood education, it is an area within or apart from a classroom where children work with art materials; also called an *art area* or *studio*; pronounced *atuh-lyey*

Building/construction toys   Toys consisting of a set of many small standardized pieces made of plastic, wood, or metal; designed to be used to construct different objects

Climbing structure   A structure of wood and/or metal and rope used by children for climbing and playing, often including platforms, tunnels, bridges, slides, ladders, nets, and ramps; sometimes called a superstructure or climbing frame

Cubbyholes or cubbies   Space for the storage of belongings in classrooms for young children for personal items

Dramatic play   A form of symbolic play identified by Smilansky in which children individually or with another child act out human relationships using symbols but without a well-defined story line

Equipment   Furniture and other large and expensive items used in early childhood programs, such as easels and climbing structures

Forest schools   A type of outdoor education, which takes place typically in the woods or a forest, as a means to build skills, independence, and self-esteem; also called *nature schools*

Glider rocker   A type of rocking chair that moves as a swing seat; because pinch points are moved away from the floor, a glider is safer for children.

Hollow blocks   Large building blocks and boards. These are typically made of wood and are big enough to use to create structures children can enter but light enough that a preschool child can carry them.

Interest center   A well-defined space in a classroom where a particular type of activity takes place; also called a *learning area or center*

Learning center   A well-defined space in a classroom where a particular type of activity takes place; also called an *area or interest center*

Learning environment   The indoor and outdoor area in which an early childhood program takes place; in Reggio Emilia called the *third teacher*

Light table or light panel   A translucent table top or panel with recessed fluorescent light bulbs or led lights. Originally a tool for photographers and graphic artists, it was popularized as classroom equipment by the educators of Reggio Emilia.

Loose parts   Materials that can be moved, carried, combined, redesigned, lined up, and taken apart and put back together in multiple ways

Manipulative–creative zone.   An area in the play yard where manipulative and creative activities like art and woodworking take place

Manipulative toys or manipulatives   Toys and games that enhance children's fine motor skills and develop fine motor strength

Materials   Small, less expensive educational items, such as puzzles, books, games, and toys

Natural elements zone   An area in the play yard where there are plants, dirt, rocks, trees, grass, water, and living creatures

Nature preschools   Preschool programs with a primary focus on nature and outdoors activities; also called *forest schools*

Open design classrooms   A classroom in which several classes of children share one large room most of the time

Partial seclusion   A learning center protected on two or three sides from foot traffic

Purpose-built   A building created to be an early childhood program and not for other purposes

Racetracks   Circular paths around shelves or tables that invite running

Rotate   As in *rotate* materials—the practice in early childhood classrooms of putting some toys and materials away and bringing others out

Self-contained classrooms   A classroom in which one class or group of children spends the bulk of the program day

Sensory table   A plastic or metal basin or tub freely standing on legs, usually with a drain or cover. It can be filled with materials (e.g., water, sand, dirt, or rice) that children can touch, scoop, pour, pile, sort, or sift, using scoops, ladles, sieves, shovels, and other toys; also called a *water table or sand table*

Social–dramatic zone   An area in the play yard where children pretend, dress-up, and use props in dramatic play

Superstructure   A structure of wood and/or metal and rope used by children for climbing and playing, often including platforms, tunnels, bridges, slides, ladders, nets, and ramps; sometimes called a *climbing frame* or *climbing structure*

Supplies   Consumables like paint, paper, glue, and tape

Third teacher   Another name for the *learning environment*

Unifix cubes   Colorful, interlocking plastic cubes designed to teach early math and reading concepts

Unit blocks   Hardwood building blocks developed by Carolyn Pratt in the early 1900s. Each block is a fraction or multiple of a standard "unit" block 5.5 inches long, 2.75 inches wide, and 1.375 inches thick.

Universal design   An environment designed so that it can be accessed, understood and used to the greatest extent possible by all people regardless of size, ability or disability. It includes entries, pathways, centers, tables, climbing structures, and play materials that are flexible and easily adapted to accommodate all children.

Visual boundaries   A border that gives a visual signal that encourages children to avoid an area that might be hazardous

Water or sand table   A plastic or metal basin or tub freely standing on legs usually with a drain or cover. It can be filled with "sensory" materials (e.g., water, sand, dirt, or rice) that children can touch, scoop, pour, pile, sort, or sift, using scoops, ladles, sieves, shovels, and other toys; also called a *sensory table*

Wheeled vehicles   Vehicles like trikes, scooters, wagons, and balance bikes that young children can propel without assistance

Workjob   A term coined by Mary Baratta-Lorton to describe a teacher-made game designed to teach a concept or develop a skill, usually using recycled materials.

Zone   A large part of a room or yard with a distinct purpose, such as a transition zone where children enter and exit the play yard that allows children to see what is available and make choices

Chapter 9

Associative play   One of the stages of play described by Parten in which children play in groups in the same area and sharing materials but with little cooperation and negotiation; dominant in young preschoolers.

Big-body play   Play fighting without intent to harm; also called *rough-and-tumble play*

Constructive play   A form of symbolic play identified by Smilansky in which the child uses real objects to build a representation of something according to a plan

Cooperative play   One of the stages of play described by Parten in which children create sustained play episodes with joint themes—characteristic of older preschool- and kindergarten/primary-age children

Decentration   The ability to consider multiple aspects of a stimulus or situation

Dramatic play   A form of play in which children individually or with another child act out human relationships using symbols

Flow   Complete and energized focus

Functional play   One of the stages of play described by Piaget in which children explore the sensory qualities of objects and practice motor skills; also called *practice play*

Game   Structured play that has a goal, rules, and a challenge

Games with rules   A form of play in which children recognize and follow preset rules that conform to the expectations and goals of the games

Intrinsic motivation   Internal rewards that prompt behavior (e.g., play) without reward or reinforcement from an outside source

Make-believe play   A form of play in which children pretend often using objects. It involves a scenario, roles, and a set of rules that evolve with the roles; also called *pretend play* or *dramatic play*

Parallel play   One of the stages of play described by Parten in which children play side by side engaged with their own play objects with little interpersonal interaction; dominant in toddlerhood

Perceptual-motor coordination   The ability to use sensory information to direct motor activity

Play   Intrinsically motivated, freely chosen activity that is pleasurable, enjoyable, engaging, and self-oriented rather than object oriented

Practice play   One of the stages of play described by Piaget in which children explore the sensory qualities of objects and practice motor skills; also called *functional play*

Role-play   Play in which a child takes on the role of another person or an animal

Rough-and-tumble play   Play fighting without intent to harm; also called *big-body play*

Sociodramatic play   A form of symbolic play identified by Smilansky in which children act out complex interactions in cooperation with others. It includes a story line, assigned roles, and negotiated changes.

Solitary play   One of the stages of play described by Parten in which children play alone and independently with objects; dominant in infancy

Stage manager   A teacher's role in children's play that includes selecting and organizing materials, space, and equipment so that they suggest play that is meaningful to the children

Symbolic play   One of the stages of play described by Piaget in which children use one object to represent another object and use make-believe actions and roles.

Chapter 10

Aesthetic appreciation   The appreciation of beauty; the ability to find, recognize, and take pleasure in beauty in the physical and social world

Alphabetic knowledge   Familiarity with the shapes and sounds of letters and awareness that there is a relationship between letters and sounds; foundational knowledge required for reading and writing

Book knowledge   Understanding of how to use books (e.g., how to hold books, how to turn pages, and read from front to back); foundational knowledge required for reading and writing and other learning

Common Core Standards   National standards for English language arts/literacy and mathematics for children in grades K through 12

Content   The subject matter or curriculum that is taught

Content standards   The goals and objectives that are determined by each state to be important for each subject area for each grade

Cooperative games   Games that encourage cooperation and do not involve competition, winners, or losers

Curriculum   Intentional learning experiences designed by a teacher or a team of teachers in response to what they know and observe about children, the academic content taught, the knowledge and skills students are expected to learn, and the specific learning standards, lessons, assignments, and materials used to organize and teach

Curriculum approach or model   An orientation toward the design of curriculum that reflects a philosophy, values, and beliefs about learners

Curriculum content standards Standards for what teachers are expected to teach in different content areas

Decontextualized speech Abstract language; talking about subjects that are removed from the here and now

Developmentally appropriate practice (DAP) A research-based framework of principles and guidelines for early childhood practice that engages children and adapts for their development, strengths, interests, and needs and that considers the social and cultural contexts in which they live

Dual Language Learners Children for whom English is not the primary home language, also referred to as *English language learners*

Early learning guidelines Outlines of what young children should know and be able to do at different stages of their development; also called *early learning standards*

Early learning standards Outlines of what young children should know and be able to do at different stages of their development; described by officially mandated bodies of state and territorial governments; also called *early learning and development guidelines*

Educational pendulum A metaphor for popular educational thought that moves from one extreme to another

Emergent literacy The evolving process by which children become literate during the span from birth until children read and write in conventional ways

Genres of children's literature Categories of literature defined by content, pattern, or structure; examples include folktales, concept books, and informational books

Gross motor curriculum Planned activity for developing skills that use the large muscles of the body; also called *large motor curriculum*.

Hand–eye coordination The coordinated control of the eye with hand movement and the processing of visual inputs that guide reaching and grasping; also known as *eye–hand coordination*

Inquiry curriculum Curriculum in mathematics, science, and social studies designed to support children's thinking and problem solving and their growing understanding of the world

Intentional Using knowledge, judgment, and expertise to organize learning experiences purposefully and to respond to unexpected situations as teaching opportunities

Literacy The developmental process of learning to write and read; also called *emergent literacy*

Literature extensions Activities that use an element from a story to enhance children's enjoyment or understanding of the story or as a springboard for learning in other subject areas; sometimes called a story stretcher

Locomotor skills Movement that transports a child from one place to another: walking, jumping, hopping, skipping, galloping, and sliding; also called *traveling movement*

Method A type of teaching activity used to deliver curriculum (e.g., reading a book); also called a *strategy*

Nonlocomotor skills Movement skills that involve bending, balancing, and twisting while staying in one place

Object control skills The use of arms, hands, and feet to move objects, such as balls; also called *gross motor manipulative skills*

Oral language The ability to talk; a foundational skill for reading and writing and other learning

Pedagogy The art or science of teaching, education, and instructional methods

Phonological awareness The understanding that the sounds of words can be changed and manipulated; foundational knowledge required for reading and writing

Print knowledge Understanding rules about using print (e.g., read from left to right and it always says the same thing); foundational knowledge required for reading and writing

Scaffolding Teaching by providing a challenge with a question or adjusting the environment to support a child's development of a skill or concept

Chapter 11

Activity plan A detailed written outline for a specific learning activity that includes objectives, teaching steps, and assessment

Aims Inspirational ideals based on philosophy and values that frame the program as a whole

Behavioral objectives Objectives that precisely describe a behavior. They describe specific behaviors, the conditions under which they take place, and the criteria for success; also called *measurable objectives*

Content The subject matter or curriculum that is taught

Curriculum web A diagram used to visually organize ideas in a way that shows relationships between pieces of the whole

Developmentally appropriate practice (DAP) Program and curriculum appropriate to children's age and individual needs, backgrounds, and interests

Direct instruction Education by explicit, guided instruction relying on specific lesson plans with little variation—not appropriate for young children

Dispositions Tendencies to respond to experiences in certain ways

Goals Broad statements of desired ends toward which teaching is directed; what a teacher or program intends to accomplish

Holistically An approach to teaching that provides many different avenues for learning about a topic using diverse modalities

Integrated curriculum An educational approach in which a topic of study provides a focus for the curriculum

Integrated plan A plan for several weeks of activities, addressing many different subject areas, based on a topic

Intended learning outcome The desired result of teaching

Intentional teaching Using knowledge, judgment, and expertise to organize learning experiences purposefully and to respond to unexpected situations as teaching opportunities

Learner-centered organization Curriculum organization based on the developmental stage, needs, and interests of children

Lesson plan A detailed written outline for a specific learning activity that includes objectives, teaching steps, and assessment

Methods Type of teaching activities used to deliver curriculum (e.g., reading a book) (*see* strategy)

Mind-map A diagram used to visually organize ideas in a way that shows relationships between pieces of the whole

Objectives Statements outlining the intended result of what a curriculum activity is designed to accomplish

Plan A detailed map or guide for teaching

Purpose In a plan, a statement of what the teacher is trying to accomplish (*see* aims, goals, objectives, and ilo

Strategy A type of teaching activity used to deliver curriculum (e.g., reading a book) (*see* methods)

Subject-centered organization Curriculum organized by subject areas focused on the attainment of knowledge sometimes referred to as *direct instruction*; not appropriate for young children

Weekly plan A calendar showing all the learning activities that will occur each day over a week

Chapter 12

Asperger syndrome   A mild autism spectrum disorder characterized by tendencies toward social isolation, communication difficulties, and eccentric behavior

Attention deficit disorder   The inability to focus and stay on task

Attention-deficit/hyperactivity disorder (ADHD)   Children with attention deficit disorder who also exhibit impulsive, out-of-control behavior and hyperactivity beyond what is appropriate for their age-group

Autism spectrum disorder   A developmental disorder that appears in the first 3 years of life and affects the brain's normal development of social and communication skills

Bilingual   Able to use two languages with equal or nearly equal fluency

Culturally, Linguistically, and Ability Diverse practices (CLAD)   Culturally responsive practices that support the full participation of children and families

Developmental delay   The condition of a child not meeting developmental milestones in one or more domains—physical, cognitive, language, social, emotional, or adaptive

Disabilities   Physical or mental impairments that limit a child's movements, senses, or activities; development outside the expected range

Dual language learners   Non–English-speaking children who are learning English while continuing to learn their home language

Free appropriate public education   The provision of IDEIA that requires that children with disabilities learn in the same environments as their typically developing peers

Gifted   A characteristic of children who have unusual strengths, abilities, or talents

Inclusion   Education and services for children with disabilities in the same learning environments as their typically developing peers

Individualized education plan (IEP)   A plan for a child who meets state disability requirements and is identified as needing special services. It has individualized objectives and is developed by a team and reviewed and revised regularly.

Individualized family services plan (IFSP)   A written plan developed by a team to guide the provision of early intervention services to children under the age of 3 and their families

Individualized health care plan   A plan developed by a team to address the needs of a child who has an acute or chronic health condition

Individuals with Disabilities Education Improvement Act (IDEIA)   U.S. federal law that governs how states should provide education and services to children (3 to 18 years of age) who have disabilities; originally called the Individuals with Disabilities Education Act (IDEA)

Learning disability   Learning problems exhibited by children with normal intelligence but below-age-level academic functioning

Least restrictive environment   The provision of IDEA that requires that children with disabilities should, to the greatest extent possible, participate in regular education classrooms with their peers who do not have disabilities and experience the same curriculum as their typically developing peers

Otitis media   Middle ear infection

People-first language   The recommended practice of speaking of the child first and the disability second

Recognition and Response (RTI Pre-K)   A similar framework to RTI for providing instructional support tailored to the needs of 3- to 5-year-olds

Response to Intervention (RTI)   A three-part instructional framework that identifies young children's learning and behavioral

problems early so that educators can intervene with specialized instruction

Sensory integration   The process by which the brain takes in information from the senses and interprets it for use

Sensory processing disorder (previously referred to as sensory integration disorder)   A condition characterized by difficulty in taking in and processing information received from the senses

Special needs   Specialized risk factors, including health or emotional health issues and physical, sensory, or cognitive impairments

Task analysis   Breaking down a complex task into its component parts and teaching them separately as a series of subskills

Universal Design for Learning (UDL)   An educational framework that guides the development of flexible learning environments that accommodate individual differences in learning

Vestibular   The system that contributes to balance and spatial orientation

Chapter 13

Confidentiality   The ethical responsibility of early childhood professionals to keep information about children and families strictly private, sharing only with those who have a legitimate, professional need for the information and/or for whom families have given written permission to receive specific information

Family Corner   An area of a school or classroom designed to be comfortable for families; these areas are separate from children's spaces, have adult seating and provide information that is meaningful to families

Family engagement   A reciprocal, strength-based partnership between families and early childhood program staff, built through mutual respect and program practices that include families in all aspects of their children's learning and school experiences

Family systems theory   A theory that suggests that families can be understood as systems of interconnected and interdependent individuals, whose roles, behaviors, and decisions influence the other members and whose actions are best understood within the context of the family system

Mandated reporter   A person who is required by law to report suspected cases of child abuse, maltreatment, or neglect to an authority designated by state statute

Open door policy   A practice required by many programs and mandated in some states that welcomes families to come into the classroom at any time and stay for as long as they wish

Chapter 14

Advocacy   Giving public support to a policy or cause that you believe to be right

Classroom Assessment Scoring System (CLASS)   An observational instrument developed to assess classroom quality and teaching interactions linked to student achievement and development

Early childhood professional   An early childhood educator who has acquired the basic knowledge and skills that are necessary to work effectively with young children, who demonstrates professional behavior, who behaves ethically, and who has personal qualities needed to nurture and care for the very young

Educational philosophy   Set of beliefs, guiding principles, and ideals that inform professional practice

Issues   Subjects of ongoing discussion and debate; discussions may go on over time and never be fully resolved

School readiness   Children's preparation to engage successfully with school learning experiences and meet school expectations

Bibliography

Chapter 1

Barnett, W. S. (2004). Better teachers, better preschools: Student achievement linked to teacher qualifications. *NIEER Preschool Policy Matters, 2*(1–11).

Bellm, D. (n.d.) Establishing teacher competencies in early care and education: A review of current models and options for California. Policy brief for Building California's preschool for all workforce. Berkeley, CA: Center for the Study of Child Care Employment.

Biber, B., & Snyder, A. (1948). How do we know a good teacher? *Childhood Education, 24*(6), 281–285.

Bredekamp, S. (1992). Composing a profession. *Young Children, 47*(2), 52–54.

Bredekamp, S. (2011). *Effective practices in early childhood education: Building a foundation.* Upper Saddle River, NJ: Pearson.

Bredekamp, S., & Copple, C. (Eds.). (2009). *Developmentally appropriate practice in early childhood programs* (3rd ed.). Washington, DC: NAEYC.

Burks, J., & Rubenstein, M. (1979). *Temperament styles in adult interaction.* New York: Brunner/Mazel.

CambridgeDictionary-dictionary.cambridge.org.

Cartwright, S. (1999). What makes good early childhood teachers? *Young Children, 54*(6), 4–7.

Colker, L. J. (2008, March). Twelve characteristics of effective early childhood teachers. *Beyond the Journal.* Available online from NAEYC. Retrieved from http://journal.naeyc.org/btj/200803/BTJColker.asp

Council for Exceptional Children. (n. d.). *CEC standards for professional practice.* Retrieved from www.cec.sped.org/content/navigation-menu/professionaldevelopment/professionalstandards/

Council for Professional Recognition. (2011). *National competency standards for CDA credential.* Retrieved from www.cdacouncil.org/the-cda-credential/about-the-cda/cda-competency-standards

Derman-Sparks, L. (1989). *Anti-bias curriculum: Tools for empowering young children.* Washington, DC: NAEYC.

Early, D. M., Maxwell, K. L., Burchinal, M., Alva, S., Bender, R. H., Bryant, D., . . . Zill, N. (2007). Teacher's education, classroom quality, and young children's academic skills: Results from seven studies of preschool programs. *Child Development, 78,* 558–580.

Epstein, A. S. (2007). *The intentional teacher: Choosing the best strategies for young children's learning.* Washington, DC: NAEYC.

Feeney, S., & Chun, R. (1985). Effective teachers of young children. *Young Children, 41*(1), 47–52.

Gardner, H. (1983). *Frames of mind.* New York: Basic Books.

Institute of Medicine and National Research Council. (2015). *Transforming the workforce for children birth through age 8: A unifying foundation.* Washington, DC: The National Academies Press. doi:10.17226/19401

Katz, L. G. (1993, April). *Dispositions: Definitions and implications for early childhood practices.* Retrieved from http://ceep.crc.uiuc.edu/eecearchive/books/disposit.html

Katz, L. G. (1995). The developmental stages of teachers. In *Talks with teachers of young children.* Norwood, NJ: Ablex.

Katz, L. G., & Ward, E. (1978). *Ethical behavior in early childhood education.* Washington, DC: NAEYC.

Kidder, R. (1995). *How good people make tough choices.* New York: Simon & Schuster.

Kipnis, K. (1987). How to discuss professional ethics. *Young Children, 42*(4), 26–33.

Kontos, S., & Wilcox-Herzog, A. (2001). How do education and experience affect teachers of young children? *Young Children, 56*(4), 85–91.

National Association for the Education of Young Children (NAEYC). (2005). *Code of ethical conduct and statement of commitment* (Rev. ed.). Washington, DC: NAEYC.

National Association for the Education of Young Children (NAEYC). (2009). *Developmentally appropriate practice* (3rd ed.)., p. 13.

National Association for the Education of Young Children (NAEYC). (2009). *NAEYC standards for early childhood professional preparation programs: Position statement.* Washington, DC: Author. Retrieved from www.naeyc.org/files/naeyc/file/positions/ProfPrep Standards09.pdf

National Board for Professional Teaching Standards (NBPTS). (2001). *Early childhood generalist standards* (2nd ed.). Retrieved from www.nbpts.org/userfiles/File/ec_gen_standards.pdf

Thomas, A., & Chess, S. (1977). *Temperament and development.* New York: Brunner/Mazel.

Chapter 2

Administration for Children and Families. (2015). *Head Start Program facts: Fiscal year 2015.* Retrieved from https://eclkc.ohs.acf.hhs.gov/hslc/data/factsheets/docs/head-start-fact-sheet-fy-2015.pdf

Administration for Children and Families. (2016). *QRIS resource guide: About QRIS.* Retrieved from https://qrisguide.acf.hhs.gov/index.cfm?do=qris

Administration for Children and Families. Early Childhood Learning and Knowledge Center. (2016). *Head Start program performance standards.* Retrieved from http://eclkc.ohs.acf.hhs.gov/hslc/hs/docs/hspps-appendix.pdf

Administration for Children and Families & Office of Head Start. *Head Start Program fact sheet: Fiscal year 2010.* Retrieved from http://www.acf.hhs.gov/programs/ohs/about/fy2010.html

Administration for Children, Youth, and Families. (2001). *Head Start FACES, Chapter 5.* Retrieved from http://www.acf.hhs.gov/programs/opre/hs/faces/reports/perform_3rd_rep/meas_99_title.html

Administration for Children, Youth, and Families. (2003). *Head Start FACES, progress report.* Retrieved from http://www.acf.hhs.gov/programs/opre/hs/faces00/reports/perform_4thprogress/faces00_title.html

Administration for Children, Youth, and Families. (2006). *Head Start FACES, progress report.* Retrieved from http://www.acf.hhs.gov/programs/opre/hs/faces/reports/research_2003_title.html

Alliance for Childhood. (2011). *Policy brief: Why we object to the K–3 Core Standards.* Retrieved from http://www.allianceforchildhood.org

Barnett, W. S. (1995). Long-term effects of early childhood programs on cognitive and school outcomes. In *The future of children: Long-term outcomes of early childhood programs,5*(3). Los Altos, CA: Center for the Future of Children, The David and Lucile Packard Foundation.

Barnett, W. S., Carolan, M. E., Fitzgerald, J., & Squires, J. H. (2012). *The state of preschool 2012: State preschool yearbook.* New Brunswick, NJ: National Institute for Early Education Research.

Barnett, W. S., Epstein, D. J., Carolan, M. E., Fitzgerald, J., Ackerman, D. J., & Friedman, A. H. (2010). *State preschoool yearbook: The state of preschool 2010.* Retrieved from http://nieer.org/yearbook

Barnett, W. S., Friedman-Krauss, A. H., Gomez, R. W., Weisenfeld, G. G., Clarke-Brown, K., & Squires J. H. (2015). *The state of preschool 2015, national institute for early education research.* Retrieved from http://nieer.org/yearbook

Barnett, W. S., Friedman-Krauss, A. H., Gomez, R. W., Weisenfeld, G. G., Clarke-Brown, K., & Squires J. H. (2015). *The state of preschool 2015-2016, national institute for early education research.* Retrieved from http://nieer.org/yearbook

Barnett, W. S., & Hustedt, J. T. (2005). Head Start's lasting benefits. *Infants and Young Children, 18*(18), 1–24.

The Build Initiative. Retrieved from http://www.earlychildhoodfinance.org/downloads/2009/QRISasSystemReform_2009.pdf

Bureau of Labor Statistics, (2015). *Women in the labor force: A databook.* Washington, DC: U.S. Department of Labor. Retrieved from http://www.bls.gov/opub/reports/womens-databook/archive/women-in-the-labor-force-a-databook-2015.pdf

Center for Law and Social Policy. (2010a). *Head Start by the numbers: 2009 PIR profile.* Retrieved from http://www.clasp.org/admin/site/publications/files/hsdata2009us.pdf

Center for Law and Social Policy. (2010b). *Early Head Start participants, programs, families, and staff.* Retrieved from http://www.clasp.org/publications/ehs_pir_2009.pdf

Common Core Standards Initiative. (2010). *Core standards.* Retrieved from http://www.corestandards.org

Department of Defense. (2008). *Overview of the military child development system.* Retrieved from http://www.militaryhomefront.dod.mil/portal/page/mhf/MHF/MHF_DETAIL_1?id=20.80.500.95.0.0.0.0.0&current_id=20.80.500.95.500.30.30.0.0

Dodge, K .A, Bai, Y., Ladd, H. F., & Muschkin, C. G. Impact of North Carolina's early childhood programs and policies on educational outcomes in elementary school. *Child Dev.* 2016 Nov 17. doi: 10.1111/cdev.12645. [Epub ahead of print]

Education Commission of the States. (2008). *Access to kindergarten: Age issues and state statutes.* Denver, CO: Author. Retrieved from http://www.ecs.org/clearinghouse/79/58/7958.pdf

Federal Interagency Forum on Child and Family Statistics. (2013). *America's children: Key national indicators of well-being, 2013, the kindergarten year.* Retrieved from http://www.childstats.gov/americaschildren/index3.asp

Hruska, K. (2009). Your updated guide to military child care. *Military Money,* Spring 2009. Retrieved from http://www.militarymoney.com/spouse/militarychildren/tabid/128/itemId/2216/Default.aspx

Kagan, S. L., Scott-Little, C., & Stebbins Frelow, V. (2003). Early learning standards for young children: A survey of the states. *Young Children, 58*(5), 58–64.

Kauerz, K. (2005, March). State kindergarten policies: Straddling early learning and early elementary school. *Young Children: Beyond the Journal.* Retrieved from http://journal.naeyc.org/btj/200503/01Kauerz.asp

Laughlin, L. 2013. *Who's minding the kids? Child care arrangements: Spring 2011.* Current Population Reports, P70-135. Washington, DC: U.S. Census Bureau. Retrieved from http://www.census.gov/prod/2013pubs/p70-135.pdf

Lewit, E. M., & Baker, L. (1995). School readiness. *The Future of Children, 5*(2), 128–139.

Minnesota Department of Education. (2014). Early childhood family education (ECFE). Retrieved from http://education.state.mn.us/MDE/StuSuc/EarlyLearn/ECFE

Morgan, G. G. (2003). Regulatory policy. In D. Cryer & R. M. Clifford (Eds.), *Early childhood education and care in the United States* (pp. 65–85). Baltimore: Brookes.

National Association of Child Care Resource and Referral Agencies. (2008). *Child care in America: 2008 state fact sheets.* Retrieved from http://www.naccrra.org/policy/docs/ChildCareinAmerica.pdf

National Association of Child Care Resource and Referral Agencies. (2011). *Number of children potentially needing child care.* Retrieved from http://www.naccrra.org/randd/docs/Children-Under-Age-6-Potentially-Needing-Care.pdf

National Association of Child Care Resource and Referral Agencies. (2013). *We can do better: (2013 Update). Child Care Aware of America's ranking of state child care center regulations and oversight.* Retrieved from http://www.naccrra.org/sites/default/files/default_site_pages/2013/wcdb_2013_final_april_11_0.pdf

National Association for the Education of Young Children. (1995). *Position statement on school readiness.* Washington, DC: Author.

National Association for the Education of Young Children. (1997). NAEYC position statement on licensing and public regulation of early childhood. *Young Children, 53*(1), 43–50.

National Association for the Education of Young Children. (2009). *Where we stand on early learning standards.* Joint position statement of NAEYC and the National Association of Early Childhood Specialists in State Departments of Education. Executive Summary. Retrieved from www.naeyc.org/positionstatements/learning_standards

National Association for the Education of Young Children Academy. (2009). *Accreditation of programs for young children.* Retrieved from http://www.naeyc.org/academy/accreditation/search

National Association for the Education of Young Children Academy. (2017). *Summary of accredited programs.* Washington, DC: Author. Retrieved from http://www.naeyc.org/academy/accreditation/summary

National Center on Child Care Quality Improvement. (2013). *Administration for children and families. State/territory early learning guidelines.* Retrieved from https://childcare.gov/sites/default/files/075_1301_state_elgs_web_0.pdf

National Center for Education Statistics. (2012). *Digest of education statistics, 2012.* Washington, DC: Department of Education, Institute of Education Sciences. Retrieved from https://nces.ed.gov/programs/digest/d12/tables/dt12_136.asp

National Center for Education Statistics. (2013a, March). *The condition of education, private school enrollment.* Retrieved from http://nces.ed.gov/pubs2013/2013037.pdf

National Center for Education Statistics, U.S. Department of Education, Institute of Education Sciences. (2013b). *Full-day and half-day kindergarten in the United States: Findings from the Early Childhood Longitudinal Study, Kindergarten Class of 1998–99.* NCES 2004-078. Washington, DC: U.S. Government Printing Office.

National Center for Education Statistics. (2015). *Digest of education statistics, 2014.* Washington, DC: Department of Education, Institute of Education Sciences. Retrieved from https://nces.ed.gov/programs/digest/d14/tables_1.asp

National Center for Education Statistics. (2016a). *Digest of education statistics, 2015.* Washington, DC: Department of Education, Institute of Education Sciences. Retrieved from https://nces.ed.gov/programs/digest/2015menu_tables.asp

National Center for Education Statistics. (2016b). *The condition of education: Charter school enrollment.* Washington, DC: Department of Education, Institute of Education Sciences. Retrieved from http://nces.ed.gov/programs/coe/indicator_cgb.asp

National Center for Education Statistics. (2016c). *State education reforms: Student readiness and progress through school.* Washington DC: Department of Education, Institute of Education Sciences. Retrieved from https://nces.ed.gov/programs/statereform/srp.asp

National Commission on Excellence in Education. (1983). *A nation at risk: The imperative for educational reform.* Washington, DC: U.S. Government Printing Office.

National Education Goals Panel. (1997). *National education goals report: Building a nation of learners.* Retrieved from http://readyweb.crc.uiuc.edu/virtual-library/1997/goals/contents.html

National Institute of Child Health and Human Development. (1997). The effects of infant child care on infant-mother attachment security. *Child Development, 68,* 860–879.

Padak, N., & Rasinski, T. (2003, April). *Family literacy programs: Who benefits?* Columbus, Ohio Literacy Resource Center, Kent State University. Retrieved from http://literacy.kent.edu/Oasis/Pubs/WhoBenefits2003.pdf

Porter, T., Paulsell, D., Nichols, T., Begnoche, C., & Del Grosso, P. (2010, March). *Supporting quality in home-based child care: A compendium of 23 initiatives.* Princeton, NJ: Mathematica Policy Research, Inc.

Pungello, E. P., Campbell, F. A., & Barnett, W. S. (2006). *Poverty and early childhood educational intervention.* New Brunswick, NJ: National Institute for Early Education Research, Rutgers University.

QRIS National Learning Network. (2009). *Quality, rating and improvement systems.* Retrieved from http://qrisnetwork.org

Ray, B. D. (2006, July). *Research facts on homeschooling.* National Home Education Research Institute. Retrieved from http://www.nheri.org/Research-Facts-on-Homeschooling.html

Schmit, S., & Ewen, D. (2012, February). *Putting children and families first: Head Start programs in 2010.* Brief No. 10. Washington, DC: Center for Law and Social Policy.

Schweinhart, L. (2007). *The High/Scope Perry Preschool Study through age 40: Summary, conclusions and frequently asked questions.* Ypsilanti, MI: High/Scope Educational Research Foundation. Retrieved from http://www.highscope.org/file/Research/PerryProject/3_special-summary%20col%2006%2007.pdf

Scott-Little, C., Lesko, J., Martella, J., & Milburn, P. (2007). Early learning standards: Results from a national survey to document trends in state-level policies and practices. *Early Childhood Research and Practice, 9*(1). Retrieved from http://ecrp.uiuc.edu/v9n1/little.html

Snow, K. L. (2006). Measuring school readiness: Conceptual and practical considerations. *Early Education and Development, 17,* 7–41.

Thorman, A., & Kauerz, K. (2011). QRIS and P-3: Creating synergy across systems to close achievement gaps and improve opportunities for young children. *Early Childhood Systems Reform Brief.* Retrieved from http://www.buildinitiative.org/files/QRIS_P-3brief.pdf

Tout, K., Starr, R., Soli, M., Moodie, S., Kirby, G., & Boller, K. (2010). *Compendium of quality rating systems and evaluations.* Washington, DC: Child Trends.

U.S. Census Bureau. (2005). *Who's minding the kids? Child care arrangements: Spring 2005, detailed tables.* Retrieved from http://www.census.gov/population/www/socdemo/child/ppl-2005.html

U.S. Charter Schools. (n.d.). *Overview.* Retrieved from http://www.uscharterschools.org/pub/uscs_docs/o/index.htm

Wood, S., Fraga, L., Dobbins, D., & McCready, M. (2015). *Parents and the high cost of child care. 2015 report.* Arlington, VA: Child Care Aware. Retrieved from http://usa.childcareaware.org/wp-content/uploads/2016/05/Parents-and-the-High-Cost-of-Child-Care-2015-FINAL.pdf

Zero to Three. (2008). *Early learning guidelines for infants and toddlers: Recommendations for states.* Washington, DC: Zero to Three. Retrieved from http://www.zerotothree.org/site/DocServer/Early_Learning_Guidelines_for_Infants_and_Toddlers.pdf?docID=4961

Zero to Three. (2012). *Successful early childhood home visiting systems.* Retrieved from http://www.zerotothree.org/public-policy/webinars-conference-calls/home-visitation-webinar.html

Chapter 3

Association of Waldorf Schools North America. (n.d.). *Why Waldorf works.* Retrieved from http://www.whywaldorfworks.org/06_Global

Beatty, B. (1995). *Preschool education in America: The culture of young children from the colonial era to the present.* New Haven, CT: Yale University Press.

Braun, S. J., & Edwards, E. P. (1972). *History and theory of early childhood education.* Belmont, CA: Wadsworth.

Brosterman, N. (1997). *Inventing kindergarten.* New York: Abrams.

Byers, L. (1972). *Origins and early history of the parent cooperative nursery school movement in America.* ERIC Document Reproduction Service No. ED091063

Cleverley, J., & Phillips, D. C. (1986). *Visions of childhood: Influential models from Locke to Spock* (Rev. ed.). New York: Teachers College Press.

Cuffaro, H. K. (1995). *Experimenting with the world: John Dewey and the early childhood classroom.* New York: Teachers College Press.

Cunningham, H. (1995). *Children and childhood in Western society since 1500.* London and New York: Longman.

Deasey, D. (1978). *Education under six.* New York: St. Martin's Press.

Dewey, J. (1972). *Experience and education.* New York: Collier Books.

Dewey, J. (2010). *My pedagogic creed.* Charleston, SC: Nabu Press. (Originally published in *School Journal, 54*(1897, January), 77–80.)

Education Commission of the States. (2011). *Access to kindergarten: Age issues in state statutes.* Retrieved from http://mb2.ecs.org/reports/Report.aspx?id=32

Edwards, C. P. (2002, Spring). Three approaches from Europe: Waldorf, Montessori, and Reggio Emilia. *Early Childhood Research and Practice, 4*(1). Retrieved from http://ecrp.uiuc.edu/v4n1/edwards.html

Edwards, C., Gandini, L., & Forman, G. (Eds.). (1998). *The hundred languages of children.* Norwood, NJ: Ablex.

Elkind, D. (2015). *Giants in the nursery: A biographical history of developmentally appropriate practice.* St. Paul, MN: Redleaf Press.

Goffin, S. G., & Wilson, C. (2001). *Curriculum models and early childhood education: Appraising the relationship* (2nd ed.). Upper Saddle River, NJ: Pearson.

Grubb, W. N., & Lazerson, A. M. W. (1988). *Broken promises: How Americans fail their children* (Rev. ed.). Chicago: University of Chicago Press.

Gutek, G. L. (1994). *A history of the Western educational experience* (2nd ed.). Long Grove, IL: Waveland Press.

High/Scope Education Research Foundation. (1989). *The High/Scope K–3 curriculum: An introduction.* Ypsilanti, MI: High/Scope Press.

Hymes, J. L. (1996). Industrial day care's roots in America. In K. M. Paciorek & J. H. Munro (Eds.), *Sources: Notable selections in early childhood education* (2nd ed., pp. 283–288). Guilford, CT: Dushkin/McGraw-Hill.

Jones, A. (2002, May). *Peabody: Kindergarten pioneer and abolitionist. Early childhood annual: Looking at history.* Champaign: University of Illinois.

Lascarides, V. C., & Hinitz, B. F. (2000). *History of early childhood education*. New York and London: Falmer.

McMillan, M. (1919). *The nursery school*. New York: Dutton.

Michel, S. (1999). *Children's interest/mothers' rights: The shaping of America's child care policy*. New Haven, CT: Yale University Press.

Montessori, M. (1965). *Dr. Montessori's own handbook*. New York: Schocken.

Montessori, M. (1967). *The absorbent mind*. New York: Holt, Rinehart and Winston.

Nager, N., & Shapiro, E. (Eds.). (2000). *Revisiting progressive pedagogy: The Developmental Interaction Approach*. Albany: State University of New York Press.

National Association for the Education of Young Children. (2011). *2010 NAEYC standards for initial & advanced early childhood professional preparation programs for use by associate, baccalaureate and graduate degree programs*. Washington, DC: NAEYC.

North American Montessori Teachers Association. (2014). *How many Montessori schools are there?* Retrieved from http://www.montessori-namta.org/FAQ/Montessori

Osborn, D. K. (1991). *Early childhood education in historical perspective* (3rd ed.). Athens, GA: Education Associates.

Prochner, L. (2009). *A history of early childhood education in Canada, Australia, and New Zealand*. Vancouver: University of British Columbia Press.

Schweinhart, L. (2007). *The High/Scope Perry Preschool Study through age 40: Summary, conclusions and frequently asked questions*. Ypsilanti, MI: High/Scope Educational Research Foundation. Retrieved from http://www.highscope.org/file/Research/PerryProject/3_special-summary%20col%2006%2007.pdf

Shapiro, M. S. (1983). *Child's garden: The kindergarten movement from Fröebel to Dewey*. University Park: Pennsylvania State University Press.

Silber, K. (1965). *Pestalozzi: The man and his work*. New York: Schocken.

Smith, T. E., & Knapp, C. E. (Eds.). (2010). *Sourcebook of experiential education: Key thinkers and their contributions*. New York: Routledge.

Steiner, G. Y. (1976). *The children's cause*. Washington, DC: Brookings Institution.

Steinfels, M. O. (1973). *Who's minding the children?* New York: Simon & Schuster.

Weber, E. (1969). *The kindergarten: Its encounter with educational thought in America*. New York: Teachers College Press.

Weber, E. (1984). *Ideas influencing early childhood education: A theoretical analysis*. New York: Teachers College Press.

Williams, C. L., & Johnson, J. E. (2005). The Waldorf approach to early childhood education. In J. L. Roopnarine & J. E. Johnson (Eds.), *Approaches to early childhood education* (4th ed., pp. 336–362). Upper Saddle River, NJ: Pearson.

Williams, L. R. (1992). Historical and philosophical roots of early childhood practice. In D. P. Fromberg & L. R. Williams (Eds.), *Encyclopedia of early childhood education* (ED #, pp. 7–98). New York: Garland. (newer edition Routledge 2012).

Wolfe, J. (2002). *Learning from the past: Historical voices in early childhood education* (2nd ed.). Alberta, Canada: Piney Branch Press Mayerthorpe.

Wortham, S. C. (1992). *Childhood, 1892–1992*. Wheaton, MD: Association for Childhood Education International.

Chapter 4

Ainsworth, M. (1979). *Patterns of attachment*. New York: Halsted Press.

Bailey, D. B., Jr., Bruer, J. T., Symons, F. J., & Lichtman, J. W. (Eds.). (2001). *Critical thinking about critical periods*. Baltimore: Brookes.

Berk, L. E. (2012). *Child development* (9th ed.). Upper Saddle River, NJ: Pearson.

Berk, L. E. (2016). *Infants and children: Prenatal through middle childhood* (8th ed.). Needham Heights, MA: Allyn & Bacon.

Bodrova, E., & Leong, D. (2007). *Tools of the mind: The Vygotskian approach to early childhood education* (2nd ed.). Upper Saddle River, NJ: Pearson.

Bowlby, J. (1969). *Attachment and loss*. New York: Basic Books.

Breslin, D. (2005). Children's capacity to develop resiliency: How to nurture it. *Young Children, 60*(1), 47–52.

Bruer, J. T., & Greenough, W. T. (2001). The subtle science of how experience affects the brain. In D. B. Bailey, Jr., J. T. Bruer, F. J. Symons, & J. W. Lichtman (Eds.). *Critical thinking about critical periods*. Baltimore: Brookes.

Center on the Developing Child at Harvard University. (2010). *The foundations of health are built in early childhood*. Retrieved from http://www.developingchild.harvard.edu

Center on the Developing Child at Harvard University. (2011). *Building the brain's "air traffic control" system: How early experiences shape the development of executive function*. Working Paper No. 11. Retrieved from http://www.developingchild.harvard.edu

Center on the Developing Child at Harvard University. (2016). *From best practices to breakthrough impacts: A science-based approach to building a more promising future for young children and families*. Retrieved from http://www.developingchild.harvard

Centers for Disease Control and Prevention. (2006). *A report of the CDC/ATSDR Preconception Care Work Group and the Select Panel on Preconception Care*. Retrieved from http://www.cdc.gov/mmwr/preview/mmwrhtml/rr5506a1.htm

Chess, S., & Thomas, A. (1996). *Temperament: Theory and practice*. New York: Brunner/Mazel.

Chess, S., Thomas, A., & Birch, H. G. (1970). The origin of personality. *Scientific American*, 102–109.

Copple, C., & Bredekamp, S. (2006). *Basics of developmentally appropriate practice: An introduction for teachers of children 3 to 6*. Washington, DC: National Association for the Education of Young Children.

Copple, C., & Bredekamp, S. (Eds.). (2009). *Developmentally appropriate practice in early childhood programs serving children from birth through age 8* (3rd ed.). Washington, DC: National Association for the Education of Young Children.

Damon, W. (1988). *The moral child*. New York: Free Press.

Dennis, W. (1973). *Children of the crèche*. New York: Appleton-Century-Crofts.

Edwards, C. P. (1986). *Promoting social and moral development in young children*. New York: Teachers College Press.

Eisenberg, N. (1992). *The caring child*. Cambridge, MA: Harvard University Press.

Erikson, E. (1963). *Childhood and society* (Rev. ed.). New York: Norton.

Galinsky, E. (2010). *Mind in the making: The seven essential life skills every child needs*. New York: Harper Collins.

Gardner, H. (1991). *The unschooled mind*. New York: Basic Books.

Gardner, H. (1993). *Multiple intelligences: The theory in practice*. New York: Basic Books.

Gardner, H. (2000). *Intelligence reframed: Multiple intelligences for the 21st century*. New York: Basic Books.

Gardner, H. (2011). *Frames of mind*. New York: Basic Books.

Gerber, M. (Ed.). (1997). *The RIE manual for parents and professionals*. Los Angeles: Resources for Infant Educators.

Gesell, A. (1940). *The first five years of life*. New York: Harper & Row.

Gesell, A., & Ilg, F. L. (1974). *The child from five to ten* (Rev. ed.). New York: Harper & Row.

Gilligan, C. (1982). *In a different voice.* Cambridge, MA: Harvard University Press.

Gonzalez-Mena, J., & Eyer, D. W. (2014). *Infants, toddlers, and caregivers* (8th ed.). New York: McGraw-Hill.

Harlow, H. F. & Zimmerman, R. (1959). Affectional responses in the infant monkey. *Science, 130,* 421–432.

Hawley, T. (2000). *Starting smart: How early experiences affect brain development.* Washington, DC: Ounce of Prevention Fund and Chicago: Zero to Three.

Healy, J. M. (1990). *Endangered minds.* New York: Simon & Schuster.

Hunt, J. M. (1961). *Intelligence and experience.* New York: Ronald Press.

Kagan, J. (1984). *The nature of the child.* New York: Basic Books.

Kagan, J., Arcus, D., Snidman, N., Feng, W., Hendler, J., & Green, S. (1994). Reactivity in infants: A cross national comparison. *Developmental Psychology, 60,* 342–345.

Kaiser, B., & Rasminsky, J. (2012). *Challenging behavior in young children: Understanding, preventing, and responding effectively* (3rd ed.). Upper Saddle River, NJ: Pearson.

Kersey, K., & Malley, C. (2005). Helping children develop resiliency: Providing supportive relationships. *Young Children, 60*(1), 53–58.

Kohlberg, L. (Ed.). (1981). *The philosophy of moral development: Moral stages and the idea of justice.* San Francisco: Harper & Row

Kohlberg, L. (1984). *The psychology of moral development: The nature and validity of moral stages.* New York: Harper & Row.

Kostelnik, M. J., Whiren, A., Soderman, A. K., Gregory, K., & Stein, L. C. (2014). *Guiding children's social development* (3rd ed.). Albany, NY: Delmar.

Lalley, R. J. (2009). The science and psychology of infant–toddler care: How an understanding of early learning has transformed child care. *Zero to Three, 30*(3), 47–53.

Lewis, M., Ramsay, D., & Kawakami, K. (1993). Differences between Japanese infants and Caucasian American infants in behavioral and cortisol response to inoculation. *Child Development, 64,* 1722–1731.

Lickona, T., Geis, G., & Kohlberg, L. (Eds.). (1976). *Moral development and behavior: Theory, research, and social issues.* New York: Holt, Rinehart and Winston.

Lin, H. L., Lawrence, F. R., & Gorrell, J. (2003). Kindergarten teachers' views of children's readiness for school. *Early Childhood Research Quarterly, 18*(2), 225–236.

Maslow, A. H. (1968). *Toward a psychology of being.* Princeton, NJ: Van Nostrand.

Maslow, A. (1970). *Motivation and personality* (2nd ed.). New York: Harper & Row.

McCall, S. G., & Plemons, B. (2001). The concept of critical periods and their implications for early childhood services. In D. B. Bailey, Jr., J. T. Bruer, F. J. Symons, & J. W. Lichtman (Eds.). *Critical thinking about critical periods.* Baltimore: Brookes.

McDevitt, T. M., & Ormrod, J. E. (2016). *Child development and education* (6th ed.). Upper Saddle River, NJ: Pearson.

Mooney, C. G. (2013). *Theories of childhood: An introduction to Dewey, Montessori, Erickson, Piaget, and Vygotsky.* (2nd ed.) St. Paul, MN: Redleaf Press.

National Association for the Education of Young Children. (2011). *2010 NAEYC standards for initial & advanced early childhood professional preparation programs for use by associate, baccalaureate and graduate degree programs.* Washington, DC: NAEYC.

National Center for Learning Disabilities (NCLD). (2010). *What is executive function?* Retrieved from http://www.ncld.org/ld-basics/ld-aamp-executive-functioning/basic-ef-facts/what-is-executive-function#top

National Institute of Child Health and Human Development. (2006). *The NICHD study of early child care and youth development (SECCYD): Findings for children up to age 4½ years.* Retrieved from http://www.nichd.nih.gov/publications/pubs_details.cfm?from=&pubs_id=5047

National Scientific Council on the Developing Child. (2007). *The timing and quality of early experiences combine to shape brain architecture.* Working Paper No. 5. Retrieved from http://www.developingchild.net

Neville, H., Stevens, C., Pakulak, E., Bell, T. A., Fanning, J., Klein, S., & Isbell, E. (2013). Family-based training program improves brain function, cognition and behavior in lower socioeconomic status preschoolers. *PNAS, Early Edition.*

Piaget, J. (1965). *The moral judgment of the child.* New York: Free Press. (Original work published 1932.)

Piaget, J. (1966). *The origins of intelligence in children* (2nd ed.). New York: International Universities Press.

Ramey, C., Campbell, F., & Blair, C. (1998). Enhancing the life course for high-risk children. In J. Crane (Ed.), *Social programs that work* (pp. 184–199). New York: Russell Sage Foundation.

Reynolds, A., & Ou, S. (2011). Paths of effects from preschool to adult well-being: A confirmatory analysis of the child-parent center program. *Child Development, 82*(2), 555–582.

Rothbart, M. K., Ahadi, B. A., & Evans, D. E. (2000). Temperament and personality: Origins and outcomes. *Journal of Personality and Social Psychology, 78,* 122–135.

Segal, N. L. (2012). *Born together—reared apart: The landmark minnesota twins study.* Boston: Harvard University Press.

Shonkoff, J., & Phillips, D. (Eds.). (2000). *From neurons to neighborhoods: The science of early childhood development.* Washington, DC: National Academy Press.

Shore, R. (1997). *Rethinking the brain.* New York: Families and Work Institute.

Smetana, J. G., Killen, M., & Turiel, E. (1991). Children's reasoning about interpersonal and moral conflicts. *Child Development, 62,* 629–644.

Stevens, C., & Neville, H. (2013) Different profiles of neuroplasticity in human neurocognition. In S. Lipina & M. Sigman (Eds.). *Cognitive Neuroscience and Education.*

Tabors, P. O. (2008). *One child, two languages: A guide for early childhood educators of children learning English as a second language.* Baltimore: Brookes.

Thomas, A., & Chess, S. (1977). *Temperament and development.* New York: Brunner/Mazel.

Thomas, A., Chess, S., & Birch, H. G. (1970). The origin of personality. *Scientific American, 223,* 102–109.

Vygotsky, L. S. (1962). *Thought and language.* Cambridge, MA: MIT Press.

Vygotsky, L. S. (1978). *Mind in society: The development of higher psychological processes.* Cambridge, MA: Harvard University Press.

Walker, L. J. (1995). Sexism in Kohlberg's moral psychology? In W. M. Kurtines & J. L. Gewirtz (Eds.), *Moral development: An introduction.* Boston: Allyn & Bacon.

Werner, E. E., Bierman, J. M., & French, F. E. (1971). *The children of Kauai: A longitudinal study from the prenatal period to age ten.* Honolulu: University of Hawaii Press.

Werner, E. E., & Smith, R. S. (1992). *Overcoming the odds: High-risk children from birth to adulthood.* Ithaca, NY: Cornell University Press.

Youngquist, J., & Martinez-Griego, B. (2009). Learning in English, learning in Spanish: A Head Start program changes its approach. *Young Children, 64*(4), 92–98

Chapter 5

Alliance for Childhood. (2001). High stakes testing. Retrieved from http://www.allianceforchildhood.org/testing_position_statement

Bentzen, W. R. (2008). *Seeing young children: A guide to observing and recording behavior* (6th ed.). Albany, NY: Delmar.

Brickman, N., & Barton, H. (Eds.). (2010). *Preschool child observation record user guide*. Ypsilanti, MI: High/Scope Press.

Brunette, L. (2013, January–February). Documenting children's work: Embracing technology with e-portfolios. *Childcare Information Exchange, 35*(1), 26–29.

Cohen, D. H., Stern, V., Balaban, N., & Gropper, N. (2008). *Observing and recording the behavior of young children* (5th ed.). New York: Teacher's College Press.

Curtis, D., & Carter, M. (2012). The art of awareness: How observation can transform your teaching (2nd ed.). St. Paul, MN: Redleaf Press.

Daniels, D. H., Beaumont, L. J., & Doolin, C. A. (2007). *Understanding children: An interview and observation guide for educators* (2nd ed). New York: McGraw-Hill Higher Education.

Dodge, D. T., Colker, L. J., & Heroman, C. (2015). *The creative curriculum for preschool* (5th ed.). Washington, DC: Teaching Strategies.

Dodge, D. T., Rudick, S., & Berke, K. (2014). *The creative curriculum for infants, toddlers, and twos* (3rd ed.). Washington, DC: Teaching Strategies.

Epstein, A. S., Schweinhart, L. J., DeBruin-Parecki, A., & Robin, K. B. (2004, July). Preschool assessment: A guide to developing a balanced approach. *Preschool Policy Matters*. New Brunswick, NJ: National Institute for Early Education Research.

Feeney, S. (2016). *Straight talk about kindergarten readiness assessment*. Jamaica Plain, MA: Defending the Early Years. Retrieved from https://www.deyproject.org.

Feeney, S., & Freeman, N. K. (2015). Smartphones and social media: Ethical implications for educators. *Young Children, 70*(1), 98–101.

Forman, G., & Hall, E. (2005). Wondering with children: The importance of observation in early education. In *Early Childhood Research & Practice (ECRP), 7*(2). Retrieved from http://www.ecrp.uiuc.edu/v7n2/forman.html

Friedman, D. L. (2012). *Creating and presenting an early childhood portfolio: A reflective approach*. Belmont, CA: Wadsworth.

Galper, A. R., & Seefeldt, C. (2009). Assessing young children. In S. Feeney, A. Galper, & C. Seefeldt (Eds.), *Continuing issues in early childhood education* (3rd ed., pp. 329–345). Upper Saddle River, NJ: Pearson.

Graves, D. H. (2002). *Testing is not teaching: What should count in education*. Portsmouth, NH: Heinemann.

Gronlund, G., & Engel, B. (2001). *Focused portfolios: A complete assessment for the young child*. St. Paul, MN: Redleaf Press.

Guddemi, M. P. (2003). The important role of quality assessment in young children ages 3–8. In Gullo, D. F. (2005). *Understanding assessment and evaluation in early childhood education* (2nd ed.). New York: Teachers College Press.

Helm, J., Beneke, S., & Steinheimer, K. (2008). *Windows on learning: Documenting young children's work* (2nd ed.). New York: Teachers College Press.

High/Scope. (2014). *The High/Scope child observation record advantage*. Florence, KY: Wadsworth.

Hughes, K., & Gullo, D. (2010). Joyful learning and assessment in kindergarten. *Young Children, 65*(3), 57–59.

Jones, J. (2004). Framing the assessment discussion. In D. Koralek (Ed.), *Spotlight on young children and assessment*. Washington, DC: NAEYC.

Kohn, A. (2000). *The case against standardized testing: Raising the scores, ruining the schools*. Pourtsmouth, NH: Heinemann.

Koralek, D. (Ed.). (2004). *Spotlight on young children and assessment*. Washington, DC: NAEYC.

Losardo, A., & Notari-Syverson, A. (2011). *Alternative approaches to assessing young children* (2nd ed.). Baltimore: Brookes.

Marion, M. (2004). *Using observation in early childhood education*. Upper Saddle River, NJ: Pearson.

Maxwell, K. L., & Clifford, R. M. (2004, January). Research in review: School readiness assessment. *Young Children: Beyond the Journal*. Retrieved from http://www.journal.naeyc.org/btj/200401/maxwell.asp

McAfee, O., Leong, D., & Bodrova, E. (2004). *Basics of assessment: A primer for early childhood educators*. Washington, DC: NAEYC.

McAfee, O., Leong, D., & Bodrova, E. (2016). *Assessing and guiding young children's development and learning* (6th ed.). Upper Saddle River, NJ: Pearson.

Meisels, S. J. (2006). *Accountability in early childhood: No easy answers*. Occasional Paper, No. 6. Chicago: Erikson Institute Herr Research Center for Children and Social Policy.

Meisels, S. J., & Atkins-Burnett, S. (2005). *Developmental screening in early childhood: A guide* (5th ed.). Washington, DC: NAEYC.

Meisels, S. J., Dombro, A. L., Marsden, D. B., Weston, D., & Jewkes, A. M. (2003). *The ounce scale: An observational assessment for infants, toddlers, and families*. New York: Pearson Early Learning.

Meisels, S. J., Marsden, D. B., Jablon, J. R., & Dichtelmiller, M. K. (2013). *The work sampling system* (5th ed.). San Antonio, TX: Pearson.

National Association for the Education of Young Children (NAEYC). (2009). *NAEYC standards for early childhood professional preparation programs: Position statement*. Washington, DC: Author. Retrieved from http://www.naeyc.org/files/naeyc/file/positions/ProfPrepStandards09.pdf

National Association for the Education of Young Children. (2011). *Code of Ethical Conduct and Statement of Commitment*. Washington, DC: National Association for the Education of Young Children.

National Association for the Education of Young Children (NAEYC) & National Association of Early Childhood Specialists in State Departments of Education (NAECS/SDE). (2003). Joint position statement. *Early childhood curriculum, assessment, and program evaluation: Building an effective, accountable system in programs for children birth through age 8*. Retrieved from http://www.naeyc.org/about/positions/pdf/CAPEexpand.pdf

Ogunnaike-Lafe, Y., & Krohn, J. (2010). Using document panels to record, reflect, and relate learning experiences. *Childcare Information Exchange 32*(3), 92–96.

Puckett, M. B., & Black, J. K. (2008). *Meaningful assessment of the young child: Celebrating development and learning* (3rd ed.). Upper Saddle River, NJ: Pearson.

Riley-Ayers, Shannon (2014). *Formative assessment: guidance for early childhood policymakers*. New Brunswick, NJ: The Center on Enhancing Early Learning Outcomes (CEELO) National Institute for Early Education Research.

SECA (Southern Early Childhood Association). (2013). *Assessing development and learning in young children, position statement*. Retrieved from http://www.southernearlychildhood.org

Seitz, H. (2008, March). The power of documentation in the early childhood classroom. *Young Children, 63*(2), 83–92.

Shillady, A. L. (2004, January). Choosing an appropriate assessment system. *Young Children: Beyond the Journal*. Retrieved from http://www.journal.naeyc.org/btj/200401/shillady.ASP

Shores, E. F., & Grace, C. (1998). *The portfolio book*. Lewisville, NC: Gryphon House.

Snow, C. E., & Van Hemel, S. B. (Eds.). (2008). *Early childhood assessment: Why, what, and how.* Washington, DC: National Academies Press.

Wortham, S. C. (2011). *Assessment in early childhood education* (6th ed.). Upper Saddle River, NJ: Pearson.

Chapter 6

American Academy of Pediatrics. (2009). Discipline and your child. *Healthy Children.* Retrieved from http://www.healthychildren.org/English/family-life/family-dynamics/communication-discipline

Bilmes, J. (2004). *Beyond behavior management: The six life skills children need to thrive in today's world.* St. Paul, MN: Redleaf Press.

Bodrova, E., & Leong, D. J. (2007). *Tools of the mind: The Vygotskian approach to early childhood education* (2nd ed.). Columbus, OH: Merrill/Prentice Hall.

Bodrova, E., & D. J. Leong. 2008. Of Primary Interest. Developing self-regulation in kindergarten: Can we keep all the crickets in the basket? *Young Children* 63(2): 56–58. www.journal.naeyc.org/btj/200803

Bowlby, J. (1982). *Attachment and loss: Vol. 1. Attachment.* London: Hogarth.

Brazelton, T. B., & Greenspan, S. I. (2000). *The irreducible needs of children: What every child must have to grow, learn, and flourish.* New York: Perseus.

Breslin, D. (2005). Children's capacity to develop resiliency: How to nurture it. *Young Children, 60*(1), 47–52.

Bronson, M. (2000). Recognizing and supporting the development of self-regulation in young children. *Young Children, 55*(2), 32–37.

CASEL Forum Report. (2011, April 13–14). *Expanding social and emotional learning nationwide: Let's go!* Collaborative for Academic, Social, and Emotional Learning. Retrieved from http://casel.org/wp-content/uploads/2011-Forum-Report.pdf

Center on the Developing Child at Harvard University. (2016). From *Best practices to breakthrough impacts: A science-based approach to building a more promising future for young children and families.* Retrieved from http://www.developingchild.harvard.edu

Christakis, E. (2016). *The importance of being little: What preschoolers really need from grownups.* New York: Viking.

Copple, C., & Bredekamp, S. (Eds.). (2009). *Developmentally appropriate practices in early childhood programs* (3rd ed.). Washington, DC: NAEYC.

Dillon, J. T. (1990). *Personal teaching: Efforts to combine personal love and professional skill.* Lanham, MD: University Press of America.

Dombro, A., Jablon, J., & Stetson, C. (2011). *Powerful interactions: How to connect with children to extend their learning.* Washington, DC: NAEYC.

Dreikurs, R. (1969). *Psychology in the classroom.* New York: Harper & Row.

Durlak, J., Weissberg, R., Dymnicki, A., Taylor, R., & Schellinger, K. (2011). The impact of enhancing students' social and emotional learning: A meta-analysis of school-based universal interventions. *Child Development, 82*(1), 405–432.

Epstein, A. S. (2009). *Me, you, us: Social-emotional learning in preschool.* Washington, DC: National Association for the Education of Young Children; Ypsilanti, MI: High School Press.

Epstein, A. S. (2014). *The intentional teacher: Choosing the best strategies for young children's learning* (Rev. ed.). Washington, DC: National Association for the Education of Young Children; Ypsilanti, MI: High School Press.

Evans, B. (2014, May). Bullying: Can it begin in preschool? *Extensions: Curriculum Newsletter from HighScope, 25*(3) 1–5. Retrieved from http://www.highscope.org/file/NewsandInformation/Extensions/ExtVol25No3_low.pdf

Fields, M. V., Perry, N. J., & Fields, D. M. (2010). *Constructive guidance and discipline: Preschool and primary education* (5th ed.). Upper Saddle River, NJ: Pearson.

Fox, L., Carta, J., Strain, P., Dunlap, G., & Hemmeter, M. L. (2009). *Response to intervention and the pyramid model.* Tampa, FL: University of South Florida Technical Assistance Center on Social Emotional Intervention for Young Children. Retrieved from http://www.challengingbehavior.org

Fox, L., Dunlap, G., Hemmeter, M. L., Joseph, G. E., & Strain, P. S. (2003). The teaching pyramid: A model for supporting social competence and preventing challenging behavior in young children. *Young Children, 58*(4), 48–52.

Galinsky, E. (2010). *Mind in the making: The seven essential life skills every child needs.* New York: HarperCollins.

Gartrell, D. (1987). Punishment or guidance? *Young Children, 42*(2), 55–61.

Gartrell, D. (1995). Misbehavior or mistaken behavior? *Young Children, 50*(5), 27–34.

Gartrell, D. (2001). Replacing time-out: Part one—Using guidance to build an encouraging classroom. *Young Children, 56*(6), 8–16.

Gartrell, D. (2002). Replacing time-out: Part two—Using guidance to maintain an encouraging classroom. *Young Children, 57*(2), 36–43.

Gartrell, D. (2012). *Education for a civil society: How guidance teaches young children democratic life skills.* Washington, DC: National Association for the Education of Young Children.

Gilliam, W. (2005). *Prekindergarteners left behind: Expulsion rates in state prekindergarten programs.* FCD Policy Brief Series No. 3. New York: Foundation for Child Development.

Ginott, H. (1972). *Teacher and child: A book for parents and teachers.* New York: Macmillan.

Gonzalez-Mena, J. (2011). *Foundations: Early childhood education in a diverse society* (5th ed.). Boston: McGraw-Hill.

Gonzalez-Mena, J., & Eyer, D. W. (2009). *Infants, toddlers, and caregivers* (8th ed.). Boston: McGraw-Hill.

Gordon, T., with Burch, N. (2003). *Teacher effectiveness training: The program proven to help teachers bring out the best in students of all ages.* New York: Three Rivers Press.

Hemmeter, M. L. (2007, July/August). We are all in this together: Supporting children's social emotional development and addressing challenging behavior. *Exchange*, 12–16.

Hitz, R., & Driscoll, A. (1988). Praise or encouragement: New insights into praise. *Young Children, 43*(5), 6–13.

Honig, A. S. (1985). Compliance, control, and discipline. *Young Children, 40*(3), 47–52.

Howes, C., & Ritchie, S. (2002). *A matter of trust: Connecting teachers and learners in the early childhood classroom.* New York: Teachers College Press.

Hyson, M. (2002). Emotional development and school readiness. *Young Children, 57*(6), 76–78.

Kaiser, B., & Rasminsky, J. S. (2012). *Challenging behavior in young children: Understanding, preventing, and responding effectively.* Upper Saddle River, NJ: Pearson.

Katz, L. G. (1984). The professional early childhood teacher. *Young Children, 39*(5), 3–10.

Kersey, K. C., & Malley, C. R. (2005). Helping children develop resiliency: Providing supportive relationships. *Young Children, 60*(1), 53–58.

Kohn, A. (2001). Five reasons to stop saying "Good job!" *Young Children, 56*(5), 24–28.

Kostelnik, M., Whiren, A., Soderman, A., Stein, L., & Gregory, K. (2014). *Guiding children's social development* (8th ed.). Belmont, CA: Cengage Wadsworth.

Livergood, N. D. (n.d.). *Social intelligence: A new definition of human intelligence.* Retrieved from http://www.hermes-press.com/socint4.htm

Meece, D., & Soderman, A. K. (2010). Positive verbal environments: Setting the stage for young children's social development. *Young Children, 65*(5), 81–86.

Mitchell, A., & Glossop, R. (2005). *Heart smarts: Contemporary family trends.* Ottawa, Canada: The Vanier Institute of the Family.

National Association for the Education of Young Children. (2009). *NAEYC standards for early childhood professional preparation programs: Position statement.* Washington, DC: Author. Retrieved from http://www.naeyc.org/files/naeyc/file/positions/ProfPrep-Standards09.pdf

National Association for the Education of Young Children. (2011). *Code of ethical conduct and statement of commitment* (Rev. ed.). Washington, DC: Author.

National Scientific Council on the Developing Child. (2004). *Young children develop in an environment of relationships.* Working paper no. 1. Cambridge, MA: Center on the Developing Child, Harvard University. Retrieved from http://www.developingchild.net

Pizzolongo, P., & Hunter, A. (2011). I am safe and secure: Promoting resilience in young children. *Young Children, 66*(2), 67–69.

Rogers, F. (2003). *The world according to Mister Rogers: Important things to remember.* New York: Hyperion.

Schreiber, M. E. (1999). Time-outs for toddlers: Is our goal punishment or education? *Young Children, 54*(4), 22–25.

Straus, M. A., Sugarman, D. B., & Giles-Sims, J. (1997). Spanking by parents and subsequent antisocial behavior of children. *Archives of Pediatric and Adolescent Medicine, 151*(8), 761–767.

Sugai, G., Horner, R. H., Dunlap, G., Hieneman, M., Lewis, T. J., Nelson, C. M., Ruef, M. (2000). Applying positive behavioral support and functional behavioral assessment in schools. *Journal of Positive Behavior Interventions, 2*(3), 131–143.

Vance, E., & Weaver, P. J. (2002). *Class meetings: Young children solving problems together.* Washington, DC: National Association for the Education of Young Children.

Willis, C., & Schiller, P. (2011). Preschoolers' social skills steer life success. *Young Children, 66*(1), 42–49.

Chapter 7

American Academy of Allergy, Asthma and Immunology. (2014). *Allergy statistics.* Retrieved from http://www.aaaai.org/about-the-aaaai/newsroom/allergy-statistics.aspx

American Academy of Child and Adolescent Psychiatry. (2014). *TV violence and young children.* Retrieved from http://www.aacap.org/aacap/families_and_youth/facts_for_families/fff-guide/Children-And-TV-Violence-013.aspx

American Academy of Pediatrics. (2015). *Sun and water safety tips.* Retrieved from https://www.aap.org/en-us/about-the-aap/aap-press-room/news-features-and-safety-tips/Pages/Sun-and-Water-Safety-Tips.aspx

American Academy of Pediatrics. (2016a). *Media and young minds. Pediatrics* 138(5) Policy Statement. Retrieved from http://pediatrics.aappublications.org/content/138/5/e20162591

American Academy of Pediatrics. (2016b). *SIDS and other sleep-related infant deaths: Updated 2016 recommendations for a safe infant sleeping environment.* Retrieved from http://pediatrics.aappublications.org/content/early/2016/10/20/peds.2016-2938

American Academy of Pediatrics, American Public Health Association, & National Resource Center for Health and Safety in Child Care and Early Education. (2013). *Stepping stones to caring for our children: National health and safety performance standards: Guidelines for early care and education programs* (3rd ed.). Elk Grove Village, IL: American Academy of Pediatrics; Washington, DC: American Public Health Association. Retrieved from http://nrckids.org

American Academy of Pediatrics Committee on Public Education. (2001). Children, adolescents, and television. *Pediatrics, 10*(2), 423–426.

Aronson, S. (Ed.). (2012). *Healthy young children: A manual for programs.* Washington, DC: National Association for the Education of Young Children.

Aronson, S., & Shope, T. (Eds.). (2013). *Managing infectious diseases in child care and schools: A quick reference guide.* Elk Grove Village, IL: American Academy of Pediatrics.

Ball, J., Bindler, R., & Cowen, K. (2011). *Principles of pediatric nursing caring for children.* Upper Saddle River, NJ: Prentice Hall.

Branum, A., & Lukacs, S. (2008). *Food allergy among U.S. children: Trends in prevalence and hospitalizations.* NCHS Data Brief No. 10. Hyattsville, MD: National Center for Health Statistics.

Brazelton, T., & Greenspan, S. (2000). *The irreducible needs of children: What every child must have to grow, learn and flourish.* Cambridge, MA: Perseus.

Carlson, F. (2006). *Essential touch: Meeting the needs of young children.* Washington, DC: National Association for the Education of Young Children.

Centers for Disease Control and Prevention. (2013a). *Lead.* Retrieved from http://cdc.gov/nceh/lead

Centers for Disease Control and Prevention. (2013b) *Voluntary guidelines for managing food allergies in schools and early care and education programs.* Washington, DC: U.S. Department of Health and Human Services. Retrieved from www.cdc.gov/HealthyYouth/foodallergies/pdf/13_243135_A_Food_Allergy_Web_508.pdf

Centers for Disease Control and Prevention: Press Release. (2014). *New CDC data show encouraging development in obesity rates among 2 to 5 year olds.* Retrieved from http://www.cdc.gov/media/releases/2014/p0225-child-obesity.html

Centers for Disease Control & Prevention. (2015). *Healthy schools: Childhood obesity facts.* Retrieved from https://www.cdc.gov/healthyschools/obesity/facts.htm

Centers for Disease Control & Prevention. (2016). *Overweight & obesity; early care & education state indicator report.* Retrieved from https://www.cdc.gov/obesity/strategies/ece-state-indicator-report.html

ChildCare Aware of America. (2016). *Child care in America 2016 state fact sheets.* Retrieved from http://usa.childcareaware.org/wp-content/uploads/2016/07/2016-Fact-Sheets-Full-Report-02-27-17.pdf

Child Welfare Information Gateway. (2013). *What is child abuse and neglect? Recognizing the signs and symptoms.* Washington, DC: U.S. Department of Health and Human Services, Children's Bureau. Retrieved from www.childwelfare.gov/

Consumer Product Safety Commission (CPSC). (2008). *Nursery product-related injuries and deaths among children under age five.* Washington, DC: U.S. Government Printing Office.

Consumer Product Safety Commission (CPSC). (2010). *16 CFR parts 1219, 1220, and 1500 safety standards for full-size baby cribs and non-full-size baby cribs; Final rule.* Retrieved from http://www.cpsc.gov/PageFiles/101628/cribfinal.pdf

Consumer Product Safety Commission (CPSC). (2015). *Public playground safety handbook.* CPSC Document No. 325. Retrieved from http://www.cpsc.gov/cpscpub/pubs/325.pdf

Copple, C., & Bredekamp, S. (Eds.). (2009). *Developmentally appropriate practices in early childhood programs* (3rd ed.). Washington, DC: NAEYC.

Eliassen, E. (2011). The impact of teachers and families on young children's eating behaviors. *Young Children, 66*(2), 84–89.

Feeney, S., & Freedman, N. The birthday cake: Balancing responsibilities to children and families. *Young Children, 68*(1).

Galinsky, E. (1971a). *School beginnings: The first day.* New York: Bank Street College of Education.

Galinsky, E. (1971b). *School beginnings: The first weeks*. New York: Bank Street College of Education.

Goodman-Bryan, M., & Joyce, C. (2010). *Touch is a form of communication*. Retrieved from http://www.urbanchildinstitute.org

Greenman, J. (2001). *What happened to the world? Helping children cope in turbulent times*. New York: Bright Horizons.

Greenman, J. (2007). *Caring spaces, learning places: Children's environments that work*. Redmond, WA: Exchange Press.

Haonkoff, J. & Phillips, D. (Eds.). (2000). *From neurons to neighborhoods: The science of early childhood development*. Washington, DC: National Academy Press.

Healthychildren.org. (2015). *Common food allergies*. Retrieved https://healthychildren.org/English/healthy-living/nutrition/Pages/Common-Food-Allergies.aspx

Hirsch, E. (n.d.). *Transition periods: Stumbling blocks of education*. New York: Early Childhood Education Council of New York.

Holland, M. (2004). "That food makes me sick!" Managing food allergies and intolerances in early childhood settings. *Young Children, 59*(2), 42–46.

Huettig, C., Sanborn, C., DiMarco, N., Popejoy, A., & Rich, S. (2004). The O generation: Our youngest children are at risk for obesity. *Young Children, 59*(2), 50–55.

Jacobs, N. L. (1992). Unhappy endings. *Young Children, 47*(3), 23–27.

Jordan, N. H. (1993). Sexual abuse prevention programs in early childhood education: A caveat. *Young Children, 48*(6), 76–79.

Marotz, L. (2015). *Health, safety, and nutrition for the young child*. Belmont, CA: Wadsworth Cengage Learning.

Maslow, A. (1968). *Toward a psychology of being*. New York: Van Nostrand Reinhold.

Moorman, J. E., Akinbami L. J., Bailey C. M., Zahran, H. S., King, M. E., Johnson, C. A., & Liu, X. (2012). National surveillance of asthma: United States, 2001–2010. National Center for Health Statistics. *Vital Health Stat 3*(35).

Moravcik, E., & Nolte, S. (2017) *Meaningful curriculum for young children*. Boston, MA: Pearson.

National Association for the Education of Young Children. (1993). *Violence in the lives of children*. Washington, DC: Author.

National Association for the Education of Young Children (NAEYC). (1996). *Prevention of child abuse in early childhood programs and the responsibilities of early childhood professionals to prevent child abuse*. Washington, DC: Author.

National Association for the Education of Young Children (NAEYC). (2005/2011). *Code of ethical conduct and statement of commitment* (Rev. ed.). Washington, DC: NAEYC.

National Association for the Education of Young Children. (2011). *2010 NAEYC standards for initial & advanced early childhood professional preparation programs for use by associate, baccalaureate and graduate degree programs*. Washington, DC: NAEYC.

National Association for the Education of Young Children. (2015). *NAEYC early childhood program standards and accreditation criteria & guidance for assessment* (Updated 2015, April 1). Washington, DC: Author.

National Association for the Education of Young Children. (2017). *NAEYC early learning standards and accreditation criteria: Revised criteria and guidance for assessment effective 1 April 2017*. Washington, DC: Author.

National Association of Child Care Resource and Referral Agencies (NACCRRA). (2010). *Child care in America: 2010 fact sheets*. Arlington, VA: NACCRRA.

National Research Council and Institute of Medicine. (2000). *From neurons to neighborhoods: The science of early childhood development*. Committee on Instituting the Science of Early Childhood Development. Jack A. Shonkoff and Deborah A. Phillips, eds. Board on Children, Youth and Families, Commission on Social Sciences and Education. Washington, DC: National Academy Press.

National Scientific Council on the Developing Child. (2010). *Persistent fear and anxiety can affect young children's learning and development*. Working Paper No. 9. Retrieved from www.developingchild.harvard.edu

Park, M., McHugh, M., & Katsiafacas, C. (2016). *Serving immigrant families through two-generation programs: Identifying family needs and responsive program approaches*. Washington. DC: Migration Policy Institute, 2015.

Pianta, R. C., Cox, M. J., Early, D., & Taylor, L. (1999). Kindergarten teachers' practices related to the transition to school: Results of a national survey. *Elementary School Journal, 100*(1), 71–86.

Pica, R. (2006). Physical fitness and the early childhood curriculum. *Young Children, 61*(3), 12–18.

Sanders, S. (2002). *Active for life: Developmentally appropriate movement programs for young children*. Washington, DC: NAEYC.

Sicherer, S., Muñoz-Furlong, A., & Sampson, H. (2003). Prevalence of peanut and tree nut allergy in the United States determined by means of a random digit dial telephone survey: A 5-year follow-up study. *Journal of Allergy and Clinical Immunology, 112*(6), 1203–1207.

Society of Health and Physical Educators. (2009). *Active start: A statement of physical activity guidelines for children birth to five years*. Reston, VA: Author.

Sorte, J., & Daeschel, I. (2006). Health in action: A program approach to fighting obesity in young children. *Young Children, 61*(3), 40–48.

U.S. Census Bureau. (2013). *Who's minding the kids? Child care arrangements: Spring 2011*. Retrieved from http://www.census.gov/prod/2013pubs/p70-135.pdf

U.S. Department of Agriculture. (2011). *My plate*. Retrieved from http://www.choosemyplate.gov

U.S. Department of Education, Office of Planning, Evaluation and Policy Development. (2017). *Resource guide: Building a bright future for all*. Washington, DC. Retrieved from https://www2.ed.gov/about/overview/focus/immigration-resources.html

U.S. Department of Health and Human Services. (2003). *Easing the transition from preschool to kindergarten: A guide for early childhood teachers and administrators*. Retrieved from headstartinfo.org/recruitment/trans_hs.htm

U.S. Department of Health and Human Services, Centers for Disease Control and Prevention, National Center for Health Statistics. (2012). *Summary health statistics for U.S. children: National health interview survey 2012*. Retrieved from http://www.cdc.gov/nchs/data/series/sr_10/sr10_258.pdf

U.S. Department of Health and Human Services, Office of Disease Prevention and Health Promotion. (2014). *Healthy People 2020*. Retrieved from http://healthypeople.gov

White House Task Force on Childhood Obesity. (2010). *Solving the problem of childhood obesity within a generation*. Executive Office of the President of the United States. Retrieved from http://www.letsmove.gov/sites/letsmove.gov/files/TaskForce_on_Childhood_Obesity_May2010_FullReport.pdf

World Health Organization. (1948, June). *Preamble to the constitution of the World Health Organization as adopted by the International Health Conference, New York*. New York: Author.

Chapter 8

American Academy of Pediatrics, American Public Health Association, National Resource Center for Health and Safety in Child Care and Early Education. (2011). *Caring for our children: National health and safety performance standards; Guidelines for early care and education programs* (3rd ed.). Elk Grove Village, IL: American Academy of Pediatrics; Washington, DC: American Public Health Association. Also available at http://nrckids.org

American Academy of Pediatrics (AAP), Committee on Public Education. (2001). Children, adolescents, and television. *Pediatrics, 107*(2), 423–426.

American Academy of Pediatrics Policy Statement. (2016). Media and young minds. *Pediatrics, 138* (5).

Aronson, S. (Ed.). (2012). *Healthy young children: A manual for programs* (5th ed.). Washington, DC: National Association for the Education of Young Children.

Bergman, R., & Gainer, S. (2002, September–October). Home-like environments. *Child Care Information Exchange, 50–52.*

Berry, P. (2001). *Playgrounds that work.* Baulkham Hills, NSW, Australia: Pademelon Press.

Bredekamp, S., & C. Copple (Eds.). (2010). *Developmentally appropriate practice in early childhood programs* (3rd ed.). Washington, DC: NAEYC.

Bronson, M. B. (1996). *The right stuff for children birth to 8: Selecting play materials to support development.* Washington, DC: NAEYC.

Bullard, J. (2014). *Creating environments for learning: Birth to age eight* (2nd ed.). Columbus, OH: Pearson.

Bunnett, R., & Kroll, D. (2000, January–February). Transforming spaces: Rethinking the possibilities—Turning design challenges into opportunities. *Child Care Information Exchange, 26–29.*

Bus, A. G., Takacs, Z. K., & Kegel C. A. (2015). Affordances and limitations of electronic storybooks for young children's emergent literacy. *Dev Rev.* 2015, 35:79–97.

Cespedes, E. M., Gillman, M. W., Kleinman, K., Rifas-Shiman, S. L., Redline, S., Taveras, & E. M. (2014). Television viewing, bedroom television, and sleep duration from infancy to mid-childhood. *Pediatrics, 133*(5). Retrieved from: www.pediatrics.org/cgi/content/full/133/5/e1163

Chandler, P. A. (1994). *A Place for me: Including children with special needs in early care and education settings.* Washington, DC: NAEYC.

Christakis, D. A., Zimmerman, F. J., DiGiuseppe, D. L. & McCarty, C. A. (2004). Early television exposure and subsequent attentional problems in children. *Pediatrics, 113*(4), 708–713.

Conn-Powers, M., Cross A. F., Traub, E. K., & Hutter-Pishgahi, L. (2006, September). The universal design of early education moving forward for all children. Young Children on the Web.

Consumer Products Safety Commission (CPSC). (2008). *Public playground safety handbook.* CPSC Document #325. Retrieved from http://www.cpsc.gov/cpscpub/pubs/325.pdf

Cordes C., & Miller, E. (Eds.). (2000). *Fool's gold: A critical look at computers in childhood.* College Park, MD: Alliance for Childhood.

Cuffaro, H. K. (1995). *Experimenting with the world: John Dewey and the early childhood classroom.* New York: Teachers College Press.

Curtis, D., & Carter, M. (2014). *Designs for living and learning: Transforming early childhood environments* (2nd ed.). St. Paul, MN: Redleaf Press.

Daly, L. (2014). *Loose parts: Inspiring play in young children.* St. Paul, MN: Redleaf Press.

Daly, L., Beloglovsky, M. (2016). *Loose parts 2: Inspiring play with infants and toddlers.* St. Paul, MN: Redleaf Press.

DeViney, J., Duncan, S., Harris, S., Rody, M. A., & Rosenberry, L. (2010a). *Inspiring spaces for young children.* Silver Spring, MD: Gryphon House.

DeViney, J., Duncan, S., Harris, S., Rody, M. A., & Rosenberry, L. (2010b). *Rating observation scale for inspiring environments.* Silver Spring, MD: Gryphon House.

Dodge, D. T., Ruddik, S., & Berke, K. (2006). *Creative curriculum for infants and toddlers* (2nd ed.). Washington, DC: Teaching Strategies.

Early Childhood Today. (2013). ECT interview: Computers and young children. Here are two points of view - one from Douglas H. Clements, Ph.D., and the other from Jane M. Healy, Ph.D. *Early Childhood Today.* Retrieved from http://www.scholastic.com/teachers/article/ect-interview-computers-and-young-children

Edwards, C., Gandini, L., & Forman, G. (Eds.). (2012). *The hundred languages of children* (3rd ed.). New York: Praeger.

Elliott, S. (Ed.). (2008). *The outdoor playspace naturally.* Castle Hills: Pademelon Press.

Feeney, S., & Moravcik, E. (1987). A thing of beauty: Aesthetic development and young children. *Young Children, 42*(6), 7–15.

Field, T. (1999). Music enhances sleep in preschool children. *Early Child Development and Care, 150*(1), 65–68.

Frost, J. L. (1992). *Play and playscapes.* Albany, NY: Delmar.

Frost, J. S., Wortham, S. C. & Reifel, S. (2008). *Play and child development* (3rd ed.). Upper Saddle River, NJ: Merrill/Prentice Hall.

Gandini, L. (1984, Spring). Not just anywhere: Making child care centers into "particular" places. *Beginnings,* 17–20.

Garner, A., Skeen, P., & Cartwright, S. (1984). *Woodworking for young children.* Washington, DC: National Association for the Education of Young Children.

Gonzalez-Mena, J., & Eyer, D. W. (2011). *Infants, toddlers, and caregivers* (9th ed.). New York: McGraw-Hill.

Greenman, J. (1998). *Places for childhoods: Making quality happen in the real world.* Redmond, WA: Exchange Press.

Greenman, J. (2005). *Places for childhood in the 21st century: A conceptual framework.* Retrieved from http://journal.naeyc=.org/btj/200505/01Greenman.pdf

Greenman, J. (2007). *Caring spaces, learning places: Children's environments that work.* Redmond, WA: Exchange Press.

Haas-Foletta, K., & Ottolini-Geno, L. (2006, March–April). Setting the stage for children's success: The physical and emotional environment in school-age programs. *Child Care Information Exchange:* 40–44.

Harms, T., & Clifford, R. (2014). *Early childhood environment rating scale* (3rd ed.). New York: Teachers College Press.

Heschong Mahone Group, Inc. (2003). *Windows and classrooms: A study of student performance and the indoor environment.* Sacramento: California Energy Commission.

Hill, D. M. (1977). *Mud, sand, and water.* Washington, DC: NAEYC.

Hirsch, E. (1996). *The block book* (3rd ed.). Washington, DC: NAEYC.

Johnson, J. E., Christie, J. F., & Wardle, F. (2005). *Play and early childhood development* (3rd ed.). Boston: Allyn & Bacon.

Jones, E., & Prescott, E. (1984). *Dimensions of teaching-learning environments: A handbook for teachers in elementary schools and day care centers* (2nd ed.). Pasadena, CA: Pacific Oaks College.

Kalyanee, V. (2011). *Block play: The creative openness.* Retrieved from http://www.phenomenologyonline.com/sources/textorium/kalyanee-vorapassu-block-play-the-creative-openness

Keeler, R. (2008). *Natural playscapes: Creating outdoor play environments for the soul.* Redmond, WA: Exchange Press.

Koralek, D. G., Colker, L. J., & Dodge, D. T. (1993). *The what, why, and how of high-quality early childhood education: A guide for on-site supervision*. Washington, DC: NAEYC.

Kuh, L. P. (2014) *Thinking critically about environments for young children: Bridging theory and practice*. New York: Teachers College Press.

Levin, D. E. (May–June 2011). Beyond remote-controlled teaching and learning: The special challenges of helping children construct knowledge today. *Child Care Information Exchange*, 59–62

Louv, R. (2008). *Last child in the woods: Saving our children from nature-deficit disorder*. Chapel Hill, NC: Algonquin Books.

Luckenbill, J. (2012). Getting the picture using the digital camera as a tool to support reflective practice and responsive care. *Young Children, 67*(2), 29–36.

Moore, R. C. (2014). *National guidelines nature play and learning places: Creating and managing places where children engage with nature*. Raleigh, NC: Natural Learning Initiative and Reston, VA: National Wildlife Federation.

National Association for the Education of Young Children (NAEYC). (1996). NAEYC position statement: Technology and young children—ages three through eight. *Young Children, 51*(6), 11–16.

National Association for the Education of Young Children (NAEYC). (2009). NAEYC standards for early childhood professional preparation programs: Position statement. Washington, DC: Retrieved from http://www.naeyc.org/files/naeyc/file/positions/ProfPrepStandards09.pdf

National Institute of Building Sciences. (2017). *Whole building design guide*. Washington, DC: Retrieved from http://wbdg.org/design/design-recommendations

Neumann-Hinds, C. (2007). *Picture science: Using digital photography to teach young children*. St. Paul, MN: Redleaf Press.

Nimmo, J., & Hallet, B. (2008). Childhood in the garden. *Young Children, 63*(1), 32–38.

Olds, A. R. (2001). *Child care design guide*. New York: McGraw-Hill.

Phillips, D. A. (1987). *Quality in childcare: What does research tell us?* Washington, DC: NAEYC.

Prescott, E. (2008, March–April). The physical environment. *Child Care Information Exchange*: 34–37.

Readdick, C. A. (1993). Solitary pursuits: Supporting children's privacy needs in group settings. *Young Children, 49*(1), 60–64.

Rosenow, N. (2008). Teaching and learning about the natural world. *Young Children, 63*(1), 10–13.

Seefeldt, C. (2002). *Creating rooms of wonder*. Beltsville, MD: Gryphon House.

Shade, D. (1996). Software evaluation. *Young Children, 51*(6), 17–21.

Sommer, R. (1969). *Personal space: The behavioral basis for design*. Upper Saddle River, NJ: Merrill/Prentice Hall.

Suglia, S. F., Duarte, C. S., Chambers, E. C., & Boynton-Jarrett, R. (2013). Social and behavioral risk factors for obesity in early childhood. *J Dev Behav Pediatr, 34*(8):549–556.

U.S. General Services Administration. (2003). *Child care center design guide*. New York: GSA Public Buildings Service Office of Child Care.

Vijakkhana, N., Wilaisakditipakorn, T., Ruedeekhajorn, K., Pruksananonda, C., & Chonchaiya, W. (2015). Evening media exposure reduces night-time sleep. *Acta Paediatr, 104*(3):306–312.

Warden, C. (2012). *Nature kindergartens and forest schools: An exploration of naturalistic learning within nature* (2nd ed.). Auchterarder, United Kingdom: Mindstretchers.

White House Task Force on Childhood Obesity. (2010). *Solving the problem of childhood obesity within a generation*. Retrieved from http://www.letsmove.gov/sites/letsmove.gov/files/TaskForce_on_Childhood_Obesity_May2010_FullReport.pdf

Zane, L. (2015) *Pedagogy and space: Design inspirations for early childhood classrooms*. St. Paul, MN: Redleaf Press.

Chapter 9

Adolph, K. E., Vereijken, B., & Shrout, P. E. (2003). What changes in infant walking and why. *Child Development, 74*, 475–497.

American Academy of Pediatrics. (2000, July 26). *Joint statement on the impact of entertainment violence on children. Congressional Public Health Summit*. Retrieved from http://www2.aap.org/advocacy/releases/jstmtevc.htm

American Academy of Pediatrics, Committee on Public Education. (2001). Children, adolescents, and television. *Pediatrics, 107*(2), 423–426.

American Journal of Play 7 (3) (2015). Excerpted from *The handbook of play studies*, copublished by The Strong and Rowman & Littlefield. Retrieved from http://files.eric.ed.gov/fulltext/EJ1070266.pdf

Bodrova, E., & Leong, D. J. (2003). Chopsticks and counting chips: Do play and foundational skills need to compete for the teacher's attention in an early childhood classroom? *Young Children, 58*(3), 10–17.

Bodrova, E., & Leong, D. J. (2007). *Tools of the mind: The Vygotskian approach to early childhood education* (2nd ed.). Upper Saddle River, NJ: Pearson.

Bedrova, E. & Leong D. J. (2015). Vygotskian and post-Vygotskian views on children's play.

Bronson, M. B. (2000). *Self-regulation in early childhood: Nature and nurture*. New York: Guilford Press.

Brown, S., & Vaughn, C. (2009). *Play: How it shapes the brain, opens the imagination, and invigorates the soul*. New York: Avery.

Carlson, F. (2009). Rough and tumble play 101. *Childcare Information Exchange, 188*, 70–72.

Carlson, F. (2011). *Big body play: Why boisterous, vigorous, and very physical play is essential to children's development and learning*. Washington, DC: National Association for the Education of Young Children.

Centers for Disease Control. (2007). *Childhood overweight*. Retrieved from http://www.cdc.gov/nccdphp/dnpa/obesity/childhood

Csikszentmihalyi, M. (2008). *Flow: The psychology of optimal experience*. New York: Harper.

Dewey, J. (1910). *How we think*. London: D. C. Heath.

Ebbeck, M., & Waniganayake, M. (Eds). (2010). *Play in early childhood education: Learning in diverse contexts*. Victoria, AU: Oxford University Press.

Elkind, D. (1981). *The hurried child: Growing up too fast too soon*. Menlo Park, CA: Addison-Wesley.

Elkind, D. (2007). *The power of play: Learning what comes naturally*. Philadelphia: Da Capo Lifelong Books.

Frost, J. L. (2008, June). *Neuroscience, play and brain development*. Paper presented at IPA/USA Triennial National Conference, Longmont, CO. ERIC Document Reproduction Service No. ED427845.

Frost, J. S., Wortham, S. C., & Reifel, S. (2011). *Play and child development* (4th ed.). Upper Saddle River, NJ: Pearson.

Ginsburg, K. R., Committee on Communications, & Committee on Psychosocial Aspects of Child and Family Health. (2007). The importance of play in promoting healthy child development and maintaining strong parent-child bonds. *Pediatrics, 119*(1), 183–196.

Gronlund, G. (2010). *Developmentally appropriate play: Guiding young children to a higher level*. St. Paul, MN: Redleaf Press.

Groos, K. (1976). *The play of man*. New York: Arno Press. (Original work published 1901.)

Hall, G. S. (1904). *Adolescence*. New York: D. Appleton.

Hassett, J. M., Siebert, E. R., & Wallen, K. (2008). Sex differences in rhesus monkey toy preferences parallel those of children. *Hormones and Behavior, 54*(3), 359–364.

Hassinger-Das, B. Hirsh-Pasek, K., & Golinkoff, R. M. (2017, May) The case of brain science and guided play: A developing story, *Young Children, 72*(2).

Hirsh-Pasek, K., Golinkoff, R. M., Berk, L. E., & Singer, D. G. (2009). *A mandate for playful learning in preschool: Presenting the evidence.* Oxford, NY: Oxford University Press.

Hughes, F. (2009). *Children, play, and development* (4th ed.). Boston: Allyn & Bacon.

Huizinga, J. (1971). *Homo Ludens: A study of the play-element in culture.* London: Maurice Temple Smith Ltd.

Isenberg, J. P., & Quisenberry, N. (2002). *Play: Essential for all children.* Position Paper of the Association for Childhood Education International. Retrieved from http://www.acei.org/wp-content/uploads/PlayEssential.pdf

Jarvis, P. (2006). "Rough and tumble" play: Lessons in life. *Evolutionary Psychology, 4,* 330–346. Retrieved from http://www.epjournal.net/filestore/ep043303462.pdf

Johnson, J. E., Christie, J. F., & Wardle, F. (2005). *Play and early childhood development* (3rd ed.). Boston: Allyn & Bacon.

Jones, E., & Reynolds, G. (1992). *The play's the thing: Teachers' roles in children's play.* New York: Teachers College Press.

Levin, D. E. (1998). *Remote control childhood: Combating the hazards of media culture.* Washington, DC: NAEYC.

Levin, D. E., & Carlsson-Paige, N. (2006). *The war play dilemma: What every parent and teacher needs to know* (2nd ed.). New York: Teachers College Press.

National Association for the Education of Young Children (NAEYC). (2009). *NAEYC standards for early childhood professional preparation programs: Position statement.* Washington, DC: Author. Retrieved from http://www.naeyc.org/files/naeyc/file/positions/ProfPrepStandards09.pdf

Nell, M. L., Drew, W. F., with Bush, D. E. (2013). *From play to practice: Connecting teachers' play to children's learning.* Washington, DC: National Association for the Education of Young Children.

Orenstein, P. (2006, December 24). What's wrong with Cinderella? *New York Times Magazine.* Retrieved from http://www.nytimes.com/2006/12/24/magazine/24princess.t.html

Paley, V. G. (1993). *You can't say you can't play.* Boston: Harvard University Press.

Paley, V. G. (2004). *A child's work: The importance of fantasy play.* Chicago: University of Chicago Press.

Parten, M. B. (1932). Social participation among preschool children. *Journal of Abnormal Psychology, 27*(3), 243–269.

Patrick, G. T. W. (1916). *The psychology of relaxation.* Boston: Houghton Mifflin.

Pellegrini, A. (1995). *School recess and playground behavior.* New York: State University of New York Press.

Pellis, S. M., & Pellis, V. C. (2007). Rough-and-tumble play and the development of the social brain. *Current Directions in Psychological Science, 16*(2), 95–98.

Pellis, S. M., & Pellis, V. C. (2009, 2013) *The playful brain: Venturing to the limits of neuroscience.* London: Oneworld Publications.

Piaget, J. (1962). *Play, dreams, and imitation in childhood.* New York: Norton.

Reifel, S., & Sutterby, J. A. (2009). Play theory and practice in contemporary classrooms. In S. Feeney, A. Galper, & C. Seefeldt (Eds.), *Continuing issues in early childhood education* (3rd ed., pp. 238–257). Upper Saddle River, NJ: Pearson.

Reynolds, G., & Jones, E. (1997). *Master players: Learning from children at play.* New York: Teachers College Press.

Rogers, S. (Ed.) (2011). *Rethinking play and pedagogy in early childhood education: Concepts, contexts, and cultures.* New York: Routledge.

Sääkslahti, A., Numminen, P., Varstala, V., Helenius, H., Tammi, A., Viikari, J., & Välimäki, I. (2004). Physical activity as a preventive measure for coronary heart disease risk factors in early childhood. *Scandinavian Journal of Medication Science and Sports, 14,* 143–149.

Saracho, O., & Spodek, B. (Eds.). (1998). *Multiple perspectives on play in early childhood education.* Albany: State University of New York Press.

Schickedanz, J. A., Schickedanz, D. I., & Forsythe, P. D. (1993). *Understanding children.* Mountain View, CA: Mayfield.

Shonkoff, J. P., & Phillips, D. A. (Eds.). (2000). *From neurons to neighborhoods: The science of early childhood development.* Washington, DC: National Academy Press.

Singer, D. G., Golinkoff, R. M., & Hirsh-Pasek, K. (2006). *Play=learning: How play motivates and enhances children's cognitive and social-emotional growth.* Oxford, NY: Oxford University Press.

Smilansky, S. (1968). *The effects of sociodramatic play on disadvantaged pre-school children.* New York: Wiley.

Smilansky, S., & Shefatya, L. (1990). *Facilitating play: A medium for promoting cognitive, socio-emotional, and academic development in young children.* Gaithersburg, MD: Psychosocial and Educational Publications.

Spencer, H. (1963). *Education: Intellectual, moral, and physical.* Paterson, NJ: Littlefield Adams. (Original work published 1861.)

Strasburger V.C., (2011). Children, adolescents, obesity, and the media. *Pediatrics.* 2011 Jul;128(1):201-8. doi: 10.1542/peds.2011-1066. Epub 2011 Jun 27.

Trawick-Smith, J. (1994). *Interactions in the classroom: Facilitating play in the early years.* Upper Saddle River, NJ: Pearson.

Trawick-Smith, J. (2010). *From playpen to playground—The importance of physical play for the motor development of young children.* Washington, DC: U.S. Department of Health and Human Services, Administration for Children and Families.

United Nations General Assembly. (1989, November 20). *Convention on the rights of the child.* New York: United Nations.

Van Hoorn, J., Monighan Nourot, P., Scales, B., & Alward, K. R. (2014). *Play at the center of the curriculum* (6th ed.). Upper Saddle River, NJ: Pearson.

Williams, A. (2007, May 20). Putting the skinned knees back into playtime. *New York Times.* Retrieved from http://www.nytimes.com/2007/05/20/fashion/20retro.html

Wolk, S. (2008). Joy in school. *The Positive Classroom, 66*(1), 8–15.

Chapter 10

Bowman, B. (Ed.). (2003). *Love to read: Essays in developing and enhancing early literacy skills of African American children.* Washington, DC: National Black Child Development Institute.

Bredekamp, S., & Rosegrant, T. (2001). *Reaching potentials: Transforming early childhood curriculum and assessment* (Vol. 2). Washington, DC: NAEYC.

Campbell, D. (2000). *The Mozart effect in children: Awakening your child's mind, body, and creativity with music.* New York: Avon.

Cazden, C. (Ed.). (1981). *Language in early childhood education* (Rev. ed.). Washington, DC: NAEYC.

Chaillé, C., & Britain, L. (2003). *The young child as scientist: A constructivist approach to early childhood science education* (3rd ed.). Boston: Allyn & Bacon.

Children's Defense Fund. (2010). *The state of America's children 2008.* Washington, DC: Children's Defense Fund.